CD-ROM TRAINING PACKAGE AVAILABLE

ExamSim

Experience realistic, simulated exams on your own computer with Osborne's interactive ExamSim software. This computer-based test engine offers both standard and adaptive test modes, knowledge-based and product simulation questions like those found on the real exams, and review tools that help you study more efficiently. Intuitive controls allow you to move easily through the program: mark difficult or unanswered questions for further review and skip ahead, and then assess your performance at the end.

Knowledge-based and **scenario-based** questions present challenging material in multiple-choice format. Use Review Mode to re-examine missed questions: answer treatments not only explain why the correct options are right, but also tell you why the incorrect answers were wrong

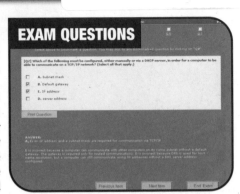

Additional CD-ROM Features

- Complete hypertext linked e-book for easy information access and self-paced study

- **DriveTime** audio tracks offer concise review of key exam topics for in the car or on the go!

- Includes Internet Explorer 5 on CD-ROM

System Requirements:

A PC running Internet Explorer version 5 or higher

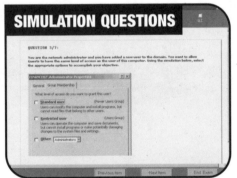

Realistic Windows 2000 product **simulation questions** test the skills you need to pass the exam—these questions look and feel like the actual exam simulations!

Detailed **Score Reports** provide score analysis and history to chart your progress and focus your study time

MICROSOFT CERTIFIED SYSTEMS ENGINEER

MCSE Windows® 2000
Server Study Guide

(Exam 70-215)

Syngress Media, Inc.

Osborne McGraw-Hill

Berkeley New York St. Louis San Francisco Auckland Bogotá Hamburg London Madrid Mexico City
Milan Montreal New Delhi Panama City Paris São Paulo Singapore Sydney Tokyo Toronto

Osborne McGraw-Hill
2600 Tenth Street
Berkeley, California 94710
U.S.A.

For information on translations or book distributors outside the U.S.A., or to arrange bulk purchase discounts for sales promotions, premiums, or fundraisers, please contact Osborne/**McGraw-Hill** at the above address.

MCSE Windows 2000 Server Study Guide (Exam 70-215)

1234567890 PBT PBT 0198765432109

Book p/n 0-07-212378-8 and CD p/n 0-07-XXXXXX-X
parts of ISBN 0-07-212386-9

Publisher	**Editorial Assistant**	**Proofreader**
Brandon A. Nordin	Tara Davis	Carol Burbo
Vice President and	**VP, Worldwide Business**	**Indexer**
Associate Publisher	**Development Global Knowledge**	Irv Hershman
Scott Rogers	Richard Kristof	
		Computer Designer
Acquisitions Editor	**Series Editors**	Roberta Steele
Gareth Hancock	Dr. Thomas W. Shinder	Lauren McCarthy
	Debra Littlejohn Shinder	
Associate Acquisitions Editor		**Illustrator**
Timothy Green	**Technical Editor**	Michael Mueller
	Ryan Sokolowski	Bob Hansen
Editorial Management		
Syngress Media, Inc.	**Copy Editors**	**Series Design**
	Darlene Bordwell	Roberta Steele
Project Editors	Adaya Henis	
Julie Smalley		**Cover Design**
Jenn Tust		Regan Honda

This book was published with Corel VENTURA™ Publisher.

Information has been obtained by Osborne/**McGraw-Hill** from sources believed to be reliable. However, because of the possibility of human or mechanical error by our sources, Osborne/**McGraw-Hill**, or others, Osborne/**McGraw-Hill** does not guarantee the accuracy, adequacy, or completeness of any information and is not responsible for any errors or omissions or the results obtained from use of such information.

FOREWORD

From Global Knowledge

At Global Knowledge we strive to support the multiplicity of learning styles required by our students to achieve success as technical professionals. In this series of books, it is our intention to offer the reader a valuable tool for successful completion of the MCSE Windows 2000 Certification exams.

As the world's largest IT training company, Global Knowledge is uniquely positioned to offer these books. The expertise gained each year from providing instructor-led training to hundreds of thousands of students worldwide has been captured in book form to enhance your learning experience. We hope that the quality of these books demonstrates our commitment to your lifelong learning success. Whether you choose to learn through the written word, computer-based training, Web delivery, or instructor-led training, Global Knowledge is committed to providing you the very best in each of those categories. For those of you who know Global Knowledge, or those of you who have just found us for the first time, our goal is to be your lifelong competency partner.

Thank you for the opportunity to serve you. We look forward to serving your needs again in the future.

Warmest regards,

Duncan Anderson
President and Chief Operating Officer, Global Knowledge

The Global Knowledge Advantage

Global Knowledge has a global delivery system for its products and services. The company has 28 subsidiaries, and offers its programs through a total of 60+ locations. No other vendor can provide consistent services across a geographic area this large. Global Knowledge is the largest independent information technology education provider, offering programs on a variety of platforms. This enables our multi-platform and multi-national customers to obtain all of their programs from a single vendor. The company has developed the unique Competus™ Framework software tool and methodology which can quickly reconfigure courseware to the proficiency level of a student on an interactive basis. Combined with self-paced and on-line programs, this technology can reduce the time required for training by prescribing content in only the deficient skills areas. The company has fully automated every aspect of the education process, from registration and follow-up, to "just-in-time" production of courseware. Global Knowledge Network through its Enterprise Services Consultancy, can customize programs and products to suit the needs of an individual customer.

Global Knowledge Classroom Education Programs

The backbone of our delivery options is classroom-based education. Our modern, well-equipped facilities staffed with the finest instructors offer programs in a wide variety of information technology topics, many of which lead to professional certifications.

Custom Learning Solutions

This delivery option has been created for companies and governments that value customized learning solutions. For them, our consultancy-based approach of developing targeted education solutions is most effective at helping them meet specific objectives.

Self-Paced and Multimedia Products

This delivery option offers self-paced program titles in interactive CD-ROM, videotape and audio tape programs. In addition, we offer custom development of interactive multimedia courseware to customers and partners. Call us at 1-888-427-4228.

Electronic Delivery of Training

Our network-based training service delivers efficient competency-based, interactive training via the World Wide Web and organizational intranets. This leading-edge delivery option provides a custom learning path and "just-in-time" training for maximum convenience to students.

ARG

American Research Group (ARG), a wholly-owned subsidiary of Global Knowledge, one of the largest worldwide training partners of Cisco Systems, offers a wide range of internetworking, LAN/WAN, Bay Networks, FORE Systems, IBM, and UNIX courses. ARG offers hands on network training in both instructor-led classes and self-paced PC-based training.

Global Knowledge Courses Available

Network Fundamentals

- Understanding Computer Networks
- Telecommunications Fundamentals I
- Telecommunications Fundamentals II
- Understanding Networking Fundamentals
- Implementing Computer Telephony Integration
- Introduction to Voice Over IP
- Introduction to Wide Area Networking
- Cabling Voice and Data Networks
- Introduction to LAN/WAN protocols
- Virtual Private Networks
- ATM Essentials

Network Security & Management

- Troubleshooting TCP/IP Networks
- Network Management
- Network Troubleshooting
- IP Address Management
- Network Security Administration
- Web Security
- Implementing UNIX Security
- Managing Cisco Network Security
- Windows NT 4.0 Security

IT Professional Skills

- Project Management for IT Professionals
- Advanced Project Management for IT Professionals
- Survival Skills for the New IT Manager
- Making IT Teams Work

LAN/WAN Internetworking

- Frame Relay Internetworking
- Implementing T1/T3 Services
- Understanding Digital Subscriber Line (xDSL)
- Internetworking with Routers and Switches
- Advanced Routing and Switching
- Multi-Layer Switching and Wire-Speed Routing
- Internetworking with TCP/IP
- ATM Internetworking
- OSPF Design and Configuration
- Border Gateway Protocol (BGP) Configuration

Authorized Vendor Training

Cisco Systems

- Introduction to Cisco Router Configuration
- Advanced Cisco Router Configuration
- Installation and Maintenance of Cisco Routers
- Cisco Internetwork Troubleshooting
- Cisco Internetwork Design
- Cisco Routers and LAN Switches
- Catalyst 5000 Series Configuration
- Cisco LAN Switch Configuration
- Managing Cisco Switched Internetworks
- Configuring, Monitoring, and Troubleshooting Dial-Up Services
- Cisco AS5200 Installation and Configuration
- Cisco Campus ATM Solutions

Bay Networks

- Bay Networks Accelerated Router Configuration
- Bay Networks Advanced IP Routing
- Bay Networks Hub Connectivity
- Bay Networks Accelar 1xxx Installation and Basic Configuration
- Bay Networks Centillion Switching

FORE Systems

- FORE ATM Enterprise Core Products
- FORE ATM Enterprise Edge Products
- FORE ATM Theory
- FORE LAN Certification

Operating Systems & Programming

Microsoft

- Introduction to Windows NT
- Microsoft Networking Essentials
- Windows NT 4.0 Workstation
- Windows NT 4.0 Server
- Advanced Windows NT 4.0 Server
- Windows NT Networking with TCP/IP
- Introduction to Microsoft Web Tools
- Windows NT Troubleshooting
- Windows Registry Configuration

UNIX

- UNIX Level I
- UNIX Level II
- Essentials of UNIX and NT Integration

Programming

- Introduction to JavaScript
- Java Programming
- PERL Programming
- Advanced PERL with CGI for the Web

Web Site Management & Development

- Building a Web Site
- Web Site Management and Performance
- Web Development Fundamentals

High Speed Networking

- Essentials of Wide Area Networking
- Integrating ISDN
- Fiber Optic Network Design
- Fiber Optic Network Installation
- Migrating to High Performance Ethernet

DIGITAL UNIX

- UNIX Utilities and Commands
- DIGITAL UNIX v4.0 System Administration
- DIGITAL UNIX v4.0 (TCP/IP) Network Management
- AdvFS, LSM, and RAID Configuration and Management
- DIGITAL UNIX TruCluster Software Configuration and Management
- UNIX Shell Programming Featuring Kornshell
- DIGITAL UNIX v4.0 Security Management
- DIGITAL UNIX v4.0 Performance Management
- DIGITAL UNIX v4.0 Intervals Overview

DIGITAL OpenVMS

- OpenVMS Skills for Users
- OpenVMS System and Network Node Management I
- OpenVMS System and Network Node Management II
- OpenVMS System and Network Node Management III
- OpenVMS System and Network Node Operations
- OpenVMS for Programmers
- OpenVMS System Troubleshooting for Systems Managers
- Configuring and Managing Complex VMScluster Systems
- Utilizing OpenVMS Features from C
- OpenVMS Performance Management
- Managing DEC TCP/IP Services for OpenVMS
- Programming in C

Hardware Courses

- AlphaServer 1000/1000A Installation, Configuration and Maintenance
- AlphaServer 2100 Server Maintenance
- AlphaServer 4100, Troubleshooting Techniques and Problem Solving

About Syngress Media

Syngress Media creates books and software for Information Technology professionals seeking skill enhancement and career advancement. Its products are designed to comply with vendor and industry standard course curricula and are optimized for certification exam preparation. You can contact Syngress via the Web at **www.syngress.com**.

Contributors

Pawan K. Bhardwaj (MCSE, MCP+I, CCNA) has spent 13 years in the IT industry, working at various systems and network support levels. He has been involved in designing and implementing LAN and WAN solutions for several small- and medium-sized companies. He taught MCSE classes for one year in India prior to relocating to the United States. Mr. Bhardwaj is currently working as Windows NT Consultant with a turnkey solution provider in New Jersey. He can be reached at pawan_bhardwaj@hotmail.com.

Lance Ecklesdafer (MCSE, MCP+I, CNP, CNE) is an Infrastructure Specialist with Electronic Data Systems in Southfield, Michigan. He has over 15 years of professional experience in networking applications, hardware, and engineering. He has been certified in Novell Netware since 1991 and Windows NT since 1998. The Certified Network Professional certification was earned in 1998 and was a goal of Lance's since it was first conceived by the NPA (Network Professional Association). Lance's other interests include the ancient artifacts of Egypt, the exploration of the planet Mars, and physical fitness activities.

Jocelyn Fowke (MCSE, MCP+I) is a Technology Solutions Associate for Clarica Life Insurance Company. Her background includes experience as a network administrator and software developer. She recently joined the Internet Strategy Team at the Clarica Corporate Head Office in Waterloo, Ontario. Jocelyn enjoys the challenges and potentials available in the IT industry. Outside of IT she enjoys traveling, hiking, music, reading, and her new-found love, scuba diving! Jocelyn lives in Mississauga, Ontario, with her partner Jason Tratch, who is employed as a Strategic Consultant for an Internet/E-Commerce company.

Eriq Oliver Neale is a systems architect and technology strategist, consulting with IT organizations to plan and implement computing infrastructures based on current and forthcoming technologies. Eriq spends some of his spare time writing on topics such as Windows 2000, Macintosh, Internet and music technologies, computer education, and antivirus issues. He also enjoys writing music for guitar and keyboard. Eriq maintains a home in North Texas with his wife, seven cats, two dogs, and dozens of fish.

Robert A. Patton (MCDBA, MCSD, MCSE+I, MCP+I) is a software engineer specializing in Microsoft Windows DNA applications utilizing Interdev and Visual Basic with Windows 2000 and SQL Server. He is currently a Senior Applications Developer at PurchasingFirst.com in Dublin, Ohio, and has done work for First Union National Bank, Corporate Strategic Services, the Midland Life Insurance Company, and Sykes Enterprises. He attended the University of Chicago, where he studied Public Policy and played varsity football. Robert earned his Bachelor of Science degree in Software Engineering from the Ohio State University and is an avid fan of Buckeye athletics. He lives in Dublin, Ohio, with his wife, Jenny, and their sons, Michael and Alex.

Mary Robinson (MCP) is a Network Administrator at the University of Victoria in Victoria, British Columbia. Along with her colleagues, she has recently been spending much of her time with Windows 2000 Server and Professional in order to upgrade her organization's Windows NT network in the near future. Mary also works with Exchange 5.5 and BackOffice 4.5. Mary has a Bachelor of Arts degree in Liberal Studies.

Thomas W. Shinder, M.D. (MCSE, MCP+I, MCT) is a technology trainer and consultant in the Dallas-Ft. Worth metroplex. Dr. Shinder has consulted with major firms, including Xerox, Lucent Technologies, and FINA Oil, assisting in the development and implementation of IP-based communications strategies. Dr. Shinder attended medical school at the University of Illinois in Chicago, and trained in neurology at the Oregon Health Sciences Center in Portland, Oregon. His fascination with interneuronal communication ultimately melded with his interest in internetworking and led him to focus on systems engineering. Tom works with his wife, Deb Shinder, to design elegant and cost-efficient solutions for small- and medium-sized businesses based on Windows NT/2000 platforms.

Holly C. Simard (MCSE, MCP+I, A+) is the Lab Network Administrator for the University of Victoria, Division of Continuing Studies. In addition to her work at UVIC and coauthoring technical books, Holly also delivers online instruction and enjoys learning new technologies. Holly loves hiking, running, playing the piano, and spending time with her "little sister". Holly lives in Victoria, British Columbia, with her husband, Hervey, who is a multimedia web designer, dogs Hubert and Hailey, and cats Daisy and Marigold.

Amy Thomson (A+, MOUS) is a Technical Writer for Core Networks, located in Halifax, Nova Scotia. The flagship product of Core Networks is CoreOS, a system designed to provide cable ISPs with tools to manage data-over-cable services. Amy also has a long history as an instructor in both computer software and A+ certification. She has more than 10 years of experience working with computer hardware and applications and holds an Honours B.Sc. in Psychology. Amy lives in Bedford, Nova Scotia, with her husband, Jeff.

Cameron Wakefield (MCSD, MCP) is a Senior Software Engineer. He works at Computer Science Innovations, Inc. (**http://www.csihq.com**) in Melbourne, Florida, where he develops custom software solutions ranging from satellite communications to data mining applications. His development work spans a broad spectrum including Visual C++, Visual Basic, COM, ADO, ASP, Delphi, CORBA, and UNIX. He does some work through his own business developing software for a Brazilian Hematology company and developing Business-to-Business web applications. He also teaches Microsoft Certification courses for Herzing College (AATP) where he teaches in the MCSE and MCSD programs. His formal education was in Computer Science with a minor in Math at Rollins College. He lives in Rockledge, Florida, with his wife, Lorraine, and daughter, Rachel. He also plays racquetball competitively. He can be contacted at cwakefield@csihq.com.

Technical Editors

Ryan Neil Sokolowski (MCSE, CCNA, CCDA, CNE, CNA, VCE) is a Senior Technical Analyst in the Design and Engineering group at a Fortune 100 company in Minneapolis, Minnesota. He also operates Onyx Consulting, an independent consulting company. Sokolowski is a participant in the Internet Engineering Task Force (IETF) and a member of the Institute of Electrical and Electronics Engineers (IEEE), the SANS Institute, the Association of Windows NT Systems Professionals, and NetWare Users International. With a true love of technology and a strong background in design, implementation, engineering and consulting services, Sokolowski's specialties include network operating systems, directory services and Cisco networking environments. He dedicates this book to his parents, who taught him everything they knew…and how to learn the rest for himself.

Ralph Crump (MCSE, CCNA, and a CNE 3.x, 4.x, and 5.x, with a Master CNE in Integrating Windows NT) manages a team responsible for a large scale Windows NT and Novell NetWare infrastructure for a major telecommunications company in Atlanta, Georgia. He specializes in Windows NT and BackOffice applications as well as Novell NetWare solutions. He is currently working in cooperation with Microsoft on Windows 2000 Rapid Deployment projects.

Series Editors

Thomas W. Shinder, M.D. (MCSE, MCP+I, MCT) is a technology trainer and consultant in the Dallas-Ft. Worth metroplex. Dr. Shinder has consulted with major firms, including Xerox, Lucent Technologies, and FINA Oil, assisting in the development and implementation of IP-based communications strategies. Dr. Shinder attended medical school at the University of Illinois in Chicago, and trained in neurology at the Oregon Health Sciences Center in Portland, Oregon. His fascination with interneuronal communication ultimately melded with his interest in internetworking and led him to focus on systems engineering. Tom works with his wife, Deb Shinder, to design elegant and cost-efficient solutions for small- and medium-sized businesses based on Windows NT/2000 platforms.

Debra Littlejohn Shinder (MCSE, MCP+I, MCT) is an instructor in the AATP program at Eastfield College, Dallas County Community College District, where she has taught since 1992. She is webmaster for the cities of Seagoville and Sunnyvale, Texas, as well as the family web site at **www.shinder.net**. She and her husband, Dr. Thomas W. Shinder, provide consulting and technical support services to Dallas-area organizations. She is also the proud mom of a daughter, Kristen, who is serving in the U.S. Navy in Italy, and a son, Kris, who is a high school chess champion. Deb has been a writer for most her life, and has published numerous articles in both technical and nontechnical fields. She can be contacted at deb@shinder.net.

ACKNOWLEDGMENTS

We would like to thank the following people:

- Richard Kristof of Global Knowledge for championing the series and providing access to some great people and information.

- All the incredibly hardworking folks at Osborne/McGraw-Hill: Brandon Nordin, Scott Rogers, Gareth Hancock, and Tim Green for their help in launching a great series and being solid team players. In addition, Tara Davis, and Jenn Tust for their help in fine-tuning the book.

- Monica Kilwine at Microsoft Corp., for being patient and diligent in answering all our questions.

CONTENTS

8 Managing, Monitoring, and Optimizing System Performance, Reliability, and Availability 379

11 Configuring and Troubleshooting Windows 2000 Network Connections 519

PREFACE

This book's primary objective is to help you prepare for the MCSE Installing, Configuring, and Administering Microsoft Windows 2000 Server exam under the new Windows 2000 certification track. As the Microsoft program transitions from Windows NT 4.0, it will become increasingly important that current and aspiring IT professionals have multiple resources available to assist them in increasing their knowledge and building their skills.

At the time of publication, all the exam objectives have been posted on the Microsoft Web site and the beta exam process has been completed. Microsoft has announced its commitment to measuring real-world skills. This book is designed with that premise in mind; its authors have practical experience in the field, using the Windows 2000 operating systems in hands-on situations and have followed the development of the product since early beta versions.

Because the focus of the exam is on application and understanding, as opposed to memorization of facts, no book by itself can fully prepare you to obtain a passing score. It is essential that you work with the software to enhance your proficiency. Toward that end, this book includes many practical step-by-step exercises in each chapter that are designed to give you hands-on practice as well as to guide you in truly learning Microsoft Windows 2000 Server, not just learning *about* it.

In This Book

This book is organized in such a way as to serve as an in-depth review for the MCSE Installing, Configuring, and Administering Microsoft Windows 2000 Server exam for both experienced Windows NT professionals and newcomers to Microsoft networking technologies. Each chapter covers a major aspect of the exam, with an emphasis on the "why" as well as the "how to" of working with and supporting Windows 2000 as a network administrator or engineer.

On the CD

The CD-ROM contains the CertTrainer software. CertTrainer comes complete with ExamSim, Skill Assessment tests, CertCam movie clips, the e-book (electronic version of the book), and Drive Time. CertTrainer is easy to install on any Windows 98/NT/2000 computer and must be installed to access these features. You may, however, browse the e-book direct from the CD without installation. For more information on the CD-ROM, please see Appendix A.

In Every Chapter

We've created a set of chapter components that call your attention to important items, reinforce important points, and provide helpful exam-taking hints. Take a look at what you'll find in every chapter:

- Every chapter begins with the **Certification Objectives**—what you need to know in order to pass the section on the exam addressing the chapter topic. The Objective headings identify the objectives within the chapter, so you'll always know an objective when you see it!

- Exam Watch notes call attention to information about, and potential pitfalls in, the exam. These helpful hints are written by authors who have taken the exams and received their certification—who better to tell you what to worry about? They know what you're about to go through!

- **Practice Exercises** are interspersed throughout the chapters. These are step-by-step exercises that allow you to get the hands-on experience you need in order to pass the exam. They help you master skills that are likely to be an area of focus on the exam. Don't just read through the exercises; they are hands-on practice that you should be comfortable completing. Learning by doing is an effective way to increase your competency with a product. The practical exercises will be very helpful for any simulation exercises you may encounter on the MCSE Installing, Configuring, and Administering Microsoft Windows 2000 Server exam.

- The **CertCam** icon that appears in many of the exercises indicates that the exercise is presented in .avi format on the accompanying CD-ROM. These .avi clips walk you step-by-step through various system configurations and are narrated by Thomas W. Shinder, M.D., MCSE.

- On The Job notes describe the issues that come up most often in real-world settings. They provide a valuable perspective on certification and product-related topics. They point out common mistakes and address questions that have arisen from on the job discussions and experience.

- **From The Classroom** sidebars describe the issues that come up most often in the training classroom setting. These sidebars highlight some of the most common and confusing problems that students encounter when taking a live Windows 2000 training course. You can get a leg up on those difficult to understand subjects by focusing extra attention on these sidebars.

- **Scenario & Solution** sections lay out potential problems and solutions in a quick-to-read format:

SCENARIO & SOLUTION

Is Active Directory scalable?	Yes! Unlike the Windows NT security database, which is limited to approximately 40,000 objects, Active Directory supports literally millions of objects.
Is Active Directory compatible with other LDAP directory services?	Yes! Active Directory can share information with other directory services that support LDAP versions 2 and 3, such as Novell's NDS.

- The **Certification Summary** is a succinct review of the chapter and a restatement of salient points regarding the exam.

 - The **Two-Minute Drill** at the end of every chapter is a checklist of the main points of the chapter. It can be used for last-minute review.

- The **Self Test** offers questions similar to those found on the certification exams. The answers to these questions, as well as explanations of the answers, can be found at the end of each chapter. By taking the Self Test after completing each chapter, you'll reinforce what you've learned from that chapter while becoming familiar with the structure of the exam questions.

■ The **Lab Question** at the end of the Self Test section offers a unique and challenging question format that requires the reader to understand multiple chapter concepts to answer correctly. These questions are more complex and more comprehensive than the other questions—they test your ability to take all the knowledge you have gained from reading the chapter and apply it to complicated, real-world situations. These questions are aimed to be more difficult than what you will find on the exam. If you can answer these questions, you have proven you know the subject!

The Global Knowledge Web Site

Check out the Web site. Global Knowledge invites you to become an active member of the Access Global Web site. This site is an online mall and an information repository that you'll find invaluable. You can access many types of products to assist you in your preparation for the exam, and you'll be able to participate in forums, online discussions, and threaded discussions. No other book brings you unlimited access to such a resource. You'll find more information about this site in Appendix B.

Some Pointers

Once you've finished reading this book, set aside some time to do a thorough review. You might want to return to the book several times and make use of all the methods it offers for reviewing the material:

1. *Re-read all the Two-Minute Drills,* or have someone quiz you. You also can use the drills as a way to do a quick cram before the exam. You might want to make some flash cards that have the Two-Minute Drill material on them.

2. *Re-read all the Exam Watch notes.* Remember that these notes are written by authors who have taken the exam and passed. They know what you should expect—and what you should be on the lookout for.

3. *Review all the S&S sections* for quick problem solving.

4. *Re-take the Self Tests.* Taking the tests right after you've read the chapter is a good idea, because the questions help reinforce what you've just learned. However, it's an even better idea to go back later and do all the questions in the book in one sitting. Pretend that you're taking the live exam. (When you

go through the questions the first time, you should mark your answers on a separate piece of paper. That way, you can run through the questions as many times as you need to until you feel comfortable with the material.)

5. *Complete the Exercises.* Did you do the exercises when you read through each chapter? If not, do them! These exercises are designed to cover exam topics, and there's no better way to get to know this material than by practicing. Be sure you understand why you are performing each step in each exercise. If there is something you are not clear on, re-read that section in the chapter.

MCSE Certification

If you are new to Microsoft certification, we have some good news and some bad. This book is designed to help you pass the MCSE Installing, Configuring, and Administering Microsoft Windows 2000 Server exam. At the time this book was written, the exam objectives for the exam were posted on the Microsoft Web site, and the beta exams had been completed. We wrote this book to give you a complete and incisive review of all the important topics that are targeted for the exam. The information contained here will provide you with the required foundation of knowledge that will not only allow you to succeed in passing the MCSE Installing, Configuring, and Administering Microsoft Windows 2000 Server exam, but will also make you a better Microsoft Certified Systems Engineer.

The nature of the Information Technology industry is changing rapidly, and the requirements and specifications for certification can change just as quickly without notice. Microsoft expects you to regularly visit their Website at **http://www.microsoft.com/mcp/certstep/mcse.htm** to get the most up to date information on the entire MCSE program.

TABLE 1-1   Windows 2000 Certification Track

Core Exams		
Candidates Who Have <u>Not</u> Already Passed Windows NT 4.0 Exams All 4 of the Following Core Exams Required:	**OR**	**Candidates Who Have Passed 3 Windows NT 4.0 Exams (Exams 70-067, 70-068, and 70-073) Instead of the 4 Core Exams on Left, You May Take:**
Exam 70-210: Installing, Configuring, and Administering Microsoft® Windows® 2000 Professional		**Exam 70-240**: Microsoft® Windows® 2000 Accelerated Exam for MCPs Certified on Microsoft® Windows NT® 4.0.
Exam 70-215: Installing, Configuring, and Administering Microsoft® Windows® 2000 Server		
Exam 70-216: Implementing and Administering a Microsoft® Windows® 2000 Network Infrastructure		The accelerated exam will be available until December 31, 2001. It covers the core competencies of exams **70-210, 70-215, 70-216, and 70-217.**
Exam 70-217: Implementing and Administering a Microsoft® Windows® 2000 Directory Services Infrastructure		

Core Exams
PLUS – All Candidates – *1 of the Following Core Exams Required:*
*Exam 70-219: Designing a Microsoft® Windows® 2000 Directory Services Infrastructure
*Exam 70-220: Designing Security for a Microsoft® Windows® 2000 Network
*Exam 70-221: Designing a Microsoft® Windows® 2000 Network Infrastructure
PLUS – All Candidates – *2 Elective Exams Required:*
Any current MCSE electives when the Windows 2000 exams listed above are released in their live versions. **Electives scheduled for retirement will not be considered current.** Selected third-party certifications that focus on interoperability will be accepted as an alternative to one elective exam.
*Exam 70-219: Designing a Microsoft® Windows® 2000 Directory Services Infrastructure
*Exam 70-220: Designing Security for a Microsoft® Windows® 2000 Network
*Exam 70-221: Designing a Microsoft® Windows® 2000 Network Infrastructure
Exam 70-222: Upgrading from Microsoft® Windows® NT 4.0 to Microsoft® Windows® 2000

*Note that some of the Windows 2000 core exams can be used as elective exams as well. An exam that is used to meet the design requirement cannot also count as an elective. Each exam can only be counted once in the Windows 2000 Certification.

Let's look at two scenarios. The first applies to the person who has already taken the Windows NT 4.0 Server (70-067), Windows NT 4.0 Workstation (70-073), and Windows NT 4.0 Server in the Enterprise (70-068) exams. The second scenario covers the situation of the person who has not completed those Windows NT 4.0 exams and would like to concentrate *only* on Windows 2000.

In the first scenario, you have the option of taking all four Windows 2000 core exams, or you can take the Windows 2000 Accelerated Exam for MCPs if you have already passed exams 70-067, 70-068, and 70-073. (Note that you must have passed those specific exams to qualify for the Accelerated Exam; if you have fulfilled your NT 4.0 MCSE requirements by passing the Windows 95 or Windows 98 exam as your client operating system option, and did not take the NT Workstation Exam, you don't qualify.)

After completing the core requirements, either by passing the four core exams or the one Accelerated exam, you must pass a "design" exam. The design exams include Designing a Microsoft Windows 2000 Directory Services Infrastructure (70-219), Designing Security for Microsoft Windows 2000 Network (70-220), and Designing a Microsoft Windows 2000 Network Infrastructure (70-221). One design exam is *required.*

You also must pass two exams from the list of electives. This includes any of the MCSE electives that are current when the Windows 2000 exams are released. In summary, you would take a total of at least two more exams, the upgrade exam and the design exam. Any additional exams would be dependent on which electives the candidate may have already completed.

In the second scenario, if you have not completed and do not plan to complete, the Core Windows NT 4.0 exams, you must pass the four core Windows 2000 exams, one design exam, and two elective exams. Again, no exam can be counted twice. In this case, you must pass a total of seven exams to obtain the Windows 2000 MCSE certification.

How to Take a Microsoft Certification Exam

If you have taken a Microsoft Certification exam before, we have some good news and some bad news. The good news is that the new testing formats will be a true measure of your ability and knowledge. Microsoft has "raised the bar" for its Windows 2000 certification exams. If you are an expert in the Windows 2000 operating system, and can troubleshoot and engineer efficient, cost-effective solutions using Windows 2000, you will have no difficulty with the new exams.

The bad news is that if you have used resources such as "brain-dumps," boot-camps, or exam-specific practice tests as your only method of test preparation, you will undoubtedly fail your Windows 2000 exams. The new Windows 2000 MCSE exams will test your knowledge, and your ability to apply that knowledge in more sophisticated and accurate ways than was expected for the MCSE exams for Windows NT 4.0.

In the Windows 2000 exams, Microsoft will use a variety of testing formats that include product simulations, adaptive testing, drag-and-drop matching, and possibly even fill-in-the-blank questions (also called "free response" questions). The test-taking process will measure the examinee's fundamental knowledge of the Windows 2000 operating system rather than the ability to memorize a few facts and then answer a few simple multiple-choice questions.

In addition, the pool of questions for each exam will significantly increase. The greater number of questions combined with the adaptive testing techniques will enhance the validity and security of the certification process.

We will begin by looking at the purpose, focus, and structure of Microsoft certification tests, and examine the effect that these factors have on the kinds of questions you will face on your certification exams. We will define the structure of exam questions and investigate some common formats. Next, we will present a strategy for answering these questions. Finally, we will give some specific guidelines on what you should do on the day of your test.

Why Vendor Certification?

The Microsoft Certified Professional program, like the certification programs from Cisco, Novell, Oracle, and other software vendors, is maintained for the ultimate purpose of increasing the corporation's profits. A successful vendor certification program accomplishes this goal by helping to create a pool of experts in a company's software and by "branding" these experts so companies using the software can identify them.

We know that vendor certification has become increasingly popular in the last few years because it helps employers find qualified workers and it also helps software vendors, like Microsoft, sell their products. But why vendor certification rather than a more traditional approach like a college degree in computer science? A college education is a broadening and enriching experience, but a degree in computer science does not prepare students for most jobs in the IT industry.

A common truism in our business states, "If you are out of the IT industry for three years and want to return, you have to start over." The problem, of course, is *timeliness*; if a first-year student learns about a specific computer program, it probably will no longer be in wide use when he or she graduates. Although some colleges are trying to integrate Microsoft certification into their curriculum, the problem is not really a flaw in higher education, but a characteristic of the IT industry. Computer software is changing so rapidly that a four-year college just can't keep up.

A marked characteristic of the Microsoft certification program is an emphasis on performing specific job tasks rather than merely gathering knowledge. It may come as a shock, but most potential employers do not care how much you know about the theory of operating systems, networking, or database design. As one IT manager said, "I don't really care what my employees know about the theory of our network. We don't need someone to sit at a desk and think about it. We need people who can actually do something to make it work better."

You should not think that this attitude is some kind of anti-intellectual revolt against book learning. Knowledge is a necessary prerequisite, but it is not enough. More than one company has hired a computer science graduate as a network administrator, only to learn that the new employee has no idea how to add users, assign permissions, or perform the other day-to-day tasks necessary to maintain a network. This brings us to the second major characteristic of Microsoft certification that affects the questions you must be prepared to answer. In addition to timeliness, Microsoft certification is also job-task oriented.

The timeliness of Microsoft's certification program is obvious and is inherent in the fact that you will be tested on current versions of software in wide use today. The job-task orientation of Microsoft certification is almost as obvious, but testing real-world job skills using a computer-based test is not easy.

Computerized Testing

Considering the popularity of Microsoft certification, and the fact that certification candidates are spread around the world, the only practical way to administer tests for the certification program is through Sylvan Prometric or Vue testing centers, which operate internationally. Sylvan Prometric and Vue provide proctor testing services for Microsoft, Oracle, Novell, Lotus, and the A+ computer technician certification. Although the IT industry accounts for much of Sylvan's revenue, the company provides services for a number of other businesses and organizations, such as FAA preflight pilot tests. Historically, several hundred questions were developed for a new Microsoft certification exam. The Windows 2000 MCSE exam pool is expected to contain hundreds of new questions. Microsoft is aware that many new MCSE candidates have been able to access information on test questions via the Internet or other resources. The company is very concerned about maintaining the MCSE as a "premium" certification. The significant increase in the number of test questions, together with stronger enforcement of the NDA (Non-disclosure agreement) will ensure that a higher standard for certification is attained.

Microsoft treats the test-building process very seriously. Test questions are first reviewed by a number of subject matter experts for technical accuracy and then are presented in a beta test. Taking the beta test may require several hours, due to the large number of questions. After a few weeks, Microsoft Certification uses the statistical feedback from Sylvan to check the performance of the beta questions. The beta test group for the Windows 2000 certification series included MCTs, MCSEs, and members of Microsoft's rapid deployment partners groups. Because the exams will be normalized based on this population, you can be sure that the passing scores will be difficult to achieve without detailed product knowledge.

Questions are discarded if most test takers get them right (too easy) or wrong (too difficult), and a number of other statistical measures are taken of each question. Although the scope of our discussion precludes a rigorous treatment of question analysis, you should be aware that Microsoft and other vendors spend a great deal of time and effort making sure their exam questions are valid.

The questions that survive statistical analysis form the pool of questions for the final certification exam.

Test Structure

The questions in a Microsoft form test will not be equally weighted. From what we can tell at the present time, different questions are given a value based on the level of difficulty. You will get more credit for getting a difficult question correct than if you got an easy one correct. Because the questions are weighted differently and the exams will likely use the adapter method of testing, your score will not bear any relationship to how many questions you answered correctly.

Microsoft has implemented *adaptive* testing. When an adaptive test begins, the candidate is first given a level three question. If it is answered correctly, a question from the next higher level is presented, and an incorrect response results in a question from the next lower level. When 15 to 20 questions have been answered in this manner, the scoring algorithm is able to predict, with a high degree of statistical certainty, whether the candidate would pass or fail if all the questions in the form were answered. When the required degree of certainty is attained, the test ends and the candidate receives a pass/fail grade.

Adaptive testing has some definite advantages for everyone involved in the certification process. Adaptive tests allow Sylvan Prometric or Vue to deliver more tests with the same resources, as certification candidates often are in and out in 30 minutes or less. For candidates, the "fatigue factor" is reduced due to the shortened testing time. For Microsoft, adaptive testing means that fewer test questions are exposed to each candidate, and this can enhance the security, and therefore the overall validity, of certification tests.

One possible problem you may have with adaptive testing is that you are not allowed to mark and revisit questions. Since the adaptive algorithm is interactive, and all questions but the first are selected on the basis of your response to the previous question, it is not possible to skip a particular question or change an answer.

Question Types

Computerized test questions can be presented in a number of ways. Some of the possible formats are used on Microsoft certification exam and some are not.

True/False

We are all familiar with True/False questions, but because of the inherent 50 percent chance of guessing the correct answer, you will not see questions of this type on Microsoft certification exams.

Multiple Choice

The majority of Microsoft certification questions are in the multiple-choice format, with either a single correct answer or multiple correct answers. One interesting variation on multiple-choice questions with multiple correct answers is whether or not the candidate is told how many answers are correct.

EXAMPLE:

Which two files can be altered to configure the MS-DOS environment? (Choose two.)

Or

Which files can be altered to configure the MS-DOS environment? (Choose all that apply.)

You may see both variations on Microsoft certification exams, but the trend seems to be toward the first type, where candidates are told explicitly how many answers are correct. Questions of the "choose all that apply" variety are more difficult and can be confusing.

Graphical Questions

One or more graphical elements are sometimes used to help present or clarify an exam question. These elements may take the form of a network diagram, pictures of networking components, or screen shots from the software on which you are being tested. It is often easier to present the concepts required for a complex performance-based scenario with a graphic than with words.

Test questions known as *hotspots* actually incorporate graphics as part of the answer. These questions ask the certification candidate to click on a location or graphical element to answer the question. For example, you might be shown the diagram of a network and asked to click on an appropriate location for a router. The answer is correct if the candidate clicks within the *hotspot* that defines the correct location.

Free Response Questions

Another kind of question you sometimes see on Microsoft certification exams requires a *free response* or type-in answer. An example of this type of question might present a TCP/IP network scenario and ask the candidate to calculate and enter the correct subnet mask in dotted decimal notation.

Simulation Questions

Simulation questions provide a method for Microsoft to test how familiar the test taker is with the actual product interface and the candidate's ability to quickly implement a task using the interface. These questions will present an actual Windows 2000 interface that you must work with to solve a problem or implement a solution. If you are familiar with the product, you will be able to answer these questions quickly, and they will be the easiest questions on the exam. However, if you are not accustomed to working with Windows 2000, these questions will be difficult for you to answer. This is why actual hands-on practice with Windows 2000 is so important!

Knowledge-Based and Performance-Based Questions

Microsoft Certification develops a blueprint for each Microsoft certification exam with input from subject matter experts. This blueprint defines the content areas and objectives for each test, and each test question is created to test a specific objective. The basic information from the examination blueprint can be found on Microsoft's Web site in the Exam Prep Guide for each test.

Psychometricians (psychologists who specialize in designing and analyzing tests) categorize test questions as knowledge- or performance-based. As the names imply, knowledge-based questions are designed to test knowledge, while performance-based questions are designed to test performance.

Some objectives demand a knowledge-based question. For example, objectives that use verbs like *list* and *identify* tend to test only what you know, not what you can do.

EXAMPLE:

Objective: Identify the MS-DOS configuration files.

Which two files can be altered to configure the MS-DOS environment? (Choose two.)

A. COMMAND.COM

B. AUTOEXEC.BAT

C. IO.SYS

D. CONFIG.SYS

Correct answers: B, D

Other objectives use action verbs like *install, configure,* and *troubleshoot* to define job tasks. These objectives can often be tested with either a knowledge-based question or a performance-based question.

EXAMPLE:

Objective: Configure an MS-DOS installation appropriately using the PATH statement in AUTOEXEX.BAT.

Knowledge-based question:

What is the correct syntax to set a path to the D: directory in AUTOEXEC.BAT?

A. SET PATH EQUAL TO D:

B. PATH D:

C. SETPATH D:

D. D:EQUALS PATH

Correct answer: B

Performance-based question:

Your company uses several DOS accounting applications that access a group of common utility programs. What is the best strategy for configuring the computers in the accounting department so that the accounting applications will always be able to access the utility programs?

A. Store all the utilities on a single floppy disk and make a copy of the disk for each computer in the accounting department.

B. Copy all the utilities to a directory on the C: drive of each computer in the accounting department and add a PATH statement pointing to this directory in the AUTOEXEC.BAT files.

C. Copy all the utilities to all application directories on each computer in the accounting department.

    D. Place all the utilities in the C: directory on each computer, because the C: directory is automatically included in the PATH statement when AUTOEXEC.BAT is executed.

    Correct answer: B

Even in this simple example, the superiority of the performance-based question is obvious. Whereas the knowledge-based question asks for a single fact, the performance-based question presents a real-life situation and requires that you make a decision based on this scenario. Thus, performance-based questions give more bang (validity) for the test author's buck (individual question).

Testing Job Performance

We have said that Microsoft certification focuses on timeliness and the ability to perform job tasks. We have also introduced the concept of performance-based questions, but even performance-based multiple-choice questions do not really measure performance. Another strategy is needed to test job skills.

Given unlimited resources, it is not difficult to test job skills. In an ideal world, Microsoft would fly MCP candidates to Redmond, place them in a controlled environment with a team of experts, and ask them to plan, install, maintain, and troubleshoot a Windows network. In a few days at most, the experts could reach a valid decision as to whether each candidate should or should not be granted MCDBA or MCSE status. Needless to say, this is not likely to happen.

Closer to reality, another way to test performance is by using the actual software and creating a testing program to present tasks and automatically grade a candidate's performance when the tasks are completed. This *cooperative* approach would be practical in some testing situations, but the same test that is presented to MCP candidates in Boston must also be available in Bahrain and Botswana. The most workable solution for measuring performance in today's testing environment is a *simulation* program. When the program is launched during a test, the candidate sees a simulation of the actual software that looks, and behaves, just like the real thing. When the testing software presents a task, the simulation program is launched and the candidate performs the required task. The testing software then grades the candidate's performance on the required task and moves to the next question. Microsoft has introduced simulation questions on the certification exam for Internet Information Server 4.0. Simulation questions provide many advantages over other testing methodologies, and simulations are expected to become increasingly important in the Microsoft certification program. For example, studies have shown that there is a very high correlation between the ability to perform simulated tasks on a computer-based test and the ability to perform the actual job tasks. Thus, simulations enhance the validity of the certification process.

Another truly wonderful benefit of simulations is in the area of test security. It is just not possible to cheat on a simulation question. In fact, you will be told exactly what tasks you are expected to perform on the test. How can a certification candidate cheat? By learning to perform the tasks? What a concept!

Study Strategies

There are appropriate ways to study for the different types of questions you will see on a Microsoft certification exam.

Knowledge-Based Questions

Knowledge-based questions require that you memorize facts. There are hundreds of facts inherent in every content area of every Microsoft certification exam. There are several keys to memorizing facts:

- **Repetition** The more times your brain is exposed to a fact, the more likely you are to remember it.

- **Association** Connecting facts within a logical framework makes them easier to remember.

- **Motor Association** It is often easier to remember something if you write it down or perform some other physical act, like clicking on a practice test answer.

We have said that the emphasis of Microsoft certification is job performance, and that there are very few knowledge-based questions on Microsoft certification exams. Why should you waste a lot of time learning filenames, IP address formulas, and other minutiae? Read on.

Performance-Based Questions

Most of the questions you will face on a Microsoft certification exam are performance-based scenario questions. We have discussed the superiority of these questions over simple knowledge-based questions, but you should remember that the job-task orientation of Microsoft certification extends the knowledge you need to pass the exams; it does not replace this knowledge. Therefore, the first step in preparing for scenario questions is to absorb as many facts relating to the exam content areas as you can. In other words, go back to the previous section and follow the steps to prepare for an exam composed of knowledge-based questions.

The second step is to familiarize yourself with the format of the questions you are likely to see on the exam. You can do this by answering the questions in this study guide, by using Microsoft assessment tests, or by using practice tests on the included CD-ROM. The day of your test is not the time to be surprised by the construction of Microsoft exam questions.

At best, performance-based scenario questions really do test certification candidates at a higher cognitive level than knowledge-based questions. At worst, these questions can test your reading comprehension and test-taking ability rather than your ability to use Microsoft products. Be sure to get in the habit of reading the question carefully to determine what is being asked.

The third step in preparing for Microsoft's scenario questions is to adopt the following attitude: Multiple-choice questions aren't really performance-based. It is all a cruel lie. These scenario questions are just knowledge-based questions with a story wrapped around them.

To answer a scenario question, you have to sift through the story to the underlying facts of the situation and apply your knowledge to determine the correct answer. This may sound silly at first, but the process we go through in solving real-life problems is quite similar. The key concept is that every scenario question (and every real-life problem) has a fact at its center, and if we can identify that fact, we can answer the question.

Simulations

Simulation questions really do measure your ability to perform job tasks. You must be able to perform the specified tasks. There are two ways to prepare for simulation questions:

1. Get experience with the actual software. If you have the resources, this is a great way to prepare for simulation questions.

2. Use the practice test on this book's accompanying CD-ROM. It contains simulation questions similar to those you will find on the Microsoft exam. This approach has the added advantage of grading your efforts, and you can find additional practice tests at **www.osborne.com** and **www.syngress.com**.

Signing Up

Signing up to take a Microsoft certification exam is easy. Sylvan Prometric or Vue operators in each country can schedule tests at any testing center. There are, however, a few things you should know:

- If you call Sylvan Prometric or Vue during a busy time, get a cup of coffee first, because you may be in for a long wait. The exam providers do an excellent job, but everyone in the world seems to want to sign up for a test on Monday morning.

- You will need your social security number or some other unique identifier to sign up for a test, so have it at hand.

- Pay for your test by credit card if at all possible. This makes things easier, and you can even schedule tests for the same day you call, if space is available at your local testing center.

- Know the number and title of the test you want to take before you call. This is not essential, and the Sylvan operators will help you if they can. Having this information in advance, however, speeds up and improves the accuracy of the registration process.

Taking the Test

Teachers have always told you not to try to cram for exams because it does no good. If you are faced with a knowledge-based test requiring only that you regurgitate facts, cramming can mean the difference between passing and failing. This is not the case, however, with Microsoft certification exams. If you don't know it the night before, don't bother to stay up and cram.

Instead, create a schedule and stick to it. Plan your study time carefully, and do not schedule your test until you think you are ready to succeed. Follow these guidelines on the day of your exam:

- Get a good night's sleep. The scenario questions you will face on a Microsoft certification exam require a clear head.

- Remember to take two forms of identification—at least one with a picture. A driver's license with your picture and social security or credit card is acceptable.

- Leave home in time to arrive at your testing center a few minutes early. It is not a good idea to feel rushed as you begin your exam.

- Do not spend too much time on any one question. You cannot mark and revisit questions on an adaptive test, so you must do your best on each question as you go.

- If you do not know the answer to a question, try to eliminate the obviously wrong answers and guess from the rest. If you can eliminate two out of four options, you have a 50 percent chance of guessing the correct answer.

- For scenario questions, follow the steps we outlined earlier. Read the question carefully and try to identify the facts at the center of the story.

Finally, we would advise anyone attempting to earn Microsoft MCDBA and MCSE certification to adopt a philosophical attitude. The Windows 2000 MCSE exam will be the most difficult MCSE exam ever to be offered. The questions will be at a higher cognitive level than seen on all previous MCSE exams. Therefore, even if you are the kind of person who never fails a test, you are likely to fail at least one Windows 2000 certification test somewhere along the way. Do not get discouraged. Microsoft wants to ensure the value of your certification. Moreover, it will attempt to do so by keeping the standard as high as possible. If Microsoft certification were easy to obtain, more people would have it, and it would not be so respected and so valuable to your future in the IT industry.

MCSE
MICROSOFT CERTIFIED SYSTEMS ENGINEER

1

Introduction to Installing, Configuring, and Administering Microsoft Windows 2000 Server

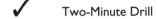
CERTIFICATION OBJECTIVES

W elcome to Windows 2000 Server. One of the most important topics you'll cover during your trek for the Windows 2000 MCSE is learning about Installing and Configuring Windows 2000 Server. In this book you'll learn how to install, configure, and troubleshoot the myriad of services and protocols included with Windows 2000.

CERTIFICATION OBJECTIVE 1.01

What Is Installing, Configuring, and Administering Microsoft Windows 2000 Server?

Windows 2000 is a major overhaul of the Windows NT 4.0 operating system. Although Windows 2000 has been built on the Windows NT 4.0 kernel, much of what you know about Windows NT 4.0 no longer applies in Windows 2000. Although the many services and protocols that were included with Windows NT 4.0 have been ported to Windows 2000, you will find their implementation has changed and the user interfaces have been altered significantly.

In addition to those services and protocols that you know and love from Windows NT 4.0, you will need to learn about the dozens of new features available only with Windows 2000. You will learn about new features such as the Remote Installation Service (RIS), Remote Storage Service (RSS), HTTP Printing, Publishing folders to the Active Directory, new Plug-and-Play features, and much more.

It might be tempting to try to draw a correlation between the NT 4.0 core exams and the new Windows 2000 core exams. In so doing, you might conclude that Exam 70-215, the core exam that covers installing and configuring Windows 2000 Server, is a replacement for the old Windows NT 4.0 Server exam. However, the Windows 2000 Server exam goes far beyond the basic "Here's how to install and how it's supposed to work" approach of the Windows NT 4.0 exams. You'll need a deep understanding of the services and protocols, how they work together, and, most important, how to troubleshoot problems when they arise.

exam
Ⓦatch

Pay close attention to the prerequisites Microsoft lists for each exam on its Web site. The exam will assume that you are already expert at the technologies that are listed as prerequisites, and the questions may come from material that is included in the prerequisite courses.

Target Audience

Microsoft's stated "target audience" for this exam is somewhat different from the intended audience for the NT Server exam from the Windows NT 4.0 MCSE track, for which Microsoft lists no prerequisites on the exam preparation Web page. There has been a lot of talk, with the advent of the Windows 2000 certification track, about Microsoft's desire to "raise the bar" and restore the MCSE to the status of a "premium" certification. This is reflected in the suggested prerequisites.

Experienced Networking Professionals

According to the Microsoft Web site and documentation, exam candidates are presumed to be networking personnel operating in medium to very large computing environments with a minimum of a year's experience in administering and implementing Windows networking components and supporting 200 or more users in five or more physical locations. It is also presumed that the exam taker is familiar with typical network services and applications, such as file and print sharing, databases, messaging services, proxy services and/or firewalls, dial-in remote access servers, Web hosting, and desktop management and control.

It is important to consider these prerequisites when you prepare for the exam and read the official Microsoft Study materials. If you do not have the requisite background in networking and in Microsoft Network operating systems, you might find the exams very difficult to pass, and find evening studying for the exams a very difficult proposition.

on the
Ü o b   *Microsoft's mission is to make Windows 2000 the Internet application platform of choice. In order to attain that goal, Microsoft Certified Systems Engineers must be expert in Internet technologies. These technologies typically include Virtual Private Networks, Web sites that tie into database servers, Internet e-mail and groupware applications, proxy services, and firewalls for security. This means, for the Windows 2000 exams, that these subjects will be considered fair game even if they are not explicitly covered within the scope of a particular class or exam.*

What If You're New to Networking?

This does not mean that if you don't have on-the-job experience as a network administrator you won't be able to pass the Windows 2000 exams. It does mean that if you don't meet the description of the exam's "target audience," you will need to study harder, and in particular you will need to get more hands-on practice in working with the products.

This book contains a large number of practical exercises that walk you through the steps of procedures common to working network professionals. In order to really understand the concepts and skills covered by the exam, it is essential that you do more than read through the exercises; you must work through them on a Windows 2000 computer. This can be done on a relatively simple home network, and we highly recommend that you consider setting up a two- or three-system lab if you don't have access to a network on the job or in a classroom situation. The cost of doing so is an investment that can quickly pay for itself in terms of time saved in obtaining the certification.

In certain scenarios you will have to be able to understand and implement configurations in a multidomain, multisegment network. If you cannot afford several computers, you can simulate a much larger network by using some very helpful software from VMware. The VMware software will allow you to install multiple instances of an operating system and allows them to run concurrently on a single machine. Each instance is network enabled and allows you to simulate much larger environments than you might otherwise be able to. For more information about VMware, check out their Web site at: **www.vmware.com**.

exam
ⓦatch

If you are new to networking or computing in general, you should make it a practice to learn the language and the issues that are important to network professionals. Seek out magazines and Web sites that focus on networking, and on Windows 2000 in particular.

Exam Questions

The Windows 2000 exams will involve questions that require a higher cognitive level to arrive at the correct solution. The emphasis in writing these questions is on scenario-based problems that a network professional could expect to face on the job, in the real world. The Microsoft exam writers are attempting to formulate questions that measure practice skills, rather than simple memorization of facts and figures. The goal is to map each test item directly to one of the stated exam objectives; this is why it is so important that test takers carefully review the objectives posted on Microsoft's Web site.

The exam questions also will be rotated in and out of the exam pool frequently in order to protect exam security. One of the major challenges Microsoft has had to face is that of "Cram and Dump" Web sites, book publishers, and practice test providers. Microsoft has been very aware of their existence, and one of their stated goals in the development of the Windows 2000 exams is to create a large and ever changing pool of test questions in an effort to thwart these individuals.

Cognitive Skills

Let's take a look at how the questions for the Windows 2000 certification exams are put together, and the objectives of those who write the test items. Microsoft has invested a great deal of time and effort in ensuring that test questions are valid, fair, and accurately measure knowledge and skills required to perform the job of network administrator.

The Windows 2000 exam questions are constructed based on the premise that job duties require different levels of cognitive skills, all the way from raw memorization to the ability to analyze a set of specifications, diagnose problems, design solutions, and evaluate the effectiveness of those solutions.

The cognitive levels, also called cognitive domain objectives by educational psychologists, are commonly organized into a hierarchy, as shown in Figure 1-1.

Knowledge (that is, knowing or memorizing factual information such as "You use an unattended text file to carry out an unattended installation") is the very lowest level of learning. It is, of course, important that a network administrator have this knowledge. However, in the field, you would not be expected to just recite an answer to the question "What type of file do I use to carry out an unattended

FIGURE 1-1

Hierarchy of
cognitive levels.

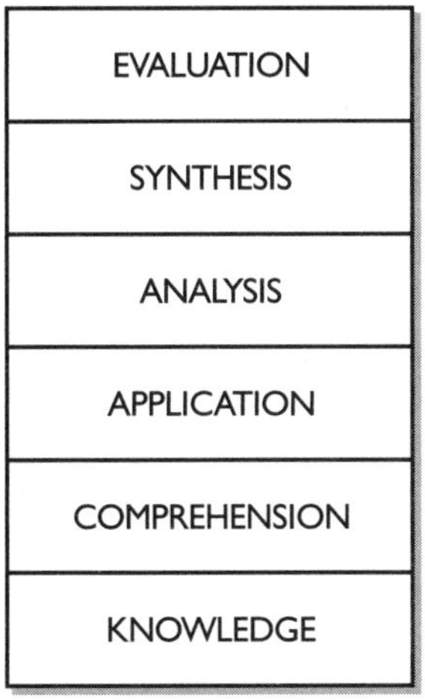

EVALUATION
SYNTHESIS
ANALYSIS
APPLICATION
COMPREHENSION
KNOWLEDGE

installation?" Rather, you would need to know how to construct and configure an unattended.txt file, a udf file, and know how to use the syntax included in those files. You will also need to understand where to place the files and how to call the files from a command-line argument.

A question that tests a higher cognitive level, while still requiring that you know the same facts, would be more effectively designed as a scenario-based item, as in this example:

You have upgraded your Windows NT 4.0 Server computer to Windows 2000 Advanced Server. You would like to create a Stripe Set with Parity on your new Windows 2000 Installation, but you do not find that option available to you. What must you do in order to allow you to create a new Stripe Set with Parity on your Windows 2000 Advanced Server Computer?

1. Uninstall Windows 2000 and create the Stripe Set with Parity on a Windows NT 4.0 installation, and then upgrade to Windows 2000.

2. You must first install the ftdisk2k.sys driver in order to create a new Stripe Set with parity on your Windows 2000 Advanced Server

3. You need at least five physical disks to create a Stripe Set with Parity in Windows 2000.

4. You must first upgrade the basic disks to Dynamic Disks to create the Stripe Set with Parity.

In this example, you must have knowledge about multiple subjects in order to answer the question correctly. You need to know about the effect of upgrading a Windows NT 4.0 computer to Windows 2000. You need to know how many disks are required to create a Stripe Set with parity. You need to understand what basic and dynamic disks are, and what the differences are between them. You need to know the names of the device drivers that run the various disk-related system services. Then, with this knowledge, you must be able to integrate what you know and be able to come up with an answer that will solve the problem. (By the way, the correct answer is 4.)

exam
🐵 a t c h

One clue as to what cognitive level you should expect to be measured in regard to specific exam topics is the verb used in the objective to which the question is mapped.

In writing exam objectives, Microsoft uses specific verbs to indicate the skill—and the cognitive level—which the exam items will measure. For instance, one of the exam objectives for Exam 70-215 is: "Monitor, configure, and troubleshoot disks and volumes."

The verbs in this objective would indicate that you will be tested at the application level, measuring your ability to implement a procedure. Verbs such as the following also suggest that the exam items will be at least at the application level of cognition:

- Customize
- Monitor
- Enable
- Manage

Table 1-1 lists some of the verbs that correspond to various cognitive levels. When an objective—or a question—contains these words, it gives you a clue as to what level is being measured by the test item.

The Windows 2000 certification exams are designed to measure the test taker's ability to perform job functions and solve real-world problems, rather than just testing knowledge. The advantage of testing at higher cognitive levels is that questions requiring those levels of cognition also incorporate knowledge gained at

TABLE 1-1	Cognitive Level	Corresponding Verbs
Cognitive Levels and Corresponding Verbs	Evaluation	Assess, summarize, weigh, decide, apply standards
	Synthesis	Design, formulate, integrate, predict, propose, generalize, show relationship
	Analysis	Analyze, compare, contrast, diagnose, diagram, discriminate, conclude
	Application	Apply, choose, demonstrate, perform a procedure, solve, plot, calculate, change, interpret, operate
	Comprehension	Distinguish between, discuss, estimate, explain, indicate, paraphrase, give examples
	Knowledge	Define, locate, recall, recognize, state, match, label, identify

the lower levels. If you are able to perform a task properly, it can be assumed that you also have the knowledge upon which that performance is based.

Question Formats

Within the parameters of the type of computerized testing used by Microsoft to administer the certification exams, there are necessarily limits on the question formats that can be used. The ideal testing environment, in terms of accurately assessing the ability to perform job duties, would probably be a set of live practical exercises in which the student is given specific tasks to perform and is evaluated based on how quickly, efficiently, and accurately they are performed. Some vendors (such as Cisco) actually use this testing model; unfortunately, it creates a situation in which exams are prohibitively expensive and time-consuming, and thus a significant number of candidates who might have mastered the skills are prevented from obtaining the certification because of the high cost or investment of time required.

The Microsoft exams attempt to evaluate the ability to perform by using scenario-based multiple-choice questions and computer simulations to emulate the hands-on environment as closely as possible. Questions are reviewed by networking professionals who are working in the field and have firsthand experience at performing the job duties being tested by the exam questions. After the proposed questions are reviewed for technical accuracy, clarity, and relevance to objectives, beta testing is done and input is solicited from those who take the beta exams. The results of the beta tests allow Microsoft to determine which questions are most relevant and the level of difficulty, and thus make the decision as to which questions will be included on the live exam.

All questions on exam 70-215 will deal with the installation, configuration, and troubleshooting of Windows 2000 Server and Advanced Server components.

CERTIFICATION OBJECTIVE 1.02

A High-Level View of Select New Windows 2000 Features Covered on the 70-215 Exam

Let's take a look at some of the most important features and services that are new to Windows 2000, which you should know about for the exam. In this section we'll take a quick high-level look at some of these new features to whet your appetite for what is to come as you read and learn the material in this book.

Remote Installation Services

The Windows 2000 Remote Installation Services allow you a way to create an image of Windows 2000 Professional you can use to install Windows 2000 Professional on your network client systems. This image actually consists of the installation files from the Windows 2000 Professional CD-ROM. You can customize this image to allow for granular control over the desktop environment the user will have after the installation.

After installing the RIS Server from the Add/Remove Programs applet in the Control Panel, you can start configuring the RIS Server and the Windows 2000 Professional images you wish to create by opening the Run command and typing:

```
Risetup
```

The Remote Installation Services Server setup program begins. You'll see the Wizard welcome you, as shown in Figure 1-2.

FIGURE 1-2

The RIS Setup Wizard welcome screen

Note that before you can configure the RIS Server you must have Active Directory installed and configured. In addition, a DHCP and a DNS Server must be up and running. Finally, you'll need the Windows 2000 Professional source media and a RIS Startup disk or PXE (Preboot eXecution Environment)-compliant network adapter. Be sure you know these requirements before starting your RIS configuration and installation!

After your RIS Server is installed and configured, you may want to create not only some customized images that provide a custom desktop environment, but also preinstalled programs that will be ready to use as soon as the installation is completed.

To create a custom distribution image you need to run the RIPprep program. You can get RIPrep started by opening the Run command and typing:

```
C:\<system_root>\system32\reminst\riprep.exe [where C: is your boot partition]
```

The RIPrep Wizard welcomes you (see Figure 1-3.)

The Wizard will walk you through the process of creating the custom image and it will copy the image to the RIS Server of choice. Be aware that you can only create images of the C: partition on a computer, so the operating system and all program files included on the images must be on drive C:

The RIPrep Installation Wizard welcome screen

Spend extra time learning how the Remote Installation Service Server works in Windows 2000. You are sure to get questions on this new feature, and the best way to understand it is to go through the practice exercises in this book on your own network.

on the **job** *The Remote Installation Service will be a great boon to the network administrator who wishes to create customized installations of Windows 2000 Professional on his or her network. This topic will not only get a lot of coverage on the Windows 2000 exams, but will also save you a lot of time and effort on the job.*

Distributed File System

The Windows 2000 Distributed File System provides you a method to centralize the organization of the shared resources on your network. In the past, shared resources were most often accessed via the Network Neighborhood applet, and users would have to wade through a number of domains and servers in order to access the shared folder or printer that they sought. Network users also had to remember where the obscure bit of information was stored, including both a cryptic server name and share name. Most frequently, there was no rhyme or reason to how servers were named, and even less so for how the shares were named.

The Distributed File System (Dfs) allows you to simplify the organization of your network resources by placing them in central shares that are accessed via a single server. The information may be located on multiple servers dispersed throughout the network, even over the expanse of thousands of miles, but the fortunate user of the Dfs tree sees only a meaningful hierarchy of folders located on a single file server.

You can create a new Dfs root by accessing the Distributed File System console from the Administrative Tools menu. The first time you open the console, you will not see any Dfs objects. Right-click Distributed File System in the left pane, go down to New, and then click Dfs Root. This starts the wizard that you see in Figure 1-4.

When creating a new Dfs root, you decide whether you want it to become a domain Dfs root or a stand-alone Dfs root. While both allow you to centrally organize the shared resources on your network, there are many advantages to creating and using the domain Dfs root in your organization. These Dfs trees are fault tolerant, and the contents are automatically replicated to other servers in the domain. Also, a domain Dfs root–based tree provides for load balancing. When a Dfs client makes a request for resources contained in the tree, the client is sent a list

FIGURE 1-4

Creating a New
Dfs root using
the Dfs Root
Wizard

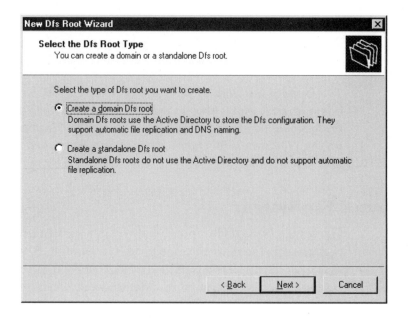

of servers that participate in the Dfs replication network. The client randomly selects
a server from the list to access the desired information.

The Distributed File System takes advantage of the new File Replication Service
(FRS). You will find the FRS to be a tremendous improvement over its poor cousin,
the Replicator Service, which you distrusted in Windows NT 4.0. Learn how to
implement both domain Dfs and stand-alone Dfs roots. Be sure to go through the
exercises about Dfs. It's something that will surely rear its head on your Windows
2000 Server exam.

Driver Signing and Resource Management

One of the most frustrating things about Windows operating systems is the fact that
any software vendors can overwrite critical system level files with their own versions.
The problem has been that sometimes the vendor's version of a system level file is
buggy or flawed, and it prevents the operating system from functioning correctly,
or in the worst case, would prevent it from starting at all. Windows 2000 uses a
procedure called Driver Signing that allows the operating system to recognize files
that have been approved by Microsoft to be functional and of high quality. With

this seal of approval, you should be confident that installing applications containing signed files will not disable your computer.

You can customize how the operating system will respond during the installation of unsigned drivers. Right-click My Computer and click the Hardware tab. Located on the Hardware tab is a button named Driver Signing. Click that button and you will see what appears in Figure 1-5.

Driver Signing allows for three responses: Warn, Block, or Ignore. You choose the level of protection you want from the list provided. The default setting is to Warn. You should be very wary of installing any unsigned files to your computer, as the results are unpredictable, as you have experienced with previous versions of Windows operating systems.

exam
ⓦatch

The Drivers are signed using a digital signature, much like the digital signatures that are used in IPSec or SSL or any other signing process that includes the creation of a digest via a hash algorithm. The signature is not added directly to the file code itself, but rather stored in a .cat file. The .inf file that is used to install the program maintains an association between the .cat file and the .inf file.

FIGURE 1-5

The Driver
Signing Options
dialog box

System Monitor

In Windows NT 4.0 you learned how to monitor your servers and the network using Performance Monitor. In Windows 2000 the Performance Monitor has transposed itself into what is now known as Performance, which can be accessed via the Administrative Tools menu. Performance actually contains two important administrative objects: the System Monitor and Performance Logs and Alerts. Figure 1-6 shows the Performance console.

The System Monitor looks very much like the Performance Monitor provided with Windows NT 4.0. However, there are some subtle differences in its functionality, so make sure to pay special attention to these differences in Chapter 8, "Managing, Monitoring, and Optimizing System Performance, Reliability, and Availability."

FIGURE 1-6

The Performance console displaying the System Monitor

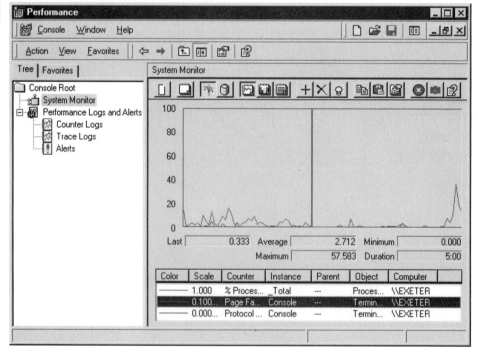

In addition to the System Monitor node in the Performance console, we now have the Performance Logs and Alerts. It is now much easier to configure network alerts during periods of noteworthy activity on your server. Counter logs are maintained in a similar fashion as they were in Windows NT 4.0, but the procedure for configuring the Counter logs is a bit different. Trace logs are much easier to configure in Windows 2000 because you now can set them up from the console, rather than having to edit the registry as you had to do in Windows NT 4.0.

Figure 1-7 displays the contents of the Alerts node, and the green icon for the Down Server alert indicates that the alert is actively monitoring for the selected performance objects.

Disk Quotas

Disk hogs are the bane of the network administrator's existence. In Windows NT 4.0 there was no way, without using third-party add-on products, to monitor and control the amount of disk usage on a per user basis. This could become extremely annoying when you tried to provide fault tolerance for your user data by having users save all their files to a central server, and then having one or two users monopolize virtually all the disk space.

FIGURE 1-7

The Performance console with the Alerts node selected

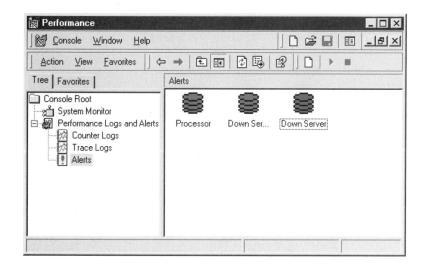

Windows 2000 comes with a disk quota feature that allows you to control users' disk consumption on a per user/per partition basis. To begin setting disk quotas for your users, right-click any partition in either Windows Explorer or the My Computer object. Click Properties and then click the Quota tab. You will see what appears in Figure 1-8.

On the Quota tab properties sheet you enable quota management for the partition and then set default values for disk space consumption limits for your users. You can also choose to log when quotas are exceeded and when they reach their warning limit.

However, you set quotas on a per user or group basis. To define the users or groups limited by quota management, click the Quota Entries button. You will see what appears in Figure 1-9.

It is here in the Quota Entries window that you add users or groups to your Quota Management scheme. Remember for the exam that the quotas are set on a

FIGURE 1-8

The Quota tab on the Partition Properties sheet

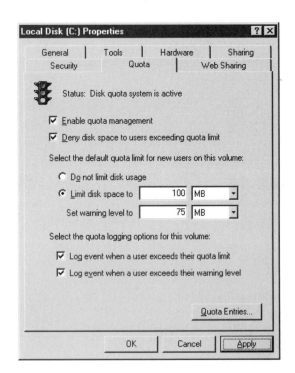

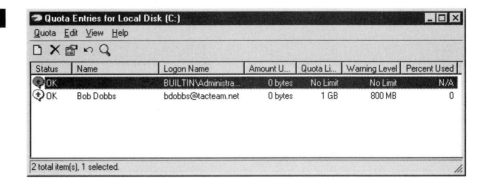

FIGURE 1-9

Defining a list of
users or groups
limited by quota
management

per partition basis and not a per server basis. It is easy to miss a question if you
forget this important fact.

Local Group Policy

Group Policy provides the key technologies for change management and desktop
control on the Windows 2000 platform. You are familiar with the control you had in
Windows NT 4.0 using System Policies. Group Policy is similar to System Policies
but allows you a much higher level of granular configuration management over your
network. Group Policy can be applied to an entire organization via its integration
with the Active Directory, or to a single machine via Local Group Policy.

The subject of Group Policy as it applies to entire organizations will get major
coverage in the Active Directory and Security Design exams. It is more likely that
you will need to be aware of the features and functionality of Local Group Policy
on the Windows 2000 Server exam.

Local Group Policy can be administered by opening the Run command and typing:

```
gpedit.msc
```

Then click OK and you'll see what appears in Figure 1-10.

Via Local Group Policy, you as an administrator on the Local Machine can lock
down the desktops of machines that are not actively participating in a Windows 2000
domain. You can control Security and software settings, Internet Explorer behavior,
log-on and log-off scripts, and a myriad of registry-based settings via Administrative
Templates that contain hundreds of customized entries allowing you finely tuned
control over users' computing environment.

FIGURE 1-10

The Local
Group Policy
management
console

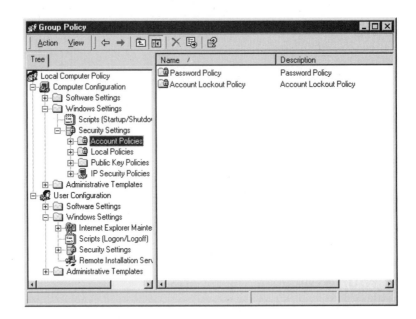

SCENARIO & SOLUTION

Will RIS be important to know for the Windows 2000 Exams?	Absolutely! Microsoft wants us to know how to plan and execute unattended and automated installations in order to reduce the total cost of ownership related to Windows 2000. Spend some extra study time learning about RIS Server and RIS client installation.
Is the Distributed File System the same in Windows 2000 as it was with Windows NT 4.0?	No! It is much better. You can now integrate the Dfs with the Active Directory and create a fault tolerant Dfs hierarchy. The Dfs tree can be copied to other servers and create a fault-tolerant directory structure for your network clients.
Can I monitor disk quotas for an entire server on a per user basis?	No. You can monitor disk quotas for users on each partition or volume. Windows 2000 does not provide a mechanism for you to track disk usages for an entire server.

CERTIFICATION OBJECTIVE 1.03

Overview of Exam 70-215

For a list of the learning objectives for Exam 70-215, see the Microsoft Web site at **http://www.microsoft.com/mcp/exam/stat/SP70-215.htm**. The objectives are somewhat broad, and you'll note that they are performance-based. This does not mean that you don't need to know any of the theory behind the concepts being tested. It does mean that knowing only the theory, without having ever put it into practice by working with the operating system, will make it difficult or even impossible for you to pass the exam.

The objectives are divided into logical categories.

Installing Windows 2000 Server

There are a number of ways you can install Windows 2000 Server and Advanced Server. You already know from your Windows NT 4.0 training that you could install via local CD-ROM, from the local hard disk, by copying the i386 folder to the local drive, or via a network install from a network installation share point. You could also install Windows NT 4.0 Server via an unattended installation by using a text-based file that would answer installation questions for you. These methods are available with Windows 2000 as well, and there are many more options available to you when installing Windows 2000 Server family operating systems.

Other automated installation options for Windows 2000 include the Remote Installation Services and Disk Imaging and preparation services. You will also need to know how to apply Windows 2000 Service packs, which will be done a lot differently than the way it was done in Windows NT 4.0. Of course, you'll need to know how to troubleshoot a failed installation.

Installing, Configuring, and Troubleshooting Access to Resources

Resource access controls were a big topic in Windows NT 4.0, and will be even more so with Windows 2000 Server. You will need to have a good understanding of NTFS 5.0, which is the version of NTFS included with Windows 2000. In addition to the access controls that you can place on files and folders via NTFS, you will need to understand how share permissions are implemented on Windows 2000 Servers. While the same general principles apply to Windows 2000 as they did to Windows NT 4.0, there are some subtle, and major differences on how both NTFS and share permissions are implemented. Know these differences.

Much of printer management is similar in Windows 2000; however, there are some interface changes of which you should be aware. In addition, the HTTP printing feature is all new with Windows 2000 and definitely something at which you will want to be an expert at for your Windows 2000 exam.

The Distributed File System (Dfs) allows you to create a central share point for shared resources located through the organization on a number of different servers. Understand how Dfs works and doesn't work, because you will definitely be tested on this new feature.

On the Windows NT 4.0 Server exam, almost all of the content was focused on LAN implementation. The Windows 2000 Server exam melts together local network and file system access controls with Web-based access controls via Internet Information Server 5.0. Web Services are an integral element of Windows 2000, and you should be able to configure access and access controls for resources via local file sharing protocols and access controls as well as Web-based protocols.

Configuring and Troubleshooting Hardware Devices and Drivers

One of the major improvements seen in Windows 2000 is the operating system's ability to protect itself from rogue drivers. These third-party drivers are frequently the source of consternation for legions of network administrators. Learn about Windows 2000 Driver Signing and how to configure the operating system's response when a third-party application tries to overwrite critical operating system files.

Windows 2000 now features one of the nicer elements of Win9x, the ability to accurately report on hardware and resource status. Learn to use the Computer Management console to optimize and troubleshoot your Windows 2000 hardware configuration.

Managing, Monitoring, and Optimizing System Performance, Reliability, and Availability

You are already acquainted with the Windows NT 4.0 Performance Monitor. Windows 2000 comes with a new and improved version of the Performance Monitor referred to as the System Monitor. The System Monitor is bundled into an MMC known as Performance that you find in the Administrative Tools menu. It looks very much like the Performance Monitor, but has many new and enhanced features. Be sure to understand how to use the new features.

Managing, Configuring, and Troubleshooting Storage Use

Throughout the history of Microsoft operating systems, we've learned about disks and partitioning. You learned about Primary Partitions, Extended Partitions, Logical Drives within Extended Partitions, and Active Partitions. You now need to add to your knowledge of drive partitioning and learn how to use Dynamic Disks. Be sure to know the difference between Basic and Dynamic Disks.

Something administrators always have to deal with on file and profile servers is how much disk space is consumed by user data. Windows 2000 allows you to enable disk quotas that will warn users about, and then prevent them from using, any more disk space than their allotted amount. They will have to delete the flotsam and jetsam they've accrued in their Internet wanderings.

Most important of all in your Storage use tasks is mastering the replacement for the Windows NT 4.0 Disk Administrator: the Windows 2000 Logical Disk Manager. The Disk Management Console is like the Windows NT 4.0 Disk Administrator on steroids. Be sure to master the differences between the two, and to know the differences in how special partitions, such as volume sets, stripe sets, and stripe sets with parity are handled on Windows 2000 machines.

Configuring and Troubleshooting Windows 2000 Network Connections

While much of the networking you learned in Windows NT 4.0 will still apply, perhaps the biggest area of change and improvement is seen in the Windows 2000 Network Services arena. There are many new and improved features that you must know and be expert at implementing in order to pass the Windows 2000 Server exam.

Know about the Internet Connection Service (ICS). If you have used Windows 98SE you may already be familiar with some of the components of ICS and how it works. If not, spend extra time with this service. Windows 2000 also includes Network Address Translation (NAT), which provides IP address translation in a similar fashion to ICS, but is more robust and is used on larger, corporate networks. Both ICS and NAT translate private IP addresses to public IP addresses so that multiple computers located on a private network can access Internet resources without needing a public IP address.

Virtual Private Networks (VPNs) are becoming so popular, and so important to businesses of virtually any size, that a thorough knowledge of how Windows 2000 handles VPNs is crucial. Know how to install and configure Windows 2000 VPNs to protect network communications over a public network.

The Windows NT 4.0 RAS Server has been expanded and fortified. In Windows 2000 it is now known as the Routing and Remote Access Service (RRAS) and provides many new features; just this service will take you many hours of study to learn and get up to date on. You can be sure that there will be a lot of questions related to the Routing and Remote Access Service, so spend extra time learning its features and functionality.

The Terminal Server required a special version of the operating system in Windows NT 4.0. In Windows 2000 you'll find Terminal Services included with the basic Server operating system. One of the great improvements of Windows 2000 Terminal Services is that it is integrated with the Windows 2000 operating system, and not an "add-on" service on top of the OS, as it was with Windows NT 4.0. Learn how to take advantage of Terminal Services so your users will have the power of a Windows 2000 desktop operating environment as well as a network management and troubleshooting tool.

Implementing, Monitoring, and Troubleshooting Security

Windows 2000 is all about centralized management. One of the things you want to be most concerned about is central management of network security. This is perhaps the most important, and the most difficult topic you will deal with in your Windows 2000 studies. The entire security infrastructure has been revamped from what you knew about in Windows NT 4.0.

FROM THE CLASSROOM

Hardware Skills Development

During the process of becoming an MCSE, you will need to learn about basic hardware concepts such as RAM, hard disks, floppy drives, CD-ROM drives, sound cards, network interface cards, motherboards, system BIOS, and other devices. A book can teach the general principles on how to work with these hardware devices, but you must get actual hands-on practice with installing and configuring hardware devices. If you are new, and even if you are an experienced system administrator, you should purchase a machine that you can build and tear down regularly. This will provide you with an excellent test bed to hone your hardware skills.

—*Thomas W. Shinder, M.D., MCSE, MCP+I, MCT*

Most of what you know about auditing and account policy is the same, but implemented in a different way. Know these differences and how to efficiently create an audit policy for your Windows 2000 network.

The Encrypting File System takes advantage of the added feature set provided by the NTFS 5.0 file system and allows users to encrypt data that can be decrypted only by themselves and selected Recovery Agents on the network.

Group Policy is similar to the System Policies you knew and loved in Windows NT 4.0. However, Group Policy allows you a level of granular control over the user environment that you never had in Windows NT 4.0. Group Policy will be a major subject covered on the Active Directory and Security Design exams, but you will need to know how it is used on the Windows 2000 Server exam as well. Focus on local policy for this exam, and know how Windows NT 4.0 System Policies work on Windows 2000 network clients (and vice versa).

exam
⚙atch

Although much of the knowledge and skill you may have gained from working with NT in the past is transferable to Windows 2000, it is imperative that you not make assumptions that similar tasks are accomplished in the same way in Windows 2000. Nothing substitutes for hands-on experience using the operating system.

CERTIFICATION OBJECTIVE 1.04

What We'll Cover in This Book

Each of the exam topics covered in the 70-215 list of objectives will be addressed in this book. However, we will go beyond the basic how-to aspect even though the certification objectives are written almost exclusively as performance-based statements. We know that to really understand what you're doing, you need to know the theory behind it. If you have many long years of on-the-job experience working with Windows NT 4.0, and have worked a great deal with extra add-on software and third-party products, you may already be familiar with the concepts behind these task-oriented objectives. Otherwise, it will benefit you both to read the explanatory text carefully and to perform the exercises contained in each chapter.

Knowledge

In the beginning of each chapter, we will give you a foundation of knowledge upon which conceptual comprehension and practices skills can be built. This includes definitions of new terms, explanations of processes, and discussion of relationships between components.

Topic Tie-ins

We will cross-reference subjects that appear elsewhere in the book, that tie in to the topic of the chapter, and/or that will aid you in understanding the material to be presented in the chapter.

For "Newbies" and "Old Pros"

For those who are brand new to the world of Microsoft network operating systems, each chapter will contain a section that provides background information that, although not specifically covered by the Windows 2000 exam objectives, is essential to understanding the chapter topic(s). For experienced administrators, there will be special tips for Windows NT 4.0 pros, pointing out the areas in which Windows 2000 differs (subtly or drastically) from its predecessor, and warning you of common pitfalls that you may encounter in making the transition to Microsoft's new way of doing things.

Concepts

In addition to basic knowledge-based information such as definitions and relationships, we will provide an overview of the concepts behind the skills-based exercises. For example, setting up a RIS server involves a skill set. The concept of Remote Installation Services requires that you understand concepts of disk partitioning, TCP/IP, DHCP, hardware addresses, and Active Directory before you can successfully implement one.

As much as possible, we will attempt to make all abstract concepts as easy to understand as possible, using analogies and graphics.

Practical Skills

The heart of Windows 2000 exam preparation is development of practical skills—the ability not just to know about the operating system, but also to use it to perform common network administration tasks. The exams are performance based, as is obvious from the wording of the exam objectives, almost all of which use action verbs such as "configure," "install," "monitor," "troubleshoot," "manage," "create," "remove," "implement," and the like.

More so than with the Windows NT 4.0 exams, it is imperative that you do the practical exercises in each chapter, that you experiment with various settings and options, that you get hands-on experience in performing the tasks about which you read.

Many of the exam questions will be relatively simple for those who have worked with the product, and almost impossible to answer for those who haven't gone through the processes themselves. There are so many different dialog boxes and wizard-based procedures, that hands-on experience cannot be adequately replaced with textbook or practice test simulations. Many wizards branch off, depending on the options selected; exam simulation software cannot possible prepare you for all the possibilities. In this book, we attempt to simulate the Windows 2000 working environment as much as possible by liberal use of screenshots and detailed descriptions of what to expect in response to particular actions or commands; however, there is no substitute for doing it yourself.

CERTIFICATION OBJECTIVE 1.05

Microsoft Operating System Terminology

For those who are beginning their study of Windows 2000 with little exposure to real-life networking and operating systems, one of the most important (and perhaps most tedious) tasks is to "learn the language." At times, as you read through the study material, you may feel as if you're floating in a sea of acronyms and unfamiliar words.

In this book, our policy is to spell out all acronyms in full the first time they appear, and to define new terms within the text whenever possible. However, a term that is well known to a networking professional may be new to you, and in a book this size, trying to flip back through the pages to find the first occurrence of a word could be a time-consuming process.

We suggest that you make liberal use of the glossary. If you run across a word or term whose meaning you're not sure of, and that's not obvious from the context, don't just skim over it and hope it will be clarified later. Taking the time to look it up may seem to slow down your study, but in actuality it's one of the best ways to ensure that you remember the meaning later.

Double Meanings

Don't despair if you find that definitions are not always absolutely consistent from one source to the next. Within the computer industry and even within the more narrowly defined networking world, there are many subspecialty areas that have their own brand of jargon.

For example, you may hear the word "segment" used to describe a length of cable, or the computers that are connected to a length of backbone cable. You will hear the same word used, in discussions of TCP/IP, to describe the "chunks" into which data is broken down to be transmitted across the network. Likewise, "cell" means one thing in the context of wireless communications, and something else in a discussion of ATM technology.

This Scenario & Solution grid lists some of the more confusing double meanings that you are likely to encounter in your studies of networking infrastructure fundamentals.

SCENARIO & SOLUTION	
What is a segment?	In discussions of TCP/IP, "segment" often refers to the group of computers located on one side of a router, or sometimes a group of computers within the same collision domain. In TCP/IP terminology, "segment" can also be used to describe the chunk of data sent by TCP over the network (roughly equivalent to the usage of "packet" or "frame").
What does "server" mean? I've seen it used in a variety of different contexts.	The word "server" can take on a variety of different meanings. A server can be a physical computer. Such as "Check out that Server over in the Accounting Department". A server can also represent a particular software package. For example, Microsoft Exchange 2000 is a mail and groupware Server application. Often server applications are just referred to as "servers," as in "Check out what the problem is with the mail server." The term "server" is also used to refer to any computer that is currently sharing its resources on the network. In this context, all computers, whether they are Windows 3x or Windows 2000 computers, can be servers on a network.
What does "remote" mean? I thought it had to do with using RAS.	The word "remote" can take on a number of different meanings depending on the context. In the case of an individual computer, the computer you are sitting in front of is sometimes referred to as being "local" while any other computer is considered "remote." In this context any machine but your own is considered a remote computer. In discussions related to network configuration and design, "remote" may refer to segments and machines that are on the far side of a router. In this context, all machines on your physical segment are considered "local" and machines located on other physical segments are referred to as "remote." "Remote" is often used in the context of the Remote Access Service, or RAS. The remote access service allows for dial-up access to networks via telephone lines. In this case, the term "remote" might refer to a network client or server that is separate from its destination via telephone lines.

SCENARIO & SOLUTION

Why does the word "gateway" seem to have two different meanings?	"Gateway" is used in networking to refer to a router or a computer functioning as one, the "way out" of the network or subnet, to get to another network. The word "gateway" is also used in regard to software that connects a system using one protocol to a system using a different protocol, such as the Systems Network Architecture (SNA) software that allows a PC LAN to connect to an IBM mainframe, or the Gateway Services for NetWare used to provide a way for Microsoft clients to go through a Windows NT or Windows 2000 server to access files on a Novell file server. You will also occasionally see the term "Gateway" used to describe a brand of computer. In this case, no specific networking technologies are referred to.
Why do they call it "Group Policy" if you can't apply it to groups?	It's sort of funny, because you could apply the Windows NT 4.0 System Policy to groups, as well as systems, but you can't directly apply Windows 2000 Group Policy to groups, although you can apply it to systems. Some of the confusion comes from the change of names applied to different groups in Windows 2000. You can apply Group Policy to sites, domains, and organizational units. Each of these represents a group of objects, so Group Policy is applied to the group of objects contained in each of these entities. Group Policy cannot be directly applied to Security Groups that are similar to the groups you are used to working with in Windows NT 4.0. However, by using Group Policy Filtering, you can successfully apply Group Policy to individual Security Groups.

For Networking Newbies

If you are new to computer networking and operating systems, we recommend that you take a course or study a good book about basic networking and operating system concepts. Even if you are following the Windows 2000 MCSE certification track, it would benefit you to study one of the NT 4.0 Networking Essentials study guides and/or take the Windows 2000 Network and Operating Systems Essentials course. If you are new to computers in general, you might also consider studying about computer hardware and software along the lines of the CompTIA A+ or Network+ curricula.

You will find that familiarizing yourself with basic networking concepts—such as physical topologies, characteristics of different cable and other media types, the popular networking architectures such as Ethernet, AppleTalk, and Token Ring, and often referenced networking standards and models such as the OSI, DoD, and

Windows models and the IEEE 802 specifications—will benefit you in many ways. Basic operating system and computing concepts such as RAM, ROM, partitions, files folders, disks, user interfaces, and programs must be second nature to you. Not only will the knowledge provide a solid foundation for the material you will be studying in the process of obtaining Microsoft certification, but also most employers will expect you, as an MCP or MCSE, to recognize these fundamental concepts.

The very best investment a Microsoft operating system and networking neophyte can make, though, is to build your own network from the ground up. Even a simple two-computer thinnet network will give you a taste of the challenges faced by Enterprise pros in the field, and many of the setup, maintenance, and troubleshooting scenarios associated with large production networks can be simulated on a smaller scale with a small home network.

There are a number of excellent books, as well as numerous Web resources, available to guide you through the challenging experience of getting those first two computers to "talk" to one another.

For NT Pros

If you are already certified and/or experienced in Windows NT 4.0, you may be able to skip some parts of this book that provide basic information about features and services with which you are already familiar. But don't skip too much! Windows 2000 is built on the NT kernel, and you will find much in the new operating system that feels like "home"—but you will also discover, as you delve deeper, that there are many fundamental changes, even to "old friends" like automated installation, WINS, DNS, and RAS.

Windows NT 4.0 professionals will need to guard against the possibility that your experience and mastery of the earlier operating system will be your biggest enemy on the Windows 2000 certification exams. Expect questions that try to "trick" you by providing solutions that would have been correct if you were using Windows NT 4.0, that measure whether you're aware of the differences between the two operating systems (just as there were traditionally questions on the NT certification exams that used a test-taker's experience with Windows 9x against him in the same way).

We certainly don't advise Windows NT 4.0 pros to "forget everything you ever knew" about network operating systems, but we do encourage you not only to study Windows 2000, but to actually use it on a day-to-day basis. If possible, upgrade your primary workstation to Windows 2000 Professional or Server so that the slightly different ways of performing routine tasks, and the subtle differences in the interface, become second nature to you. Work with Windows 2000 Server or Advanced Server—on the job if you can, at home or in the classroom if not. It's in the server products that the major differences between Windows NT 4.0 and Windows 2000 show themselves. You will find many unexpected problems in using Windows 2000 Professional if you don't have experience with the new user interface.

Your NT experience can put you a step ahead of the networking newcomers—if you remember not to make too many assumptions (generally a good policy to follow in all areas of life).

CERTIFICATION SUMMARY

In this introductory chapter we covered some important concepts related to how the Microsoft Certification exams are created, and what is expected of you as a Microsoft examinee in your quest for the Windows 2000 MCSE Certification.

We saw that Microsoft is attempting to raise the bar on the Windows 2000 MCSE, and now requires a level of experience and knowledge that is equivalent to at least one year in the industry. In order to pass these new exams, you need the insight of a person with extensive on-the-job experience.

Although you might not have a year of experience in the field supporting enterprise network, you can simulate a reasonable facsimile of an enterprise network for your own home lab with just a few computers. You can gain the experience required on your own if you perform all the exercises in this book over and over until you really understand what you are doing, and why you are doing it.

The exams are very different from the Windows NT 4.0 exams. No longer will the tests focus primarily on basic knowledge of facts and statistics. The new Windows 2000 Exams will concentrate on how you apply your knowledge in a variety of real-world, complex scenarios that will not only require the material that you learn specifically for the Windows 2000 Server exam, but will draw on your resources from your years of experience with other Microsoft operating systems, especially your experience with Windows NT 4.0.

You got a short introduction to some of the most important new services and features in Windows 2000, including the Remote Installation Service, the Distributed File System, Driver Signing, the System Monitor and Performance Console, Disk Quotas, and Local Group Policy. Since these all represent new or improved components in Windows 2000, you need to be on special alert for these subjects, as they are likely to be covered on your Windows 2000 Server exam.

We covered the exam objectives published by Microsoft. Although they seem broad and vague at first, you will find as you move through the book that there is a logical sequence that can be broken down into manageable chunks that will allow you to study and learn about Windows 2000 in a way that is actually easier and more efficient than if you just installed the monster and started playing with it. By focusing your efforts on the Microsoft exam objectives, you will be learning what Microsoft thinks is important for a Certified Engineer to know at work, and on the exams.

The key to your success will be to study the concepts and understand them to the best of your ability, and then perform the numerous practice exercises in this book. The practice exercises are geared to helping you become expert at working with the operating system. If the exercise doesn't work, undo what you did and try again. Your very best learning will come when you use the troubleshooting process to evaluate what has happened when a particular procedure doesn't work correctly.

If you ever have any problems with the exercises, or something in the book doesn't make sense, the panel of Windows 2000 experts who wrote this book is glad to help you in your studies.

TWO-MINUTE DRILL

What Is Installing, Configuring, and Administering Microsoft Windows 2000 Server?

❑ The Microsoft Windows 2000 Exams will be more difficult and demanding than those you encountered during your Windows NT 4.0 Certification.

❑ The Windows 2000 Exams are aimed at networking professionals who have at least one year of on-the-job experience and who understand how LANs and WANs work together in simple and complex connectivity environments.

❑ You can learn the concepts of enterprise-level networking with due diligence and hard work. If you set up your own test network and perform the exercises in this book repeatedly, you should be able to attain the level of knowledge that you need to pass the Windows 2000 Server examination.

A High-Level View of Select New Windows 2000 Features Covered on 70-215

❑ The Remote Installation Service allows you to create images of Windows 2000 Professional that you can use to install Windows 2000 network clients in an automated fashion.

❑ The Distributed File System helps you centralize your network resource management and simplifies the task of locating network resources for your users.

❑ Windows 2000 Driver Signing helps protect your operating system against rogue programs created by third-party developers. Driver Signing can warn you when an approved operating system file is about to be replaced by a third-party file.

❑ Disk quotas provide you with control of how much disk space is consumed on a per user/per partition basis.

❑ Local Group Policy allows you to control user desktops even in environments that do not employ the Windows 2000 domain model.

Overview of Exam 70-215

❏ Installing Windows 2000 Server will cover unattended installations, and the new methods of installation such as Remote Installation Services and sysprep.

❏ Resource Management will be a big part of the Windows 2000 Server exam. Be sure you thoroughly understand both share and NTFS permissions and how they interact. Pay close attention to how permissions are inherited in Windows 2000 environments.

❏ Windows 2000 now supports Plug-and-Play. You should know how Plug-and-Play works, and then be able to troubleshoot problems when Plug-and-Play devices fail to work as advertised.

❏ While Windows 2000 is a highly tuned operating system right out of the box, you will need to learn how to improve it even further by using the tools provided to tune and optimize the operating system for your particular environment. Become expert at the System Monitor and Performance console for your Windows 2000 Server exam.

❏ Windows 2000 introduces an entirely new vocabulary related to how information is stored on physical disks. Understand the difference between basic and dynamic disks, and when to use and not use either one. Get a solid understanding of the "special" partitions, such as volume and stripe sets, as well as RAID-5 volumes. Pay close attention to the differences between how they were handled in Windows NT 4.0 and Windows 2000.

❏ The Windows 2000 networking infrastructure represents a major overhaul of the Windows NT 4.0 networking services. Although much of what you have learned about networking protocols still applies, the user interfaces have changed dramatically and there are many new networking services available. Learn the changes to the interface and the new networking services. They will likely to covered heavily on the exam.

❏ Security is the most important job in Windows 2000. The Security infrastructure of Windows 2000 is the most changed of all the components of Windows 2000 compared to Windows NT 4.0. Learn about Kerberos, Certificates, and Public Key Infrastructure. Learn how to monitor and assess when you have adequate and inadequate security measures in place.

What We'll Cover in This Book

❑ When topics are covered in more detail in other sections of the book, we'll refer you to those chapters for a more in-depth coverage of the topic.

❑ Newbies to Windows Network Operating Systems should refer to the glossary whenever they encounter a new term or phrase with which they are unfamiliar. Half the battle is learning the new language.

❑ For Windows NT 4.0 pros, much of what you know will help you in your Windows 2000 MCSE endeavor; however, be careful that your Windows NT 4.0 knowledge doesn't get in the way. Pay special attention to how things are done differently in Windows 2000.

Microsoft Operating System Terminology

❑ Many words encountered in the network arena are used differently depending on the context. Learn to recognize what is meant by terms such as "segment," "server," and "remote," depending on the context in which they are used.

❑ If something doesn't make sense, check out the glossary, or fire off a letter to the writer for clarification.

❑ Be sure to check out the help files that come with Windows 2000 if a term seems obscure and you require further definition. The Windows 2000 Help files are especially informative and may point you in the direction you seek.

SELF TEST

The following questions will help you measure your understanding of the material presented in this chapter. Read all of the choices carefully, as there may be more than one correct answer. Choose all correct answers for each question.

What Is Installing, Configuring, and Administering Microsoft Windows 2000 Server?

1. Which of these are the types of questions you are likely to encounter in the Windows 2000 Exams?

   A. Questions like this one, in which you are asked to make a simple choice from a list of definitions

   B. Knowledge-based questions like most of those in the Windows NT 4.0 exam

   C. Complex troubleshooting and scenario questions that test your ability to use and apply the knowledge and experience you have gained

   D. Totally convoluted, meaningless questions that are based on the esoteric interests of Microsoft Certified Trainers

2. Who is the target audience for the Windows 2000 exams?

   A. High school teachers who want to migrate from teaching art to network engineering

   B. Accountants who have been power users for years and have managed their own NetWare 2.x network for years and want to get into the IT business full-time

   C. People who heard there was a lot of money to be made in the computer business and figured that the MCSE was a fast track to wealth

   D. People who have been working in the IT industry for at least a year, and have worked on networks with at least five locations and over 200 users

3. What are some things you can do to develop the skills required to pass the Windows 2000 exams?

   A. Purchase two or three low-end computers that meet the minimum hardware requirements for Windows 2000 and create a home network.

   B. Purchase the VMware program to help simulate an enterprise computing environment.

   C. Just read about how to do the practice exercises, but don't actually do them yourself, because the pictures are good enough for you to pass.

   D. Scour the Web for brain dump sites and memorize the answers to the exams.

A High-Level View of Select New Windows 2000 Features Covered on 70-215

4. What are the requirements for Remote Installation Services to work correctly?

    A. A DHCP Server that has been installed and configured on the network

    B. A DNS Server that has been installed and configured on the network

    C. A domain controller with Active Directory installed and configured on the network

    D. A WINS Server that has been installed and configured on the network

5. What are the advantages of using a domain Dfs root over a stand-alone Dfs root?

    A. Fault tolerance

    B. Load balancing

    C. Central location for accessing resources distributed throughout the network

    D. Ease of use for network users

6. Driver Signing is done on the actual file itself.

    A. True

    B. False

7. What Windows 2000 utility could you use to baseline and monitor the performance of your computer locally and on the network?

    A. System Monitor

    B. WINS Management console

    C. SMTP

    D. DHCP Server

8. You have a small group of users that abuse the amount of disk space on the file server that you use to store user profiles on your network. What tool would help you in controlling the harmful activities of these users?

    A. Set NTFS permissions to prevent users from saving information in their profiles.

    B. Use the Performance console to send an alert to you when the amount of disk space consumed by a particular users exceeds a threshold value.

    C. Disk Quota Management can help control the amount of disk space the abusers consume.

     D. Disable the Workstation Service on the machines that the abusive users use to access network resources.

9. What can you use to control the desktop environment for users and computers that do not participate in a Windows 2000 domain?

     A. The Computer Management console

     B. The Distributed File System console

     C. The Routing and Remote Access console

     D. Local Group Policy

Overview of Exam 70-215

10. Which of the following are methods you can use to install Windows 2000 Server?

     A. A scripted install using an answer file

     B. A local installation for the CD-ROM drive on the computer on which it is being installed

     C. Using the Remote Installation Services

     D. Booting using the Emergency Repair Disk and starting a local installation

11. You would like to create a stripe set with parity on your Windows 2000 Server computer, but find that you are not given the option in the Disk Management console. What might be the reason for this?

     A. You must use only SCSI disks for stripe sets with parity, and you are trying to create the set using IDE disks only.

     B. You are attempting to create a stripe set with parity on a mix of IDE and SCSI disks, and all disks in the set must use the same type of interface.

     C. You must use only basic disks to create a stripe set with parity in Windows 2000.

     D. You can create stripe sets with parity only on dynamic disks in Windows 2000.

12. You have only one public IP address available to your organization and would like to connect all the computers on your internal network to the Internet. What Windows 2000 Server technologies can you use to allow all your internal computers a connection to the Internet?

     A. Certificate Server

     B. Internet Connection Services (ICS)

C. Network Address Translation (NAT)

D. Remote Access Dial-In User Service (RADIUS)

What We'll Cover in This Book

13. You are a Windows NT 4.0 Pro and read about a lot of services and features that are the same in Windows 2000 and Windows NT 4.0. Because of this, you feel that you don't need to spend much time on studying those areas, such as DNS, DHCP, and WINS, that were also available in Windows NT 4.0. Is this the correct approach to take when studying for your Windows 2000 exams?

A. Yes

B. No

Microsoft Operating System Terminology

14. Which of the following definitions apply to the term "segment"?

A. A piece of cable joined by a RJ45 coupler

B. A part of the network where all of the computers are on the same side of a router

C. A chunk of data received from Application Level processes that is broken down by the Transport level and passed to Internet Layer processes

D. The part of a Metropolitan Area Network that is located in the South part of the city

15. To which of the following situations does the term "remote" refer?

A. A machine is using the telephone lines to connect to a server at the corporate network.

B. You are trying to connect to a machine on another segment.

C. You are trying to connect to a machine on the same segment.

D. You are dealing with a machine that is shy and doesn't share its feelings.

SELF TEST ANSWERS

What Is Installing, Configuring, and Administering Microsoft Windows 2000 Server?

1. ☑ **C.** You can expect to see a number of complex troubleshooting and scenario-based questions on the exam to test the limits of your skills at practical application of your knowledge.

    ☒ **A** is incorrect, because simple "select the definition" questions will be deemphasized in the Windows 2000 exams. **B** is incorrect, because the new Windows 2000 exams will expect you to have a large foundation of knowledge from your studies, and will aim to test you on your ability to apply that knowledge. **D** is incorrect, because one of Microsoft's stated goals is to improve the quality of the questions and reduce the number of "Guess what I'm thinking" questions.

2. ☑ **B and D. B** is correct, because the accountant, while not working officially in the capacity of a network administrator in a large corporation, has been working as a power user and maintaining his own mission-critical network for his office. He likely is aware of important troubleshooting and maintenance issues. With dedicated study, he could pass the Windows 2000 exams. **D** is correct, because Microsoft expects you to have at least one year of experience before taking the exams.

    ☒ **A** is incorrect, because the Windows 2000 exams will expect a higher level of knowledge of networking infrastructures than is held by someone who has not worked with computer on a regular basis for a long time. **C** is incorrect, because it takes years of hard study and experience before you can make a modest wage in the IT business. High salaries accrue to people with a large practical knowledge base that they can apply at work and that provides value added for their employer.

3. ☑ **A and B. A** is correct, because you can set up a home lab with just a few computers and you create relatively complex scenarios that you are likely to see on the job in enterprisewide networks. Remember that no matter how many machines are located on the network, similar principles still apply. **B** is correct, because you can use the VMware program to increase the number of machines on your network. The VMware program allows you to run multiple operating systems simultaneously on a single computer, for essentially the price of a RAM upgrade.

    ☒ **C** is incorrect, because you need to actually perform the exercises on a real networked machine to see how Windows 2000 works. While the pictures in the book are good at helping you orient yourself while you work on the exercises, you should always perform the actual exercises to gain skill with the product. **D** is incorrect, because Microsoft will be frequently seeding the exam pool with many new questions, and the brain dump sites on the Web will likely be behind the curve. The best way to pass the exams is to learn the product well by studying this book closely.

A High-Level View of Select New Windows 2000 Features Covered on 70-215

4. ☑   **A, B,** and **C. A** is correct, because RIS requires a DHCP Server to assign an IP address to the RIS Client. **B** is correct, because the DNS Server is used to locate a domain controller on Windows 2000 networks. **C** is correct, because information about how RIS Clients are installed is contained in the Active Directory that is stored on all Windows 2000 domain controllers for the domain.

    ☒   **D** is incorrect, because WINS is not required for RIS to work correctly.

5. ☑   **A** and **B** are correct. **A** is correct, because when the Dfs tree is integrated with Active Directory you can take advantage of the File Replication Service to copy the contents of the tree from one location to another. **B** is correct, because Active Directory integrated Dfs trees that are replicated will send a list of servers that can be contacted to the Dfs client, and then the client will select a server randomly from the list.

    ☒   **C** is incorrect, because both Active Directory and non-Active Directory integrated Dfs roots allow for centralized access to distributed network resources. **D** is incorrect, because both types of Dfs roots make life simpler for the user who is trying to locate a network resource.

6. ☑   **B.** When Microsoft tests and approves a file, it will sign that file or driver. This is a digital signature that is the result of a specific hash function. However, the actual file is never affected, and the signature for the file is saved to a special file with the .cat file extension.

7. ☑   **A.** You can baseline and monitor your computer's functioning using the System Monitor, which is contained in the new Windows 2000 Performance console.

    ☒   **B** is incorrect, because WINS maintains a database of NetBIOS name to IP address mappings and does not perform baselining. **C** is incorrect, because SMTP (Simple Mail Transfer Protocol) is used for mail systems, not as a performance monitor and assessment tool. **D** is incorrect, because a DHCP Server is used to automatically assign IP addressing information to DHCP client machines, and does not perform operating system baselining and real-time monitoring.

8. ☑   **C.** On NTFS partitions, you can use disk quotas to control how much space a particular user or group can use on a particular partition.

    ☒   **A** is incorrect, because you cannot control the amount of disk space used by setting NTFS permissions. **B** is incorrect, because there are no counters in System Monitor that would allow you to control the amount of disk space used by a particular user or group. **D** is incorrect, because if you disable the workstation service on a Microsoft Network Client, that computer will no longer be able to participate in network activity, which could seriously hamper the users' job functioning.

9. ☑ **D.** You can use Local Group Policy to lock down local users' desktop environment.
   ☒ **A** is incorrect, because you cannot use the Computer Management console to lock down desktop environment. **B** is incorrect, because you cannot control the user environment via the Distributed File System. **C** is incorrect, because you cannot mediate the desktop environment via the RRAS console.

Overview of Exam 70-215

10. ☑ **A and B. A** is correct, because you can use an unattend.txt file, which is an answer file, to accomplish an unattended installation of a Windows 2000 Server operating system. **B** is correct, because you can always use the local CD-ROM and install Windows 2000 Server locally.
    ☒ **C** is incorrect, because you can only install Windows 2000 Professional using the Remote Installation Service. **D** is incorrect, because you cannot boot from the Emergency Repair Disk.

11. ☑ **D.** The only way to create a new array on a Windows 2000 Server is to first upgrade basic disks to dynamic disks.
    ☒ **A** is incorrect, because you can create RAID-5 sets on either SCSI or IDE drives, not just SCSI drives. **B** is incorrect, because you can mix any combination of IDE and SCSI drives in your RAID-5 array if you like. **C** is incorrect, because you cannot create new RAID-5 arrays in Windows 2000 using basic disks; you must convert them to dynamic disks. Note that if you upgrade a Windows NT 4.0 Server that has a RAID-5 array already in place, the upgraded array will exist on a basic disk; you just cannot create a new array on a basic disk.

12. ☑ **B and C. B** is correct, because the Internet Connection Service allows small networks without DNS or DHCP Servers to connect to the Internet using a single point of access. **C** is correct, because Network Address Translation (NAT) allows large corporations to use a single point of access, typically a network interface card connection to a dedicated connection to the Internet, to connect to the Internet. While NAT solves some problems regarding Internet access for machines on an internal network that use private IP addresses, one limitation of NAT is that you cannot take advantage of L2TP/IPSec.
    ☒ **A** is incorrect, because Certificate Server is used to create and distribute digital certificates for security purposes; it cannot provide a central access point to the Internet. **D** is incorrect.

What We'll Cover in This Book

13. ☑ **B.** Even if you are a Windows NT 4.0 Pro and have been working with all versions of Windows NT 4.0 since the first time you saw the Windows NT 3.1 Box in the Egghead Software Store in the early 1990s, you should still be studying those areas in intensity in Windows 2000. Although there are many familiar services in Windows 2000 that have been part of Windows NT since its inception, many of the old services have been improved, and the user interface has changed. Microsoft will surely try to trip up the test taker by mixing up old Windows NT 4.0 concepts with how they are implemented in Windows 2000. So, if you're already an expert, don't lull yourself into a sense of false security! Study all areas included in this book, and do all the exercises so that you become expert with the new Windows 2000 interface.

Microsoft Operating System Terminology

14. ☑ **B and C. B** is correct, because a group of computers on the same side of a router interface, and typically part of the same collision domain, is referred to as a network segment. A segmented network typically includes multiple logical subnets where each physical segment has its own logical network ID. **C** is correct, because when chunks of data are passed to Transport Layer Protocols such as TCP, TCP can break down the data into smaller chunks and deliver those chunks to Internet Layer Protocols such as the Internet Protocol. These manageable chunks are often referred to as TCP segments.

    ☒ **A** is incorrect because two pieces of cable joined with an RJ45 coupler are not typically referred to as a segment. **D** is incorrect, because the Southern part of a MAN is not typically referred to as a segment.

15. ☑ **A, B, and C. A** is correct, because "remote access" is the term frequently used when machines are connecting to each other via public telephone lines. **B** is correct, because the term "remote network" is often used to communicate information about a network located on a different physical segment. **C** is correct, because a machine that is not the machine you're sitting in front of is sometimes referred to as remote, as in the concept of "remote control."

    ☒ **D** is incorrect, because although this would define a person who seemed remote, the definitions would not apply to computers.

2

Attended Installation of Windows 2000 Server

I n this chapter we will discuss how to perform an attended installation of Windows 2000 Server. In Windows 2000, installation has been made easier than it was in Windows NT 4.0, and some additional features have been added. Before actually starting the installation process, you should plan ahead.

You should prepare for installation before you start. You need to determine whether your computer meets the minimum hardware requirements. You will need to decide how to partition your hard drive and what file system to use. During installation, you will have to choose a licensing mode, so you should determine ahead of time which one is best for your situation. You also have to decide whether to join a domain or a workgroup. Also during installation, you need to choose which optional components to install and how to configure the computer to operate on the network.

You can perform an attended installation of Windows 2000 Server from a CD-ROM or across the network from a distribution server. When you install over the network, you have many options for customizing the installation process. It is important to understand these options.

CERTIFICATION OBJECTIVE 2.01

Perform an Attended Installation of Windows 2000 Server

When you perform an attended installation of Windows 2000 Server, you will have to make many choices. By planning for installation ahead of time, you will be prepared to make these choices. You should make sure that you meet the hardware requirements, determine how to partition the hard disk, select the file system and licensing mode to use, decide whether to join a domain or workgroup, and decide which components to install. For attended installation, you can install from the CD-ROM or across the network.

Preparing for Installation

There are some options that you will be required to choose from during installation, and things will go more smoothly if you determine which choices to make ahead of time. You will need to have considered the following factors: Ensure that your computer has the minimum required hardware, determine how to partition your hard disk, choose a file system, choose a licensing mode, and decide whether to join a domain or a workgroup.

Hardware Requirements

Before starting installation, you need to check to make sure that your hardware meets the minimum requirements and that it is compatible with Windows 2000. See the list below for the minimum requirements for running Windows 2000 Server.

- 133 MHz Pentium or higher CPU
- Only up to four CPUs supported
- 64MB of RAM required, with 128MB of RAM recommended as the minimum. 4GB of RAM is the maximum.

To install Windows 2000 Server, the Setup process needs approximately 1GB of free space. You need a minimum of 671MB of free space with 2GB recommended on the partition on which Windows 2000 Server is to be installed. Once Setup is complete, the temporary files will be deleted and less free space is then required by Windows 2000 Server. You might need more than the minimum space required depending on your configuration and options. See the following list for cases in which more disk space is needed:

- You will need additional space for each additional component you install.
- If you use the FAT file system, you will need an additional 100–200MB of free space.
- If you install across the network, you will need as much as 100–200MB of additional free space for additional driver files required for the network installation.
- If you are upgrading, you will need additional space to import the existing user account database.

exam
ⓦatch

There are usually some questions pertaining to the hardware requirements. Make sure you know what they are and how to determine whether an existing computer meets the requirements.

Keep in mind that your computer will be severely limited by using the bare minimum hardware requirements. You should always perform some analysis and testing to determine what hardware is needed for your computer. You will need to take into account the applications that will be run, and how much network traffic your server will handle.

You also need to make sure your hardware and BIOS is compatible with Windows 2000 Server. Before installation, verify that all of your hardware is on the Hardware Compatibility List (HCL). The HCL is a listing of all the hardware that has passed the Hardware Compatibility Tests (HCTs) and the devices that are supported by Windows 2000 Server. The testing is performed by Windows Hardware Quality Labs (WHQL) and by hardware vendors to prove compatibility with Windows 2000 Server. If your hardware is not on the HCL, your computer may not work correctly after Windows 2000 Server is installed. The HCL can be found on the Windows 2000 Server CD-ROM in the Support directory, or you can access the latest version of the HCL on the Microsoft Web site. It is also important to ensure that your BIOS is compatible. If it is not compatible, you might not be able to use the advanced power management or Plug-and-Play features of Windows 2000 Server, or your computer may not work correctly. If your hardware is not found on the HCL, contact the hardware vendor to see whether it has any updates to make the hardware compliant with Windows 2000.

on the **job**

Windows 2000 has updated the serial port configuration. If your BIOS is not updated, your COM ports may not function.

Partitioning the Hard Disk

When you perform a new installation, you need to decide how to configure your hard disk. The hard disk contains one or more partitions. A primary partition can be seen as a logical drive, whereas an extended partition can contain multiple logical drives. Each partition can be assigned a drive letter such as C: or D: and can use different file systems, such as FAT, FAT32, or NTFS. You can create partitions prior to installation, during the setup process, or after Windows 2000 Server is installed. During setup, you should create and size only the partition on which you are installing the operating system. You can use the Disk Management tool to configure other partitions after installation. The partition on which you installed the Windows 2000 Server operating system files is called the boot partition. It contains all the files you need to run Windows 2000 Server. When the computer boots up, the active partition (normally the C:\ drive) searches for the files needed to load Windows 2000 Server (Ntldr, Ntdetect.com, Boot.ini). These files load the Windows 2000 Server operating system from the system partition. If Windows 2000 Server is installed on the boot partition, this partition is both the system partition and the boot partition.

exam
ⓦatch

The partition on which Windows 2000 is installed is called the boot partition.

It is important to remember that if you delete an existing partition, you cannot access the information that was previously stored on that partition. Before deleting a partition, if there is any data that you need on that partition, make sure you back up the data. Actually, it is recommended that you back up all of your data before changing your partition configuration.

When you create a partition on which to install Windows 2000 Server, you need to make sure the partition is large enough for the operating system, applications, and data that will be stored on the partition. To install Windows 2000 Server, Setup needs at least 1GB of free disk space with 671MB of free space on the partition where Windows 2000 Server will be installed. If you are going to configure your computer for multiple operating systems, you need to install Windows 2000 Server on its own partition. This prevents setup from overwriting files needed by other operating systems.

Choosing a File System

Once you have decided how to partition your hard disk and which partition to install Windows 2000 Server on, you need to decide which file system to use for the partition. Windows 2000 supports the NTFS, FAT, and FAT32 file systems. In most configurations, the NTFS file system is the best choice. The only reason to use FAT or FAT32 is for a dual-boot configuration in which you have more than one operating system that can be run on a computer. Microsoft does not recommend using the dual-boot configuration on a server. During setup, you can convert an existing FAT or FAT32 partition to the new NTFS. This allows you to keep your existing data on the partition. If you do not need to keep the existing data on the partition, it is recommended that you format the drive with NTFS rather than converting it. This will erase all existing data on the partition, but the partition will have less fragmentation and thus better performance.

exam
Ⓦatch

The only reason to use the FAT or FAT32 file system is for dual-booting configurations. Microsoft recommends NTFS and does not recommend dual-boot configurations for servers.

NTFS   The NTFS file system provides these features:

- **Security at the file and folder level**   This allows you to control access down to the file level.

- **File compression**   This allows you to compress folders, subfolders, and files to increase the amount of file storage, but slows down access to the files.

- **Disk quotas**   This allows you to limit the amount of disk space used by each user.

- **File encryption**   Folders, subfolders, and files can be encrypted and decrypted automatically by the operating system.

- **Active Directory**   This allows domain-based security.

With Windows 2000 using NTFS, you can use remote storage, dynamic volumes, and mounting volumes to folders. These features will be discussed later in the book. Partitions that use the NTFS file system can be accessed only by Windows NT and Windows 2000. However, if you use any of the new NTFS features provided by Windows 2000, you will not be able to access it from Windows NT. NTFS is the best choice when security is an issue.

on the
Ⓙob

You can use important features such as Active Directory and domain-based security only by choosing NTFS as your file system.

FAT and FAT32   FAT (or FAT16) allows access from multiple operating systems, including Windows 2000, Windows NT, Windows 95/98, MS-DOS, and OS/2. It is a less efficient file systems with fewer features than NTFS and does not offer any built-in security. FAT32 enhances the FAT file system by allowing larger partition sizes and smaller cluster sizes. FAT partitions are limited to 4GB. With hard disks commonly larger than 8GB, FAT32 was introduced in Windows 98 to extend the partition sizes. FAT32 is compatible with Windows 98 and Windows 2000. Windows NT cannot use FAT32 partitions.

So how do you choose which file system to use on partitions? It depends on how your server will be configured. Microsoft recommends the NTFS partition with single boot operating system for servers. Also, NTFS is the only file system that supports the new Active Directory introduced with Windows 2000. If you want to dual-boot with Windows 2000 and Windows 95/98, you will need to choose the FAT or FAT32 file system. Also, some new features have been added to NTFS by Windows 2000. For example, if you used the new encryption feature on a file, that file would not be readable when you booted up into Windows NT. For configuring a computer for dual-booting between Windows 2000 and Windows NT 4.0, Microsoft recommends using a FAT partition (not FAT32 because Windows NT 4.0 does not recognize it). This ensures that when the computer is booted up into Windows NT 4.0, it will have access to all of the files on the computer. Windows NT 4.0 with Service Pack 4.0 or later can access NTFS 5.0 volumes. However, it cannot access files that have been encrypted or use volumes that use NTFS 5.0 compression and other specific features.

Multiboot Configurations

With many versions of the Windows operating system now available, some users will need to have multiple operating systems installed on the same computer. The user can choose which operating system to load. During installation, you can upgrade an existing Windows operating system to Windows 2000, but when you do, you cannot load it. When you configure your computer for multiboot operations, consider the following things:

- To upgrade an existing Windows operating system to Windows 2000, you must install Windows 2000 in the same directory. To dual-boot with the existing Windows operating system and Windows 2000, you must install Windows 2000 in a different directory so it doesn't overwrite the existing files.

- When dual-booting Windows 2000 with MS-DOS or Windows 95/98, install Windows 2000 last, because older operating systems overwrite the Master Boot Record and you won't be able to boot into Windows 2000.

- You cannot install Windows 2000 in a compressed drive that is not compressed with NTFS.

FROM THE CLASSROOM

Installation Problems

The installation process for Windows 2000 is much improved over Windows NT, as Microsoft integrated some of the features used in the Windows 98 Setup program to enhance installation. Despite these improvements, however, one can still encounter problems during Setup.

One of the most common Setup problems I have seen has to do with hardware problems. This is why checking your hardware for compatibility with Windows 2000 is one of the most important steps in the installation process. Specifically, many people have asked me questions about COM ports that don't work after installing Windows 2000. This is because Windows 2000 actually uses COM ports differently than Windows NT. The fix for this problem is to upgrade the computer's BIOS with a version that is compatible with Windows 2000.

Other problems have to do with understanding the installation process, the settings and options that are available in the process, and how to choose them. I have heard people ask why FAT32 cannot be selected for a partition's file system during Setup. This is not a problem, per se, but a feature. Setup will choose between FAT (sometimes called FAT16) and FAT32 based on the partition's size. If a partition is less than 2 GB in size, then Setup automatically chooses FAT. If the partition is greater than or equal to 2 GB in size, then Setup chooses the FAT32 file system.

When entering your computer name, some users complain that the name contained an underscore (_), but later they found it to be replaced by a dash (-). This is also a feature, not a problem. Active Directory is based on DNS, and some DNS servers do not allow the underscore character (Microsoft DNS servers do). If you wish, you can change the name so that you can use the underscore after installation. Setup does allow you to enter other characters that are not compliant with DNS and you are given a warning when you do. It is recommended that you do not use any characters that were previously compliant with NetBIOS (but not DNS) in a Windows 2000 network because of the move to DNS for name resolution.

These are just a few of the problems that may arise during Setup. Remember to check out your hardware and software for compatibility and be sure to understand the Setup processes. Determine ahead of time the options you will choose, and learn the differences between Windows 2000 and Windows NT.

—*Cameron Wakefield, MCSD, MCPS*

■ All applications must be reinstalled on Windows 2000 when you do not upgrade from the existing operating system. To save disk space, you can install most applications to the same directory that they are currently installed in.

■ With Windows NT 4.0 Service Pack 4 and later, NT 4 is able to read data on NTFS partitions, but it cannot read files encrypted in Windows 2000.

exam
ⓦatch

You will probably see several questions on the exam asking you to determine which file system to use for a given scenario. This includes configurations for dual-booting.

Choose Licensing Mode

When you install Windows 2000 Server, you will have to choose a licensing mode. This determines where the Client Access License (CAL) will reside. The CAL allows clients to access the Windows 2000 Server's network services, shared folders, and printers. The licensing modes are the same as under Windows NT 4.0. It important to understand the difference between the two modes: Per Seat and Per Server. When you use the Per Seat mode, each computer that accesses the server must have a CAL.

SCENARIO & SOLUTION	
What type of file system should I use if I am dual-booting between MS-DOS and Windows 2000?	FAT is the only file system that MS-DOS recognizes.
What types of file systems should I use if I am dual-booting between Windows 98 and Windows 2000?	FAT and FAT32 are the only file systems that you can use with Windows 98. FAT32 is a better choice if your partition is greater than 2GB.
What types of file system should I use if I am dual-booting between Windows NT 4 and Windows 2000?	FAT or NTFS. Windows NT 4 does not recognize FAT32. You should be concerned about the new NTFS 5, since some features in the new version of NTFS, such as file and folder encryption, won't function correctly in version 4.
What types of file system should I use if I am dual-booting between Windows 95 and Windows 2000?	FAT or FAT32 are the only file systems that you can use with Windows 95. FAT32 is only available on Windows 95 OSR2. FAT32 is a better choice if you are running OSR2.*x* and your partition is greater than 2GB.

The Per Server mode requires a CAL for each connection to the server. This is a subtle but significant difference.

The difference is in where the license resides. When you use the Per Seat mode, a client can access multiple Windows 2000 Servers with the same license. This mode is the most common when a network has more than one Windows 2000 server. Use this mode when clients need to access more than one server. When the Per Server mode is used, each concurrent connection requires a license on the server. That means there is a limit on how many simultaneous connections a Windows 2000 Server can have. For example, if you are using the Per Server mode with five concurrent connections, five computers can simultaneously access the server without additional licenses on the client. Once the number of concurrent connections reaches the maximum, Windows 2000 will reject any further access attempts until the number of concurrent connections goes below the maximum. This is the preferred mode if there is only one server on the network or for Internet/RAS computers when clients don't need to be licensed. If you are not sure which mode to use, choose the Per Server mode, because you can change to the Per Seat mode at no cost. However, you cannot change from the Per Seat mode to the Per Server mode.

on the **Job**

If you are not sure which type of licensing mode to use, choose the Per Server mode. When you choose Per Server, you can convert to Per Seat later if needed. You cannot convert from the Per Seat to the Per Server mode.

SCENARIO & SOLUTION

Which licensing mode should I use when there are many servers on the network and clients will be accessing multiple servers?	Per Seat, so the clients can access multiple servers with the same Client Access License (CAL).
Which licensing mode should I use when there is only one server on the network?	Per Server, so you don't have to have a license for each client. You will be limited only to the number of simultaneous connections to the server.
Which licensing mode should I use when I am not sure which mode is best for my server?	Per Server, because you can change to the Per Seat mode at no cost later. You cannot change from the Per Seat mode to the Per Server mode later.

Domain or Workgroup Membership

A domain is a collection of accounts and network resources that are grouped together using a single domain name and security boundary. All user accounts, permissions, and other network details are all stored in a centralized database on the domain controllers. A single login gives the users access to all resources they have permissions for. Domains are recommended for all networks with more than ten computers or for networks that are expected to grow to larger than ten computers in the near future. There are a few requirements for joining a domain. You will need to know the domain name. You must have a computer account for the computer you are installing Windows 2000 Server on. This account can be created either by the administrator before installing Windows 2000 Server or during setup with the username and password of an account with the permissions to create a computer account. You will also need at least one domain controller and Domain Name Server (DNS) online when you install Windows 2000 Server. You can add the server as a member server or as a domain controller. A member server is a member that does not have a copy of the Active Directory. A member server does not perform security functionality for the domain.

A workgroup is a logical grouping of resources on a network. It is generally used in peer-to-peer networks. This means that each computer is responsible for access to its resources. Each computer has its own account database and is administered separately. Security is not shared between computers, and administration is more difficult than in a centralized domain. It is intended only as a convenience to help find resources. When you browse the network, the resources in your same workgroup are found first. It does not provide any security. In a workgroup, you might have to remember a different password for every resource you want to access. To join a workgroup during installation, all you need is a workgroup name. This can be the name of an existing workgroup or a new one. You must join a workgroup or a domain during installation, but you can change these memberships later as needed.

Optional Components

When you install Windows 2000 Server, there are some optional components you can install. You need to determine how your server will be utilized so you can decide which optional components to install. These optional components extend the functionality of Windows 2000 Server. If you do not install a component that you determine a need for later, you can add any optional components later, after installation, through the Add/Remove Programs application in Control Panel. The more components you install, the more functionality your server will have. However, do not install components you know you will not need, as they will just take up disk space. Table 2-1 shows the available optional components.

Networking Components

Most of the time, a Windows 2000 Server will need just the TCP/IP network protocol. This is the protocol used on the Internet. Prior to installation, you need to determine whether you will use the automatic settings for TCP/IP. If you need to manually configure TCP/IP, you should determine the settings before starting installation. The TCP/IP settings can be changed after installation. If you are going to be using a different protocol, you need to ensure that you know how to configure it and the settings you will be using.

TABLE 2-1	Optional Components for Windows 2000 Server
Option	**Description**
Accessories and Utilities	Includes desktop accessories such as Wordpad, Paint, Calculator, and CD Player, as well as games such as Solitaire. To select individual items, click Details and select from the list.
Certificate Services	Provides security and authentication support, including secure e-mail, Web-based authentication, and smart card authentication.
Indexing Service	Provides indexing functions for documents stored on disk, allowing users to search for specific document text or properties.
Internet Information Services (IIS)	Provides support for Web site creation, configuration, and management, along with Network News Transfer Protocol (NNTP), File Transfer Protocol (FTP), and Simple Mail Transfer Protocol (SMTP).
Management and Monitoring Tools	Provides tools for communications administration, monitoring, and management, including programs that support development of customized client dialers for remote users and implementation of phone books that can be automatically updated from a central server. In addition, includes the Simple Network Management Protocol (SNMP).
Message Queuing Services	Provides a communication infrastructure and a development tool for creating distributed messaging applications. Such applications can communicate across heterogeneous networks and with computers that might be offline. Message Queuing provides guaranteed message delivery, efficient routing, security, transactional support, and priority-based messaging.

| TABLE 2-1 | Optional Components for Windows 2000 Server *(continued)* |

Option	Description
Networking Services	Provides important support for networking, including the items in the following list. For information about network monitoring, see "Management and Monitoring Tools," in this table. For background information about IP addresses and name resolution, see Networking: TCP/IP, IP addresses, and name resolution. **COM Internet Services Proxy** Supports distributed applications that use HTTP to communicate through Internet Information Services. **Domain Name System (DNS)** Provides name resolution for clients running Windows 2000. With name resolution, users can access servers by name, instead of having to use IP addresses that are difficult to recognize and remember. **Dynamic Host Configuration Protocol (DHCP)** Gives a server the capability of assigning IP addresses dynamically to network devices. These devices typically include server and workstation computers, but can also include other devices such as printers and scanners. With DHCP, you do not need to set and maintain static IP addresses on any of these devices, except for intranet servers providing DHCP, DNS, and/or WINS service. **Internet Authentication Service (IAS)** Performs authentication, authorization, and accounting of dial-up and VPN users. IAS supports the RADIUS protocol. **QoS Admission Control** Allows you to control how applications are allotted network bandwidth. You can give important applications more bandwidth, less important applications less bandwidth. **Simple TCP/IP Services** Supports Character Generator, Daytime Discard, Echo, and Quote of the Day. **Site Server ILS Service** Supports IP telephony applications. Publishes IP multicast conferences on a network, and can also publish user IP address mappings for H.323 IP telephony. Telephony applications, such as NetMeeting and Phone Dialer in Windows Accessories, use Site Server ILS Service to display user names and conferences with published addresses. Site Server ILS Service depends on Internet Information Services (IIS). **Windows Internet Name Service (WINS)** Provides NetBIOS name resolution for clients running Windows NT and earlier versions of Microsoft operating systems. With name resolution, users can access servers by name, instead of having to use IP addresses that are difficult to recognize and remember.
Other Network File and Print Services	Provides file and print services for the Macintosh operating system, as well as print services for UNIX.

| TABLE 2-1 | Optional Components for Windows 2000 Server *(continued)* |

Option	Description
Remote Installation Services	Provides services that you can use to set up new client computers remotely, without the need to visit each client. The target clients either must support remote startup with the Pre-Boot eXecution Environment (PXE) ROM, or else must be started with a remote-start floppy disk. On the server, you will need a separate partition for Remote Installation Services. For more information, see Planning disk partitions for new installations.
Remote Storage	Provides an extension to your disk space by making removable media such as tapes more accessible. Infrequently used data can automatically be transferred to tape and retrieved when needed.
Script Debugger	Provides support for script development.
Terminal Services	Offers two modes: remote administration mode or application server mode. In application server mode, Terminal Services provides the ability to run client applications on the server, while "thin client" software acts as a terminal emulator on the client. Each user sees an individual session, displayed as a Windows 2000 desktop, and each session is managed by the server, independent of any other client session. If you install Terminal Services as an application server, you must also install Terminal Services Licensing (not necessarily on the same computer). However, temporary licenses can be issued for clients that allow you to use Terminal servers for up to 90 days. In remote administration mode, you can use Terminal Services to remotely log on and manage Windows 2000 systems from virtually anywhere on your network (instead of being limited to working locally on a server). Remote administration mode allows for two concurrent connections from a given server and minimizes impact on server performance. Remote administration mode does not require you to install Terminal Services Licensing.
Windows Media Services	Provides multimedia support, allowing you to deliver content using Advanced Streaming Format over an internetwork or the Internet.

Four-Step Process from CD-ROM

When you install Windows 2000 Server from a CD-ROM, you will need to boot the server either from the CD-ROM or from floppy disks. During installation, you will use some Setup Wizards to guide you through the process. This process is similar to the installation of Windows NT 4.0. The installation of Windows 2000 Server has four basic steps: running the setup program, running the Setup Wizard, installing networking, and completing installation.

You have several options for starting the installation. On the Windows 2000 Server CD-ROM, you can run Setup.exe to launch the installation. Setup will then run either Winnt.exe or Winnt32.exe, depending on which operating system you are currently running. If you are running MS-DOS or Windows 3.x, Setup will run Winnt.exe. If you are running Windows 95/98 or Windows NT, Setup will run Winnt32.exe. You can also run Winnt.exe or Winnt32.exe directly. The Winnt.exe and Winnt32.exe files are located in the /i386 directory on the CD-ROM.

Step One: Run the Setup Program

The first step for installing Windows 2000 Server is the text mode portion of setup. This is very similar to the Windows NT 4.0 text mode portion of setup. This portion of setup copies the minimum version of Windows 2000 Server to memory to begin the setup. You will have the option to run setup, to repair an existing Windows 2000 Server installation, or to exit setup. Then you will have to agree to the terms of the license agreement in order to continue with setup. The next step is to select a partition on which to install Windows 2000 Server. You can choose an existing partition, create a new partition from free space, and even delete a partition to create free space. When you delete a partition, keep in mind that you will lose all the data on that partition. After you have selected a partition to install to, you will have to decide whether to use the FAT or NTFS file system. Then setup will copy files to the hard disk and reboot the computer. Exercise 2-1 shows the steps for this phase of setup.

CertCam 2-1

EXERCISE 2-1

Starting the Installation

1. To start installation from the CD_ROM, you can boot from the Windows 2000 Server CD-ROM. Place the CD-ROM in the drive and reboot the computer. Make sure your BIOS is set up to boot from the CD-ROM drive. When you boot from the CD-ROM, Setup will copy the minimum version of Windows 2000 Server to memory and start the text mode portion of setup. If you have any third-party disk controller drivers you need to use (such as Small Computer System Interface [SCSI], Redundant Array of Independent Disks [RAID], or additional IDE-based devices on the computer), press F6 to install the drivers for these devices.

2. You will come to the Welcome to Setup screen. You have three options to choose from:

   ■ Run Windows 2000 setup. Press ENTER for this option.

   ■ Repair an existing Windows 2000 installation. Press R for this option.

   ■ Exit setup without installing Windows 2000. Press F3 for this option.

3. If the hard disk contains an operating system that is not compatible with Windows 2000, a screen will appear notifying you that you could lose data if you continue with setup. You have two options at this point:

   ■ Continue setup. Press C for this option.

   ■ Quit setup. Press F3.

4. Read the license agreement and then choose to agree or to not agree with the licensing agreement. If you do not agree to the terms, you will not be able to continue with setup. You can use the Page Down key to read the entire agreement. To accept the conditions of the agreement, press the F8 key. If you do not accept the terms of the agreement, press the ESC key and setup will quit.

5. The next screen will show you the existing free space and/or existing partitions on the hard disk. You will have three options:
   1. To set up Windows 2000 Server on the selected partition, press ENTER.
   2. To create a new partition in the unpartitioned space, press C. When you select this option, you will have the option of choosing how large to make that partition or going back to the previous screen without creating a new partition. Either accept the default size of all remaining free space or type in the size you want for the new partition. Then press ENTER to create the partition or ESC to cancel creating the partition.
   3. To delete the selected partition, press D. Be careful when you delete any partitions. Any files stored on those partitions will be lost.

6. After you press ENTER to install Windows 2000 Server on the selected partition, you will come to the screen for formatting the partition. You can choose from NTFS or FAT. NTFS is the default. (Note: if the partition size is larger than 2GB, it will automatically use the FAT32 file system.) Choose the file system to format the partition and press ENTER. Since you are installing Windows 2000 Server, you should always choose NTFS.

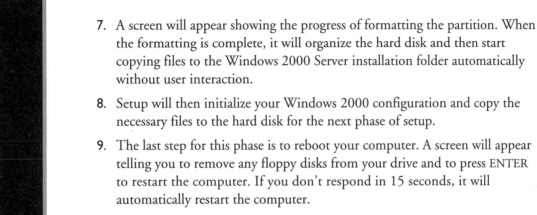

7. A screen will appear showing the progress of formatting the partition. When the formatting is complete, it will organize the hard disk and then start copying files to the Windows 2000 Server installation folder automatically without user interaction.

8. Setup will then initialize your Windows 2000 configuration and copy the necessary files to the hard disk for the next phase of setup.

9. The last step for this phase is to reboot your computer. A screen will appear telling you to remove any floppy disks from your drive and to press ENTER to restart the computer. If you don't respond in 15 seconds, it will automatically restart the computer.

10. When the computer boots up, there will be a progress bar at the bottom that says "Starting Windows." You can press F8 for troubleshooting options. When the computer boots up, you will be in the Setup Wizard phase of the Windows 2000 Server installation.

Step Two: Run the Setup Wizard

The second step for installing Windows 2000 Server uses the Setup Wizard. This begins the Windows or GUI portion of setup. You will have to provide some information for setting up Windows 2000 Server. Setup will perform some initial hardware detection and will allow you to customize your keyboard and locale configuration. Then you will need to enter name and company information. This allows you to personalize the software on the computer. You will need a product key in order to continue with setup. The product key can be found on the Windows 2000 Server CD-ROM case. Next you will need to choose the licensing mode. You will have to choose between Per Server and Per Seat. If you choose the Per Server mode, you will have to enter the number of simultaneous connections allowed to the server. The default is five. A unique computer name needs to be entered and a password for the Administrator account needs to be entered. The computer name is a NetBIOS name that can be up to 15 characters in length. Setup will automatically generate a 15-character computer name for you. You can either accept this or enter your own. The NetBIOS name must be different from other computer names, workgroup names, and domain names on the network. The Administrator account password can be up to 127 characters in length. Although it is strongly recommended not to do it, you can leave the password space blank. Then you need to choose which optional components to install. Finally, you need to set up the date, time, and time zone for the computer. Exercise 2-2 shows the steps for this phase of setup.

CertCam 2-2

Running the Setup Wizard

1. After completing the text-mode portion of the installation, your computer will reboot. After reboot, the first screen will welcome you to the Windows 2000 Setup Wizard. Click Next to continue.

2. The Setup Wizard will detect and configure some of the devices on your computer such as the keyboard and mouse.

3. Select your Regional settings. You can customize your locale and keyboard settings. Either customize the settings or accept the default and click Next to continue.

4. This screen allows you to personalize your software by entering your name and organization information. After you have entered your information, click Next to continue.

5. Enter your product key. This key can be found on the Windows 2000 CD-ROM case. Enter the number and click Next to continue.

6. The next screen allows you to select which licensing mode you will use for Windows 2000 Server. You can choose either Per Server and enter the number of concurrent connections, or Per Seat, for which each client must have a Client Access License. Choose the mode and click Next to continue.

7. This screen allows you to enter a name for your computer and the password for the Administrator account. The computer name will need to be unique on the network. You will have to enter the Administrator password twice. When you have entered this information, click Next to continue.

8. Decide which optional components of Windows 2000 Server you would like to install.

9. Last, you can set the date, time, and time zone. Setup now moves into the network portion.

Step Three: Install Windows 2000 Networking

Now that Setup has finished gathering information about your computer, it is time to install the Windows 2000 networking components. You will need to decide which networking components to install. By default, Setup will install the Client for Microsoft Networks, File and Print Sharing for Microsoft Networks, and TCP/IP with automatic addressing. You can install other components if you need them. In this phase you will also join a domain or workgroup. If you join a domain, you will need to have a computer account on the domain. If you don't already have an account for your computer, you can add one from Setup. Exercise 2-3 shows the steps for this phase of setup.

CertCam 2-3

EXERCISE 2-3

Installing the Networking Components

1. The Network Settings screen allows you either to choose the typical settings or to customize the settings. The Typical settings option will install Client for Microsoft Networks, File and Print Sharing for Microsoft Networks, and TCP/IP with automatic addressing. The Customize settings option allows you to install and configure the networking components to your requirements, such as specifying TCP/IP addresses and choosing other components to install.

2. The Workgroup or Computer Domain screen allows you choose between joining either a workgroup or a domain. To join a workgroup, select No and enter the workgroup name. To join a domain, select Yes and enter the name of the domain you want to join.

3. The Join Computer to Domain dialog box allows you to enter the username and password of an account that has the proper permissions to join the computer to the domain.

4. The networking components will now be installed. The networking portion of setup is now complete.

Step Four: Complete the Setup Program

Setup has a few more tasks left to complete the installation of Windows 2000 Server. It will finish copying files to the hard disk, and save the configuration you have chosen to hard disk. Then it will remove the temporary files and restart the computer. Exercise 2-4 shows the steps for this phase of setup.

CertCam 2-4

EXERCISE 2-4

Completing the Setup Program

1. Setup will complete the installation. Setup will finish copying files, such as accessories and bitmaps, to the computer.

2. Setup will apply and save to hard disk the configuration settings you entered earlier.

3. Setup removes the temporary setup files and restarts the computer.

4. Windows 2000 Server is now installed on your computer.

Installing over the Network

Installing Windows 2000 Server over the network is similar to installing it from the CD-ROM, except the source location is different and the process will be slower since the files have to be transferred across the network. When Windows 2000 Server is installed on multiple computers, installing over the network is easier and more efficient than installing each one separately from a CD-ROM. The installation can be performed on identical computers or computers with different configurations. The setup program will be run from a shared folder on the network. The setup program will then copy the needed files to the client computer to start installation. The installation can be customized by using different setup options available from command-line switches.

Distribution Server

The first requirement for network installation is a distribution server that contains the installation files. The distribution server can be any computer on the network that the clients have access to. To set up the distribution server, create a shared folder to hold the setup files. For Intel-based installations, copy the /I386 directory from the Windows 2000 Server CD-ROM to the shared folder.

Second, the computer that Windows 2000 Server is to be installed on needs to have a 850MB (or more as necessary) partition. In Windows NT 4.0, network installations required a FAT partition. In Windows 2000, you can perform a network installation to either a FAT or a NTFS partition.

Third, the client computer that you are installing to needs a networking software client that allows it to connect to the distribution server. If the client has an existing operating system with a network client, you can connect to the distribution server and start the installation from it. Otherwise, you need to create a boot disk that includes a network client that can connect to the distribution server.

Exercise 2-5 shows the basic steps for installing Windows 2000 Server using a network installation.

EXERCISE 2-5

Network Installation of Windows 2000 Server

1. Boot from the network client on the target computer.

2. Connect to the shared folder on the distribution server.

3. Run Winnt.exe from the shared folder on the distribution server. Setup starts and creates a temporary folder named Win_nt.~bt on the system partition and copies the Setup boot files to the folder.

4. Setup creates a temporary folder named Win_nt.~ls and then copies the installation files from the distribution folder to this folder. Setup does not create the Setup floppy disks as it did in Windows NT 4.0.

5. You will then be prompted to restart the computer. When the computer restarts, you can proceed with the installation as described above.

6. Setup restarts the client computer and starts the Windows 2000 installation.

Modifying Setup Using WINNT.EXE

You can customize the network installation process for Windows 2000 Server by changing how the setup program runs. This can be accomplished by using command-line switches when you run the Winnt.exe program. The Winnt.exe program is used for network installations that use an MS-DOS network client.

Enumerate the Switches   The options available for customizing setup can be seen in Table 2-2. It lists the available options for running Winnt.exe. Notice that there aren't any switches for creating Setup disks. To create the Setup disks, you must use the Makeboot.exe program located on the Bootdisk folder of the Windows 2000 Server installation CD-ROM. To create the Setup disks using floppy drive A, just run makeboot a:.

TABLE 2-2   The Winnt.exe Switches

Switch	Description
/a	Enables the accessibility option.
/e[:command]	Executes a command before the final phase of setup.
/I:[:inf_file]	The filename of the setup information file (without the path). The default filename is DOSNET.INF.
/r[:folder]	Creates an additional folder within the system root folder (where the Windows 2000 system files are located).
/rx[:folder]	Also creates an additional folder within the system root folder, but Setup deletes the files after installation is completed.
/s[:sourcepath]	Specifies the location of the Windows 2000 installation files. It must contain the full path using drive letter (i.e., f:\path) or UNC (\\server\shared_folder\path).
/t[:tempdrive]	The drive that contains the temporary setup files. If you do not use this switch, Setup will decide for you by using the partition with the most available space.
/u[:answer_file]	Performs an unattended installation by using an optional answer file. When you use the unattended installation option, you are required to use the /s switch.
/udf:id[,*UDF_file*]	Indicates an identifier (*id*) that Setup uses to specify how a Uniqueness Database File (UDF) modifies an answer file (see the /u entry, above). The UDF overrides values in the answer file, and the identifier determines which values in the UDF file are used. For example, /udf:RAS_user,Our_company.udf overrides settings specified for the identifier RAS_user in the Our_company.udf file. If no *UDF_file* is specified, Setup prompts the user to insert a disk that contains the $Unique$.udf file.

SCENARIO & SOLUTION

To specify which drive to use to store the temporary files during setup, which Winnt command-line switch should you use?	The /t switch allows you to specify the drive to use to store the temporary files during Setup.
To specify an unattended installation of Windows 2000 Server and answer file to use, which Winnt command-line switch should you use?	The /u[:answer_file] performs an unattended installation using the specified answer file.

e x a m
ⓦ a t c h

It is important to know the command-line switches for Winnt.exe to pass the exam, as most exams contain several questions pertaining to them.

Modifying Setup Using WINNT32.EXE

The Winnt32.exe program is used to customize the process for upgrading existing installations. The Winnt32.exe program is used for installing Windows 2000 from a computer that is currently running Windows 95/98 or Windows NT. As with the Winnt.exe program, you can use command-line switches to customize the setup process. The options available for Winnt32.exe are listed in Table 2-3.

e x a m
ⓦ a t c h

It is important to know the difference between command-line switches for Winnt.exe and Winnt32.exe. Most of the switches have similar functionality with a different syntax. Make sure that you know the different syntaxes for each.

CERTIFICATION SUMMARY

Installing Windows 2000 Server is easier than it was in Windows NT 4.0. Some of the administrative overhead that was required in Windows NT 4.0 has been removed. Before starting the installation process, there is some preparation you should do first. You should check the computer for meeting the minimum hardware requirements. Check that all of the hardware is on the Hardware Compatibility List. You must decide how to partition the hard disk and which file system to use. You should decide which licensing mode to use, whether to join a workgroup or a domain, and whether to configure the computer for single or multiboot operations.

Windows 2000 is most commonly installed from the CD-ROM. The CD-ROM installation has four basic stages: running the setup program, running the Setup

TABLE 2-3	The Winnt32.exe Switches
Switch	**Description**
/copydir[:folder_name]	Creates an additional folder within the system root folder (where the Windows 2000 system files are located).
/copysource[:folder_name]	Also creates an additional folder within the system root folder, but Setup deletes the files after installation is completed.
/cmd[:command_line]	Executes a command before the final phase of setup.
/cmdcons	Installs additional files to the hard disk that are necessary to load a command-line interface for repair and recovery purposes.
/debug[level][:file_name]	Creates a debug log at the level specified. By default, it creates C:\Winnt32.log at level 2 (the warning level).
/s[:source_path]	Specifies the location of the Windows 2000 installation files. It must contain the full path using drive letter (i.e., f:\path) or UNC (\\server\shared_folder\path). To simultaneously copy files from multiple paths, use a separate /s switch for each source path.
/syspart[:drive_letter]	Copies Setup start files to a hard disk and marks the partition as active. You can then install the hard disk in another computer. When you start that computer, Setup starts at the next phase. Use of this switch requires the /tempdrive switch.
/tempdrive[:drive_letter]	Places temporary files on the specified drive and installs Windows 2000 on that drive.
/unattend[number] [:answer_file]	Performs an unattended installation. The answer file provides the custom specifications to Setup. If you do not specify an answer file, all user settings are taken from the previous installation.
/udf:id[,udf_file]	Indicates an identifier (*id*) that Setup uses to specify how a Uniqueness Database File (UDF) modifies an answer file (see the /u entry, above). The UDF overrides values in the answer file, and the identifier determines which values in the UDF file are used. For example, /udf:RAS_user,Our_company.udf overrides settings specified for the identifier RAS_user in the Our_company.udf file. If no *UDF_file* is specified, Setup prompts the user to insert a disk that contains the $Unique$.udf file.

Wizard, installing networking, and completing installation. Phase one, running the setup program, is the text mode portion of Setup. You will choose the partition for installing to and choose which file system to use. Then Setup will copy files to the hard disk and reboot the computer. Phase two, running the Setup Wizard, will configure the licensing mode. You can choose Per Seat or Per Server. If you choose Per Server, you must enter the maximum number of concurrent connections. You must enter a unique computer name and password for the Administrator account. Then you choose the optional components to install. Phase three, installing networking, configures the computer to use the network. It installs the protocols and networking services. If you join a domain, your computer must have an account on the domain. Phase four, completing installation, finishes copying files to the hard disk, saves the settings to hard disk, removes temporary files, and restarts the computer.

Installing Windows 2000 Server from the network is much like installing from the CD-ROM, except that the source is located in a different place. When installing Windows 2000 to a large amount of computers, installing over the network is more efficient. For network installations, a distribution server must be used. A distribution server is a computer on the network that can be accessed by the client computers. It needs a shared folder that contains the /I386 folder from the Windows 2000 Server CD-ROM. You can customize the installation using command-line switches.

TWO-MINUTE DRILL

❑ Before you start the Windows 2000 installation, you must do some preparation.

❑ You should check your existing hardware against the Hardware Compatibility List (HCL).

❑ The HCL is provided by Microsoft for all hardware that is supported by Windows 2000.

❑ The hard disk can be partitioned before, during, or after installation.

❑ Windows 2000 can be installed on a FAT, FAT32, or NTFS partition. For single boot configurations, it is recommended to use NTFS. For dual-booting with Windows 95/98, you may choose the Fat or FAT32 file system.

❑ NTFS provides enhancements over FAT such as security, encryption, compression, and the Active Directory.

❑ You can perform an attended installation of Windows 2000 Server from a CD-ROM or across the network.

❑ You can upgrade existing Windows operating systems to Windows 2000, or install it separately for single or multiboot configurations.

❑ Microsoft recommends a single boot configuration for Windows 2000 Servers.

❑ There are many command-line switches available to customize the Setup program.

❑ To create the Setup floppy disks, you must use the Makeboot.exe program.

❑ When a large number of installations are required, you may choose to install Windows 2000 Server over the network.

❑ There are two licensing modes: Per Seat and Per Server. Per Seat mode requires the client to have a license. Per Server mode holds the licenses, but there is a maximum number of simultaneous connections allowed to the server.

❑ A Windows 2000 Server must join either a workgroup or a domain.

❑ During Setup, you must provide a unique name for the computer.

❑ To install Windows 2000 Server over the network, you need to set up a distribution server.

❑ To set up the distribution server, copy the /I386 folder from the CD-ROM to the shared folder on the distribution server.

❑ In Windows 2000, you can perform a network installation to a client with a FAT or NTFS partition. In Windows NT 4.0, you could only perform a network install to a client with a FAT partition.

❑ The client you are installing across the network to must have network client software that allows it to connect to the distribution server.

❑ You can customize the network installation process by using the command-line switches for Winnt.exe and Winnt32.exe.

SELF TEST

The following questions will help you measure your understanding of the material presented in this chapter. Read all of the choices carefully, as there may be more than one correct answer. Choose all correct answers for each question.

1. Which of the following is NOT a minimum hardware requirement for Windows 2000 Server?

   A. 133 MHz Pentium CPU

   B. At least two CPUs

   C. 64MB RAM

   D. 671MB partition

2. You have a computer on which you want to install Windows 2000 Server. You are preparing for installation and you want to determine if your hardware is compatible with Windows 2000 Server. Where can you find out whether you hardware is compatible?

   A. Windows 2000 Compatibility List

   B. Hardware Vendors List

   C. Hardware Compatibility List

   D. Hardware Abstraction Layer

3. You are preparing to install Windows 2000 Server on your computer. You check your hardware on the HCL, and your network card is not on the list. What should you do?

   A. Install Windows 2000 Server and see whether it works.

   B. Check the hardware vendor's Web site.

   C. Use the Windows 98 driver that came with the card.

   D. Do not install Windows 2000 until you get a network card on the HCL.

4. Which of the following file systems are supported by Windows 2000? (Choose all that apply.)

   A. FAT

   B. FAT32

   C. HPFS

   D. NTFS

5. You are installing Windows 2000 Server on a computer. You want to configure the computer to be as secure as possible. When you choose the file system during Setup, which file system should you use?

A. FAT

B. FAT32

C. HPFS

D. NTFS

6. You are installing Windows 2000 Server and Windows 98 on the same computer with a dual-boot configuration. After installing Windows 2000, you realize that all of the applications you installed on Windows 98 are not available on Windows 2000. What should you do?

A. Create shortcuts to the executables for the applications.

B. Import the application settings in the Windows 98 registry to the Windows 2000 registry.

C. Reinstall all of the applications.

D. Export the Windows 2000 registry to the Windows 98 registry.

7. You want to install Windows 2000 Server on a computer that currently is running Windows 98. You want to be able to run both operating systems with a dual-boot configuration. Currently, the computer has a hard disk with one partition that is 4GB. Which file system should you choose when installing Windows 2000?

A. FAT

B. FAT32

C. NTFS

D. You must install the NTFS upgrade to Windows 98 and then convert the partition to NTFS.

8. You are installing Windows 2000 Server on a network with many servers. Most of the client computers will need to access multiple servers. Which licensing mode should you choose during installation?

A. Per Client

B. Per Seat

C. Per Server

D. Per CAL

9. You are installing Windows 2000 Server on a network that doesn't have any servers. This will be the only server on the network. During installation, you must select the licensing mode. Which licensing mode should you choose?

    A. Per Client

    B. Per Seat

    C. Per Server

    D. Per CAL

10. You are an administrator installing Windows 2000 Server on a computer, and you just remembered that you forgot to add the computer account to the domain. The Windows 2000 Domain controller is in another building, and you don't want to walk over there to add it to the domain. What should you do?

    A. You must walk over to the domain controller to create a computer account.

    B. Enter your administrator account's username and password when prompted.

    C. Nothing. Windows 2000 Server is automatically added to the domain by the Setup program.

    D. Add the computer to a workgroup with the same name as the domain, and the domain controller will automatically add it to the domain when it sees it on the network.

11. You are installing Windows 2000 Server on a computer that is already running Windows 98. You want to be able to load both operating systems. How should you install Windows 2000 Server?

    A. Install Windows 2000 Server in the same directory that Windows 98 is installed in.

    B. Install Windows 2000 in a separate directory.

    C. Install Windows 2000 in the same directory, but update the BOOT.INI file to allow dual-booting.

    D. You cannot dual-boot between Windows 2000 and Windows 98.

12. Which of the following components would allow you to select and install Wordpad during the installation of Windows 2000 Server?

    A. Windows Media Services

    B. Management and Monitoring Tools

    C. Accessories and Utilities

    D. Office programs

13. During installation of Windows 2000 Server, you are prompted to enter a name for your computer. Which of the following is a requirement for the computer name?

A. You must use your own name for the computer name.

B. The computer name must be unique on the network.

C. The computer name must be the same as the domain name.

D. The computer name must be the same as the workgroup name.

14. During installation of Windows 2000 server, you choose the Typical option for Network components to install. Which of the following will NOT be installed?

A. Client for Microsoft Networks

B. File and Print Sharing for Microsoft Networks

C. NetBEUI

D. TCP/IP

15. You are performing a Windows 2000 Server installation over the network with the Winnt.exe. Which switch should you use to specify the source of the installation files?

A. /a

B. /r

C. /rx

D. /s

16. What folder do you copy from the Windows 2000 Server CD when you need to perform network installations on Intel-based x86 computers?

A. i386

B. x386

C. xIntel

D. Alpha

17. Which of the following commands should you use to create the Setup disks using floppy drive A?

A. Winnt /b

B. makeboot a:

C. Winnt /ox

D. Makeboot /b

18. You want to execute a command before the final phase of Setup. Which switch should you use with the Winnt program to accomplish this?

A. /exe

B. /Execute

C. /e

D. /run

19. You seem to be having trouble when you run the Windows 2000 Server Setup program. You decide to try to debug the installation. Which switch can you use with the Winnt32.exe program to accomplish this?

A. /d

B. /debug

C. /log

D. /troubleshoot

20. What is the default filename used for the setup information file with Winnt32.exe command-line switch /I?

A. SETUP.INF

B. INFO.INF

C. SETUPINFO.INF

D. DOSNET.INF

LAB QUESTION

You are tasked with starting a network for a new company. You want to use Windows 2000 for all of your servers. You have to give a presentation to management explaining the issues involved with installing Windows 2000 Server on the network. Below is a list of topics to cover in the presentation. Write about the areas of concern of each of the topics listed.

1. System requirements

2. Hardware compatibility

3. Optional device inventory

4. Mass storage devices

5. BIOS

6. Important files to review

7. What licensing mode to use

8. What file system to use

9. Planning disk partitions

10. Choosing components to install

11. Networking: TCP/IP, IP addresses, and name resolution

12. Deciding between workgroups and domains

13. Planning for domain controllers and member servers

SELF TEST ANSWERS

1. ☑ **B.** Only one CPU is required in order to install Windows 2000 Server.
   ☒ **A** is incorrect, because a 133 MHz Pentium CPU is the minimum requirement for the CPU. **C** is incorrect, because 64MB of RAM is the minimum requirement for memory. **D** is incorrect, because a 671MB partition is the minimum requirement for disk space.

2. ☑ **C.** The Hardware Compatibility List (HCL) contains a listing of all the hardware that has been tested and verified to be compatible with Windows 2000. If the hardware is not on the HCL, your computer may not operate correctly.
   ☒ **A** is incorrect, because there is no such thing as the Windows 2000 Compatibility List. **B** is incorrect, because there is no such thing as the Hardware Vendors List. **D** is incorrect, because the Hardware Abstraction Layer (HAL) is a function of the operating system, not a list of valid hardware.

3. ☑ **D.** If it is not on the Hardware Compatibility List (HCL), it has not been tested and proven to be compatible with Windows 2000 Server. If it is not on the HCL, your computer may not operate correctly.
   ☒ **A.** is incorrect, because you should not install Windows 2000 if any of your hardware is not on the HCL. **B** is incorrect, because even if the vendor says it is compatible, you cannot be completely sure unless it is on the HCL. **C** is incorrect, because most drivers designed for Windows 98 will not work correctly on Windows 2000. You should never use drivers not specifically designed for Windows 2000.

4. ☑ **A, B, D.** Windows 2000 supports the FAT, FAT32, and NTFS file systems.
   ☒ **C** is incorrect, because the High Performance File System (HPFS) is not supported by Windows 2000.

5. ☑ **D.** NTFS provides security features such as file and folder level security.
   ☒ **A** and **B** are incorrect, because FAT and FAT32 do not support security. **C** is incorrect, because Windows 2000 does not support HPFS.

6. ☑ **C.** If you install Windows 2000 to a separate directory from that of the existing operating system, you will then have to reinstall all of the applications over again.
   ☒ **A** is incorrect, because creating a shortcut does not configure the application. Most applications require some registry settings and system files copied to the system directory. **B** is incorrect, because you cannot import registry settings from Windows 98 to Windows 2000. The two registries are not compatible with each other. **D** is incorrect, because you cannot export the Windows 2000 registry to Windows 98. Also, even if you could, it would not configure Windows 2000 registry with the settings for the applications.

7. ☑ **B.** Windows 98 can use only the FAT and FAT32 file systems. Since the partition is larger than 2GB, it is likely that the FAT32 file system is being used. In order to dual-boot with Windows 98 and Windows 2000, you must use FAT32. Windows 98 cannot use the NTFS file system.

☒ **A** is incorrect because FAT is the file system that would normally be used for partitions larger than 2GB. **C** is incorrect, because Windows 98 cannot use NTFS. If you convert the partition to NTFS, Windows 98 will no longer be functional. **D** is incorrect, because there is no such thing as a Windows 98 NTFS upgrade. Windows 98 cannot use NTFS.

8. ☑ **B.** The Per Seat license mode allows a client to access multiple servers with the same license. This is the preferred mode when there are multiple servers on the network.

☒ **A** is incorrect, because there is no such thing as a Per Client licensing mode. **C** is incorrect, because you would need multiple licenses for each client who was going to access multiple servers. This mode is preferred when there is only one server on the network. **D** is incorrect, because there is no such thing as a Per CAL licensing mode.

9. ☑ **C.** The Per Server mode is the best licensing mode when there is only one server on a network. This way you do not need a CAL for each client, just for the number of concurrent connections.

☒ **A** is incorrect, because there is no such thing as a Per Client licensing mode. **B** is incorrect, because the Per Seat mode would require a CAL for each client. This is the preferred mode when clients will access multiple servers. **D** is incorrect, because there is no such thing as a Per CAL licensing mode.

10. ☑ **B.** You can create a computer account in a domain during Setup if you have a valid username and password for an administrator account.

☒ **A** is incorrect, because you can create the computer account from the computer on which you are running Setup. You don't have to do it from a domain controller. **C** is incorrect, because no computer accounts are automatically added to a domain controller. An administrator must create the account. **D** is incorrect, because a domain controller does not automatically add computer accounts to the domain. An administrator must add it to the domain.

11. ☑ **B.** In order to dual-boot between Windows 98 and Windows 2000, you must install them in different directories. If you install Windows 2000 in the same directory, it will overwrite files required for Windows 98.

☒ **A** and **C** are incorrect, because if you install Windows 2000 in the same directory as Windows 98, it will overwrite files required by Windows 98. **D** is incorrect, because you are able to dual-boot between Windows 98 and Windows 2000 if you install them in different directories.

12. ☑ **C.** Wordpad is part of the Accessories and Utilities optional component. To select Wordpad, click Details and select Wordpad.

☒ **A** is incorrect, because the Windows Media component provides multimedia support, allowing you to deliver content using Advanced Streaming Format over an internetwork or the

Internet. **B** is incorrect, because the Management and Monitoring Tools provide tools for communications administration, monitoring, and management, including programs that support development of customized client dialers for remote users and implementation of phone books that can be automatically updated from a central server. **D** is incorrect, because Office Programs is not an optional component.

13. ☑ **B**. Each computer on the network must have a unique computer name.
    ☒ **A** is incorrect, because you are not limited to using your own name as a computer name. A computer name should be descriptive, but it is not required to be. **C** is incorrect, because if all computers in a domain used the domain name as their computer name, the computer names would not be unique. **D** is incorrect, because if all computers on a network used the workgroup name as their computer name, the computer names would not be unique.

14. ☑ **C**. The only network protocol installed by default is TCP/IP. NetBEUI is not installed.
    ☒ **A**, **B**, and **D** are incorrect, because the default network components that are installed are Client for Microsoft Networks, File and Print Sharing for Microsoft Networks, and TCP/IP.

15. ☑ **D**. The /s switch specifies the location of the Windows 2000 installation files.
    ☒ **A** is incorrect, because the /a switch enables the accessibility option. **B** is incorrect, because the /r switch Creates an additional folder within the system root folder (where the Windows 2000 system files are located). **C** is incorrect, because the /rx switch creates an additional folder within the system root folder, but Setup deletes the files after installation is completed.

16. ☑ **A**. The i386 directory on the Windows 2000 server CD-ROM contains the installation files needed to install Windows 2000 Server on Intel-based x86 computers.
    ☒ **B** and **C** are incorrect, because these directories do not exist on the Windows 2000 Server CD-ROM. **A** is incorrect, because Microsoft dropped support for the Alpha line of hardware after Windows 2000 Release Candidate 1 and the final release of Windows 2000 has no Alpha-based support (and no Alpha directory on the CD-ROM).

17. ☑ **B**. With Windows 2000 you use the makeboot.exe program to create the Setup disks. The Makeboot program takes the drive letter for the floppy drive as a command-line property.
    ☒ **A** and **C** are incorrect, because with Windows 2000, you have to use the Makeboot program. **D** is incorrect, because the Makeboot program takes a command-line parameter for the drive letter of the floppy drive.

18. ☑ **C**. The /e switch will execute a command prior to running the final phase of setup.
    ☒ **A**, **B**, and **D** are incorrect, because they are not valid command-line switches for the Winnt.exe program.

19. ☑ **B.** The /debug switch allows you to turn debugging on. You can also set the level of debugging and the filename to hold the debug log. By default, it uses the file C:\Winnt32.log at level 2 (the warning level).

☒ **A, C,** and **D** are incorrect, because they are not valid command-line switches for the Winnt.exe program.

20. ☑ **D.** If you do not specify a setup information filename with the /I switch, it will use the file DOSNET.INF by default.

☒ **A, B,** and **C** are incorrect, because the correct filename is DOSNET.INF.

LAB ANSWER

System Requirements

You have to ensure that the computers on which you are going to install Windows 2000 Server have the adequate resources. Not only does the computer have to meet the minimum requirements, but it also must be able to handle the load that will be placed on it. Some of the components to look at are the CPU, RAM, hard-disk controller, hard-disk space, and network card. You also want to ensure the computer has a CD-ROM drive and/or DVD drive and a floppy-disk drive.

Hardware Compatibility

You should make sure that the computers on which you are installing Windows 2000 Server are compatible with Windows 2000 Server. During Setup, your hardware will be checked for compatibility and any conflicts will be reported. However, you should check your hardware against the HCL before running Setup to prevent problems during installation. You should also make sure you have device drivers for your hardware that are designed for Windows 2000.

Optional Device Inventory

Windows 2000 now supports Plug-and-Play, so your devices will be detected, configured, and installed automatically. If any of your hardware is not Plug-and-Play compatible, you need to take some extra steps to prevent conflicts. Take an inventory of all the devices in the computer. Take note of the IRQ and memory address each device uses. This can help prevent conflicts that cannot be resolved during Setup. For instance, if two devices use the same IRQ and one of the devices does not use Plug-and-Play, you can either remove one of the adapters before installation and install it after setup or modify the IRQ setting of one of the devices before setup using the jumpers if available. Table 2-4 suggests some information to gather.

TABLE 2-4	Device	Information
Device Inventory Information	Video	Adapter or chipset type and how many video adapters
	Network	IRQ, I/O address, DMA (if used) connector type (for example, BNC or twisted pair), and bus type
	SCSI controller	Adapter model or chipset, IRQ, and bus type
	Mouse	Mouse type and port (COM1, COM2, bus, or PS/2) or USB
	I/O port	IRQ, I/O address, and DMA (if used) for each I/O port
	Sound adapter	IRQ, I/O address, and DMA
	Universal serial bus (USB)	Devices and Hubs attached
	PC Card	What adapters are inserted and in which slots
	Plug-and-Play	Whether enabled or disabled in BIOS
	BIOS settings	BIOS revision and date
	External modem	Com port connections (COM1, COM2, and so on)
	Internal modem	Com port connections; for nonstandard configurations, IRQ, and I/0 address
	Advanced Configuration and Power Interface (ACPI); Power Options	Enabled or disabled; current setting
	PCI	What PCI adapters are inserted and in which slots

Mass Storage Devices

If you are going to be using a mass storage device (i.e., SCSI or RAID) for your hard disk, you need to make sure the hard-disk controller is on the HCL. If it is not on the HCL, check the vendor for an updated driver designed for Windows 2000 Server that has been tested for compatibility. If there is one available, put it on a floppy disk and have it available during Setup.

BIOS

The basic input/output system (BIOS) of a computer is software that the operating system can use to communicate with the hardware devices. The current BIOS standard is called the Advanced Configuration and Power Interface (ACPI). Windows 2000 supports this standard as well as the older Advanced Power Management (APM) standard. You need to make sure that the BIOS is compatible with Windows 2000. You should check the HCL and you should check with the vendor to see if there is a BIOS upgrade for Windows 2000.

Important Files to Review

On the Windows 2000 server CD-ROM, there are some files in the root directory that you should read prior to installation. The file READ1ST.TXT contains notes that can be critical to the success of your installation. The file README.DOC contains information about the usage of hardware, networking, applications, and printing.

What Licensing Mode to Use

When you install Windows 2000 Server, you will have to choose a licensing mode. This determines where the Client Access License (CAL) will reside. The CAL allows clients to access the Windows 2000's network services, shared folders, and printers. You have to choose between Per Seat and Per Server. When using the Per Seat mode, each computer that accesses the server must have a CAL. The Per Server mode requires a CAL for each connection to the server.

The difference is where the license resides. When you use the Per Seat mode, a client can access multiple Windows 2000 Servers with the same license. This mode is the most common where a network has more than one Windows 2000 Server. Use this mode when clients need to access more than one server. When the Per Server mode is used, each concurrent connection requires a license on the server. That means there is a limit on how many simultaneous connections a Windows 2000 Server can have. For example, if you are using the Per Server mode with five concurrent connections, five computers can simultaneously access the server without additional licenses on the client. Once the number of concurrent connections reaches the maximum, Windows 2000 will reject any further access attempts until the number of concurrent connections goes below the maximum. This is the preferred mode if there is only one server on the network or for Internet/RAS computers when clients don't need to be licensed. If you are not sure which mode to use, choose the Per Server mode, because you can change to the Per Seat mode at no cost. You cannot change from the Per Seat mode to the Per Server mode.

What File System to Use

Windows 2000 supports the FAT, FAT32, and NTFS file systems. Since you are installing Windows 2000 Server, it is recommended that you use the NTFS file system. NTFS is a more powerful file system than FAT and FAT32. NTFS supports the Active Directory as well as built-in domain-based security and other features not available in FAT and FAT32. Since this is a new installation, you should not configure the servers for multiboot, so there is no good reason to choose FAT or Fat32.

Planning Disk Partitions

Since this will be a new installation, you should plan how you will partition your disk prior to starting installation. You need to determine the size of the partition on which you will be installing Windows 2000 Server. There aren't any hard-and-fast rules, but you should make the partition big enough for the operating system, applications that will be installed on this partition, and any other files that will be stored on it. Setup requires at least 1GB of free space with 671MB of free space on the partition you are installing to, but you should provide a much larger partition. With hard disks becoming so inexpensive, it is not uncommon to have 10GB partitions. This allows space for a variety of items, including optional components, user accounts, Active Directory information, logs, future service packs, the page file used by the operating system, and other items.

During Setup, create and size only the partition on which you want to install Windows 2000. After Windows 2000 is installed, you can use Disk Management to manage new and existing disks and volumes. This includes creating new partitions from unpartitioned space; deleting, renaming, and reformatting existing partitions; adding and removing hard disks; and upgrading and reverting hard disks between basic and dynamic formats. Setup examines the hard disk to determine its existing configuration, and then offers the following options:

- If the hard disk is unpartitioned, you can create and size the Windows 2000 partition.

- If the hard disk is partitioned but has enough unpartitioned disk space, you can create the Windows 2000 partition by using the unpartitioned space.

- If the hard disk has an existing partition that is large enough, you can install Windows 2000 on that partition, with or without reformatting the partition first. Reformatting a partition erases all data on the partition. If you don't reformat the partition but you do install Windows 2000 where there was already an operating system, that operating system will be overwritten, and you will have to reinstall any applications you want to use with Windows 2000.

- If the hard disk has an existing partition, you can delete it to create more unpartitioned disk space for the Windows 2000 partition. Deleting an existing partition also erases any data on that partition.

Choosing Components to Install

When you install Windows 2000 Server, there are some optional components you can install. You need to determine how your server will be utilized so you can determine which optional components to install. These optional components extend the functionality of Windows 2000 Server. If you do not install a component that you determine a need for later, you can add any optional components later, after installation, through the Add/Remove Programs in Control Panel. The more components you install, the more functionality your server will have. However, do not install components you know you will not need. They will just take up disk space. There are also some components that are specific to Windows 2000 Server. You can choose from the following components:

■ **Dynamic Host Configuration Protocol (DHCP)** Used for dynamic IP addressing.

■ **Domain Name Service (DNS)** Used for converting domain names to IP addresses.

■ **Windows Internet Name Service (WINS)** Used for converting NetBIOS names to IP addresses.

■ **Remote Installation Services** Provides services that you can use to set up new client computers remotely, without the need to visit each client.

■ **Terminal Services** Provides the ability to run client applications on the server, while "thin client" software acts as a terminal emulator on the client.

■ **Certificate Services** Provides security and authentication support, including secure e-mail, Web-based authentication, and smart card authentication.

■ **Indexing Service** Provides indexing functions for documents stored on disk, allowing users to search for specific document text or properties.

■ **Internet Information Services (IIS)** Provides support for Web site creation, configuration, and management, along with Network News Transfer Protocol (NNTP), File Transfer Protocol (FTP), and Simple Mail Transfer Protocol (SMTP), and so on.

■ **Windows Media Services** Provides multimedia support, allowing you to deliver content using Advanced Streaming Format over an internetwork or the Internet.

Networking: TCP/IP, IP Addresses, and Name Resolution

To set up TCP/IP on your servers, each server needs to have an IP address. This can be provided automatically by DHCP or manually by assigning a static IP address. Because these addresses are numbers and can be hard to remember, you will also have to provide users with names that can be resolved to IP addresses by DNS and WINS.

When TCP/IP is used, an IP address must be provided for each computer. This list describes the methods you can use to provide an IP address:

■ For a limited number of servers (five or fewer) on a small private network, you can use the Windows 2000 Server feature called Automatic Private IP Addressing (APIPA) to automatically assign IP addresses for you.

■ If your network has more than one subnet, choose one server on which to install and configure the Dynamic Host Configuration Protocol (DHCP) component. It must itself be assigned a static IP address (so other computers can locate it). In this situation, in order to support clients, you might also need one or more servers with the DNS component and/or the Windows Internet Name Service (WINS) component.

■ If a particular server will be directly providing access to users on the Internet, you must assign that server a static IP address.

To make it easier for users, you can allow them to use names instead of IP addresses. These names can be translated to IP addresses by DNS or WINS. DNS is a hierarchical naming system used for locating computers on the Internet and on private TCP/IP networks. DNS is required for Internet e-mail, Web browsing, and Active Directory. DNS is also required in domains with clients running Windows 2000. DNS is installed automatically when you create a domain controller unless the Windows 2000 software detects that a DNS service already exists for that domain.

Deciding Between Workgroups and Domains

A domain is a collection of accounts and network resources that are grouped together using a single domain name and security boundary. All user accounts, permissions, and other network details are stored in a centralized database on the primary domain controller and replicated to the backup domain controllers. A single login gives the user access to all resources for which they have permissions. Domains are recommended for all networks that have more than ten computers or that are expected to grow to larger than ten computers in the near future. There are a few requirements for joining a domain: You need to know the domain name. You must have a computer account for the computer on which you are installing Windows 2000 Server. This account can be created either by the administrator before installing Windows 2000 Server or during setup with the username and password of an account with the permissions to create a computer account. You also need at least one domain controller and Domain Name Server (DNS) Service online when you install Windows 2000 Server. You can add the server as either a member server or a domain controller. A member server is a member that does not have a copy of the Active Directory and does not perform security functionality for the domain.

A workgroup is a logical grouping of resources on a network. It is generally used in peer-to-peer networks. This means that each computer is responsible for access to its own resources. Each computer has its own account database and is administered separately. Security is not shared between computers, and administration is more difficult than in a centralized domain. It is intended only as a convenience to help you find resources. When the computer is browsing the network, the resources in your same workgroup are found first. It does not provide any security. In a workgroup, you might have to remember a different password for every resource you want to access. To join a workgroup during installation, all you need is a workgroup name. This can be the name of an existing workgroup or a new one. You must join a workgroup or a domain during installation, but you can change these memberships later as needed.

Planning for Domain Controllers and Member Servers

Windows 2000 Servers in a domain can have one of two roles: domain controllers, which contain matching copies of the user accounts and other Active Directory data in a given domain; and member servers, which belong to a domain but do not contain a copy of the Active Directory data. (A server that belongs to a workgroup, not a domain, is called a stand-alone server.) With Windows 2000, it is possible to change the role of a server back and forth from domain controller to member server (or stand-alone server), even after Setup is complete. However, it is recommended that you plan your domain before running Setup, and change server roles only when necessary.

You should determine names for your domain controllers before running Setup. You cannot change the name of a server while it is a domain controller. Instead, you must change it to a member or stand-alone server, change the name, and finally make the server a domain controller once again.

If you have multiple domain controllers, you can provide better support for users than if you have only one. Multiple domain controllers provide automatic backup for user accounts and other Active Directory data, and they work together to support domain controller functions (such as validating logons).

3

Unattended Installation of Windows 2000 Server

T he attended installation methods for Windows 2000 Server consume a significant amount of time, and the administrator must answer a lot of setup questions. In a large organization with hundreds of servers, it is neither a desired method of installation nor it is it recommended to perform attended installations. Attended installations can cost the organization a significant amount of time and money and can delay projects. Windows 2000 Server comes with some tools and utilities that help you automate the installation process, thereby reducing the time and deployment costs for implementation. These methods also help in standardizing the server configurations throughout the organization.

This chapter describes how the automated and customized installations can be performed on computers with similar or different hardware configurations using these tools. This chapter also discusses the installation and configuration of Remote Installation Services for deployment of Windows 2000 Professional.

CERTIFICATION OBJECTIVE 3.01

Understanding the Difference Between Unattended Installations and Prepared Images

The unattended installation of any operating system is the preferred method of installation when you have a large number of computers. Disk imaging systems have become popular because they save the network administrator from a number of hardships while rolling out any operating system. These installation methods drastically reduce the costs incurred and time spent in deployment.

But before you decide on some method of automated deployment of an operating system, it is necessary that you understand all the ups and downs of using a particular method. Windows 2000 Server includes some tools to automate the installation process. The Setup Manager is one such interactive graphical wizard that helps you create custom answer files. To create such answer files, you need not be an expert in writing long scripts.

The basic difference between unattended installations and prepared images lies in the requirements of each method and its usage. The imaging methods discussed later in this chapter are the System Preparation (SysPrep) tool and the Remote Installation Preparation (RIPrep) wizard. These can be part of your completely automated installation plans. The method that you use for automating the Windows 2000 Server installations depends on the results that you want to get when the installation process is over. The following methods can be used to perform unattended installations:

- The WINNT32.EXE command used with the /unattend switch specifying an answer file

- The bootable CD-ROM method, which requires a prepared answer file that is to be stored on a floppy disk

- Installations using the Systems Management Server (SMS)

The imaging tools that can be used are as follows:

- The System Preparation (SysPrep) tool

- The WINNT32.EXE command used with the /syspart switch

- The Remote Installation Preparation (RIPrep) utility, which uses the Remote Installation Services (RIS); this method can be used for installing Windows 2000 Professional only

The details of each of these methods are given in the following sections. The use of SMS for automating installations is not covered in the MCSE Windows 2000 Server exam.

Extracting Deployment Tools

Before we can use any of these tools, we need to find out where they are located in the Windows 2000 Professional CD with the exception of the Remote Installation Preparation (RIPrep) tool, which comes with Windows 2000 Server. You will find the SysPrep tool and the Setup Manager in the DEPLOY.CAB file of the Support\Tools folder on your Windows 2000 Professional CD. The process of writing installation scripts or answer files using the Setup Manager is discussed later in this chapter. In Exercise 3-1, which follows, we learn how to extract these files.

CertCam 3-1

EXERCISE 3-1

Extracting the Windows 2000 Deployment Tools

1. Select a computer where you want to extract the deployment tools. Log on as administrator.

2. Insert the Windows 2000 Server CD in the CD-ROM drive. Close the window that pops up immediately after inserting the CD.

3. Open Windows Explorer and create a folder named DEPTOOLS in the C: drive. You will use this folder to keep the files you extract from the Support\Tools folder on the CD-ROM.

4. Considering that D: is the drive letter for your CD-ROM, double-click the DEPLOY.CAB folder icon, located in the D:\Support\Tools folder:

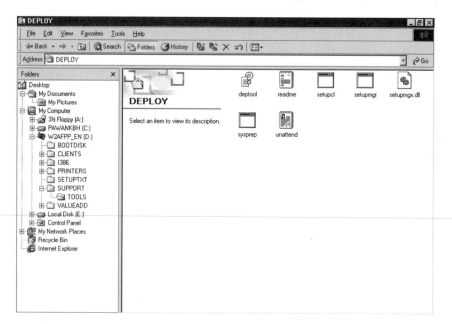

5. From the File menu, click Edit | Select All. All the files are selected. Right-click on any of the files and click Extract.

6. In the Browse for Folder window, select the Deptools folder under the C: drive. Click Deptools, and then click OK.

7. The file extraction takes only a few seconds. Check the contents of the Deptools folder in the Windows Explorer. You will notice that seven files have been copied to this folder.

CERTIFICATION OBJECTIVE 3.02

Creating and Configuring Automated Methods for Installation

You might be familiar with the unattended installation of Windows NT Server 4.0 using the customized answer files. The Setup Manager still remains an excellent choice for generating custom answer files in Windows 2000, and it has been vastly improved. We now have other deployment utilities such as the SysPrep tool and the Remote Installation Service (RIS). The RIS uses RIPrep to duplicate disks. These tools are disk-cloning systems that help prepare the images of fully configured computers with the operating system and all applications. Although SysPrep can be used for both Windows 2000 Server and Windows 2000 Professional operating systems, RIS supports deployment of Windows 2000 Professional on client computers only.

What Is RIPrep?

Remote Installation Preparation (RIPrep) is a disk duplication tool included with Windows 2000 Server. It is an ideal tool for creating images of fully prepared client computers. RIPrep helps in fast deployment of the operating system and applications on a large number of client computers using the RIS of a Windows 2000 Server. It is notable that the RIPrep can only prepare the images of fully configured client computers that are running the Windows 2000 Professional operating system. The deployment of images created by RIPrep does not need the client computer hardware to be identical.

RIPrep requires that the RIS and its associated services be configured and running on one or more servers on the network. The client computers are first configured with an operating system and all standard or custom-built business applications. The RIPrep wizard is run on the client computer to create an image of the computer. This image is uploaded to a Windows 2000 Server running the RIS for further distribution to other client computers.

What Is SysPrep?

The *System Preparation tool*, or *SysPrep,* provides an excellent means of saving installation time and reducing installation costs. Like RIPrep, SysPrep is a disk duplication method that works for creating images of both Windows 2000 Server and Windows 2000 Professional operating systems. It is also helpful in standardizing the desktop environment throughout the organization. A single SysPrep image cannot typically be used as a standard in different departments of an organization due to differences in applications used by each department, even if the computers have identical hardware. SysPrep can be used to create multiple images. Besides standardizing the server environment, you can use SysPrep to implement uniform policies in the organization.

For creating system images using SysPrep, one computer is fully configured with the operating system and all the applications. This computer serves as the master or model computer that has the complete setup of the operating system, application software, and any service packs. The SYSPREP.EXE file is executed to prepare the hard disk for imaging on a master computer. The image, called the *master image,* is copied to a CD-ROM or put on a network share for distribution to many computers. Any third-party disk-imaging tool can then be used to replicate the image to other identical computers. Some of the image-copying tools are Drive Image from Power Quest and Norton Ghost from Symantec.

exam
ⓦatch

Note that the SysPrep tool can be used only for clean installations. It cannot be used for upgrading a previous operating system.

When to Use UNATTEND.TXT Instead of SysPrep or RIPrep

The decision of using a particular method of automating installation for an operating system largely depends on the host organization's requirements. A number of factors must be taken into account. All deployment methods have certain requirements as well as their own advantages and disadvantages.

The creation of customized UNATTEND.TXT answer files is the simplest form of providing answers to setup queries and unattended installation of Windows 2000. This can either be done using the Setup Manager or by editing the sample UNATTEND.TXT file using Notepad or the MS-DOS text editor. The UNATTEND.TXT file does not provide any means of creating an image of the computer. This method works for both Server and Professional versions of Windows 2000. It is independent of the computer hardware and can be used for clean installations as well as upgrades.

The SysPrep and RIPrep methods of disk duplication require considerable planning and preparation before you can create and distribute system images. SysPrep works on both Windows 2000 Server and Professional and can be used only for clean installations, when all the computers have nearly identical hardware. The prepared images must be distributed using a third-party utility. On the other hand, using RIPrep requires a fully configured RIS server and its associated services such as Active Directory, DNS, and DHCP to be functional on the network. RIPrep can deliver only Windows 2000 Professional images and does not support the use of third-party disk imaging tools.

Table 3-1 will help you understand and decide on the method of unattended installation of Windows 2000 that's right for you.

Preparing and Deploying Images Using SysPrep and RIPrep

As we have observed, SysPrep and RIPrep are utilities that prepare master images of fully configured computers. SysPrep only prepares a master computer for creating an image; RIPrep works with the RIS to complete the image creation and distribution job. The preparation and distribution of operating system images needs a careful study of available methods of deployment. This also requires that you take into account all the hardware-related factors. The choice of an imaging method depends on the type of installation you need. SysPrep and RIPrep can be used only for clean installations. These methods will not work if you want to upgrade a previous version of an operating system such as Windows NT 4.0.

Remember that although SysPrep can be used for preparing images of both Windows 2000 Server and Windows 2000 Professional, RIPrep can be used only for Windows 2000 Professional. Again, neither of these tools can be used for upgrading any previously installed operating system.

TABLE 3-1 Comparison of Automated Installation Methods

Installation Requirements	UNATTEND.TXT	SysPrep	RIPrep
Clean installation	Yes	Yes	Yes
Upgrade	Yes	No	No
Similar hardware	Yes	Yes	Yes
Dissimilar hardware	Yes	No	Yes
Windows 2000 Server	Yes	Yes	No
Windows 2000 Professional	Yes	Yes	Yes

Requirements for Running SysPrep

As we have observed, the SysPrep tool is an ideal imaging solution for computers that have identical hardware configurations. The following points describe the various requirements that must be met in order to use SysPrep:

- In order to use SysPrep, you must ensure that the master and destination computers have identical Hardware Abstraction Layer (HAL) and Advanced Configuration and Power Interface (ACPI) support as well as mass storage device controllers. The hard drive capacity required on the destination computers must be at least equal to or higher than the hard drive capacity on the master computer. For example, SysPrep will not help if the master computer has a SCSI hard drive and the destination computer has an IDE hard drive.

- There is an exception for Plug-and-Play devices. These devices need not necessarily be identical. Examples of such devices are video cards, network adapters, sound cards, and modems. The SysPrep master image automatically runs full Plug-and-Play device detection on the destination computer.

- The SysPrep tool only prepares the hard disk of a master computer for imaging. You need some third-party utility to distribute the master image. There is no limit on the number of master images that you can create. For example, if your company has five different hardware configurations, you can create five master images.

- You need to have administrative privileges on the master computer where you want to run SysPrep. It is also advisable that you test the applications thoroughly and apply all necessary service packs before creating a master image.

- The most important and mandatory requirement for running SysPrep is that you must have a volume licensing agreement from Microsoft. Besides that agreement, you must ensure that you are not violating license agreements of any other application that you want to distribute.

exam
ⓦatch

SysPrep cannot be used in environments in which every other desktop has its own custom configuration.

Components of SysPrep

The SysPrep utility has the four components associated with it. These are SYSPREP.EXE, SYSPREP.INF, SETUPCL.EXE, and the Mini-Setup wizard. The function of each component is covered in this section.

SYSPREP.EXE SYSPREP.EXE is the main SysPrep executable file. This command has the following syntax:

```
Sysprep.exe [-quiet] [-nosidgen] [-reboot]
```

- **-quiet** This option runs SysPrep in a quiet mode and does not generate any messages on the screen.
- **-nosidgen** This option runs SysPrep without regenerating any security IDs (SIDs). This allows the user to test and customize the computer's image. This function is particularly useful when you do not want to clone the master computer on which SysPrep is being run.
- **-reboot** This option forces a reboot of the master computer after the image has been created.

SYSPREP.INF SYSPREP.INF is an answer file. When you want to automate the Mini-Setup wizard by providing predetermined answers to all setup questions, you must use this file. This file needs to be placed in the %Systemroot%\Sysprep folder or on a floppy disk. When the Mini-Setup wizard is run on the computer on which the image is being distributed, it takes answers from the SYSPREP.INF file without prompting the user for any input.

SETUPCL.EXE The function of the SETUPCL.EXE file is to run the Mini-Setup wizard and to regenerate the security IDs on the master and destination computers. The Mini-Setup wizard starts on the master computer when it is booted for the first time after running SysPrep.

The Mini-Setup Wizard The purpose of this wizard is to add some user-specific parameters on the destination computer. These parameters include the following information:

- End-user license agreement (EULA)
- Product key (serial number)
- Username, company name, and administrator password
- Network configuration
- Domain or workgroup name
- Date and time zone selection

The information in the Mini-Setup wizard can be automated using the SYSPREP.INF file. The syntax and structure of the SYSPREP.INF file is similar to the answer file created by Setup Manager. You can also use the Setup Manager to create an answer file for the Mini-Setup wizard.

exam
ⓦatch

Using SYSPREP.INF file gives you an option to provide answers to all or some of the user input required by the Mini-Setup wizard. The user is prompted for any answers that are not included in the SYSPREP.INF file.

The SysPrep Process: Preparing a Master Image

Let's look at the process of preparing a master computer for imaging using SysPrep. The following description will help you understand the various steps involved in this process:

1. Select a computer that has the hardware identical to all or many of the other computers involved in the installation. Install Windows 2000 Professional on this computer. (For a description of how to install Windows 2000 Server, refer to Chapter 2 of this book.) It is recommended that you do not make the computer a member of any domain. In addition, keep the local administrator password blank.

2. When the Windows 2000 Server setup is complete, log on to the computer as administrator. Make necessary changes to the Windows configuration that you want to standardize throughout your organization. Install any custom or business applications on this computer. Apply service packs, if any.

3. Test all the components of the operating system and the applications on the master computer for reliability. When you are ready, delete any unwanted files, such as setup and audit logs.

4. Prepare the master image by running the SysPrep utility. Exercise 3-2 describes how to run SysPrep. When the image has been created, the system either shuts down automatically or prompts you that it is safe to shut down.

5. The next step is disk duplication. This needs to be done using a third-party imaging tool, such as Drive Image from Power Quest or Norton Ghost from Symantec. This step needs to be done prior to restarting the master computer, similar to the way a Mini-Setup wizard starts running on the master computer when you restart it. This happens because the SysPrep process takes off the security ID of the computer, and this SID needs to be restored.

6. The final step is image distribution. This can be accomplished using any third-party utility. When the destination computer is started for the first time, a Mini-Setup wizard is run. SysPrep adds this wizard to the master image.

EXERCISE 3-2

Running SysPrep from the Command Prompt

This method of running SysPrep gives you the option of using any or all the optional switches associated with SysPrep. In this exercise, we use the /reboot switch:

1. Log on to the master computer as an administrator.

2. Select Start | Run and type **cmd**. The MS-DOS prompt window opens.

3. Change to the system root by typing **cd **. Create a directory named SysPrep by typing **md SysPrep**.

4. Change to the SysPrep folder by typing **cd SysPrep**.

5. Insert the Windows 2000 Server setup CD-ROM in the CD-ROM drive. Double-click the DEPLOY.CAB file in the \support\tools folder.

6. Copy the SYSPREP.EXE and the SETUPCL.EXE files to this folder.

7. Run SysPrep from the c:\Sysprep directory by typing the following command:

```
Sysprep -reboot
```

8. A warning message appears on the screen, as shown in the illustration below, telling you that the execution of SysPrep may change some security settings of this computer. Click OK.

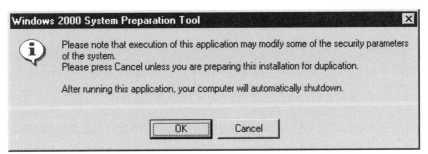

9. Since we used the -reboot option with SYSPREP.EXE, the master computer prepares the image and restarts automatically.

on the
job

It is best to perform the SysPrep installation when you have a large number of computers that need a clean installation. Usually this is not the case. You might have computers that are already running some other operating system and applications. Even in networked environments where users have their home and data folders on the servers, data is still stored locally. Be sure to ask your users about the importance of their data and make backups before you go ahead with your plans for a mass deployment using any of these tools.

The Remote Installation Preparation Wizard

The RIS supports two types of images: CD-ROM-based images and those prepared using the RIPrep wizard. The CD-ROM-based image is similar to installing Windows 2000 Professional from the setup CD-ROM. The only difference is that the installation files are stored on the RIS server.

The RIPrep wizard enables the network administrator to distribute to a large number of client computers a standard desktop configuration that includes the operating system and the applications. This not only helps in maintaining a uniform standard across the enterprise; it also cuts the costs and time involved in a large-scale rollout of Windows 2000 Professional.

The limitation of RIPrep is that it can replicate images of only a single disk with a single partition. But the flip side is that the client computers need not have identical hardware configurations. The RIPrep utility automatically detects the difference between the source and destination hardware configurations using the Plug-and-Play support.

How does RIPrep work? First you need to install Windows 2000 Professional on a client computer that is chosen to act as a model. This installation is performed as a remote installation using an existing RIS server on the network. Next, all the required applications as defined in the enterprise standards are installed locally on this computer. The operating system and the applications are tested for reliability in all respects. The RIPrep is then run on this computer to create an image of the operating system and the applications. This image is uploaded to the RIS server for further distribution to the clients that need a similar configuration. When RIS is installed on a Windows 2000 Server, the Single-Instance Store (SIS) service is also added to the server. This service is utilized to reduce the hard disk space requirements for the volumes that hold the RIS images. The SIS service keeps a check on any duplicate files; if duplicates are found, SIS replaces them with a link. This practice helps save disk space.

EXERCISE 3-3

Running the Remote Installation Preparation Wizard

1. Select a client computer as a model and install Windows 2000 Professional from an existing RIS server on the network.

2. Install any applications on this computer that meet the requirements of your desktop standards. Configure the operating system and the applications. Test all aspects of the client computer for reliability.

3. Connect to the RIS server to run the RIPrep wizard. Click Start | Run and type in the correct path of the RIPREP.EXE file, as follows:

   ```
   \\RISserver_name\RemoteInstallshare_name\Admin\i386\RIPrep.exe
   ```

4. The Remote Installation Preparation wizard starts with a welcome screen. Click Next.

5. When prompted, type in the name of the RIS server to which the image is intended to be copied. By default, the same RIS server is chosen that is running the RIPrep wizard. Click Next.

6. You will be prompted for the name of the directory to which the image is to be copied. Type in the name and click Next.

7. The Friendly Description and Help Text prompts appear. In case you plan to create more than one image, it is recommended that you type in the correct name and description of the image. This is helpful for identifying an image when the other clients are presented with image selection options.

8. The next window displays a summary of the selections you have made. In case you need to change any setting, click the Back button and review the settings.

9. If everything seems fine, click Next.

The image preparation and replication to the RIS server takes a few minutes. Once the image is copied to the RIS server, any remote boot client can use the image for installation.

Advantages and Disadvantages of SysPrep

Any new feature in an operating system comes with added benefits to the user. Automating the Windows 2000 installation using SysPrep has associated with it certain advantages and disadvantages.

Advantages of SysPrep   The following are the advantages of SysPrep:

- SysPrep is the quickest way to prepare the image.
- SysPrep is ideal for clean installations.
- SysPrep requires low administrative overheads.
- SysPrep saves installation time and money.
- SysPrep works for Windows 2000 Server as well as Windows 2000 Professional.

Disadvantages of SysPrep   The following points outline the disadvantages of SysPrep:

- The master and destination computers need to be identical in the hardware, except Plug-and-Play devices.
- SysPrep cannot be used for upgrading a previously installed operating system.
- A third-party tool is required for creating and delivering images, accruing additional deployment costs.
- The computer on which the image is created must be reconfigured using the Mini-Setup wizard.

Advantages and Disadvantages of RIPrep

RIPrep is another method of preparing images for computers running Windows 2000 Professional. The following advantages and disadvantages are important to study before deciding to use RIPrep.

Advantages of RIPrep   Some of the advantages of using RIPrep are:

- The RIPrep utility is bundled with Windows 2000 Server, and no third-party tool is required for creation or delivery of images.
- RIPrep's Single-Instance Store (SIS) saves a good deal of hard drive space, eliminating duplicate copies of setup files.

- RIPrep is independent of hardware configuration.
- RIPrep helps standardize the Windows 2000 Professional-based desktop environment in an organization.

Disadvantages of RIPrep   The following points highlight some disadvantages of using RIPrep:

- RIPrep accumulates high administrative costs and needs trained professionals to implement.
- RIPrep is dependent on several other services, such as RIS, Active Directory, DNS, and DHCP. These must be running on the network.
- RIPrep can be used for clean installations only. Upgrades are not supported.
- RIPrep can be used to prepare images of Windows 2000 Professional only.
- RIPrep can duplicate images of a single hard drive consisting of a single partition only.
- Only some PCI network adapters or PXE-ROM version .99 or later are supported for booting the remote client.

Now that you have some idea of automating Windows 2000 Server operating system, let's consider some real-life scenarios.

SCENARIO & SOLUTION

Three different vendors have supplied the server hardware in my office. Can I use SysPrep to create one standard image for these servers?	No, SysPrep requires the hardware to be identical for all servers.
I am already running Windows NT 4.0 on seven servers. What is the best way to upgrade in unattended mode?	Use the scripted method. Create custom answer files using Setup Manager.
Can I use Remote Installation Service to deploy Windows 2000 Server in my organization?	No, RIS can deliver only Windows 2000 Professional.
Is it necessary for the hardware to be identical if I want to use RIPrep for creating images of my Windows 2000 Professional computers?	No. RIPrep is independent of hardware.

CERTIFICATION OBJECTIVE 3.03

Using Setup Manager to Automate the Installation Process

The Setup Manager is an interactive graphical wizard that makes it easy to create or modify customized answer files for unattended setup of Windows 2000 Server. It provides you with the option of either creating a fresh answer file or modifying an existing file. You can also choose to copy the configuration of the computer on which you are running the Setup Manager. This wizard makes it easy to indicate the computer- and user-specific information in the answer files and create a distribution folder. When you create answer files using the Setup Manager, the following three files are created:

- **UNATTEND.TXT** This is the actual answer file.
- **UNATTEND.BAT** This file is used to run the UNATTEND.TXT file.
- **UNATTEND.UDF** This file is the Uniqueness Database File, which provides customized settings for each computer using the automated installation.

Answer files help automate the installation process as all the queries presented to you during installation are answered by the answer files. With careful planning, you can prepare answers that eliminate the possibility of incorrect answers typed in by the person performing the installation, thus reducing the chances of setup failure. The Setup Manager wizard can be used to quickly create a customized answer file. This technique minimizes the chances of committing syntax-related errors while manually creating or editing the sample answer files.

When you need to customize automated installation of each computer, you can use the Uniqueness Database Files. These files have a .UDB extension. A UDF file allows the automated installation with unique settings contained in the UDF file. The data contained in the UDF file is merged into the answer file during setup.

Creating Answer Files for Unattended Installation

Answer files can be created by any of the following methods:

- By writing a fresh script using the correct syntax required using the Notepad or the MS-DOS editor program

- By editing the sample answer file that is located in the \i386 folder of the Windows 2000 Server Setup CD-ROM

- By using the Setup Manager wizard; this is the fastest and most accurate method and can also create a distribution folder

The unattended method for Windows 2000 Server installation uses the answer file to specify various configuration parameters. This method eliminates user interaction during installation, thereby automating the installation process and reducing the chances of input errors. Answers to most of the questions asked by the setup process are specified in the answer file. In addition, the scripted method can be used for clean installations and upgrades.

The Windows 2000 Server CD-ROM includes a sample answer file, UNATTEND.TXT, which is located in the \i386 folder. This file can be edited and customized for individual installation needs. Once the answer file is ready, the Windows 2000 Server installation can be started in unattended mode using the WINNT.EXE or WINNT32.EXE command with /u switch.

Creating a Custom Answer File

The UNATTEND.TXT answer file included in the Windows 2000 Server CD-ROM may not be suitable for all unattended installations. You can create custom answer files by either using the Notepad or modifying the UNATTEND.TXT file. In case you decide to use Notepad, be careful to follow the correct syntax. It is also not mandatory to name the answer file *UNATTEND.TXT*. If you want to create several answer files, you can name the files as suits your requirements. The other option is to use the Setup Manager to create a customized answer file.

The following is an edited version of the UNATTEND.TXT file that comes with Windows 2000 Server CD-ROM:

```
; This file contains information about how to automate the installation
; or upgrade of Windows 2000 Professional and Windows 2000 Server so the
; Setup program runs without requiring user input.
  [Unattended]
Unattendmode = FullUnattended
OemPreinstall = NO
TargetPath = WINNT
Filesystem = LeaveAlone
```

```
[UserData]
FullName = "PBHARDWAJ"
OrgName = "First MCSE, Inc."
ComputerName = "TestComp"

[GuiUnattended]
; Sets the Timezone to the Pacific Northwest
; Sets the Admin Password to NULL
; Turn AutoLogon ON and login once
TimeZone = "004"
AdminPassword = pass
AutoLogon = No
AutoLogonCount = 15
 [GuiRunOnce]
; List the programs that you want to launch when the machine is logged into for the first time

 [Display]
BitsPerPel = 8
XResolution = 800
YResolution = 600
VRefresh = 70

[Networking]
; When set to YES, setup will install default-networking components. The components to be set are
; TCP/IP, File and Print Sharing, and the Client for Microsoft Networks.
InstallDefaultComponents = YES

[Identification]
JoinWorkgroup = Workgroup
; In order to join a domain, delete the line above and add the following lines
; JoinDomain = DomainName
; CreateComputerAccountInDomain = Yes
; DomainAdmin = Administrator
; DomainAdminPassword = AdminPassword
```

After the study of scripted installation methods, you must be able to understand the utility of customized answer files and ways to create or edit them. Let's look at a quick review.

SCENARIO & SOLUTION

If an answer file comes with Windows 2000 Professional, why can't I use it for all installations?	The answer file included with Windows 2000 Professional is basically intended to help administrators understand the program's use and syntax and is in its most generalized form using many default parameters. Many setup parameters in this file might not suit your requirements. The file has to be edited before you can use it.
Why do I need to create a network share when I can use the CD-ROM for installations?	You need a network share when you want to install Windows 2000 Professional or any other operating system simultaneously on many computers. One CD-ROM can be used at one computer only. If you have many computers running Setup and notice that the server holding the network share is very slow, you might need to create more network shares.
I hate using Notepad or WordPad and typing the tough syntax for editing or creating a custom answer file. Is there any other option that can help me create an answer file?	Yes. Use the Windows 2000 Setup Manager wizard. This graphical tool helps you create custom answer files or scripts for many computers at a time without much effort.

EXERCISE 3-4

Using Setup Manager to Create Answer Files

1. Log on as administrator on a computer running Windows 2000 Professional. In Windows Explorer, change to the folder in which the deployment tools are located.

2. Double-click on the SETUPMGR.EXE file. The Windows 2000 Setup Manager welcome screen opens. Click Next to continue.

3. You are prompted to select a type of answer file. Click the radio button for the option Create a new answer file, as shown in the illustration below. Doing so opens another screen, where you are prompted to select an operating system.

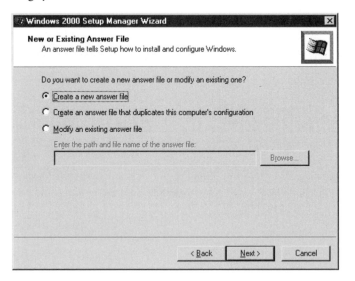

4. Select Windows 2000 Unattended Installation, as shown in the next illustration. Click Next. In the next screen, select Windows 2000 Server.

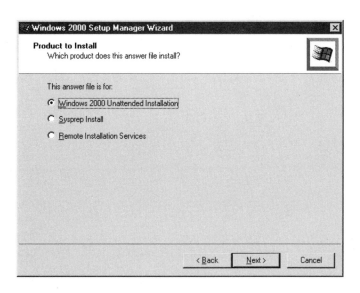

5. The User Interaction Level screen appears. You are presented with the following five options:

- **Provide Defaults**   To accept or modify the default answers.
- **Fully Automated**   The setup is fully automated. The user is not allowed to change any answers.
- **Hide Pages**   The pages for which the answers are supplied by the script are not shown to the user.
- **Read Only**   The user can see the answers on any unhidden setup pages but cannot change them.
- **GUI Attended**   In this case only the text-mode phase of the setup is automated. The user must type in the answers in the graphics phase of the setup.

For the purpose of this exercise, select the Fully Automated option, as shown:

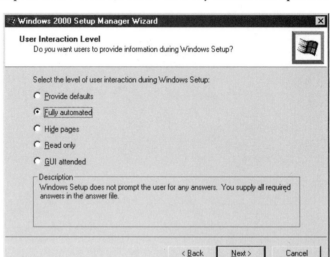

Click "I accept the terms of the License Agreement." Click Next. This brings up the Customize the Software screen.

6. Type in your name and the name of your organization. Click Next.

7. The next screen is where you assign computer names. You can elect to create answer files for one computer or for many computers. Create two answer files for use with two computers. You can either type in the names yourself or enter the name of a text file that contains the computer names. The latter option is useful when you have a large number of computers that will use this answer file. The Setup Manager can also generate the computer names automatically. Type **TestComp1** and click Add. Then type **TestComp2** and click Add. As shown in the following illustration, these names are added in a separate box that shows the names of the computers to be installed. Click Next.

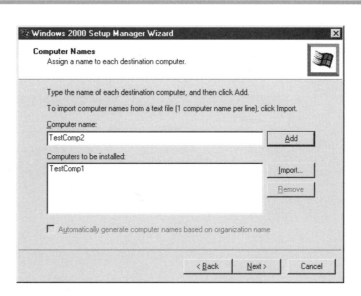

8. The next window is for supplying the administrator password. There are two options: prompt the user to supply a password or use the following administrator password. Notice in the illustration below that the first option is grayed out because you selected a fully automated installation earlier. Leave the password blank for this exercise.

9. The next screen is where you select display settings, as shown in the illustration below. Change colors to display 256 colors and screen area to 800 by 600 pixels. Click Next.

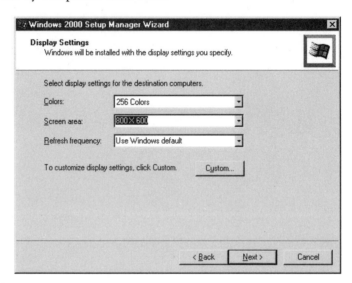

10. Next comes the Network Settings window. If you select the typical settings, the TCP/IP protocol will be installed, DHCP will be enabled, and the Client for Microsoft Networks protocol will also be installed. Click Custom Settings because we will not use DHCP in this exercise.

11. In the next screen, select One Network Adapter, which is the default, and click Next. Select Internet Protocol (TCP/IP) and click Properties. Enter the appropriate parameters for the target workstation's IP configuration and click Next.

12. Accept the default Workgroup option in the next screen, as shown:

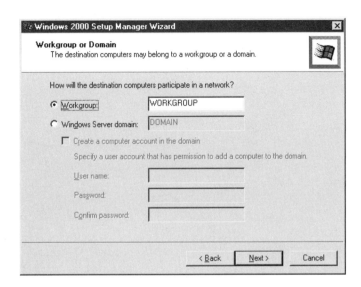

13. The next screen prompts you to select the time zone. Select the appropriate zone and click Next.

14. The next screen prompts you to choose whether or not you want to edit the additional settings offered through Setup Manager, such as telephony, regional settings, languages, browser and shell settings for Internet Explorer, installation folder, printers, and run-once commands. Select "No, do not edit the additional settings." Click Next.

15. The Distribution Folder screen appears. You can either specify the name of the distribution folder or have the Setup Manager create a folder on a local computer. The default is "Yes, create or modify a Distribution folder." Click Next. In the next screen, shown in the next illustration, select the default "Create a new distribution folder" and confirm the path and share names. Click Next.

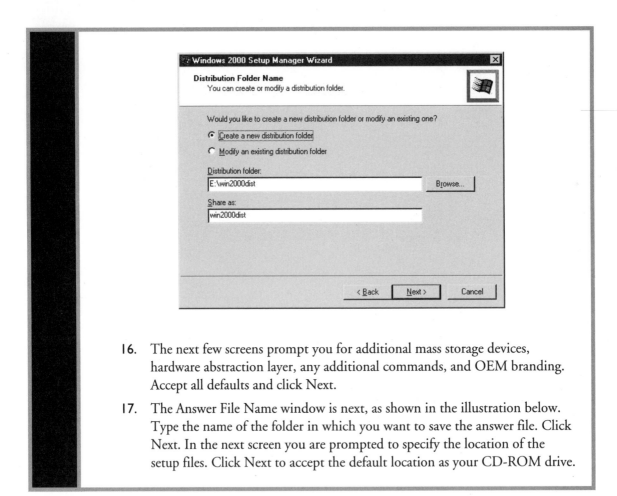

16. The next few screens prompt you for additional mass storage devices, hardware abstraction layer, any additional commands, and OEM branding. Accept all defaults and click Next.

17. The Answer File Name window is next, as shown in the illustration below. Type the name of the folder in which you want to save the answer file. Click Next. In the next screen you are prompted to specify the location of the setup files. Click Next to accept the default location as your CD-ROM drive.

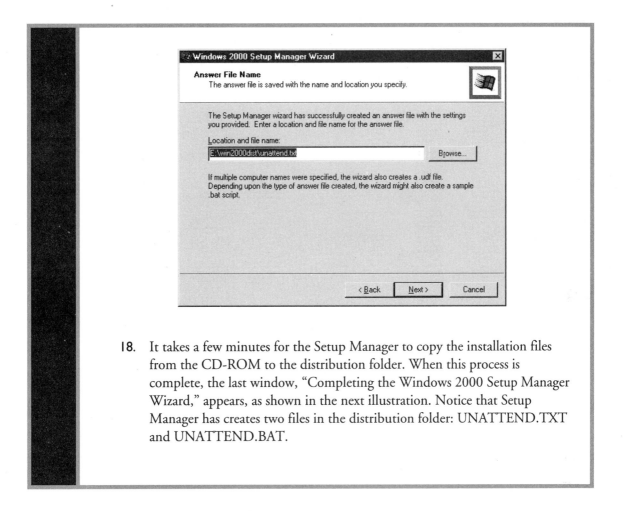

18. It takes a few minutes for the Setup Manager to copy the installation files from the CD-ROM to the distribution folder. When this process is complete, the last window, "Completing the Windows 2000 Setup Manager Wizard," appears, as shown in the next illustration. Notice that Setup Manager has creates two files in the distribution folder: UNATTEND.TXT and UNATTEND.BAT.

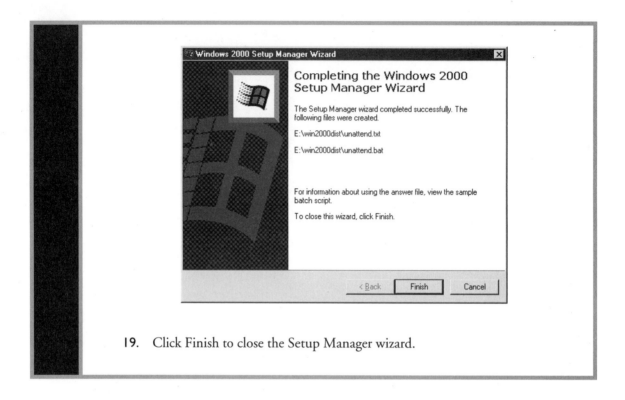

19. Click Finish to close the Setup Manager wizard.

exam
ⓦatch

If a fully automated installation mode is selected in the answer file, the user is not prompted for an administrator password.

Creating and Using UDFs for Multiple Users

When you use the WINNT32.EXE command with the /unattend option, you can also specify a Unique Database File (UDF), which has a .UDB extension. This file forces Setup to use certain values from the UDF file, thus overriding the values given in the answer file. This is particularly useful when you want to specify multiple users during the setup. The syntax for using a UDF with WINNT32.EXE is as follows:

```
/udf:ID[,UDB_File]
```

An identifier (ID) in this switch tells Setup how to modify the values given in the answer file. When you use the /udf option without specifying the .UDB file, Setup prompts you to insert a disk that contains such a file.

FROM THE CLASSROOM

Setup Manager Guidelines

The Setup Manager is the best tool to use when you have no idea of the answer file syntax or when you do not want to get into the time-consuming task of creating or modifying the sample answer file. When you choose to use the Setup Manager for unattended installations, you need to do a lot of planning beforehand. It is understood that you will not be using Setup Manager for automating installations on one or two computers; that would be a waste of effort. Setup Manager is useful for mass deployments only. Installation needs vary from one network environment to the other, but here are some general guidelines that will be helpful to you while using Setup Manager:

Know the present network setup, including computer hardware and installed applications. Make a list of the computer names. Decide whether you need to upgrade or do a clean installation.

1. Make a note of all network-related information such as the TCP/IP addressing scheme and the names of the domain controller, DHCP server, DNS server, and so on.

2. Arrange for any service packs or application upgrades to address any compatibility issues with Windows 2000 Server.

3. Document each and every piece of information you collect.

4. When you create scripts for unattended answer files, test one or two installations using your script files before applying them to mass setup. It is recommended that you take a hard copy of some scripts and check for any irregularities.

In practice, it is a bit difficult to have a complete automated installation process that does not ask for any user intervention. The Setup Manager helps you automate it to an extent, wherein very little user intervention is needed. One final piece of advice: Do not leave your first few unattended installations "unattended." Watch each and every step being completed automatically.

—*Pawan K. Bhardwaj, MCSE, MCP+I, CCNA*

CERTIFICATION OBJECTIVE 3.04

Understanding Remote Installation Services (RIS)

The *Remote Installation Service (RIS)* is a part of the Windows 2000 Server operating system. It is installed as an optional service on the Windows 2000 Server and facilitates installation of Windows 2000 Professional remotely on a large number of computers with similar or dissimilar hardware configurations. This not only reduces the installation time but also helps keep the deployment costs low.

RIS is an excellent utility provided by Microsoft, but it requires careful study and planning before it can be used successfully. RIS needs services such as Active Directory, DNS, and DHCP to be running on the network. The client computers need to have either one of the supported network adapters or must have a PXE-based Boot ROM that supports booting from the network.

How Does RIS Work?

To gain an understanding of the remote installation process, consider that a client computer boots using either the Remote Boot Disk prepared by a RIS server or a compatible Boot ROM on the network interface card. While a *BootP* message is displayed on the client, it connects to the DHCP server that is preconfigured to allocate an IP address to this client. The Boot Information Negotiation Layer (BINL) extensions on the DHCP server redirect the client computer to the RIS server on the network.

A Client Installation wizard (CIW) is downloaded to the client. This utility prompts the user to log on. Once the user has successfully logged on, the RIS server contacts the Active Directory to determine what options of the CIW are to be displayed to the user. It also checks with the Active Directory to find out what images the user is authorized to select. Active Directory uses Trivial File Transfer Protocol (TFTP) to transfer the first few required files to the client. The DNS server plays its role in locating the Active Directory server on the network. Once the user selects an image, Setup starts running on the client computer. It is evident that the sequence of protocol activities is DHCP, BINL, and TFTP.

The image that is to be distributed to the client can be prepared by any of the disk duplication methods. The *Remote Installation Preparation (RIPrep)* is one such wizard that is more or less similar to the SysPrep tool. The difference is that RIPrep removes not only the security ID from the master computer; it also removes all the hardware-specific settings. This makes the image independent of the hardware configuration. RIS as a whole is a useful utility aimed at reducing deployment time, administrative efforts, and costs.

exam
ⓦatch

RIS can be used only to distribute Windows 2000 Professional operating system images. You cannot use it to deploy any version of Windows 2000 Server or any other operating system.

Components of the Remote Installation Service

Let's see what components make up the RIS service. Primarily, there are five parts of the RIS service:

■ **RIS on the server running Windows 2000 Server operating system** The RISETUP.EXE file is run from the Start menu.

■ **Administration of RIS**

■ **Client Installation wizard** The executable file is OSCHOOSER.EXE.

■ **Remote Installation Preparation wizard** RIPREP.EXE is the executable file for this wizard and has to be run from the RIS server.

■ **Remote Installation Boot Disk** This disk is used to boot the client and connect to the RIS server to get an initial IP address from the DHCP server. This disk also starts the Client Installation wizard.

exam
ⓦatch

RIS can be used to duplicate only a single hard drive and a single partition, usually the C: drive.

The Single-Instance Store Volume

As we observed earlier while discussing RIPrep, RIS creates a Single-Instance Store (SIS) volume. What is the SIS for? When you have more than one image on the RIS server, each holding Windows 2000 Professional setup files, there will definitely be duplicate copies of hundreds of files. This duplication can consume significant hard drive space on the RIS server. To overcome this problem, Microsoft introduced a new feature, the SIS, which works on NTFS partitions. The SIS helps eliminate duplicate files, thus saving hard drive space.

To give you an idea of the exact requirements of the hard drive volume used for RIS, the following points need to be highlighted: the volume chosen to hold the images must be formatted with NTFS; the volume on the RIS server must be different from the one that runs RIS server; the RIS server must have enough free hard drive space to hold at least one Windows 2000 Professional image (this space is roughly 800MB to 1GB); and this volume must be shared on the network.

In many cases, when you are planning to use RIS, you may need to create as many images as the number of different desktop configurations used in your organization. For example, the configuration of a computer used in the accounting department may be entirely different from one in your marketing or production department.

Installing the Remote Installation Server

Now that you are familiar with the RIS service and the various components that make it up, let's see how can we set up the RIS server. First, we need to know the requirements that must be met in order to set up the RIS server.

RIS needs the following additional network services running on the RIS server or elsewhere on the network:

- **Domain Name Service (DNS)**   RIS is dependent on the DNS for locating the directory services and the machine accounts for the client computers.

- **Dynamic Host Configuration Protocol (DHCP)**   The DHCP services are used to provide initial IP addresses to the client computers when they start up. An IP address is necessary to continue participating in a TCP/IP network.

- **Active Directory Service**   This service provides the means for locating the RIS servers and the client computers on the network. The RIS server must have access to the Active Directory.

EXERCISE 3-5

Installing the Remote Installation Service

Select the Windows 2000 Server (in case you have many servers running on the network) and log on as an administrator.

Insert the Windows 2000 Server CD-ROM in the CD-ROM drive. Close the dialog box that pops up after inserting the CD-ROM. Then do the following:

1. Click Start | Settings | Control Panel. The Control Panel Window opens.

2. Click Add/Remove Programs. The Add/Remove Programs Window opens.

3. Click the Windows Components tab. It takes a while for this window to open.

4. Click the Remote Installation Service checkbox. Click Next.

5. At this point, the Remote Installation Service is installed. Click Finish to complete the installation.

6. A dialog box appears that says that the systems settings have changed and that you must restart your computer. Remove the Windows 2000 Server CD-ROM from the CD-ROM drive.

7. Click Yes to restart.

on the Job

In Exercise 3-4, you simply clicked Yes to reboot the server. In practice, you must be very careful while rebooting any server that is live on the network. If you are performing this exercise on a live server or you are not the network administrator, you must ask the network administrator whether it is safe to reboot the server. At a minimum, you must send a message to all the connected users that the server will be rebooted in the next five minutes or so and that they must save their work.

Once the RIS service has been installed on a Windows 2000 Server, it needs to be configured. In the following exercise, we learn how to configure this service.

CertCam 3-6

EXERCISE 3-6

Configuring the Remote Installation Service

1. Click Start | Run and type **RISetup.exe**. Press ENTER. This starts the Remote Installation Services Setup wizard. A welcome screen appears.

2. In the Remote Installation Folder Location window, you are prompted to type the path name of the volume that will hold the remote installation images. Type the correct path of the folder, as shown in the illustration below. (You could also click the Browse button to locate the folder). Click Next.

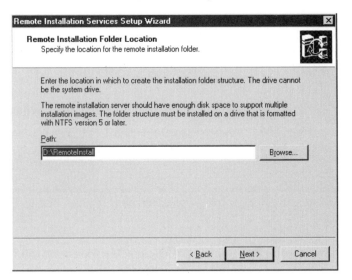

3. The Initial Settings window opens (see the next illustration). In this window you can specify how the RIS server will respond to the clients. By default, the RIS server will not respond to the clients until it is configured to do so. Here you may choose for the RIS server to respond or not to respond to the unknown clients requesting the RIS service. For the purpose of this exercise, click the checkbox opposite "Respond to client computers requesting service." Click Next.

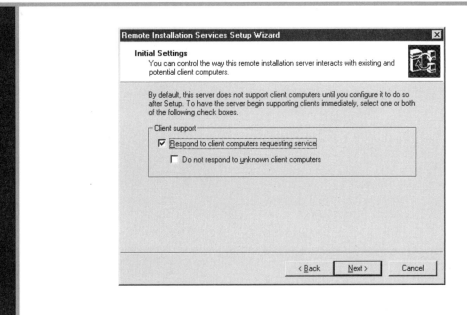

4. The Installation Source Files Location window appears. As shown in the next illustration, you are prompted to specify the location of Windows 2000 Professional files. These files are located in the \i386 folder of the CD-ROM drive. Check for the correct drive letter of the CD-ROM drive and type the path name. If you are unsure about the CD-ROM drive letter, click the Browse button to locate the correct path. We are using F:\i386 in this exercise. Make sure that the Windows 2000 Professional CD-ROM is inserted in the CD-ROM drive.

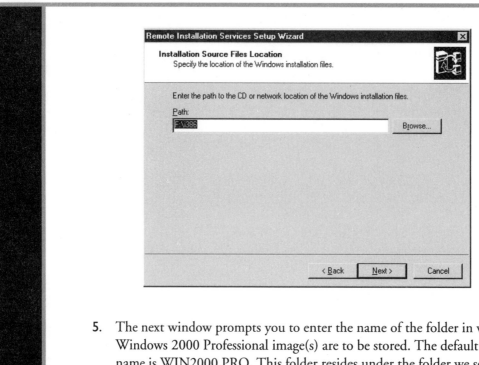

5. The next window prompts you to enter the name of the folder in which the Windows 2000 Professional image(s) are to be stored. The default folder name is WIN2000.PRO. This folder resides under the folder we selected in step 2 earlier in this exercise.

6. The Friendly Description and Help Text window is the next to appear on your screen. You can give a description to the image so that users can identify the image when the Client Installation wizard runs. The default friendly description of the image is "Microsoft Windows 2000 Professional" (see the next illustration) and the default help text is "Automatically installs Windows 2000 Professional without prompting the user for input." You can type in any custom friendly description and help text that suits the requirements of your organization. This is particularly useful when you have more than one image meant for various departments in your company. If there is only one image, it is best to keep the defaults.

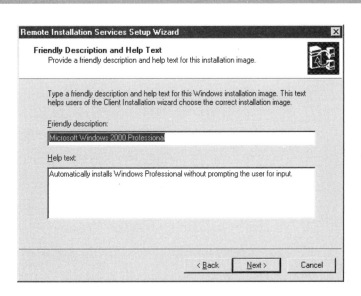

7. The illustration below shows the Review Settings window, which appears next in the RIS configuration wizard. The Review Settings screen shows the various settings you have chosen. If you see anything that is incorrect, click the Back button and make necessary corrections. Otherwise, click Finish.

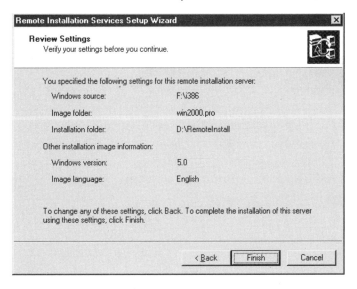

8. It takes a while for the wizard to install the settings of the RIS that you have selected. When it's finished, a window appears that shows each of the services. The following tasks are shown as they are completed:

■ A remote installation folder is created.

■ The necessary files needed by the service are copied into the above folder.

■ The Windows installation files are copied to the WIN2000.PRO folder.

■ The screen files for the Client Installation wizard are updated.

■ An unattended Setup answer file is created.

■ The remote installation services are created.

■ The registry of the RIS server is updated with new and/or modified entries.

■ A Single-Instance Store volume is created.

■ The required RIS is started.

9. This finishes the initial configuration for RIS. A check mark appears before each of the tasks when it is complete. You are prompted to click the Done button. Why wait? Click it and you are finished! The server does not reboot after this configuration.

Authorizing the RIS Server

The next step in establishing the RIS server is to authorize it in the Active Directory in order for the RIS server to serve the client computers. If this step is skipped, the RIS clients will not be able to get a response from the RIS server. In Exercise 3-6, we authorize the RIS server in the Active Directory to respond to the requesting RIS clients and provide IP addresses. This authorization is done from the DHCP Manager MMC snap-in on a server that is running the DHCP service. By default, this service is disabled.

EXERCISE 3-7

Authorizing the RIS Server

1. Log on to the server as a domain administrator where the DHCP services are running. This may or may not be the same server as the RIS server.

2. Click Start | Programs | Administrative Tools | DHCP.

3. The DHCP Manager window opens, as shown in the illustration below. Right-click DHCP in the left pane and click Add Server.

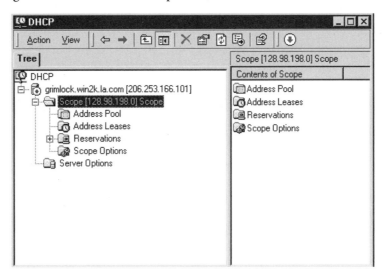

4. The Add Server dialog box appears. Type in the IP address of the RIS server and click OK.

5. Right-click DHCP again and click Manage Authorize Servers.

6. Select the RIS server and click Authorize. Click OK.

In order to authorize the RIS server in the Active Directory, you must have domain administrator rights.

Hardware Requirements for RIS

In order to use RIS for automating the deployment of Windows 2000 Professional in your organization, you need to fulfill certain hardware requirements for the RIS server and the RIS client. These requirements are described in this section.

Hardware Requirements for the RIS Server

The server that is selected to host RIS must have the following minimum hardware components:

- A Pentium 166MHz processor. It is recommended that you use a 200MHz. Pentium II or a later processor with higher speed.

- A minimum of 64MB RAM if RIS is the only service hosted by the server. If the server is hosting any additional services such as Active Directory, DNS, or DHCP, a minimum of 128MB RAM is required.

- Free hard drive space of 2GB, which should be dedicated to the RIS directory. The partition chosen for RIS must not be the boot partition of the server.

- A network adapter with 10Mbps data transfer speed. A 100Mbps adapter is recommended.

Hardware Requirements for the RIS Client

The client computers requesting RIS must have the following minimum hardware components:

- A Pentium processor, 166MHz or faster

- A minimum of 32MB RAM minimum, 64MB recommended

- A hard disk with a minimum capacity of 800MB

- A PCI Plug-and-Play adapter supported by RIS or a PXE-based Remote Boot ROM version .99 or later.

When you create a boot disk using the Remote Boot Disk Generator utility, as discussed later in this section, you are able to view a list of the supported network adapters.

PXE-Capable BIOS

The *Preboot Execution Environment (PXE)* is a new DHCP-based technology used to help client computers boot from the network. The Windows 2000 RIS uses the PXE technology along with the existing TCP/IP network infrastructure to implement the RIS-based deployment of Windows 2000 Professional. The client computer that has the PXE-based ROM uses its BIOS to contact an existing RIS server and get an IP address from the DHCP server running on the network. The RIS server then initializes the installation process on the client computer.

PXE-Capable Network Interface Cards

Any computer with a network interface card that has a PXE-based ROM can use RIS for initializing the installation process. When such a computer starts, the PXE ROM contacts an existing RIS server and requests an IP address using the normal DHCP process. The RIS server that is preconfigured to respond to client computers in the Active Directory responds and provides an IP address to the client.

A *boot ROM* is a chip on the network adapter that helps the computer boot from the network. Such a computer need not have a previously installed operating system. The BIOS of the computer that has a PXE-based boot ROM must be configured to boot from the network. Windows 2000 Server RIS supports PXE ROM versions .99 or later.

NetPC

A computer that meets NetPC specifications is another kind of computer that can be a RIS client. The following are some additional requirements for computers with NetPC configuration:

- The network adapter must be configured as the primary boot device.
- The user account for performing the installation must have rights to log on as a batch job.
- The users who will use NetPC computers must have permission to create computer accounts in the domain.

How do you know which PXE ROM version you running? This is a typical question that arises when we talk about the PXE ROMs. There are two methods to find out the correct version of the PXE ROM. The first is to check the documentation. This is the best method; it will tell you which version of PXE ROM is run by your system. Windows 2000 supports only version .99 or later. The second is from the startup messages. When the PXE ROM-based computer starts, a PXE ROM boot sequence is run. The PXE ROM code messages displayed on the screen will tell you the version of PXE ROM you are running.

RIS Support for Laptops

RIS with Windows 2000 Professional is not supported on laptop computers that have PC Cards or PCMCIA network cards. Some laptop computers can be addressed by RIS when used in docking stations that use supported network adapters. Since the number of laptops and docking stations tested by Microsoft is very limited, you must check the documentation of such computers before attempting to install Windows 2000 remotely.

The Remote Installation Boot Disk

When the client computer starts, it needs to contact the RIS server. It can accomplish this task in two ways. One, the client must have a PXE-based boot ROM on the network adapter. Second, the client must boot using a remote installation boot disk. The remote installation boot disk simulates the PXE boot process. This helps the client get an IP address from any DHCP server on the network. Once the client gets the IP address, it can communicate with other computers on the network.

For client computers that do not have a PXE boot ROM, RIS includes a boot disk generator utility. This disk can be used to initiate the remote installation process.

Creating a Boot Disk

The boot disk generator utility RBGF.EXE currently supports only 25 PCI-based network adapters. Many of the popular adapters are supported, so there's no need to purchase new adapters for hundreds of client computers. The RBGF.EXE utility can be run from any of the following computers:

- The RIS server

- A client computer that has a connection to the RIS server

- Any client connected to the RIS server on which the Windows 2000 Server Administrative Tools are installed

exam
ⓦatch

The Remote Boot Disk generator program supports only PCI network adapters.
PCMCIA, ISA, EISA, or Token Ring network adapters are not supported.

EXERCISE 3-8

Creating a Remote Installation Boot Disk

1. Ensure that the RIS server is up and running. Log on as an administrator.

2. Click Start | Run and type in RBGF.EXE. Click OK. If you are running this command from another computer, type in the following command and click OK:

   ```
   \\RISServer_name\RemoteInstall\Admin\i386\RBGF.exe
   ```

3. The Windows 2000 Remote Installation Boot Disk Generator window opens, as shown:

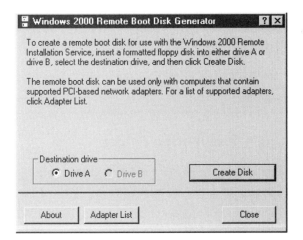

4. Check the path of the destination disk. It is usually drive A:. Insert a blank formatted floppy disk into drive A:.

5. To see a list of supported adapters, click the Adapter List button. Make sure that the adapters you have are in the list.

6. Click Create Disk. This creates a remote installation boot disk. Remove the disk and close the Windows 2000 Remote Boot Disk Generator window.

Creating a Distribution Server

The distribution server is a centralized location for storing the installation files and any additional driver files. There may be more than one distribution server in the network; they help balance the load in case of simultaneous multiple installations. Windows 2000 supports up to eight locations of source installation files when you use the WINNT32 command with the /s switch. The advantage of having a distribution folder is that you need not have multiple copies of the Windows 2000 setup CD-ROM or third-party driver CD-ROMs when a large-scale deployment is planned. In addition, many of the computers on the network may not have CD-ROM drives.

The distribution server contains a distribution folder and is shared on the network. The distribution folder has a hierarchical structure containing the Windows 2000 setup files as well as other necessary files used for automating the installation process. This folder also holds the necessary service packs or upgrades for the applications. The distribution folder can be created using the Setup Manager, as discussed later in this chapter. The following exercise explains the steps to manually create a distribution folder.

EXERCISE 3-9

Creating a Distribution Folder

1. Log on to a server that has been selected to act as a distribution server. Ensure that it has sufficient free hard-disk space.

2. In Windows Explorer, create a folder named Win2kPro.

3. Share the folder as Installs.

4. Insert the Windows 2000 Server CD-ROM in the CD-ROM drive. Copy the entire \i386 folder to the Installs folder.

5. Create another folder named *OEM* under the Installs folder. Copy any driver files you might need during setup. The Windows 2000 setup automatically copies the contents of this folder to a temporary folder during the text mode of setup.

Deploying Windows 2000 Using Remote Installation Service

As observed earlier in this chapter, RIS can be used only for deployment of the Windows 2000 Professional operating system. This service requires that other services such as Active Directory, DNS, and DHCP are also running on the network. These services may reside on the same server that is hosting the RIS service or any other server that is part of the domain. Once the RIS server is fully configured, you can start the Client Installation wizard on any of the client computers. The remote boot disk can be used to boot and start the network services on the client computer.

The Client Installation Wizard

It's time now to turn to the client side. When a client computer boots using either the Remote Boot Disk or the PXE-based Boot ROM, it tries to establish a connection to the RIS server. If the RIS server is preconfigured to service the RIS clients, it helps the client to get an IP address from the DHCP service. The Client Installation wizard is then downloaded from the RIS server. This wizard has four installation options. The options that are presented to the user depend on the group policy set in the Active Directory. In starting an automatic setup, a user might get all four options or none of the options. The four installation options are as follows:

- **Automatic Setup**   Automatic Setup is the default option. This is also the easiest installation method. It allows the user to select the operating system image. No more questions are asked of the user. The various configuration parameters are predetermined.

- **Custom Setup**   This option is a bit more flexible, allowing the user to override the process of automatically naming a computer. This option also allows the user to select a location in the Active Directory where the computer account will be created. This option requires significant administrative effort because almost every aspect of the installation can be customized.

- **Restart a Previous Setup Attempt**   As its name suggests, this option enables the user to restart a failed setup attempt. The user is not prompted for any input that he or she has already entered. This option is particularly useful when for some reason the user loses connection to the RIS server during setup or in case there is accidental shutdown of the client computer.

■ **Maintenance and Troubleshooting** This option provides access to any third-party maintenance tools that you may want to use before the installation starts. Since this option is not meant for every other user, the administrator can restrict access to this option in the group policy set in the Active Directory.

After making a selection from the above options, a list of available image options is displayed to the user. When a selection has been made, the user is presented with a summary screen. The installation begins immediately after this screen appears.

exam
ⓦatch

If the domain administrator has authorized the user for only one image, the user is not prompted for image selection and the installation starts as soon as the user selects the Automatic Setup option.

Troubleshooting Using Remote Installation Service

RIS is dependent on many other services running on the network. The complete RIS setup itself is not an easy operation for any network administrator. To have a fully functional RIS system, you must ensure the following:

1. The RIS server is up and running.

2. The DHCP server is authorized to service RIS clients in the Active Directory.

3. An IP address scope has been created in the DHCP server for RIS clients and has been activated.

4. If there is a router on the network between the RIS server and the clients, configure it to forward BootP broadcasts.

We have discussed the Remote Installation Service in detail. Let's have a quick look at some of the important questions that you could face on the job.

SCENARIO & SOLUTION

I want to use the RIS service. Is it necessary that the Active Directory, DNS, and DHCP are installed on the same server?	No. The Active Directory, DNS, and DHCP may reside anywhere on the network, but these should be functional before you configure RIS.
I need to install Windows 2000 on 50 computers. How do I ensure that the distribution server is not overloaded when simultaneous installations are running?	Create more than one distribution folder to balance the load.
Is there any way to know online that the Remote Installation Service supports the network adapters in the client computers?	Yes. When you run the RBGF.EXE utility, you can click the Adapter List tab to view a list of supported adapters.
When I was running the Client Installation wizard, someone pulled the wire and the setup aborted. What should I do?	Run the Client Installation wizard again and, when prompted, choose the "Restart a previous setup attempt" option.

CERTIFICATION OBJECTIVE 3.05

Performing an Unattended Installation of Windows 2000 Server

An automated or unattended installation of any software product means that the person performing the job does not have to answer any questions that the setup programs generally ask. Answer files, also known as *installation script files,* usually provide the answers automatically. Disk duplication methods provide another way to automate the installation.

The simplest form of performing the unattended installation is by using the WINNT32.EXE setup command with the /unattend switch. This method uses the answer file that you already have created. The WINNT.EXE command uses the /u switch.

WINNT32 or WINNT?

Two different commands can be used from the command prompt for initializing the setup process of Windows 2000 Server, depending on the previously installed operating system on the computer:

■ The command WINNT.EXE is used for starting the setup from a computer running MS-DOS or Windows 3.x. This command cannot be used for upgrading the previous operating system to Windows 2000.

■ The WINNT32.EXE command is used to start the setup from a computer running Windows 95, Windows 98, or Windows NT.

Remember that direct upgrade to Windows 2000 Server of any Windows NT Server prior to version 3.51 is not supported. In case you still want to install on such a computer, you must either do a clean installation or first upgrade it to Windows NT 3.51 or 4.0.

The setup can be run from either a local CD-ROM drive or the network. In order to run the unattended installation on a computer running MS-DOS or Windows 3.x from the network, you must first connect to the network share containing the Windows 2000 Server installation files. You can choose to use the share created on the distribution server.

Running Unattended Setup with the WINNT.EXE Command

The WINNT.EXE command has the following syntax:

```
Winnt    /s:x:\i386 /u:x:\i386\unattend.txt /t:c
```

- /s specifies the location of the source containing the installation files; in this case, *x* points to the drive that contains the i386 folder

- /u tells the setup that this is an unattended installation and specifies x:\i386 as the location of the custom answer file UNATTEND.TXT

- /t is used to specify a folder for storing any temporary files used during the setup process

Running an Unattended Setup with the WINNT32.EXE Command

When you are running the setup from within Windows 9x or Windows NT, the WINNT32.EXE command is used. The following is the syntax of this command:

```
Winnt32  /s:x:\i386 /unattend 5:X:\i386\unattend.txt /tempdrive:c
```

This command is different from the WINNT.EXE command in only minor ways. You might have noted that this time we are using the /unattend switch instead of /U. Furthermore, we used a number 5, which specifies the time that the computer will wait before rebooting when the file copy phase is over. This wait time works only on computers running Windows NT and Windows 2000 but is ignored in Windows 9x. All other switches and their syntax are similar to those used in WINNT.EXE command.

exam
ⓦatch

The two commands WINNT32.EXE and WINNT.EXE use the unattend switch differently. WINNT32.EXE uses the /unattend switch, while the WINNT.EXE command uses /u.

EXERCISE 3-10

Running an Unattended Installation Using the WINNT32.EXE Command

This exercise assumes that you have already created a custom answer file called UNATTEND.TXT. The Windows 2000 Server setup files are on a network file server share named Installs. The UNATTEND.EXE and the UNATTEND.BAT files are placed in the \i386 folder of the Installs share. This exercise needs a running network and you must be able to connect to the network file server. Now do the following:

1. From the Start menu, click Run | cmd. Click OK. The MS-DOS window opens.

2. Connect to the file server using the following command:

   ```
   net use x: \\server name\installs
   ```

3. You will notice that a message is displayed on the screen saying that the command completed successfully. This means that the x: drive is now connected to the Installs share on the file server.

4. Change to the x: drive by typing the following at the command prompt:

   ```
   cd x:
   ```

5. Type the following command again at the prompt to initiate the setup:

   ```
   winnt32 /b /s:x:\i386 /unattend:X:\i386\unattend.txt /tempdrive:c
   ```

6. The installation starts. Very little or no interaction is needed from you during the setup, depending on the parameters specified in the answer file.

7. If a fully automated method has been selected for installation when using the Setup Manager, you will not be able to select the local administrator password.

Installing Optional Programs

Unattended setup can be used to install optional application programs during the GUI phase of the setup. The CMDLINES.TXT file can be used for such an installation. The CMDLINES.TXT file can have some commands that run the files with an .INF extension. In order to use this feature, you need to copy the application in the OEM subfolder in the distribution folder.

Multiple commands can be used in the [Command] section of the UNATTEND.TXT file. The following is the syntax for using CMDLINES.TXT:

```
[Commands]
"command_1"
"command_2"
....
"command_3"
```

You need to place all the commands in double quotation marks. This feature has certain limitations:

- You must place the applications in the distribution folder.

- The installation must run in fully unattended mode. Any interaction by the user will stop the execution of the command.

- The CMDLINES.TXT runs as a service rather than using any user account.

Unattended Installation Using a Bootable CD-ROM

This method of unattended installation can be used on computers with BIOS that supports booting from a CD-ROM. You must create an answer file and store it on a floppy disk before starting the setup program. The following are the requirements for running such an installation:

- The BIOS of the computer should support the El Torito Bootable CD-ROM (no emulation mode) format.

- The previously created answer file must be named WINNT.SIF and stored on a floppy disk.

- The answer file must include a [Data] section that contains the required keys.

When you are sure that you have the Windows 2000 Server CD-ROM and the floppy containing the customized answer file named WINNT.SIF ready, you can start the setup process as explained in the following exercise.

EXERCISE 3-11

CertCam 3-11

Running Unattended Installation from a CD-ROM

1. Insert the Windows 2000 Server CD-ROM in the CD-ROM drive and recycle the computer power.

2. As soon as the blue-colored text-mode screen appears, insert the floppy disk.

3. You will notice that the computer reads the answer file from the floppy disk. The floppy disk indicator remains lit during this time.

4. When the computer has loaded the WINNT.SIF answer file from the floppy disk, the floppy disk indicator goes off. Remove the floppy disk at this point.

5. The installation continues from the CD-ROM in an unattended mode and all the answers are read from the loaded WINNT.SIF file.

exam
ⓦatch

The bootable CD-ROM method can be used for clean installations only. It is not possible to perform an upgrade installation using this method. It is also not possible to specify any UDF files with this method.

CERTIFICATION SUMMARY

Windows 2000 Server ships with many utilities that facilitate unattended installation of the operating system. The unattended installations make the rollout fast and reduce the cost for medium-sized and large organizations. Unattended installations also help standardize the desktop environment throughout the organization.

The unattended installations use an answer file that supplies answers to various questions prompted by the Setup Manager wizard. The sample answer file, UNATTEND.TXT, can be edited using Notepad. The Setup Manager wizard helps you create customized answer files for one or many of the computers for fully automated installations.

Once the answer file is ready, the installation can be started in an unattended mode using the WINNT or WINNT32 command and the /u or /unattend switch and specifying the location of the installation files and the answer file. Unattended mode can be used for either a clean installation or an upgrade.

Disk duplication tools such as the System Preparation tool (SysPrep) and the Remote Installation Preparation (RIPrep) wizard are used to prepare replicas of a completely configured Windows 2000 Professional computer. The Remote Installation Service (RIS) is included with Windows 2000 Server and is quite useful in delivering Windows 2000 Professional installations to multiple clients. The Setup Manager wizard is used to create custom answer files for unattended setup.

The system images prepared by SysPrep must be created and distributed to other computers using some third-party imaging utility. This utility also requires that all the destination computers have hardware identical to the master computer. When an image of the system is created using SysPrep, the user-specific settings of the master computer are copied. A Mini-Setup wizard that runs on the next reboot can help restore all these settings. It is recommended that the master computer be tested in all respects before running SysPrep to create an image.

The image prepared by the RIPrep utility is independent of the destination computer hardware. You also need not have a third-party utility to distribute the prepared image. The RIS server handles the job of distribution. RIS requires fully functional Active Directory services, DHCP services, and DNS running on the network. The client computers must have a PXE-based boot ROM or must boot from the remote boot disk prepared using the RBGF.EXE utility. This remote boot disk starts the Client Installation wizard on the destination computers. The administrator can control access to the Client Installation wizard options and the images that a user can select.

TWO-MINUTE DRILL

Understanding the Difference Between Unattended Installations and Prepared Images

■ Windows 2000 Server installation can be automated using scripted answer files that provide the answers to many or all the setup questions. The unattended installation method can be used for a clean installation or to upgrade a previously installed operating system.

■ The disk duplication methods that come with Windows 2000 operating system reduce the rollout time and save costs incurred on deployment as well as help standardizing the desktop environment throughout the organization.

■ It is important that you understand the requirements, advantages, and disadvantages of each method of unattended installation before making a final decision on which type is right for you.

Creating and Configuring Automated Methods for Installation

■ The disk duplication methods can be used for clean installations only. These methods do not support upgrading from a previous operating system. System Preparation (SysPrep) is used to prepare an image of a computer fully configured with the operating system and the applications.

■ SysPrep requires that the source master computer and all the destination computers have identical hardware, but Plug-and-Play devices are exempted from this condition. The image creation and distribution is handled by a third-party utility.

■ RIPrep is a RIS-based disk-cloning utility that can be used to create images of fully configured Windows 2000 Professional computers. RIS is then used to deliver the images to other computers that might or might not be identical in hardware.

Using Setup Manager to Automate the Installation Process

■ The UNATTEND.TXT file is the default answer file that comes with Windows 2000. This file can be modified to suit individual installation needs using Notepad.

- The Setup Manager wizard is used to create custom answer files that provide various configuration parameters. The installation can be fully automated, wherein the user is not prompted for any input.

- The Setup Manager can either create a new answer file or can modify an existing file. It can also create an answer file that duplicates the configuration of the computer on which the wizard is being run.

Understanding Remote Installation Services

- The Remote Installation Service (RIS) is included with Windows 2000 Server for remote installation of Windows 2000 Professional. This service is dependent on Active Directory, DHCP, and DNS running on the network.

- RIS can deliver images prepared by the Remote Installation Preparation (RIPrep) wizard. The image is stored in the RIS server.

- The Client Installation wizard runs on the RIS client computer when booted using a PXE-based boot ROM or a remote boot disk that is prepared using the RBGF.EXE utility. This utility supports many PCI-based network adapters.

Performing an Unattended Installation of Windows 2000 Server

- The unattended installation of Windows 2000 Server is done using the WINNT or WINNT32 command with the /u switch and specifying the location of the installation files and the answer file.

- The user who wants to do an unattended setup can modify the default answer file using Notepad or create a custom answer file using the Setup Manager wizard.

- If a fully automated installation mode is selected in the answer file, the user is not prompted for an administrator password.

SELF TEST

The following questions will help you measure your understanding of the material presented in this chapter. Read all of the choices carefully because there may be more than one correct answer. Choose all correct answers for each question.

Understanding the Difference Between Unattended Installations and Prepared Images

1. When do you need a customized answer file in unattended setup? Select all that apply.

   A. When you want to have more control over the installation process

   B. When you want to process custom upgrade packs

   C. When all of the computers in the network have different settings

   D. All of the above

2. Which of the following methods can be used to create an image of a fully configured computer running Windows 2000 Server and applications?

   A. SysPrep

   B. RIPrep

   C. Systems Management Server

   D. Setup Manager

3. You are planning to use one of the deployment tools included with Windows 2000 Server. Where can you find the DEPLOY.CAB file that contains these tools?

   A. In the Windows 2000 Server Resource Kit

   B. In the \i386 folder of the setup CD-ROM

   C. In the \support\tools folder on the setup CD-ROM

   D. Any of the above

4. Which of the following are the deciding factors when you want to select a method for unattended installation of Windows 2000 Server? Select all that apply.

   A. The computer hardware

   B. Network configuration

   C. Administrative costs

   D. Upgrade or clean installation

   E. Applications

Creating and Configuring Automated Methods for Installation

5. You are creating custom answer files using the Setup Manager wizard for automated installations of Windows 2000 Professional. You selected the "Create a new answer file" option. What kind of answer files can you create?

   A. Windows 2000 unattended installation

   B. Remote Installation Service

   C. SysPrep installation

   D. All of the above

6. You want to use the SysPrep tool from the command prompt for creating an image of your computer. Which option can you use with the SYSPREP.EXE command so that no messages are displayed on the screen?

   A. -nodisplay

   B. -quiet

   C. -q

   D. -nosidgen

Using Setup Manager to Automate the Installation Process

7. What does the Setup Manager that is included in the Windows 2000 Server CD-ROM do? Select all that apply.

   A. Helps in automating Windows 2000 Server installations

   B. Creates scripts for multiple computers that are similar or dissimilar in hardware

   C. Lowers the cost of operating system deployment

   D. All of the above

8. You want to generate computer names automatically during unattended setup of Windows 2000 Server. How can you ensure that the answer file you create using the Setup Manager does this job for you?

   A. Provide a text file with the computer names

   B. Select the Automatically Generate Computer Names Based on Organization Name option

   C. This is not possible; you must provide computer names to the Setup Manager wizard when it prompts

   D. Use a third-party tool to generate and provide computer names

9. Matt created some setup scripts using the Setup Manager and selected the Read Only installation option. He wanted the users to choose their own passwords for the local administrator account. When one of the users started installation using the script, he could not change the default password. This happened to a few other users as well. Can you tell Matt what the problem is?

   A. Windows 2000 supports strong security. The users are not allowed to specify or change administrator passwords.

   B. Even if the password option is not displayed, users will still be able to select their administrator passwords at a later stage.

   C. With the Read Only installation option, users are not allowed to type in the local administrator passwords.

   D. None of the above

10. You have created an answer file using the Setup Manager and the Installs share on a file server as the distribution folder. What is the name of the answer file, and where does the Setup Manager store it?

    A. UNATTEND.TXT, in the distribution folder

    B. WINNT.TXT, in the distribution folder

    C. UNATTEND.BAT, in the i386 folder

    D. WINNT.SIF, stored on a floppy disk

Understanding Remote Installation Service

11. You want to use RIS for preparing and distributing images of the client containing the operating system and application files. Which of the following computers can become RIS clients? Select all that apply.

    A. All kinds of Intel-based computers and laptops

    B. Computers with a single network adapter supported by RIS

    C. Computers with network adapters having PXE-based boot ROMs on them

    D. NetPCs with or without network adapters configured as the primary boot devices

12. Which of the following options is used to install third-party maintenance utilities from the Client Installation wizard?

    A. Automatic setup

    B. Custom setup

C. Restart a previous setup attempt

D. Maintenance and troubleshooting

13. While trying to boot from the RIS boot disk after preparing the RIS server, you find that it is not responding. The computer times out and displays an error message: "No boot file received from DHCP, BINL or BootP." You know that the RIS server is online. What must you do to resolve the problem?

A   Restart the client computer.

B   Restart the RIS server.

C   Stop and restart the BINL service.

D   Restart the DHCP server.

14. A client computer has been powered on using a remote boot disk. This computer is supposed to contact a preconfigured RIS server for installation of Windows 2000 Professional. What is the correct sequence of activities taking place on initialization?

A. DHCP, BINL, and TFTP

B. BINL, DHCP, and TFTP

C. TFTP, BINL, and DHCP

D. TFTP, DHCP, and BINL

Performing an Unattended Installation of Windows 2000 Server

15. Considering that you have already created a custom answer file, which of the following methods can you use for performing an unattended installation of Windows 2000 Server, specifying a uniqueness database file for each user? Select all that apply.

A. WINNT32.EXE command file

B. WINNT.EXE command file

C. CD-ROM based method

D. RIS-based installation

16. What are the requirements for performing an unattended installation using the CD-ROM-based method? Select all that apply.

A. An answer file named WINNT.SIF stored on a floppy disk

B. A functional Active Directory

C. A remote boot disk

D. Computer BIOS supporting El Torito bootable CD-ROM format

17. You want to upgrade your Windows NT 4.0 server to Windows 2000 Server in unattended mode. You have created an answer file using the Setup Manager and named it UNATTEND.TXT. The file has been placed in the \i386 folder of a file server named Master. The folder containing the setup files is shared as Installs. You have mapped the x: drive of your server to \\Master\Installs. Which of the following is a correct command to run setup in unattended mode?

    A. winnt /s:x:\i386 /unattend:x:\i386\unattend.txt /t:c

    B. winnt32 /s:x:\i386 /unattend:x:\i386\unattend.txt /tempdrive:c

    C. winnt32 /s:x:\i386 /u:x:\i386\unattend.txt /tempdrive:c

    D. None of the above

LAB QUESTION

Consider that you are the network administrator of a company called My Company, Inc. The company has six Windows 2000 servers that were upgraded from Windows NT 4.0 last month. There are seven departments within the company; the total number of client computers is nearly 175 at a single location, all running Windows NT 4.0 Workstation on different hardware configurations.

Your current project requires you to install Windows 2000 Professional and business applications on all 175 workstations. The software configuration is almost the same on all departmental computers except the accounting department, which has some custom-built software for accounting functions. For data security reasons, the company's managers would like to avoid hiring anyone from outside to do the upgrade. You have decided to use the remote installation method to accomplish this task.

Some steps that could help you perform a successful RIS-based deployment of Windows 2000 Professional follow. Can you tell whether some steps are missing or are incorrect?

1. Install Remote Installation Service on one of the servers using Control Panel | Add Remove Programs | Add Remove Windows Components.

2. Ensure that you have a DNS server running on the network.

3. Create a DHCP scope on the DHCP server and activate it.

4. Install Windows 2000 Professional on a computer using RIS.

5. Install all business and custom applications on this computer and test it.

6. Run RIPrep on the test computer to make an image of the system and copy it to the RIS server.

7. Make remote boot disks for the clients using the RBGF.EXE utility.

8. Boot the client computers using the remote boot disk to run the client Installation wizard.

9. When given a choice, select the image appropriate to the department.

SELF TEST ANSWERS

Understanding the Difference Between Unattended Installations and Prepared Images

1. ☑ **D.** All the conditions listed in the answer options need a customized answer file. The UNATTEND.TXT answer file that comes with Windows 2000 cannot be used in any of the given situations. This file can be edited using a text editor or Notepad.

2. ☑ **A.** The SysPrep tool is used to create an image of a fully configured Windows 2000 Server.
   ☒ **B** is incorrect because RIPrep works with RIS to deliver the Windows 2000 Professional operating system only. **C** is incorrect because the System Management Server is employed for managed installations, not for creating images. **D** is incorrect because the Setup Manager is used to create or modify custom answer files.

3. ☑ **C.** The deployment tools are contained in compressed form in the DEPLOY.CAB file in the \support\tools folder on the setup CD-ROM.
   ☒ **A** is incorrect because you need not purchase the Resource Kit to obtain these tools. **B** is incorrect because the \i386 folder does not contain any installation tools. It has only the UNATTEND.TXT sample file. **D** is inappropriate because only one of the given answers is correct.

4. ☑ **A, C, and D** are correct. In selecting a method for unattended installation, the computer hardware and administrative costs are major factors. In addition, the decision to perform a clean installation or an upgrade also affects method selection. For example, the Setup Manager can be used to create scripts for both clean and upgrade installations, but SysPrep restricts its use to clean installations on computer hardware that is identical.
   ☒ **B** is not a suitable option because the network configuration does not affect the decision of an installation method. **E** is inappropriate because the applications can be installed later or can be integrated into any method.

Creating and Configuring Automated Methods for Installation

5. ☑ **D.** All of the above. The Setup Manager can create custom answer files for all the given choices: Windows 2000 unattended installation, RIS installation, and SysPrep installation. But you must note that the RIS method does not support installation of the Windows 2000 Server operating system.

6. ☑ **B.** In order to avoid displaying any messages on the screen while running the SysPrep utility, we specify the -quiet switch. This runs SysPrep in quiet mode, and no user interaction is required.

☒ **A** and **C** are incorrect because there are no such options with the SysPrep command. **D** is incorrect because the -nosidgen switch is used to avoid generation of security identifiers.

Using Setup Manager to Automate the Installation Process

7. ☑ **D.** All of the above. The Setup Manager is helpful in automating the Windows 2000 Server deployment by creating answer files or scripts for multiple computers. This reduces the time and costs involved in the deployment.

8. ☑ **B.** In order to generate computer names automatically during setup, you can select the Automatically Generate Computer Names Based on Organization Name option in the Setup Manager wizard.

☒ **A** is incorrect because this is not an option while using Setup Manager. **C** is incorrect because the Setup Manager can generate the computer names automatically. **D** is an invalid choice because you need not use a third-party tool.

9. ☑ **C.** The setup will not prompt the user for a local administrator password when the fully automated installation option is selected in Setup Manager. The purpose of a fully automated setup is defeated if the user is prompted for input every now and then during the setup. This is the reason no option is displayed.

☒ **A** is incorrect because security is not an issue here. However, it is, of course, true that Windows 2000 supports strong security. **B** is incorrect, although it seems correct. The user can change the password, but this is not what the question asks. **D** is incorrect.

10. ☑ **A.** The default name of the answer file is UNATTEND.TXT, and it is stored in the distribution folder.

☒ **B** is incorrect because the name of the answer file is not WINNT.EXE unless you have specified this name. **C** is incorrect because the UNATTEND.BAT file is not the actual answer file. UNATTEND.BAT file is used to run the UNATTEND.TXT file. **D** is incorrect because the answer file will be named WINNT.SIF and stored on a floppy disk only when you select these options in the Setup Manager. Since the question does not tell us anything about such a situation, we cannot consider it the best answer. Remember that the answer file, when saved as WINNT.SIF and stored on a floppy disk, can be used for CD-ROM-based unattended installations.

Understanding Remote Installation Service

11. ☑ **B** and **C**. The client computers must have a supported adapter or an adapter with a PXE-based boot ROM configured as the primary boot device.
☒ **A** is incorrect because simply being an Intel-based computer does not satisfy the requirements to become an RIS client. Laptop computers have PC Cards and cannot be RIS clients. **D** is an incorrect statement because NetPCs must be configured to boot from the network.

12. ☑ **D**. When the Client Installation wizard starts on a client computer, the user is given four setup options. The maintenance and troubleshooting option enables installation of third-party tools that could be helpful to the user.
☒ **A** is incorrect because the automatic option is used for a fully automated setup. **B** is incorrect because the custom setup option cannot be selected to install any third-party utility. This option enables the user to configure the operating system in a desired way. **C** is also incorrect because the restart option is used when a setup attempt has failed or aborted due to any reason. When selected, the setup does not prompt the user for any answers that were previously provided.

13. ☑ **C**. Stop and restart the BINL service. The possible cause of this timing out is that the BINL service on the RIS server is not responding. This happens after the computer has received an IP address from the DHCP server. Stopping and restarting the BINL service on the RIS server will help resolve the problem.
☒ **A** is incorrect; restarting the client computer will not help because the problem is not at the client end. **B** is not a good choice because if stopping and restarting only the BINL service can help resolve the problem, there is no need to restart the RIS server. **D** is incorrect; DHCP server is not an issue, because the client has already got the IP address.

14. ☑ **A**. DHCP, BINL, and TFTP. When a computer is started using a remote boot disk, it first tries to contact the DHCP server to locate an IP address. After getting an IP address, the computer contacts the RIS server to get the boot file. This is accomplished by the BINL service running on the RIS server. TFTP is then utilized to transfer the necessary boot files from the RIS server to the client computer.
☒ **B** and **C** are incorrect because BINL and TFTP do not initialize before the DHCP. DHCP must first provide an IP address to the client. **D** is incorrect because TFTP works after DHCP and BINL.

Performing an Unattended Installation of Windows 2000 Server

15. ☑ **A, B.** If you want to run unattended installation of Windows 2000 Server, WINNT32.EXE and WINNT.EXE can be used with the /udf switch and by specifying the location of the UNATTEND.TXT file. The choice of WINNT32 or WINNT depends on the previous operating system you are using on your computer.

    ☒ **C** is incorrect because the CD-ROM-based method does not allow you to specify the uniqueness database files for unattended installations. **D** is incorrect because RIS can be used only for Windows 2000 Professional installations.

16. ☑ **A, D.** An answer file named WINNT.SIF stored on a floppy disk, and computer BIOS supporting El Torito bootable CD-ROM format. For running the setup in unattended mode using the CD-ROM-based method, the computer BIOS must support the El Torito bootable CD-ROM format. In addition, the answer file must be stored in a floppy disk and named WINNT.SIF. This disk is inserted when the text phase of setup starts.

    ☒ **B** is incorrect because you do not need a functional Active Directory for a CD-ROM-based unattended installation. **C** is incorrect because a remote boot disk is required when you are running the setup from the network. In a CD-ROM-based installation, you boot from the CD-ROM itself.

17. ☑ **B,** winnt32 /s:x:\i386 /unattend:x:\i386\unattend.txt /tempdrive:c, is correct. You use the WINNT32 command because this is an upgrade from Windows NT 4.0. The drive x: is \\Master\Installs, specified in the /s switch and the /unattend switch.

    ☒ **A** is incorrect for two reasons: WINNT.EXE cannot be used for upgrade installations, and /unattend is not used with WINNT.EXE. **C** is incorrect because the /u switch is invalid for WINNT32.EXE command. **D** is incorrect.

LAB ANSWER

These steps seem perfect, but in fact, they are not. The following important steps are missing:

1. After installing Remote Installation Services on the Windows 2000 Server, the server must be configured. To configure RIS, run RISETUP.EXE from the command prompt. This is an important step whereby the RIS server is configured to respond to the client computers requesting RIS. Without this configuration, the clients will get no response from the RIS server when they start up using the remote boot disk. A remote installation folder is also configured in this step.

2. Authorize the RIS server in the Active Directory. This must be done from Start | Programs | Administrative Tools | DHCP.

3. The next important missing step is that you must check whether or not the client computers have supported network adapters. Run the RGBF.EXE utility and click the Adapter List tab to view a list of supported adapters.

4. The steps in the question mention that only one image is to be created; this is incorrect. There must be two different images.

This procedure assumes that you have the domain administrator rights and are the only one performing the remote installations. If some other people will help you carry out the deployment, you need to give them rights so that they can create computer accounts in the domain.

4

Upgrading from Windows NT

I n this chapter, we discuss upgrading your network from Windows NT to Windows 2000.
There are many tasks involved in this upgrade. The most important task is your plan to
upgrade. You need to determine your networking requirements and how to handle IP
addressing and name resolution. Then you should design a strategy for upgrading your Windows
NT domains to Windows 2000 domains. Will you leave them as they are, merge multiple domains
into one, or split up domains?

When upgrading your Windows NT servers to Windows 2000, you need to
determine the role each of them will serve in the Windows 2000 network. In Windows
2000, a server can act as a domain controller, member server, or stand-alone server.
Unlike roles for Windows NT Servers, roles for Windows 2000 Servers can be changed
after installation, so your decision doesn't have to be permanent. There are several ways
to upgrade your server; you need to choose the best method for your enterprise. You
should also develop a rollback plan in case of problems during the upgrade.

Periodically, Microsoft releases fixes to its operating systems; these fixes are known as
service packs. Service packs contain bug and security fixes. Normally, you want to have
your computers running the latest service pack that is available. However, you should
test the service packs for your environment prior to deploying them.

On occasion, the installation of Windows 2000 Server will fail. When it does fail,
you need to be prepared to solve the problems causing the failure. You should know
the common problems that can occur and understand that Setup creates log files
that can be used to help with troubleshooting.

CERTIFICATION OBJECTIVE 4.01

Planning a Network Upgrade to Windows 2000

As with just about anything you do, you should plan ahead. This includes upgrading
your network to Windows 2000. You need to determine your network requirements
and map out how you will fulfill those requirements in Windows 2000. You should
determine how to configure Transmission Control Protocol/Internet Protocol
(TCP/IP), how to provide IP addresses (dynamically or statically), and how to

implement name resolution. You should determine how you will structure your domains using the new features of Windows 2000 such as forests and trees. In addition, you should determine what role each of your Windows NT servers will play in the Windows 2000 environment. You should figure these things out before you start the upgrade.

Networking Requirements

When you are determining the network requirements for Windows 2000, some areas to consider are the network protocol requirements and name resolution. When you use TCP/IP as the network protocol, decide whether to provide automatic or manual assignment of IP addresses. For name resolution, determine your DNS requirements and whether you need to use Windows Internet Name Service (WINS).

TCP/IP Requirements

The TCP/IP network protocol is the protocol used across the Internet. The Windows 2000 Setup program makes it easier to configure TCP/IP. Each Windows 2000 server should be given an IP address. This IP address can be assigned dynamically through Dynamic Host Configuration Protocol (DHCP), automatically by Windows 2000 Server, or manually by assigning a static IP address. If you have a small number of servers (five or fewer) on a small network, you can allow Windows 2000 Server to automatically assign an IP address to the server using Automatic Private IP Addressing (APIPA). For larger networks, especially networks with more than one subnet, you should dynamically assign IP addresses using DHCP for workstations. The DHCP server must be assigned a static IP address so that other computers can locate it and so that other servers will be assigned an IP address dynamically by the DHCP server.

If a Windows 2000 Server is to be accessed directly across the Internet, it should have a static IP address. A static IP address allows users to use a domain name that can be translated into an IP address. The static IP address allows the server to always have the same IP address, so the domain name always translates to the correct IP address. If the address was assigned dynamically and it occasionally changed, users might not be able to access the server across the Internet using the domain name.

In Exercise 4-1, we take a look at your current TCP/IP configuration. This exercise should be performed using Windows NT 4.0. However, most of the exercise will also work on Windows 95 or 98.

Determining the Current TCP/IP Configuration

1. On the desktop, right-click the Network Neighborhood icon and select Properties from the context menu to bring up the Network dialog box.

2. By default, the Identification tab is displayed. This tab shows your current computer name and domain name. Click the Protocols tab. The Protocols screen is shown:

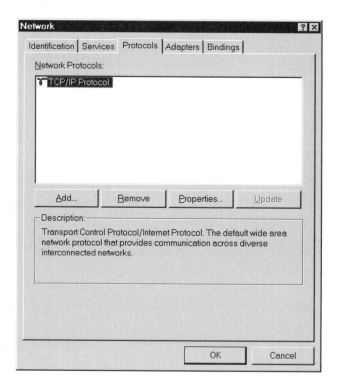

3. Select TCP/IP Protocol and click the Properties button. This brings up the Microsoft TCP/IP Properties dialog box.

4. By default, the IP Address tab is selected, as shown:

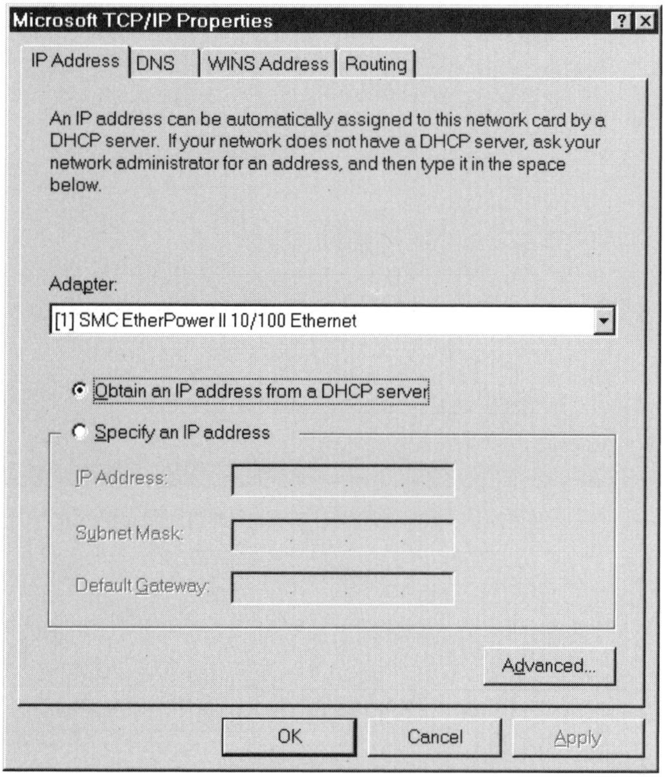

5. In the illustration above, notice that the option for "Obtain an IP address from a DHCP server" is selected. This means it is configured for automatic

IP addressing using DHCP. With the Specify an IP address selection, you can manually configure your IP address, as shown:

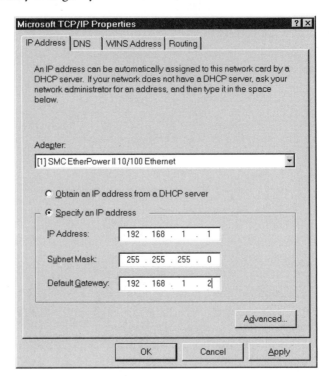

6. Click the DNS tab. Doing so displays your DNS settings, as shown in the next illustration. Since we used DHCP here, most of the settings are left blank. If your computer is manually configured, you should document the current settings.

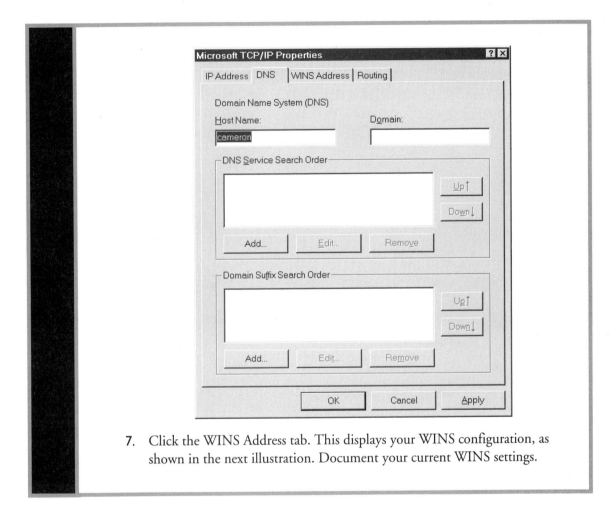

7. Click the WINS Address tab. This displays your WINS configuration, as shown in the next illustration. Document your current WINS settings.

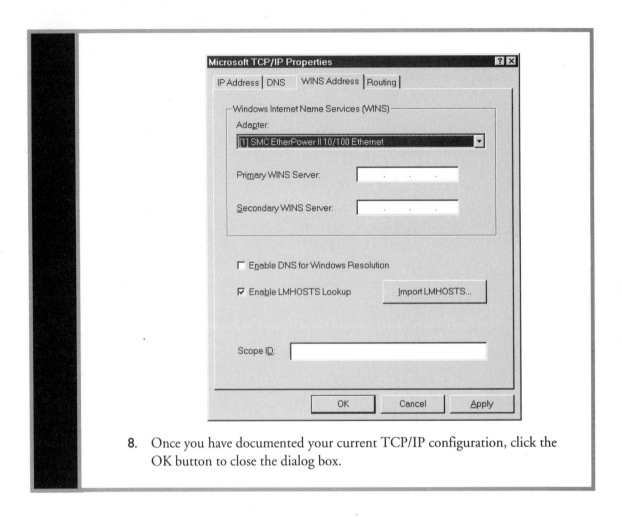

8. Once you have documented your current TCP/IP configuration, click the OK button to close the dialog box.

Domain Name Service

Now that your server has an IP address, we need to discuss name resolution. Since an IP address is a group of numbers (e.g., 192.168.1.1), you need to provide a way for users to use names rather than IP addresses to access computers. Name resolution allows users to use a name that is easier to remember than an IP address to access a computer on a network or the Internet.

One type of name resolution is the *Domain Name Service (DNS)*. DNS maps a domain name to an IP address. Windows 2000 uses DNS as the primary name resolution method. DNS is part of the TCP/IP protocol suite and comes with Windows 2000 Server. DNS services are required for Internet e-mail, Web browsing, and support for clients running Windows 2000 and Active Directory Services. When you install Windows 2000 Server as a domain controller or when you promote a member to a domain controller, DNS is installed automatically. DNS can also be installed during or after setup for member servers. DNS servers should be assigned a static IP address. This allows clients to find the DNS server by its IP address. A client cannot find the DNS server by name because it needs to know where the DNS server is in order to translate the name into an IP address.

exam

ⓦatch

When installing Windows 2000 Server as an upgrade to an NT domain controller or NT member server that you are upgrading to a domain controller, DNS is installed automatically, by default.

Windows Internet Name Service

If your network will support clients that are running Windows NT or Windows 95 or 98, you should install the *Windows Internet Name Service (WINS)* to support them. WINS is used to map NetBIOS computer names to IP addresses. This allows users to access other computers on the network by computer name. WINS servers should be assigned a static IP address, which allows clients to be able to find the WINS servers. Clients cannot find a WINS server by name because they need to know where the WINS server is in order to translate the name into an IP address.

Creating a Naming Strategy

When you are planning names for your computers and domains, it is important to use names that are descriptive. Use names that are immediately indicative to whom the computer or domain belongs. Using computer names such as Comp1, Comp2, and so on is not very descriptive. With such a naming scheme, each time the network administrator (i.e., you) needed to find the computer, you would have to look up where it was and to whom it belonged—that is, of course, assuming you have documentation available.

SCENARIO & SOLUTION

You are upgrading a server that will be a Web server running IIS. Should the IP address be dynamic or static?	Any server that will be accessed across the Internet should be configured with a static IP address. A Web site has a domain name that is registered to an IP address, so the IP address cannot be changed.
You are upgrading your servers to Windows 2000. Many of your clients will still be running Windows NT and Windows 98. Should you use WINS?	Although Windows 2000 does not need WINS because it has been replaced in the DNS server, legacy operating systems could still require WINS. Therefore, you should install WINS if you have clients that are not running Windows 2000.

A common approach to naming is to use the department name, title, and user's name. For example, say John Smith is the vice president of engineering. Rather than using a name such as Comp1 for Smith's computer, use *EngVPjsmith*.

The computer name is a NetBIOS name. A NetBIOS name can be up to 15 characters long. The name must contain only legal characters. You can use letters, numbers, and extended characters. Do not use spaces in your computer name. Although a name containing spaces might appear to work initially, it can cause problems with browsing in some versions of Windows.

However, ultimately, the use of extended characters can cause problems when you move away from NetBIOS names to a true DNS-compliant environment. Therefore, it is best to stick with the characters A to Z, a to z, 0 to 9, and the hyphen (-).

Domain Upgrade Strategy

Upgrading a domain is accomplished by upgrading your Windows NT primary and backup domain controllers to Windows 2000 Server. By upgrading your existing domain, the settings and configuration of the existing domain are preserved. You should plan the upgrade of the domain prior to starting any upgrade process.

A domain consists of a logical grouping of accounts and resources within a security boundary. As with Windows NT, a domain is needed to provide domain user accounts and domain security. Part of upgrading your Windows NT servers to Windows 2000 Server is determining the role the servers will perform. Windows 2000 servers can have one of three roles: domain controller, member server, and stand-alone server. A *domain controller* provides user login authentication and security functions via Active Directory (AD) for the domain. A *member server* belongs to the domain but doesn't contain a copy of the AD database or provide login authentication or security for the domain. A *stand-alone server* is not part of a domain but is part of a workgroup.

In order to have a domain, you must have at least one domain controller. Additional domain controllers can be added to provide fault tolerance and load balancing for the AD.

You should plan the role of your servers prior to upgrading them. However, unlike Windows NT, the role of the server can be changed without reinstalling Windows 2000 Server. Table 4-1 contains a list of the upgrade paths that are available for the Windows 2000 Server roles.

When upgrading a Windows NT domain to Windows 2000, you don't have to upgrade all the servers at the same time. Windows 2000 domain controllers can operate in a mode (mixed mode) that allows them to be backward compatible with Windows NT backup domain controllers. This structure allows you to upgrade the domain incrementally and test the functionality at each step, solving problems as they come along. When you upgrade the domain, the existing functionality will be preserved, as well as the new features available in Windows 2000 added. (Mixed mode is discussed later in the chapter.)

When upgrading a Windows NT domain to a Windows 2000 domain, you should perform the upgrade in steps:

1. Plan the upgrade from Windows NT to Windows 2000.

2. Start preparing for the upgrade from Windows NT to Windows 2000.

3. Upgrade the primary domain controller.

4. Upgrade the backup domain controllers.

5. Upgrade the member servers.

TABLE 4-1	Role in Windows NT Domain	Role in Windows 2000 Server Domain
Windows 2000 Server Upgrade Paths	Primary domain controller	Domain controller
	Backup domain controller	Domain controller or member server
	Member server	Member server or stand-alone server
	Stand-alone server	Member server or stand-alone server

There are several areas you should consider when planning the upgrade from Windows NT to Windows 2000. You need to develop a plan for the DNS domain name structure, develop a plan for consolidating existing domain structures, and determine the location of user and machine accounts in Windows 2000.

The next step is to prepare for the upgrade. The first thing you should do is back up all hard disks of the servers that will be upgraded. You should also take one of the backup domain controllers offline in case of an upgrade failure. This way, you can always bring the backup domain controller back online, if necessary, to revert back to the Windows NT domain. Prepare a test environment or pilot. In the test environment, test the following: user and group policies, user profiles, and logon scripts. When setting up the test environment, create scenarios that are easy to verify. Create users and groups similar to the existing Windows NT domain.

The last steps involve upgrading the servers in the domain. The primary domain controller needs to be upgraded first. Then upgrade the backup domain controllers. Finally, upgrade the member servers in the domain. When these steps are complete, you can put the domain controllers in a mode (native mode) that makes it purely a Windows 2000 domain. (Native mode is discussed later in the chapter.)

Importance of the Root Domain of the Forest

When organizing your current enterprise, you need to decide how to organize the Active Directory. The Active Directory comprises components that allow you to structure the AD so that it is logical and intuitive to users and administrators. The components are domains, organizational units (OUs), trees, forests, and schema.

Organizational units, or OUs, are units used to organize objects within a domain. These objects can include user accounts, groups, computers, printers, and even other OUs. The hierarchy of OUs is independent of other domains. Each domain can have its own OU structure. This gives you the flexibility to organize each domain to match the purpose of the domain instead of a general structure to be used by all domains.

A *tree* is a grouping of one or more domains. It allows you to create a hierarchical grouping of domains that share a common contiguous namespace. This hierarchy allows global sharing of resources among domains in the tree.

All the domains in a tree share information and resources with a single directory. There is only one directory per tree. However, each domain manages its own subset of the directory that contains the user accounts for that domain. So, when a user logs into a domain, the user has global access to all resources that are part of the tree, providing the user has the proper permissions.

FROM THE CLASSROOM

Changing the Role of the Server

One of the common questions asked is, how do you decide to make a Windows 2000 server a domain controller or a member server? Fortunately, in Windows 2000 Server, you can change the role of the server after installation. In Windows NT, you must reinstall the operating system in order to change the role of the server. Now, with Windows 2000, you can make a server a member server if you don't think you need it to act as a domain controller. Then, if your domain's load changes and you need another domain controller, you can simply promote one of your member servers to a domain controller. You no longer have to plan for this possibility far in advance. If your network appears to be operating nominally, you should make any new servers member servers, and as your load on the domain controllers increases, simply promote the appropriate servers.

Also in Windows 2000, you no longer have to make the decision as to which domain controller will be the primary domain controller. Windows 2000 does not make a distinction between primary and backup domain controllers. They are considered basically equal with an updatable copy of the Active Directory.

—*Cameron Wakefield, MCSD, MCP*

The tree allows the domains to share a namespace as well as a hierarchical naming structure. When you add a domain to a tree that already exists, it becomes a *child* domain of one of the existing *parent* domains, to give you a *tree* structure. For example, say you had a tree that consisted of one root domain named *syngress.com*. When you added a new domain named *author*, *author* would become a child domain of the existing domain *syngress.com*.

The naming structure follows the DNS standards so that the domain name for the child domain uses a relative path name. So, in our example, the *author* domain would be accessed using *author.syngress.com*. When creating the tree, the domain tree name should map to your Internet domain name if it is to be accessed across the Internet.

As you might guess, a *forest* is a grouping of one or more trees. This group of trees does not share a common namespace; in fact, it forms a noncontiguous (or *discontiguous*) namespace. However, the trees in a forest share a common configuration, global catalog, and directory schema. All trees within a forest have a two-way transitive trust between root domains. A trust allows all the trees to share resources and have common administrative functions. Such sharing capability allows the trees to operate independently of each other, with separate namespaces, yet still be able to communicate and share resources through trusts.

When you upgrade to Windows 2000, the first domain controller that is upgraded becomes the root domain of the forest. This domain contains the configuration and schema for the entire forest. This structure is normally created when you install the Active Directory services.

The root domain of the forest is the top of the hierarchical namespace. Once the forest root domain is created, it cannot be deleted, changed, or renamed without completely starting your Active Directory structure over again. The root domain of the forest contains the Enterprise Administrators and Schema Administrators groups. These groups are forestwide groups and reside in the forest's root domain. The decision as to which domain will be the root domain should be considered carefully. In an extreme case in which all the domain controllers for the root domain crashed and could not be restored, the Enterprise Administrators and Schema Administrators group would be lost, and you would not be able to reinstall the forest root domain.

You have two basic options for choosing the root domain. You can either use an existing domain or create a new domain that serves only as the forest root. If you choose to use an existing domain, select the most critical domain in your enterprise, because that should be the domain with the highest level of fault tolerance. If it isn't, choose as your root domain the domain that does have the highest level of fault tolerance.

Choosing to create a new domain for the root domain of the forest has some advantages and disadvantages. The most obvious disadvantage is the overhead costs associated with a domain. In some cases, the advantages outweigh the overhead costs. Since the Enterprise Administrators and Schema Administrators groups reside in this domain, the domain administrators will be able to change the membership of these groups. If you have domain administrators who you do not want to have access to these groups, you should consider a separate domain.

Another reason for choosing to create a new domain is obsolescence. If you choose an existing domain and you later decide to remove the domain, you will not be able to completely remove it. Another reason is since the domain will be small, it will not take a large amount of resources to replicate it on the network, even across slow links in your enterprise. So, if you have a catastrophe in one location, the domain would still be available in the location to which it was replicated.

If you have a catastrophe and you lose all your domain controllers for the forest's root domain and you cannot restore any of them, you will lose the Enterprise Administrators and Schema Administrators groups. Furthermore, you cannot reinstall the forest's root domain, so make sure you have good fault tolerance and backups available.

Restructuring Domains: Merging or Splitting

When you upgrade your Windows NT domain to Windows 2000, as much of your current domain configuration and settings are preserved as is possible. *Domain restructure,* also referred to as *domain consolidation,* is the method of changing the structure of your domains. Restructuring your domains can allow you to take advantage of the new features of Windows 2000, such as greater scalability. Windows 2000 does not have the same limitation as the SAM account database in Windows NT. Without this limitation, you can merge domains into one larger domain. Using Windows 2000 OUs, you have finer granularity in delegating administrative tasks.

Administration in Windows 2000 is also easier than in Windows NT. Using OUs and the domain trees with trusts, you can simplify the administration of the domains. Domain restructure could mean anything from changing the logical structure and/or hierarchy of your domains to merging and/or splitting existing domains. In Windows NT, you must use third-party tools to restructure your domains.

The two basic functions you can perform in Windows 2000 are moving user accounts from one domain to another while still maintaining access to the same resources you had prior to the move and moving domain controllers from one domain to another without reinstalling the operating system. Now, with Windows 2000, you can restructure your domains from within Windows. You need to decide if you want to leave the domain structure as it is or restructure it. So, when do you need to restructure? If you want to change some or all of your structure or if you cannot migrate to Windows 2000 without impacting your enterprise too much, you should probably consider restructuring your domains.

The next question is, when should you restructure your domains? If you can migrate the domains as they are, you should go ahead and migrate to Windows 2000 and then restructure the domains after the upgrade. If you cannot migrate the domains as they are and still be able to use the new features available with Active Directory or if the impact from migrating is too great on your enterprise, you should restructure the domains during the migration to Windows 2000. This allows you to create a fresh new domain structure without any latency problems. Restructuring your domains is not an easy task and should be planned carefully. You can also restructure your domains later, after migration is complete. This option allows you to change the structure as your organization changes.

When you decide to restructure your domains, one of the important decisions will be whether or not to merge or split existing domains. In Windows 2000, there isn't a simple operation that simply splits a domain. You must first create a new, empty domain and move the objects from the domain you want to split into the new domain. When moving a user from one domain to another, you must create a temporary password for the user in the new domain because user passwords are not preserved when they are moved. The user can change the password back to the original password, if desired. To create a new domain, you can either promote a Windows 2000 member server to a domain controller or upgrade a Windows NT 3.51 or 4.0 primary domain controller to a Windows 2000 Server domain controller.

Merging domains is similar to splitting domains in that you are moving user, group, and computer accounts to another domain. Merging domains allows easier administration by decreasing the number of trusts that must be created and can reduce the number of domain controllers required. Windows 2000 domains can contain significantly more user, group, and computer accounts. To merge domains, you simply move all the objects from one domain to another.

Windows 2000 facilitates domain restructuring by providing the following capabilities:

- User and group accounts can be moved from one domain to another with their security identity preserved.

- You can move a domain controllers to another domain by first demoting it to a member server.

- Remote administration tools (MOVETREE, SIDWALK, NETDOM, etc.) are available to move computers from one domain to another.

CERTIFICATION OBJECTIVE 4.02

Upgrading a Server from Microsoft Windows NT

When you have existing Windows NT servers on your network, you have to decide whether to upgrade the servers or install Windows 2000 Server as a new installation for dual-booting. In this section, we talk about upgrading an existing Windows NT server to a Windows 2000 Server. When you upgrade an existing operating system, you install it in the same partition and folder in which the existing operating system is installed. When you elect to perform an upgrade, Windows 2000 automatically installs in the same folder as the existing operating system. When upgrading from Windows NT, you can upgrade from the following versions: Windows NT 3.51, Windows NT 4.0, and Windows NT 4.0 Terminal Server.

exam
ⓌatcH

If you have an existing Windows NT 4.0 Server Enterprise Edition, you cannot upgrade to Windows 2000 Server; you must upgrade it to Windows 2000 Advanced Server or Windows 2000 Datacenter Server.

Prior to any type of installation, you should verify that the computer hardware meets the minimum requirements and is on the HCL. You also need to verify that the software you are using is compatible. To help determine the compatibility, you can use the Windows 2000 Compatibility Tool to generate a hardware and software compatibility report. This tool is run during setup, but you should run it before running Setup so you can fix any potential problems ahead of time.

There are two ways to use the Compatibility Tool. First, you can type **Winnt32 /checkupgradeonly**. This will start Setup to generate a compatibility report without starting installation of Windows 2000. This command generates a report named WINNT32.LOG in the <systemroot> folder. Or you can run the Windows 2000 Readiness Analyzer, which generates the report without running Setup. This tool can be downloaded from Microsoft at **www.microsoft.com/windows2000/ upgrade/compat**. The report provides a listing of the hardware and software that is found to be incompatible with Windows 2000. However, the Readiness Analyzer will not work if you have a dual-boot configuration with Windows 95, Windows 98, and Windows NT.

exam

ⓦatch

If your existing server is running a version of Windows NT earlier than 3.51, you cannot upgrade it directly to Windows 2000 Server. You must first upgrade it to Windows NT 3.51 or Windows NT 4.0 Server.

Upgrade Paths

When upgrading a Windows NT server, you have several options as to how to perform the upgrade. You can upgrade from the Windows 2000 Server CD-ROM, from a distribution server on the network, or using the UNATTEND.TXT answer file. Remember, only Windows NT 3.51 Server, Windows NT 4.0 Server, and earlier (beta) versions of Windows 2000 Server can be upgraded to Windows 2000 Server or Advanced Server.

Upgrading with a Compact Disc

To upgrade an existing version of Windows NT to Windows 2000 Server, insert the Windows 2000 Server CD-ROM in the CD-ROM drive and, if Autorun is on, it will automatically start Setup. Alternatively, you can run WINNT32.EXE from the i386 folder on the CD-ROM. You cannot upgrade using the boot disks or when booting from the CD-ROM. You must upgrade by starting Setup from Winnt32 or using Autorun on the CD-ROM. When you start using Autorun, you will see the window shown in Figure 4-1.

When you click the Yes button to upgrade to Windows 2000 Server, the program will check to see if you can upgrade. For example, if you are running Windows 98, you cannot upgrade to Windows 2000 Server. If you try, you will get the message box shown in Figure 4-2.

If you click OK, Windows will bring you to the Setup screen, but the only option available will be to perform a clean installation, as shown on the screen in Figure 4-3.

If your computer can be upgraded, you can choose the upgrade option and run Setup to upgrade your computer to Windows 2000 Server.

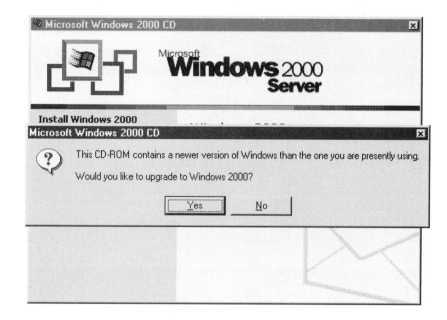

FIGURE 4-1

Upgrading to
Windows 2000
Server

Upgrading from a Network Distribution

Upgrading to Windows 2000 Server is basically the same as from the CD-ROM,
except you start the installation by running the WINNT32.EXE program from a
distribution server. You still have the same limitations and requirements as with the
CD-ROM installation, plus you have to be able to access the shared folder where the
Setup files are located.

FIGURE 4-2

The message
that you cannot
upgrade from
Windows 98

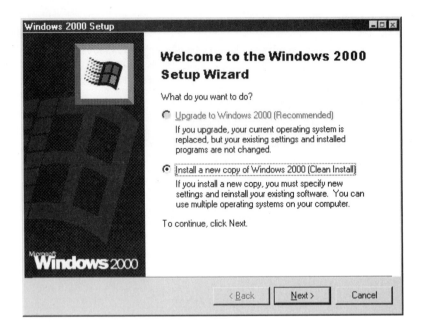

FIGURE 4-3

The screen giving you the ability to install a new copy of Windows 2000

Upgrading Using UNATTEND.TXT

You can also upgrade to Windows 2000 Server with an unattended installation. Instead of prompting the user, Setup retrieves answers to the questions from an answer file called UNATTEND.TXT. You can use the WINNT.EXE and WINNT32.EXE programs to perform an unattended installation of Windows 2000 Server, as detailed in Chapter 3.

Minimum Hardware Requirements

The hardware requirements for upgrading to Windows 2000 Server are basically the same as for performing a clean installation of Windows 2000 Server. The primary difference is that if you are upgrading a Windows NT domain controller, you have to allow additional hard-disk space for upgrading the domain. How much space is needed depends on the size of the domain you are upgrading. You should also ensure that the hardware is on the Hardware Compatibility List (HCL). The following is a list of the basic hardware requirements for upgrading to Windows 2000 Server. For the complete hardware requirements, refer to Chapter 2.

■ A 133MHz Pentium or higher CPU.

- Only up to four CPUs are supported.

- 256MB of RAM is the recommended minimum. 128MB of RAM is the minimum supported; 4GB of RAM is the maximum.

- To install Windows 2000 Server, the Setup process needs approximately 1GB of free space. You need a minimum of 671MB of free space, with 2GB recommended on the partition on which Windows 2000 Server will be installed. Once Setup is complete, the temporary files are deleted and less free space is required by Windows 2000 Server. Remember to allow additional disk space for upgrading the domain user account database and any additional components you install.

Rollback Strategy

As with any upgrade, problems can arise that sometimes require going back to the previous state. This possibility also applies to upgrading your domain to Windows 2000. You need to create a plan to roll back your network to its previous state if the upgrade to Windows 2000 fails.

When upgrading the domain controllers, do not upgrade the backup domain controller (BDC) that has the current directory database. Make sure the BDC is synchronized with the primary domain controller (PDC), and then take it offline. Leave the BDC as is until the upgrade is successful. If you run into problems during the upgrade, you can bring the BDC back online, promote it to the PDC, and recover the Windows NT state. If this process is successful, you can upgrade the BDC to Windows 2000.

Determining a Strategy and Performing Upgrades of Domain Controllers to Windows 2000

Prior to upgrading a domain controller to Windows 2000, you should prepare for the upgrade. If you have any third-party network services or virus programs, remove them prior to the upgrade. If you have an uninterruptible power supply (UPS) connected to the computer, remove the serial cable prior to the upgrade, because the detection process can have adverse affects on some UPS devices. Finally, set up your BIOS. If you have any ISA bus devices that are not Plug-and-Play compliant, reserve their IRQs in the BIOS prior to upgrading. If you don't, you will sometimes get IRQ conflicts.

Prior to upgrading the domain controllers, you need to perform the following tasks: If the WINS service is running, disable it so that the WINS database can be converted to Windows 2000. If the DHCP service is running, disable it so that the DHCP database can be converted to Windows 2000.

In Windows 2000 networks, there is no distinction between primary and backup domain controllers. All domain controllers have equal status. In Windows NT, only the primary domain controller has a domain database that can be updated. The backup domain controllers have only a copy of the domain database. In Windows 2000, all the domain controllers have a writable domain database that can be updated. Furthermore, in Windows 2000, all domain controllers should use the NTFS file system.

on the
Job

If the server has any partitions that are using the FAT or FAT32 file system, it will not be able use many security features available in Windows 2000. You will not be able to use file-level security or prevent local access to files. It is recommended that you convert all partitions to NTFS.

Upgrading Primary Domain Controllers

When upgrading your domain to Windows 2000, the PDC must be upgraded first. It is also recommended that you synchronize all the BDCs prior to upgrading the PDCs. When the PDC is upgraded, the Active Directory will be installed. Part of installing the AD is choosing between creating the first tree in a forest or creating a new tree in an existing forest. You must also choose between creating a new domain or a child domain. Also during the upgrade, you have the option to select where tree files are located. These files are the database that contains the user accounts, the log file, and the system volume, or SYSVOL. The user account database and the log file should be stored on a partition using the NTFS file system. The system volume must be stored on a partition with NTFS.

When the PDC is upgraded to Windows 2000 Server, it is backward compatible with other servers and clients that are not running Windows 2000. It emulates the Windows NT 4.0 PDC for these computers and acts as a Windows 2000 domain controller for Windows 2000 servers and clients. The contents of the Windows NT account database and Security Account Manager (SAM) are copied into the AD during the upgrade. Even if you made changes to user accounts or groups, these changes are replicated to any existing Windows NT BDCs that still exist in the domain.

exam
Watch

When upgrading your domain from Windows NT to Windows 2000, you must upgrade the PDC first.

Upgrading Backup Domain Controllers

Upgrading BDCs to Windows 2000 is the same process you used for the PDC. You do not have to upgrade all the BDCs at the same time. You can upgrade them incrementally, as needed. Make sure you back up the server prior to upgrading. When you upgrade, make sure the PDC that was upgraded is running and available on the network. This server is used as a template to copy for the BDCs when they are upgraded. After upgrading each BDC, make sure it is working correctly before upgrading the next BDC.

When upgrading domain controllers, allow more free disk space than the minimum, because additional space is required for the user account database. The actual amount needed depends on the size of the database.

Switching from Mixed to Native Mode

Windows 2000 domains can operate in two modes: Mixed Mode or Native Mode. *Mixed Mode* allows Windows NT domain controllers to still operate in a Windows 2000 domain. The Windows NT domain controllers can be version 3.51 or version 4.0. The PDC has to be upgraded first when you are upgrading to Windows 2000 Server. Mixed Mode allows the remaining BDCs to still operate as domain controllers. The PDC uses the AD but exposes the data as a flat store, as in Windows NT.

When in Mixed Mode, the domain still uses master replication with a Windows 2000 PDC. The Windows NT BDCs replicate from the Windows 2000 server, as did the Windows NT PDC. When you are operating in Mixed Mode, some Windows 2000 functionality will not be available. You will not be able to use group nesting. You can still use transitive trusts; however, NT domain controllers will not be able to use Kerberos authentication—it will only be available between Windows 2000 computers. (These topics are covered later in the book.) Mixed Mode is the default mode.

Native Mode allows only Windows 2000 domain controllers to operate in the domain. When all domain controllers for the domain are upgraded to Windows 2000 Server, you can switch to Native Mode. This allows you to use transitive trusts and the group-nesting features of Windows 2000. When switching to Native Mode, ensure you no longer need to operate in Mixed Mode, because you cannot switch back to Mixed Mode once you are in Native Mode.

The Mixed and Native Modes refer only to the domain controllers. When you switch to Native Mode, clients that are not running a Windows 2000 operating system can still be part of the domain. When you switch to Native Mode, the domain uses Active Directory exclusively. This means you are not able to add

Windows NT backup domain controllers to the network. You are able to add only Windows 2000 Server domain controllers. Now all domain controllers have a master replicated copy of Active Directory. This means that there is no longer a PDC. All the domain controllers are able to update the directory.

exam

ⓦatch

Once you switch to Native Mode, you cannot switch back to Mixed Mode.

There may be situations in which you cannot switch to Native Mode. There may be cases when a BDC cannot be upgraded. Such an instance could be caused by an application that has to run on a domain controller but that is not compatible with Windows 2000 domain controllers. Another possible reason is physical security. Say a BDC is stored in a location that could be subject to attack. In a Windows NT BDC, it has only a read-only copy of the user account database and SAM. In Windows 2000, all domain controllers have a master copy of the Active Directory and therefore can be updated. If you determine this situation is an unnecessary security risk, you could leave the domain controllers in Mixed Mode. However, you should consider moving the computer to a more secure location.

Switching to Native Mode is a manual operation performed by the administrator. You perform it via the Active Directory Domains and Trusts dialog box. See Exercise 4-2 on how to switch mode.

EXERCISE 4-2

Switching from Mixed Mode to Native Mode

1. From the Start menu, select Programs | Administrative Tools | Active Directory Domains and Trusts.

2. Right-click the domain and select Properties. This will bring up the Properties dialog box.

3. Click the General tab to open it.

4. Click the Change Mode button. You are given a warning that when you change to Native Mode, you cannot switch back to Mixed Mode.

5. Click the Yes button on the warning message box.

6. Click the OK button to close the Properties dialog box.

Upgrade and Promote Member Servers to Windows 2000

When you are upgrading an existing domain to Windows 2000, you can upgrade existing Windows NT member servers before, during, or after the domain upgrade process. To upgrade, you must be currently running the Windows NT 3.51 or 4.0 Server operating system. If the computer has a dual-boot configuration, you must be running the operating system that you want to upgrade when you begin installation.

To start installation, insert the Windows 2000 Server CD-ROM. When prompted, click "upgrade to Windows 2000" and follow the instructions to upgrade the existing server. When you have finished the upgrade, the member server will still be a member of the domain or workgroup of which it was previously a member. The local user and group accounts are stored in the registry of the server and are not moved to the Active Directory. In the final phase of setup, all applications and operating system configuration settings from Windows NT will be available in Windows 2000.

on the *job*

If the member server you are upgrading is a DHCP server, you must authorize the DHCP Server service in Active Directory or the service will not start. Authorization is not automatically granted when you upgrade to Windows 2000.

Once a member server has been upgraded to Windows 2000 Server, it can be promoted to a domain controller. To promote it, use the Active Directory Installation Wizard (DCPROMO.EXE). When you have promoted the server to a domain controller, all the local user and group accounts are then added to the Active Directory while maintaining permissions to local resources. In Windows NT, you had to reinstall the operating system to "promote" a member server to a domain controller. Exercise 4-3 walks you through upgrading a member server to a domain controller. This exercise demonstrates how to create a new domain from an existing member server.

CertCam 4-3

EXERCISE 4-3

Upgrading a Member Server to a Domain Controller

1. From the Start menu, select Run.

2. In the Run dialog box, type **dcpromo,** as shown in the illustration below, and click the OK button.

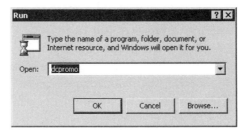

3. When the Welcome to the Active Directory Installation Wizard screen appears, as shown below, click Next.

4. Now you will decide whether to make the server a domain controller for a new domain or make it a domain controller for an existing domain. For this exercise, we will create a new domain. Select "Domain controller for a new domain," as shown in the next illustration, and click Next.

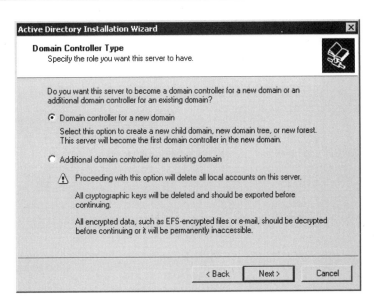

5. Next you have to choose between creating a new tree or adding the new domain as a child domain to an existing tree. In this exercise, we will create a new tree. Make sure the "Create a new domain tree" option is selected, as shown in the illustration below, and click Next.

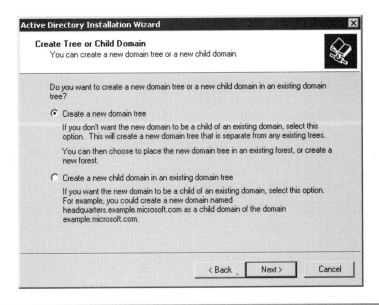

6. You can either create a new forest or add the new tree to an existing forest. For this exercise, we will create a new forest. Make sure the "Create a new forest of domain trees" option is selected, as shown in the illustration below, and click Next.

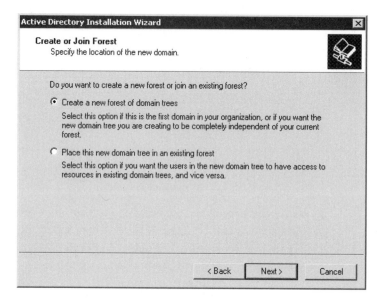

7. Now enter the NetBIOS name for the domain. Enter **CAMERON**, as shown in the next illustration, and click Next.

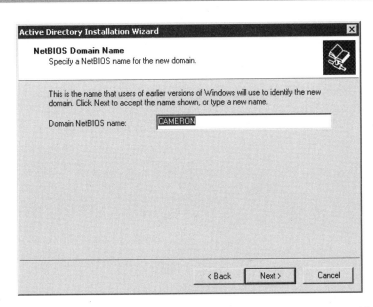

8. The next screen allows you to choose where to store the database and log.
    These can be stored on any partition. Accept the defaults, as shown in the
    illustration below, and click Next.

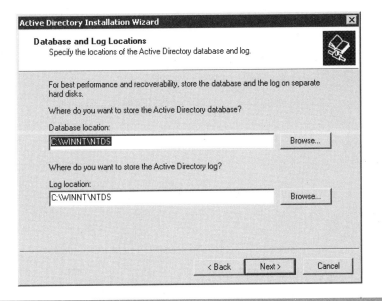

9. The Sysvol folder contains the domain's public files. It can be stored only on a partition formatted with NTFS 5.0. Ensure that the path shown is on an NTFS partition, as shown in the illustration below, and click Next.

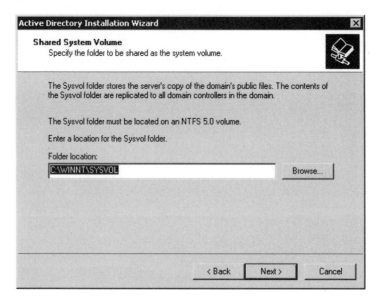

10. Now you must choose whether or not you want the permissions to be backward compatible. Make sure the "Permissions compatible with pre-Windows 2000 servers" option is selected, as shown in the next illustration, and click Next.

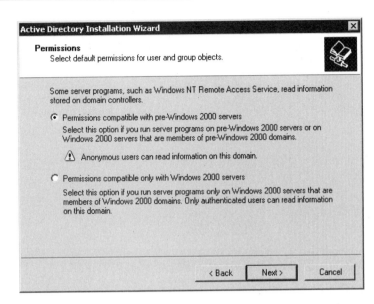

11. Enter a password to use when you are restoring the directory. (This password is used for the local Administrator account in the Recovery Console.) Type in a password of your choice and click Next, as shown:

12. A summary of your choices is displayed. Review the options, as shown below, and click Next.

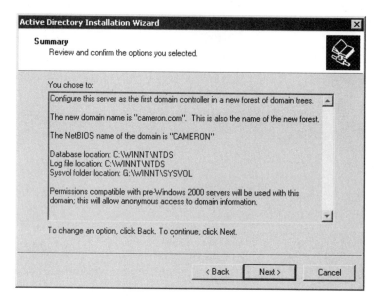

13. A splash screen is displayed while the Active Directory is installed, as shown:

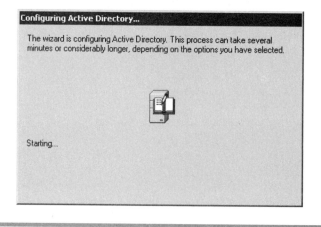

14. When the installation is complete, the Completing the Active Directory Installation screen appears, as shown below. Click Finish.

15. The last step is to restart the computer. Click Restart Now, as shown:

SCENARIO & SOLUTION

You have a domain that you upgraded to Windows 2000 that has users from two different departments. You decide to split up the domain. How can you accomplish this?	First, create a new domain. Once the domain is created, you can move users to the new domain, and they will still have their security IDs.
You are preparing to install Windows 2000 and you want to determine if your computer is compatible with Windows 2000. How can you do this?	You can run the WINNT32.EXE program with the /checkupgradeonly switch. This starts Setup to generate a compatibility report without starting installation of Windows 2000. It generates a report named WINNT32.LOG in the <systemroot> folder.

CERIFICATION OBJECTIVE 4.03

Deploying Service Packs

Periodically, Microsoft releases service packs for its operating systems. A service pack typically contains bug fixes, security fixes, systems administration tools, drivers, and additional components. Microsoft recommends installing the latest service packs as they are released. In addition, as a new feature in Windows 2000, you do not have to reinstall components after installing a service pack, as you did with Windows NT. You can also see what service pack is currently installed on a computer by running the WINVER utility program. WINVER brings up the About Windows dialog box. It displays the version of Windows and the version of the service pack you are running.

To install a service pack, use the UPDATE.EXE program. When a service pack is applied, Windows 2000 tracks which service pack was installed and which files were added and/or replaced. This way, when a component or service is added or removed, if any of the required files were included in the service pack, the operating system automatically retrieves those files from the service pack. This feature prevents you from having to reinstall the service pack.

Testing Service Packs

Prior to deploying service packs to the enterprise, you should perform some testing. Some applications have problems running after new service packs are installed.

To test new service packs, create test environments for each computer configuration in your enterprise. Make sure the test computers have the same hardware and are running the same software and performing the same operations as the computers in the enterprise. Testing a service pack this way allows you to find potential errors prior to deploying a service pack throughout your enterprise.

Integrating Service Packs with Distribution Images

You can include service packs with a distribution image. This feature is called *service pack slipstreaming*. Using slipstreaming, you can install Windows 2000 with the service pack already applied to the installation files on a CD-ROM or distribution folder. You do not have to apply the service pack after installation of Windows 2000 Server. To apply a service pack to distribution files, use the UPDATE.EXE file with the /slip switch. This combination overwrites the existing distribution files with the service pack files.

CERTIFICATION OBJECTIVE 4.04

Troubleshooting Failed Installations

Once in a while, you will have some problems trying to install Windows 2000 Server. Problems can also occur when you are restarting the computer for the first time after installation is complete. When these problems occur, you need to be able to detect and resolve them.

Resolving Common Problems

If the CD-ROM you are installing from has errors on it, you will not be able to install from it. You must obtain another CD-ROM. If you don't have an additional copy, contact Microsoft or your vendor. Some CD-ROM drives are not supported by Windows 2000 Server. If this is the case, you must either replace the CD-ROM drive with a drive that is supported or choose a different installation method, such as a network installation. When you install Windows 2000 Server, you must ensure that you have enough free disk space. If you don't, the Setup program can create a new partition if there is any space on the hard disk. If there is no space, you can delete and create partitions as needed so that you can create a partition large enough to install Windows 2000 Server. To free some space, you can also add another hard drive or delete some applications that are not being used.

When installing Windows 2000 Server, you can sometimes get an error message when trying to locate the domain controller. Check that you entered the correct domain name and that a domain controller is running on the network. In addition, verify that the DNS server is running. If you cannot locate a domain controller, join a workgroup and then later, after installation, when you can locate a domain controller, join the domain.

Sometimes problems show up after installation is complete and you are starting Windows 2000 Server for the first time. If Windows 2000 Server fails to start, verify that all the hardware is on the HCL and that all hardware is being detected. Sometimes a dependency service fails to start. If this occurs, verify that the correct network adapter is being installed and check the configuration settings (e.g., the transceiver setting). In addition, verify that you have installed the correct protocol and that the computer name is unique on the network.

Setup Logs

During the GUI phase of setup, log files are created. These log files are located in the directory to which Windows 2000 is being installed. Four log files are created:

- **SETUPACT.LOG**   The Action log file contains details about the files that are copied during setup.

- **SETUPERR.LOG**   The Error log file contains details about errors that occurred during setup.

- **SETUPAPI.LOG**   This log file contains details about the device driver files that were copied during setup. This log can be used to facilitate troubleshooting of device installations. The file contains errors and warnings along with a time stamp for each issue.

- **SETUPLOG.TXT**   This log file contains additional information about the device driver files that were copied during setup.

Let's take a look at the contents of your setup logs in Exercise 4-4.

Looking at the Setup Logs

1. Open My Computer.

2. Open the C: drive. (If you installed Windows 2000 Server on a different drive, open that drive instead. The rest of the exercise assumes you're using drive C:. As you read, replace references to drive C: with the appropriate drive as necessary.)

3. Open the Winnt folder. (Again, this exercise assumes you used Winnt as the installation folder name. You can replace it if you installed to another folder name.)

4. Open the SETUPACT.LOG file for review. An example of the first few lines of the log file follows. When you double-click the log files, the log file is opened in Notepad by default:

```
GUI mode Setup has started.
C:\WINNT\Driver Cache\i386\driver.cab was copied to
C:\WINNT\System32\storprop.dll.
C:\$WIN_NT$.~LS\i386\SPOOLSV.EX_ was copied to
C:\WINNT\System32\SPOOLSV.EXE.
```

5. Close SETUPACT.LOG.

6. Open the SETUPAPI.LOG file for review. The following is an example of the first few lines of the log file:

```
[2000/02/21 13:25:25 324.12]
Munged cmdline: setup -newsetup
EXE name: C:\WINNT\system32\setup.exe
Installing Device Class:
{6BDD1FC1-810F-11D0-BEC7-08002BE2092F} 1394.
Class install completed with no errors.
[2000/02/21 13:25:26 324.15]
Installing Device Class:
{72631e54-78a4-11d0-bcf7-00aa00b7b32a} Battery.
Class install completed with no errors.
[2000/02/21 13:25:26 324.20]
Installing Device Class:
{4D36E965-E325-11CE-BFC1-08002BE10318} CDROM.
Class install completed with no errors.
```

EXERCISE 4-4

7. Close SETUPAPI.LOG.

8. Open the SETUPERR.LOG file for review. If there weren't any errors during setup, this file is empty.

9. Close SETUPERR.LOG.

10. Open the SETUPLOG.TXT file for review. The following is an example of the first few lines of the log file:

```
13:24:58.559 syssetup.c @ 1214 Setup: (non-critical error):
Failed load of ismif32.dll.
13:24:59.510 ctls.c @ 807 SETUP: Enter RegisterOleControls
13:24:59.520 ctls.c @ 860 SETUP: back from OleInitialize
13:24:59.520 ctls.c @ 879 SETUP: filename for file to
register is rsabase.dll
13:24:59.520 ctls.c @ 433 SETUP: loading dll...
13:24:59.560 ctls.c @ 504 SETUP: ...dll loaded
13:24:59.560 ctls.c @ 533 SETUP: registering...
13:24:59.560 ctls.c @ 581 SETUP: ...registered
```

11. Close SETUPLOG.TXT.

SCENARIO & SOLUTION

You have a distribution server from which clients upgrade to Windows 2000. After they upgrade, they install a service pack from another network location. What can you do to simplify this process?	Service packs can be integrated or slipstreamed into a distribution image using the Service Pack UPDATE.EXE program. This program installs the service pack files during setup.
You are trying to install Windows 2000 with a dual-boot configuration. The partition to which you want to install is not big enough, but you have 2GB of unpartitioned disk space. What can you do to make the partition large enough?	During setup, you can delete the partition that is not large enough, and then create it again but make it larger using the unpartitioned space of the hard disk.

CERTIFICATION SUMMARY

In this chapter, we talked about upgrading your existing Windows NT network to Windows 2000. The most important task in upgrading your network is planning ahead. Plan your networking requirements such as your network protocol and naming services. You also need to make sure you understand the new features available in Windows 2000 so that you can decide how to structure your domains. You need to decide on a root domain and whether or not to restructure your domains.

When upgrading your Windows NT Server to Windows 2000 Server, you can use a variety of methods: the Windows 2000 Server CD-ROM, install across the network, and even perform unattended installations. One crucial aspect of upgrading is verifying that your hardware is compatible with Windows 2000. You should check the HCL for compatibility. Prior to starting your upgrade, create a rollback plan in case of a failure while upgrading.

When upgrading your domain controllers, you must upgrade the primary domain controller (PDC) first. Once the PDC is successfully upgraded, you can upgrade your backup domain controllers (BDCs). You don't have to upgrade them all at once. Windows 2000 Server domain controllers can operate in Mixed Mode to allow Windows NT BDCs to still operate in the domain. Once all your Windows NT domain controllers are upgraded to Windows 2000, you should switch to Native Mode, which allows you to utilize all the features of Windows 2000. In addition, you can promote and demote Windows 2000 Server between the member server role and domain controller role using the DCPROMO.EXE command-line utility.

Windows 2000 has made using service packs easier. You can use slipstreaming to integrate service packs with Windows 2000 distribution images. Another new feature is that you don't have to reinstall a service pack after adding components or installing applications. Windows 2000 automatically uses the existing service packs files.

On the rare occasion that a Windows 2000 installation fails, you should understand the common causes of failure and how to solve the problems. In the event of more complicated failures, you can use the Setup log files to assist you in troubleshooting.

TWO-MINUTE DRILL

Planning a Network Upgrade to Windows 2000

- ❑ Plan your upgrade in detail prior to starting.
- ❑ Determine your DHCP and WINS requirements.
- ❑ You can provide a dynamic IP address using either DHCP or APIPA.
- ❑ DNS provides name resolution to IP addresses.
- ❑ DNS allows users to remember names rather than IP addresses.
- ❑ You should provide WINS when you are supporting clients not running Windows 2000.
- ❑ Create a naming strategy that is intuitive and easy to use.
- ❑ You should determine the role your Windows NT servers will play in Windows 2000.
- ❑ Prepare for the upgrade.
- ❑ Back up all data on computers prior to upgrading.
- ❑ Synchronize and take a BDC off-line prior to upgrading the domain.
- ❑ Upgrade the PDC first.
- ❑ A tree contains one or more domains with global access.
- ❑ A forest contains one or more trees.
- ❑ The root of the forest contains the forestwide groups.
- ❑ The first domain controller upgraded becomes the root of the forest.
- ❑ Existing domains can be merged into a larger domain or split into multiple domains.

Upgrading a Server from Windows NT

- ❑ Only Windows NT 3.51 and 4.0 Servers can be upgraded to Windows 2000 Server.

❑ You can upgrade using the CD-ROM, a network distribution server, or unattended.

❑ Make sure the computer meets the minimum hardware requirements.

❑ Make sure that all the hardware and software is compatible with Windows 2000.

❑ Create a plan to roll back to Windows NT if you run into problems during the upgrade.

❑ The user account database and the log file can be stored on a partition using the FAT, FAT32, or NTFS file system.

❑ The System volume (SYSVOL) must be stored on an NTFS 5.0 partition.

❑ The BDCs can be upgraded incrementally. You do not have to upgrade them all at once.

❑ Mixed Mode makes your domain backward compatible with Windows NT BDCs.

❑ Native Mode allows you to use all the features of Windows 2000 domains and supports only Windows 2000 domain controllers.

❑ You can switch from Mixed Mode to Native Mode, but you cannot switch from Native Mode to Mixed Mode.

❑ Windows 2000 member servers can be promoted to domain controllers, and Windows 2000 domain controllers can be demoted to member servers.

❑ In Windows 2000, there isn't a distinction between primary and backup domain controllers.

Deploying Service Packs

❑ Microsoft periodically releases updates to Windows operating systems.

❑ These updates, called *service packs,* contain bug and security fixes.

❑ Service packs are installed using the UPDATE.EXE program.

❑ You don't have to reinstall service packs after adding or deleting components or services.

❑ You should test your service pack for software compatibility prior to deploying it.

❑ You can include a service pack in a distribution image.

❑ You can deploy service packs using group policies.

Troubleshooting Failed Installations

❑ If the installation CD-ROM is damaged, you have to replace it.

❑ Ensure there is enough free disk space on the computer prior to installation.

❑ Make sure the domain controller is on-line and available.

❑ Verify that the DNS server is running.

❑ SETUPACT.LOG contains details about the files that are copied during setup.

❑ SETUPERR.LOG contains details about errors that occurred during setup.

❑ SETUPAPI.LOG contains details about the device driver files that were copied during setup.

❑ SETUPLOG.TXT contains additional information about the device driver files that were copied during setup.

SELF TEST

The following questions will help you measure your understanding of the material presented in this chapter. Read all of the choices carefully because there may be more than one correct answer. Choose all correct answers for each question.

Planning a Network Upgrade to Windows 2000

1. You are planning to upgrade your domain to Windows 2000. In case you have problems during the upgrade, you want to be able to restore your network to the original Windows NT domain. Which of the following will allow you to do this?

    A. Demote one of the domain controllers that are already upgraded to Windows 2000 to a Windows NT domain controller.

    B. Take the primary domain controller off-line and upgrade the backup domain controllers first.

    C. Synchronize and take a backup domain controller off-line.

    D. Once you start the upgrade, you cannot revert to Windows NT domains.

2. What is the difference between a forest and a tree?

    A. A forest is a group of domains, and a tree is a group of forests that share the same namespace.

    B. A tree is a group of domains with the same namespace, and a forest is a group of trees that also share the same namespace.

    C. A tree is a group of domains with the same namespace, and a forest is a group of trees that do not share the same namespace.

    D. A forest is a group of domains with the same namespace, and a tree is a group of forests that do not share the same namespace.

3. Which of the following is *not* a role a Windows 2000 Server can perform?

    A. Domain controller

    B. Member server

    C. Master controller

    D. Stand-alone server

4. You have an existing Windows NT domain that you have decided to upgrade to Windows 2000. When you upgrade a Windows NT domain to Windows 2000, which of the following must be upgraded first?

A. Primary domain controller

B. Backup domain controller

C. Member servers

D. Stand-alone servers

Upgrading a Server from Windows NT

5. You will upgrade your existing Windows NT servers to Windows 2000 Server on your network. Which of the following is not a valid upgrade path from Windows NT Server to Windows 2000 Server?

A. Windows NT domain controller to Windows 2000 domain controller

B. Windows NT member server to Windows 2000 domain controller

C. Windows NT member server to Windows 2000 member server

D. Windows NT stand-alone server to Windows 2000 member server

6. You want to upgrade an existing Windows NT 4.0 member server to a Windows 2000 domain controller. The computer is currently configured to dual-boot with Windows 98, so all the partitions are formatted with FAT. Which of the following requirements prevents you from making this computer a domain controller?

A. The log file must be stored on a FAT32 partition.

B. The user account database can be stored on a FAT partition.

C. The system volume must be stored on an NTFS 5.0 partition.

D. The system volume must be stored on a FAT partition.

7. You have upgraded your network to Windows 2000. All your domain controllers are now running Windows 2000. The domain controllers are running in Mixed Mode. You are considering switching to Native Mode. Which of the following is *not* a consideration when switching from Mixed to Native Mode?

A. Once in Native Mode, you cannot switch back to Mixed Mode.

B. The existing Windows NT Workstation computers will no longer be able to be a part of the domain and must be upgraded to Windows 2000.

C. Any new Windows NT domain controllers added to the domain will not be able to participate in the domain.

D. You will no longer be able to add Windows NT backup domain controllers to the domain.

8. You have a Windows 2000 Server that is a member server. Your domain is growing and you want to add another domain controller to it. Which of the following programs is used to upgrade a member server to a domain controller?

A. PROMOTE.EXE

B. DCPROMO.EXE

C. DCUPGRADE.EXE

D. You cannot upgrade a member server to a domain controller

Deploying Service Packs

9. Which of the following methods *cannot* be used to deploy service packs in Windows 2000?

A. Using the UPDATE.EXE program

B. Including the service pack in a distribution image

C. Using the SPINSTALL.EXE program

D. Using group policies

10. You want to install Windows 2000 on some new computers. However, a new service pack was just released. You want to include the service pack as part of the distribution image. Which of the following command-line switches is used to integrate the service pack with a distribution image?

A. /slip

B. /s

C. /integrate

D. /copy

11. Your computer is running Windows 2000. You have installed the latest service pack. After installing the service pack, you add a Windows component. Which of the following must you do after adding the component to keep the service pack files current?

A. Reinstall Windows 2000.

B. Add the service pack to a Windows 2000 distribution image and then reinstall Windows 2000.

C. Reinstall the service pack.

D. You don't have to do anything.

Troubleshooting Failed Installations

12. During the installation of Windows 2000 Server, you are trying to join a domain. You receive an error that Setup cannot locate a domain controller. Which of the following do you *not* need to do?

    A. Check that you entered the correct domain name.

    B. Verify that a domain controller is available.

    C. Verify that a WINS server is running.

    D. Verify that a DNS server is running.

13. You are trying to install Windows 2000 on an older computer. You find that your CD-ROM drive is not supported by Windows 2000. Which of the following can you do to resolve the problem to allow you to install Windows 2000 Server? Choose all that apply.

    A. Replace the CD-ROM drive with one that is supported by Windows 2000.

    B. Use a different Windows 2000 CD-ROM.

    C. Install Windows 2000 from a distribution server on the network.

    D. Boot the computer from the Windows 2000 Server CD-ROM.

14. You installed Windows 2000 on a new computer to the default location on the C: drive. You are encountering some strange errors, and it was recommended that you review the Setup log files. In which directory would these log files be found?

    A. C:\

    B. C:\Winnt

    C. C:\Winnt\System

    D. C:\Winnt\Log

15. Which of the following is *not* a log file created by Windows 2000 Setup?

    A. SETUPACT.LOG

    B. SETUP.LOG

    C. SETUPERR.LOG

    D. SETUPLOG.TXT

16. You installed Windows 2000 Server on a computer. You are having some trouble with one of the devices on the computer. Which of the following Setup files should you use for troubleshooting to find errors that might have occurred while installing this device?

    A. SETUPACT.LOG

B. SETUPERR.LOG

C. SETUPAPI.LOG

D. SETUPDEVICEERR.LOG

LAB QUESTION

You have been given the task of upgrading your existing Windows NT domain to Windows 2000. You must generate a report outlining the process you will take to perform the upgrade. Write a report to detail the upgrade process using these steps:

1. System requirements

2. Read READ1ST.TXT, README.DOC, and hardware compatibility information

3. Operating system upgradeable to Windows 2000

4. Review concepts for upgrading an existing domain

5. Choose file system to use

6. Prepare your system for upgrading

7. Check applications for compatibility

SELF TEST ANSWERS

Planning a Network Upgrade to Windows 2000

1. ☑ **C.** Synchronize and take a backup domain controller off-line. Prior to upgrading a Windows NT domain, you should first synchronize a backup domain controller and then take it off-line. That way, if you cannot upgrade your domain, you can bring the BDC back on-line to revert to the Windows NT domain.
   ☒ **A** is not correct because a Windows 2000 Server cannot be demoted to a Windows NT domain controller. **B** is not correct because the primary domain controller must be upgraded to Windows 2000 Server first. **D** is not correct because you can revert to a Windows NT domain if the upgrade to Windows 2000 fails.

2. ☑ **C.** A tree is a group of domains that share a DNS namespace. A forest is a group of trees that allow transitive trusts between the trees.
   ☒ **A** is not correct because a tree is not a group of forests, it is a group of domains. **B** is not correct because the trees in a forest do not necessarily share a namespace. Each tree can have its own separate namespace. **D** is not correct because a forest is a group of trees, not domains.

3. ☑ **C.** A master controller is not a role that a Windows 2000 Server performs.
   ☒ **A, B,** and **D** are not correct because a Windows 2000 Server can serve as a domain controller, a member server, or a stand-alone server.

4. ☑ **A.** A primary domain controller for a domain must be upgraded first since it has the master copy of the domain information.
   ☒ **B, C,** and **D** are not correct because you must upgrade the primary domain controller prior to upgrading the backup domain controller(s), member server(s), and stand-alone server(s).

Upgrading a Server from Microsoft Windows NT

5. ☑ **B.** Windows NT member server to Windows 2000 domain controller. Only existing Windows NT domain controllers can be directly upgraded to Windows 2000 domain controllers. However, Windows 2000 member servers can be promoted to domain controllers after installation.
   ☒ **A** is not correct because you can upgrade Windows NT domain controllers to Windows 2000 domain controllers. **C** is not correct because you can upgrade Windows NT member servers to Windows 2000 member servers. **D** is not correct because you can upgrade Windows NT stand-alone servers to Windows 2000 member servers.

6. ☑ **C.** The system volume must be stored on an NTFS 5.0 partition. Since the computer only has FAT partitions, it would not meet this requirement. One of the partitions would have to be upgraded to NTFS prior to making the computer a domain controller. The computer could be upgraded to a Windows 2000 member server.

   ☒ **A** is not correct because even though the log file can be stored on a FAT32 partition, it can also be stored on FAT and NTFS partitions, so this would not prevent you from upgrading. **B** is not correct because even though this is a correct statement, it would not prevent you from upgrading because the user account database can be stored on a FAT, FAT32, or NTFS partition. **D** is not correct because the system volume cannot be stored on a FAT partition. It must be stored on an NTFS 5.0 partition.

7. ☑ **B.** The existing Windows NT Workstation computers will no longer be able to be a part of the domain and must be upgraded to Windows 2000. When you switch to Native Mode, your existing clients that are not running Windows 2000 can still function in the domain. The mode refers only to domain controllers and how they operate, not the clients.

   ☒ **A** is not correct because once you are in Native Mode, you cannot switch back to Mixed Mode. **C** is not correct because any new Windows NT backup domain controllers in the domain would not be able to participate as domain controllers in the domain. **D** is not correct because once you switch to Native Mode, you cannot have any Windows NT domain controllers in the domain.

8. ☑ **B.** The DCPROMO.EXE program is used to promote member servers to domain controllers.

   ☒ **A** and **C** are not correct because there are no Windows programs called PROMOTE.EXE and DCUPGRADE.EXE to promote member servers to domain controllers. **D** is not correct because a member server can be promoted to a domain controller.

Deploying Service Packs

9. ☑ **C.** Using the SPINSTALL.EXE program. There is no such thing as a SPINSTALL.EXE program to install service packs. The UPGRADE.EXE program is used to install service packs.

   ☒ **A** is not correct because the UPGRADE.EXE program can be used to install service packs. **B** is not correct because you can integrate service packs into distribution images. **D** is not correct because group policies can be used to deploy service packs.

10. ☑ **A.** The UPDATE.EXE program uses the /slip switch to specify that you want to integrate a service pack with an existing distribution image.

   ☒ **B, C,** and **D** are not correct because these are not valid switches for the UPGRADE.EXE program The /slip switch is used.

11. ☑ **D.** You don't have to do anything. When you install a service pack in Windows 2000, it updates Windows with the files updated in the service pack. This way, when a component or service is added or deleted, it can get the updated file from the service pack. In Windows NT, it retrieves the file from the Windows installation media and then you need to reinstall the service pack.

☒ **A** is not correct because you do not have to reinstall Windows 2000. The files included in the service pack are automatically retrieved. **B** is not correct because you don't have to reinstall Windows. This is a good method for new installations or upgrades. **C** is not correct because you do not have to reinstall the service pack. The files included in the service pack are automatically retrieved.

Troubleshooting Failed Installations

12. **C.** Verify that a WINS server is running. You do not need WINS to locate a domain controller. Windows 2000 uses only DNS for name resolution.

☒ **A** is not correct because you do need to enter the correct domain name in order to join a domain. **B** is not correct because you do need to verify that a domain controller is on-line and running in order to join a domain. **D** is not correct because you do need to verify there is a DNS server on-line and available to locate a domain controller.

13. **A and C.** Replace the CD-ROM drive with one that is supported by Windows 2000, and install Windows 2000 from a distribution server on the network. If your CD-ROM drive is not supported, you should replace the CD-ROM drive. You could also perform a network installation, but you should still replace the CD-ROM drive so that you can install other applications.

☒ **B** is not correct because using a different CD-ROM will not solve the problem with the CD-ROM drive. **D** is not correct because if the CD-ROM drive is not supported, you still will not be able to install from it.

14. ☑ **B.** C:\Winnt\System. The Setup log files are created in the system root folder, which is the directory in which you installed Windows 2000.

☒ **A, C,** and **D** are incorrect because the Setup log files are created in the system root folder.

15. ☑ **B.** Setup does not create a log file called SETUP.LOG.

☒ **A** is not correct because Setup creates the SETUPACT.LOG file. **C** is not correct because Setup does create the SETUPERR.LOG file. **D** is not correct because Setup does create the SETUPLOG.TXT file.

16. ☑ **C.** The SETUPAPI.LOG file contains details about device driver files that were copied as well as errors and warnings that have occurred during setup.

☒   **A** is not correct because the SETUPACT.LOG file is used to log details about the files that are copied during setup. **B** is not correct because the SETUPERR.LOG contains details about general errors that occur during setup, not device driver installation errors. **D** is not correct because a SETUPDEVICEERR.LOG file is not created by setup.

LAB ANSWER

I.   *System Requirements*

The minimum requirements for upgrading to Windows 2000 Server are as follows:

- A 133MHz Pentium or higher CPU.
- Only up to four CPUs are supported.
- 64MB of RAM required, with 128MB of RAM recommended as the minimum; 4GB of RAM is the maximum.
- To install Windows 2000 Server, the Setup process needs approximately 1GB of free space. You need a minimum of 671MB of free space, with 2GB recommended on the partition on which Windows 2000 Server will be installed. Once setup is complete, the temporary files are deleted and less free space is then required by Windows 2000 Server. You will need additional free space to upgrade the domain's user account database. How much space depends on the size of the domain. Additional free space is also required for any components you install or if you install across the network.

However, the minimum requirements are not sufficient in most cases. You should do some performance testing to determine the exact needs for your environment. You should also verify that the existing hardware is compatible with Windows 2000, including the BIOS. The hardware should be included in the HCL.

2.   *Read READ1ST.TXT, README.DOC, and Hardware Compatibility Information*

On the Windows 2000 server CD-ROM, there are some files in the root directory that you should read prior to installation. The file READ1ST.TXT contains notes that can be critical to the success of installation. The file README.DOC contains information about the usage of hardware, networking, applications, and printing.

3.   *Server Operating System Upgradeable to Windows 2000*

There are two things to consider when determining whether or not your servers can be upgraded to Windows 2000 Server. First, only Windows NT Server 3.51 and 4.0 can be upgraded directly to

Windows 2000 Server. If you have an earlier version of Windows NT, you must first upgrade it to Windows NT 3.51 or 4.0 Server. Microsoft recommends upgrading it to Windows NT 4.0. Next, you must determine which role the server currently plays in the domain and what role you want it to play in Windows 2000. Refer to the list in Table 4-1, which shows the upgrade paths for Windows NT roles. Keep in mind that if you want to use a role that isn't in the path shown, you can change the server's role after upgrading to Windows 2000 Server.

4. *Review Concepts for Upgrading an Existing Domain*

When upgrading a domain, you should always use the NTFS file system for your domain controller. If you use FAT or FAT32, you will lose the security benefits associated with NTFS. Check all the current software for compatibility with Windows 2000 prior to the upgrade. When you start upgrading the domain controllers, the primary domain controller must be upgraded first.

5. *Choose the File System to Use*

Once you have decided how to partition your hard disk and on which partition to install Windows 2000 Server, you need to decide which file system to use for the partition. Windows 2000 supports the following file systems: NTFS, FAT, and FAT32. In most configurations, the NTFS file system is the best choice. The only reason to use FAT or FAT32 is for a dual-boot configuration in which you have more than one operating system that can be run on a computer. Microsoft does not recommend using the dual-boot configuration on a server. During setup, you can convert an existing FAT or FAT32 partition to the new NTFS. This allows you to keep your existing data on the partition. If you do not need to keep the existing data on the partition, it is recommended that you format the drive with NTFS rather than converting it. Doing so erases all existing data on the partition, but the partition will have less fragmentation and thus better performance.

The NTFS file system provides the following features:

- **Security at the file and folder level**   This feature allows you to control access down to the file level.

- **Disk compression**   This feature allows you to compress folders, subfolders, and files to increase the amount of file storage but slows down access to the files.

- **Disk quotas**   This feature allows you to limit the amount of disk space used by each user.

- **File encryption**   Folders, subfolders, and files can be encrypted and decrypted automatically by the operating system.

- **Active Directory**   This feature allows domain-based security.

With Windows 2000 using NTFS, you can use remote storage, dynamic volumes, and mounting volumes to folders. These features are discussed later in the book. Partitions that use the NTFS file system can only be accessed by Windows NT and Windows 2000. However, if you use any of the new NTFS features provided by Windows 2000, you will not be able to access it from Windows NT. NTFS is the best choice when security is an issue.

The FAT (or FAT16) allows access from multiple operating systems, including Windows 2000, Windows NT, Windows 95 and 98, MS-DOS, and OS/2. It is a less efficient file system with fewer features than NTFS and does not offer any built-in security. The FAT32 enhanced the FAT file system by allowing larger partition sizes and smaller cluster sizes. FAT partitions were limited to 2GB. With hard disks commonly larger than 8GB, FAT32 was introduced in Windows 98 to extend the partition sizes. FAT32 is compatible with Windows 98 and Windows 2000. Windows NT cannot use FAT32 partitions.

So, how do you choose which file system to use on partitions? It depends on how your server will be configured. Microsoft recommends the NTFS partition with single boot operating system for servers. In addition, NTFS is the only file system that supports the new Active Directory introduced with Windows 2000. If you want to dual-boot with Windows 2000 and Windows 95 or 98, you might want to choose the FAT or FAT32 file system. Furthermore, some new features have been added to NTFS by Windows 2000. For example, if you used the new encryption feature on a file, that file would not be readable when you booted up into Windows NT. When configuring a computer for dual-booting between Windows 2000 and Windows NT 4.0, Microsoft recommends using a FAT partition (not FAT32 because Windows NT 4.0 does not recognize FAT32). This ensures that when the computer is booted up into Windows NT 4.0, it will have access to all files on the computer.

With many versions of the Windows operating system now available, some users need to have multiple operating systems installed on the same computer. The user can choose which operating system to load. During installation, you can upgrade an existing Windows operating system to Windows 2000, but when you do, you cannot load it. When configuring your computer for multiboot operations, consider the following things:

- To upgrade an existing Windows operating system to Windows 2000, you must install Windows 2000 in the same directory. To dual-boot with the existing Windows operating system and Windows 2000, you must install Windows 2000 in a different directory so it doesn't overwrite the existing files.

- When dual-booting Windows 2000 with MS-DOS or Windows 95 or 98, install Windows 2000 last because older operating systems overwrite the Master Boot Record and you won't be able to boot into Windows 2000.

- You cannot install Windows 2000 in a compressed drive that is not compressed with NTFS.

- All applications must be reinstalled on Windows 2000 when you do not upgrade from the existing operating system. To save disk space, you can install most applications to the same directory in which they are currently installed.

6. *Prepare Your System for Upgrading*

Prior to upgrading any of your servers, you should prepare your servers for upgrading. This includes backing up data, decompressing any compressed drives, turning off disk mirroring, and disconnecting any UPS devices.

You should back up all data on your servers prior to upgrading. Back up all the hard disks on the servers that will be upgraded. In addition, take one of the backup domain controllers off-line in case of an upgrade failure. This way, you can always bring the BDC back on-line, if necessary, to revert back to the Windows NT domain. Prepare a test environment or pilot. In the test environment, test the following: user and group policies, user profiles, and logon scripts. When setting up the test environment, create scenarios that are easy to verify. Create users and groups similar to the existing Windows NT domain.

If any of your drives are compressed with DriveSpace or DoubleSpace, you should decompress them before the upgrade. Furthermore, if you are using disk mirroring, disable it before the upgrade. Once the installation is complete, you can reenable disk mirroring. If you have a UPS connected to the computer, disconnect the serial cable prior to upgrade, because the hardware detection features of Windows 2000 Setup can damage the UPS.

7. *Check Applications for Compatibility*

Some applications need to be removed or disabled prior to running Setup. The README.DOC file discussed earlier has information about any applications that can potentially cause problems and how to minimize the risk.

5

Network Services

Microsoft has changed the focus of networking in the Windows 2000 arena from a mixture of NetBEUI, IPX/SPX, and TCP/IP to one of TCP/IP almost exclusively. This shift has occurred for a number of reasons, but there is no doubt that the increase in the number of Internet-aware applications and people's reliance on the World Wide Web has forced the networking infrastructure to rely on TCP/IP. Unfortunately, TCP/IP networking is still a fairly complex entity that can be difficult to maintain at best.

One of the reasons for this complexity is our increased reliance on laptop computers. Individuals with laptops require the ability to hook up anywhere in the world and have the same connectivity as their counterparts who use desktop computers. Managing TCP/IP environments in this dynamic, mobile environment is becoming a job requirement of systems administrators, not just a project to consider on the weekends.

This chapter covers three tools that systems administrators can use in a Windows 2000 environment to ease the management of the TCP/IP infrastructure for the entire network, not just the mobile community. For each of these tools, we present a brief explanation of the tool's purpose, a description of how to install and configure the tool on a Windows 2000 server, and an exercise that walks you through the process. At the end of the chapter, we provide a number of questions that will test your knowledge about the material presented here. By working through the entire chapter, you will gain an understanding of the fundamentals of these tools and be better prepared to use them in a production environment.

CERTIFICATION OBJECTIVE 5.01

Installing, Configuring, and Administering Dynamic Host Configuration Protocol

There are two ways of assigning TCP/IP configurations to computers on an IP network: manually assigning a static address or automatically providing a dynamic address. Even in small network environments, maintaining static addressing can be a huge amount of work. To ease this burden, you can use the Dynamic Host

Configuration Protocol (DHCP) service to centrally manage and maintain the allocation of TCP/IP addresses for small and large network environments. The DHCP service can be run on a Windows 2000 server to help manage the assignment of addresses to Windows 2000 Professional and other clients.

DHCP provides key networking information to clients: an IP address, a subnet mask, and values for default gateways, Domain Name Service (DNS) server addresses, or Windows Internet Naming Service (WINS) server addresses. The DHCP server is configured with a pool of IP addresses that it can assign to DHCP clients. It is up to the client to request an address from the server. That process is outlined in the following sections.

The DHCP Lease Process

The assignment of an IP address to a DHCP client computer is a temporary one. The client submits a request to "borrow," or lease, the address from the DHCP server. The process to request the address lease has four steps. Figure 5-1 illustrates these steps, which are *discover, offer, request,* and *acknowledge,* also known as the *DORA broadcast process.* Let's take a closer look at DORA.

Discover

A DHCP client begins the lease process with a DHCPDISCOVER message. The client broadcasts this message after loading a minimal TCP/IP environment. The

FIGURE 5-1

discover,
offer, request,
acknowledge
(DORA)

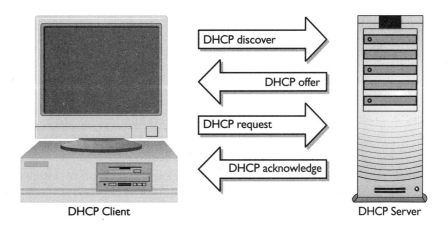

DHCP discover

DHCP offer

DHCP request

DHCP acknowledge

DHCP Client

DHCP Server

client does not know the address of the DHCP server, so it sends the message using a TCP/IP broadcast, with 0.0.0.0 as the source address and 255.255.255.255 as the destination address. The DHCPDISCOVER message contains the client's network hardware address (a MAC address), its computer name, a list of DHCP options the client supports, and a message ID that will be used in all messages between the client and the server to identify the particular request.

Offer

After the DHCP server receives the DHCPDISCOVER message, it looks at the request to see if the client configuration request is valid. If the request is valid, the server sends back a DHCPOFFER message to the client's network hardware address and includes an IP address available for lease, the length of time the lease is valid, and the IP and MAC addresses of the server that provided the DHCP information. This message is also a TCP/IP broadcast (255.255.255.255), because the client does not yet have an IP address. The server then reserves the address it sent to the client so that the address is not offered to another client making a request. If there is more than one DHCP server on the network, all servers respond to the DHCPDISCOVER message with a DHCPOFFER message.

Request

After the client receives the DHCPOFFER message and accepts the IP address, it sends a DHCPREQUEST message to all DHCP servers, indicating that it has accepted an offer. The broadcast message contains the IP address of the DHCP server that made the accepted offer, and all other DHCP servers release the addresses they had offered back into their available address pool.

Acknowledge

When the DHCP server that made the successful offer receives the DHCPREQUEST message, it responds to the client with an acknowledgment broadcast. If the request message is accepted, the server broadcasts a successful acknowledgment with a DHCPACK message. This message contains a valid lease for the IP address and can contain other configuration information. At this point, the client finishes initializing its TCP/IP network environment with the information provided by the DHCP server.

If the request is not successful, possibly because the client is trying to lease a previous address that is no longer available or the IP address is not correct because the client is on a different subnet, the server broadcasts a negative acknowledgment with a DHCPNACK message. If the client receives a DHCPNACK message, it starts the DHCP lease process again.

Lease Renewal

To help keep the IP address pool fresh, the client must attempt to renew its lease halfway (50 percent) through the length of the lease. The server defines the length of the lease; for Windows 2000 servers, the default lease length is eight days. This value can be customized to match the needs of the environment. To renew a lease, the client sends up to three DHCPREQUEST messages (at 4-, 8-, and 16-second intervals) directly to the server that provided the DHCP lease. If the server is available, it renews the lease and sends a DHCPACK message back to the client with updated lease and configuration information. The client updates its configuration when it receives the DHCPACK from the server.

If the client is unable to renew its lease with the original server, it broadcasts a DHCPREQUEST to all DHCP servers at 87.5 percent of the lease time, with up to three retries at 4-, 8-, and 16-second intervals. Any server can renew the lease with a DHCPACK message, or it can reject the lease with a DHCPNACK message, forcing the client to restart the lease process. Upon receiving a DHCPNACK message or when the lease on the address expires, the client must release the address from its configuration and attempt to gain a new one.

on the
❶ o b

Microsoft DHCP clients do not send a DHCPRELEASE message when the system is shut down. Microsoft clients always try to keep the same IP address from session to session by not releasing the address at shutdown. This can cause problems in environments in which the pool of available addresses is not much larger than the number of computers that need addresses. If a laptop client receives a DHCP lease on a Friday but does not connect to the network again for more than a week, the address assigned remains locked until the end of the lease, even though it is not being used.

Windows 2000 Professional DHCP clients can manually request a lease renewal by using the IPCONFIG command with the /renew switch. This command sends a DHCPREQUEST message back to the DHCP server and attempts to update the lease, as described above. Windows 2000 clients can also release the IP configuration information with the /release switch on the IPCONFIG command. This command sends a DHCPRELEASE message to the DHCP server, and the client is unable to communicate with the TCP/IP network until a new address is requested.

exam
ⓦatch
At boot time, a DHCP client that has never obtained an IP address or does not have an active IP address because of a release starts the lease process from the beginning. When the client boots within the lease period for its last IP address, it sends a DHCPREQUEST message instead of a DHCPDISCOVER message. This is a way for the client to see if it has moved subnets and needs a new address. If the client has been moved, the renewal request is denied, and the client requests a new address.

DHCP Server Configuration

A Windows 2000 Server that is to provide DHCP services must be configured with the following items:

- A static IP address, a subnet mask, a default gateway (if needed), and other necessary TCP/IP options
- The DHCP service installed
- A range (or pool) of IP addresses that can be leased to clients
- Authorization with Active Directory services

The server running DHCP services can be configured as a domain controller or as a stand-alone server. The DHCP server must have a static IP address, because the DHCP server *cannot* also be a DHCP client.

DHCP Scopes

The range of IP addresses that the DHCP server can assign is called a *scope*. Each DHCP server must have at least one scope, which contains all the IP addresses to be made available for that subnet.

Each subnet must have a scope defined on a server. A subnet can have DHCP services provided by more than one DHCP server, but the IP addresses in the scope on each server cannot overlap. For instance, one DHCP server can have a scope that includes the addresses 10.10.1.50-10.10.1.150, and a second server can include the range 10.10.1.151-10.10.1.200. This arrangement helps provide fault tolerance for a subnet if one of the DHCP servers becomes unavailable. The DHCP server does not need to be on the same subnet as its clients.

Any static addresses in a subnet must be excluded from the scope. This includes addresses for static servers, such as DHCP, DNS, and WINS servers. Excluded addresses are not made available to DHCP client requests.

Each scope contains the following information: scope name, starting and ending IP addresses, lease duration, and subnet mask. Other optional information that can be contained within the scope is detailed in the following section.

DHCP Options

A number of options can be configured within a DHCP scope. Options exist for servers, clients, scopes, and vendors or users. Table 5-1 lists the most common DHCP options available.

TABLE 5-1	Option	Description
DHCP Scope Options	003 Router	The IP address of the router or default gateway. A locally defined gateway address takes precedence over the DHCP option, so the Default Gateway field on the client computer should be empty.
	006 DNS Servers	The IP address of a DNS server. A locally defined DNS server address takes precedence over the DHCP option.
	015 DNS Domain Name	The DNS domain name for the client.
	044 WINS/NBNS Servers	The IP address of a WINS server. A locally defined WINS server address takes precedence over the DHCP option.
	046 WINS/NBT Node Type	The NetBIOS node type: 1 = B-node (broadcast), 2 = P-node (peer), 4 = M-node (mixed), and 8 = H-node (hybrid).
	047 NetBIOS Scope ID	The local NetBIOS scope ID.

DHCP Relay Agents

Since the DHCP lease request process relies on broadcast messages to get client configuration information from a server, setting up DHCP services in a routed environment presents a significant problem. In general, routers that interconnect TCP/IP subnets do not forward broadcast messages between subnets. The reason for this is clear: Keeping broadcast traffic limited to the local subnet cuts down on unnecessary traffic. However, adhering to this approach means that you have to set up a DHCP server in each subnet on your network. This can be costly and difficult to manage.

However, there are two ways that DHCP servers can be set up to deliver configuration information to clients on different subnets, minimizing the effort needed to deliver DHCP in a routed environment. The first approach is to configure your routers to provide broadcast message support through a DHCP/BOOTP *relay agent,* described in RFC 1542. A router that is RFC 1542 compliant, when enabled, recognizes DHCP and BOOTP broadcasts and relays those messages to the other subnets connected to the router.

Figure 5-2 shows a network diagram featuring a router that is acting as a DHCP/BOOTP relay agent. A client on Subnet 2 sends a DHCPDISCOVER

FIGURE 5-2

Network segments with a router providing DHCP/BOOTP relay services

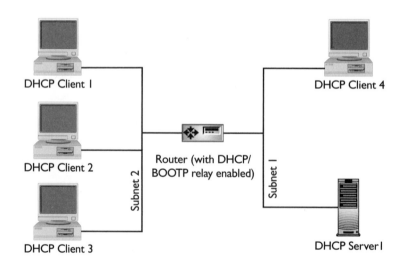

DHCP Client 1

DHCP Client 2

DHCP Client 3

Subnet 2

Router (with DHCP/ BOOTP relay enabled)

Subnet 1

DHCP Client 4

DHCP Server1

broadcast to get its configuration. The router recognizes the broadcast message and forwards that message to Subnet 1. The DHCP server on Subnet 1 receives the message, determines the appropriate configuration to send back to the requesting client, and broadcasts a DHCPOFFER message on Subnet 1. The router recognizes this broadcast and forwards it to Subnet 2, where the client receives the message. This process follows in turn for the DHCPREQUEST and DHCPACKNOWLEDGE messages.

Another approach for handling DHCP configuration requests across subnets is to set up a DHCP relay agent on each subnet that is configured to communicate with a DHCP server elsewhere on the network. Figure 5-3 shows a network diagram with a DHCP relay agent. When a client on Subnet 2 broadcasts a DHCPDISCOVER message, the broadcast is intercepted by the DHCP relay agent. The relay agent is configured with the IP address of a DHCP server that provides configuration information for Subnet 2, and it passes the request to that server. Note that the DHCP server in this example has been previously configured with valid address scopes for both Subnet 1 and Subnet 2. The DHCP server receives the request and directs its responses to the DHCP relay agent, which in turn passes the information back to the requesting client.

FIGURE 5-3

A network
segment with a
Windows 2000
DHCP relay
agent

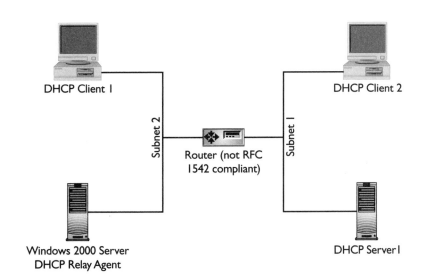

FROM THE CLASSROOM

DHCP Relay Agents Versus BOOTP Forwarders

Remember that a DHCP relay agent and a BOOTP forwarder are two different entities. I have found in the classroom that students often confuse these two, and think they are just two terms for the same thing. They are not! A DHCP relay agent is typically, on a Windows 2000 network, a computer that is configured to intercept DHCP messages and forward them to a specific DHCP server. BOOTP forwarding is done at the router.

The router can be a multihomed Windows 2000 machine configured as a router, or a dedicated hardware router. When BOOTP forwarding is enabled, DHCP broadcast messages are passed through the router interface to the next network. In order for BOOTP forwarding to work correctly, all router interface between the source of the DHCP broadcast and the destination must have BOOTP forwarding enabled.

—*Thomas W. Shinder, M.D., MCSE, MCP+I, MCT*

Installing and Managing DHCP

Exercise 5-1 walks you through the steps of installing and configuring a DHCP scope on a Windows 2000 server. This brief overview of the DHCP service is followed by a Scenario & Solution grid that expands upon the information provided.

EXERCISE 5-1

Installing and Configuring a DHCP Scope

Before beginning the exercise, you will need a Windows 2000 server configured with a static IP address. The figures in this example use a server with a static IP address of 10.10.2.111 and a subnet mask of 255.255.255.0. The range of IP addresses that are used for DHCP clients is 10.10.2.101 to 10.10.2.120. The IP addresses from 10.10.2.111 to 10.10.2.114 are excluded from the scope. The DHCP option for a default gateway is configured, but no other options are set.

1. Open the Control Panel folder.

2. Open Add/Remove Programs.

3. Click Add/Remove Windows Components.

4. Scroll down the list of components and select Networking Services, then click Details:

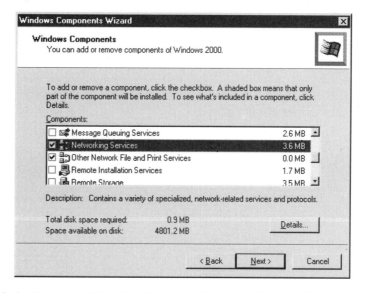

5. Check the Dynamic Host Configuration Protocol (DHCP) box, as shown in the next illustration, and click OK.

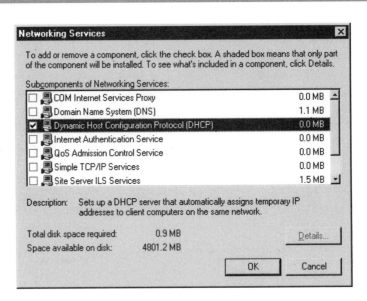

6. Click Next. The DHCP service then proceeds through installation. You might need to insert the Windows 2000 Server CD for the installation to complete.

7. When the installation finishes, click Finish in the Windows Completion wizard window.

8. Click Close to close Add/Remove Programs.

9. Open Start | Programs | Administrative Tools | DHCP to launch the DHCP manager.

10. Double-click your server name in the left-hand pane.

11. Right-click the server name and select New Scope... from the pop-up menu, as shown:

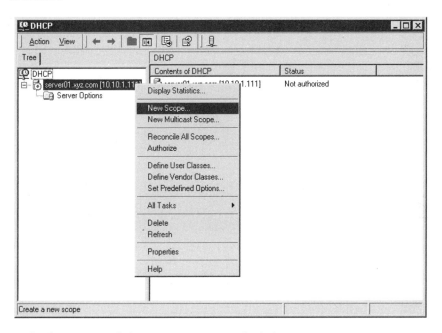

12. At the first screen of the New Scope wizard, click Next.

13. In the Name: field, enter the name of the scope, such as Server1 Scope, and click Next.

14. Complete the IP Address Range window as shown in the next illustration. Click Next.

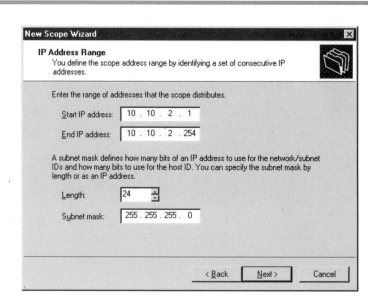

15. In the "Start IP address:" field, enter 10.10.2.111; in the "End IP address:" field, enter 10.10.2.114, and then click Add. The window should now look like the illustration below. Click Next.

16. Click Next to accept the default lease time of 8 days.

17. Click Next to configure DHCP options.

18. In the "IP address:" field, enter 10.10.2.1, then click Add. The window should now look like the illustration below. Click Next.

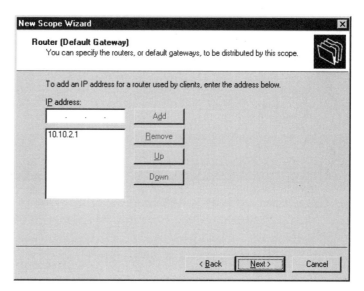

19. Click Next to skip DNS options configuration.

20. Click Next to skip WINS options configuration.

21. Click Next to activate the scope.

22. Click Finish to complete the New Scope wizard.

23. To authorize the DHCP server in Active Directory, right-click the server and select Authorize from the pop-up menu, as shown in the illustration below. Note that prior to authorizing the scope, the server displays a red down-arrow icon in the MMC window to indicate that the DHCP server is down or not active.

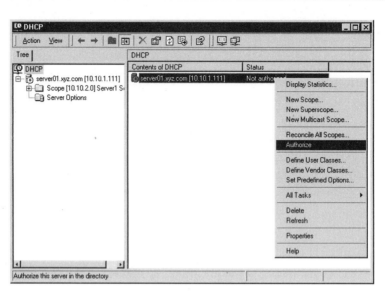

24. When the server is authorized, the DHCP manager window should look like the illustration below. Note that after authorizing the scope, the server now displays a green up-arrow icon in the MMC window to indicate that the DHCP server is up and now active.

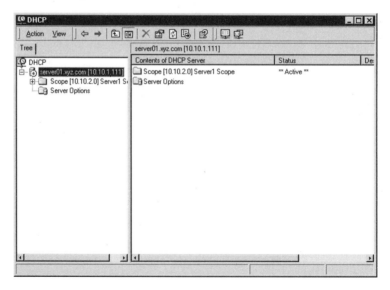

25. Close the DHCP manager.

SCENARIO & SOLUTION

Are there other DHCP messages than those mentioned in this chapter?	Yes. The DHCPINFORM message is used by the DHCP client service to communicate to DHCP servers various types of information, such as querying for the name and location of a domain controller for purposes of rogue DHCP server detection. There is also the DHCPDECLINE message, which a DHCP client sends to a DHCP server if the DHCP client detects that the IP address it has been assigned is already in use.
Do I have to create Scope options?	No. You do not have to create or use any of the DHCP options if you don't want to. You can use just server options. However, you probably want to create at least the default gateway option for each scope, since each subnet needs to use a different default gateway, and you don't want to have to manually configure the gateway address on all the DHCP client computers.
How do I determine the ideal lease duration time for my DHCP environment?	If you have a large, stable network with a large address space, you can probably safely increase the lease duration interval. If you have a sufficient number of addresses and the environment stays fairly stable, increasing the lease duration reduces the number of lease renewal queries, which in turn reduces the amount of broadcast traffic on your network. On the other hand, if you have few available addresses and a dynamic environment in which configurations change regularly or computers move freely around the network, you may want to reduce the lease duration. Shorter leases more quickly free unused addresses for reassignment to other DHCP clients. This is especially useful in an organization in which employees frequently travel with laptops.

CERTIFICATION OBJECTIVE 5.02

Installing, Configuring, and Administering Windows Internet Naming Service

In a pure Windows 2000 environment, all network interconnectivity is handled through standard Internet tools, such as DNS for address name resolution.

However, any network environment that interacts with clients other than Windows 2000 clients will have to continue to rely on Network Basic Input/Output System (NetBIOS) for resolving computer names to network addresses.

Prior to Windows 2000, this name lookup was achieved through a local LMHOSTS file, which contained a static list of computer names and network addresses, or through Windows Internet Naming Service (WINS) servers. In a dynamic network environment, the use of LMHOSTS for name resolution is all but eliminated because it requires constant updating of the file. Using WINS, however, is still practical and useful.

This section of the chapter covers the WINS name resolution process; configurations for WINS servers, clients, and proxies; and an exercise that walks through the installation and configuration of WINS on a Windows 2000 server.

The WINS Name Resolution Process

The WINS name resolution process is an interactive one between WINS clients and a WINS server. The client and server go through four steps in the resolution process: registration, renewal, release, and query.

WINS Name Registration

Each WINS client has one or more WINS servers identified in its network configuration, either through static assignment or through DHCP configuration. When the client boots and connects to the network, it registers its name and IP address with the WINS server by sending a registration request directly to the server. This is not a broadcast message, since the client has the address of the server. If the server is available and the name is not already registered, the server responds with a successful registration message, which contains the amount of time the name will be registered to the client, which is called the *time to live (TTL)*. Then the server stores the name and address combination in its local database.

If the name requested is already registered in the database with a different address, the server attempts to verify the name registration by sending a challenge to the registered machine. If the challenged client responds, the server responds to the requesting client with a negative registration response, and the client is informed that a machine with that name is already present on the network. If the challenged client does not respond after three challenge attempts, the server removes the previous registration for the name, sends a successful registration message to the requesting client, and registers the name and address of the requesting client in the local database. If the name requested is already registered in the database with the same address, the server treats the request as a renewal request, as described in the following section.

WINS Name Renewal

As with DHCP, WINS name registrations are temporary and must be renewed to continue to be valid. The client attempts to renew its registration when half (50 percent) of the TTL has elapsed. If the WINS server does not respond, the client repeatedly attempts to renew its lease at 10-minute intervals for an hour. If the client still receives no response, it restarts the process with the secondary WINS server, if one is defined. The client continues attempting to renew its lease in this manner until it receives a response from a server. At that time, the server sends a new TTL to the client and the process starts over.

WINS Name Release

When a WINS client shuts down properly, it sends a name release request to the WINS server. This request releases the name from the WINS server's database so that another client can use the name, if necessary. The release request contains the WINS name and address of the client. If the server cannot find the name, it sends a negative release response to the client. If the server finds the matching name and address in its database, it releases the name and marks the record as inactive. If the name is found but the address does not match, the server ignores the request.

WINS Name Resolution/Query

When a WINS client wants to locate another computer on the network, it performs the following steps to resolve a NetBIOS name to an address:

1. The client first checks its local NetBIOS name cache to locate the name and address of the computer.

2. If the NetBIOS name is not in the local cache, the client submits a request to the WINS server. The client makes three attempts to contact each WINS server in its configuration.

3. When a WINS server is contacted, it sends a positive or negative query response, depending on whether or not it finds the name in its WINS database.

4. If the client receives a negative query response from a server or no response at all, it attempts to locate the computer by sending a network broadcast.

WINS Servers

WINS services must be installed on a computer running Windows 2000 Server, although the server does not have to be a domain controller. Two servers acting as primary and secondary WINS servers can easily handle registration of up to 10,000 computers. Microsoft strongly recommends limiting the number of WINS servers in a network to fewer than 20. Even for large networks, this number should be sufficient.

New and Improved WINS Features

WINS services with Windows 2000 have a number of new and improved features to provide a more robust and easier-to-manage NetBIOS name management solution. The new WINS provides a distributed WINS database for registering and querying dynamic NetBIOS names on a routed network, which includes interaction with DHCP services.

Other new WINS features include:

- **Persistent connections** This feature allows WINS servers to maintain constant connections with one or more replication partners, increasing the speed of replication by eliminating the overhead of opening and closing connections between the partners.

- **Manual tombstoning** This feature allows a record to be marked for deletion across all WINS servers, preventing undeleted copies of the record from being used or repropagated back to the other servers.

- **Burst handling** This feature allows WINS servers to handle large numbers of NetBIOS registration requests, such as when systems are restarted after a power outage.

A *tombstoned record* is a WINS database record that is marked for deletion. It is better to tombstone a record, because the record will not be replicated as active again throughout the network.

Static Mappings

At times, a computer needs to resolve the NetBIOS name of a system that is not a WINS client. The way to get around this situation is to manually enter a record for the system in the WINS database, a process referred to as *static mapping*. Some database services running on NetWare or UNIX servers can respond to NetBIOS calls but do not participate in the WINS process. Creating a static mapping in the WINS database allows a WINS client to resolve the NetBIOS names of these servers for connectivity.

This method is preferred over entering the NetBIOS information in the LMHOSTS file of the client, especially when the address of the non-WINS computer changes. The mapping in the WINS database can be changed once, and all clients trying to connect to the computer are then able to resolve the name through WINS, as opposed to manually changing the LMHOSTS file on all computers trying to connect to the non-WINS client.

WINS Clients

WINS clients can be run on the following operating systems:

- Windows 2000
- Windows NT 3.5 or later
- Windows 98
- Windows 95
- Windows for Workgroups version 3.11
- MS-DOS with LAN Manager version 2.2c
- MS-DOS with Microsoft Network Client version 3.0 with real-mode TCP/IP driver

A WINS client must also have the IP address of at least one WINS server in its network configuration.

WINS Proxies

A WINS *proxy agent* is similar to a DHCP relay agent. A proxy agent "listens" for requests for non-WINS network clients and redirects those requests to a WINS server. A WINS proxy operates in two modes:

- **NetBIOS name registration**   When a WINS proxy agent receives a name registration request from a non-WINS client, it forwards the request to a WINS server to verify that the name has not been registered by another WINS client. The name is not registered in WINS; the proxy agent only verifies that the name is not already in use.

- **NetBIOS name resolution**   When a WINS proxy agent receives a name resolution broadcast from a non-WINS client, it intercepts the request and attempts to resolve the name. The proxy agent checks its local name cache, and if the name is not present in the cache, it forwards a resolution request to a WINS server, which returns a success or failure message, which is in turn sent back to the requester by the proxy agent.

A WINS client can be configured to be a WINS proxy agent by editing the registry on the client. The value of the EnableProxy key, which is in HKEY_LOCAL_MACHINE\SYSTEM\CurrentControlSet\Services\NetBT \Parameters, is set to 1 to enable the agent.

Installing and Managing WINS

WINS is not part of the standard Windows 2000 Server installation. Exercise 5-2 walks you through the process of installing and configuring WINS. A section on managing WINS services follows the exercise.

CertCam 5-2

Installing and Configuring WINS

Follow these steps to install and configure WINS on the server:

1. Open the Control Panel folder.

2. Open Add/Remove Programs.

3. Click Add/Remove Windows Components.

4. Scroll down the list of components and select Networking Services, then click Details....

5. Scroll down the list of services and click the check box next to Windows Internet Name Service (WINS) and click OK.

6. Click Next to install WINS. You might need the Windows 2000 Server CD in your drive to complete installation.

7. When the installation is complete, click Finish to close the Installation wizard.

8. Open the TCP/IP Properties dialog box in your network configuration and click the Advanced... button.

9. Click the WINS tab, and then click the Add... button.

10. Enter the IP address of your server in the WINS server: box to have the server point to itself for WINS services, then click Add.

11. Click OK to close the Advanced TCP/IP Settings dialog box, and close the remaining network configuration windows.

12. Open Start | Programs | Administrative Tools | WINS to launch the WINS manager.

13. Click the Server Status icon in the left pane to verify that WINS services are operating normally, as shown:

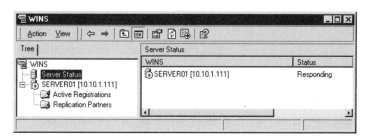

EXERCISE 5-2

Managing WINS

Management of WINS is handled through the *WINS snap-in*. The snap-in can be accessed directly from Start | Programs | Administrative Tools | WINS or through the MMC as a Computer Management snap-in, listed under Services and Applications.

With the snap-in, you can view the active WINS entries under the Active Registrations folder. In addition, you can supply static mappings for non-WINS clients on the network through the snap-in. To configure a static mapping, select the Active Registrations folder and the select New Static Mapping from the Action menu. Once a static mapping is entered into the WINS database, it cannot be edited. If changes need to be made to a static mapping, the entry must be deleted and re-created.

Now that we have covered some basic information about WINS provided by Windows 2000, here are some scenarios and solutions to provide some additional understanding of the topic.

SCENARIO & SOLUTION

Do I have to have a WINS server on my network? Can't I just use DNS?	You are not required to have a WINS server on your network, but if you run distributed NetBIOS applications, WINS is the most effective method of name resolution. DNS can be used to resolve NetBIOS names, but because of the way NetBIOS name resolution is processed, it isn't the fastest or most efficient way to proceed.
Should I place more than one WINS proxy agent on a segment for fault tolerance?	It is generally not considered a good idea to place more than one WINS proxy agent on a single segment. This is because each WINS proxy agent will intercept all NetBIOS name query request broadcasts and forward them to the WINS server. This increases the amount of traffic sent to the WINS server for identical name resolution requests. However, if you have only a single WINS proxy agent, you have no fault tolerance. Since a limited number of segments will require a WINS proxy agent, your own baselining is the best indicator of the most prudent action.
When should I create static mappings, and what is the best way to create them?	Create static mappings for computers that run NetBIOS applications but are not WINS clients. Some database applications run on UNIX or NetWare servers as NetBIOS application servers and require NetBIOS client software. You are likely using LMHOSTS files to resolve these NetBIOS names. It is easy to import entries in LMHOSTS files to make static mapping via the WINS Management console.

Installing, Configuring, and Administering Domain Name System

WINS services have been used to provide name-to-address translations for NetBIOS networks, but the Domain Name System (DNS) must be used to provide the same service for an Internet-based network. DNS is the standard way to translate Internet names on an IP network. However, DNS has a different structure from that of WINS; this structure requires different organization and implementation than WINS.

The DNS Namespace

Whereas NetBIOS names exist in essentially a flat namespace, DNS names exist in a hierarchical structure, divided into multiple domains. The first division, called the *top-level domain,* contains major address groups, such as .com, .gov, .net, .edu, and .org. Those domains are further divided into subdomains called *second-level domains,* such as microsoft.com, apple.com, nasa.gov, pbs.org, and so on. Each second-level domain can then be divided into further subdomains. The Internet name given to a computer identifies how it can be found. For instance, the Web server www.jpl.nasa.gov is a computer named *www* that exists in the *jpl* subdomain of the *nasa* subdomain of the *gov* domain. To find the server, you would traverse the name in reverse order, first looking in the *gov* domain to find the *nasa* subdomain, then looking there to find the *jpl* subdomain, then looking there to find the *www* server.

Domain and Host Name Specifications

The following guidelines are widely accepted as standard conventions for creating and maintaining domain names:

- **Keep the number of subdomains small, usually no more than three or four levels** Not only does www.web.admin.production.corporate. yourcompany.com increase the number of steps it takes to resolve the name, which makes it harder on name servers, but it's also difficult for your potential audience to type and remember, possibly driving away the very people you want to attract to your Web site.

■ **Keep names unique**   Each object within a domain or subdomain must have a unique name to ensure identifying each object within the namespace exactly. Domain names are not case sensitive, so the names www.irs.gov and www.IRS.gov are the same.

■ **Keep domain names short**   Even though each domain name can have up to 63 characters, the total length of a fully qualified domain name cannot exceed 255 characters. Besides, no one really wants to type www.bobsmeatmarketandcoffeeshopindowntowndallas.com into a Web browser.

■ **Use standard characters in domain names**   DNS names can contain letters (A–Z and a–z), numbers (0–9), and a hyphen (-) in the domain name. DNS also supports Unicode characters, which are required for languages such as Spanish, German, and French.

A *fully qualified domain name (FQDN)* is a combination of the host name and the host's domain location.

Zones of Authority

The DNS namespace is divided into zones, and each zone must have one name server that is the authority for the name mapping for the zone. Depending on the size of the namespace, a zone can be subdivided into multiple zones, each with its own authority, or there can be a single authority for the entire zone. For instance, a small company with only 200–300 computers could have one DNS server handle the entire namespace. On the other hand, a larger company might want or need to divide its namespace into multiple zones: one for the top level of the domain, one for the sales division, one for the development division, one for the human resources division, and so on.

All these zones of authority do not have to exist on the public Internet. Some of these zones might be only for internal access within the company, but the process is handled in the same way as though the namespace were available to the public. In addition, more than one DNS server can handle requests for a zone. In fact, this is a good idea, because it provides redundancy in case of a network outage or system failure or for load balancing for a heavily trafficked domain.

Resource Records

Each DNS server has a number of *resource records* that can be assigned, in addition to the regular name and address mappings. Two records that are added automatically when a DNS server is created are the Start of Authority (SOA) and the Name Server (NS) records. The *SOA record* identifies the address of the name server that is the authority for the zone, and it is the first record in the zone database. *NS records* identify the addresses for name servers for specific domains. These records are used to instruct the name servers as to whom to contact if the server cannot process a request locally.

on the
() o b

Additional information about the structure and definition of the DNS name resolution process can be found in RFC 1034 and RFC 1035. Information about using Unicode characters in domain names appears in RFC 2044. Information about additional resource records used by DNS servers is in RFC 2052 and RFC 2065. Information about Dynamic DNS can be found in RFC 2136 and RFC 2137.

DNS Name Resolution Process

The process of resolving DNS names is much like finding a name in a telephone book. You don't just pick up the phone book and start looking for the desired name on the first page and keep turning pages until you find it. Like a phone book, the DNS name structure is broken down into smaller categories that can be searched more easily and logically for a name.

Following a DNS Query from Request to Resolution

There are two types of DNS name lookup queries: forward and reverse. A *forward lookup query* resolves a name into an IP address. A *reverse lookup query* resolves an IP address to a name. The process is described in the next two sections.

Forward Lookup Queries   A forward lookup query occurs when a computer needs to get the IP address for a computer with an Internet name. The local computer sends a query to a local DNS name server, which resolves the name or passes the request to another server for resolution. For example, the following steps would be taken to resolve the Internet name www.nasa.gov:

- The client sends a forward lookup query to its local name server for **www.nasa.gov**.

- The local name server looks in its database for the address. If it does not already have the address, and since the server is probably not the name authority for the nasa.gov domain, it passes the request to a root DNS server. That server responds with the address of a DNS server for the .gov domain.

- The local name server forwards the request to the .gov name server, which responds with the address of a name server for the nasa.gov domain.

- The local name server sends the request to the nasa.gov name server, which services the request by returning the IP address for www.nasa.gov to the local name server.

- The local name server responds to the client request by providing the client with the IP address for www.nasa.gov. The client then is able to open a connection to the Web server directly, using its IP address.

To reduce network traffic generated by going through this process for every name lookup, the local DNS server caches the query results it receives from the other name servers. These results are kept for a specified amount of time (the TTL), then the server removes the entry from its cache. Longer TTL times result in fewer resolution requests for frequently accessed names, but they also result in delays when a name or address mapping changes down the line. Shorter TTL times ensure that the name or address map is more accurate, but they generate more network traffic.

Reverse Lookup Queries   A reverse lookup query resolves an IP address to a DNS name and can be used for a variety of reasons. The process is different from that of the forward lookup query, though, because the reverse lookup uses a special domain called *in-addr.arpa*. This domain is also hierarchical, but it is based on IP addresses, not names. The subdomains are organized by the *reverse* order of the IP address. For instance, the domain 16.254.169.in-addr.arpa contains the addresses in the 169.254.16.* range; the 120.129.in-addr.arpa domain contains the addresses for the 129.120.*.* range.

Windows 2000 DNS Server Roles

The implementation of DNS in Windows 2000 allows a DNS server to act in one of several roles. A Windows 2000 DNS server is frequently used as a primary or secondary DNS server, but other roles include DNS forwarder, caching-only server, DNS slave server, and dynamic update server.

Primary DNS Server

The *primary DNS server* maintains the master copy of the DNS database for the zone. This copy of the database is the only one that can be modified, and any changes made to its database are distributed to secondary servers in the zone during a zone transfer process. The server can cache resolution requests locally so a lookup query does not have to be sent across the network for a duplicate request. The primary server contains the address mappings for the Internet root DNS servers. Primary servers can also act as secondary servers for other zones, as described in the next section.

Secondary DNS Server

Secondary DNS servers provide fault tolerance and load balancing for DNS zones. A secondary server contains a read-only copy of the zone database that it receives from the primary server during a zone transfer. A secondary server responds to a DNS request if the primary server fails to respond because of an error or a heavy load. Since secondary servers can resolve DNS queries, they are also considered authoritative within a domain and can help with load balancing on the network. Secondary servers can be placed in remote locations on the network and configured to respond to DNS queries from local computers, potentially reducing query traffic across longer network distances. Whereas there can be only one primary server in a zone, multiple secondary servers can be set up for redundancy and load balancing.

Other DNS Server Roles

Caching-only DNS servers do not contain a copy of the zone map for a domain, but they do store external DNS queries in their caches, making those external lookups available to local clients for a predetermined period of time. A special type of caching server is a *DNS forwarder*. This server handles recursive queries from another server, not from DNS clients. A client sends a request to its preferred DNS server, called the *forwarding* server, which then passes the request on to the *forwarder* server, which actually performs the DNS query.

exam
ⓦatch
Be aware of questions on the exam regarding forwarding and forwarder servers. Be sure to read the questions carefully.

One other type of DNS server, new with Windows 2000, is the *Dynamic DNS server*. As the use of DHCP for address configuration becomes more popular, the process of maintaining a static database of IP names and addresses for DNS resolution becomes much more difficult. With a Dynamic DNS server, the zone database can be modified automatically, much as the WINS database is updated in the NetBIOS world. Dynamic DNS integrates tightly with DHCP services so that as an address is assigned through DHCP, the DNS database is updated with the name associated with that address.

Integrating Windows 2000 DNS Server with Active Directory

DNS is required for Windows 2000 domains. In fact, the Windows 2000 domains are based on the DNS zone structure, so an integration of DNS with Active Directory is only natural. Primary zone data can be stored in Active Directory, automatically replicating the data through the Active Directory structure. With Active Directory, all domain controllers for the domain can modify the zone and replicate the updates to the other controllers, a process called *multimaster replication*. Standard zone transfers can still be performed with standard secondary DNS servers.

Integrating Windows 2000 DNS with Active Directory has the following benefits:

- **Fault tolerance** Multimaster replication eliminates the possibility of a single point of failure for zone updates.

- **Security** Access can be limited for zone and record updates, preventing any unwanted or insecure dynamic updates.

- **Ease of management** Since Active Directory handles zone replication, a separate zone transfer process does not have to be maintained.

- **Efficient replication of large zones** Active Directory replicates only relevant changes to the zone information, a quicker process than a full zone transfer.

DNS Clients

Windows 2000 DNS clients can be configured in one of two ways: manually or through DHCP. The DHCP configuration process requires that the DHCP server is set up to provide DNS server information, a primary and at least one secondary, to the client during the DHCP process. In addition, the client must not have any DNS server entries configured locally, because the local configuration will override the DHCP settings.

Manual configuration settings for the DNS client are in the DNS tab of the Advanced TCP/IP Settings dialog box, shown in Figure 5-4. Each client should have two DNS servers entered. Up to three DNS servers can be entered in the dialog box, and the client uses the servers in the order listed. The dialog box also allows you to specify how to resolve partial DNS names by listing DNS suffixes to append to a partial address for resolution. The "Register this connection's addresses in DNS" check box allows the computer to participate in Dynamic DNS by attempting to update the Dynamic DNS server with its DNS information.

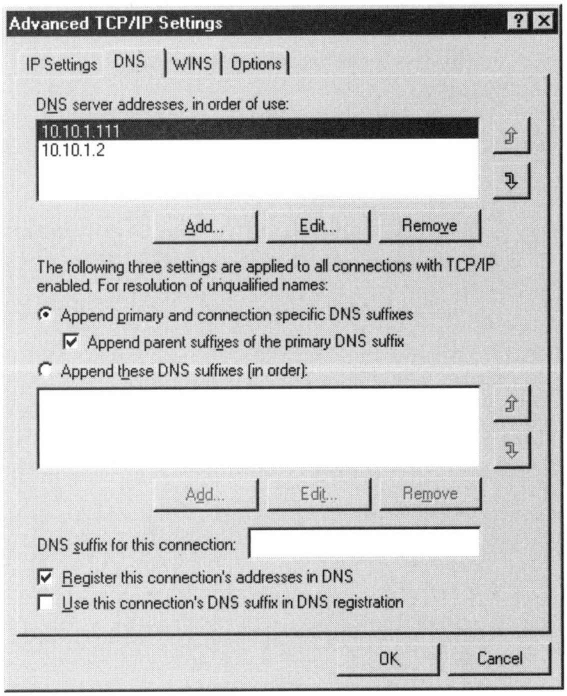

FIGURE 5-4

The Advanced TCP/IP Settings dialog box with manual DNS settings

Installing and Managing DNS

DNS is not part of the default Windows 2000 Server installation process. Exercise 5-3 walks you through the process of installing and configuring DNS on a Windows 2000 server. A section dealing with management of DNS services follows the exercise.

CertCam 5-3

Installing and Configuring DNS

For this exercise, we create a primary DNS server that is Active Directory integrated. The server will be the authority for our fictitious xyz.com domain that exists on a private network with the address range of 10.10.1.x through 10.10.254.x. In addition to the Active Directory-integrated zone, we create a reverse lookup zone.

1. Open the Control Panel folder.

2. Open Add/Remove Programs.

3. Click Add/Remove Windows Components.

4. Scroll down the list of components and select Networking Services, then click Details....

5. Scroll down the list of services and click the check box next to Domain Name System (DNS) and click OK.

6. Click Next to install DNS. You might need the Windows 2000 Server CD in your drive to complete installation.

7. When the installation is complete, click Finish to close the Installation wizard. The DNS installation process creates a *systemroot*\System32\Dns folder, which can contain the following DNS configuration files:

   ■ *domain_name*.dns   This is the zone database file that stores the host names and IP addresses for computers in the zone.

- *z.y.x.w*.**in-addr.arpa**   This is the reverse name lookup file (present only if configured).

- **Cache.dns**   This is the cache file that contains host information for resolving names outside of authoritative domains. The default file contains records for name servers that host the Internet root zone.

8. Open the DNS manager from Start | Programs | Administrative Tools | DNS.

9. Select the server icon in the left pane of the window and select Configure the server...from the Action menu or by right-clicking the icon, as shown in the illustration below. This starts the Configure DNS Server wizard.

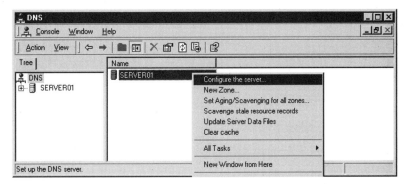

10. Click Next to start the wizard.

11. Click Next to create a forward lookup zone.

12. Click the Active Directory-integrated radio button, as shown in the next illustration, then click Next.

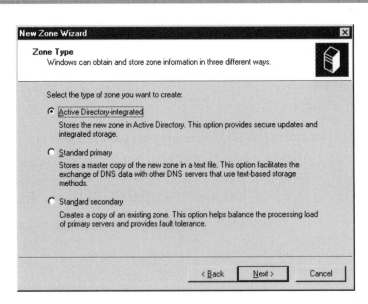

13. Enter **xyz.com** for the name of the zone, then click Next.

14. Click Next to create a reverse lookup zone.

15. Click the Active Directory-integrated radio button, then click Next.

16. Click the Network ID: radio button and enter 10.10 in the field, as shown in the next illustration. The Reverse lookup zone name: field is modified automatically. Click Next to continue.

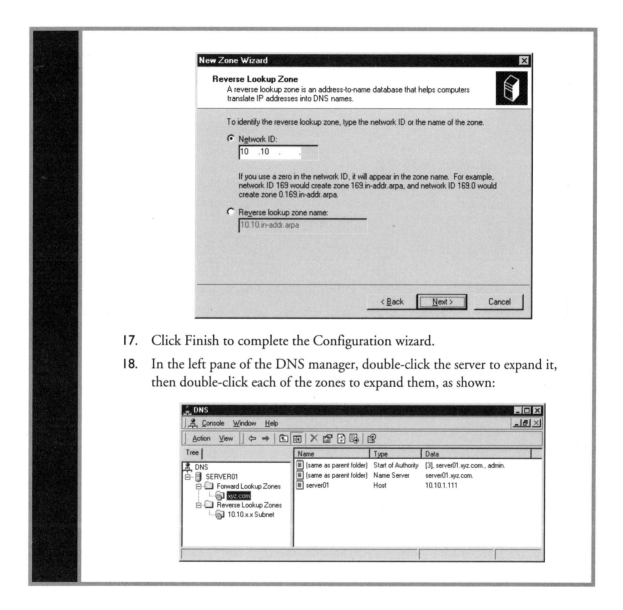

17. Click Finish to complete the Configuration wizard.

18. In the left pane of the DNS manager, double-click the server to expand it, then double-click each of the zones to expand them, as shown:

19. Open the Properties of the forward lookup zone xyz.com and click the General tab, as shown in the illustration below. In the "Allow dynamic updates?" pop-up menu, select "Only secure updates," then click OK.

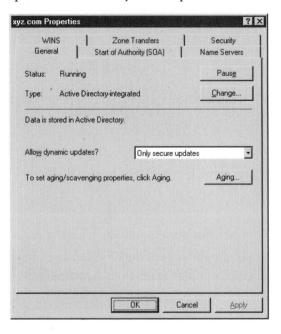

The Windows 2000 DNS server includes service (SRV) resource records for identifying network resources, such as domain controllers. Configuring SRV records for domain controllers in the DNS server allows clients to perform resource-specific queries to the DNS server to locate the appropriate domain controller for network access. SRV records can be added to standard zones in addition to Active Directory-integrated zones. Other DNS servers, such as UNIX-based DNS servers, might not have the capability of using SRV records, making it almost a requirement to add a Windows 2000 DNS server to the network for this purpose alone.

Managing DNS

Even if you choose to configure your DNS server with an Active Directory-integrated zone and dynamic updates, you will still need to perform some maintenance and monitoring to ensure that your DNS services are working correctly.

The DNS Snap-in   The DNS snap-in can be loaded from Start | Programs | Administrative Tools | DNS or by manually loading the snap-in into MMC. Once the DNS manager is open, you can monitor the server's zone activity by opening the Monitoring tab of the server's Properties dialog box, shown in Figure 5-5. The DNS name server can be tested with two types of queries:

- **Simple query**   This test performs a local query to the DNS server.
- **Recursive query**   This test performs a recursive query by forwarding a lookup request to another DNS server.

Selecting a DNS query test in the Monitoring tab of the DNS server's Properties dialog box

SCENARIO & SOLUTION

I am having problems with my DNS clients not being able to resolve Internet names when using my DNS server. What might be the problem?	When you install the Windows 2000 DNS server, you might see an entry for ".". Delete that entry, and your lookups will use the Internet root servers rather than treating your second-level domain as the root of the DNS namespace.
I am installing a Windows 2000 DNS server for our organization, but our organization already uses a UNIX server for DNS services. Do I need to create a second domain for my Windows 2000 domain?	Windows 2000 computers require a DNS server that supports SRV records. The UNIX DNS server might support these records. If it does not, you might want to consider creating a subdomain, such as win2k.*yourdomainname*.com, for your Windows computers that require SRV records for service location and domain registration.

To perform a test, select one or both of the query types and click Test Now. The results of the test appear in the field at the bottom of the window. Click the "Perform automatic testing at the following interval:" check box to perform repeated tests on the server at intervals as short as 30 seconds.

This section of the chapter introduced you to the Windows 2000 implementation of DNS. The following scenarios and solutions provide some additional insight into the topic.

CERTIFICATION SUMMARY

This chapter provided a basic look at three key network services for Windows 2000: DHCP, WINS, and DNS. Successful implementation of these services in a Windows 2000 environment is important as Windows networking moves toward TCP/IP as the foundation. Furthermore, the implementation of these services with Windows 2000 adds some features and functionality not found in other implementations.

DHCP services provide dynamic network configuration information to network clients. Dynamically assigning IP addresses and network resource information eases the workload on network administrators when changes need to be made to the underlying network structure. DHCP services not only provide an IP address, subnet mask, and gateway IP to DHCP clients, but information about WINS and DNS servers can be provided to the client as well. The DHCP client obtains this information through the DORA broadcast process—discover, offer, request, and acknowledge—with a DHCP server. DHCP servers maintain scopes, which contain pools of IP addresses, subnet masks, lease duration, and other optional configuration settings. DHCP relay agents aid in the DHCP request process by "listening" for DHCP request broadcasts and forwarding those requests directly to a DHCP server on a different subnet.

WINS provides machine name lookups for pre-Windows 2000 computers that rely on NetBIOS for machine-to-machine communication. When connecting to the network, a WINS client informs a WINS server of its name and IP address. When a WINS client needs to find another computer on the network, it first looks in its local name cache, then queries a WINS server, and finally broadcasts a request on the network. WINS proxies act as gateways between WINS servers and non-WINS clients that rely on NetBIOS name access.

DNS provides machine name lookups for IP-based clients and will eventually eliminate the need for WINS. A computer is assigned a name in a DNS server manually or through the DHCP process. When a computer needs to locate another system through DNS, it first looks in its local name cache, then sends a request to its primary DNS server. The DNS server then looks in its local cache, forwarding the request to another DNS server if the address is not found locally. The DNS server has the job of querying all the necessary external DNS servers to locate the address and send it back to the client. DNS servers share information through a zone transfer process, by which the primary DNS server sends the contents of its database to secondary DNS servers. Windows 2000 DNS servers can integrate with Active Directory, which provides a more efficient transfer process and redundancy.

You should now have a basic understanding of how each of these three services works, and you have also seen the installation and configuration process to get each of these services active on a Windows 2000 server. As a result, you should now be better prepared to implement these services in a real-world environment.

✓ TWO-MINUTE DRILL

Installing, Configuring, and Administering Dynamic Host Configuration Protocol

❑ You can remember the lease process by thinking of DORA: *discover, offer, request, acknowledgment.*

❑ DHCP clients first attempt to renew their lease at 50 percent of their lease period. If unable to renew the lease at the 50 percent mark, they try again at 87.5 percent of their lease period.

❑ Using DHCP relay agents that intercept broadcasts and forward broadcast requests as unicast messages to a remote DHCP server, DHCP broadcast messages can be conveyed without forwarding broadcasts to remote DHCP servers.

❑ DHCP servers store groups of IP addresses to hand out to DHCP clients in scopes. Each scope represents a different subnet, and only a single subnet can be included in a scope.

❑ In addition to assigning an IP address and subnet mask, the DHCP can provide other information such as WINS server, DNS server, and default gateway addresses. These are configured as DHCP options.

Installing, Configuring, and Administering Windows Internet Naming Service

❑ WINS servers register the NetBIOS names and IP addresses of WINS clients. WINS servers also respond to requests for NetBIOS name resolution.

❑ A WINS client is a computer that can be configured to register its NetBIOS name with a WINS server and that can query a WINS server for the IP address of a particular NetBIOS name.

❑ The four main interactions between WINS servers and clients are NetBIOS name registration, NetBIOS name query request, NetBIOS name release, and NetBIOS name refresh.

❑ The WINS proxy agent intercepts NetBIOS name resolution request broadcasts on a local segment and forwards them to a WINS server for name resolution.

WINS proxy agents are typically used to allow NetBIOS name resolution via WINS for non-WINS clients.

❏ The Windows 2000 WINS server supports persistent connections, which allow WINS replication partners to maintain an open channel at all times and reduce the overhead related to establishing and tearing down sessions during each replication event.

❏ A tombstoned record is a WINS database record that is marked for deletion. It is better to tombstone a record because the record will not be replicated as active again throughout the network.

Installing, Configuring, and Administering Domain Name Service

❏ The NetBIOS namespace is flat; the DNS namespace is hierarchical.

❏ A fully qualified domain name (FQDN) is a combination of the host name and the host's domain location.

❏ A single DNS server can contain multiple zone database files, and a single zone can contain multiple domains.

❏ A forward lookup zone resolves host names to IP addresses.

❏ A reverse lookup zone resolves IP addresses to host names and uses the special in-addr.arpa domain to store its resource records.

❏ The only read/write copy of the zone database file is stored on a primary DNS server. Secondary DNS servers contain read-only copies.

SELF TEST

The following questions will help you measure your understanding of the material presented in this chapter. Read all the choices carefully because there might be more than one correct answer. Choose all correct answers for each question.

Installing, Configuring, and Administering Dynamic Host Configuration Protocol

1. Which of the following messages are passed between a DHCP server and a DHCP client? Choose all that apply.

    A. DHCPDISCOVER

    B. DHCPOFFER

    C. DHCPREQUEST

    D. DHCPACK

2. You are performing a Network Monitor session and you see several DHCP messages included in your capture. While following the message IDs in your capture, you notice a conversation between a DHCP client and DHCP server that includes only a DHCPREQUEST and a DHCPACK message. What might cause the conversation to include only these two messages? Choose all that apply.

    A. There has been an error in the DHCP client's TCP/IP protocol stack.

    B. The DHCP client has a valid lease and is booting up.

    C. The DHCP client has reached one-half of its lease period.

    D. DHCP clients issue DHCPDISCOVER messages only the first time they ever boot; they never issue any subsequent DHCP messages.

3. The Windows 2000 DHCP server default lease period is:

    A. Two days

    B. Four days

    C. Six days

    D. Eight days

4. You have recently implemented a new network that has 3,500 client machines. You are still in the "shakedown" period for several segments; the IP addresses of the WINS server, DHCP

servers, and default gateways are likely to change frequently during this period. You will use DHCP to assign IP addressing information during this shakedown period. What should you do with your DHCP leases during this period to make change management easier?

A. Keep the lease period relatively short.

B. Increase the lease period as long as possible to introduce a level of stability to this unstable network.

C. Manually configure all your clients' IP addressing information until everything is stable and you have no other alternatives.

D. Use WINS server to assign IP addressing information until your DHCP lease information can be permanently defined.

5. Which of the following are requirements for running the Windows 2000 DHCP server service? Choose all that apply.

A. The computer must have a static IP address.

B. The computer must be running Windows 2000 Server configured as a domain controller.

C. The DHCP service must be authorized within Active Directory services.

D. The service must have at least one scope defined with a range or pool of IP addresses that can be leased to clients.

6. You recently changed the default gateways for the machines on your network. All the machines use DHCP to obtain IP addressing information. In order to deliver the new information to your DHCP clients, you remotely reboot all the computers on the network so that they receive their new default gateway addresses. However, you receive multiple calls from a department regarding their inability to access remote subnets. You check the scope settings on the DHCP server that handles the department's subnets and everything looks good. What do you think is preventing these clients from accessing remote locations?

A. You must install a DHCP relay agent in order for the machines to obtain new gateway parameters.

B. A remote reboot will not allow the DHCP client machines to issue DHCPREQUEST messages when they start up again.

C. The engineers have manually entered the default gateway information on their workstations.

D. You cannot set gateway options on the DHCP server.

Installing, Configuring, and Administering Windows Internet Naming Service

7. The maximum number of WINS servers you should have on your network is:

A. 5

B. 10

C. 15

D. 20

8. You have set up a small TCP/IP network for your company. As your network grows with additional computers, the network begins to experience a more significant increase in broadcast traffic than you expected. Which of the following tasks would be the best way to help cut the amount of broadcast traffic on your network?

A. Divide your network into multiple physical segments, separated by bridges.

B. Divide your network into multiple logical segments, installing gateways between the segments.

C. Install a DHCP server on the network.

D. Install a WINS server on the network.

9. A single WINS server and a backup WINS server should be able to accommodate how many WINS clients?

A. 100

B. 1,000

C. 10,000

D. 50,000

10. You have two subnets separated by a router. These subnets are 192.168.1.0 and 192.168.2.0, both with 24-bit subnet masks. You have a WINS server on 192.168.1.0 and a WINS proxy agent on 192.168.2.0. On each subnet, you have non-WINS client UNIX servers that run NetBIOS applications and need to resolve NetBIOS names to IP addresses. The UNIX machines on 192.168.2.0 have no problems resolving NetBIOS names to IP addresses, but the UNIX machines on the same subnet as the WINS server are not able to successfully resolve NetBIOS names. Why can't the UNIX machines resolve the NetBIOS names?

A. The UNIX machines on the same subnet as the WINS server must be configured with the IP address of the WINS server.

B. You must open the WINS proxy port UDP 140 on the router for the UNIX servers on 192.168.1.0 to communicate with the WINS proxy agent.

C. The WINS server does not respond to NetBIOS name query request broadcast messages.

D. You must install the WINS proxy agent software on the UNIX NetBIOS client machines.

11. Which of the following are requirements for installing the Windows 2000 WINS Server service? Choose all that apply.

A. The computer operating system must be a member of the Windows 2000 Server family of products.

B. The computer must have a static IP address.

C. The computer must have at least two network cards.

D. The computer must be a member of the same Windows 2000 domain for which it will service registration and query requests.

12. What happens to a WINS database record if it not renewed at one-half of the time to live it received when it registered with the WINS server?

A. The record remains active until 87.5 percent of the TTL has passed.

B. The record is marked inactive or released.

C. The record is tombstoned.

D. The record is removed from the WINS database via scavenging.

Installing, Configuring, and Administering Domain Name Service

13. You are planning a TCP/IP-based Windows 2000 network. What service should you install to allow host name resolution on your network?

A. NNTP

B. RIPv2

C. DNS

D. RIS

14. After installing a primary DNS server for a Windows 2000 standard zone, you decide you should have some fault tolerance built into your corporate DNS solution. What kind of DNS servers can you implement in order to provide both fault tolerance and load balancing of host name resolution for your network?

    A. A secondary DNS server

    B. A DNS forwarder

    C. A zone infrastructure server

    D. A second primary DNS server for the zone

15. Some advantages of using caching-only DNS servers include which of the following? Choose all that apply.

    A. They do not generate zone transfer traffic.

    B. They can be configured as secure DNS forwarders.

    C. You can store your external zone files on them for Internet user access.

    D. They can be placed at remote office locations to reduce the amount of traffic over the slow WAN link.

16. You work in an organization that has more than 7,000 computers. The network has been upgraded to all Windows 2000 Professional or Windows 2000 Server computers. DNS is the only name resolution service on your network, because NetBIOS is no longer required and your WINS servers have been decommissioned. Users are allowed to share desktop resources with each other. What would you do to enable efficient name resolution while making your life as systems administrator as easy as possible?

    A. Create a centralized LMHOSTS file and tell users to point to it.

    B. Create a HOSTS file and have each user install it on his or her computer.

    C. Allow your DNS server to accept dynamic updates from all DNS clients in the organization.

    D. Configure the DNS servers to perform WINS lookups.

17. Which of the following are benefits of integrating Windows 2000 DNS services with Active Directory? Choose all that apply.

    A. Efficient replication of large zones

    B. Ease of management

    C. Security

    D. Fault-tolerance

LAB QUESTION

You just hired on with a startup company (pre-IPO, of course) that needs you to build a network infrastructure from the ground up. You are given the task of setting up several Windows 2000 servers, including an Exchange server, a SQL server, a RAS server, and a file server for network data storage.

All the desktop computers the company will use are to be purchased new, but the sales force for the company, which has been at work for several months now, is using older laptops with a mixture of Windows 95 and Windows 98. While on the road, the sales force will dial in to check e-mail on the Exchange server, but in the office, they will directly connect to the LAN to access the resources you will provide. The sales force will expand, but your boss wants to keep Windows 95 and Windows 98 as the operating systems for the laptops they will use. The company, expecting massive growth over the first two years, has already leased enough office space to handle up to 2,000 employees, even though there are only 20 employees right now.

As you plan the construction of your new company's network, how would you implement the basic network services? Would you implement a Windows 2000 Active Directory model or a Windows NT domain model? Would you configure DHCP, WINS, and DNS, or would you make the network function without them?

SELF TEST ANSWERS

Installing, Configuring, and Administering Dynamic Host Configuration Protocol

1. ☑ **A, B, C,** and **D.** The DHCP lease process includes the DHCPDISCOVER message, which the DHCP client sends when it attempts to obtain a new lease. The DHCPOFFER message is returned by all DHCP servers that received the DHCPDISCOVER message. The DHCPREQUEST message that the DHCP client sends to the DHCP server requests that it keep the lease in the DHCPOFFER message, and the DHCPACK message sent from the DHCP server confirms the lease and provides DHCP options information.

2. ☑ **B** and **C.** The DHCP client has a valid lease and is booting up, and the DHCP client has reached one-half of its lease period. A DHCP client always issues a DHCPREQUEST message to renew its lease when it boots up in order to assess whether it is still on the same network. The DHCP client issues a DHCPREQUEST message after one-half of its lease period in order to renew its lease.
   ☒ **A** is incorrect because its unlikely that a TCP/IP protocol stack error would cause a selective disruption of only the DHCPDISCOVER message on the DHCP client. **D** is incorrect because DHCP DHCPREQUEST messages can be delivered during bootup and during lease renewal.

3. ☑ **D.** The default lease period for the Windows 2000 DHCP server is eight days. This is in contrast to the default lease period for the Windows NT 4.0 DHCP Server, which was six days.
   ☒ **A, B,** and **C** are incorrect because the correct answer is eight days.

4. ☑ **A.** Keep the lease period relatively short. If you keep your leases short, the DHCP clients issue DHCPREQUEST messages more frequently. When the DHCP client's lease is renewed, it also receives new option parameters such as WINS, DNS, and gateway addresses.
   ☒ **B,** increase the lease period as long as possible to introduce a level of stability to this unstable network, is incorrect because if you make the lease periods longer, the clients will not receive updated option information on a timely basis. **C,** manually configure all your clients' IP addressing information until everything is stable and you have no other alternatives, is incorrect because manually reconfiguring client IP addresses will end up causing more work for the administrator. **D,** use WINS server to assign IP addressing information until your DHCP lease information can be permanently defined, is incorrect because WINS servers do not assign IP addressing information.

5. ☑ **A, C,** and **D.** The DHCP service, like WINS and DNS, must be running on a computer with a static IP address. The Windows 2000 DHCP service cannot respond to DHCP requests until it is authorized in Active Directory. Finally, a DHCP server must have a set of IP addresses to lease out to clients, and those addresses must be defined within a scope.

   ☒ **B** is incorrect because the DHCP service can be run on any flavor of Windows 2000 Server, with no requirements as to how that server is configured to participate in a domain or in an Active Directory structure. It can be a domain controller, a member server, or the like.

6. ☑ **C.** The engineers have manually entered the default gateway information on their workstations. Locally configured options override any options you configure at the DHCP server.

   ☒ **A** is incorrect because you do not need a DHCP relay agent simply to renew IP addressing information. If the DHCP client did not need a relay agent previously, it should not need one now. BOOTP forwarding could be enabled in order to pass DHCP messages to remote DHCP servers instead. **B** is incorrect because it doesn't matter how you reboot the machine, the DHCP client always issues a DHCPREQUEST message during bootup. **D** is incorrect because you can set default gateway (router) options on a DHCP server.

Installing, Configuring, and Administering Windows Internet Naming Service

7. ☑ **D.** 20. Microsoft recommends that you never install more than 20 WINS servers on your network. If you feel that you need more than 20 WINS servers, Microsoft recommends that you install Microsoft Consulting Services for an analysis of your situation.

   ☒ **A, B,** and **C** are incorrect because 20 is the maximum number of WINS servers you should have installed on your network.

8. ☑ **D.** Install a WINS server on the network. If there is no WINS server, each of the computers on the network must send broadcast messages to try to locate other computers on the network. As the network grows, the amount of broadcast traffic grows, too, since there are more computers that each member of the network needs to locate. Installing a WINS server greatly reduces the amount of broadcast traffic on the network because each client sends the name lookup request directly to the WINS server, instead of sending the request as broadcast traffic on the network.

   ☒ **A** is incorrect because dividing your network into multiple physical subnets will not remove the source of the broadcast traffic, although it might help reduce the total amount of broadcast traffic carried on each segment. As your network continues to grow, however, the amount of broadcast traffic will continue to increase as well, because the source for the traffic has not been addressed. **B** is incorrect for essentially the same reason. The gateway could help reduce the amount of traffic that passes between the subnets, but it does not address the cause of the traffic. **C** is incorrect because adding a DHCP server to your network will not cut broadcast traffic. In fact, if the computers on your network have their TCP/IP settings configured manually, adding a DHCP server to dynamically configure the TCP/IP settings will actually increase the broadcast traffic on the network, but not to the degree described in this question. Adding a DCHP server would not address the source of the broadcast traffic.

9. ☑ **C.** 10,000. Microsoft recommends a single WINS server and a backup for every 10,000 WINS clients. You might want to deploy more WINS servers than this, depending on the nature of the links between your organization's sites. In actual practice, it's likely that your ratio of WINS clients to servers will be higher than this due to the way most networks are segmented. Microsoft makes this recommendation to remind administrators and architects that often, far too many WINS servers are implemented than are needed.
   ☒ **A, B,** and **D** are incorrect because the correct answer is 10,000.

10. ☑ **C.** The WINS server does not respond to NetBIOS name query request broadcast messages. WINS servers do not respond to broadcast NetBIOS name query requests. Since the UNIX servers on the same subnet are non-WINS clients, they cannot directly communicate with the WINS server and can only resolve names via broadcasts.
   ☒ **A** is incorrect because non-WINS clients cannot be configured with the IP address of a WINS server. **B** is incorrect because there is no WINS proxy agent port. **D** is incorrect because there is no WINS proxy agent software to install on UNIX clients.

11. ☑ **A** and **B.** The computer operating system must be a member of the Windows 2000 Server family of products, and the computer must have a static IP address. You can install Server services only on Server operating systems. The Windows 2000 WINS Server service cannot be installed on Windows 2000 Professional. Furthermore, a WINS server must have a static IP address to which WINS clients can connect.
   ☒ **C** is incorrect because a WINS server does not require two network interface cards. **D** is incorrect because a WINS server does not need to be a member of the same Windows 2000 domain as the WINS clients that it services.

12. ☑ **B.** The record is marked inactive or released. If the record is not renewed at 50 percent of its TTL, it will be marked as inactive (released). An inactive record can be dynamically updated without being challenged by the WINS server.
   ☒ **A** is incorrect because the record doesn't remain active after 50 percent of the TTL unless it is renewed. **C** is incorrect because a record is tombstoned only after the passage of the extinction interval. **D** is incorrect because the record is not removed until the extinction time-out has expired.

Installing, Configuring, and Administering Domain Name Service

13. ☑ **C.** DNS. DNS servers can resolve host names to IP addresses and IP addresses to host names.
☒ **A** is incorrect because Network News Transfer Protocol (NNTP) is used to transmit information to and from newsgroup servers. **B** is incorrect because RIPv2 is a routing protocol that can be installed via the Routing and Remote Access Console. **D** is incorrect because Remote Installation Services (RIS) is a service new to Windows 2000 that allows you to install Windows 2000 Professional remotely over the network.

14. ☑ **A.** A secondary DNS server. A secondary DNS server provides for both load balancing and fault tolerance for the zone. A secondary DNS server contains a read-only copy of the zone database file; a primary DNS server contains a read/write copy of the zone file.
☒ **B** is incorrect because a DNS forwarder is a DNS server that receives DNS queries from another DNS server and returns the result to the DNS server that issued the query. **C** is incorrect because there is no such thing as a zone infrastructure server. There is such a thing as an infrastructure master, which is one of the five Operations Masters in Windows 2000 domains. The infrastructure master is responsible for updating the group-to-user references whenever the members of groups are renamed or changed. At any time, there can be only one domain controller acting as the infrastructure master in each domain. **D** is incorrect because standard zones can have only a single primary DNS server. Active Directory integrated zones are multimaster and support multiple primary DNS zones.

15. ☑ **A, B,** and **D.** They do not generate zone transfer traffic, they can be configured as secure DNS forwarders, and they can be placed at remote office locations to reduce the amount of traffic over the slow WAN link. Caching-only servers do not contain zone files; therefore, there is no need for zone transfer traffic. Caching-only servers are ideal as secure DNS forwarders because hackers are not able to access any zone data on them, since there are no zone files to access. Finally, you obviate the need for large zone transfer traffic with caching-only DNS servers; therefore, remote offices can benefit from having a cache of successfully resolved queries build up over time on the caching-only server.
☒ **C** is incorrect because caching-only forwarders do not contain zone files, and therefore they would not be useful in providing name resolution for your external, Internet-accessible resources.

16. ☑ **C.** Allow your DNS server to accept dynamic updates from all DNS clients in the organization. When NetBIOS is disabled on all machines on the network, the only method of name resolution is host name resolution. Therefore, all names are resolved using DNS servers. You could create host records for each machine on the network, but that would be a very time-consuming task, and you would have a tough time keeping track of machines that receive IP addresses via DHCP (if DHCP is enabled on the network). In this environment, where users are allowed to share their desktop resources with each other, the users must have a mechanism in place that will allow their WinSock applications to resolve host names to IP addresses. The easiest route here is to enable dynamic updates to your DNS zones so all machines automatically update the DNS zone database.

☒ **A** is incorrect because asking users to do anything is unwise at best and disastrous at worst. In addition, the LMHOSTS file is used to resolve NetBIOS names to IP addresses. However, an LMHOSTS file can be used during the host name resolution sequence if the other methods have failed. **B** is incorrect because you do not want users doing anything with their computers other than the work they've been assigned. In addition, the HOSTS file suffers the same limitations as the LMHOSTS file. **D** is incorrect because you have disabled NetBIOS on all the machines on the network, and therefore you have no need for WINS servers. Even if WINS servers were installed, there would be no registrations since there are no NetBIOS WINS clients on the network.

17. ☑ **A, B, C,** and **D.** Active Directory replicates only relevant changes to the zone information, which is a quicker process than performing a full zone transfer, as is done in standard DNS servers. A separate zone transfer process does not have to be maintained, since Active Directory handles the zone replication process between Active Directory-integrated DNS servers. Restrictions can be placed on access for zone and record updates, which helps to prevent insecure dynamic updates. The multimaster replication feature of Windows 2000 DNS removes the single point of failure for zone updates within a DNS server system.

LAB ANSWER

There are many different approaches to planning this network, but a few decisions seem fairly obvious right up front. Since the company is small now, it may seem easier to set up the network under an NT domain model to get services active quickly. However, since you have Windows 95 and Windows 98 laptops in the mix, and since you plan on running Windows 2000 servers, you should go ahead and implement an Active Directory model with DHCP, WINS, and DNS services. Here are a few reasons that this is the way to go:

- **IP addresses** Since the network is starting small, you might be tempted to manually assign IP addresses for the computers. As the company grows, however, maintaining static addresses for the nonserver computers will become a huge task. In addition, the expected growth of the company in the short term means that your network will probably expand into multiple segments and multiple subnets. Enter the laptops: With a static IP address, laptop users would be limited to where they could connect to the network. So, not only would it make sense to configure DHCP services for the laptops, but all end-user computers in the company would benefit from using DHCP for configuring the network interface. If you need to change basic network information, such as segment addresses or gateways, this is easier to perform automatically with DHCP services than by visiting each affected machine individually and changing the configuration by hand. Running DHCP services on a Windows 2000 server requires authorization in Active Directory, so you will need to implement Active Directory instead of an NT domain model.

■ **Machine lookups**   Since Windows 2000 networking is based on TCP/IP and not NetBIOS, Windows 2000 computers expect DNS to be available for machine lookups. Since you will use DHCP on the network, you will want to implement Dynamic DNS on your DNS servers so that as IP addresses change for computers on the network, the DNS tables will be kept up to date for machine lookups. Integrating your DNS servers with Active Directory gives added benefits for fault tolerance and faster zone updates, another reason to go with the Active Directory model over an NT domain model. In addition, though, you will also want to implement WINS on your network for the laptops running Windows 95 and Windows 98. Those computers will still expect to use NetBIOS services for name lookups through WINS, so until the laptops are all moved to Windows 2000, you will want to maintain WINS. Fortunately, setting up and maintaining two WINS servers (for fault tolerance) is a relatively minor issue.

6

Installing, Configuring, and Troubleshooting Access to Resources

CERTIFICATION OBJECTIVES

6.01	Monitor, Configure, Troubleshoot, and Control Access to Files, Folders, and Shared Folders
6.02	Monitor, Configure, Troubleshoot, and Control Access to Dfs Resources
6.03	Monitor, Configure, Troubleshoot, and Control Access to Printers
✓	Two-Minute Drill
Q&A	Self Test

Providing access to file and print resources is an essential function of a network. This chapter will introduce you to or reacquaint you with basic file and folder sharing, setting up a Dfs sharing tree, and print resource sharing and configuration. While the focus of this chapter is on Windows 2000 Server, some of these functions can be performed on Windows 2000 Professional as well, and there may be appropriate times to do so.

Windows 2000 provides all the necessary tools to configure and maintain these services. No third-party tools are necessary for administering these resources, even though some third-party tools may make management of these resources easier. This chapter will focus solely on the default tools provided with Windows 2000 Server to help you prepare for certification.

CERTIFICATION OBJECTIVE 6.01

Monitor, Configure, Troubleshoot, and Control Access to Files, Folders, and Shared Folders

Windows 2000 provides a greater file system security model than has been available in most other Microsoft operating systems. Many of the security features in Windows 2000 were introduced in Windows NT, but these features are more mature in Windows 2000, and new features have been added to further solidify the security model.

Windows 2000 file security is available only on volumes that have been formatted as NTFS volumes. Even though Windows 2000 can access FAT16 and FAT 32 volumes, only NTFS partitions provide any security features. This section of the chapter will cover the use of NTFS permissions for local folder and shared folder security.

Local Security on Files and Folders

Even though Windows 2000 provides different profile settings for each user who logs on to a Windows 2000 computer, file system security is not contained within the profile. In other words, unless specific NTFS permissions have been set for local folders on a Windows 2000 workstation, any user who logs in on the workstation can access the entire file system on the computer. Windows 2000 does provide some protection for the WINNT folder on the system volume so that non-administrator logins cannot modify certain system files.

NTFS Folder Permissions

NTFS folder permissions define a user's access to a folder and its contents. Table 6-1 lists the various NTFS folder permissions and their functions.

NTFS File Permissions

NTFS file permissions are applied to individual files within a folder and can be more restrictive or more lenient than the permissions set on the parent folder. Table 6-2 lists the various NTFS file permissions and their functions.

TABLE 6-1	Permission	Function
NTFS Folder Permissions	Read	Read file/folder contents Read attributes and extended attributes on files and folders Read permissions on files and folders
	Write	Create, write to, and append to files Create new folders Write attributes and extended attributes on files and folders Read permissions on files and folders
	List Folder Contents	Same as Read Traverse folders
	Read & Execute	Same as List Folder Contents Execute applications
	Modify	Same as Read & Execute All permissions for Write Delete files
	Full Control	Same as Modify Delete subfolders and files Change permissions Take ownership

TABLE 6-2	Permission	Function
NTFS File Permissions	Read	Read file contents Read attributes and extended attributes on files Read permissions on files
	Write	Create, write to, and append to files Write attributes and extended attributes on files Read permissions on files
	Read & Execute	Same as Read Execute applications
	Modify	Same as Read & Execute All permissions for Write Delete files
	Full Control	Same as Modify Change permissions Take ownership

Assigning NTFS Permissions

NTFS permissions can be applied at the user or group level. Generally, it is best to use group memberships to assign NTFS permissions, but that does not preclude setting individual user permissions on a file or folder. When a user is a member of multiple groups that have different NTFS permissions on a file or folder, the effective permissions are cumulative. For instance, if a user is a member of one group that has Read permissions on a folder and is also a member of another group that has Write permissions to the same folder, the user has both Read and Write permissions to that folder.

NTFS permissions are assigned in the Security tab of the Properties window for a file or folder. Figure 6-1 shows the permissions on the Author Files folder. In this example, the Everyone Group has Read permission on the folder, but no others. Thus, anyone who logs in on this computer would be able to view the contents of the files in this folder but would not be able to save changes to any existing files, create any new files or folders, or modify any attributes or permissions on any of the files. However, members of the Administrators Group have all permissions in this folder, and since the permissions are cumulative, the members of the Administrators Group, who are members of the Everyone Group by default, have all permissions to the folder and are not limited to just the Read permission.

FIGURE 6-1

Folder
permissions

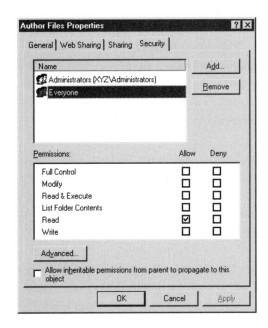

Permissions in a folder can be changed by clicking the appropriate check box in the Allow column to turn the permission on or off. Additional group permissions can be added by clicking the Add... button and selecting a group to add to the permissions list. When the permissions are set correctly, click Apply, then OK to enable the permissions configuration and close the window.

Deny Permissions   Unlike the Allow permission, the Deny permission overrides all other permissions set for a file or folder. If a user is a member of one group that has the Deny Write permission for a folder and is a member of another group that has the Allow Full Control permission, the user will be unable to perform any of the tasks the Write permission allows, because it has been Denied. The Deny permission should be used with extreme caution, as it can actually lock out all users, even administrators, from a file or folder. The proper way to remove a permission from a user or group on a file or folder is to uncheck the Allow permission for that user or group, not to check the Deny permission.

NTFS Special Access Permissions

In addition to the basic NTFS permissions, there are several special access permissions that provide extended functions. These special permissions are found in the Advanced window of the Security tab of the file or folder Properties window, as shown in Figure 6-2. Two important special access permissions, Change Permission and Take Ownership Permission, are described below.

Change Permission This permission can be used to allow users the ability to change permissions on files and folders without giving them the Full Control permission. This permission can be used to give a user or group access to modify permissions on file or folder objects without giving them the ability to have complete control over the object.

Take Ownership Permission This permission can be given to allow a user to take ownership of a file or folder object. Every file and folder on an NTFS drive has an owner, usually the account that created the object. However, there are times when ownership of a file needs to be changed, perhaps because of a change in team membership or a set of new responsibilities for a user.

FIGURE 6-2

Access Control
Settings for a
folder

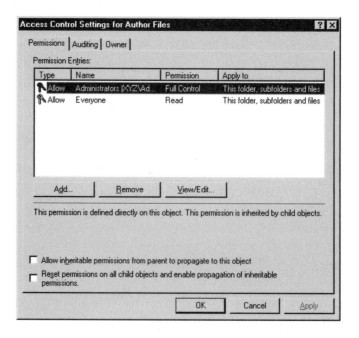

Object ownership in Windows 2000 cannot be explicitly assigned. Ownership can be changed only when a user object takes ownership of a file or folder object. By default, only administrators can take ownership of a file or folder object, but the Take Ownership permission can be assigned to a user for a file or folder so that the user can independently take ownership and become the owner of the file or folder object. When an administrator takes ownership of an object, the Administrators Group becomes the owner of the object so that anyone in the Administrators Group can access the object as owner.

Other Special Permissions   Table 6-3 describes the remaining special access permissions. In many cases, use of these special access permissions can more effectively control access to file system objects and should at least be considered when file system security is planned.

NTFS Permissions Inheritance

By default, all permissions set for a folder are inherited by the files in the folder, the subfolders in the folder, and the contents of the subfolders. When the permissions on a folder are viewed in the Security tab of the file or folder Permissions window, inherited permissions are indicated with a gray check box, as shown in Figure 6-3.

TABLE 6-3	Special Access Permission	Function
Special Access Permissions	Traverse Folder/Execute File	Browse folder contents or execute an application
	List Folder/Read Data	View the contents of a file or folder
	Read Attributes	View the attributes of a file or folder
	Read Extended Attributes	View the extended attributes of a file or folder
	Create Files/Write Data	Create a new file
	Create Folders/Append Data	Create a new subfolder or append data to a file
	Write Attributes	Set the attributes of a folder or file
	Write Extended Attributes	Set the extended attributes of a folder or file
	Delete Subfolders and Files	Remove files or subfolders from a folder
	Read Permissions	View permissions of a file or folder

FIGURE 6-3

Folder with
inherited
permissions

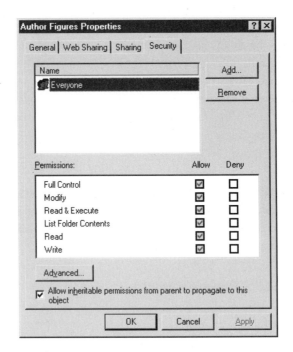

Allowing Permissions Inheritance   To ensure that an object will inherit
permissions from its parent object, turn on the Allow inheritable permissions from
parent to propagate to this object check box in the Security tab of the object's
Properties dialog. This setting is on by default unless it has been previously removed.
This check box is also visible in the Access Control Settings window of the object,
which can be opened by clicking the Advanced… button in the Security tab.

Preventing Permissions Inheritance   There may be times when you want to
assign a new set of permissions for an object and prevent any permissions from a
parent object from being inherited. To "start over" with a new set of permissions for
a file or folder, turn off the Allow inheritable permissions from parent to propagate
to this object check box in the Security tab. When you do so, you will be prompted
to choose how to assign new permissions for the object. You can either copy the
inherited permissions to the object, or you can remove the permissions altogether
and start clean. Either way, at the end of the task, you will be able to set specific
permissions for the object, regardless of the permissions of the parent object.

Conflicting file and folder permissions are not only a common problem in a real-world environment; they are a favorite topic in exam questions. Be sure you understand how conflicting file and folder permissions are resolved.

Copying or Moving Files and Folders

NTFS permissions assigned to a file or folder are not necessarily kept intact when the file or folder is moved or copied to a new location. When files and folders are moved or copied from an NTFS volume to a FAT16 or FAT32 volume, all permissions are lost, as FAT16 and FAT 32 volumes do not support NTFS permissions. It is important to know the results of moving or copying files and folders to other NTFS volumes.

Copying Files and Folders   In order for a user account to copy files and folders to NTFS volumes, the user account must have permissions to write to the destination location. When the file or folder is copied, it is created as a new file in the destination, and the user copying the file or folder becomes the owner of the newly created items.

NTFS permissions assigned to the new objects depend on the destination where the objects are created. Table 6-4 describes the results.

Moving Files and Folders   Before a user account can move files and folders from one location to another, the user must have permissions to create objects at the new location, and must also have permission to delete the objects from the original location. When moving files and folders, the original objects will be deleted after they have been successfully created in the destination location. The user account moving the objects will become the owner of the objects in the new location.

NTFS permissions assigned to the new objects depend on the destination where the objects are created. Table 6-5 describes the results.

TABLE 6-4	Destination	Permissions
NTFS Permissions Applied to Copied Files and Folders	Objects copied within the same NTFS volume	Objects inherit the permissions of the new location
	Objects copied to a different NTFS volume	Objects inherit the permissions of the new location

	Destination	Permissions
	Objects moved within the same NTFS volume	Objects retain their original NTFS permissions in the new location
	Objects moved to a different NTFS volume	Objects inherit the permissions of the new location

TABLE 6-5

NTFS Permissions Applied to Moved Files and Folders

exam
ⓦatch

You may encounter one or more questions involving permissions on files or folders that have been moved or copied within and across volumes. These questions are designed to test your understanding of how permissions are handled in these situations.

Access to Files and Folders in a Shared Folder

Shared folders present an additional level of security to the files and folders within the share. In addition to needing permissions to access the files and folders on the NTFS volume, users must also have permissions to access the share on the network.

Shared Folder Permissions

As only folders, not files, can be shared, shared folder permissions are a small subset of standard NTFS permissions for a folder. However, securing access to a folder through share permissions can be more restrictive or more liberal than standard NTFS folder permissions. Table 6-6 describes the permissions that apply to shared folders.

Shared folder permissions are applied in the same manner as NTFS permissions. Permissions can be allowed or denied to groups or individual users, although denied permissions override any allow permissions applied. Shared folder permissions are cumulative when multiple permissions are applied. If a user is a member of two groups, one that has Read permission on a shared folder and another that has Change permission on the same folder, then the user has Change permissions to that folder.

There are some significant differences between shared folder permissions and NTFS permissions:

■ Shared folder permissions apply only when the folder is accessed through the share. If the shared folder exists on the local computer, only the NTFS permissions will apply to the folder if it is accessed locally. The folder must be accessed through the share before the share permissions will apply.

■ Shared folder permissions are the only way to provide security to folders on FAT16 or FAT32 volumes. The protection applies only through the share.

■ When both Share permissions and NTFS permissions are applied to a folder, the more restrictive permission will determine access to the contents of the folder. In other words, if a user has Full Control NTFS permissions on a folder but only Read permissions on the share, that user has read-only access to the contents of the folder when it is accessed through the share. However, if the user has only the NTFS Read permission on a folder but has Full Control on the share, that user still has only Read access to the contents of the folder.

■ The default permission applied to new shares is Full Control, which is assigned to the Everyone Group.

TABLE 6-6	Permission	Description
Shared Folder Permissions	Read	Users can: View file names and folder names View file contents and attributes Execute program files Traverse folders within the shared folder
	Change	Users can: Create folders Add files to folders Change content of files Change file attributes Delete folders and files Perform tasks allowed with Read permission
	Full Control	Users can: Change file permissions Take ownership of files Perform tasks allowed with Change permission

on the

I've been caught more than once not setting share and NTFS folder permissions correctly. Several times I have needed to share out some space on my server to an individual for temporary storage or backup. Knowing that I wanted that person only to see the share, I removed all permissions from the Everyone Group on the share and gave the individual's account Change permission on the share so the individual could read and write to the contents of the share. Then, when I needed to access the share from a remote location to verify the contents or perform maintenance on the contents, I was unable to access the share because I had forgotten to give share permissions to my account. How embarrassing!

Copying or Moving Shared Folders   When a shared folder is copied to a new location, the original folder remains shared, but the new folder is not shared. When a shared folder is moved, it is no longer shared.

Sharing Folders in the Active Directory

Folders can be shared from a Windows 2000 workstation or server, and they can also be created in the Active Directory. The advantage of sharing a folder in the Active Directory is that users can search the Active Directory for a particular share as opposed to needing the name of the server hosting the share in order to open it. Instructions for sharing a folder through Active Directory are contained in Exercise 6-1.

EXERCISE 6-1

Creating a Shared Folder in the Active Directory

In this exercise, you will go through the steps of creating a folder, setting permissions on the folder, sharing the folder, setting permissions on the share, and placing the share in the Active Directory.

1. Create a new folder in the root of the system volume called Public.

2. Right-click the folder and select Sharing from the pop-up menu. This opens the Properties dialog to the Sharing tab, as shown in the illustration below. Click the Share this folder radio button and type **Public** in the Share name: text field. Type a description in the Comment: text field.

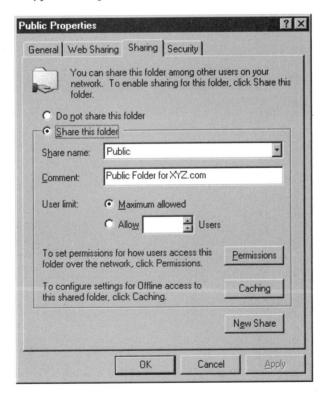

3. Click the Permissions button to open the Share Permissions window, illustrated below. Verify that the Everyone Group has been given Full Control permission on the share. Click OK when done.

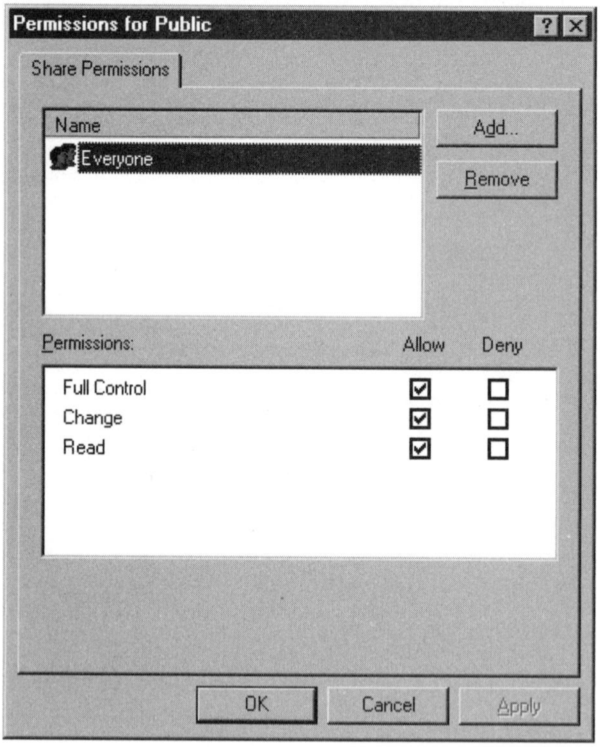

4. Click the Security tab in the Properties dialog for the Public folder. This will bring up the NTFS configuration settings window. Turn off the Allow inheritable permissions check box. This will generate the notification window shown in the illustration below. Click Copy to copy the current permissions settings to the object.

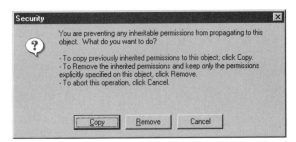

5. Assign permissions to the Everyone Group, as illustrated below. Users accessing this folder will be able to read the contents of any files in the folder, execute applications in the folder, but not make any changes to any of the contents of the folder.

6. Add access permissions for the Administrators Group to this folder by clicking the Add button. This will open the Select Users, Computers, or Groups window shown in the illustration below. Select the Administrators Group from the group list in the top window and click Add. The Administrators Group is added to the bottom window. Click OK.

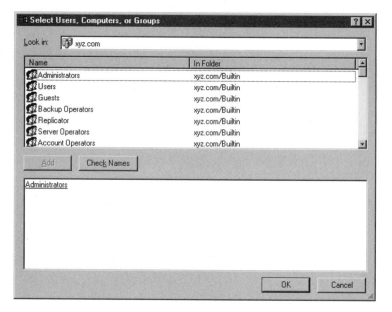

7. Give Full Control permission to the Administrators Group, as shown in the next illustration. Click OK to close the Properties dialog and activate the NTFS and Share permissions for the Public folder.

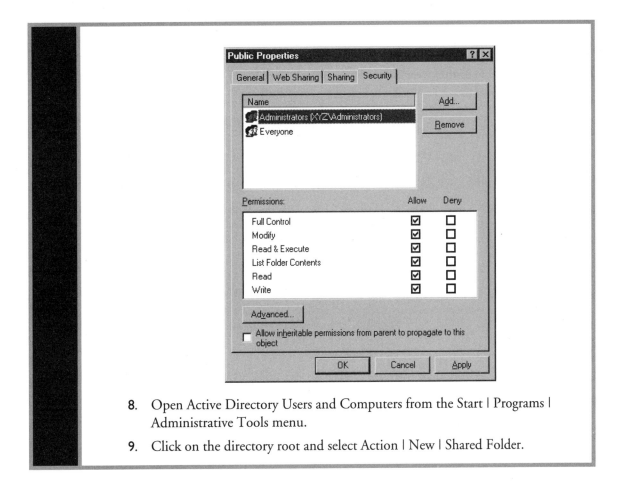

8. Open Active Directory Users and Computers from the Start | Programs | Administrative Tools menu.

9. Click on the directory root and select Action | New | Shared Folder.

10. In the New Object —Shared Folder window, illustrated below, type **Public** in the Name: text field, and type the path to your Public share from your server in the Network path text field. Click OK.

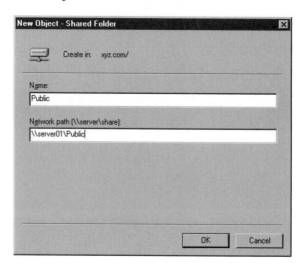

11. Verify that the shared folder now displays in the Active Directory Users and Computers window, as shown:

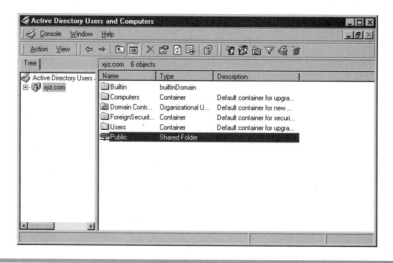

12. Open the Properties window for the share by double-clicking or right-clicking and choosing Properties.... Type a description for the share in the Description: text field, as shown in the illustration below. Click OK and close Active Directory Users and Computers when finished.

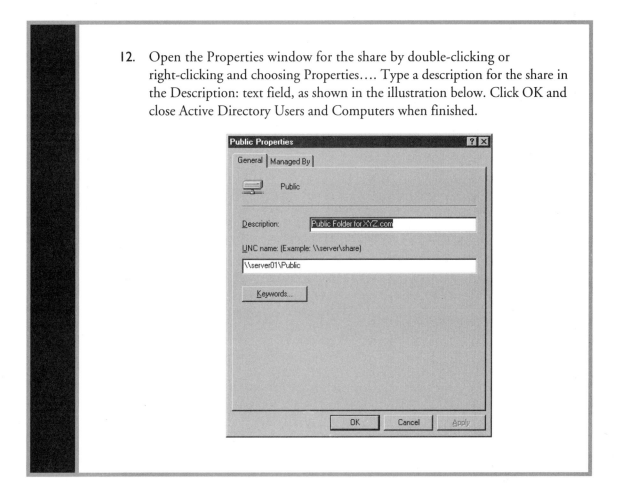

Troubleshooting Access to Shared Folders

Table 6-7 describes some common problems you may encounter with user access to folders and folder shares.

Now that you have a better understanding of how Windows 2000 handles NTFS file and folder permissions and share permissions, the scenario & solution grid on the next page offers some real-world and exam scenarios that you may encounter.

TABLE 6-7	Problem	Solution
Common Shared Folder Access Problems	User cannot access a file or folder	Check the NTFS permissions on the folder. The user needs to be a member of a group that has permission to access the folder, or a group the user belongs to must be given permission to access the folder. See whether a group has been given the Deny permission on the folder; the Deny permission overrides all other permissions and may lock the user out of the resource. If the folder being accessed is a shared folder, make sure the share permissions are set correctly. When a folder is accessed through a share, the more restrictive of the share and NTFS permissions are applied to the user object. If the user has Read access to the share but needs to be able to write to files in the share, the user's permissions on the share should be Change instead. It is almost always advisable to give the Everyone Group Change or Full Control permission on a share and configure access to the folder contents with NTFS permissions to make sure the correct permissions are being applied.
	User has been added to a group to gain access to a folder or file, but the user still cannot access the resource.	Group memberships and related access rights are assigned at login time. The user will not be able to access resources dependent upon the new permissions until the user logs out and logs back in.
	Users are able to delete files, even though they do not have permissions to delete the files.	Check the permissions applied to the user at the folder level. If the user's effective permissions are Full Control, consider having more restrictive permissions for the folder. To prevent users from deleting files in a folder, all permissions except Full Control can be granted for the folder

SCENARIO & SOLUTION

When a user accesses one of my folders through the network share, the user can access the contents only in the way that I want. However, when the user logs in on the machine locally, the account has full access to the folder. What's wrong?	One of two things may be happening here. First, the folder may not have the correct NTFS permissions set locally. Remember that share permissions override NTFS permissions only when the folder is accessed through the share. Second, the folder being shared may be on a FAT or FAT32 volume, which cannot have NTFS permissions set, so when users access the folder locally, they effectively have full control over the folder and its contents.
I have a share that I want only a certain group to access. I turned off the permissions for the Everyone Group, and now no one can access the share, not even me. What's wrong?	In all likelihood, you selected the Deny permissions for the Everyone Group instead of just removing the Allow permissions for the share. Fortunately, you can access the share locally and reset the permissions, making sure that the Everyone Group does not have any permissions assigned, Allow or Deny.
I needed to free up some disk space on one of my volumes and I moved several folders to another volume that has ample free space. Now users are complaining that they cannot access certain shares and folders anymore. What's wrong?	Remember that when you move files and folders to a new volume, the files and folders take the default permissions of the destination folder. You will need to reset the permissions on the files and folders in their new location to match the settings you had before the move. If any of the folders were shared, you will need to re-create the share as well.

CERTIFICATION OBJECTIVE 6.02

Monitor, Configure, Troubleshoot, and Control Access to Dfs Resources

The Distributed File System (Dfs) allows system administrators to logically manage a collection of network resources and present those resources to the user community as a single, hierarchical structure. Instead of forcing your users to remember that the retirement planning forms are stored on the Human Resources server, the direct deposit forms are on the Payroll server, the latest product presentations are on the

Marketing server, and the latest Netscape installer is on one of the central application servers somewhere, you can configure these resources in a logical tree with Dfs. Not only can this simplify the location of resources for the user community, it can also ease your administration of these resources, allowing you to move resources around among various servers without affecting user access to the resources.

There are a number of advantages to using Dfs:

- **Resource administration** If a server fails, a network link becomes temporarily unavailable, a resource needs to be moved or replaced, or there is any other reason that access to a resource would be interrupted in a traditional network environment, the network link in the Dfs tree can be modified to point to a replacement resource without interruption to user access. The Dfs link to the resource can be remapped to the equivalent resource while the map of the Dfs tree is maintained. Users continue to access the resource with the same Dfs path as before.

- **Drive mappings** Drive mappings can be all but eliminated with a Dfs structure in place. Instead of mapping a drive letter to a shared resource on each server, the user accesses multiple resources through a single Dfs tree.

- **Fault tolerance and load balancing** Since Dfs can be configured to have multiple providers for a specific resource, the load on any single resource provider is not higher than the load on any other provider, as Dfs randomly selects from the list of providers when a resource is accessed. In this same way, if a resource provider becomes unavailable, user access to the resource is handled through the alternates, ensuring that the resource is always available.

- **Network permissions** Dfs makes use of existing network permissions for shared resources. No additional security configuration is required to access a resource through Dfs.

- **Integration with Internet Information Services (IIS)** IIS can be configured to use file resources through a Dfs tree. In the same way resource administration is provided to users, IIS directories and links can benefit from the load balancing, fault tolerance, and high reliability of access with Dfs.

Sharing Folders Using Dfs

Dfs services are automatically installed with Windows 2000. While the service can be started, stopped, and suspended on the server, it cannot be removed. Access to the Dfs services is provided through a Dfs root. The Dfs root contains nodes that point to shared resources on the network.

There are two types of Dfs roots: stand-alone and fault-tolerant.

Stand-alone Distributed File System (Dfs) Root

Stand-alone Dfs roots have the following characteristics:

- Stand-alone Dfs information is stored in the registry of the server hosting the Dfs root.

- Stand-alone Dfs roots are limited to a single level of Dfs nodes.

- Stand-alone Dfs roots are not fault-tolerant, as they are a single point of failure in the network. These roots have no replication or backup services.

Installing Dfs on a Single System   A stand-alone Dfs root is created with the New Dfs Root Wizard. The wizard can be started with the Distributed File System Snap-in. Here are the steps to complete the wizard.

- At the Select the Dfs Root Type screen, select the Create a stand-alone Dfs root radio button.

- At the Specify the Host Server for the Dfs Root screen, specify the network connection for the resources in the Dfs tree. Any Windows 2000 server can host a Dfs root.

- At the Specify the Dfs Share screen, select an existing share from the root server or create a new share in a new or existing folder.

- At the Name the Dfs Root screen, modify the name of the Dfs tree, if necessary, and type a description of the share in the Comment text box.

- At the Completing the New Root Wizard screen, verify that the information presented about the share is correct. Click Back to make changes to the configuration, or click Finish to complete the wizard.

Fault-Tolerant (Domain-Based) Distributed File System Root (Dfs)

Fault-tolerant (domain-based) Dfs roots have the following characteristics:

- Fault-tolerant Dfs roots exist in the Active Directory and rely on multiple servers to respond to requests for Dfs resources.

- Changes to a Dfs tree are automatically synchronized and published with Active Directory services, which ensures that a Dfs root structure can be recovered in the event of a catastrophic failure.

- Fault-tolerant Dfs roots must reside on an NTFS 5.0 disk partition and must be hosted on a Windows 2000 domain controller.

exam

ⓌＡｔｃｈ

Make sure you understand the difference between a stand-alone Dfs server and a fault-tolerant Dfs server.

Dfs Child Nodes

Dfs child nodes are the links that connect the user browsing the Dfs tree to the shared resource elsewhere on the network. Each node appears as a folder within the Dfs tree, but opening the node in the tree actually makes the network connection to the remote resource. The location of the actual resource cannot be determined from the Dfs hierarchy; all open resources maintain their Dfs path when path information is requested or displayed.

Designing a Dfs Shared Folder System

Designing an efficient Dfs system requires planning on your part and input from your user community. First, identify resources that will be accessed by a majority of clients in your user community. Specifically target geographically distributed common information shares, such as Human Resources documentation that is stored on multiple servers that are positioned physically and logically close to large groups of clients. If possible, you may want to set up servers centrally located near large clusters of users solely for the purpose of providing Dfs shares. Next, poll your user community to learn what shared resources they access frequently. Include these resources in your Dfs plan as well. Finally, request that your user community provide you with regular updates for resources they use. Including these resources in the Dfs system will make them easier for your users to access, and getting feedback from your user community helps you to be aware of their needs and activities.

In a small computing environment, you can set up a stand-alone Dfs root on a server in your network and create all Dfs nodes on that server. You will need to make sure this server is available during all times that your user community would be using it to access Dfs resources. Depending on your environment, you may not need multiple levels of Dfs links or the added reliability of a domain-based Dfs root.

In a larger environment, specifically one that is geographically dispersed, you would set up a domain-based Dfs root. This would store the Dfs root information in the Active Directory, meaning that users could locate the Dfs root quickly no matter what part of the network they are on. Also, since the Dfs information is stored in the Active Directory and not on a specific server, when a Directory server goes down, the Dfs information is not lost.

FROM THE CLASSROOM

The Ideal Dfs System

Let's examine a fictitious organization that has set up an ideal Dfs system. This organization, the XYZ Company, has offices in New York, Chicago, and Los Angeles. Its Dfs system is set up as a domain-based root, storing the root information in the Active Directory, so it is replicated to Directory servers in each of the cities. In addition, information that is important to all employees of the company is stored on a set of servers, one set in New York, one set in Chicago, and one set in Los Angeles. These servers are replicating their file systems so that when Human Resources in New York changes a document on the server in New York, that change is automatically replicated to the servers in Chicago and Los Angeles. The Dfs links for Human Resources are set up to point to the shares for the servers in New York, Chicago, and Los Angeles so that when

an employee in New York tries to access a document, it is served to him off a New York server. Should that New York server go down, however, the request would be serviced by either the Chicago or Los Angeles servers, and the employee would not be aware of any problems. In addition, local resources specific to each of the offices can be grouped under Dfs links specific to that area. The real advantage to this is when an executive from the New York office is in the Los Angeles office for a week, she uses the same Dfs tree to access resources back in her home office. Any companywide resources she may access are delivered to her off the local servers, cutting down on network traffic across the wide-area links. Also, any specific resources she needs to access from her home office are still available and presented to her as usual.

—Eriq Oliver Neale

How Clients Access and Use Dfs Shared Folders

Dfs resources can be accessed by a number of Microsoft client platforms. Table 6-8 lists the supported platforms and the way in which the appropriate client software is obtained.

Dfs roots can be served off of Windows NT servers as well, but these roots can only be stand-alone roots, as Windows NT 4.0 does not participate in the Active Directory model. Windows 2000 servers can host stand-alone or domain-based Dfs roots.

Clients access the resources in the Dfs tree by accessing the Dfs root via the UNC path to the root or by mapping a drive to the Dfs root share. Either way, the client sees the Dfs resources as folders in the share and is not necessarily aware that the folder contents being used are not on the Dfs root server.

TABLE 6-8	Platform	Dfs Client
Dfs Client Availability for Microsoft Platforms	DOS, Windows 3.x, Windows for Workgroups, NetWare server	No Dfs client available.
	Windows 95	Client version 4.x and 5.0 can be downloaded.
	Windows 98	Includes 4.x and 5.0 client for stand-alone Dfs roots. Client version 5.0 for domain-based roots can be downloaded.
	Windows NT 4.0 with Service Pack 3 or later	Client version 4.x and 5.0 included for stand-alone Dfs roots. Cannot access domain-based Dfs roots.
	Windows 2000	Client version 5.0 included.

CertCam 6-2

EXERCISE 6-2

Creating and Publishing a Dfs Root

This exercise will lead you through the steps of setting up a domain-based Dfs root on a server and adding Dfs links to the root. The exercise will use the shared folder created in Exercise 6-1 as the root for the Dfs tree, so you will need to complete the steps in Exercise 6-1 now if you have not already done so.

1. Open the Dfs snap-in from Start | Programs | Administrative Tools | Distributed File System.

2. Highlight Distributed File System in the left window, then select Action | New Dfs Root....

3. Select the Create a domain Dfs root radio button, as shown:

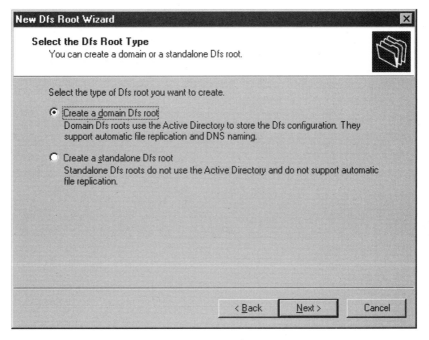

4. Select the host domain for the Dfs root. Accept the default domain selected (xyz.com in these figures).

5. Type the name of the host server for the Dfs root, **server01.xyz.com** for this exercise. You can click the Browse... button to search the network for the server to use.

6. Click the Use an existing share: radio button and select Public from the pop-up menu, as shown in the illustration below. You can also create a new share on the server in this window.

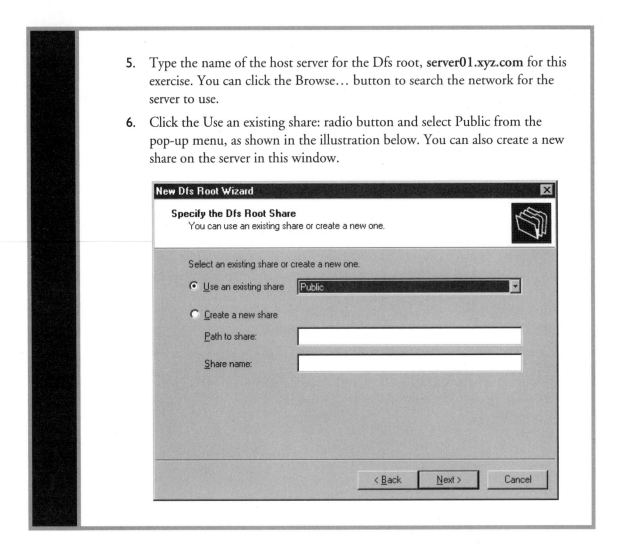

7. Type the name and comment for the Dfs root, as shown in the illustration below. This name is how the Dfs root will be accessed on the network. The UNC path for the Dfs root is displayed in the top portion of the window.

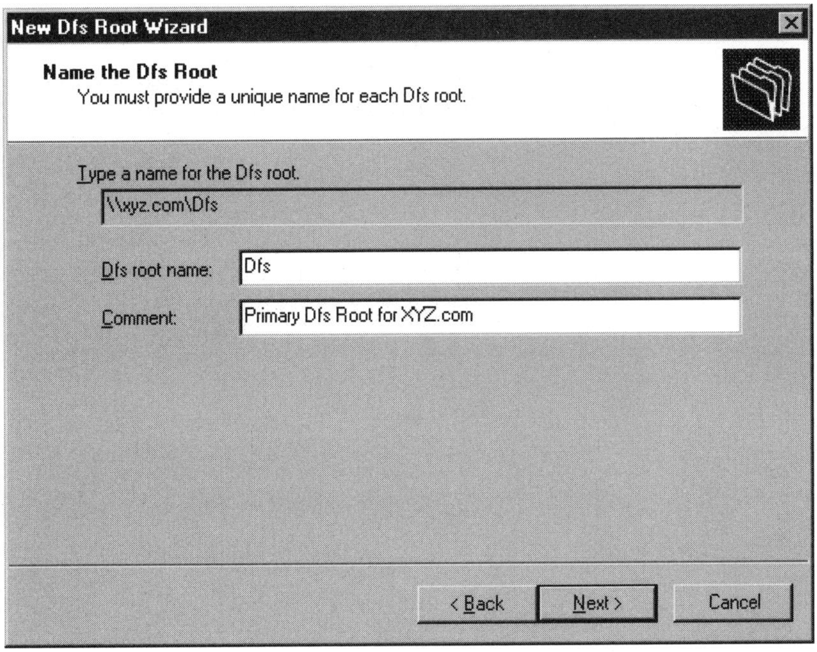

8. Verify the information in the wizard is correct before finishing the process. The illustration below shows that the Dfs root Dfs will be created in the xyz.com domain using the Public share off the server01.xyz.com server.

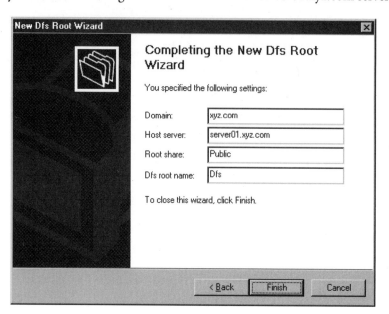

9. The new Dfs root is now visible in the Distributed File System snap-in display, as seen in the illustration below. The Dfs contents can now be accessed with the UNC path \\xyz.com\Dfs. In addition, accessing the \\Server01\Public share will also navigate the Dfs tree.

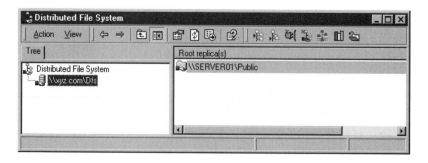

10. Create three additional shares on your server according to Table 6-9.

TABLE 6-9	Share Name	Description
Server shares	HR	Human Resources
	MKTG	Marketing
	R&D	Research & Development

11. Highlight the Dfs root entry and select Action | New Dfs Link....

12. Create a link for the HR share, as shown:

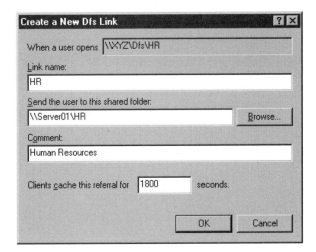

13. Repeat steps 11 and 12 for the MKTG and R&D shares.

14. When all the links are complete, the Distributed File System snap-in window should look like the illustration below, with the R&D link selected.

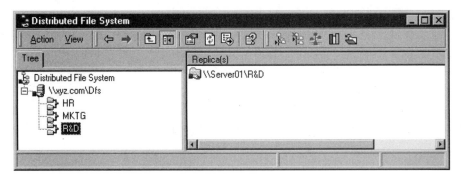

15. Open the Run... window and type *domain_name**dfs_root* (**xyz.com****Dfs** in this example) to open the Dfs root. Your window should look similar to the following:

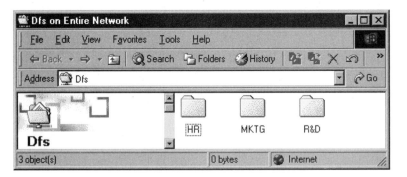

Now that you have a better understanding of how Windows 2000 implements distributed file systems, here are some real-world and exam scenarios you may encounter.

SCENARIO & SOLUTION

I've set up a Dfs root on one of my servers and have it configured to point to multiple shares for each Dfs node I have configured. I had to take the server down for emergency maintenance last week for about an hour, and my entire Dfs tree disappeared from the network. What happened?	The Dfs root you set up was a stand-alone root, not a fault-tolerant root. When the server hosting the stand-alone root went down, the entire Dfs tree went with it. Using a fault-tolerant Dfs root will store the Dfs tree information in the Active Directory, sharing the information among multiple servers. Then, when one of the servers goes off-line, the Dfs tree is still available to the user community.
I had a fault-tolerant Dfs root set up on one of my servers that I took out of service. I moved the Dfs root folder to a new server and fixed the configuration in the Active Directory to point to this new server. I have a few users who now say they cannot access the Dfs tree. What happened?	Your users were probably accessing the Dfs tree off the direct server share instead of the Active Directory share. Remember that pointing to the direct share provides the same Dfs access as pointing to the Active Directory root. When you took down the server, the share they were using disappeared. Have them re-create their access to the Dfs root through the Active Directory share so this won't happen again.

CERTIFICATION OBJECTIVE 6.03

Monitor, Configure, Troubleshoot, and Control Access to Printers

Microsoft Windows 2000 Server provides network printing services for a variety of computer platforms, not just Windows 2000 clients. The server routes print jobs from client computers to printers connected directly to the server through a serial or parallel port, or to printers connected through a network interface. Either way, the services and utilities provided with Windows 2000 Server ease administration of large numbers of printers in a network environment. This section of the chapter will introduce you to the printing terminology used with Windows 2000, show you how to set up and configure a variety of printer devices on a Windows 2000 server, and introduce you to tools and techniques for monitoring and troubleshooting printer issues.

Windows 2000 Printing Terminology

In order to work efficiently with the Windows 2000 printing environment, you must first understand the terminology used to describe the printing process. Here are a few key terms that will be used extensively in this section.

- **Print Device** The hardware that actually does the printing. A print device is one of two types as defined in Windows 2000: local or network-interface. A local print device connects directly to the print server with a serial or parallel interface. A network-interface print device connects to the printer across the network and must have its own network interface or be connected to an external network adapter.

- **Print Server** A computer that manages printing on the network. A print server can be a dedicated computer hosting multiple printers, or it can run as one of many processes on a nondedicated computer.

- **Print Driver** A software program used by Windows 2000 and other computer programs to connect with printers and plotters. It translates information sent to it into commands that the print device can understand.

■ **Printer**   The software interface between the document and the print device. The logical interface between the user and the print device allows the user to specify a print job's destination, the time it will be printed, and how other aspects of the process will be handled by the print server.

Network Printing Environment

Configuring the ideal printing environment can be almost as complicated as planning the ideal network environment for client computers. Here are a few issues you will need to consider in planning the printing environment.

Dedicated and Nondedicated Servers

A dedicated printer server is a Windows 2000 server whose only role is to provide printing services. The server does not provide directory space for users other than storage for spooled print jobs. It does not provide authentication services, does not host database services, does not act as a DNS server, and so on. A dedicated print server can host several hundred printers and print queues, however. Though it may not be obvious, the printing process does have an impact on the performance of the server providing the printing services. Spooling several dozen large print files to network printers can affect the performance of other tasks running on a print server, and those other tasks can slow down the printing process in turn as well. An environment with a large number of printers or print jobs should strongly consider using at least one dedicated print server.

A nondedicated print server is a Windows 2000 server that hosts printing services in addition to other services. A domain controller, database server, or DNS server can provide printing services as well, but should be used only for a smaller number of printers or for printers that are not heavily used. Anyone setting up a nondedicated print server should monitor the performance of the printing process and the other tasks running on the server and be prepared to modify the server configuration if the performance drops below acceptable levels.

A Windows 2000 Professional workstation could also be used as a nondedicated print server. This solution can be used if a user has a local printer that he or she would like to share with other nearby users. Due to the limitation of the number of connections supported by Windows 2000 Professional and the other types of applications running on a Windows 2000 Professional workstation, printing performance will not be very efficient. In addition, only DOS, Windows, and some UNIX computers can print to printers served by Windows 2000 Professional. Configuring other types of printers requires Windows 2000 Server.

Network Printing Configurations

A number of different printing configurations are possible with Windows 2000 Server and local and network printers. Four basic configurations will serve most printing needs.

- **Local Printer** A print device that is directly attached, via a parallel or serial cable, to the computer that is providing the printing services (see Figure 6-4). For a Windows 2000 Professional workstation, a local printer is one that is connected to the workstation. For a Windows 2000 Server, a local printer is one that is connected to the server. Drivers for the print device must reside on the computer that connects to the printer.

- **Network Printer** A print device that has a built-in network interface or connects directly to a dedicated network interface (see Figure 6-5). Both workstations and servers can be configured to print directly to the network printer, and the network printer controls its own printer queue, determining which jobs from which clients will print in which order. Printing clients have no direct control over the printer queue and cannot see other print jobs being submitted to the printer. Administration of a network printer is difficult. Drivers for the print device must reside on the computer that connects to the printer.

FIGURE 6-4

Local printer connection

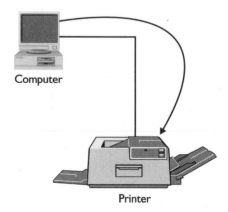

Computer

Printer

FIGURE 6-5

Network printer
connection

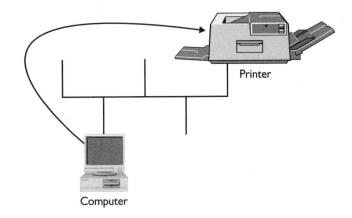

- **Remote Local Printer** A print device connected directly to a print server but accessed by another print server or by workstations (see Figure 6-6). The queue for the print device exists on the server, and the print server controls job priority, print order, and queue administration. Client computers submit print jobs to the server and can observe the queue to monitor the printing process on the server. Drivers for the print device are loaded onto the client computer from the print server.

- **Remote Network Printer** A network printer connected to a print server that is accessed by client workstations or other print servers (see Figure 6-7).

FIGURE 6-6

Remote local
printer
connection

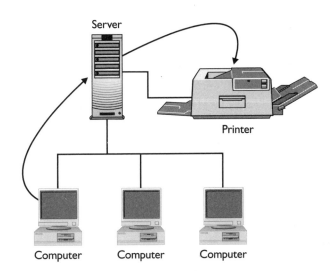

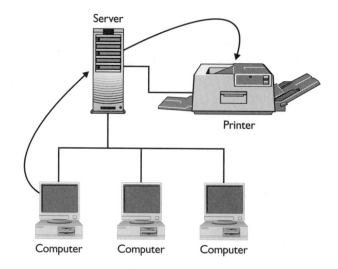

FIGURE 6-7

Remote network printer connection

Like the remote local printer, the printer queue is controlled by the print server, meaning that the client computers submit their print jobs to the print server, rather than to the print device directly. This allows for server administration and monitoring of the printer queues. Drivers for the print device are loaded onto the client computers from the print server.

In most cases when print servers are used, client computers will see the printers as remote local printers or remote network printers, giving network administrators better control over the printing environment.

Even though Microsoft's terminology relating to the printing process can be confusing, it is a common topic on exams. Be sure you are comfortable with the terminology before taking the exam.

Installing and Sharing Printers

Printers must be installed and shared on a server before other clients can access the print device. The Add Printer Wizard is used to create local and network print objects on a server, which can then be shared out to the network.

Installing a Local Printer

Local printers are the easiest types of printers to set up on a Windows 2000 Professional workstation or Windows 2000 Server. To install a local printer, start the Add Printer Wizard, and select Local Printer rather than Network Printer in the wizard (see Figure 6-8). Then follow the instructions in the wizard to select the local port used to connect the printer. Most modern printers can be detected and configured automatically by Windows 2000. If your printer is not automatically detected, you will be asked to provide drivers for the printer before configuration can continue. Once the printer is configured, print a test page to verify proper communication between the computer and the printer.

Installing a Network Printer

Network printers are more common in larger computing environments and generally perform better than local printers. Setting up network printers is more involved than setting up a local printer in that there are many types of network interfaces that can be used to communicate with the printer.

FIGURE 6-8

Select Local or Network Printer

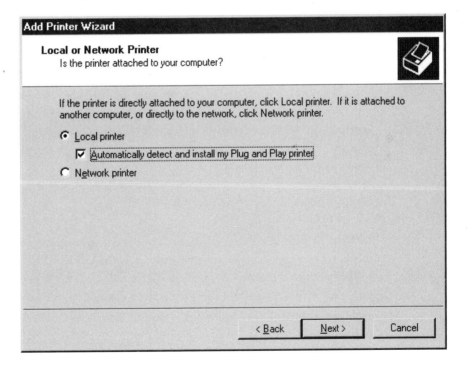

Add Printer Wizard

Local or Network Printer
Is the printer attached to your computer?

If the printer is directly attached to your computer, click Local printer. If it is attached to another computer, or directly to the network, click Network printer.

- ⦿ Local printer
    - ☑ Automatically detect and install my Plug and Play printer
- ○ Network printer

< Back   Next >   Cancel

TCP/IP Printer Ports Many modern large-capacity printers provide a network interface that uses TCP/IP for communication. One popular printer manufacturer that does this is Hewlett-Packard with its LaserJet series printers and the JetDirect network cards. These devices must be configured to communicate with the TCP/IP network just like the client computers.

To set up a TCP/IP port connection for a printer, you will still define the printer as a local printer in the Add Printer Wizard. Instead of selecting one of the hardware ports, however, you will select the Create a new port: button and choose the Standard TCP/IP Port option from the Type: pop-up menu, as shown in Figure 6-9. Hewlett-Packard, Lexmark, and other printer vendors will provide additional TCP/IP interface drivers for communicating with their network devices. When those drivers are installed on the server, the network device will appear in the pop-up menu in addition to the Standard TCP/IP Port option. If you are creating an interface to a Hewlett-Packard printer with a JetDirect interface, use the JetDirect port option instead of the Standard TCP/IP Port option in the Type: pop-up menu, and likewise for other printer vendors. Next, you will specify the IP address of the printer; then Windows 2000 should autodetect the type of printer and autoconfigure the settings for it. Otherwise, you will be prompted to provide drivers for the printer to proceed with the configuration. Once the printer is configured, print a test page to ensure that the communication between the computer and the printer is correct.

It is important to note that if the print server can create a TCP/IP printing connection to the print device, so can other TCP/IP clients. Having multiple clients print directly to the print device negates the management of the printer queue centrally and adds unneeded complexity to the troubleshooting process. In a large printing environment, it is best to make printing through the print server the easiest way of getting printing services; otherwise knowledgeable users will bypass the print server and print directly to the print device, increasing problems for all users and administrators.

LPR/LPD Printer Port One type of remote printing that may be encountered in a cross-platform computing environment is the UNIX LPR/LPD printing service. LPR (line printer remote) is a process that spools a print job to a remote print spool that is advertised by LPD. LPD (line printer daemon) is the server process that advertises printer queues and accepts incoming print submissions, which are then routed to the print device.

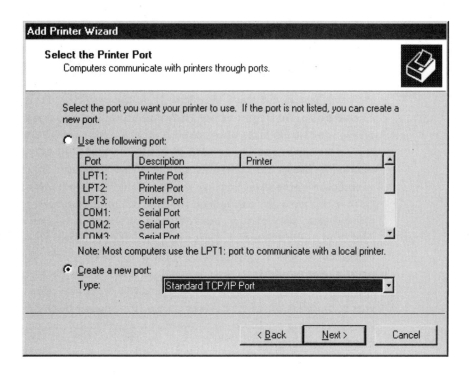

FIGURE 6-9

Select Standard
TCP/IP Port

Microsoft Windows 2000 can use LPR/LPD to print to an existing UNIX LPD server or act as an LPD server for incoming UNIX print jobs. If an existing UNIX print server is already in place, it is preferable to create a printer that points to the LPD server, allowing Windows clients to print to the existing server, rather than re-create the printer configuration and have Windows 2000 act as the LPD server for the UNIX clients. The implementations of LPR vary widely among UNIX vendors, and a given LPR system on a UNIX client is not guaranteed to communicate correctly with the LPD service on a Windows 2000 server.

To set up an LPD printer on a Windows 2000 server, open the Add Printer Wizard, click the Local Printer radio button, and uncheck the Automatically detect and install my Plug and Play printer check box, then click Next. In the next window, click the Create a new port radio button and select LPR Port under the Type: pop-up menu. In the next window you will specify the name or IP address of the LPD host and the name of the print queue for the print device on that host. After the connection is verified, you will follow the remainder of the standard printer installation process.

on the job

At one site where I worked, we relied very heavily on LPR printing from our Windows servers. Even though we were using primarily Hewlett-Packard printers equipped with JetDirect cards, we did not use the JetDirect interface because of the excessive network traffic generated by the cards. Using an LPR interface to the print devices cut down significantly on the traffic on the network.

At one point, we began experiencing seemingly random hangs with the printer queues. We set up a scheduled script that would shut down and restart the print spooler service on the servers at 2:00 A.M. to clear out any conflict in the queues, but this improved the situation only minimally. After spending months investigating the problem, we finally discovered that several printer drivers were configured for bidirectional communication with the print device, even though the LPR print service is one-way communication. The driver, and therefore the server, would encounter a situation in which it expected to hear a response from the print device, and all activity on that print queue would stop until it received a response from the print device or the spooler service was restarted. Since the print device recognized that it was connected via LPR, it never sent any response back to the print server. Turning off the bidirectional communication setting in the drivers fixed the problem.

Unfortunately, some drivers we encountered enabled bidirectional communication by default, and this was set when a new printer with the driver was added. We were hoping that the new printer drivers for Windows 2000 would not behave this way. Unfortunately, some still do. So when these printers are set up on these servers, every printer configuration must be checked to ensure that bidirectional communication is turned off for each queue.

AppleTalk Printing Devices   Another type of remote printer is the AppleTalk printing device. Like a TCP/IP printer, an AppleTalk printer can be connected directly to an AppleTalk network or shared across the network through an AppleShare print server. Like the TCP/IP printers, a large number of modern, high-capacity PostScript printers can be configured to communicate with an AppleTalk network as well as a TCP/IP network. In fact, many Hewlett-Packard LaserJet printers have JetDirect cards that will speak TCP/IP and AppleTalk at the same time.

The advantage of having native support for AppleTalk printing devices in Windows 2000 is that printing services can be established in a multiplatform environment with a single printing interface. In other words, a single print queue can be established that will support both Windows clients and AppleTalk clients so that all users of the printer can monitor all activity to the printer from one location. Administration and maintenance of the printer queue is also simplified by having one printer interface support multiple client platforms.

Setting up AppleTalk print services requires that the AppleTalk protocol be installed and configured on the server. This installation does not occur by default when the server is installed, so the protocol usually must be added after the server is up and running. The process is the same as for TCP/IP printing in the Add Printer Wizard. After selecting a Local Printer install, create a new port using the AppleTalk printer port, as shown in Figure 6-10. You will then have to browse your AppleTalk network to locate the printer. Once the printer is selected, you have the option to "capture" the printer on the AppleTalk network. Capturing an AppleTalk printer means that only the Windows 2000 print server can speak directly to the printer. The captured printer advertises itself only to the print server and not to any other clients on the AppleTalk network, rendering it "invisible" to other AppleTalk devices. All AppleTalk clients would have to submit print jobs to the print server, because that would be the only printing device advertised on the network. This has the advantage that all printing to the AppleTalk printer is routed through the print server, meaning that all print queue management can take place on the server. The disadvantage is that if the print server goes down, the AppleTalk printer begins advertising itself on the network again, and AppleTalk clients can, and usually will, create new printer interfaces to the printer directly, leading to mass confusion if and when print server problems are encountered. In a stable printing environment, though, this occurs very rarely.

Sharing Printers

Once a printer has been created on a print server, it must be shared before any clients can use the service. Sharing a printer is very similar to sharing a folder on a server, and many of the same permissions concepts apply to both printer shares and folder shares. Printer shares can be set up during the printer installation process, which is detailed in Exercise 6-3. Otherwise, all printers share creation, and maintenance is performed in the Share tab of the printer's Properties dialog.

There are four elements in the Share tab of a printer's Properties dialog. The Not shared: button, when enabled, deactivates all sharing features for the printer. The Shared as: button, when enabled, turns on sharing for the printer and allows you to specify the share name for the printer in the adjacent text field. When a share name is specified for a printer, the name should be descriptive enough that a user can easily identify the location of the printer by the name, but it should be short enough that it can be found by all flavors of the Windows OS. Windows 95 and Windows

FIGURE 6-10

Creating an
AppleTalk printer
port

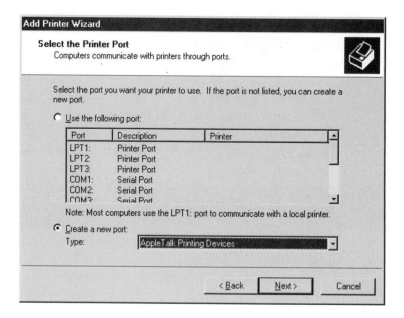

98 cannot see printer shares that have very long names or contain spaces within the share name.

When the Shared as: button is enabled, the List in the Directory check box becomes active. Turning on this check box will advertise the printer in the Active Directory, making it easier for users to locate the printer when they know the printer name. Otherwise, users must search for the printer name by searching through the print server's shares to locate the desired printer.

The Additional Drivers... button opens a dialog where print drivers for additional Windows operating systems can be loaded on the server. In an environment with multiple versions of the Windows OS accessing printing services, it is best to load the print drivers for those OSs on the server so the client can automatically download the appropriate driver when installing a printer for the first time. If the driver for a printer is not loaded on the server, the client will have to locate and install the driver manually before being able to print to the printer on the server. Windows 2000 clients do not load printer drivers locally when connecting to server shares. Like earlier Windows NT clients, the Windows 2000 workstation client uses the print drivers on the server instead of downloading the drivers locally.

In addition to setting up the share name for the printer, the printer can be given specific network permissions to allow or prevent printing for users or groups of users on the network. Additional information about the specific printer security permissions is detailed in Managing Printers and Print Servers section later in the chapter.

EXERCISE 6-3

Installing and Sharing a TCP/IP Network Printer

In this exercise, you will set up a local printer connected via a TCP/IP port that will then be shared out on the network. This exercise will use the Standard TCP/IP port to identify the network printer.

1. Open the Printers folder and double-click the Add Printer icon.

2. Click the Local Printer radio button and turn off the Automatically detect my printer check box. Click Next.

3. Click the Create a new port radio button and select Standard TCP/IP Port from the Type: pop-up menu. Click Next.

4. The Add Standard TCP/IP Port Wizard starts. In the Printer Name or IP Address: field, type the IP address of the printer as **10.1.1.101.** The Port Name: field will automatically adjust its value to IP_10.1.1.101, as shown in the illustration below. Click Next.

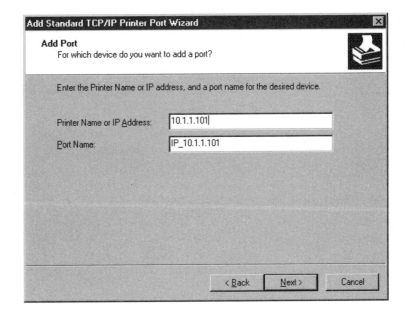

5. At this point, you will get an error that the wizard cannot connect to the printer, because the IP address specified does not exist. Click Next. Now you will see the summary page of the Add Standard TCP/IP Port Wizard, as shown in the illustration below. Click Finish.

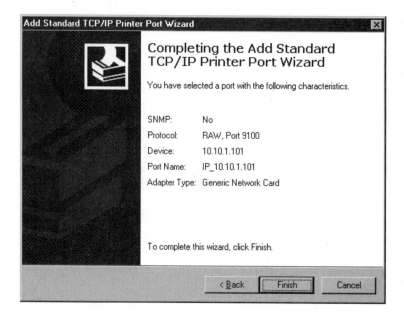

6. Select the printer manufacturer as HP under Manufacturers: and the printer type as HP LaserJet 4000 Series PCL under Printers: as shown in the following illustration. Click Next.

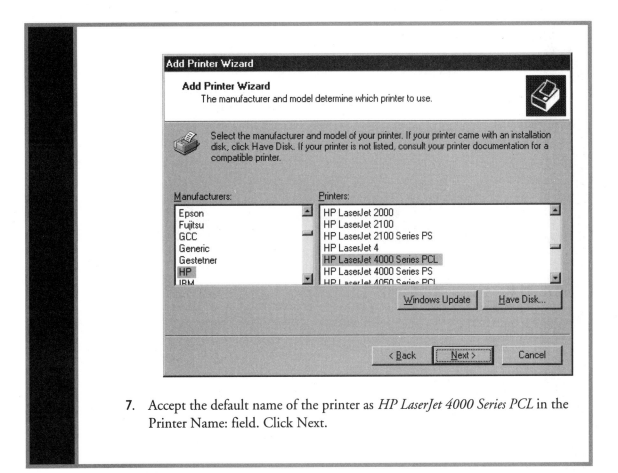

7. Accept the default name of the printer as *HP LaserJet 4000 Series PCL* in the Printer Name: field. Click Next.

8. Click the Share as: radio button and specify the share name of the printer as **HPLJ4000** in the field, as shown in the following illustration. Click Next.

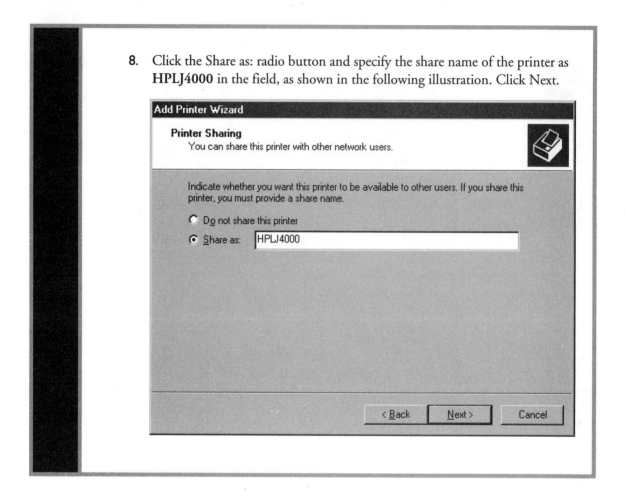

9. In the Location: text box, type text that describes the location of the printer, such as **Second Floor Public Printer Area.** In the Comment: text box, type text that describes the printer, such as **Second Floor Public Laser Printer,** as shown in the following illustration. Click Next.

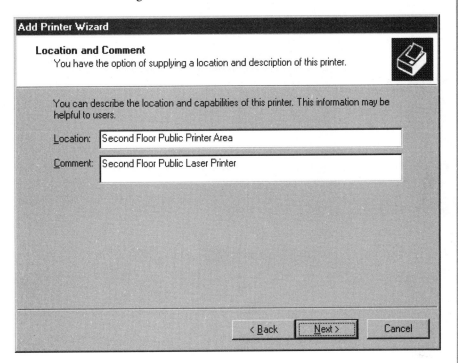

10. Click the No radio button in the Print Test Page window and click Next.

11. Review the information displayed in the Completing the Add Printer Wizard window, shown in the following illustration, and click Finish.

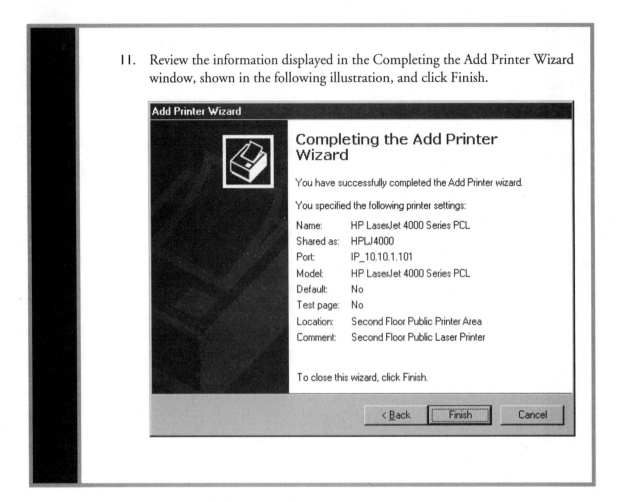

Now you will see a printer icon named HP LaserJet 4000 in the Printers window, similar to Figure 6-11. The icon will have a hand beneath the printer, indicating that the printer is shared. Other clients on the network will see the printer shared as HPLJ4000.

Publishing Printers in the Active Directory

Advertising printers in the Active Directory makes it easier for clients to locate printers on the network. A well-planned printing environment will be very easy for

Printers window
after new printer
is added

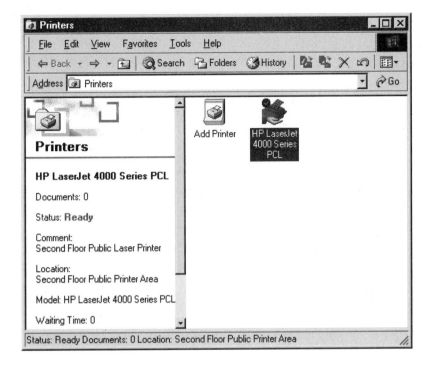

clients to browse and easily locate printers geographically close to them for use. Here
are a few key points regarding printers and the Active Directory.

- Print servers must publish information for their own printers in the Active
  Directory.

- When printers are updated on the print server, the print server automatically
  updates the information in the Active Directory and those changes propagate
  through the entire directory.

- Printers are entered into the Active Directory as printQueue objects.

- By default, any printer shared by a print server is advertised in the Active
  Directory.

- The printQueue object is located in the print server's computer object in the
  Active Directory.

- When a print server disappears from the network, its printers are removed
  from the Active Directory.

When printers are shared with the Add Printer Wizard, the shared printer is listed in the Active Directory by default. In order to remove a printer listing from the Active Directory, turn off the List in the Directory check box in the Sharing tab of the printer's Properties dialog box.

How Clients Locate Published Printers

Once a printer has been shared by a print server, it must be set up on the client before the client can print. This process involves locating the printer on the network, setting up the logical printer interface on the client, and installing printer drivers on the client. For Microsoft clients, these processes are straightforward and, for the most part, automatic. Other steps must be performed to set up printers on non-Microsoft clients.

There are several ways to locate a printer to set up on the client workstation.

Add Printer Wizard   All clients running a version of the Windows operating system (Windows 2000, Windows NT, Windows 98, and Windows 95) can use the Add Printer Wizard to create a printer entry on the client. This is the same Add Printer Wizard described earlier to create and share a printer on a print server. The Windows 2000 version of the Add Printer Wizard has more options than the wizard in other versions of Windows, but many of the same methods can be used to get the printer set up on the client.

To create a printer with the Add Printer Wizard, you will start the wizard and select the Network Printer radio button in the Local or Network Printer window of the wizard. You will then choose how to locate the printer on the network. (The three search options are shown in Figure 6-12.) You can search the Active Directory for the printer object, or you can type the UNC name or URL for the printer, if known. Once you have found the printer on the network, the printer object will be created locally and any necessary printer drivers will be downloaded to the client. As with printer installation on a print server, you will have the option of printing a test page to confirm the successful creation of the printer object.

Searching the Active Directory   In addition to using the Add Printer Wizard, you can locate the printer object on the network yourself and install the printer directly. If you know the name of the printer in the Active Directory, you can search for it using the Start | Search | For Printers interface in Windows 2000. Only Windows 2000 clients can search the Active Directory for printers. In addition

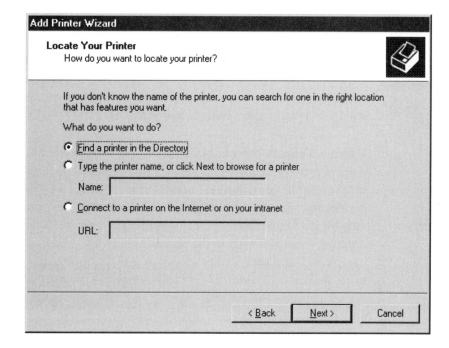

FIGURE 6-12

Three methods
for locating a
printer in the
Add Printer
Wizard

to searching for a printer by name, you can also search on printer location or capabilities. Once the printer is located, you can right-click the printer and select Install from the pop-up menu.

UNC Name   If you know the full network path to the printer, you can connect to the printer using the Run command on the Start menu from any Windows 95 or newer client. Type the UNC name of the printer in the Open box, and click OK. If the printer has not already been installed on your system, you will see a note that the printer must be set up before it can be accessed. Clicking OK in the note window will proceed to install the printer on the client.

If you know only the UNC name of the print server hosting the printer, you can open the server the same way as was described earlier. This will open a window listing all the public shares on the server, if any, and all the shared printers. Once you locate the correct printer in the window, you can double-click it, which will have the same result as typing the full UNC name in the Run command, or you can right-click the printer icon and select Install from the pop-up menu. Either method will install the printer, but the latter choice will yield one less warning window.

Browsing the Network   Another method for installing a printer is to browse through My Network Places. You can navigate through the network map to locate the print server, then open the server to choose from the printer shares listed. This method for locating and installing a printer can be helpful if you do not already know what server a printer is on. Otherwise, it makes more sense to use one of the more direct methods for locating a printer.

Using a Web Browser   Clients running Windows 2000 can use a Web browser to locate and install printers off the print server. Type the URL for the print server as **http://<servername>/printers** to see a list of all printers supported by the print server, similar to the list shown in Figure 6-13. You can also use the share name of the printer in the URL, such as **http://<servername>/<printername>** to open the browser directly to the printer. Click the Connect link in the browser window to install the printer connection. In either case, you must have permission to use the printer in order to view and install the printer via the Web interface, as the Web browser will use your network authentication to determine your access to the printer.

The print server must be configured to accept printer requests via the Web interface. If the printer is served on a Windows 2000 server, the server must have Microsoft Internet Information Server (IIS) installed and running. If the printer is served on a Windows 2000 Professional workstation, the workstation must be running Microsoft Peer Web Services (PWS).

FIGURE 6-13

Viewing available printers through a Web interface

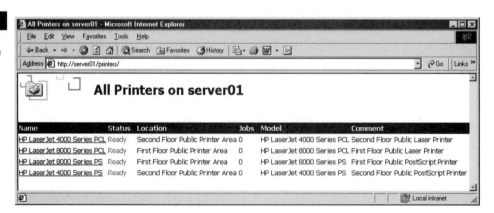

e x a m
ⓦa t c h

Be sure you know the various ways for locating printers on the network.
Questions about locating printers are common.

Managing Printers and Print Servers

Managing printing services is more than just creating printer objects on a server and establishing printer shares. For a variety of reasons, access to certain printers may need to be limited to certain groups or individuals. It may be necessary to redirect print jobs to different printers when printer or server maintenance is performed. You may also be called upon to clear hung jobs from a printer queue when other users are unable to print as a result.

Printer Permissions

Printer permissions are established through the Security tab in the printer's Properties dialog. The security settings for printer objects are similar to the security settings for folder shares. The default permissions for a printer are shown in Figure 6-14.

FIGURE 6-14

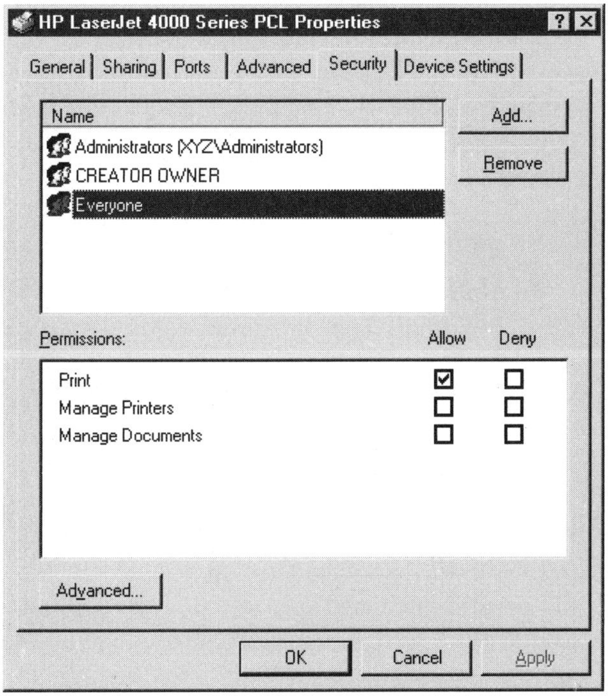

Default printer
security settings

HP LaserJet 4000 Series PCL Properties

General | Sharing | Ports | Advanced | Security | Device Settings

Name	
Administrators (XYZ\Administrators)	Add...
CREATOR OWNER	Remove
Everyone	

Permissions:	Allow	Deny
Print	☑	☐
Manage Printers	☐	☐
Manage Documents	☐	☐

Advanced...

OK | Cancel | Apply

The Everyone Group is given Print permissions by default, meaning that all users can submit print jobs to the printer. In addition, the Creator Owner Group has the Manage Documents permission, meaning that the account that submitted a job to the print queue can modify the settings on the job while it is still in the queue. However, no other users can modify document settings for print jobs they did not submit themselves. The exception to this is the Administrators Group, which is given the Manage Documents permission as well. In addition, the Administrators Group has the Manage Printers permission, which allows administrators to change settings on the printer object itself. Users who have permission to use the printer can see the settings for the printer object but cannot make changes to the configuration.

Administrators may want to delegate management of printers to additional groups of users by creating a Printer Administrators Group, adding those users to that group, and giving that group permissions on the printer to manage the printer and the documents in the queue.

Printer Management

Modern printers are quite complex devices and have many options that can be configured. The majority of the configuration and management of a printer takes place in the Device Settings tab of the printer's Properties dialog, as shown in Figure 6-15.

One important printing feature, configuring separator pages, is not located in the Device Settings tab. A separator page is a document that contains commands sent to the print device for one of two reasons:

- Separating print jobs and identifying the owner of the job
- Switching between printing modes. Many modern printers support at least two printer languages, usually PostScript and the vendor's printer language (such as PCL). The separator page can send instructions to the printer telling the printer what language the following print job uses if the printer cannot automatically detect the language used in the print job.

Windows 2000 comes bundled with four separator page files, stored in the %systemroot%\System32 folder. The files and their functions are described in Table 6-10.

Printers do not have to be set up on the server so that only one queue points to only one print device. Multiple queues can point to the same print device, and

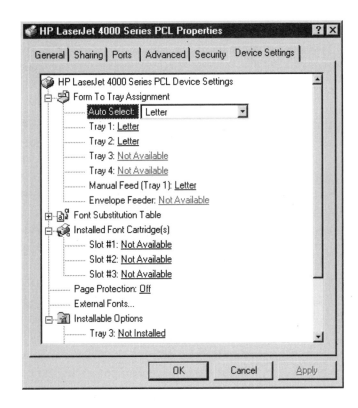

FIGURE 6-15

Print device
options in the
Device Settings
tab

multiple print devices can service the same queue. Depending on your printing
needs, you may set up one or both of these configurations in your environment. The
first scenario is useful to help establish multiple priority queues for a single print

TABLE 6-10	Separator Page File	Description
Description of Bundled Separator Pages	Pcl.sep	Switches the printer to PCL printing mode and prints a page preceding each document.
	Pscript.sep	Switches the printer to PostScript printing mode and prints a page preceding each document.
	Sysprint.sep	Prints a PostScript-compatible page preceding each document.
	Sysprtjp.sep	Prints a PostScript-compatible page preceding each document using Japanese characters.

device (see Figure 6-16). If a print device is shared by a VP, regular employees, and workers who produce large volume printouts, you may set up three queues. The first queue could be set up with normal priority settings and would be usable by everyone. A second queue could be established with high priority settings so that only the VP and his or her delegates could submit jobs to that queue. A third queue could be configured as very low priority and the only one that accepts large document submissions. In this configuration, everyone in the area would have the regular queue set up as the default printer on their computers. If the VP needed to generate a print document quickly and there were a large number of print jobs already in the queue, the document would be placed in the high-priority queue and would begin printing on the print device immediately following the current document. A large job would be printed in the low-priority queue, which would keep it from printing until all other jobs in the normal and high-priority queue finished.

To set the priority on a print queue, open the printer's Properties dialog and click the Advanced tab. This will display the information shown in Figure 6-17. The Priority: picklist contains values from 1 to 99, with 1 being the lowest priority. The queue set up for long print jobs would have a low priority, probably 1. The queue set up for the VP would have a high priority, probably 99. The regular queue would have a priority somewhere between the two values, possibly around 50.

The second scenario is called printer pooling and is ideal for high-volume printing environments. There is no default designation of priorities in this scenario other than that all print jobs need to be printed as quickly as possible. To set up a printer pool, you would need several identical printers and configure them to service the same print queue, which is illustrated in Figure 6-18. When several jobs

FIGURE 6-16

Priority queues printing to a single print device

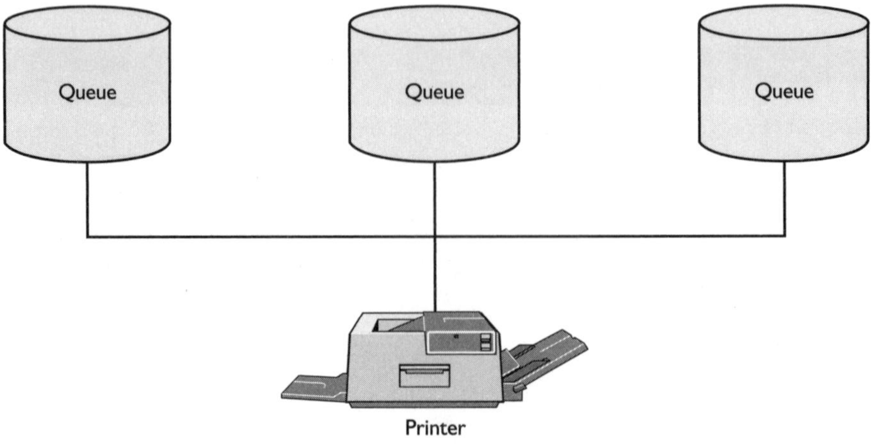

Printer

FIGURE 6-17

Printer
Properties
Advanced tab
Priority setting

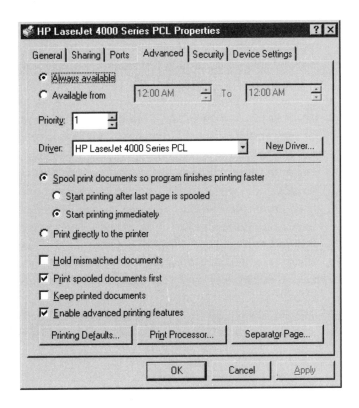

FIGURE 6-18 Printer pooling from a single queue

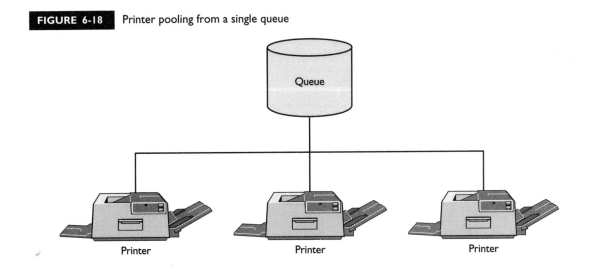

are submitted to the queue, the first job goes to one of the printers. The next job, seeing that one of the printers is already in use, starts printing on the next printer in the pool, and so on. Ideally, you would set up at least two or three high-speed print devices in the same physical location to support this type of print scenario.

To create a printer pool, open the printer's Properties dialog and click the Ports tab, as shown in Figure 6-19. Normally, only one port can be selected in this dialog for each printer. However, turning on the Enable printer pooling check box will let you select multiple ports, and therefore multiple print devices, for a single queue. The print queue will then automatically redirect print devices through all the selected ports, spreading the print load among the print devices connected. Identical print devices must be used, however, as only one print driver can be loaded for the queue, and all the settings for the queue will be applied to all connected print devices. For instance, if one printer does not have a duplexing unit installed but the driver is configured to print duplex by default, any jobs sent to that printer will not print in duplex, and the owner of the job may get understandably upset.

FIGURE 6-19

Printer
Properties Ports
tab with Enable
printer pooling
check box

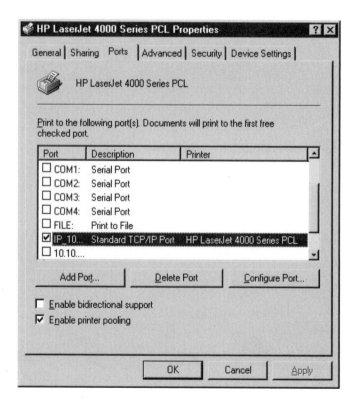

Document Management

Providing printer support is more than connecting the print devices to the network and making them available through printer shares on the print server. In most cases, printer administrators must manage documents in the print queues as well. There may be times when a large job is preventing other users from printing documents, or a document is hung in the queue waiting for a particular form to be loaded at the printer. For these and other reasons, you may need to manipulate the documents in the queue directly.

Managing Documents from Windows 2000   There are several ways to manage print jobs in the queues. The first is to open the printer object on the server and manipulate the jobs in the queue directly. Within the print queue window, you can double-click a print job and modify settings on that job, as shown in Figure 6-20. In this window, you can modify the priority of the specific print job, change the

FIGURE 6-20

Print Job
Properties
General tab

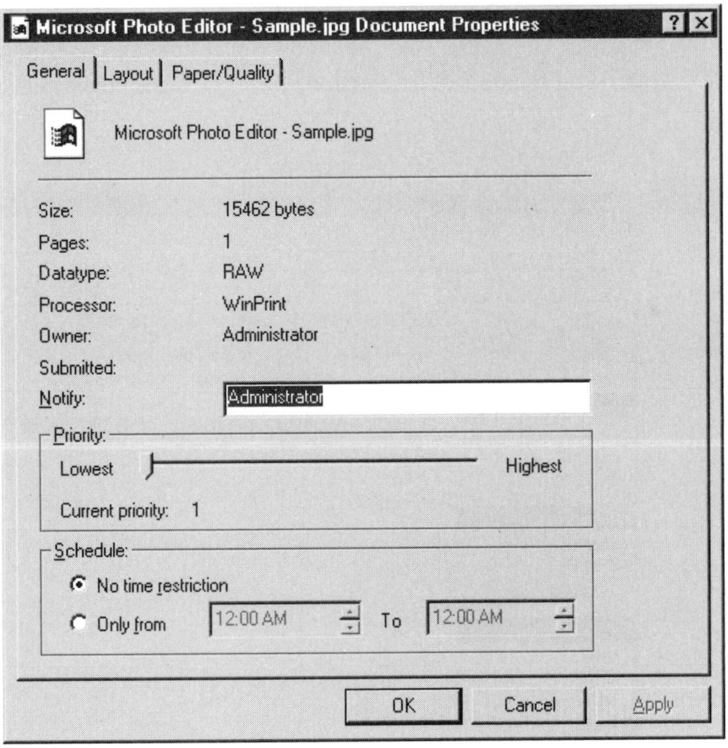

account to be notified when the job has printed, and specify a time restriction on the job. In the Layout and Paper/Quality tabs, you can modify the settings particular to the print device being used.

In addition to modifying the properties on the print job, you can also Pause, Resume, and Cancel the print job from the Document menu in the print queue window. Pausing the job will place the job "on hold," allowing other jobs in the queue to print ahead of it. You can take the job "off hold" by Resuming the job. Canceling the job deletes it from the queue, and the job will not be printed.

Managing Documents with a Web Browser   From a Windows 2000 workstation or server, a Web browser can also be used to manage documents in a Windows 2000 print queue. When you are logged into the Windows 2000 network with an account that has permissions to manage the print queue, you can point your Web browser to the print server's printer URL, usually **http://<servername>/printers**. Then you can click the print queue name to list the jobs active in the queue, as shown in Figure 6-21. Selecting a job in the queue will activate the Pause, Resume, and Cancel links in the Document Actions area of the browser window. These actions have the same effect as the actions just described.

FIGURE 6-21

Windows 2000
Web interface
to print job
management

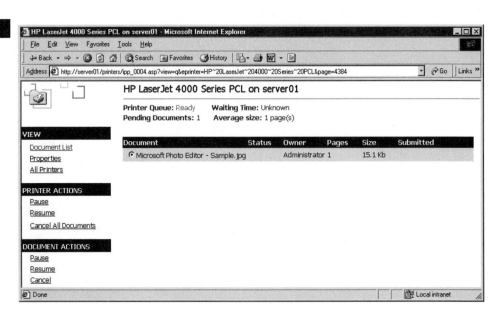

Troubleshooting Printing Problems

There are a number of problems that you can encounter in the printing environment, but most of them are minor in nature and can be resolved easily. The first class of problems deals with the print device itself and will not be detailed here. Essentially, if the printer is unable to perform its own self-checks correctly, it will need to be serviced before any troubleshooting can occur for other related printing problems on the server.

Here are some guidelines for identifying other problems with the printing process.

- Verify that the print device is plugged in and powered on, and that the network connection, if any, to the printer is active.

- Print from a different document or application to rule out issues with the document or program. Problems with a document or application generally revolve around driver conflict or incompatibilities.

- Print to the print device from a different user account to rule out problems with the user account. Problems with the user account generally revolve around permissions.

- Verify that the correct driver is loaded on the server and workstation for the print device. Incorrect drivers can generate garbled printouts or no printouts at all, especially when a PCL driver is used to print to a PostScript printer.

- Verify that the print server can communicate with the print device by printing a test page from the server.

- Verify that the Print Spooler service is enabled and active on the print server.

- Verify that there is enough disk space on the server for print jobs to spool.

- If a print queue appears to be hung and the print device is working properly, stop and restart the print spooler service.

Now that you have a better understanding of how Windows 2000 manages the printing process, here are some real-world and exam scenarios you may encounter.

SCENARIO & SOLUTION

I've set up priority queues for a print device so that a VP and his admin can print high-priority documents ahead of other users. Sometimes jobs printed to the priority queue come out before other documents; sometimes they do not. What's happening?	Several situations could lead to this scenario. First, make sure that each queue does have a different priority set. The high priority queue should have a priority of 99, and the other queue should have a priority of 50 or less (1 being the lowest priority). If the priorities on the queues are the same, the spooler will alternate between the queues, meaning some jobs in the "low" priority queue would print before jobs in the other queue. Another possibility is that the high-priority queue has not been restricted so that only the VP and his admin can print to it. If the queue is unrestricted, other users could find the queue, realize it is a high priority queue, and print their nonpriority jobs to it if they didn't want to wait. Check the permissions on the queues as well as the priority settings to make sure the configuration matches your desired behavior.
A VP asked me to set up a color printer to be shared off his admin's computer so that only he and his staff can print to it. It is an expensive printer to maintain, and they don't want everyone in the company printing to it. I set up the share on the admin's workstation, and everything was working fine for several weeks. Then people outside his department started printing to the printer, and now he's angry with me. What happened?	Again, this is probably a permissions problem. Just because the printer has been shared off a workstation and not a server, this does not mean that it is hidden from the rest of the company. To ensure that only the desired people can print to the printer, you will need to set up a group on the workstation with the accounts who should have access to the printer and then restrict the printer to that group only. Users outside that group may still locate the printer, but without the appropriate permissions applied they won't be able to print to it. Connecting the printer to the admin's workstation and not to the network was a good idea, though, as it will prevent anyone else from creating a print object that connects with the printer directly across the network.

CERTIFICATION SUMMARY

Windows 2000 provides many default tools for managing shared resources such as file folders, Dfs, and printers. Files and folders on NTFS volumes can be protected by NTFS file and folder permissions. Folders that are shared out on the network can be further protected by share permissions. Management of file and folder permissions can be performed with several tools, most often Windows 2000 Explorer or the Microsoft Management Console.

Commonly used folder shares can be collected into a Distributed File System (Dfs) tree for easy access by all network users. The Dfs tree is a collection of Dfs nodes that point to network shares on multiple servers. Users see the shares as part of one file system tree and may not be aware that file resources are being served off multiple servers. Configuring multiple network shares to point to the same Dfs node can provide fault-tolerant and load-balanced access to those resources.

Printing resources can be shared off Windows 2000 servers or workstations. Print server shares can be advertised in the Active Directory, making it easier for users to find and use network printers. Printers can be set up to connect to print devices with a number of different network connection protocols. Printer configurations and queued documents can be managed through a Web browser if the print server has Internet Information Services or Peer Web Services configured and active.

TWO-MINUTE DRILL

Monitor, Configure, Troubleshoot, and Control Access to Files, Folders, and Shared Folders

❑ Files and folders on NTFS volumes can be protected with NTFS file and folder permissions. The permissions are Read, Write, Read & Execute, Modify, and Full Control. NTFS folder permissions have an additional permission, List Folder Contents.

❑ Folder shares are protected with share permissions. The permissions are Read, Change, and Full Control.

❑ NTFS and Share permissions are cumulative. If a user has Read permission from one group and Write permission from another, the effective permissions are Read and Write.

❑ The more restrictive permission is the effective permission when Share and NTFS permissions are combined. If a user has Read permission on a share but Full Control on the NTFS folder, the effective permissions are Read.

❑ Share permissions protect folders shared from any volume type (FAT, FAT32, NTFS), but NTFS permissions apply only to NTFS volumes.

Monitor, Configure, Troubleshoot, and Control Access to Dfs Resources

❑ Distributed File System (Dfs) provides access to a variety of network shares on multiple servers from a single, logical tree structure on the network. Users accessing resources via Dfs are not aware that resources from one Dfs node may be stored on a different server than resources from another Dfs node.

❑ Dfs provides fault tolerance and load balancing for network resources. A Dfs node can point to multiple shares that contain the same information. When the source for one share becomes unavailable because it is offline or busy, users are automatically redirected to another source.

❑ Dfs stand-alone roots are entirely stored on a single server. Information about the Dfs tree is stored in that server's registry, and if the server goes offline, the Dfs tree becomes unavailable.

❑ Dfs fault-tolerant roots make use of the Active Directory. Information about the root is stored in the Active Directory and remains available when the host server goes offline.

❑ Dfs resources are managed with the Distributed File System Snap-in.

Monitor, Configure, Troubleshoot, and Control Access to Printers

❑ The four types of printer configuration are local printer, whereby the printer is connected directly to the computer; network printer, whereby the printer is connected via the network; remote local printer, whereby the printer is directly connected to a remote print server; and remote network printer, whereby the printer is connected via the network to a remote print server.

❑ Remote printers can be connected in a number of ways, including TCP/IP, LPR/LPD, JetDirect, NWLink, and AppleTalk.

❑ Windows 2000 stores print drivers on the print server. Windows 2000 print clients do not have to download and install print drivers locally when they print through a print server. Windows 2000 print servers can store print drivers for other clients that the clients must download and install locally before printing to the Windows 2000 print server.

❑ Windows 2000 print servers can advertise printers to Windows 2000 clients through the Active Directory. Windows 2000 clients can search the Active Directory for shared printers so users do not need to know the name of the print server hosting the printer.

❑ Windows 2000 print services can be administered through a Web interface if IIS or Peer Web Services are installed on the server or workstation sharing the printers.

SELF TEST

The following questions will help you measure your understanding of the material presented in this chapter. Read all of the choices carefully because there may be more than one correct answer. Choose all correct answers for each question.

Monitor, Configure, Troubleshoot, and Control Access to Files, Folders, and Shared Folders

1. Your department needs a shared folder set up so that the entire company can read the files in the folder but not make any changes to the folder contents or add new files or folders to the shared folder. Only the members of your departmental staff should have access to make changes to the contents of the folder. What is the best strategy for setting permissions for the Everyone Group on the share and/or folder to achieve this goal?

   A. Set both the share permissions and the NTFS permissions on the folder to Read for the Everyone Group.

   B. Set the share permissions on the folder to Read for the Everyone Group and the NTFS permissions on the folder to Full Control for the Everyone Group.

   C. Set the share permissions on the folder to Full Control for the Everyone Group and the NTFS permissions to Read for the Everyone Group.

   D. Set both the share permissions and the NTFS permissions on the folder to Full Control for the Everyone Group.

2. Which of the following permissions apply to network shares? (Choose all that apply.)

   A. Read

   B. Write

   C. Change

   D. Modify

   E. Full Control

3. File permissions can be assigned to volumes formatted with what type(s) of file system? (Choose all that apply.)

   A. NTFS

   B. FAT

   C. FAT32

   D. HPFS

4. Which of the following describe how NTFS permissions are applied when files are moved and copied on NTFS volumes? (Choose all that apply.)

   A. Moving files within the same NTFS volume will retain the permissions on the files.

   B. Copying files within the same NTFS volume will retain the permissions on the files.

   C. Files moved to a different NTFS volume will inherit the permissions of the destination folder.

   D. Files copied to a different NTFS volume will inherit the permissions of the destination folder.

5. User TheBoss is a member of the Management Group and the Accounting Group. The Management Group has NTFS Read permissions on a folder shared as AnnualReports, and the Accounting Group has NTFS Full Control permissions on the same folder. To keep all other user accounts from seeing the contents of the share, you have given the Read Deny permission to the Everyone Group on the share. What access does TheBoss have to the contents of the AnnualReports share? (Choose all that apply.)

   A. No Access

   B. Read and Execute

   C. Read, Write, Execute, and Delete

   D. Full Control

Monitor, Configure, Troubleshoot, and Control Access to Dfs Resources

6. Which of the following are characteristics of stand-alone Dfs roots? (Choose all that apply.)

   A. Stand-alone Dfs information is stored in the Active Directory.

   B. Stand-alone Dfs roots are limited to a single level of Dfs nodes.

   C. Stand-alone Dfs roots have replication and backup services.

   D. Stand-alone Dfs roots are not fault-tolerant.

7. Your department supports a Windows 2000 server that is hosting a stand-alone Dfs tree with nodes pointing to servers around the rest of the company. You need to take down the server to perform a maintenance upgrade. Which scenario describes the access the user community will have to the information in the Dfs tree while the server is offline?

   A. Users will be able to access the Dfs tree and all the resources in the Dfs nodes while the server is offline.

   B. Users will be able to access the Dfs tree but will not see any of the Dfs nodes in the tree.

C. Users will be unable to access the Dfs tree but will be able to access the Dfs nodes from their source shares.

D. Users will be unable to access the Dfs tree and will be unable to access the Dfs nodes, even from the source shares.

8. Which of the following are characteristics of fault-tolerant Dfs roots? (Choose all that apply.)

A. Fault-tolerant Dfs information is stored in the Active Directory.

B. Fault-tolerant Dfs roots can support multiple levels of Dfs nodes.

C. Changes to a fault-tolerant Dfs tree are automatically replicated across the Active Directory.

D. Fault-tolerant Dfs roots may reside on NTFS, FAT, or FAT32 volumes.

9. A server that hosts several shares that are pointed to by a Dfs tree is being decommissioned. The data that is on the server will be hosted on a new server. Which scenario describes the best way for performing this transition with the least impact on the user base?

A. Back up the data from the old server onto tape, take down the server, bring up the new server with the same name as the old server, and restore the data from tape onto the new server.

B. Bring up the new server, copy the data from the old server to the new server, take down the old server, and add the share points from the new server to the Dfs tree.

C. Bring up the new server, copy the data from the old server to the new server, add the share points from the new server to the existing nodes in the Dfs tree, then take down the old server and remove its share points from the nodes in the Dfs tree.

10. When a Dfs system is planned, what factors should be considered when resources are chosen to be published in the Dfs tree? (Choose all that apply.)

A. Include resources you want to make available to your entire user community.

B. Include geographically specific resources in the root of your Dfs tree.

C. Include resources that are duplicated on multiple servers across the network for fault tolerance.

D. Seek input only from your peers when deciding which resources to include.

E. Establish multiple shares that link to the same Dfs node to provide fault-tolerant access to mission-critical resources.

Monitor, Configure, Troubleshoot, and Control Access to Printers

11. Which of the following are network printer communication methods supported by Windows 2000? (Choose all that apply.)

A. TCP/IP

B. AppleTalk

C. LPR

D. JetDirect

12. Several users are trying to print to a printer on a Windows 2000 print server. The users have started to call you, complaining that nothing is printing on the print device and that they cannot remove their jobs from the print queue. Which task provides the best solution to resolve this problem?

A. Delete and re-create the printer on the print server. Tell the users to resubmit their jobs.

B. Delete all jobs from the spool directory on the server and tell the users to resubmit their jobs.

C. Shut down the server hosting the printer and restart it.

D. Shut down and restart the print spooler service on the server hosting the printers.

13. Which of the following describe how users can locate printers on the network? (Choose all that apply.)

A. Add Printer Wizard

B. Searching the Active Directory

C. Browsing the network

D. Using a Web browser

14. You have just installed a new printer on your print server, but when you send a test page from the server to the print device, the output is garbled. What is the likely cause of the problem?

A. An incorrect print driver is installed on the server.

B. The wrong network communication protocol is configured for the printer.

C. There is not enough disk space on the print server.

D. The print spooler service is hung.

15. Which of the following software tools can be used to manage the documents in a print queue? (Choose all that apply.)

    A. Microsoft Internet Explorer

    B. Active Directory Users and Computers

    C. Windows 2000 Explorer

    D. Netscape Navigator

16. A VP in your company is complaining that his time-critical printouts are not getting printed in a timely manner. He wants you to provide a way for him and his admin to print his documents without having to wait for other print jobs. Your boss tells you to make this happen, but not to spend any money on the solution. Which scenario provides the best solution to this situation?

    A. Take a print device from elsewhere in the building and set it up near the VP and his admin. Create a new printer on the print server for this print device, and give access only to the VP and his admin for the print queue.

    B. Tell the VP you'll be happy to fix his problem, but your department has no money to spend on a new printer, so he will have to purchase a printer out of his budget. Once the new printer arrives, you will set it up for him and his admin to use, keeping other users from printing to it.

    C. Change the permissions on the printer used by the VP so that only he and his admin have access to print to it. Tell all the other users who print to the printer to find a new printer to use.

    D. Set up a new print queue for the printer, and give access only to the VP and his admin for the new queue. Set the priority on the new queue to 99. Change the priority on the old queue to 1.

17. You have been asked to create a printer pool to handle a high-volume print department. Which conditions must be present in order for you to create this pool? (Choose all that apply.)

    A. All print devices must be the same model with the same configuration.

    B. All print devices must use the same network protocol to communicate with the print server.

    C. All print devices must point to the same printer queue on the server.

    D. All print devices must be connected to the same port on the print server.

    E. All print devices must support PostScript.

LAB QUESTION

You have been asked to set up a shared folder tree for three departments in your company. Each department wants its own folder within the share, and each wants special access privileges set up on the folders so that only certain groups have access to the folders. Draw a diagram of the folder tree, labeling each folder with the permissions assignments necessary to meet each department's wishes. Then describe the reasoning behind each permissions assignment. Here is the information for the folder tree.

1. Set up a Shared folder on the server and assign it the share name Shared.

2. **Marketing** Set up a Marketing folder in the Shared folder and make sure that everyone in the company can read the contents of the folder but cannot make any changes in it. Members of the Marketing Group should be able to fully manage the Marketing folder.

3. **Finance** Set up a Finance folder in the Shared folder and make sure everyone in the company can read the contents of the folder but cannot make any changes in it. Members of the Management Group should be able to write to the contents of the folder to update budgets and project plans. Members of the Finance Group should be able to fully manage the Finance folder.

4. **Development** Set up a Development folder in the Shared folder and make sure that only members of the Development Group have access to the folder. Members of the Development Group should be able to fully manage the contents of the Development folder.

SELF TEST ANSWERS

Monitor, Configure, Troubleshoot, and Control Access to Files, Folders, and Shared Folders

1. ☑ **C.** When the share permissions and NTFS permissions on a folder are different, the more restrictive permission takes effect. In this case, the setting of the NTFS permission to Read for the Everyone Group will result in all users' having read-only access to the folder contents, even though the Everyone Group has Full Control permissions on the share. Setting additional NTFS permissions on the folder for your department will allow members of your department to modify the contents of the folder either through the share or when they are logged in locally. The suggested guidelines for creating folder shares is to give the Everyone Group Full Control permissions on the share and apply the necessary NTFS permissions to the folder to restrict access as necessary.

   ☒ **A** is incorrect, because assigning the Read permission on the share to the Everyone Group would allow read-only access to the contents of the share by any user, no matter what NTFS permissions were set on the folder. This would prevent members of your department from modifying the contents of the folder through the share. **B** is incorrect for the same reasons that **A** is incorrect; also, it would allow anyone logged in locally to have full access to the folder, which is not a desired result. **D** is incorrect, because it allows everyone on the network full access to the folder contents through the share and when logged in locally on the machine.

2. ☑ **A, C,** and **E** are correct. They are the three permissions that can be set on folder shares.
   ☒ **B** and **D** are incorrect, because they are NTFS permissions that do not apply to shares.

3. ☑ **A** is correct. NTFS permissions can be applied to volumes formatted with the NTFS file system.
   ☒ **B, C,** and **D** are incorrect, because those file systems do not support NTFS security.

4. ☑ **A, C,** and **D** are correct. They describe how permissions are applied to files being moved or copied on NTFS volumes.
   ☒ **B** is incorrect, because any files that are copied will inherit the permissions of the destination folder. Copying files always creates a new version of the files in the destination folder, and all new files inherit the permissions of the parent folder.

5. ☑ **A** is correct. Despite the NTFS permissions assigned to the groups for the folder, the Everyone Group has been given the Deny Read permission, which means that no one in the Everyone Group can access the share. Therefore, TheBoss has no access to the contents of the folder through the share.

☒ **B, C,** and **D** are incorrect, because the Deny Read permission has been assigned to the share. If TheBoss were accessing the files locally instead of through the share, he would have Full Control access to the contents. Since he is trying to access the contents through the share, he has no access.

Monitor, Configure, Troubleshoot, and Control Access to Dfs Resources

6. ☑ **B** and **D** are correct. Stand-alone Dfs roots are limited to a single level of Dfs nodes. They are not fault-tolerant because the information about the Dfs tree is stored only on the stand-alone server, and if it becomes unavailable, the Dfs tree is also unavailable.
   ☒ **A** is incorrect, because the Dfs information is stored in the registry of the Dfs root server and not stored in the Active Directory. **C** is incorrect, because stand-alone Dfs roots do not have replication or backup services.

7. ☑ **C** is correct. Since the Dfs tree is a stand-alone root, information about the tree is unavailable while the server is offline. Users will still be able to access the resources in the tree from the source shares, if they know how to locate those shares.
   ☒ **A** is incorrect, because the server is hosting a stand-alone Dfs tree. **B** is incorrect, because taking down the stand-alone Dfs root server will prevent anyone from accessing the tree. **D** is incorrect, because users will be able to access the Dfs node resources from the source shares. Taking down the Dfs tree server does not affect the servers hosting the shares being pointed to by the Dfs server, except when the Dfs server is also hosting one or more of the shares. Then those shares will be unavailable as well.

8. ☑ **A, B,** and **C** are correct. Fault-tolerant Dfs roots are stored in the Active Directory, can support multiple levels of Dfs nodes, and replicate changes automatically to the Active Directory.
   ☒ **D** is incorrect, because fault-tolerant Dfs roots can reside only on NTFS 5.0 volumes.

9. ☑ **C** is correct. When the new server is brought up and added to the Dfs tree before the old server is taken down, the information in the nodes is made available to the user community with no interruption.
   ☒ **A** and **B** are incorrect, because they both require a time period when the data from the Dfs node shares is unavailable to the user community.

10. ☑ **A, C,** and **E** are correct. Resources that are used by the majority of the user community should be included in the Dfs tree. Resources that are already set up on multiple servers for fault tolerance should be included. Mission-critical resources should be mirrored on multiple servers and linked to the same Dfs node to provide uninterrupted access when network access or the hosting server goes offline.

☒ **B** is incorrect, because geographically specific resources should be included in geographically organized areas of the Dfs tree, not in the root of the tree. **D** is incorrect, because you should query your entire user community to learn what resources they need made available in the Dfs tree.

Monitor, Configure, Troubleshoot, and Control Access to Printers

11. ☑ **A, B, C,** and **D** are correct. Windows 2000 supports all of these printer network connections.

12. ☑ **D** is correct. The fact that users cannot delete their print jobs indicates that the print spooler is hung. Stopping and restarting the spooler will correct the problem and will not affect the jobs in the print queue.
☒ **A** is incorrect, because the hung print spooler is affecting all printers on the server, and will affect new printers created as well. **B** is incorrect, because removing the files from the spool directory will not release the spooler process. Both **A** and **B** ask the users to resubmit their print jobs, which you should never do. **C** is incorrect, because shutting down the entire server is an extreme way of restarting the print spooler service. Even though it has the same outcome, shutting down an entire server is never a good idea unless it is absolutely the only way to resolve a problem.

13. ☑ **A, B, C,** and **D** are all correct. They describe some of the methods users can use to locate printers on the network.

14. ☑ **A** is correct. The print driver is responsible for converting the print job into codes that the printer can understand. If the wrong driver is installed, the wrong codes will be sent to the printer, and the output will be garbled.
☒ **B** is incorrect, because the print server would be unable to send any print information to the print device if the connection were not configured correctly. **C** is incorrect, because a lack of disk space on the print server would prevent a job from spooling to the printer at all, resulting in nothing coming out of the printer. **D** is incorrect, because a hung spooler service would not send any information to the printer.

15. ☑ **A, C,** and **D** are correct. Microsoft Internet Explorer and Netscape Navigator are Web browsers that can be used to manage the documents in a print queue if Internet Information Services (IIS) or Peer Web Services (PWS) are installed and running on the computer sharing the printer. Windows 2000 explorer can be used to open the Printers control panel and manage the documents in the print queue.
☒ **B** is incorrect, because Active Directory Users and Computers can be used to advertise a printer share in the Active Directory, but it cannot manage any of the printer settings or documents in the printer queue.

16. ☑ **D** is correct. Setting up priority queues for the printer will ensure that the VP's documents are printed before any other documents, except for any documents that are actively printing when his documents enter the queue. This does not cost any money, and no users are displaced as a result.

    ☒ **A** is incorrect, because you do not want to remove any existing printing services from any users. Either they will riot and get you fired, or they will demand that a new printer be purchased, and your boss said not to spend any money. **B** is incorrect, because your boss said not to spend any money, not just your departmental money, and a VP is not going to like being told to spend his own money to fix a problem. **C** is incorrect, because you are again removing a printer resource from the user community. Even if the user community was comfortable with this solution, you would be the one going to every desk to change default printer settings.

17. ☑ **A** and **C** are correct. Printers in a pool must be the same model and have the same configuration so that a document will come out the same from any of the printers in the pool. If different printer models are used, they will need different print drivers, which means that print jobs may print correctly on one printer in the pool but not another. The print devices must point to the same print queue so that the print server can spool jobs to all the printers in the pool.

    ☒ **B** is incorrect, because there is no requirement that printers in a pool speak the same network protocol. Some of the printers in the pool may be connected locally to the server while others are connected via TCP/IP, and the server would use two different communication methods to speak to the printers in the pool. **D** is incorrect, because only one print device can connect to a server port. **E** is incorrect, because the PostScript printer language has nothing to do with printer pooling.

LAB ANSWER

On the Shared folder, the Everyone Group is given the Read NTFS permission and the Full Control share permission. This will allow anyone connecting to the share to have read-only access to the contents of the share unless additional NTFS permissions are assigned on the folders later in the directory tree. The NTFS permissions also govern the access of user accounts that log in locally on the machine hosting the share.

On the Marketing folder, the NTFS permissions for the Everyone Group are left alone, so the Read permission is inherited from the parent folder. This will give everyone in the company read-only access to the contents of the folder. In addition, the Marketing Group is given the NTFS Full Control permission on the folder so that any member of the Marketing Group can perform any file or folder task necessary on the contents of the folder.

On the Finance folder, the NTFS permissions for the Everyone Group are left alone, so the Read permission is inherited from the parent folder. Members of the Finance Group are given the NTFS Full Control permission on the folder so that any member of the Finance Group can perform any file or folder task necessary on the contents of the folder. In addition, the Management Group is given the NTFS Read & Execute, Write, and Modify permissions on the folder. This will allow any member of the Management Group the ability to read the contents of the folder and make changes to the contents by writing to existing files or creating new files. Members of the Management Group will not be able to delete files and folders or change any of the permissions on the contents of the folder.

On the Development folder, the NTFS permissions for the Everyone Group are removed so that no permissions are inherited from the parent folder and user accounts that are not members of the Development Group cannot access the folder. Members of the Development Group are given the NTFS Full Control permission so those accounts can perform any file or folder task necessary on the contents of the folder.

7

Configuring and Troubleshooting Hardware Devices and Drivers

W indows 2000 brings with it some exciting new features for configuring and troubleshooting hardware devices and drivers. The troubleshooting wizards will help walk users through most common hardware problems. Installation and configuration is made much easier with Plug-and-Play technology, and the risk of incompatible drivers is certainly lowered with digital signing.

In addition to numerous new features, Windows 2000 provides some familiar tools such as Device Manager and Hardware Profiles. Device Manager offers an organized interface for managing your hardware devices and drivers. Hardware Profiles helps manage different hardware configurations on a single machine.

The following sections of this chapter will take you on a journey through configuring, managing, and troubleshooting hardware devices and drivers.

CERTIFICATION OBJECTIVE 7.01

Configure Hardware Devices

Windows 2000 has made it relatively easy to configure hardware devices. Plug-and-Play technology was available in Windows 95/98, but not in Windows NT 4.0. Windows 2000 marks the first operating system built on NT technology to support Plug-and-Play devices. When there is Plug-and-Play technology in place, there is generally little involved in configuring a hardware device. However, you must also be aware that there are some Non-Plug-and-Play devices that the operating system will not configure, leaving it up to you to install and configure the device properly on your own.

This section will discuss how to minimize problems before you begin, how to configure and troubleshoot Plug-and-Play and Non-Plug-and-Play devices, and how to properly utilize the Hardware Profiles.

Minimizing Hardware Problems Before They Begin

Although Windows 2000 Setup has built-in checks for hardware resources on your computer, you may want to take extra precautions to ensure a successful installation. Microsoft publishes a document called the Hardware Compatibility List (HCL).

The HCL lists all devices that Microsoft deems compatible with their operating systems. You will find the most updated version of the HCL on the Web at **www.microsoft.com/hcl/default.asp**. The version that was released with Windows 2000 can also be found on the Windows 2000 CD-ROM in the Support folder in a file called HCL.TXT.

To determine whether or not you have the most current drivers for your hardware devices, check with the manufacturer of the device. For the most recent information on your device, check the manufacturer's Web site or give them a call.

In addition to verifying the drivers and devices for your computer configuration, it may be useful to take an inventory of them. Although Windows 2000 automatically takes an inventory of your hardware devices upon setup, taking your own inventory will also be helpful. Useful information would include IRQ (interrupt request) designations, COM (communications) port connections, I/O (input/output) addresses, DMA (direct memory access), and drivers. Knowing what resources each device is using will help prevent resource conflicts.

Plug-and-Play and Non-Plug-and-Play Installations

Once you have physically installed your hardware device, it needs to be configured to work properly with your system. Configuring a hardware device requires two basic steps: 1) loading drivers and 2) configuring device properties and settings. If the installed hardware device is Plug-and-Play and the computer you are installing it on is an Advanced Configuration and Power Interface (ACPI) machine running in ACPI mode (most new computers on the market do), Windows 2000 will take care of the two basic configuration steps for you. On startup, Windows will perform an inventory of your system and detect any new hardware. Once it finds a new device, it will load the necessary drivers, configure the device, allocate resources, and update the system. Windows 2000 manages all the resources to ensure that each hardware device runs properly with other resources. This feature makes managing hardware very simple!

on the job

Windows 2000 Server may not immediately recognize some older Plug-and-Play devices. In such cases, you will be required to reboot before configuration is complete.

If the hardware device is Non-Plug-and-Play, you will need to load the drivers and configure the properties and settings for the device manually. You must be logged on as an Administrator or a member of the Administrators Group to manually configure a machine. Setup will differ for each Non-Plug-and-Play device based on the device and its manufacturer. Follow the instructions in the manual that came with the device. A word of caution: Microsoft does not generally recommend manually setting resource assignments. This is because the manually set resource assignments become fixed, giving Windows 2000 Server less flexibility when new Plug-and-Play devices are installed.

Troubleshooting Plug-and-Play Installations

Although Windows 2000 Server promotes the ability to install and configure Plug-and-Play devices with the greatest of ease, it is still possible that problems will arise once in a while. The most common problem in installing a Plug-and-Play device is a resource conflict. The conflict often stems from a previous Non-Plug-and-Play device installation. Because Non-Plug-and-Play devices are manually configured, there is a good chance that one of the resources it is using is actually preferred by the Plug-and-Play device you are trying to install, so you will likely be left to adjust the resource assignments manually. Again, Microsoft does not recommend manually changing resource settings. Try to avoid this if possible by checking your devices on Microsoft's HCL, taking an inventory of your hardware and resources, and diligently planning for new additions.

Adjusting Resource Assignments for a Non-Plug-and-Play Device

Only those with expert knowledge and experience in hardware should adjust resource assignments. Improper adjustments could cause your system to fail and become inaccessible, resulting in potential loss of data or extended periods of downtime. Windows 2000 Server will allow only Administrators or members of the Administrators Group to adjust resource settings.

Resource settings for a particular device are found in the Properties dialog of that device under the Resources tab. Figure 7-1 displays the Resources tab for COM Port 1.

Be sure to clear the box labeled "Use automatic settings." This will make the Change Settings button and Settings based on drop-down box available (otherwise they would be grayed out). Select the appropriate Hardware Profile to base your resource changes on. (Hardware Profiles are covered in the next section.) Select the resource type you are interested in changing, such as: DMA, IRQ, I/O Port, or Memory address. Click Change Setting and type in the new value.

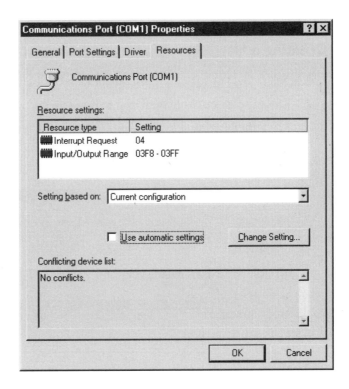

FIGURE 7-1

Resources tab for
COM Port 1

___

on the
Job *It may seem as though this is a repeat of information, but it is very important to remember that only experts in hardware should attempt to adjust these settings!*

Using Hardware Profiles

A Hardware profile is a set of instructions that tells your computer how to boot the system properly, based on the setup of your hardware. Hardware profiles are most commonly used with laptops. This is because laptops are frequently used in at least two different settings; stand-alone and in a docking station on a network. For example, when the laptop is being used at a docking station, it requires the network adapter. However, when the laptop is used away from the network, it does not. The Hardware Profile dialog manages these configuration changes. If a profile is created for each situation, the user will automatically be presented these choices on Windows startup.

Exercise 7-1 illustrates how to create a hardware profile.

EXERCISE 7-1

Creating a Hardware Profile

1. Select Start menu/Settings/Control Panel.

2. Double-click on the System icon to bring up the System Properties dialog box.

3. Click the Hardware Profiles button located in the Hardware Profiles section of the System Properties dialog to bring up the Hardware Profiles dialog box, as shown:

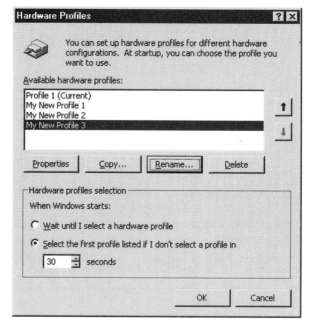

4. Highlight the current profile and click Copy.

5. Enter a name for your new profile. This is the name that will appear in the list of profile choices when the user boots up. Click OK.

6. Highlight your new profile from the list of Available Hardware Profiles and click Properties to bring up the Properties page for your profile, as shown:

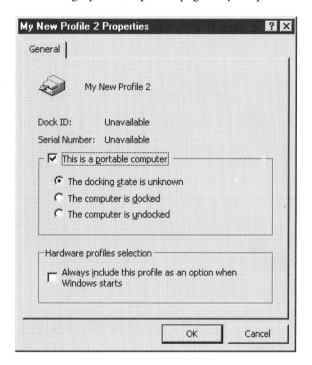

7. If you are creating a profile for a laptop computer, select the status "This is a portable computer." Mark the check box in the Hardware Profiles selection section if you always want this profile as an option. This would mean, for example, that if the profile is for a docked laptop and the laptop were booted away from the docking station, this profile would still show up as an option. Click OK to go back to the main Hardware Profiles dialog page.

8. Configure the Hardware Profiles Selection section to tell Windows 2000 Server what to do on startup.

9. Click OK to save your new profile and exit.

SCENARIO & SOLUTION

I am not sure whether my new device is compatible with Windows 2000.	Check Microsoft's HCL to see whether your device is listed.
I need to manually adjust a resource for a new device.	Go to the Resources tab of the Properties dialog for the device.
I will be using Windows 2000 on a laptop at a docking station connected to a network and off site without a docking station.	Create hardware profiles for each of the two settings.

Now that you have learned about planning, configuring, and troubleshooting hardware devices, drivers, and profiles in Windows 2000 Server, the preceding table offers a quick reference for possible scenario questions and the appropriate answers.

CERTIFICATION OBJECTIVE 7.02

Configure Driver Signing Options

Driver Signing (also known as *code signing*) is Microsoft's way of ensuring that only the highest-quality drivers are used. Windows 98 was the first Microsoft operating system to use digital signatures, but Windows 2000 marks the first Microsoft operating system based on NT technology to do this. By promoting Driver Signing for certain device classes, Microsoft intends to increase driver quality and decrease vendor costs in the area of support. Driver developers can submit their drivers to the Windows Hardware Quality Lab (WHQL) for testing with Windows 2000 products. Windows 2000 includes support for many different types of devices and their corresponding drivers, including keyboards, modems, mice, and network adapters. Windows 2000 Server also includes support for new devices, such as Smart Card Readers and USB devices.

Drivers that pass the WHQL testing are given a Microsoft digital signature certifying that the driver will not destabilize the user's system. The signature does not appear directly in the binary driver (.BIN) file. Instead, the signature appears in the catalog driver file (.CAT) that is created for each driver package. The information driver file (.INF) directs the operating system to the catalog file to read the digital signature.

FROM THE CLASSROOM

Exam Tips

For the exam it is important to remember that Microsoft will want to test you on new features of Windows 2000 Server. Make sure you understand the concepts surrounding Driver-Signing Options, Windows 2000 Hardware Troubleshooter, and how Plug-and-Play affects the Windows 2000 Platform. In addition, Microsoft is bound to include some questions around the "tried and true" features that Windows 2000 has inherited from older NT technology. Be sure to familiarize yourself with the Device Manager MMC Snap-In and how Hardware Profiles work.

—Jocelyn Fowke, MCSE, MCP+I

Setting Driver-Signing Options

Windows 2000 gives you three options for managing your certified drivers. These three options are:

- Ignore
- Warn
- Block

Ignore will install the driver files whether they are digitally signed or not. Warn will provide a message if you are about to install a driver that is not signed. The Warn message gives you the option of proceeding with the install or canceling at that point. Block will prohibit the installation of any driver that is not digitally signed. The default for Windows 2000 systems is Warn mode. Warn is provided as default so that users are not prevented from applying urgent driver updates before vendors are able to get them tested by WHQL.

Exercise 7-2 illustrates how to configure Driver Signing options as described above. It is important to remember that you must be logged on as the Administrator or a member of the Administrators Group in order to decrease the security of Driver Signing Options from Block to Warn or Warn to Ignore. All members of the Users group, however, have access to increase the security of Driver Signing Options from Ignore to Warn or Warn to Block.

CertCam 7-2

EXERCISE 7-2

Configuring Driver Signing Options

1. Select Start menu/Settings/Control Panel.

2. Double-click on the System icon to bring up the System Properties dialog box.

3. Select the Hardware tab on the System Properties dialog.

4. Click the Driver Signing button located in the Device Manager section of the System Properties dialog to bring up the Driver Signing Options dialog box, as shown:

5. Pick one of the three options in the File signature verification section of the dialog.

6. If you want to apply the setting as system default then click in the Administrator option check box.

7. Click OK in the Driver Signing Options dialog box to apply your selection.

8. Click OK in the System Properties dialog to exit.

Keep an eye open for the security context of the user who is performing the operation. In order to decrease the security of Driver Signing Options from Warn to Ignore, you must be logged on as the Administrator or a member of the Administrators Group. All members of the Users Group have access to increase the security from Warn to Block.

CERTIFICATION OBJECTIVE 7.03

Update Device Drivers

There may come a time when you need to update a driver. For example, the company that developed your hardware may release an updated driver for a particular device, or an older machine on your network may be due for updated drivers. Sometimes devices need to be removed or disabled if they are no longer in use. This section will describe how you can manage, update, remove, or disable devices and their drivers.

Getting Familiar with Device Manager

The first step in managing your device is to locate the Device Manager. The Device Manager is an MMC Snap-in included in the Computer Management console that is provided by Windows 2000 Server. The Computer Management console is preconfigured and saved in the Administrative Tools applet of the Control Panel. Although Snap-Ins is a new feature of Windows 2000 Server, you will already by familiar with the look and feel of Device Manager if you have used Windows NT 4.0. In the Device Manager, you can view and manage all the information about devices and their drivers such as connections, status of a device, and driver files.

Exercise 7-3 shows you how to open Device Manager.

EXERCISE 7-3

How to Open Device Manager

1. Select Start menu/Settings/Control Panel.

2. Double-click the System icon to bring up the System Properties dialog box.

3. Select the Hardware tab.

4. Click Device Manager to open the Device Manager and display what you see:

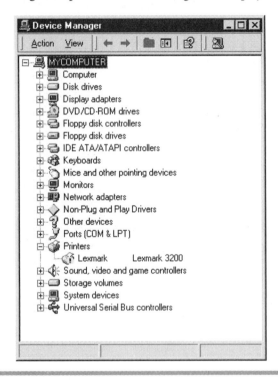

exam

ⓦatch

It is important to remember that you can also access Device Manager by right-clicking My Computer and selecting Properties. Once the Properties page pops up, select the Hardware tab and then the Device Manager button.

The Device Manager displays all the devices installed on your computer in one of four views. These views can be selected from the view menu, including:

- Devices by type
- Devices by connection
- Resources by type
- Resources by connection

Windows 2000 defaults to the "Devices by type" view.

You can also choose to show Hidden Devices from the View menu. Selecting Hidden Devices will add your Non-Plug-and-Play devices to the view. These are usually devices that have had drivers manually installed to the system. The Customize option from the View menu allows you to manage your menu and toolbar options.

Getting Details about a Device Driver

Details about a device driver that has been installed are found in the Properties dialog for each device. Exercise 7-4 shows you how to open the properties for a specific device.

Opening Properties for a Device

1. From Device Manager, locate the device you want more information on. You may need to click a plus sign next to the device type in order to view the complete list of devices available.

2. Select the Device and click the Properties button on the toolbar. Another way to open the properties dialog is to right-click the device and select Properties from the pop-up menu. Alternatively, you can double-click the device in the list.

You are now in the Properties dialog for the device you selected. Note the various tabs including a combination of General, Drivers, Resources, and so on. The Properties dialog for a hard disk drive:

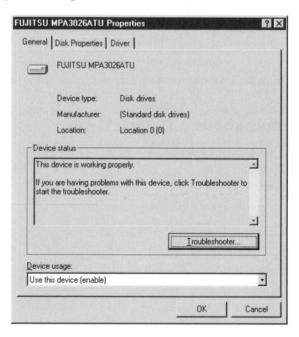

You will find various combinations of tabs in the Properties dialog, but driver-specific information is found in the Driver tab, where you will find general information about the driver such as Provider and Digital Signer. Three buttons are located at the bottom of the Driver tab:

- Driver Details
- Uninstall
- Update Driver

These buttons will be discussed more fully in the following two sections.

exam
ⓦatch

It is important to remember that Device Manager manages the local computer only and has read-only access to remote computers.

Device Driver Updating

A driver can be updated easily by clicking the Update Driver button, which is found on the Driver tab of the Property dialog for any given device. Figure 7-2 shows the Driver tab for a CD-ROM drive.

Clicking the Update Driver button will execute the Upgrade Device Driver Wizard. This wizard will walk you through the required steps for upgrading your driver. Be sure to have your new driver software ready, because the wizard will cue you when it is needed in your disk drive.

FIGURE 7-2

Driver tab for a
CD-ROM drive

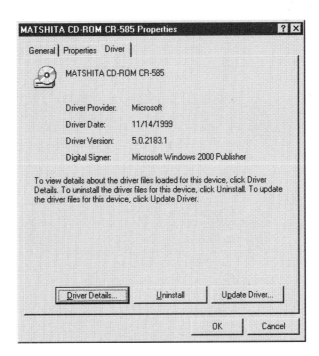

Exercise 7-5 walks you through the Upgrade Device Driver Wizard.

Walk through the Upgrade Device Driver Wizard

1. Click Update Driver. This will bring up the Welcome screen.

2. Click Next to bring up a screen with detection options, as shown:

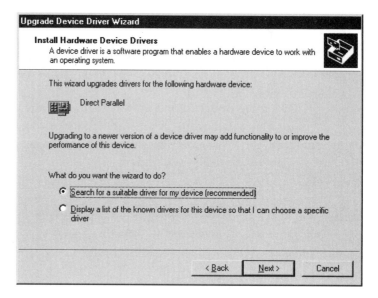

3. One option will allow Windows to detect the updated drivers and the other will allow you to manually pick the driver from a list. Microsoft recommends that you let the operating system do the detection. Select your choice and click Next.

4. The Locate Driver Files screen allows you to add additional search locations (floppy-disk drive, CD-ROM drive) if you chose the first option in step 2. Select the options you wish to search and click Next.

5. Windows 2000 will now start searching for an updated driver. Once it has found the new driver it will display the path where it found the driver.

6. Click Next and then Finish to complete the Update.

on the !ob *If you want to update all the system drivers on your computer, visit Microsoft's Windows Update page on the Web at www.windowsupdate. microsoft.com and click Product Updates. There you will find a catalog of drivers as well as other items such as patches, help files, and more.*

Removing a Device

Most Plug-and-Play devices can be removed by simply disconnecting or removing the device from your system. Be sure to check your device manufacturer manual for special instructions such as turning off the computer before removing the device or rebooting after it is removed.

You can remove Non-Plug-and-Play devices by using one of these two tools:

1. **Device Manager**   Clicking the Uninstall button on the Driver tab of the device you wish to remove (found on the device Properties page) will invoke a warning to confirm device removal. Click OK to immediately uninstall the device. Some devices may require a reboot after this step. Click Cancel to quit without uninstalling.

2. **Add/Remove Hardware Wizard**   The Add/Remove Hardware Wizard is found by clicking Start menu/Settings/Control Panel and then double-clicking the Add/Remove Hardware applet. The wizard will walk you through the steps required to uninstall a device.

Exercise 7-6 takes you through the Add/Remove Hardware Wizard.

Walk through the Add/Remove Hardware Wizard

1. Select Start menu/Settings/Control Panel and double-click on Add/Remove Hardware. This will bring up the Welcome screen. Click Next.

2. The Wizard will now ask you to choose a hardware task. Select Uninstall/Unplug a Device and click Next.

3. The Wizard will ask you to choose a removal task. Select Uninstall a Device and click Next.

4. Now the Wizard will display a list box of devices (see the illustration below). Select the device you want to uninstall and click Next. The check box on this screen provides the option to Show Hidden Device (Non-Plug-and-Play devices).

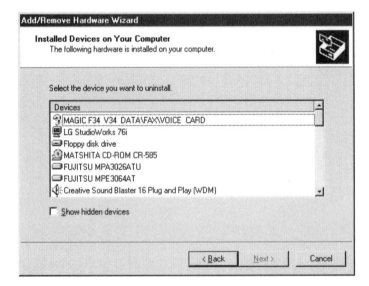

5. The Uninstall a Device dialog that is displayed next will ask you to confirm your wish to uninstall the device. You can still back out at this point by selecting "No, I don't want to uninstall this device." Select "Yes, I want to uninstall this device" and click Next.

6. Click Finish to complete the Uninstall.

e x a m
ⓦa t c h

The device drivers remain on your hard disk even after removing a device physically, through Device Manager or Add/Remove Hardware. Contact your manufacturer if you want to remove these files from your hard disk. To see a list of driver files on your hard disk, click the Driver Details button of the Driver tab in the Properties dialog for that device.

Disabling a Device

Windows 2000 Server gives you the option to temporarily remove a device by disabling it. Disabling allows you to keep the device attached to the computer but prevents its drivers from loading on startup. Disabling a device is more or less asking the computer to temporarily ignore the device. In turn, when the device is required again in the future, enabling the device makes the driver available once again at startup. There are three ways to enable/disable your device:

1. Select your device from Device Manager and click on Disable/Enable from the Action menu.

2. Select your device from Device Manager, right-click, and select Disable/Enable from the pop-up menu.

3. From the Properties dialog for your device, select Do Not Use this device (disable)/Use this device(enable) from the Device usage drop-down box.

Now that you have become familiar with Digital Signing and updating devices and drivers in Windows 2000 Server, here is a quick reference for possible scenarios and the appropriate solutions.

SCENARIO & SOLUTION

I don't want to install any drivers that aren't digitally signed by Microsoft.	Set your Driver Signing Options to Block.
I'm in Device Manager but can't see my Non-Plug-and-Play devices.	Select Hidden Devices from the View menu.
I want to remove my modem but plan on reinstalling it after a couple of weeks.	Disable the device instead of uninstalling it.

CERTIFICATION OBJECTIVE 7.04

Troubleshoot Problems with Hardware

No matter how well you plan your device configuration, problems are bound to arise, especially if you are working with a complex set of servers. If you have some experience in the IT industry, you have been exposed to troubleshooting at one time or another. It is important to remember that troubleshooting is not an exact science. It includes continuous forms of trial and error and, most important, patience! This section will take you through some common steps toward solving hardware problems.

Identifying Problem Devices

If you suspect you have a problem with one of your devices, your first step should be to investigate and identify the problem device. Which device is not working properly? There are two tools to help you identify a device as a problem: Device Manager and System Information. Both of these tools are found in the System Tools section of the Computer Management console, seen in Figure 7-3.

As previously noted in this chapter, the Computer Management console is preconfigured and saved by Windows 2000 Server in Administrative Tools found in the Control Panel. As its name suggests, the Computer Management console is designed to help the user manage the computer by providing an easily accessible view of the system and all its pieces, including not only hardware but storage devices, services, and applications as well.

The fundamental difference between Device Manager and System Information tools is their access level to information. Device Manager includes more detailed information about devices, including resources and drivers. It also provides access to edit or change these items. The System Information tool provides a more general overview of the hardware components and allows you only to view general information about the hardware on your system, not to edit or change it.

When a device has failed or it isn't working properly it will be marked with an exclamation mark in a yellow circle in Device Manager. Figure 7-4 shows us that a Lexmark printer isn't working properly. Whenever you see this symbol in Device Manager, you should take note, because it indicates that something isn't working properly.

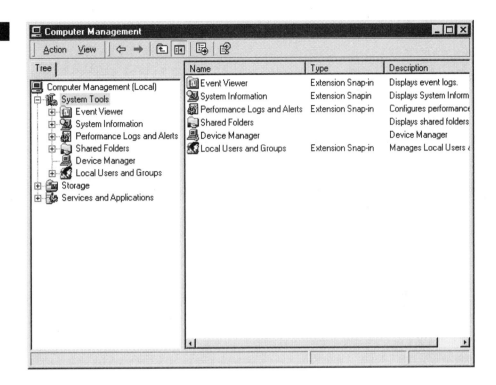

FIGURE 7-3

Computer
Management
console

To identify a problem device using System Information, open the Components folder and select the folder called Problem Devices. There you will find a list of all the current problem devices. Figure 7-4 shows a Lexmark printer as a problem device with error code 28. Figure 7-5 shows the Problem Devices folder.

exam
ⓌatCh
The Computer Management Console, where System Tools is found, can also be accessed by selecting Start | Programs | Administrative Tools | Computer Management.

Checking the Status of a Device

When you have identified a device as a problem device, checking the status will provide you with the information you need about why the device isn't working and how to go about troubleshooting the problem. Exercise 7-7 shows you how to check the status of a printing device.

FIGURE 7-4

Failed printer in
Device Manager

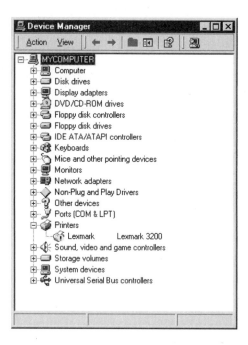

FIGURE 7-5

Failed Printer—
Problem Devices
folder of System
Information

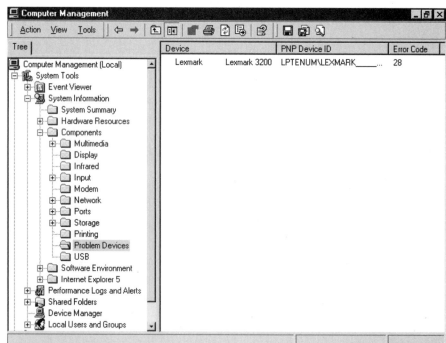

Checking the Status of a Device

1. From Device Manager, locate the device you want more information on. You may need to click a plus sign next to the device type in order to view the complete list of devices available.

2. Select the Device and click the Properties button on the toolbar. You are now in the Properties dialog for the device you selected. By default, Windows 2000 brings you to the General tab of the Properties dialog:

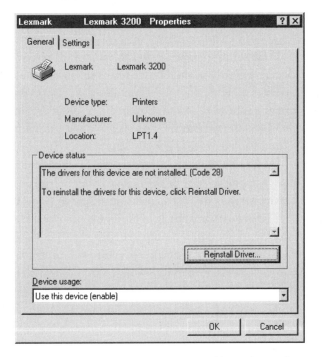

3. You will find the Device status section about halfway down the Properties dialog. The text provided in this section will indicate whether or not the device is working properly and may include information such as an Error code to help start the troubleshooting.

Troubleshooting a Device That Isn't Working Properly

When you have identified and checked the status of a problem device, you should have enough information to start troubleshooting the problem. There are many different possible error codes you might find in the Device status section but the solution to these codes can be summarized in four basic methods of troubleshooting:

- Reinstall the device driver
- Restart the computer
- Update the device driver
- Use the Windows 2000 Troubleshooter

If the solution requires you to reinstall or restart the system, it will generally state that very clearly in the Device status section of the General tab. Reinstalling a device driver is usually called for if the driver was improperly installed initially or if the driver has been removed. Restarting is usually required when the device installation required a restart but the user didn't bother to restart. Restart is also required if Windows is removing a faulty device.

Updating the device driver can fix problems such as incorrect configuration, the device failing to start or the device being corrupt. See the section labeled Updating Device Drivers for instructions on where to find the Update Driver button.

The Windows 2000 Troubleshooter is a new feature included in NT technology. The Windows 2000 Troubleshooter wizard is a self-guided tool that uses a question-and-answer format that directs you to solutions for your hardware devices. Even if you are not clear on exactly where the problem is, the troubleshooter will help you narrow it down by asking some very general questions up front and then getting progressively more detailed as you move through the wizard.

There are a variety of troubleshooters included with Windows 2000 Server. The Hardware Troubleshooter covers devices such as cameras, CD-ROM drives, game controllers, hard disks, keyboards, mice, network adapters, and scanners. Other devices, such as display or video adapters, sound cards, and modems, have their own separate Troubleshooters.

To access the Windows 2000 Hardware Troubleshooter Wizard, go to the Properties dialog of the device you want to troubleshoot and click the Troubleshooter button on the General tab. You can also start the Troubleshooter by double-clicking the Add/Remove Hardware Applet in Control Panel and selecting Add/Troubleshoot a

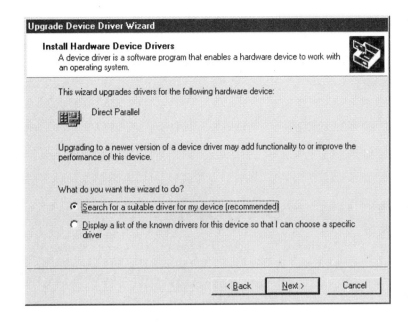

FIGURE 7-6

The Hardware
Troubleshooter

device when asked to select a Hardware Task. Figure 7-6 displays the Hardware Troubleshooter.

When the installation or configuration of a device prevents your system from starting or continuing to run properly, there are a couple of options: Safe Mode and Last Known Good Configuration. Safe Mode allows you to start up the machine with minimal necessary services that would allow you to go in and fix the changes you made with the latest installation or configuration changes. Last Known Good Configuration restores your machine to the way it was last successfully booted. If you are lucky, that was just before you installed the device that is giving you trouble. Safe Mode and Last Known Good Configuration are covered in Chapter 9, "Systems Recovery and Protection."

The Microsoft Web site is a wealth of knowledge in terms of troubleshooting problems. Go to **www.microsoft.com** and select Knowledge Base from the Support menu. This will bring you to a helpful search engine for information on Windows 2000 and other Microsoft products.

Now that you have explored the details related to troubleshooting hardware devices in Windows 2000 Server, the top of the next page offers a quick reference for possible scenarios and the appropriate solutions.

SCENARIO & SOLUTION

I want to check the status of my device.	Go to your Computer Management console and check in Device Manager or System Information.
I want to troubleshoot my network adapter.	Use the Windows 2000 Hardware Troubleshooter Wizard.
I have just installed a device and now my computer will not start properly.	Try to start up in Safe Mode or with the Last Known Good Configuration.

CERTIFICATION SUMMARY

This chapter has walked you through the various features that support hardware devices and drivers in Windows 2000 Server. Configuration and troubleshooting hardware devices and drivers is made easy with old familiar tools like Device Manager and Hardware Profiles but also through features that are new to Windows 2000 Server such as Plug-and-Play, Digital Signing, and Hardware Troubleshooting wizards.

The addition of Plug-and-Play support on the Windows 2000 Server platform has made it much easier for hardware installation and configuration. However, Windows 2000 still provides the ability to manually adjust hardware settings in order to support Non-Plug-and-Play devices that still exist on the market. Whether you are installing Plug-and-Play or Non-Plug-and-Play devices and drivers, it still makes a lot of sense to plan ahead using the Microsoft HCL and to perform a personal inventory.

The new addition of Digital Signing functionality to Windows 2000 Server promotes increased quality of drivers while decreasing device conflicts. With the default setting of Warn, users are not prevented from applying hot fixes that haven't yet completed WHQL testing.

Device Manager has worked very well for previous Microsoft operating systems, so it continues to be featured in Windows 2000 Server. Management of hardware devices and drivers is centralized here for those with Administrators Group access rights. Although System Information gives a nice clear overview of hardware configuration for a given system, Device Manager is still the main focus for identifying problem devices. The addition of Hardware Troubleshooters keeps troubleshooting time to a minimum.

TWO-MINUTE DRILL

Configure Hardware Devices

❑ To ensure the successful installation and configuration of hardware devices and drivers, it is a good idea to take an inventory of your hardware devices and drivers and to check that your devices are listed on the HCL.

❑ Windows 2000 Server supports Plug-and-Play hardware. The server takes care of configuring hardware settings for those devices and their drivers.

❑ In case device conflicts arise, resource assignments can be adjusted manually using Device Manager; however, this is not recommended by Microsoft.

❑ Hardware Profiles are most often used for laptops that are used on and off the network and therefore require at least two different hardware configurations.

Configure Driver Signing Options

❑ A Digital Signature is the "stamp" that Microsoft gives to device drivers that have passed the WHQL testing.

❑ Driver Signing Options can be set to Ignore, Warn, or Block, with Warn being the default setting.

❑ While any user can increase the security of the Driver Signing Option from Ignore to Warn or Warn to Block, only Administrators or members of the Administrators Group can decrease the Driver Signing Option from Block to Warn or Warn to Ignore.

Update Device Drivers

❑ The tool used to manage/update devices and drivers is Device Manager.

❑ The Drivers tab of the Properties dialog provides information about drivers and ways to change them.

❑ Windows 2000 Server provides a wizard for upgrading device drivers.

❑ Windows 2000 Server provides a wizard for adding and removing devices/drivers.

❑ Disabling a device allows you to temporarily remove a device from system startup, which makes it very easy to add it again down the road.

Troubleshoot Problems with Hardware

❑ The System Information Extension Snap-In provides a good overview of hardware, including Problem Devices.

❑ Checking the status of a device in Device Manager will indicate whether a device is working properly or not and usually provides error codes to aid in finding a solution.

❑ The Hardware Troubleshooter is a tool for solving hardware-related problems.

SELF TEST

The following questions will help you measure your understanding of the material presented in this chapter. Read all of the choices carefully, as there may be more than one correct answer. Choose all correct answers for each question.

Configure Hardware Devices

1. You are responsible for adding a second CD-ROM drive to each of your six servers that are running your network of 50 PCs. The operating system being used is Windows 2000 Server. Which of the following would help minimize risk?

   A. Check to make sure the CD-ROM is on the HCL.

   B. Check with the manufacturer to see that you have the correct driver.

   C. Take an inventory of devices and drivers on each machine.

   D. All of the above

2. What groups or users have access to adjusting the resource settings for Non-Plug-and-Play resources?

   A. The Administrator

   B. The Administrator and members of the Administrators Group

   C. The Administrator, members of the Administrators Group, and members of Server Operators Group

   D. None of the above

3. You have just added a Plug-and-Play device to your Windows 2000 Server. Unfortunately, a device conflict arose due to an older Non-Plug-and-Play device that is using the IRQ setting that is being requested. Assuming you are an expert in hardware devices and configuration, and are a member of the Administrators Group, what are the preferred steps that you should take?

   A. Adjust the IRQ setting for the Non-Plug-and-Play device using System Tools.

   B. Adjust the IRQ setting for the Plug-and-Play device using System Tools.

   C. Adjust the IRQ setting for the Non-Plug-and-Play device using Device Manager.

   D. Adjust the IRQ setting for the Plug-and-Play device using Device Manager.

4. What would you check to see whether your device is compatible with Windows 2000 Server?

   A. WHQL

    B. HCL

    C. IRQ

    D. Windows 2000 Hardware Troubleshooter

5. You come into work one morning and find that a group of new users are not able to logon to the network. You have checked the physical connections, and all are correctly attached to the network. You open the Hardware Profiles dialog for one of the users, and what you find is illustrated in Figure 7-7.

   What changes should you make in the Hardware Profile dialog to allow your users to log on to the network?

    A. Click the down arrow button to move the "network-enabled" profile to the top of the list.

    B. In the Hardware Profiles Selection section, increase the number of seconds to 30 or select Wait until I select a hardware profile.

    C. In the Hardware Profiles Selection section, increase the number of seconds to 30.

    D. Add a new profile that is network-enabled and move it to the top of the list in the Available Hardware Profiles section.

FIGURE 7-7

Hardware
Profiles dialog
box

Configure Driver Signing Options

6. If the Driver Signing Options are set to Warn, who has permission to change them?

  A. The Administrator

  B. The Administrator and the Administrators Group

  C. The Administrator, the Administrators Group, and the Users Group

  D. None of the above

7. What is the Windows 2000 Server default setting for Driver Signing Options?

  A. Ignore

  B. Warn

  C. Block

  D. None of the above

8. You are new to the Network Administration Team at your company and have been asked to change Driver Signing Options to Ignore. When you try to change the setting, you have no luck, however, you find you can change the setting to Block without any problem. What is the best explanation for this situation?

  A. The system policy is preventing you from applying changes.

  B. You have not yet been added to the Administrators Group.

  C. You are not logged on as an Administrator.

  D. The Apply setting as System Default option is checked

9. In which applet do you change the Driver Signing Options?

  A. System

  B. System Tools

  C. Device Manager

  D. Add/Remove Hardware

10. You are trying to install a driver on a new Windows 2000 server, but it fails to install. You know it is not digitally signed, but you have had no trouble installing it on other machines. What is wrong?

  A. You do not have Administrators Access.

  B. The Driver Signing Option for that server is Block.

C. The Driver Signing Option for that server is Warn.

D. You are not a member of the Administrators Group.

Update Device Drivers

11. You have been asked to collect detailed information on all the Disk Drives on your local computer. What is the best way to do this?

A. Open System Information and view the Hardware Resources.

B. Open Device Manager and view devices by type.

C. Open System Information and view Components folder.

D. Open Device Manager and view devices by connection.

12. You would like to remove the modem from use but plan on needing it again in a couple of weeks. What is the best strategy to accomplish this task?

A. Run the Add/Remove Hardware Wizard each time you need to add or remove the modem.

B. Click the Uninstall button to remove it, then use the Add/Remove button when you need to reinstall it.

C. Disable the device and then enable it when you need it again.

D. None of the above

13. Which of the following is a way to get into Device Manager?

A. Start Menu/Settings/Control Panel/System Applet

B. Right-click My Computer and select Properties. Then select the Hardware tab.

C. Start Menu/Programs/Administrative Tools/Computer Management

D. All of the above

14. What is the default view setting in Device Manager?

A. Devices by type

B. Devices by connection

C. Resources by type

D. Resources by connection

15. What buttons are available on the Driver tab of the Properties dialog for a hardware device?

A. Uninstall, Update Driver

B. Uninstall, Update Driver, Driver Details

C. Uninstall, Update Driver, Troubleshoot

D. Uninstall, Update Driver, Change Settings

Troubleshoot Problems with Hardware

16. You suspect a device driver conflict. Where should you first look to find information on the status of a driver?

A. Hardware Resources folder in System Tools

B. Problem Devices folder in System Tools

C. The General tab of Device Properties dialog in Device Manager

D. The Driver tab of Device Properties dialog in Device Manager

17. How is a problem device identified in Device Manager?

A. A yellow question mark

B. An exclamation mark in a yellow circle

C. The device name is typed in red bold lettering

D. The device name is typed in blue bold lettering

18. You come across an error code from a keyboard that you have not seen before. There is no extra information in the Device Status frame. What is the first logical step to begin troubleshooting this problem?

A. Run the Windows 2000 Hardware Troubleshooter.

B. Run the Keyboard Troubleshooter.

C. Go online and check the Microsoft Web site.

D. Restart the machine in Safe Mode.

19. Which of the following devices has its own separate Troubleshooter apart from the general Windows 2000 Hardware Troubleshooter?

A. CD-ROM drive

B. Network adapter

C. Hard disk

D. Sound card

20. Where could you look to find the error code for a problem device?

A. General tab of the Property dialog

B. Problem Devices folder

C. General tab of the Property dialog and the Problem Devices folder

D. None of the above

LAB QUESTION

Your company's network has had a bit of a facelift including the addition of some new third-party software on the Windows 2000 Servers. Although there was planning around the new additions, your servers have experienced a number of crashes since the facelift. You immediately wonder about the status of your new drivers. Although you suspect that some of the new drivers may not have been digitally signed, you were not warned that an unsigned device had been installed during the installation of third-party software. Describe the correct actions to take to investigate this situation.

SELF TEST ANSWERS

Configure Hardware Devices

1. ☑ **D.** All of the steps included in **A, B,** and **C** are the correct ways to minimize risk when adding additional hardware to a server.

2. ☑ **B.** The Administrator and members of the Administrators Group are the only ones with this access.
☒ **A** is incorrect, because it is missing members of the Administrators Group. **C** is incorrect, because it includes the Server Operator Group, which does not have access (Server Operators have rights to shut down the System, back up files and directories, and so on). **D** is incorrect because **B** is correct.

3. ☑ **C.** Microsoft recommends adjusting the resource setting for the Non-Plug-and-Play device because Microsoft prefers letting Windows 2000 Server configure the hardware. Device Manager is where Windows 2000 allows you to adjust resource settings.
☒ **A, B,** and **D** are incorrect, because you can't adjust resource settings in System Tools, and Microsoft recommends against adjusting Plug-and-Play device settings.

4. ☑ **B.** The HCL (Hardware Compatibility List) is a list published by Microsoft to identify hardware devices that are compatible with Windows products. The most up-to-date version is found on the Web at **www.microsoft.com/hcl/default.asp**.
☒ **A** is incorrect, because the WHQL (Windows Hardware Quality Lab) is where drivers are tested and then digitally signed by Microsoft. **C** is incorrect, because IRQ (Interrupt Request) is how hardware devices communicate to the CPU. **D** is incorrect, because the Hardware Troubleshooter is used to troubleshoot hardware problems.

5. ☑ **B.** Increasing the number of seconds will allow the user time to select the appropriate profile before it automatically selects the first one. Selecting Wait until I select a hardware profile will not default to any profile and in doing so forces the user to select the appropriate profile.
☒ **A** is incorrect, because although it will select the network-enabled profile for the users by default, when the users attempt to work while they are not connected to the network or while they are "undocked," they will not have the correct profile selected on startup. **C** is incorrect, because although it will allow the users to select the network-enabled hardware profile, it ignores the other option included in answer **B. D** is incorrect, because you already have a network-enabled profile so there is no need to create a new one. In addition, because you aren't changing the Hardware profiles

selection section, when users try to use their machines while off of the network, they won't be able to choose the Undocked profile.

Configure Driver Signing Options

6. ☑ **C.** Although only the Administrator and the Administrators Group have access and are able to decrease the security of Driver Signing Options (for example, from Block to Warn), the Users Group is able to increase the security (for example, from Warn to Block).
☒ **A** and **B** are incorrect, because they do not include the Users Group. **D** is incorrect.

7. ☑ **B.** Microsoft sets the default to Warn so that users are not prevented from adding a hot fix that is not yet through WHQL testing.
☒ **A** and **C,** the other two options available, are not the default settings, and **D** is incorrect because **B** is correct.

8. ☑ **B.** Since you are new to the Network Administration Team, it is likely they have not added you to the Administrators Group yet. Any member of the general Users Group has the ability to change the driver signing options to become more secure, but only an administrator can lower the security.
☒ **A** is incorrect, because although it is a possible explanation, it is not the best explanation because the behavior we are seeing is the default behavior; the default behavior is that members of the general Users Group can increase security but cannot decrease security). System policies can essentially "lock down" a user's workstation to prevent the user from doing certain tasks. For example, the system policy may prevent users from changing the Driver Signing Options. System policies are used to make support easier by hiding certain functions from the users. (System Policies are covered more thoroughly in Chapter 12.) **C** is incorrect, because any member of the Administrators Group has the same access. **D** is incorrect, because this setting has nothing to do with user access.

9. ☑ **A.** From the System applet, you find the Hardware tab and on it is a button for Driver Signing Options.
☒ **B** is incorrect, because it is an extension snap-in found in Computer Management. **C** is incorrect, because it provides no access to Driver Signing Options. **D** is incorrect, because it is for adding or removing hardware devices.

10. ☑ **B.** You were able to install on other machines, so it can't be your access level. Instead, it is due to a Driver Signing Option of Block, which prevents any drivers from being installed if they are not digitally signed.

☒   **A** and **D** are incorrect, because you were able to install on other servers, so it isn't an issue of access rights. **C** is incorrect, because Warn would still allow you to install.

Update Device Drivers

11. ☑   **B.** Viewing devices by type will display all the disk drives (for example, floppy, hard) on your machine, and Device Manager provides more details than the System Information.
☒   **A** and **C** are incorrect, because they do not provide as detailed information as Device Manager. **D** is incorrect, because viewing devices by connection will not display disks in an easy-to-find manner.

12. ☑   **C.** You wanted to remove it only temporarily, so this is the easiest and most efficient strategy.
☒   **A** and **B** are incorrect, because you are not temporarily removing the device, it is permanent and more time consuming. **D** is incorrect because **C** is correct.

13. ☑   **D.** You can access Device Manager by all of the above methods.

14. ☑   **A.** Devices by type is the Windows 2000 default view.
☒   **B, C,** and **D** are incorrect, because although they are also options available from the view menu in Device Manager; none of them are the default view.

15. ☑   **B.** Uninstall, Update Driver, and Driver Details are all buttons found on the Driver tab.
☒   **A** is incorrect, because it is missing Driver Details. **C** is incorrect, because Troubleshoot is not found on the Driver tab but on the General tab. **D** is incorrect, because it includes Change Settings, which is a button found on the Resources tab.

Troubleshoot Problems with Hardware

16. ☑   **C.** The General tab is where you will find the Device Status frame.
☒   **A** is incorrect, because it does not provide the status of a device. **B** is incorrect, because although it displays problem devices, there are no details on the status. **D** is incorrect, because the Driver tab does not provide any status information.

17. ☑   **B.** The problem device is identified by an exclamation mark in a yellow circle.
☒   **A** is incorrect, because a yellow question mark denotes Other Devices (a device that is working properly but is not recognized by Windows 2000 Server). **C** and **D** are incorrect, because you will not find red or blue text in Device Manager.

18. ☑   **A.** The best practice is to try the Hardware Troubleshooter when you have few or no clues to go on. The Troubleshooter will help narrow in on a solution.

    ☒   **B** is incorrect, because there is no such thing as the Keyboard Troubleshooter (other devices do have their own troubleshooter, but keyboard is included in the general Hardware Troubleshooter). **C** is incorrect. Although it is a valid place to look for information, you should try the Windows 2000 Hardware Troubleshooter first. **D** is incorrect, because Safe Mode is used if a device conflict prevents you from rebooting normally.

19. ☑ **D.** There is a troubleshooter in Windows 2000 Server specifically designed for sound cards.
    ☒   **A, B,** and **C** are incorrect, because these devices are covered in the Windows 2000 Hardware Troubleshooter.

20. ☑ **C.** Both the General tab and the Problem Devices folder identify and display the error code for a problem device.
    ☒   **A** and **B** are incorrect, because they include only one of two places to find the error code. **D** is incorrect because **A** and **B** are incorrect.

LAB ANSWER

A new feature of Windows 2000 Server is its ability to manage the quality of drivers being installed on your server. Doing so reduces the risk of device conflicts. By default, Windows 2000 Server assigns the Driver Signing Option to Warn so that before an unsigned driver can be installed, the user is informed. The Administrator or a member of the Administrators Group can change these settings. In cases in which this setting has been changed, complete the following steps to configure the Driver Signing Option back to Warn:

1. Right-click My Computer and select Properties from the pop-up menu.

2. Select the Hardware tab.

3. Click the Driver Signing button in the Driver Signing Frame to bring up the Driver Signing Options dialog, as shown in Figure 7-8, on the next page.

4. Choose Warn from the File Signature verification section of the Driver Signing Options dialog.

5. Click OK to exit.

FIGURE 7-8

Driver Signing
Options dialog
box

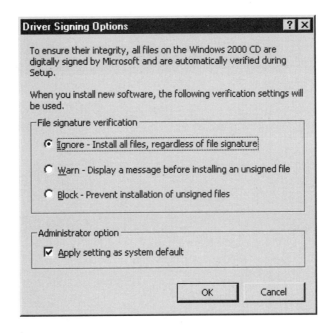

8

Managing, Monitoring, and Optimizing System Performance, Reliability, and Availability

Monitoring your system resources might seem like wasted effort sometimes, but it isn't. By continuously monitoring your system, you can create a baseline for it, so you'll know when performance starts to degrade. Monitoring also allows you to fix problems before they devastate your system, by finding bottlenecks and fixing them before they cause significant harm. You can use System Monitor to help find bottlenecks.

In this chapter, we also talk about how to manage processes. We discuss starting and stopping processes and setting priorities. Then we see how to use the Disk Defragmenter to keep our hard disks running at optimal performance. Finally, we discuss performance logs and alerts.

CERTIFICATION OBJECTIVE 8.01

Monitoring and Optimizing Usage of System Resources

Part of keeping your Windows 2000 Server operating at peak performance is monitoring the performance of your server. In order to understand how your computer is operating, you need to establish a *baseline*. A baseline tells you how various aspects of the computer are running when the server is running at normal levels. By continuously monitoring the server, you can watch for performance degradation and solve any problems before they impact your network.

Using System Monitor

Part of administering your network includes monitoring the health of your servers. In order for your network to operate efficiently, you need to make sure your servers' performance is good enough to handle the load the network places on them. By monitoring the performance of your server, you can see how the load placed on it affects your server's resources. You can monitor resource usage to see when upgrades are required. You can also create test environments to demonstrate the effects of changes to the network.

One of the tools to aid you in these monitoring activities is *System Monitor*. System Monitor replaces the Performance Monitor used in Windows NT. System Monitor allows you to collect information about your hardware's performance as well as network utilization. It also gives you the ability to view this data in many different ways. System Monitor is a snap-in to, and is installed automatically with, Performance Console. *Performance Console* is a Microsoft Management Console (MMC), accessed through the Administrative Tools program group.

System Monitor can be used to measure various aspects of a computer's performance. It can be used on your own computer or other computers on the network. System Monitor can collect data for memory usage, processor utilization, network activity, and more. This data can be displayed as a graph, a histogram, or a report.

System Monitor can perform many tasks. It can collect real-time data, measuring various aspects of performance and allowing you to view this information or save it or print it for later viewing. System Monitor comprises three basic areas: the Graph area, the Legend, and the Value Bar. Figure 8-1 shows an example of System Monitor in the Performance Console. The example shows processor utilization.

FIGURE 8-1

System Monitor displaying processor utilization data

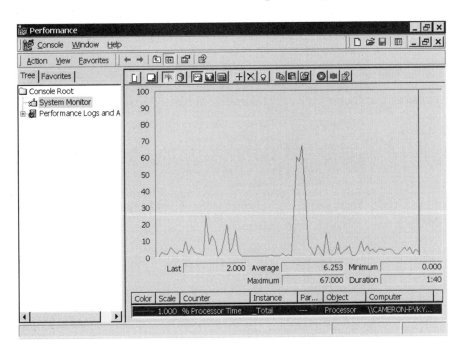

The type of data you can collect in System Monitor is extensive. There are two basic types of item on which you can collect data: objects and counters. An *object* is a component of the system, such as memory, a processor, or a hard disk. An object contains data measuring a component's tasks. As a component performs various tasks, the system collects performance data on those tasks. Generally, the object is named after the component it measures. *Counters* are the specific data of an object to be measured.

Objects can contain many different counters. Objects can also have multiple *instances*. If there are multiple objects in a computer, the objects are distinguished by instances. For example, in a computer that has multiple processors, you would use instances to differentiate between the objects for each processor. An example of a counter is the Available Bytes counter from the Memory object. See Table 8-1 for a listing of the most common objects and their functions.

The Graph Area

As mentioned earlier, the data that is collected by System Monitor can be viewed in several ways. You can view it as a chart, a histogram, or a report. By default, the Graph view is displayed when you open System Monitor. When you are creating

TABLE 8-1	Object	Function
System Monitor Objects and Their Function	Cache	Measures the disk cache usage.
	Memory	Measures memory usage and/or performance of physical and virtual memory.
	Objects	Measures miscellaneous data such as events, processes, and threads.
	Paging file	Measures page file usage.
	Physical disk	Measures hard disk utilization.
	Process	Measures running processes.
	Processor	Measures processor usage.
	Server	Measures server performance.
	System	Measures overall system performance.
	Thread	Measures thread usage.

FIGURE 8-2

The System
Monitor Graph
toolbar

baselines for your systems, you should create the baseline in the report format so that you can easily determine specific values.

Figure 8-1 showed an example of the graph display. When configuring a graph, you can choose settings for many attributes. Figure 8-2 shows the toolbar to configure a graph. Table 8-2 contains a description of the buttons in the toolbar. The toolbar buttons are described as they appear from left to right.

TABLE 8-2

System Monitor
Toolbar Buttons

Button	Function
New Counter Set	Removes counters and collected data.
Clear Display	Removes all collected data.
View Current Activity	Views live data.
View Log File Data	Views data saved to a log file.
View Chart	Views data in a chart.
View Histogram	Views data in a histogram.
View Report	Views data in a report.
Add	Adds object counter(s).
Delete	Deletes object counter(s).
Highlight	Highlights a counter.
Copy Properties	Copies counter data.
Paste Counter List	Pastes counter data.
Properties	Views System Monitor properties.
Freeze Display	Stops collecting data.
Update Data	Collects a sample of data.
Help	Help.

The data that is collected by System Monitor can be updated automatically or on demand. To collect data on demand, stop the data collection by clicking the Freeze Display button on the toolbar; when you want to collect data, click the Update Data button on the toolbar. Each time you click the Update Data button, one sample of data is collected. The solid vertical line in the graph shown in Figure 8-1 is called the *timer bar*. It moves across the graph as data is collected. The graph can display up to 100 samples at a time.

Some of the attributes that can be set for the graph include background color, font for text, and line style. You can also highlight a particular counter's data. To highlight a selected counter, either press CTRL-H or click the highlight button. When the data is highlighted, it is displayed in white.

The Value Bar

The *value bar* is positioned below the graph area. For a selected sample, it displays data such as the last sample value, the average of the counter samples, the maximum and minimum of the samples, and the duration of time the samples have been taken over. Figure 8-3 shows an example of the value bar.

FIGURE 8-3

The System Monitor value bar

| Last | 100.000 | Average | 51.871 | Minimum | 0.000 |
| Maximum | | | 100.000 | Duration | 1:40 |

The Legend

The *legend* displays information about the counters that are being measured. The legend is the set of columns at the bottom of System Monitor. The legend displays the following information:

- **Color**   The color in which the counter is displayed.
- **Scale**   The scale of the counter in the graph.
- **Counter**   The counter being measured.
- **Instance**   The instance of the object being measured.
- **Object**   The object being measured.
- **Computer**   The computer on which the counter is being measured.

You can select the counters in the legend. Notice in Figure 8-4 that the %Processor Time counter is selected. The value bar displays information about the selected counter. By clicking any of the columns, you can sort the list based on that column category.

Now that we have talked about System Monitor, let's do an exercise to see how we can use it.

FIGURE 8-4

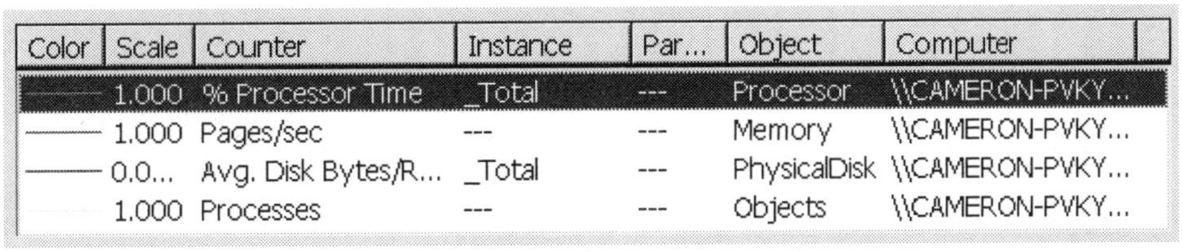

The System Monitor legend

Color	Scale	Counter	Instance	Par...	Object	Computer
———	1.000	% Processor Time	_Total	---	Processor	\\CAMERON-PVKY...
———	1.000	Pages/sec	---	---	Memory	\\CAMERON-PVKY...
———	0.0...	Avg. Disk Bytes/R...	_Total	---	PhysicalDisk	\\CAMERON-PVKY...
	1.000	Processes	---	---	Objects	\\CAMERON-PVKY...

CertCam 8-1

EXERCISE 8-1

Using System Monitor

1. To start System Monitor from the Start menu, select Start | Programs | Administrative Tools | Performance. This choice brings up System Monitor in the Performance Console.

2. Now let's add some counters to measure. Click Add, or right-click the graph area and select Add Counters...from the context menu.

3. The Add Counters dialog box appears. Select the "Use local computer counters" option button.

4. From the Performance object list, select Processor.

5. From the "Select counters from list" box, select %Processor Time. Your settings should look like the ones shown:

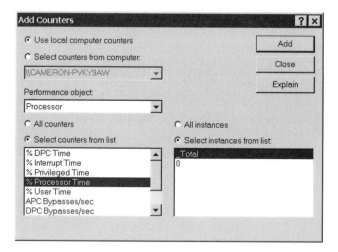

6. Click Add to add the counter.

7. Now let's add another counter. From the "Performance object" list, select Memory.

8. From the "Select counters from list" box, as shown in the next illustration, select Pages/sec and click Add. Click Close to exit the dialog box.

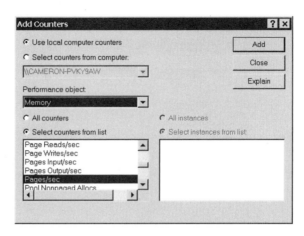

9. Notice the counters have been added to the Legend, and data is being displayed in the chart. Let's highlight the %Processor Time counter. In the Legend, select the %Processor Time counter and click the Highlight button on the toolbar. System Monitor should now show this counter highlighted in white.

10. Let's take a look at the histogram view. Click the View Histogram button. Your System Monitor should look like:

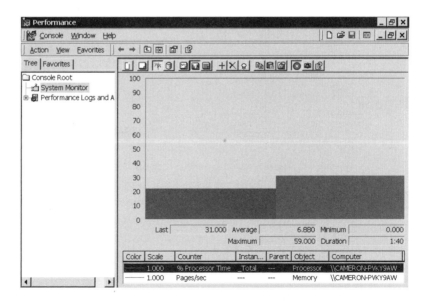

11. Now let's take a look at the report view. Click the View Report button. Your System Monitor should look like:

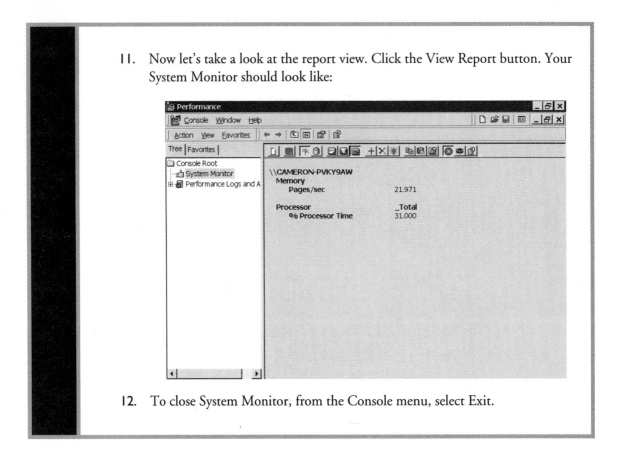

12. To close System Monitor, from the Console menu, select Exit.

Bottlenecks

Now that we have learned how to use System Monitor, what exactly do we use it for? One of the main reasons we use System Monitor is to find bottlenecks in our systems. A *bottleneck* is just what it sounds like: A bottle's neck restricts the flow from or into the bottle. A bottleneck in computer terms is a component of the system as a whole that restricts the system from operating at its peak. When a bottleneck occurs, the component that is blocking the system's functioning has a high rate of usage, and other components have a low rate of usage. In this section we discuss common computer system bottlenecks and how to find and fix them.

Identifying Bottlenecks in Processor, Memory, Disk Storage, or Network Performance

The most common causes of computer system bottlenecks are the processor, the memory, the hard disk, and the network. Let's look at how to measure for bottlenecks in these basic areas.

First, let's examine processor bottlenecks. If your applications perform large or many calculations, they can consume a great deal of processor time. If your processor cannot fulfill all these requests for processor time, it can become a bottleneck. With System Monitor, you can measure the Processor object's %Processor Time counter. When this counter reaches a sustained level of 80 percent, you need to fix the problem. This counter occasionally spikes to 100 percent, possibly when applications start or when certain operations are performed. Occasional spikes to 100 percent CPU utilization are not a cause for concern. If your processor is a bottleneck, however, you can either upgrade to a faster processor or add additional processors to the computer.

Memory issues are also prevalent bottlenecks. Arguably, memory is the most important component for system performance. Memory can be broken into two categories: physical memory and virtual memory. *Physical memory* is the actual random access memory (RAM) in the computer. When the physical memory becomes full, the operating system can also use space on the hard disk as *virtual memory*. When memory becomes full, rather than locking up the computer, the operating system stores unused data on the hard disk in a page file (in a process that is also called *paging* or *swap file*; it is known as paging because *pages* of memory are swapped at a time). Windows 2000 separates memory into 4KB pages to help prevent fragmentation. Data is swapped back and forth between the hard disk and physical memory as needed for running applications. If memory is needed that is in virtual memory, it is swapped back into physical memory.

Memory is a common cause of bottlenecks when your computer doesn't have enough memory for the applications and services that are running. When this is the case, too many pages of memory can be swapped from physical memory to the hard disk, slowing the system down. Swapping can get so frequent and cumbersome that you can hear your hard disk running constantly.

So, how do we know if memory is running low? The main counters to watch in System Monitor are the Memory object's Available Bytes and Pages/sec counters. The *Available Bytes counter* indicates the number of bytes of memory that are currently available for use by applications. When the available bytes of memory drop below 4MB (the size of the pages in which Windows 2000 stores memory), you should add more memory to the computer. The *Pages/sec counter* provides the number of pages that were either retrieved from disk or written to disk. When the Pages/sec counter reaches 20, you should look at your paging activity and consider adding more memory.

When a bottleneck occurs in memory, the most common solution is to add more memory. You can also create multiple swap files so that they are on different hard disks to increase performance. If possible, you can off-load memory-intensive applications to other servers.

The hard disk can also be a bottleneck due to the many different operations it performs. For instance, when you boot your computer, the operating system is loaded from the hard disk. The operating system swaps between physical and virtual memory using the hard disk. Furthermore, applications are loaded from the hard disk, and many applications read and write data to the hard disk. Because the hard disk is such a workhorse, the rate at which the hard disk can read and write data can have a large impact on the performance of your computer.

You can use System Monitor to determine the performance of your hard disks, using the PhysicalDisk and the LogicalDisk objects. These objects measure the transfer of data to and from the hard disk. The *PhysicalDisk object* measures the transfer of data for the entire hard disk. The *LogicalDisk object* measures the transfer of data for a logical drive (e.g., C: or D:) or storage volumes. You can use the PhysicalDisk object to determine which hard disk is causing the bottleneck. Then, to narrow the cause of the bottleneck, you can use the LogicalDisk object to determine which, if any, partition is the specific cause of the bottleneck.

Enabling the disk objects can cause a drain on system performance because the counters interrupt the processor during disk operations. These objects should be enabled only when they are in use. By default, the PhysicalDisk object is enabled and the LogicalDisk object is disabled on Windows 2000 Server. You can enable and disable these objects using the DISKPERF command. The changes won't take effect until the computer is rebooted. The following is a list of the command-line switches available for DISKPERF:

- ■ **-Y**   Enables all the disk performance counters.
- ■ **-YD**   Enables the PhysicalDisk object performance counters.
- ■ **-YV**   Enables the LogicalDisk object performance counters.

- ■ **-N**   Disables all the disk performance counters.
- ■ **-ND**   Disables the PhysicalDisk object performance counters.
- ■ **-NV**   Disables the LogicalDisk object performance counters.
- ■ **\\Computername**   Allows you to set the counters for remote computers.

When measuring the performance of your hard disk, some of the commonly measured counters are %Disk Time, Current Disk Queue Length, Disk Reads/sec, and Disk Writes/sec. If the %Disk Time reaches 90 percent or higher, your hard disk may be a bottleneck. You should check the transfer rates that are specified by the hard disk's vendor to ensure that the rates are not higher than the specification. The disk queue length should not be more than the number of spindles (normally one spindle per disk) on the hard drive, plus 2. You should measure the disk queue length by the average.

If your hard disk becomes a bottleneck, there are several things you can do to alleviate the problem. You can upgrade the hard disk to a higher-speed disk or add disks on different disk controllers. You can create striped volume sets across different physical disks, which will allow multiple I/O operations to be executed simultaneously. Try to put some of the load on another server, if possible. If a program has heavy disk utilization, you can have that program use a hard disk that is not used by the operating system or other programs. See if the drives are fragmented, and defragment them as needed. You can also consider using RAID.

e x a m
ⓦ a t c h

Increasing the size of the hard disk will not solve a performance bottleneck. It will help only if you are running out of disk space.

The performance of your network can be affected by your servers. To analyze your network, you should monitor the resources on the servers and overall network traffic. System Monitor also allows you to monitor network activities. When monitoring network performance of your server, you should monitor the services provided at each layer of the Open Systems Interconnection (OSI) model. OSI is a model that breaks networking tasks into layers. Each layer is responsible for a specific set of functions. Performance objects are available in System Monitor for analyzing network performance. See Table 8-3 for the performance objects at each layer of the OSI model.

If you suspect your server is a bottleneck on the network, start monitoring the objects at the lower layers first. One of the counters you should measure is the %Net

TABLE 8-3	OSI Layer	Performance Objects
Open Systems Interconnection Performance Objects for Monitoring Network Activities	Application, Presentation, Session	Browser, Server, Redirector, and Server Work Queues for NBT Connection.
	Transport	TCP, UDP, NetBEUI for NetBIOS, and AppleTalk.
	Network	Network Segment, IP, and NWLink IPX/SPX.
	Data Link, Physical	Network Interface.

Utilization of the Network Segment object. This counter shows you at what percentage your network capacity is operating. On Ethernet networks, the recommended threshold is 30–40 percent. Once utilization reaches this range, you can start running into problems with collisions.

From the Server object, you should monitor the Bytes Total/sec counter. If the sum of this counter for all servers on the network is close to the maximum throughput of your network, you should consider segmenting your network. Network counters that are above or below normal could be caused by the servers' resources. You should also monitor a server's memory, processor(s), and hard disk(s).

You can do many things to increase network performance. For one thing, you can segment your network. For another, if you have any protocols that aren't used, you should remove the binding for the protocol or uninstall the protocol entirely. You can also place the most used protocol first in the binding list. If you have a network adapter that is not being used, remove the binding for the network adapter. If necessary, replace your network adapter with a higher-performance network adapter. For instance, if you have a 16-bit network adapter, replace it with a 32-bit network adapter.

SCENARIO & SOLUTION

You have a server that you suspect is under-performing. What are the common resources that you should analyze?	When looking for bottlenecks on your server, monitor the processor, memory, hard disks, and network activity.
Which tools can be used to monitor your system resources?	System Monitor and Task Manager can be used to monitor your system resources.
How do I turn on my hard disk counters?	You use the DISKPERF command-line utility to enable the hard disk counters.

FROM THE CLASSROOM

Monitoring Your System for Bottlenecks

Students commonly ask, "Why bother with a baseline?" They claim that if a bottleneck occurs, it will be easy to spot. This is often true, but not always. Besides, it would be better to *prevent* the bottleneck. Creating a baseline takes some time, but the time is well worth it in the long run. You can use System Monitor to measure performance data to create the baseline against which you can compare your system's performance over time and be alerted when performance degradation occurs.

This chapter, and most classes that are taught, cannot cover everything that can be measured by System Monitor. Only the most important and common counters are discussed. The performance data that can be measured is quite extensive. You should start with these main counters to create your baseline and continue to monitor them over time. This allows you to see when performance is degrading.

At times, a bottleneck is not immediately apparent; in these cases, you need to add some counters to determine the bottleneck. To find out which ones to use, you can look in the *Windows 2000 Resource Kit* and on Microsoft TechNet for more detailed information on monitoring your system for bottlenecks.

One last thing to keep in mind is that you don't want to always measure every counter you can think of. When you are monitoring performance counters, it takes resources to measure them, and that can cause a drain on your system resources. It is best to use a main set of counters for your baseline and normal monitoring and use other counters when needed.

—*Cameron Wakefield, MCSD, MCP*

CERTIFICATION OBJECTIVE 8.02

Managing Processes

At times, you need to manage the processes that are running on your server. Sometimes a process stops responding, or it might not be getting enough CPU time. In this section, we talk about how to deal with these management tasks.

Setting and Configuring Priorities and Starting and Stopping Processes

As in Windows NT, Windows 2000 has a Task Manager. Task Manager can be used for a variety of tasks. It allows you to monitor applications, processes, and performance statistics. Task Manager can be started by pressing CTRL+ALT+DEL and selecting Task Manager, or pressing CTRL+SHIFT+ESC. You also can start Task Manager by right-clicking on the taskbar and selecting it from the context menu.

Task Manager has three tabs: Applications, Processes, and Performance, as shown in Figure 8-5. By default, the Task Manager Performance tab displays CPU and memory usage. It also displays the number of handles, threads, and processes that are running, as well as total KB for physical, kernel, and committed memory.

The Applications tab displays all the applications that are running. From this tab you can end an application, switch to an application, or start an application.

The Processes tab displays all the processes, services, and drivers that are running, as well as the process name, process ID (PID), percentage of CPU time being used, and elapsed time using the CPU and memory. You can also select other columns to be displayed. See Figure 8-6 for the columns that can be displayed in the Processes tab.

FIGURE 8-5

Windows Task Manager's Applications, Processes, and Performance tabs

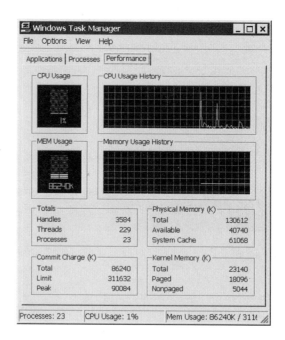

FIGURE 8-6

The Task
Manager
Processes tab
column options

FIGURE 8-6

The Task
Manager
Processes tab
column options

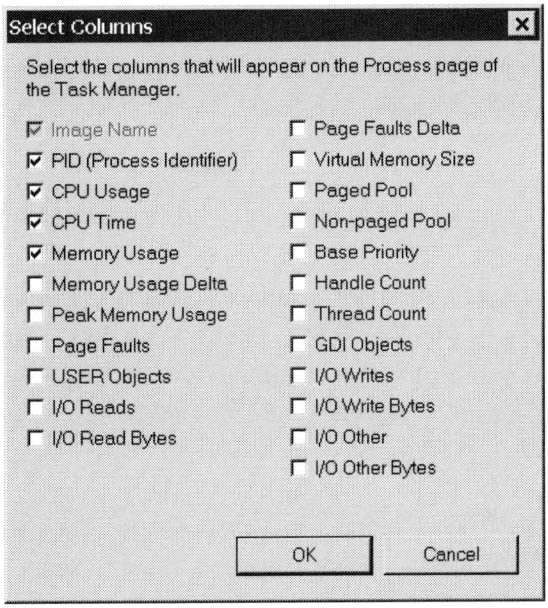

From Task Manager, you can stop applications and processes from running using the Applications tab's End Task button. To stop an application, select the application you want to stop and click End Task.

You can also stop individual processes from running from the Processes tab. To stop a process, select the process and click the End Process button, or right-click the process and select End Process.

Yet another option, useful for applications that comprise multiple processes, is called *End Process Tree;* it stops all processes related to the process you want to stop. Furthermore, if you have multiple processors on your computer, you can assign a process to a processor or processors using the SET AFFINITY command, which is available only on multiple-processor computers. You should be careful using this command, because it limits the process to running only on those processors.

Exercise 8-2 gives you a chance to practice using Task Manager.

on the
ⓘ o b

From Task Manager, you cannot stop processes that are critical to running Windows 2000.

EXERCISE 8-2

Using Task Manager to Manage Processes

1. To start Task Manager, press CTRL+ALT+DEL. Then click the Task Manager button. (You can also press CTRL+SHIFT+ESC to bring up Task Manager.)

2. Go to the Applications tab to see the applications running on your computer. Let's start an application.

3. From the Start menu, select Run. Enter **winver** and click OK. Notice that the About Windows application is now running. Now let's stop it.

4. Select the About Windows application in the Task Manager Applications window and click the End Task button. Notice that the window no longer appears in the Applications tab.

5. Now let's end a process. Let's start the Winver program again. From the Start menu, select Run. Enter **winver** and click OK. Notice that the About Windows application is now running. Now let's stop it.

6. Select the WINVER.EXE process. Notice that it is using little or no CPU time. Also notice that it is using about 912KB of memory. While the process is selected, click the End Process button.

7. To close Task Manager, from the File menu, select Exit Task Manager.

Windows 2000 uses preemptive multitasking, whereby each process is given a slice of processor time. How much processor time a process receives depends on its *priority*. When processes are started, Windows 2000 assigns them levels of priority. There are 32 priorities, ranging from 0–31. Priority 31 is the highest. User applications and noncritical operating system functions use priority levels 0–15. Critical, real-time applications such as the operating system kernel use priority levels 16–31.

There are four base process priority levels: Real-time, High, Normal, and Idle. The priority levels between these are reserved for thread priority levels that are added to the processes' basic priority levels. A thread's priority is based on its base priority. A thread can be given one of the following priorities: Highest, Above Normal, Normal, Below Normal, and Lowest. A thread's overall priority is determined by adding the thread's priority to the process's base priority. Table 8-4 displays thread priorities by the four base process priority levels.

You can change the default priority level for a process from the command line or from Task Manager. To change a process's default priority from the command line, use the START command with one of these switches: /low, /normal, /high, or /realtime. When you use the priority switches, the threads have a default Normal priority. Therefore, the switches set the program's priority as follows: Real-time 24, High 13, Normal 8, Low 4.

In Exercise 8-3, you learn how to use the START command.

TABLE 8-4	Thread Priorities	Real Time	High	Normal	Idle
	Highest	26	15	10	6
Thread and Process Priority Levels	Above normal	25	14	9	5
	Normal	24	13	8	4
	Below normal	23	12	7	3
	Lowest	22	11	6	2
	Idle	16	1	1	1

Using the START Command to Set a Process's Priority

1. From the Start menu, select Programs | Accessories | Calculator.

2. Now let's see what the default priority is. To open Task Manager, press CTRL+SHIFT+ESC.

3. Go to the Processes tab and find the CALC.EXE process. Right-click it and select Set Priority. The default priority is Normal, as shown:

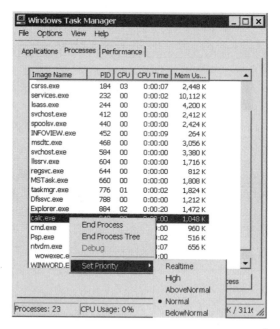

4. Close the Calculator program.

5. Now let's set the priority. From the Start menu, select Programs | Accessories | Command Prompt.

6. At the command prompt, enter **start /high calc** to start the Calculator program.

7. Now let's see what the priority level is. Go to the Processes tab of Task Manager and find the CALC.EXE process. Right-click it and select Set Priority. The priority is now set to High, as shown:

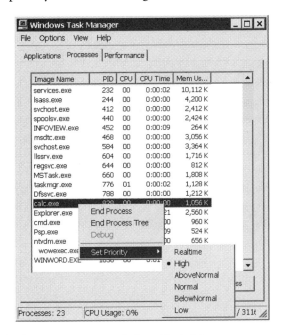

8. Close the Calculator program, and close Task Manager.

SCENARIO & SOLUTION

How can I change the default priority level for a program at startup?	You can use the START command to specify the process base priority using the priority switches.
How can I stop processes from running using Task Manager?	From the Applications tab, select a process and click the End Task button to stop it. From the Processes tab, right-click a process and select the End Process or End Process Tree option.
How can I change the priority of a running process inside Task Manager?	From the Processes tab of Task Manager, right-click a process, select Set Priority, and then select the new priority level from the context menu.

CERTIFICATION OBJECTIVE 8.03

Optimizing Disk Performance

Hard disk performance can degrade over time due to fragmentation of files. A file is *fragmented* when it is not stored in physically contiguous spaces on the hard disk. Fragmentation can happen as a file grows larger and the contiguous space near it is already in use by another file, so part of the file is stored elsewhere on the disk. When files become fragmented, additional reads and disk head movements are necessary to read or write the fragmented parts of the file. This, of course, means it takes longer to read from or write to a file.

Another result of fragmented existing files is that new files you create also become fragmented, because files are created in the first available free space and there is not enough contiguous space to store them in a defragmented condition. As you can guess, this process continues as files are created and deleted and as files are edited—and it just keeps getting worse, negatively impacting your system's performance.

The *Disk Defragmenter tool* can help alleviate this problem. Windows NT did not come with a defragmenter tool; the Defragmenter is new in Windows 2000. This tool can move and rearrange files so that they are stored in contiguous space on a hard disk. The task of finding fragmented files and moving them into contiguous space is called *defragmentation*.

Disk Defragmenter can analyze your volumes and make recommendations as to whether or not you should defragment your hard disk. Disk Defragmenter also gives you a graphical display showing you the fragmented files, contiguous files, system files, and free space. However, you wouldn't use this process lightly or without the Defragmenter's recommendation, because defragmentation can take hours, depending on several factors: the size of the volume, the number of files, the severity of the fragmentation, and the amount of free space available.

Disk Defragmenter moves all the files in the volume so that they are stored in contiguous space. It also moves the files to the front of the volume, which gives the added benefit of making the free space contiguous so that all newly created files can also be stored contiguously. Disk Defragmenter can defragment volumes formatted with FAT, FAT32, and NTFS. However, you can defragment system volumes only on the local computer. Furthermore, you can run only one instance of the Disk Defragmenter program at a time. You must have Administrator privileges to run Defragmenter.

Disk Defragmenter does not always completely defragment free space, which would have little benefit, anyway. It does move free space into just a few contiguous areas of the disk, which gives improved performance. Several factors prevent free space from being completely defragmented. For one thing, the paging file can become fragmented as it grows to meet the virtual memory requirements. The paging file is always opened exclusively by Windows 2000. This means that it cannot be defragmented using Disk Defragmenter, thus preventing free space from being completely defragmented.

Defragmenting the page file could improve the performance of your server. The only way to effectively defragment the page file is to move it to another volume. Microsoft also recommends placing the paging file on its own volume, if that's possible. Doing so prevents the paging file from becoming fragmented, and it can also increase performance if the volume that contains the paging file is low on free space. However, Microsoft also recommends leaving a small paging file on the boot partitions for recovery purposes. (System and recovery options and configurations are covered in Chapter 9, "Systems Recovery and Protection.")

exam
Watch

Remember that the paging file cannot be defragmented using Disk Defragmenter. It is locked for exclusive use by Windows 2000. To remove the fragmentation of a paging file, move the paging file to another volume, preferably its own volume with no other data files on it, to prevent future fragmentation.

On NTFS volumes, Windows 2000 reserves some free space for the *master file table (MFT)*. The MFT stores the information needed by the operating system to retrieve files from the volume. Part of the MFT is stored at the beginning of the volume and cannot be moved. In addition, if the volume contains a large number of directories, it can prevent the free space from being defragmented.

on the
Job

Often, you can defragment the same drive multiple times and receive better defragmentation results than the previous time.

The Disk Defragmenter has three main areas of display. The top area lists the volumes that can be defragmented. The middle area displays the fragmentation of the volume selected in the upper portion. The bottom portion displays the volume during and after defragmentation. The Disk Defragmenter is shown in Figure 8-7. The display shows fragmented files in red, contiguous files in blue, system files that cannot be moved by Disk Defragmenter in green, and free space in white. After running the Defragmenter, you can see the improvement in the fragmentation of the volume by comparing the Analysis display to the Defragmentation display.

FIGURE 8-7

The Disk Defragmenter tool

When you analyze a volume, Disk Defragmenter generates a report. This report gives detailed information about your volume. The top of the report contains information such as volume information, volume fragmentation, file fragmentation statistics, page file fragmentation, and directory fragmentation statistics. The bottom of the report displays information on a file-by-file basis, showing the name of the file, its size, and the number of fragments. An analysis report is shown in Figure 8-8.

on the
job

You should always analyze your volumes before defragmenting them. Analyzing your volumes will allow the system to see whether defragmentation is needed for the volume.

When should you run Disk Defragmenter? You should determine a working schedule to run the tool periodically. Note that the version that comes with Windows 2000 cannot be scheduled to run automatically; it has to be run manually. How often

FIGURE 8-8

A Disk Defragmenter analysis report

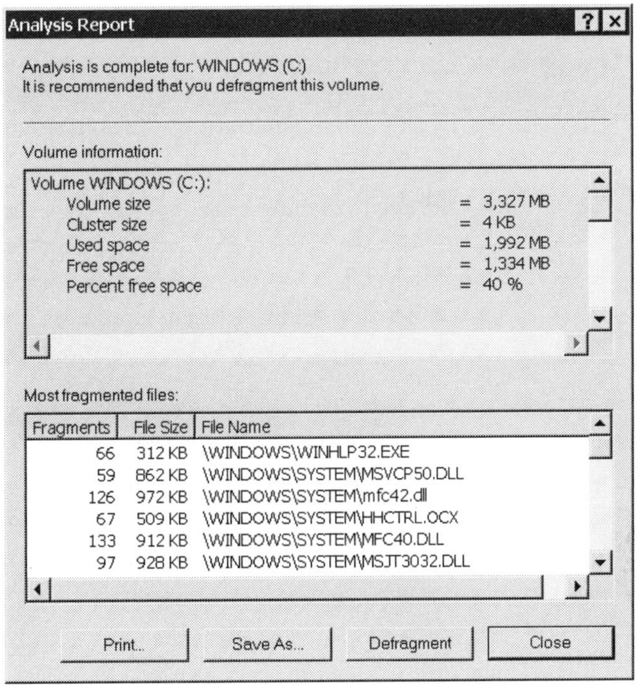

you run Defragmenter depends on how many file operations are generally performed on your computer.

You should run Defragmenter whenever you delete a large file or when a large number of files are created or deleted. Defragmentation is generally required on volumes on file servers more often than on workstations. For general-use workstations, Microsoft recommends defragmenting volumes once a month. Furthermore, since running the Defragmenter uses file I/O resources, you should run it during low-volume times. Disk Defragmenter places an additional load on the server and can significantly degrade performance.

exam Watch

To run Disk Defragmenter, you must be logged in with an account that has Administrator privileges.

Exercise 8-4 shows you how to use Disk Defragmenter.

CertCam 8-4

Using Disk Defragmenter

1. To start Disk Defragmenter, from the Start menu, select Programs | Accessories | System Tools | Disk Defragmenter.

2. When Disk Defragmenter starts, the Analysis and Defragmentation displays are blank. Let's see if volume C: needs defragmenting. Select volume C: and click the Analyze button. When analysis is complete, a message box appears, telling you whether or not defragmentation is needed. If defragmentation is needed, the message box will be similar to the one shown:

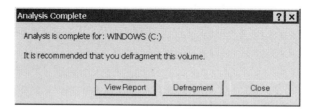

If defragmentation isn't needed, the message box will be similar to the one shown:

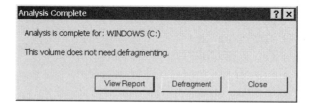

3. Click the View Report button.

4. Scroll through the top section to see the detailed information for your volume.

5. Click the Defragment button to start defragmenting the volume. As the defragmentation takes place, you should start seeing the red portion in the Analysis display become blue in the Defragmentation display. When the process is complete, a message box appears, as shown:

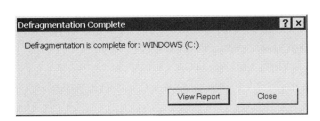

6. Your window should look similar to that shown in the illustration below. Notice that not all free space is consolidated and that the system files were not moved.

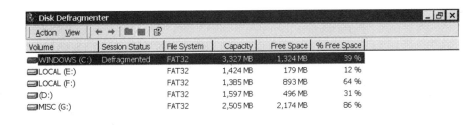

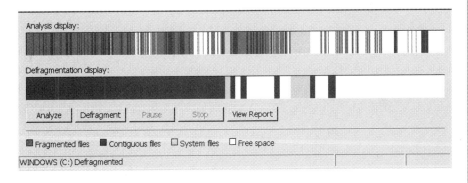

7. Close Disk Defragmenter.

Performance Logs and Alerts

Another useful item that is preconfigured with the Computer Management MMC is the Performance Logs and Alerts snap-in. It allows you to collect data from the local and remote computers to measure performance. This data can be logged and viewed in System Monitor, or it can be exported to Excel or a database. This flexibility allows you to use the tool of your choice to analyze this data and create reports.

You can set thresholds for specified counters, and if any of the thresholds set are reached, an alert can be sent to you via the Messenger service.

on the **Job** *Since the logging feature runs as a service, data can be collected even when there aren't any users logged in.*

Performance logging has many features. The collected data is stored in a comma-delimited or tab-delimited format, which allows it to be exported to spreadsheet and database applications for a variety of tasks such as charting and reports. The data can also be viewed as it is collected. You can configure the logging by specifying start and stop times, the name of the log files, and the maximum size of the log. You can start and stop the logging of data manually or create a schedule for logging. You can even specify a program to automatically run when logging stops. You can also create trace logs. *Trace logs* track events that occur rather than measuring performance counters.

The Performance Logs and Alerts snap-in is shown in Figure 8-9.

You can use the Performance Logs and Alerts MMC snap-in to configure your logging and alerts. You can configure multiple alerts and logs to run simultaneously. If you want to configure performance counter logs, select Counter Logs in the tree on the left side of the Computer Management MMC, as shown in Figure 8-10. Counter Logs displays the name of the log. A sample log file called *System Overview* is provided by default. Counter Logs also displays a comment describing the log or alert, the type of log, and the name of the log file.

From the Action menu, you can create logs. When you create a log, the first thing you do is give it a name, preferably one that is intuitive. Then you can add performance counters to the log. These are the same counters we used in System Monitor. You also

FIGURE 8-9

The Performance
Logs and Alerts
snap-in's logs

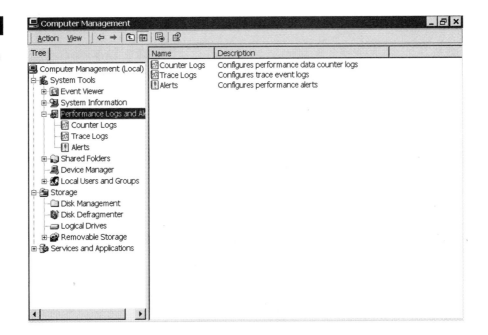

specify the interval at which the data should be collected. By default, the interval is set to 15 seconds. Next, you need to configure the log filename. The following list shows parameters you can use to specify the log filename:

- **Location**   Specify the folder where the log file will be created.

- **Filename**   Type in the base name for the log file. Do not type in the extension.

- **End filenames with**   Allows you to specify the end of the filename, which is added to the specified filename. By default, this parameter uses a six-digit number. You can also choose from date and time options.

- **Start numbering at**   When you choose the numbering scheme for the filename ending, you can specify where the automatic numbering starts.

FIGURE 8-10

Viewing
counter logs in
Performance Logs
and Alerts

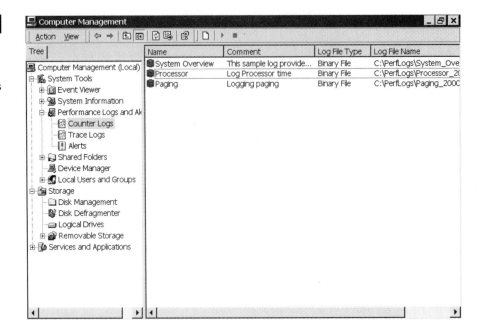

After you have configured the log filename, you need to choose the type of log
file to create. The log file type can be one of the following:

- **Binary**   This is a counter log file that stores the data in a binary format. It
  has a .BLG extension.

- **Binary circular**   This is a counter log file that stores the data in a binary
  format. However, when the log reaches a specified size, it starts overwriting
  the oldest data, rather than allowing the file to continue growing It also has a
  .BLG extension.

- **Text-CSV**   This is a counter log file in which the data is stored in a
  comma-delimited format, which is a common format that can be read by
  spreadsheet and database applications. It has a .CSV extension.

- **Text-TSV**   This is a counter log file in which the data is stored in a tab-delimited format, which is a common format that can be read by spreadsheet and database applications. It has a .TSV extension.

- **Circular trace file**   This is a trace log file. When the log reaches a specified size, it starts overwriting the oldest data, rather than allowing the file to continue growing. It has an .ETL extension.

- **Sequential trace file**   This is a trace log file that saves data until it reaches the maximum size. When the maximum size is reached, it creates a new file. It also has an .ETL extension.

The next configuration option is the comment. The *comment* allows you to enter a description of the log file you are creating. Finally, you select the file size limit. You can either choose the maximum size for the log file allowed by the operating system or disk quotas, or you can specify a maximum size. For counter logs, you specify the size in kilobytes, with a maximum of 2 gigabytes for counter logs. For trace logs, you specify the size in megabytes. When you use the binary circular log type, you must specify the size of the log.

exam
ⓦatch   *When setting the maximum size of a log file, be careful that it is not larger than the free space on the drive or larger than your disk quota. If the log runs out of disk space, an error will occur.*

You can also schedule logging. To start the log file, you can elect to start it manually or specify a time and date for the process to begin. To stop the logging, you can elect to stop it manually, after a duration, at a specified time, or when the file reaches the specified size limit. When you select the duration or size to stop the logging, you can select the option to start a new log file when the current one is closed. You can also specify a program to be run when the log file is closed. A common use for this option is to copy the log file to a remote location for archiving.

Now let's do an exercise to see how to perform these tasks.

Configuring Logs

1. To start the Performance Logs and Alerts, from the Start menu, select Programs | Administrative Tools | Performance.

2. In the tree view in the left pane, select Performance Logs and Alerts.

3. Now let's create a new log. In the right pane, select Counter Logs. From the Action menu, select New Log Settings...

4. When the New Log Settings dialog box comes up, enter **Exercise5** in the Name field.

5. Click OK to bring up the log properties, as shown:

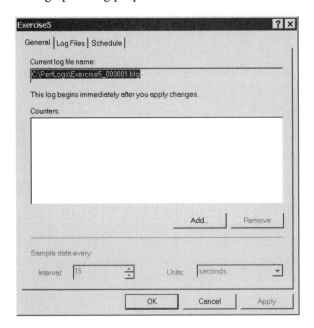

6. From the General tab, in the Counters section, click Add… to add a counter and bring up the Select Counters dialog box.

7. Select the "Use local computer counters" option.

8. In the Performance Objects list, select Processor.

9. In the Select Counters list, select the %Processor Time counter, as shown:

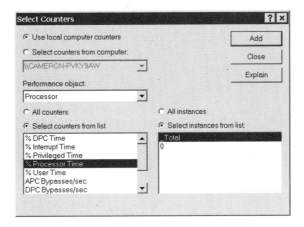

10. Click Add to add the counter.

11. Click Close to close the dialog box.

12. Leave the interval at the default of 15 seconds and click the Log Files tab.

13. Leave the location and filename at their defaults. From the "End file names with" list, select yyyymmddhh. This choice adds the date and hour to the end of a filename. Notice the example filename.

14. From the "Log file type" pull-down list, select Text File-CSV.

15. In the Comment field, enter **This is a log from Exercise 8-5.**

16. In "Log file size," select the "Limit of" option and set the size to 500KB. Your settings should look like the ones shown:

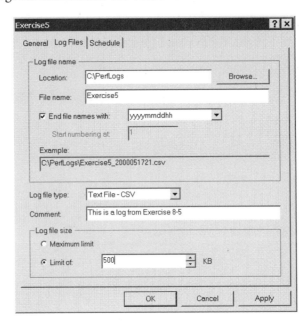

17. Go to the Schedule tab.

18. In the "Start log" section, select the At option. For the time, enter **3:26:25 PM**. For the date, use the drop-down calendar to choose 7/1/2000.

19. In the "Stop log" section, choose the "When the 500-KB log file is full" option.

20. Select the "Start a new log file" check box. Your settings should look like the ones shown:

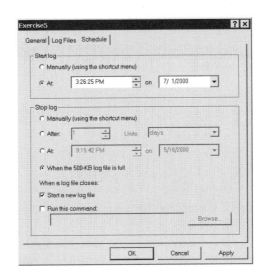

21. Click OK to create the log file.

22. The log file now appears in the right-hand pane, as shown:

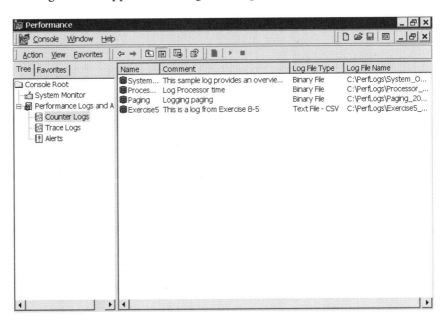

23. Close the Performance Console.

Alerts

Alerts allow some action to be performed when a performance counter reaches a particular threshold. A common action is to log an event in the application event log. You can also send a network message to a specified computer. You can have the alert trigger a performance log to start logging when the alert occurs. Finally, you can configure an alert to start a program.

When you create an alert, some of the settings are similar to creating a log. The first thing you do is give the alert a name. As with logs, you should give an alert an intuitive name. Then you can enter a comment and choose the counter or counters for the alert. One difference between an alert and a log is that you have to set a threshold for the alert. You choose a value and whether you want the alert to occur when the value is over or under the threshold. Then you also specify the interval. The default for alerts is 5 seconds.

You have some options as to what happens when an alert occurs. You can write the alert to the application event log, send a network message to a specified computer, start a log, or run a program. You can also specify the command-line parameters for the program. You have the same basic options for scheduling alerts. You can specify the start and stop options. For continuous alert scanning, you can also have the alert start a new scan when it finishes. From the Performance Logs and Alerts console, you can start and stop alerts by right-clicking them and selecting Start or Stop from the context menu.

SCENARIO & SOLUTION

When I ran the Disk Defragmenter, I noticed that the free space was still in several segments. Does this mean that my hard disk will still have a performance hit?	No, having the free space in several contiguous fragments will not have a noticeable performance hit. In fact, there is very little additional benefit from having all the free space in one contiguous space.
I created a new log file, and now my computer is running very slowly. How could this happen?	One common way this could occur is if the sample rate is set too low. For instance, setting it to less than 5 seconds can use a significant amount of resources. Try increasing the sample rate until the performance of your computer is at an acceptable level.
I don't want to continuously run logs, but I do want to know when my resources reach certain levels. How can I accomplish this?	You can use alerts. Alerts can be configured to automatically start logs and notify you when a threshold is reached.

exam
ⓦatch

Make sure you know the settings for configuring logs and alerts, including sample rates, log file options, and scheduling options.

CERTIFICATION SUMMARY

In this chapter, we discussed ways to monitor and optimize your server's resources. Creating a baseline is crucial to determining bottlenecks. A baseline allows you to easily determine which resource has become overburdened by comparing current resources to the baseline. You should monitor your server's resources continuously. This practice allows you to monitor for degradation of performance and fix it before it becomes a bottleneck. System Monitor can be used to measure the performance of your server and even other computers. Some of the common sources of bottlenecks include the processor, memory, hard disk, and network. You must use the DISKPERF utility to enable and disable the disk counters.

You can manage processes using Task Manager. You can stop or start processes and applications. This ability is useful when an application stops responding. If a process is not getting enough CPU time or if it is getting too much CPU time, you can also change the priority of the process using Task Manager. You can use the START command to set the priority of a process.

When a disk volume becomes fragmented, it can affect performance. New to Windows 2000 is the Disk Defragmenter, which you can use to defragment your volumes. When your volumes are defragmented, your system will exhibit better performance. You should run the Disk Defragmenter periodically to keep your hard disks running at peak performance.

You can use Performance Logs and Alerts to monitor performance without continuously logging data. You can create alerts with thresholds to notify you when your system meets a threshold, and you can have it start logging when an alert occurs. You can create logs for specific data and schedule them to save data as desired.

✓ TWO-MINUTE DRILL

Monitoring and Optimizing Usage of System Resources

❑ The MMC has a Performance snap-in that includes System Monitor and Performance Logs and Alerts.

❑ You can use System Monitor to analyze the health of your system.

❑ System Monitor can be used to collect data for memory usage, processor utilization, network activity, and more.

❑ System Monitor can display this data as a graph, a histogram, or a report.

❑ A bottleneck is a system component that restricts the system from operating at its peak.

❑ To properly resolve or, preferably, avoid problems, you need to monitor the processor, memory, hard disk, and the network for bottlenecks.

❑ Network bottlenecks are sometimes the result of running low on processor and memory resources.

Managing Processes

❑ You can use Task Manager to administer and configure processes.

❑ From Task Manager, you can start and stop processes and process trees, as well as set their priorities.

❑ You can assign a process to a processor or processors using the Set Affinity command.

❑ Process priorities range from 0–31, with 31 being the highest priority.

❑ There are four basic priority levels: Real-time, High, Normal, and Idle.

❑ You can set a process's priority from the command line using the START command.

Optimizing Disk Performance

❑ The performance of your hard disk can be degraded due to fragmentation.

❑ Fragmentation occurs when a file is not stored in contiguous space on a hard disk.

❑ The Disk Defragmenter can remove the fragmentation of your files.

❑ The paging file cannot be defragmented using Disk Defragmenter.

❑ To defragment a paging file, you would have to move it to another volume.

SELF TEST

The following questions will help you measure your understanding of the material presented in this chapter. Read all the choices carefully because there could be more than one correct answer. Choose all correct answers for each question.

Monitoring and Optimizing Usage of System Resources

1. You want to monitor processor and memory utilization on your computer. What utilities can you use to monitor the processor and memory utilization? Choose all that apply.

   A. Task Manager

   B. System Monitor

   C. Memory and Processor Monitor

   D. System Analyzer

2. You suspect that one of your server volumes is becoming a bottleneck in your system. You decide to monitor it in System Monitor but find that the performance counters for the volume are missing. How can you make the appropriate disk performance objects available?

   A. Reinstall Windows 2000 Server and select the disk performance components.

   B. Add the objects using Add/Remove Programs in Control Panel.

   C. Use the DISKPERF command with the /Y switch.

   D. Use the DISKPERF command with the /N switch.

3. Windows 2000 divides memory into pages of memory to help prevent memory fragmentation. What is the size of a *page* of memory in Windows 2000?

   A. 1KB

   B. 2KB

   C. 4KB

   D. 8KB

4. You have been using System Monitor to analyze memory usage. One of the counters you are measuring is the Pages/sec counter. You notice that the value for this counter seems to be stabilizing around 21. What should you do to resolve this problem?

   A. Add more memory

   B. Increase the size of the page file

    C. Split the page file over several volumes

    D. Nothing

5. You have added a server to your network, and everything seems to be operating at peak performance. You decide to create a baseline of your system using System Monitor so that you can prevent bottlenecks from occurring in the future. You are monitoring counters for CPU, memory, hard disk, and network utilization, and you want to archive this data. In what format should you generate and save this data?

    A. Report

    B. Chart

    C. Histogram

    D. Baseline log

6. Some of your users have been complaining that their disk access seems slow. You decide to monitor the hard disk in System Monitor. One of the counters you are measuring is the %Disk Time. What is the threshold for this counter when the hard disk is considered a bottleneck?

    A. 75 percent

    B. 80 percent

    C. 90 percent

    D. 100 percent

Managing Processes

7. How do you start Task Manager? Choose all that apply.

    A. By pressing CTRL+ALT+DEL and clicking the Task Manager button

    B. By pressing CTRL+SHIFT+ESC

    C. From the Start menu, select Programs I Administrative Tools I Task Manager.

    D. From the Start menu, select Programs I System Tools I Task Manager.

8. You decide you need to start a program with a priority that is higher than its default priority. You start a process from the command line using the Start command, as shown below:

```
Start /high Clock
```

What will be the priority level of the clock process?

    A. 8

    B. 10

    C. 13

    D. 15

9. You have been monitoring your processor utilization and have determined that an application is causing a bottleneck. You decide to have the application run on only one of the processors on your computer. What command do you use to specify an application to run on only a specific processor?

    A. SET PROCESSOR

    B. MOVE APPLICATION

    C. SET AFFINITY

    D. SET APPLICATION

10. What is the range of priorities to which a process can be set, and what is the highest priority?

    A. 1–32, with 1 the highest priority

    B. 1–32, with 32 the highest priority

    C. 0–31, with 1 the highest priority

    D. 0–31, with 31 the highest priority

11. Microsoft Word has stopped responding to mouse and keyboard strokes. You decide to use Task Manager to stop Word from running. Word is a large application that consists of multiple processes. You find the WINWORD.EXE process in the Processes tab of Task Manager. Which of the following commands should you use to stop WINWORD.EXE before restarting Word?

    A. END PROCESS

    B. STOP PROCESS

    C. END PROCESS TREE

    D. STOP TREE

Optimizing Disk Performance

12. Your Windows 2000 Server is acting as a file server. Users have started to complain that access to files on the server seems to be getting slower and slower. The number of users on the server hasn't increased, and there aren't any additional applications running on the server. What should you do to help increase the performance of the file access?

    A. Add memory to the client computers.

B. Defragment the volumes.

C. Add another processor to the server.

D. Restrict users to different times of the day to access the server.

13. You are using the Disk Defragmenter program to defragment the volumes on your computer. Which of the following file systems can Disk Defragmenter defragment? Choose all that apply.

A. FAT

B. FAT32

C. HPFS

D. NTFS

14. You are using Disk Defragmenter to defragment a volume on your computer. You notice that not all the free space has been consolidated into one contiguous space. Which of the following could be a cause of this lack of consolidation? Choose all that apply.

A. The page file is fragmented.

B. It would take too long.

C. Some free space is reserved for the MFT.

D. There are a large number of directories on the volume.

15. Defragmenting a volume can take hours to complete on larger volumes. To save time, you want to see whether a volume needs to be defragmented before you start defragmenting it. How can you determine whether or not the task needs to be accomplished?

A. Disk Defragmenter will display only the volumes that need to be defragmented.

B. Use the Analyze feature of Disk Defragmenter.

C. Use the Check Volume feature of Disk Defragmenter.

D. You cannot determine it ahead of time.

16. You are writing a memo detailing when volumes should be defragmented. According to best practices, which of the following are times when volumes should be defragmented? Choose all that apply.

A. When a large file is deleted

B. When a computer has been shut down for an extended period of time

C. When a directory that contains a large number of files is deleted

D. At least once a month

17. You have decided to create a performance log to check for bottlenecks.
    Required Result: The log must monitor the %Processor Time counter.
    Optional Results: The log must sample every 30 minutes. It must automatically stop running after 24 hours. When it stops running, it must automatically start another log file.
    Proposed Solution: You have created a new performance log with the settings shown in Figures 8-11 and 8-12. Which of the following best describes the performance log settings?

FIGURE 8-11

Performance log
General tab
settings

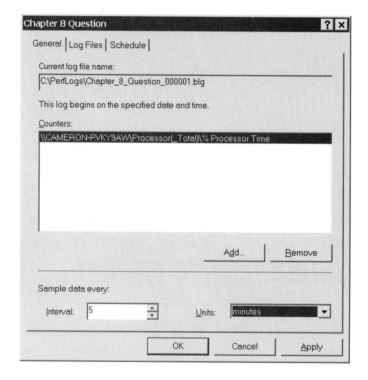

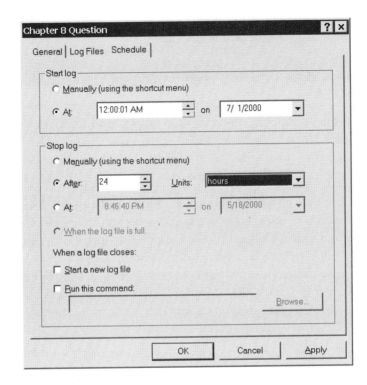

FIGURE 8-12

Performance log
Schedule tab
settings

A. The proposed solution meets the required result and all of the optional results.

B. The proposed solution meets the required result and two of the optional results.

C. The proposed solution meets the required result and one of the optional results.

D. The proposed solution does not meet the required result.

LAB QUESTION

You have a Windows 2000 server that appears to be degrading in performance. You decide to monitor it to see whether there are any bottlenecks. First, you want to view summary information to get a feel for the server's overall performance. Then you want to monitor more specific details based on what you found in the summary information. Once you have resolved any problems, you want to set some thresholds for when to start monitoring again and be notified when any threshold has been reached. What steps should you take to accomplish this goal?

SELF TEST ANSWERS

Monitoring and Optimizing Usage of System Resources

1. ☑ **A and B.** Task Manager can be used to view summary information about processor and memory usage, and System Monitor can be used to analyze detailed information about the utilization of the processor and memory resources.

   ☒ **C and D** are not correct because Windows 2000 has no utilities called Memory and Processor Monitor or System Analyzer.

2. ☑ **C.** Use the DISKPERF command with the /Y switch. DISKPERF is a command-line utility that is used to turn the hard disk counters on and off. The /Y switch turns on all the physical and logical disk counters. You could also use the –YV switch.

   ☒ **A** is not correct because there isn't an option to select the hard disk performance objects during installation. The PhysicalDisk object is enabled and the LogicalDisk object is disabled by default on Windows 2000 Server. **B** is not correct because objects cannot be added from Add/Remove Programs in Control Panel. **D** is not correct because the /D switch for the DISKPERF program disables all the hard disk performance counters.

3. ☑ **C.** Windows 2000 uses a 4KB page size for memory.

   ☒ **A, B, and D** are incorrect because Windows 2000 uses 4KB pages of memory.

4. ☑ **A.** Add more memory. When the Pages/sec counter reaches 20, memory has become a bottleneck, indicating that your system needs more memory.

   ☒ **B and C.** are not correct because optimizing your page file will not lower the amount of paging being performed; it will simply help increase the performance of paging. **D** is not correct because when the Pages/sec counter reaches 20, it is an indication that your memory is a bottleneck and you need to take some corrective action.

5. ☑ **A.** Report. When you create a baseline, you should save the data in the report format because it allows you to view specific values for the counters. When you are viewing a large number of counters in the chart view, it can be difficult to determine the values of some of the counters.

   ☒ **B and C** are not correct because these views can make it hard to discern specific values of some counters. This is especially true when you have a large number of counters with a large span of values. **D** is not correct because System Monitor does not have a baseline log option for saving data.

6. ☑ **C.** When the %Disk Time counter reaches 90 percent, it is considered a bottleneck, and Microsoft recommends taking action to lower this performance counter.
☒ **A, B,** and **D** are not correct because Microsoft considers the hard disk a bottleneck when the %Disk Time counter reaches 90 percent.

Managing Processes

7. ☑ **A and B.** You can start Task Manager by pressing either CTRL+ALT+DEL or CTRL+SHIFT+ESC.
☒ **C and D** are not correct because in the Start menu, there isn't an item for Task Manager under Administrative Tools or System Tools.

8. ☑ **C.** 13. If the base priority class is High and the thread's priority class is Normal, the overall priority is 13.
☒ **A** is not correct because an overall priority of 8 would be the case when the process's base priority class was Normal. **B** is not correct because an overall priority of 10 would also be the case when the base process priority class is Normal and the thread priority class is Highest. **D** is not correct because even though this would be a base process priority class of High, the thread priority class would have to be Highest.

9. ☑ **C.** SET AFFINITY. If you have multiple processors on your computer, you can assign a process to a processor or processors using the Set Affinity command, which is available only on multiple-processor computers.
☒ **A, B,** and **D** are incorrect because you can assign a process to a processor or processors on a multiple-processor system using the SET AFFINITY command.

10. ☑ **D.** There are 32 priority levels ranging from 0 to 31, with 31 the highest priority.
☒ **A and B** are not correct because process priorities range from 0–31, not 1–32. **C** is not correct because although process priorities do range from 0–31, the highest priority is 31, not 0.

11. ☑ **C.** If an application that contains multiple processes stops responding, you should use the END PROCESS TREE command to stop all related processes before restarting the application.
☒ **A** is not correct because even though END PROCESS will stop the WINWORD.EXE process from running, it won't stop the other dependent Word processes from running. This could potentially cause problems when you restart the application. **B and D** are not correct because the Task Manager does not have a STOP PROCESS or STOP TREE command.

Optimizing Disk Performance

12. ☑ **B.** Fragmentation of the volume can degrade performance of the hard disk over time. Use the Disk Defragmenter to defragment the volumes.
    ☒ **A** is not correct because adding memory to the client computers will have no effect on file access from a server. **C** is not correct because adding another processor will not necessarily increase file access performance. The utilization of the server hasn't increased, so it is not a matter of resources not being able to handle the additional load. **D** is not correct because even though restricting user access to different times of day might help, it is not acceptable in most work environments. Users need to be able to perform their duties as needed, not on some schedule imposed by computer system demands.

13. ☑ **A, B, and D.** You can use the Disk Defragmenter program on volumes that are formatted with FAT, FAT32, and NTFS.
    ☒ **C** is not correct because the HPFS file system cannot be defragmented with Disk Defragmenter. In fact, the HPFS file system is not even supported within Windows 2000.

14. ☑ **A, C, and D.** If the page file is fragmented, Disk Defragmenter cannot move this file because it is locked by the operating system. If a volume is NTFS, some free space is reserved at the beginning of the volume for the MFT and it cannot be moved. A large number of directories in a volume can also prevent free space from being consolidated.
    ☒ **B** is not correct because Disk Defragmenter does not limit operations by how long they will take. Some volumes can take hours to defragment.

15. ☑ **B.** The Analyze feature checks your hard disk to see whether it needs to be defragmented. It also generates a detailed report of the status of fragmentation on the volume.
    ☒ **A** is not correct because Disk Defragmenter displays all the volumes on the computer. You can defragment a volume even if it is determined by the Analyze feature that defragmentation is not needed. **C** is not correct because there isn't a Check Volume feature in Disk Defragmenter. **D** is not correct because you can determine whether or not a volume needs to be defragmented ahead of time using the Analyze feature.

16. ☑ **A, C, and D.** When a large file is deleted or a large number of files are deleted, you should defragment the volume, because new files will be created using the first available free space; defragmenting the volume will allow the new files to be created in contiguous space. Microsoft also recommends defragmenting volumes at least once a month, or more frequently for busy file servers.
    ☒ **B** is not correct because if a computer has been shut down, the volumes were not being fragmented.

17. ☑   **C.** The proposed solution meets the required result and only one of the optional results. It meets the required result because the %Processor Time counter is being measured by the log. It does meet the second optional result because the log is set to stop after running for 24 hours.

☒   **A** and **B** are not correct because the proposed solution does not meet two of the optional results. It doesn't meet the first optional result because the log is set to sample data every 5 minutes, not every 30 minutes. It doesn't meet the third optional result because it is not set to automatically start a new log file when the current one stops. To do this, you would have to check the "Start a new log file" check box. **D** is not correct because the proposed solution does meet the required result.

LAB ANSWER

The first step is to monitor summary information to determine the server's overall performance. You can use Task Manager's Performance tab, which graphically displays the CPU and memory usage as well as some other summary statistics. This information can sometimes give you quick insight into what the problem may be or where to start looking.

For more detailed information, you can use System Monitor to measure detailed information about the resources on your computer. When you find a bottleneck, resolve the problem. Then you should continue to monitor the server to ensure that you completely resolved the bottleneck.

Now that the bottleneck has been resolved, you can use Performance Logs and Alerts. Create some logs for the various resources on your computer, then create alerts with the thresholds you have determined to use, and have these alerts automatically start the appropriate log and send a message to you that the alert's threshold has been reached.

9

Systems Recovery and Protection

System availability and data safety are two of the primary concerns of any systems administrator. It is embarrassing for the administrator when for some reason the system does not start up or when data that is required urgently just vanishes. This chapter deals with methods used to fix system startup problems, and data backup and restore utilities included with Windows 2000 Server. The first part walks you through various advanced startup options in case of system boot-up failure, and explains the recovery console and some important issues that arise with the recovery of system state data.

The second part details the Windows backup and restore utilities. You will learn how to configure these two wizards. We will also discuss the backup and restore procedures for Active Directory data, which is hosted by every Windows 2000 domain controller.

CERTIFICATION OBJECTIVE 9.01

Manage and Optimize Availability of System State Data and User Data

In earlier versions of Windows NT, the Emergency Repair Disk was the only tool available for the system administrators to fix the system startup problems. The only safe startup mode was the VGA mode, which was helpful in overcoming potential display related problems. The administrator had to depend on third-party utilities to get access to the NTFS partitions. Windows 2000 has been built on strong foundations and comes loaded with numerous tools to ensure that the system downtime remains at a minimum.

The Recovery Console is a wonderful inclusion in the Windows 2000 family of operating systems. This utility not only gives access to all NTFS volumes on the system but can also re-create disk partitions. Another useful tool is the Task Scheduler, which was not available in graphical form in Windows NT 4.0. We will discuss these in detail later in this chapter.

Advanced Startup Options

If for some reason you are not able to start your system in a normal way, Windows 2000 Server gives you some advanced startup options. You can use these options to start the system and look for the problem that is preventing your system from starting. The advanced startup options are helpful in starting the operating system in a basic mode and help in diagnosing and fixing the problem.

Pressing F8 from the initial boot menu can access the advanced startup options. You have to be pretty quick in this action so that the wait time specified in the boot.ini file does not expire. In case the wait time is very low, you may press F8 during the initial startup phase. This will invoke the advanced boot options menu.

When you do not make any selection, the default operating system is started. In case you are not able to press F8 quickly, you still have a chance to do it during the initial startup phase of Windows 2000. The Windows startup screen is shown, and a small blue progress bar is shown saying that "Windows is starting up." Press F8 at this moment. The Advanced Boot Options menu has the following startup choices, which will be discussed in the following sections:

- Safe Mode
- Safe Mode with Networking
- Safe Mode with Command Prompt
- Enable Boot Logging
- Enable VGA Mode
- Last Known Good Configuration
- Directory Services Restore Mode (Windows 2000 domain controllers only)
- Debugging Mode
- Boot Normally
- Use + and - to move the highlight to your choice
- Press ENTER to choose

Safe Mode, Safe Mode with Networking, and Safe Mode with Command Prompt

The first three options give you the choice of starting the system in any of the safe modes. You may chose to start in simple Safe Mode, Safe Mode with Networking, or Safe Mode with command prompt. The choice depends on the problem you are facing with the system startup.

Safe Mode   Safe Mode starts Windows 2000 using only some basic files and device drivers. These devices include monitor, keyboard, mouse, basic VGA video, CD-ROM, and mass storage devices. The system starts only those system services that are necessary to load the operating system. Networking is not started in this mode. The Windows background screen is black in this mode, and the screen resolution is 640 by 480 pixels with 16 colors (see Figure 9-1).

You may notice that a "Safe Mode" caption is displayed on all four corners of the screen. The dialog box tells you that this mode helps you in diagnosing and fixing any startup problems.

Safe Mode with Networking   This mode is similar to the Safe Mode, but networking devices, drivers, and protocols are loaded. You may choose this mode when you are sure that the problem in the system is not due to any networking component.

Safe Mode with Command Prompt   This option starts the operating system in a safe mode using some basic files only. The Windows 2000 command prompt is shown instead of the usual Windows desktop.

<table>
<tr><td>

FIGURE 9-1

The Windows desktop in Safe Mode

</td><td>

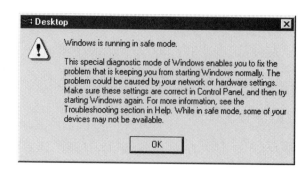

</td></tr>
</table>

The choice of a safe startup mode largely depends on the type of startup problem you are facing. In case you are not sure about the cause of the problem, use the simple Safe Mode. If this mode works, try the Safe Mode with Networking. But if the simple Safe Mode is not able to start the system, you may have to use the emergency repair process.

Enable Boot Logging

This mode tries to start Windows 2000 in a normal way and writes the startup events to a log file. This log file collects the sequence of all installed devices and drivers as they are loaded by the system successfully. The drivers that fail to load are also listed in the log file. This mode works best when you want to know exactly what is preventing the system from starting. The log file is named ntbtlog.txt and is stored in the %SystemRoot% folder.

Enable VGA Mode

This mode starts Windows 2000 using the basic video driver. When you are sure that the startup problem is due to a bad video driver or improper display settings, you can use this mode. Video problems occur when you try to install a new video driver for your display adapter or when the installed video driver file becomes corrupted. The three safe modes discussed previously use this mode when trying to start up the system. This mode uses 16 colors and 640 by 480 screen resolution.

Last Known Good Configuration

This mode starts the system using the configuration that was saved in the registry during the last system shutdown. This startup option is useful when you have changed some configuration parameters and the system fails to boot. When this mode is used to start the system, all changes that were made after the last successful logon are lost. Use this option when you suspect that some incorrect configuration changes are causing the system startup failure. This mode does not help if any of the installed drivers have been corrupted or any driver files are deleted by mistake.

Directory Services Restore Mode

This startup mode is available on Windows 2000 Server domain controller computers only. This mode can be used to restore the SYSVOL directory and Active Directory on the domain controller.

Debugging Mode

This is the most advanced startup option of all. To use this option you will need to connect another computer to the problematic computer through a serial cable. With proper configuration, the debug information is sent to the second computer. The people associated with software development projects will most often use this mode.

on the

ⓘob *Which mode to use? Inclusion of so many startup options in Windows 2000 is a welcome development on the part of Microsoft. These options were not available in Windows NT 4.0. You had to contend with only VGA mode, Last Known Good Configuration, and the Emergency repair disk. With Windows 2000 if you have even the slightest idea of what is preventing your system from starting up, you may select the particular startup option and diagnose the problem. For example, if you find out from the Web site of your video card manufacturer that a new driver can enhance the graphics capability dramatically, you may wish to download and install the new driver immediately. Forgetting to check whether the new driver is compatible with Windows 2000 or not, you may install it and get into trouble. The Enable VGA Mode can help you in such a situation. Start the system using the VGA mode and replace the incompatible driver.*

Now that you have learned some of the advanced startup options for the Windows 2000 Server, let us consider some real-life questions:

SCENARIO & SOLUTION

My Windows 2000 computer is not starting up. How can I access the Advanced boot options?	Press the F8 function key when the initial operating systems menu is displayed.
What is the best option to start the system when some configuration changes are causing the system to fail at startup?	Start the system using the Last Known Good Configuration.
I deleted two directories by mistake. Can I use the Directory Services Restore Mode to get back these directories?	Sorry. The Directory Services Restore Mode is for restoring Active Directory and not for user data directories. In any case, it works only on domain controllers.
In what circumstances should I use the Safe Mode with Networking?	When you are sure that none of the networking components are preventing the system startup.

Recovery Console

The Recovery Console is a new command-line interpreter program feature in Windows 2000 that helps in system maintenance activities and resolving system problems. This program is separate from the Windows 2000 command prompt. The following tasks can be accomplished with the help of Recovery Console:

- Start a Windows 2000 computer that is having startup problems.

- Get limited access to local NTFS, FAT32 and FAT16 partitions, and replace damaged files.

- Repair the Master Boot Record in case it is corrupted.

- Format partitions.

- Start and stop system services and drivers.

Using the Recovery Console is a secured process that allows only authorized users to access local system drives. You must have local administrative rights to start the Recovery Console on any Windows 2000 Server. The Recovery Console can either be started from the local hard disk or from the Windows 2000 CD-ROM. It requires approximately 7MB of free hard disk space.

Installing and Starting the Recovery Console

The Recovery Console can be started either from the Windows 2000 CD-ROM or from the local hard drive. In order to start the Recovery Console from the CD-ROM, the computer must be able to boot from the CD-ROM drive. Another way to start the Recovery Console is by using the Setup floppy disks. The recovery console can be installed from the Windows 2000 Server CD-ROM. Exercise 9-1 explains the steps necessary to install the Recovery Console on a computer that is running Windows 2000 Server.

The process given in this exercise assumes that you do not have mirrored drives in the computer where you are performing the installation. In order to install the Recovery Console on computers that have mirrored drives, the mirror set has to broken first. This can be reestablished after the Recovery Console is installed.

EXERCISE 9-1

Installing Recovery Console

1. Insert the Windows 2000 Server CD-ROM in your CD-ROM drive.

2. The dialog box appears, which prompts you to upgrade to Windows 2000 Server. Click No and close the window that appears.

3. From the Start menu click Start | Run. Type the following command:
   d:\i386\winnt32.exe /cmdcons
   where D is the letter of the CD-ROM drive.

4. A message is displayed on the screen, as shown:

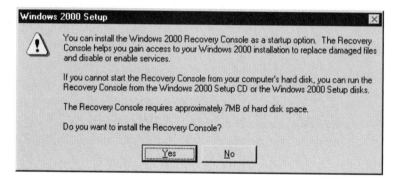

5. Click Yes to install the Recovery Console.

Starting the Recovery Console from Hard Disk   When the Recovery Console is installed on a local hard disk, an option is added to the Startup menu. You may start the Recovery Console from this menu if the master boot record of the computer is not corrupted. These steps are taken to start the Recovery Console from the boot menu:

1. Shut down and restart your computer.

2. Select Windows 2000 Recovery Console from the menu of operating systems.

3. The Recovery Console displays a command prompt. If you have more than one version of Windows installed, you are given an option to select a

particular system. Note that you can use the Recovery Console only to access installations of Windows 2000.

4. Select the operating system and press ENTER.

5. This starts the Recovery Console. You can now make the necessary changes in your system.

Starting the Recovery Console from Setup Media If you are not able to even see the Startup menu you have to use the setup floppy disk or the CD-ROM method. To use the Recovery Console, using either the Windows 2000 setup floppy disks or the CD-ROM, follow the steps given in Exercise 9-2.

Remember that use of Recovery Console requires the local administrative password. If you type an incorrect password three times or press ENTER, the Recovery Console quits and restarts the computer. Typing a correct password gives you access to the local drives. You may then start the necessary repair process.

In order to quit the Recovery Console at any time and restart the computer, type **exit** and press ENTER.

CertCam 9-2

Starting Recovery Console from Setup Media

EXERCISE 9-2

1. Start the computer with either the Window 2000 Setup floppy disks or the CD-ROM. Press ENTER when the Setup notification appears.

2. The Welcome to Setup screen appears. Press R to select Repair a Windows 2000 Installation.

3. Press C to use the Recovery Console.

4. You are prompted to select an installation in case you have more than one version of Windows 2000 running on the system. Select the installation to repair by pressing the number key corresponding to the displayed installations and press ENTER.

5. You are prompted to log on to this installation of Windows 2000 with the local administrator password. Type the password and press ENTER.

exam
ⓦatch

You must be the local administrator to use the Recovery Console. The Recovery Console will ask you for the administrator password when you start it. If you type an incorrect password three times, the Recovery Console quits and restarts the computer.

Recovery Console Commands

Once the Recovery Console has started, you can access the following directories on the NTFS drive:

- %SystemRoot%
- %Windir% and subfolders of this Windows 2000 installation (see exceptions below)
- %SystemRoot%\Cmdcons and subfolders

You also gain access to CD-ROM and floppy drives. The access to the floppy drive is limited because by default, you cannot copy files to the floppy disk. The floppy disk write access is disabled by default and has to be enabled using the **set** command. Once you are logged into a particular installation of Windows 2000, you cannot access other local installations without explicitly logging into another installation, using the **logon** command. Access is also restricted to other local folders, such as Program Files and the Documents and Settings folders.

You can use the **help** command to get a list of available commands in the Recovery Console. To get help on a particular command syntax and its usage, the /? switch can be used, which works with all commands. The Recovery Console keeps a history of previously used commands and can be accessed using the up and down arrow keys. This is similar to the DOSkey function in MS-DOS. Most of the other Recovery Console commands are similar to MS-DOS commands.

A complete listing of the Recovery Console commands, their functions and syntax is out of the scope of this book. For getting help on usage and syntax of any command, type the command name followed by the /? switch. One important command in the Recovery Console is **fixmbr**, which can be used to repair a bad master boot record.

on the
job

In case you have even a little suspicion that some sort of virus is present in the master boot record, do not use the fixmbr command. The fixmbr command can damage the partition of your computer if the master boot record is infected by a virus. Microsoft recommends that you use the built-in AVBoot antivirus program to fix the master boot record. The AVBoot is located in the \Valueadd\3rdparty\Ca-antiv folder of the Windows 2000 Server CD-ROM.

The Recovery Console has some environment variables set by default. These can be viewed and changed using the **set** command. This command is a configuration command for the Recovery Console. The syntax for this command is: **set [variable = value]**. The **set** command supports the following environment variables:

- **AllowWildCards**   This enables the use of wildcard for commands such as **copy, del,** and so on. By default, wildcards are not supported.
- **AllowAllPaths**   This provides access to all files and directories on the computer.
- **AllowRemovableMedia**   Allows copying of files and folders to removable media such as floppy disks and writeable compact disks.
- **NoCopyPrompt**   Disables the prompt that appears when an existing file is overwritten.

The value of these variables can be either enable or disable. You will need to enable the full functionality of the **set** command from the Group Policy Snap-in of the Microsoft Management Console (MMC). Exercise 9-3 explains the necessary steps to enable full functionality of the **set** command.

EXERCISE 9-3

Using Group Policy to Enable Set Command

1. Click Start | Run and type **mmc**. Press ENTER. This opens an empty Microsoft Management Console labeled as Console1.

2. From the Console menu, select Add/Remove Snap-in. The Add/Remove Snap-in window appears. Click Add.

3. Select Group Policy and click Add again, as shown:

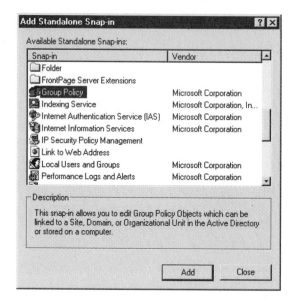

4. In the Select Group Policy Object, select Local Computer. Click Finish.

5. Click Close in the Add Standalone Snap-in window.

6. Click OK in the Add/Remove Snap-in window.

7. Click the + sign before Local Computer Policy to expand it.

8. Click the + sign before each of the following to expand: Computer Configuration | Windows Settings | Security Settings | Local Policies.

9. Click Security Options. The Local Security Policy Settings appear on the right side of the console, as shown:

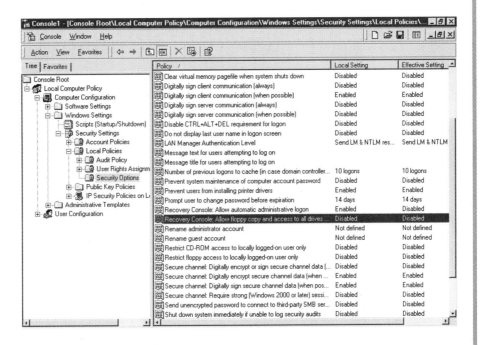

10. Double-click the policy Recovery Console: Allow floppy copy and access to all Files and all Folders.

11. This opens the Local Security Policy Setting window. Click the Enabled radio button. Click OK as shown:

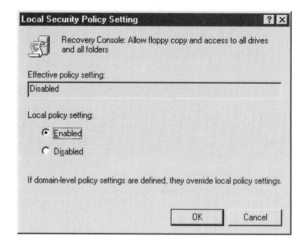

12. Click the Console menu and select Exit. Click No to exit without saving the console.

Using Recovery Console to Start and Stop Services

When you have logged on to the system successfully using the Recovery Console, you may start, stop, or change the start type of any driver or system service. The **enable** and **disable** commands are used to perform these functions.

To Stop a Service   If you need to disable a service on system startup, you can use the **disable** command from the Recovery Console prompt in the following syntax: **disable service_name.**

When you press ENTER, this command first displays the previously set startup type of the service or driver. After this the startup type is changed to disabled.

To Start a Service   The **enable** command can be used to start a system service in the following syntax: **enable service_name [start_type].**

"start_type" specifies the startup type of the service. The valid values for this option are:

- service_boot_start
- service_system_start
- service_auto_start
- service_demand_start

Another Recovery Console command that is helpful in starting and stopping services and drivers is the **listsvc** command. This command displays a list of available system services, drivers, and their startup type settings.

Using Recovery Console to Copy Files onto NTFS Drives

The Recovery Console can be used to replace corrupted files on FAT16, FAT32, and NTFS partitions of the installed disk drives. This is a useful tool for copying original files when system or driver files become corrupted or get deleted by mistake. The source of the original file may be a floppy disk, a CD-ROM, or any of the local disks or partitions. The following Recovery Console commands are helpful in file copy operations: **attrib –R |+R |-S |+S |-H |+H |-C |+C file_name.** This command is similar to the MS-DOS **attrib** command used to change the attributes of a single file.

Copy source [destination] copies a single file from the source to the destination. The destination is optional because if it is not specified, the file is copied to the current directory. When you use this command to copy any compressed files, these are uncompressed before copying.

- **del [drive_name:][path]file_name** deletes a single file from the specified drive and path.
- **dir [drive_name:][path]** gives a listing of all the files and subdirectories. This command displays even the system and hidden files.

Other useful commands that are similar to MS-DOS command are **cd/chdir, md/mkdir,** and **rd/rmdir,** which are used to change, make, and remove directories respectively.

SCENARIO & SOLUTION

Can I use the Recovery Console if I have not installed it on my hard disk?	Yes. You can start the Recovery Console from either the Windows 2000 setup floppy disks or the setup CD-ROM.
The master boot record (MBR) of one of my servers has been infected with a virus. Is it possible to fix it using the Recovery Console?	No. The **fixmbr** command in the Recovery Console repairs only the boot code in the boot partition and cannot fix the MBR virus problems. Use an antivirus program to remove the MBR virus.
Can I copy some files to a floppy disk from the NTFS drive?	No and Yes. No, because by default the Recovery Console does not allow you to copy files to a floppy drive or removable media. Yes, because you can modify the Group Policy Settings to enable this option.
I am having system startup problems due to a faulty system service. Is there any way to stop this service so that it does not prevent the system from starting?	Yes. Use Recovery Console to change the system startup setting for the particular service. You must first know the exact service that is causing the problem.

e x a m
ⓦ a t c h

You must note that the Recovery Console commands listed above do not support any wildcards by default. This means that if you want to copy all files with .exe extension, you cannot use the copy *.exe command. You will have to copy the files one by one or use the set command to enable wildcards.

After discussing various aspects of the Recovery Console usage, review the real-life scenarios and solutions in the table, above.

Active Directory Data Considerations

Microsoft has tested Active Directory for over 40 million objects. Theoretically speaking, as the number of objects grows, the size of Active Directory grows and the performance of the domain controller should tend to slow down. Practically, this does not happen. Tests have shown that the performance remains consistent when the data size increases. The size of the Active Directory database does not affect the server performance.

When you build a server as a domain controller, make sure that you have enough disk space to hold the Active Directory database. The Active Directory database is stored in the NTDS.DIT file. This will ensure that as the number of objects in Active Directory grows with the passage of time, you don't have to rebuild the server again from scratch. This is particularly important when you have limited resources.

The availability of system data on a domain controller relies on availability of the Active Directory services. The following are some of the best practices:

■ Keep at least twice the disk space estimated for the database. This takes care of future growth.

■ Make a clear estimate of the database, allocating 3.6KB per user object or other security principle, 1.1KB per nonsecurity principle, and 75 bytes per Access Control entry per object.

■ Allocate additional space for domain controllers that are also hosting Global Catalogs.

Active Directory File Structure

The Active Directory database is stored in a file named NTDS.DIT. In case you wish to perform the database sizing tests, you will need to find the size of the NTDS.DIT file. If you use Windows Explorer to check the size of NTDS.DIT file, you will notice that the size does not change even when multiple write operations are performed on the file. The reason for this is that on NTFS volumes, the size is determined when the file is opened and it is not refreshed until the file is closed.

The Active Directory database is opened when the domain controller computer starts up. It remains open while the computer is running. It is closed only when the computer is shut down. This means that using Windows Explorer or command prompt are not the correct ways to monitor the size of the NTDS.DIT database file.

The following two ways can be used to determine the size of the NTDS.DIT file:

■ Restart the domain controller. This will close the file during shut down and reopen it during startup. This method is not always recommended. Use this when it is extremely necessary to monitor the database. The file size is shown in Figure 9-2.

■ Use Windows Explorer Properties on the partition that contains the NTDS.DIT file. This reports the correct size of used and free space on the partition. Make a note of the free space before and after the tests.

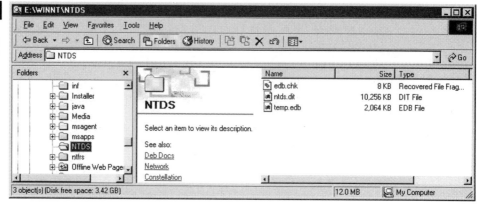

FIGURE 9-2

Checking the size
of the NTDS.DIT
file

Placement of Log Files and System Files

Active Directory resides only on Windows 2000 Server domain controllers. The
domain controllers in a network usually attract more network traffic than other
servers. The larger the network, the busier is server. To achieve best performance
from the server hosting Active Directory, it is recommended that the Active
Directory data files are placed on a separate drive from the system root. If possible,
also keep all the Active Directory log files separate from both the system and Active
Directory data files. When you install Active Directory, you are given an option to
select the location of the NTDS.DIT file and the log files (see Figure 9-3).

FIGURE 9-3

Selecting the
location of Active
Directory files

Active Directory Installation Wizard

Database and Log Locations
Specify the locations of the Active Directory database and log.

For best performance and recoverability, store the database and the log on separate hard disks.

Where do you want to store the Active Directory database?

Database location:

`D:\WINNT\NTDS`   Browse...

Where do you want to store the Active Directory log?

Log location:

`G:\WINNT\NTDS`   Browse...

< Back   Next >   Cancel

Backup and Recovery Systems and User Data

Data backup and restoration are important elements of the system recovery process in times of emergency. In spite of available tools for system recovery such as disk mirroring and implementing RAID 5, the data must be backed up on a regular basis for protection against disasters. The two types of data are systems data, which is necessary for the system to keep running, and the user data, which may contain the important files for the whole organization, covering nearly all kinds of data.

It is important to understand the importance of data backups. Backups are important not only in case of catastrophic system failure, but to also address less severe situations. Consider a user who deletes some important system files and causes the system to go down. Implementation of any type of RAID will not help in this case. You will definitely need a source from which you can recover the files. This is where data backup comes to the rescue of a system administrator.

Windows Backup

Windows Backup is a built-in Backup and Restore utility, which has many more features than the backup tool provided in Windows NT 4.0. It supports all five types of backup: Normal, Copy, Differential, Incremental, and Daily. Windows Backup allows you to perform the backup operation manually or you may schedule it to run at a later time in unattended mode. Included with the operating system, it is a tool that is flexible and easy to use.

Backup Strategies

Whether you use any third-party backup program or choose the built-in Windows Backup, there are some issues that you must consider. Before you can use any of the backup programs, you will need to do some planning. Some of the important planning issues for Windows Backup are discussed next.

What to Back Up?   The first important issue is to determine what data needs to be backed up. This depends on the importance of data and the time it would take to re-create it if it were lost. For example, some organizations may have databases containing several years' worth of information.

Who Will Back Up?   The next question to decide is who will be responsible for running the backup program and what rights and permissions will be required. This depends on the volume and location of data existing in an organization. If the data is spread on many workstations, the users can back up their own files. If the data is server based, then it is better to have a dedicated operator to perform the backup jobs. In Windows 2000, the Administrators, Backup Operators, and Server Operators can backup and restore files on servers or workstations, irrespective of any NTFS permissions set on files and folders. In addition, any user who has Read, Read and Execute, Modify, or Full Control Permissions can perform backups. Every user is the creator/owner of his/her files by default and can perform backup of all such files.

How Often to Back Up?   The answer to this question depends on how often the data changes. You have the choice of performing backups on a daily, weekly, or monthly basis. You may also have some other schedule.

When to Back Up?   This also concerns the way you run the backup. There are two ways: attended mode and unattended mode. This depends on the availability of personnel, servers, and network bandwidth. It is always better to run backup jobs at night when there are few files open and the network traffic is also very low. Most backup programs allow you to schedule the backup jobs to be run at a later time.

What Media to Use?   The data can be stored on tapes or other file systems. Tapes are inexpensive and are typically high-capacity but have a limited life. Data backed up to other file systems are stored in a single file containing all of the files and folders selected for backup. This file has a .bkf extension and can be stored on tape, Zip drives, writeable compact disks, optical disks, or another network server.

Once you have made a comprehensive plan, you are ready to use any backup program.

Using Windows Backup

The Windows Backup program contains four tools: the Backup Wizard, the Restore Wizard, the Job Scheduler, and the Emergency Repair Disk creation tool. The Windows Backup can be started in either of these ways:

- From the Start menu, select Programs | Accessories | System Tools | Backup.
- From the Start menu, click Run and type **ntbackup.exe.** Press ENTER.

Figure 9-4 shows the Windows 2000 Backup and Recovery Tools welcome screen. The Windows Backup tool can be used to back up the data on any media: files, tapes, recordable compact disks, or Zip drives. The backed-up data can be restored at a later date using the Restore Wizard. These are some of the permissions and rights that are required for performing backup or restore operations on a Windows 2000 Server:

- Administrators, Backup Operators, and Server Operators have the Backup Files and Directories and Restore Files and Directories rights assigned to them by default. The persons in these groups can back up and restore all files and folders, regardless of the NTFS permissions.

- Any user can back up and restore files and directories for which he/she is the owner. Users can also back up files and directories for which they have Read, Read and Execute, Modify, or Full Control permissions.

- Write, Modify, or Full Control permissions are required for any user performing the restore operation.

FIGURE 9-4

Windows Backup and Recovery Tools welcome screen

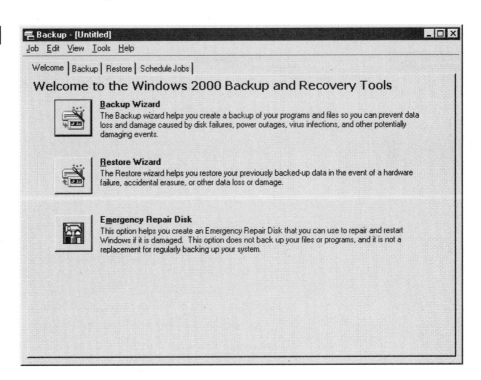

exam
ⓦatch

From the exam point of view, it is important that you remember which of the user groups have the rights to perform backup and restore on Windows 2000 servers.

Backup Options

The Windows Backup program has some default settings for data backup and restore. You can modify any of these settings to suit your requirements. To view these settings click Options from the Tools menu. The General tab of the Options screen appears, as shown in Figure 9-5.

- **General** This is the opening tab of the options menu. You may notice from Figure 9-5 that most of the settings are made by default. One important setting is Verify data after the backup completes. This helps in verifying that the backed-up data is not corrupted.

- **Restore** This tab has some data restore settings.

- **Backup Type** This tab is used to specify the type of backup required. Windows Backup allows you to select a backup type for a particular job. The types include Normal, Copy, Differential, Incremental, and Daily.

FIGURE 9-5

Windows Backup
options screen

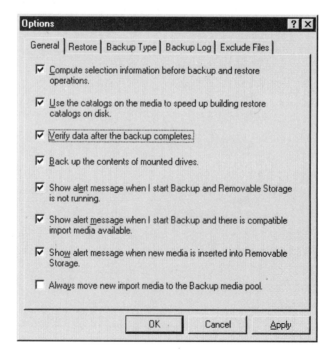

- **Backup Log**   The settings under this tab allow you to specify what information should be stored in the backup log files.
- **Exclude Files**   This tab is used to specify the types of files that you do not want to be backed up.

Backup Types

The requirement of backup jobs varies from one organization to the other. Some organizations prefer to perform a normal backup every day, while others may prefer only incremental backups on a daily basis and a full backup on the weekend. In addition, the availability of a particular server and network bandwidth also affect the choice of a backup type. Windows Backup supports five different types of backup: Normal, Copy, Differential, Incremental, and Daily. Figure 9-6 shows the backup screen where you can select the backup type.

- **Normal backup**   This is the most common type and is also known as a full backup. The Normal backup operation backs up all files and folders that are selected irrespective of the archive attributes of the files. This provides the easiest way to restore the files and folders but is expensive in terms of the time it takes to complete the backup job and the storage space it consumes.

FIGURE 9-6

Selecting backup type

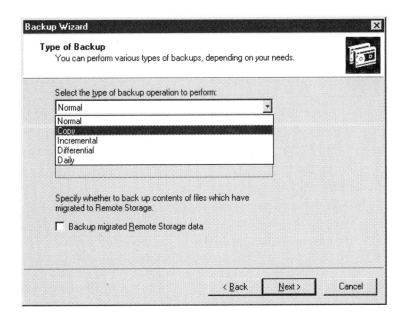

The restore process from a Normal backup is less complex because you do not have to use multiple tape sets to completely restore data.

- **Copy backup** This type of backup simply copies the selected files. It neither looks for any markers set on files nor does it clear them. The Copy backup does not affect the other Incremental or Differential backup jobs and can be performed along with the other types of backup jobs.

- **Differential backup** This backup process is relatively fast. The Differential backup checks and performs a backup of only those files that are marked. It does not clear the markers after the backup, which means that any consecutive differential backups will backup the marked files again. When you need to restore from a Differential backup you will need the most current full backup and the Differential backup performed after that.

- **Incremental backup** This backup process is similar to the Differential backup, but it clears the markers from the selected files after the process. Because it clears the markers, an incremental backup will not back up any files that have not changed since the last incremental backup. This type of backup is fast during the backup but is very slow while restoring the files. You will need the last full backup and all of the subsequent incremental backups to fully restore data. The positive side of this backup type is that it is fast and consumes very little media space.

- **Daily backup** This type of backup does not use any markers to back up selected files and folders. The files that have changed during the day are backed up every day at a specified time. This backup will not affect other backup schedules.

You may have noticed the term "marker" in the previous discussion. This is also known as Archive Bit, which is used to tell the backup program whether or not to back up a particular file.

Backup Logs

Windows Backup generates a backup log file for every backup job. These files are the best place to review the backup process in case some problem is encountered by the program. The backup log is a text file that records all the events during the backup process. The log files can be configured from the Backup Logs tab of the backup Options screen.

When you are restoring some files from a backup that was done using an incremental backup, you will need the last full backup and all the subsequent incremental backups. When you restore from a differential backup set, you need to restore the last full backup and only the last differential backup. Because of this, differential backups are typically quicker to restore.

Backup Files and Folders

Considering the importance of data backups, it is always better to plan things in advance. The backup operation requires you to consider all aspects of the job, which include speed, cost, availability of servers, network bandwidth, and data type. The local backups are not dependent on network bandwidth, but other factors such as the importance of data must be considered during planning.

First of all, you will need to select the files and folders you are planning to back up. The Windows Backup program cannot back up any files that are open or locked at the time of backup. If this is the case, you can send a notification to all the users to close any open files that are to be backed up. If the backup is to be performed during nonworking hours, this may not be required.

Using the Backup Wizard   After you have decided on a particular backup type, the next step is to select the files and folders that you wish to back up. You can use the Windows Backup Wizard to proceed. The Backup Wizard is listed in Figure 9-7. When you start the Backup Wizard, the What to Back Up screen gives these three options:

- Back up everything on my computer.
- Back up selected files, drives, or network data.
- Back up only the System State data.

You can make a choice and click Next to proceed. In the next illustration we have selected Back up selected files, drives, or network data. This is the option you may be frequently using because it is the most flexible one. You can also include the System State data on the local computer. Exercise 9-4 explains the steps you must take to perform a backup using this option.

CertCam 9-4

EXERCISE 9-4

Backing Up Selected Files and Folders

1. Log on to the server as an administrator. Click Start | Run.

2. Type **ntbackup** in the dialog box. Click OK. This opens the welcome screen of the Windows 2000 Backup and Recovery Tools. Click the Backup Wizard tab.

3. The Backup selection window appears. You will notice another dialog box where you can select Backup selected files, drives, and network data, as shown in the illustration below. Click Next.

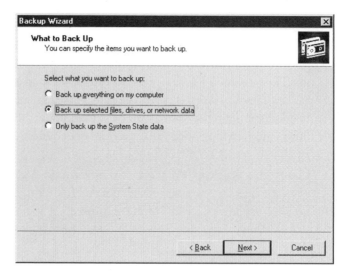

4. The Backup (Untitled) window appears next. Click My Computer to expand it. Select the files you wish to back up. Make sure you select the System State check box if you wish to include this:

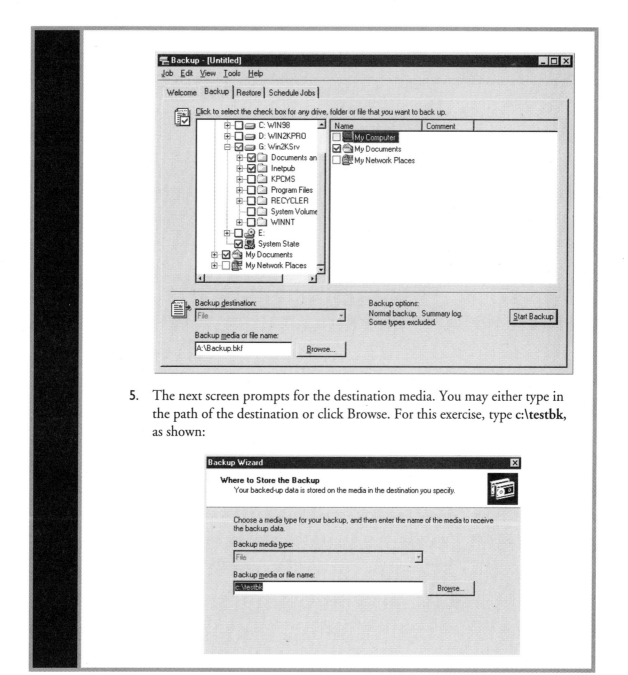

5. The next screen prompts for the destination media. You may either type in the path of the destination or click Browse. For this exercise, type **c:\testbk**, as shown:

6. The next screen is the Completing the Backup Wizard, as shown:

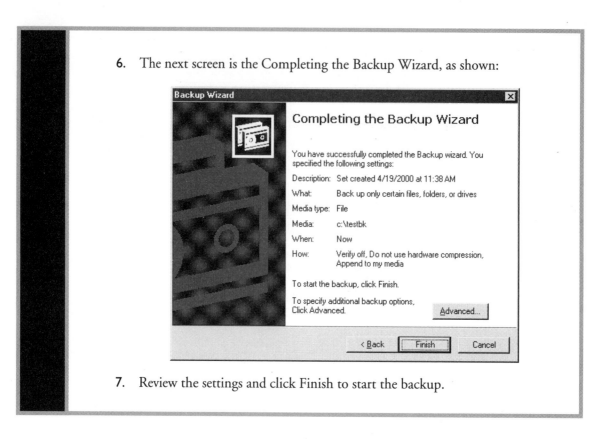

7. Review the settings and click Finish to start the backup.

Advanced Backup Options You may have noticed an Advanced tab in the Completing the Backup Wizard screen. The advanced settings allow you to make these selections:

- **Type of Backup** Normal, Copy, Differential, Incremental, or Daily
- **How to Backup** You can choose to verify the data after backup.
- **Media Options** You may choose to append data to the media or replace the old data already stored.
- **Backup Label** To specify a label

After selecting any advanced settings, you are prompted to choose whether to back up now or later. If you select Backup Now, the backup starts. If you select Backup Later, additional dialog boxes appear so that you can schedule the backup to start at a specified data and time.

Back Up and Restore System State Data

The System State data contains data that is essential in keeping Windows 2000 Server running. This data can be backed up on local computers only. It is not possible to backup System State data on remote computers. On a Windows 2000 Server, the System State data essentially contains:

- System Registry database
- COM+ Class registration database
- System startup files

Depending on other services running on the server, the System State data may contain the following additional items:

- Certificate Services database if the server is a Certificate Server
- Active Directory services and the SYSVOL directory if the server is a domain controller
- Resource registry check points (Cluster database) if the server is running Cluster Services

When you select to back up or restore the System State data, all the components are automatically selected. It is not possible to perform a backup of the System State data by selecting individual components. You need to be an administrator or a member of the Backup Operators Group in order to back up or restore the System State data.

Schedule a Backup

Backup schedules are required when you want to run the backup in an unattended mode. The Windows Backup utility includes a backup scheduling program. This can be selected from the Schedule tab of the Backup program. It is best to perform backup on a busy server when there is a lesser load on the server and network traffic is also low.

To run the backup at a later time, you will first need to configure the Backup Wizard, as described in Exercise 9-4. Choose the option Later in the When to Back Up dialog box. This activates the task scheduler. You will be prompted to select a user account and password that will be used to perform the backup job. After the username and password are confirmed, you are prompted to select the date and time when you wish the backup to start (see Figure 9-7).

FIGURE 9-7

Scheduling the
backup time

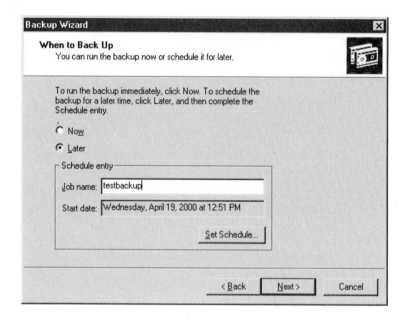

Type the name of the job. The Start date shows the current date and time as
default start time. Click Set Schedule to specify a different date and time. When you
finish entering the information, the job is put in the schedule and run later at the
specified time.

on the
job

***When you are using a centralized backup server, it is always recommended
that you run large backup jobs during the time when the network is having
relatively little traffic—for example, during the nights when you have plenty
of network bandwidth available. This will also ensure that the backup servers
do not face extra load.***

Restore Files and Folders

The backed-up data is useless unless you know how to restore it when the need
arises. You may need to restore data in case of disaster or when some data becomes
corrupted. When there is no need to run the data restore process, you must run trial
restores to see whether everything works fine. This will make sure that the backup
media is working properly and that the data will be available when it is required.

The Windows 2000 Backup program includes the Restore Wizard. This can be used to restore data from the backup archives. The first important thing is to decide what data needs to be restored. If the data is on tapes or Zip drives, you must keep these items handy. These steps explain how to run the Restore Wizard:

1. From the Windows Backup program select the Restore Wizard. The Restore window opens.

2. Select the media type from which the data is to be restored. Make sure the media contains the required data.

3. Click the media type to expand it. Select the files or folders you wish to restore. Click Next.

4. The default settings appear where the data will be restored. Check and verify that the location selected is appropriate. Click Next.

This starts the data restoration from the selected media to the specified destination on the computer.

Restore Active Directory Services

In order to restore Active Directory data, you must have domain administrative rights. You must also have the most current backup of the Active Directory data or the System State data. You must also decide beforehand whether the restore should be authoritative or nonauthoritative. The default method of Active Directory data restore is nonauthoritative. Authoritative Active Directory data restore ensures that the data is replicated to other domain controllers in the network. This requires you to run the Ntdsutil utility.

The Windows Backup Wizard can be used to restore the Active Directory data when the system is run in Restore Directory Services Mode. Since the Active Directory data is contained in the System State data, you will need to restore the System State data in order to restore it. Exercise 9-5 lists the steps needed to restore the Active Directory data.

exam
ⓦatch

Remember that when you need to restore the data in Authoritative Mode, you will need to run the Ntdsutil utility after restoring the System State data from the most current backup.

Restoring Active Directory

1. Restart the computer and press the F8 key when the operating systems menu is displayed.

2. Select Restore Directory Services Mode.

3. Log on to the system as domain administrator.

4. From the Start menu click Run. Type in **ntbackup.exe** and press ENTER. The Windows Backup program starts.

5. Click Restore. This opens the Restore window.

6. Click the check box named System State. You may also select any other data that you wish to restore:

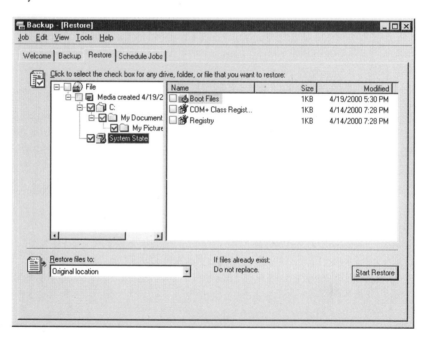

7. You will notice that the default mode of restore is Nonauthoritative. Select Authoritative Restore. Run the Ntdsutil utility.

8. This finishes the authoritative restore of Active Directory. Restart the computer and use the normal startup mode.

exam
ⓦatch

The System State data contains the Active Directory database on domain controllers and can be backed up and restored on local computers only. You must have domain administrator rights to perform the restore.

The following table will help you find answers to some of the common questions that you may encounter on the job.

SCENARIO & SOLUTION

Is it possible to run Windows Backup when nobody is present in the office?	Yes. You can schedule the backup job to run at any time you wish. When you configure the backup job you will get a dialog box that asks you to specify when you wish to start the backup.
I have only one domain controller. What kind of Active Directory restore do I need to perform: authoritative or nonauthoritative?	Nonauthoritative. This is because the Active Directory data is not replicated to any other domain controller. Be sure to use the most current backup.
I don't have much data to back up. What kind of backup should I perform?	If you do not have much data to back up, choose the Normal backup type.
When I run the Normal backup on a database server, it becomes very slow and the backup also takes very long to complete. What should I do?	This probably means that the server is experiencing excessive load during the backup and that the database size is very large. Switch to incremental backups or schedule the backup job for a time when the database is not in use.
How do I make sure that the data I am going to backup will be good?	Use the Verify option from the backup options screen.

FROM THE CLASSROOM

Planning Backup Policies

So, finally you have a backup tool that includes a graphical scheduling feature that ensures the backup will kick off at night while you are asleep. Excellent, but there are many factors that you should take care of while planning the backup policies, especially when you are responsible for a large company with gigabytes of data. Here are some important points:

1. Check the volume of data that needs backup. Use a dedicated backup server with the fastest tape devices available.

2. Decide on the backup type. In the case of large databases, do an incremental backup from Monday to Friday and a Normal (full) backup on Fridays.

3. Schedule the backup job when network traffic is low. A window between 10.00 P.M. and 4.00 A.M. is usually the best slot.

4. Prioritize the data based on importance. Start those jobs first that have incurred the most changes during the day.

5. Store the tapes off site, preferably out of town. Never keep the tapes in the same room where the servers are installed.

6. When you notice that the backup jobs are consuming a significant portion of your time, delegate your responsibilities. Two are always better than one.

7. Perform test restores to check that the backed-up data is in good condition and can be used in case of emergency situations. This will also ensure that the media works fine.

8. Document everything and keep a history of the changes.

One final word: You must perform backups at regular intervals, even if you will never need to do any restores. Don't worry about the media; it is reusable.

—Pawan K. Bhardwaj, MCSE, MCP+I, CCNA

CERTIFICATION SUMMARY

System availability and data safety are very important functions of a systems administrator. Windows 2000 comes with many tools that are helpful to keep the system downtime to a minimum. The Advanced Startup Options help in resolving system startup problems. The safe modes, Last Known Good Configuration, and the Enable VGA Mode are some of the advanced options available. The Directory Services Restore Mode is available on domain controllers to restore the Active Directory services. The Boot Logging Mode writes the startup events to a log file.

The Recovery Console is a new command-line tool in Windows 2000 that gives limited access to FAT and NTFS partitions on a hard disk. You can create, delete, or format partitions and fix the master boot record if it is corrupt. Being secure, it requires logon to the local system and does not allow you to copy files to any removable media by default. Any faulty services or drivers that are preventing the system from starting in the normal way can be stopped or restarted. The Recovery Console can be started from the setup media or from the hard disk if it is previously installed.

Windows 2000 comes with a built-in interactive backup and recovery utility. Five types of supported backup are: Normal, Copy, Differential, Incremental, and Daily. The graphical task scheduler allows you to run backup jobs at a specified time. Any user with Read, Read and Execute, Modify, or Full Control permissions can run a backup job. You must perform backups of system and user data on a regular basis and run test restores to check that the stored data is intact. Backups can be performed to file or tape. Most of the common backup media such as tape devices, Zip drives, and writeable compact disks are supported.

The System State data in a computer includes the Registry, system startup files, and COM+ class registration database. In addition, this data contains the Active Directory and the SYSVOL folder if the computer is a domain controller. The System State data cannot be backed up on remote computers through Windows Backup. The Active Directory restore can be done in Authoritative or Nonauthoritative Modes, and the person performing this restore must have domain administrator rights. The *Ntdsutil* is run to update Active Directory data on other domain controllers when an Authoritative restore is done.

TWO-MINUTE DRILL

Manage and Optimize Availability of System State Data and User Data

❑ The Advanced Startup Options are systems repair tools included with Windows 2000 for fixing system startup problems. You can access the Advanced Startup Options menu by pressing F8 when the initial operating systems menu is displayed.

❑ The three safe modes are Safe Mode, Safe Mode with Networking, and Safe Mode with Command Prompt. All safe modes use only the basic system files and a basic VGA driver for the display. The Safe Mode with Command Prompt starts the system in MS-DOS mode.

❑ The Last Known Good Configuration starts the system using the saved configuration values in the registry when the system was last shut down normally. The Directory Restore Mode is used on domain controllers to restore the Active Directory.

❑ The Recovery Console in Windows 2000 is a command line utility that can be started from either the setup floppy disks or the setup CD-ROM. It can also be started from the operating systems options menu if it is installed on the hard disk.

❑ You need to be a local administrator in order to start the Recovery Console. You can start and stop services, fix the MBR, work with partitions, and get limited access to the FAT and NTFS volumes on the hard drive. By default, you cannot copy files from hard disk to any removable media such as floppy disks.

❑ The **set** command is used in the Recovery Console to configure the environment variables for the console. You can also modify these settings using the Group Policy.

❑ The **enable** and **disable** commands are used to start and stop system services and drivers respectively. The **listsrv** command displays a list of available system services.

❑ The Active Directory data is stored in the NTDS.DIT file on the domain controller. It is not possible to check the size of this file on the fly. For best performance, it is recommended that the system files, the NTDS.DIT database and the log files be placed on separate hard drives.

Backup and Recovery Systems and User Data

❑ The Windows Backup and recovery tools can be started by running NTBACKUP.EXE or from the Start menu by selecting Programs | Accessories | System Tools | Backup.

❑ You must back up your system and user data on a regular basis. Even if you will never need to restore, test restores should be done to check the integrity of data. You should have a concrete plan in place to perform backup jobs.

❑ Windows 2000 supports five types of backup: Normal, Copy, Differential, Incremental, and Daily. Normal and Copy do the full backup. The main difference between Differential and Incremental is that the latter clears the archive bits (markers).

❑ The General tab of the backup options allows you to verify the data after the backup job is over. The Exclude tab can be used to specify which files should not be included in the backup.

❑ Any user who has Read, Read and Execute, Modify, or Full Control permissions can run a backup job. If you want to delegate the backup responsibilities, you must make the person to whom you give this job a member of the Backup Operators Group.

❑ The Backup and Restore Wizards are easy to use tools for performing these jobs. You can run the backup job immediately or schedule it to run later at a specified time. Backups can be done to either file or tape.

❑ The System State data contains the system Registry, COM+ class registration database, and the startup files. On domain controllers the Active Directory data and the SYSVOL folder are also contained in the System State data.

❑ Active Directory can be restored in either Authoritative or Nonauthoritative Mode. You must be a domain administrator to restore Active Directory. When you run the Authoritative restore, you need to run the NTDSUTIL utility to update other domain controllers.

SELF TEST

The following questions will help you measure your understanding of the material presented in this chapter. Read all of the choices carefully, as there may be more than one correct answer. Choose all correct answers for each question.

Manage and Optimize Availability of System State Data and User Data

1. What option do you have to repair a system that does not start in the Safe Mode when you select the Advanced Boot Options?

   A. Use the Safe Mode with Networking.

   B. Use the Enable VGA Mode.

   C. Use the Debugging Mode.

   D. Use the Emergency Repair Disk.

2. Under what circumstances you would try to start a system using the Safe Mode with Networking when you have startup problems?

   A. When the Safe Mode fails to start the system

   B. When Safe Mode works and you know all network components are working

   C. When you have installed an incorrect video driver

   D. When you want to restore the Active Directory data

3. What privileges are required to restore and update Active Directory on a domain controller computer?

   A. Log on as Service

   B. Domain Administrator

   C. Member of Administrators Group

   D. Member of Power Users Group

4. What is one of the most important requirements for restoring the Active Directory data on a domain controller?

   A. You must have local administrator rights on the domain controller.

   B. The restore must be done using Authoritative Mode.

   C. The System State data must have been backed up earlier.

   D. You must start the computer using the Safe Mode.

5. Your boss has asked you to tell him how the Recovery Console can help in times of emergency. Choose all the correct options from the options given below.

   A. It can fix a corrupted MBR.

   B. It can create, delete, and format partitions.

   C. It can upgrade basic disks to dynamic disks

   D. It can start and stop system services.

   E. It can install and uninstall drivers.

6. The network in your office has five Windows 2000 servers configured as domain controllers. Replication has been set on all servers so that the Active Directory database is synchronized among all. You are wise enough to perform regular backups of all these servers on a regular basis on a network backup server, running Windows Backup. One of these servers crashes one day when you are not in the office, and no one else fixes it. You return to the office after two days and want to fix the problem. Here is what you have to do:
   Required Result: Repair the server and restore the user data.
   Desired Optional Result: Restore the System State data. Make the Active Directory database in synch with other domain controllers. Proposed Solution: Fix the server problem using either the Safe mode or by using the Emergency Repair Disk. Restore the server data from the most current backup set.
   What results does the proposed solution produce?

   A. The proposed solution does not produce the required result.

   B. The proposed solution produces the required result but none of the optional results.

   C. The proposed solution produces the required result and only one of the optional results.

   D. The proposed solution produces the required result and both of the optional results.

7. One of the servers on your network is not starting up due to a failed system service, and you want to use the Recovery Console to fix the problem. What command can you use to view all the services that you can enable or disable?

   A. listsvc

   B. enable service_name

   C. disable service_name

   D. help service

8. You are using the Recovery Console to fix some problems on a server that is not starting up. You need to copy two files to a floppy disk so that you can examine them on another computer. Every time you try to copy the files to the floppy disk, you get an Access Denied message. What must you do so that you are able to copy the files to the floppy disk?

    A. Format the floppy with NTFS.

    B. Clean the MBR of the floppy.

    C. Use the **set** command to allow floppy copy access.

    D. Use Windows Explorer to check and set permissions on the files.

9. Which of the following startup modes will help you start a server using the last saved registry values when the problem is due to misconfiguration?

    A. Enable VGA

    B. Last Known Good Configuration

    C. Enable Boot Logging

    D. Any of the above

Backup and Recovery Systems and User Data

10. What command can you use to start the Windows Backup Wizard from the command prompt?

    A. Ntdsutil

    B. Ntbackup.exe

    C. Winback.exe

    D. Win AT

11. The database servers in your network host very large databases. The backup operation takes nearly eight hours to complete, and it is done every day in Normal Mode. What is your best option to reduce the backup time?

    A. Purchase faster devices that can reduce backup time.

    B. Perform the backup on a separate backup server.

    C. Switch to Incremental backup type.

    D. Switch to Copy backup type.

12. Your boss has complaints from some users that when backup operations are in progress during working hours, they experience system performance problems. He has asked you to look for

some method so that the backup does not affect the work of other users. What is your best option considering that a lot of data gets changed every day?

A. Stay late in the office to do the backups.

B. Schedule the backup to start during nonoffice hours or at night.

C. Perform the backups on alternate days.

D. Perform the backups once a week during the weekends.

13. You want the users in your office to take care of backing up their own files. What privileges do you need to assign them?

A. Backup Operators

B. Server Operators

C. Domain Administrators

D. None; they can do it without having any privilege.

14. You are currently performing incremental backups of a server on weekdays from Monday to Friday and a full backup on Friday evening. Due to an emergency on Wednesday, you are required to perform another backup of the data that has changed since that morning. What backup type will you select to ensure that the backup you will perform on Wednesday does not alter the routine backup configuration?

A. Normal backup

B. Incremental backup

C. Differential backup

D. Copy backup

15. What data on your computer must you back up in order to ensure that when you need to restore, you are able to restore the system Registry also?

A. The %SystemRoot% folder

B. The System State data

C. The COM+ class registration database

D. The system startup files

16. What is contained in the backup job when you perform a backup of the System State data on a stand-alone server? Select all that apply.

A. The Active Directory database

    B.   The COM+ class registration database

    C.   The SYSVOL folder

    D.   The system Registry

    E.   System startup files

17. You plan to run a backup of a complete folder on a server but do not want three large files to be included in the job. What can you do to make sure that these files are not backed up when the backup job runs?

    A.   Move the files to another folder.

    B.   Delete the files and then restore then from the Recycle bin.

    C.   Use the Exclude Files tab from the backup options screen.

    D.   Use the Advanced tab to specify the files.

18. You had scheduled a backup job to run at 11.00 P.M. When you came in the next morning you noticed that the job had stopped in the middle. How can you determine how much of the job was completed before it stopped running?

    A.   Check the backup log file.

    B.   Check the files and folders manually.

    C.   Click the Verify option in the backup options screen.

    D.   Run the restore utility.

LAB QUESTION

You are the systems administrator of a busy network in your office, which has nearly 100 users. You have six servers, of which two are the domain controllers and two database servers; one file server has the home directories of users. The databases are very large and have been built up gradually. You have purchased a sixth server and installed Windows 2000 Server on it. This will work as a backup server. You have to chalk out a disaster recovery plan so that the data is available when there is an emergency. Here is what you have to do:

■   Select a backup program suitable for data backup and restoration jobs. Run backup jobs on this server to backup the databases and user directories.

■   There should not be any effect on the network performance when the backup jobs are running.

- The cost of media should remain as low as possible, and the backup jobs must run fast.
- The Registry and startup files of all servers should be available for restore when any of the servers crash.
- There should be adequate arrangements to back up and restore Active Directory data.

These are the steps that we propose to complete the job. You are to find any incorrect or missing steps.

1. Use Windows Backup utility to back up the databases and the user directories.

2. On the backup server, map the servers hosting the databases and user directories.

3. When running the Backup Wizard, select Back up selected files, drives, or network data in the What to Back Up screen.

4. While selecting the data from other servers, select the System State data also so that the Active Directory data is included in the backup.

5. Perform an Incremental backup from Monday to Thursday and a differential backup on Friday.

6. Schedule the backup jobs to run at night so that the users do not experience performance degradation problems.

SELF TEST ANSWERS

Manage and Optimize Availability of System State Data and User Data

1. ☑ **D.** When the system fails to start using the simple Safe Mode, you have no option but to use the emergency repair disk.

   ☒ **A** is incorrect, because if the simple Safe Mode does not work, the Safe Mode with Networking will also not be able to start the system. **B** is incorrect, because the VGA Mode is used to fix display related problems. **C** is incorrect, because the debugging mode is used by software developers.

2. ☑ **B.** You may try to use the Safe Mode with Networking when the Safe Mode works and you are sure that none of the networking components are causing the system startup problems.

   ☒ **A** is incorrect, because the Safe Mode with Networking will not work if the Safe Mode fails to start the system. **C** is incorrect, because if you have video problems, the Enable Video Mode is a better option. **D** is incorrect, because Active Directory cannot be restored using the Safe Mode with Networking.

3. ☑ **B.** You need to be a domain administrator in order to restore and update Active Directory on a domain controller.

   ☒ **A** is incorrect, because Log on as Service rights are not required and are insufficient to perform the given task. **C** is incorrect, because the Administrators Group is local to the computer. **D** is incorrect, because the Power Users Group does not exist on domain controllers.

4. ☑ **C.** The basic requirement of any data restore is that you must have backed up the data previously. No restore is possible without first backing up. This holds good for Active Directory also, because unless you have a backup copy of the System State data, you will have no source to restore.

   ☒ **A** is incorrect, because we have a better answer option. **B** is incorrect, because this is a secondary consideration. **D** is incorrect, because you have to start the computer in Directory Services Restore Mode for restoring the Active Directory data.

5. ☑ **A, B,** and **D.** The Recovery Console, apart from its other benefits, can fix a corrupted MBR and, create, delete, and format partitions. Besides this, it is possible to start and stop system services using the Recovery Console.

   ☒ **C** and **E** are incorrect, because it is not possible to upgrade disks or install/uninstall drivers using the Recovery Console.

6. ☑ **B.** The proposed solution produces the required result and none of the desired results. This is because the server will get the most recent copy of its data from the most recent backup.

☒ **A** is incorrect because the proposed solution does, in fact, repair the server and restore the user data. **C** and **D** are incorrect because the System State data will not be restored because you are using the remote backup server for restoration of data, which does not contain the System State data. The System State data can be backed up and restored on a local computer only. In order to restore the System State data during an emergency, you must back up this data on the local computer. The Active Directory data will be backed up automatically. Later you can restore the Active Directory in Authoritative or Nonauthoritative Mode. The mode you select depends on the state of restored data. If other domain controllers have the current data, you need to use Nonauthoritative Mode. The replication from other domain controllers will bring this domain controller in synch with them.

7. ☑ **A.** The **listsvc** command in the Recovery Console gives you a list of available services that can be started or stopped from within the console.

☒ **B** and **C** are incorrect, because these commands are used to start and stop the services respectively. **D** is incorrect, because this is an invalid command. The **help** command works with the name of any other command and **service** is not a valid command.

8. ☑ **C.** By default, the Recovery Console does not allow you to copy files to any removable media such as floppy disks. You can use the **set** command to change this setting so that you can copy the files to floppy disk.

☒ **A** is incorrect, because a floppy disk cannot be formatted using the NTFS file system. Moreover, formatting the floppy disk will not resolve the problem. **B** is incorrect, because the problem is not due to a corrupt MBR in the floppy disk. Floppy disks do not have an MBR. **D** is incorrect, because setting permissions using the Windows Explorer will not help resolve the problem. You will be able to access it only when the computer is able to start. The question clearly states that the computer is having startup problems.

9. ☑ **B.** When the system configuration goes bad and the system is not able to start in a normal way, you can use the Last Known Good Configuration Mode to start the system. This mode uses the registry that was saved the last time the system was shut down normally.

☒ **A** is incorrect, because this mode is used when the display driver is causing a startup problem. **C** is incorrect, because the boot logging method does not use the last registry values to start the system. **D** is incorrect, because we have only one correct answer.

Backup and Recovery Systems and User Data

10. ☑ **B.** The **Ntbackup.exe** command can be used to start the Windows Backup Wizard from the command prompt. You can also start it from the Start menu by selecting Programs | Accessories | System Tools | Backup.
☒ **A, C,** and **D** are incorrect, because none of these is an appropriate command to start the backup program.

11. ☑ **C.** To reduce the backup time of large databases, it is best to switch to Incremental backup type. The backup will be done quickly and will also save space on storage media.
☒ **A** is incorrect, because we have a better option that can solve the problem. **B** is not the best option, because performing the backup on a separate backup server will not necessarily help reduce the backup time. **D** is incorrect, because switching to copy type will still back up the full database every day and will take the same amount of time.

12. ☑ **B.** It is best to schedule the backups to start after the office hours or at night. You can use the Windows task scheduler to configure the backup jobs to start at a specified time.
☒ **A** is incorrect, because you need not stay back for backups. **C** and **D** are incorrect, because changing the daily backups to alternate days or weekly backups may be harmful, as any emergency may occur at any time.

13. ☑ **D.** When the users have to back up their own files, you need not give them any special privilege. All users are creator/owners of their files by default, and this privilege is enough for backing up files.
☒ This makes answers **A, B,** and **C** incorrect.

14. ☑ **C.** Differential backup is the best option under the given conditions. This type of backup will take a backup of the data that has changed since morning but will not clear any archive bits (markers). This way, the routine incremental backups will continue in a normal way.
☒ **A** and **D** are incorrect, because the Normal and Copy backups will take a full backup of the data, which is not desired. **B** is incorrect, because the Incremental backup will clear the markers, which will upset your routine backup procedure.

15. ☑ **B.** The System State data must be backed up for later use in case you need to restore the Registry.
☒ **A** is incorrect, because the backup of the %SystemRoot% is not the correct way to back up the Registry. **C** and **D** are incorrect, because these items are included in the System State data and need not be backed up separately.

16. ☑ **B, D,** and **E.** When you choose to back up the System State data on a stand-alone server, the system Registry, COM+ class registration database, and system startup files are included in the backup job.

   ☒ **A** and **C** are incorrect, because the Active Directory data and the SYSVOL folder do not exist on a stand-alone server.

17. ☑ **C.** You can specify any files to be excluded from the backup job using the Exclude Files tab in the backup options screen.

   ☒ **A** and **B** are incorrect, as these are not the best solutions. **D** is incorrect, because the Advanced tab of the backup wizard does not give you any option to exclude files.

18. ☑ **A.** The Backup log is the best method to check the status of the backup job.

   ☒ **B** is incorrect, because this is a cumbersome job and may take a long time if the number of files is very large. **C** is incorrect, because the Verify option does not work after the job is over. **D** is incorrect, because checking the files by restoring is not a solution to the given problem.

LAB ANSWER

Check the required results and the solution provided. You will definitely find what is wrong with the given steps. Take the wrong steps first: In step 4, you are performing an Incremental backup from Monday to Thursday and a Differential backup on Friday. This step is wrong. You need to perform a Normal backup on Friday. In step 5, you are selecting the System State data from the servers. This is incorrect, as the System State data cannot be backed up from the network. You need to do a local backup on all servers individually.

Let us take the missing steps: When you plan a disaster recovery, you must store the tapes off site. Secondly, you must do a test restore to ensure that the backup media is intact and will work fine when you need it. The given solution does not mention any of these steps.

10

Managing, Configuring, and Troubleshooting Storage Use

P roper management of storage media and timely recovery from disk failures are critical elements in the availability of a network's server. Windows 2000 Server, with its focus on less down time, includes support for dynamic disks and the new NTFS 5 file system. It also supports data compression and disk quota features that allow administrators to make the best use of available server storage space. This chapter describes the proper use of Windows 2000 Server's disk administration tools, as well as how to avoid, or recover from, disk failures.

CERTIFICATION OBJECTIVE 10.01

Monitor, Configure, and Troubleshoot Disks and Volumes

The performance and management of a server's storage media begins with the initial selection of an appropriate disk, volume, and file system configuration. The configuration you use will play a large role in the availability, security, and fault tolerance of the server.

To begin, Windows 2000 allows you to choose either a basic or dynamic disk configuration, depending on the server's resources and the desired level of availability. Windows 2000 supports a variety of fault tolerance methods, including striping, mirroring, and striping with parity. You can also select among a variety of file systems, including FAT16, FAT32, and NTFS 5. The file system you choose will determine the server's compatibility with older programs, and will affect the disk's security, space management, and recovery abilities.

Each of the disk, volume, and file system types are described here, as well as how to create or change storage configurations using the Windows 2000 Disk Manager utility.

Basic Storage

By default, Windows 2000 Server will configure storage devices as basic disks. Basic storage uses the traditional method of dividing physical disks into primary partitions and extended partitions with logical drives. Because this format can be recognized and accessed by DOS, Windows 9x, and Windows NT, it is a good choice to use when backward compatibility is an issue.

Partitioning Basic Disks

Before a basic disk can store information, it must first be partitioned, then formatted to use a particular file system. If only one partition is created, the disk appears as a single drive letter, usually C:. However, multiple partitions (divisions) can be created on a disk. Each partition can then be formatted with a different file system, and each will be assigned a different drive letter, just as if there were multiple hard disks in the computer. See Figure 10-1 for examples of single and multiple-partition disks.

Dividing a hard disk into partitions allows you to create a multiboot configuration with operating systems that use different file systems. It also allows you to logically separate types of data among drives without having to purchase and install extra physical disks.

Windows 2000 allows you to create, delete, or change the partition structures on basic disks, and it will recognize partition structures created by older operating systems, such as DOS, Windows 9x, and Windows NT. Most changes to the partition structure do not require a reboot to take effect.

A Windows 2000 basic disk can include up to four partitions on one physical hard disk, one of which may be an extended partition. The partition information of a disk is kept in a partition table, located on the first sector of the disk. If the first sector becomes corrupt, or otherwise unreadable, all data on the drive is effectively lost, since the partition information is inaccessible.

Primary Partitions   Primary partitions are typically used to create bootable drives. Each primary partition represents one drive letter, up to a maximum of four on a single hard disk. One primary partition must be marked as active in order to boot the system, and most operating systems must place a few boot files on the primary active partition, although the operating system itself can usually be stored on a different partition.

| FIGURE 10-1 | A Windows 2000 basic disk can contain between one and four partitions (only one can be an extended partition.) In a multipartition hard disk, each partition is assigned a different drive letter, and each can be formatted with a different file system. |

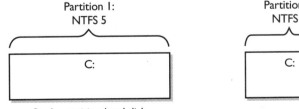
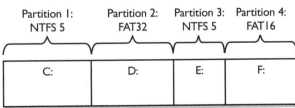

Single-partition hard disk   Multiple-partition hard disk

Extended Partitions   Although extended partitions can't be used to host operating systems, they can store other types of data, and provide an excellent way to create more drives above the four-partition limit. Here's how it works: Extended partitions do not represent one drive; rather, they can be subdivided into as many logical drives as there are letters in the alphabet. Therefore, one extended partition can contain several logical drives, each of which appears as a separate drive letter to the user. Figure 10-2 demonstrates the use of an extended partition to create extra drive letters.

Set Types on Basic Storage

Hard disk sets are groups of disks that work together to provide extra storage or fault tolerance. Basic disks support volume, stripe, and mirror sets and stripe sets with parity, all of which are described later. Each of these basic disk sets is supported by, but cannot be created within, Windows 2000. In other words, Windows 2000 will recognize basic disk sets that were created in older operating systems, but Windows 2000 does *not* allow you to create new ones. You must upgrade from basic to dynamic disk in order to create extra storage or fault tolerance sets.

exam
ⓦatch   *Although Windows 2000 will recognize existing basic disk sets (those created in older operating systems), it does not allow you to create new ones.*

Volume Set   The term "volume" indicates a single drive letter. One physical hard disk can contain several volumes, one for each primary partition or logical drive. However, the opposite is also true. You can create a single volume that spans more than one physical disk. This is a good option when you require a volume that

---

FIGURE 10-2   An extended partition can contain multiple logical drives, each assigned a separate drive letter

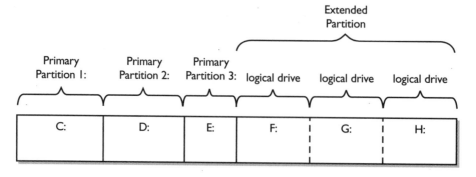

exceeds the capacity of a single physical disk. You can also create a volume set when you want to make use of leftover space on several disks by piecing them together as one volume. Refer again to Figure 10-1, which illustrates one disk with four volumes. Figure 10-3 demonstrates one volume spanning four disks.

Mirror Set In a mirror set, all data on a selected partition or drive is automatically duplicated onto another physical disk. The main purpose of a mirror set is to provide fault tolerance in the event of missing or corrupt data. If one disk fails or contains corrupt files, the data is simply retrieved and rebuilt from the other disk.

A trade-off for this fault tolerance is decreased drive performance. In a mirror set, one disk controller is responsible for writing data to both disks, so these operations can take twice as long to perform. An alternative is to use disk duplexing, in which each disk uses its own disk controller to create duplicate data. The most common implementation of disk mirroring is RAID-1. RAID is an acronym for Redundant Array of Independent Disks. Mirror sets can be migrated to Windows 2000 from Windows NT Server.

Stripe Set The term "striping" refers to the interleaving of data across separate physical disks. Each file is broken into small blocks, and each block is evenly and alternately saved to the disks in the stripe set. In a two-disk stripe set, the first block of data is saved to the first disk, the second block is saved to the second disk, and the third block is saved to the first disk, and so on. The two disks are treated as a single drive, and are given a single drive letter. Figure 10-4 illustrates the concept of disk striping.

FIGURE 10-3   Drive E: represents a 5 GB volume set that spans four physical hard disks

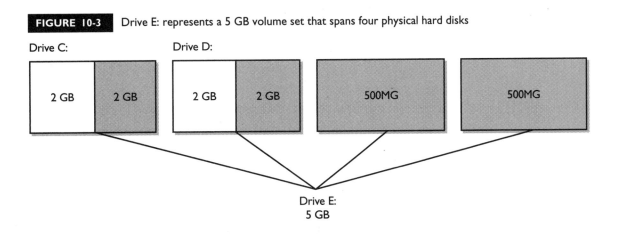

FIGURE 10-4

Striped data
is evenly
interleaved
across physical
disks

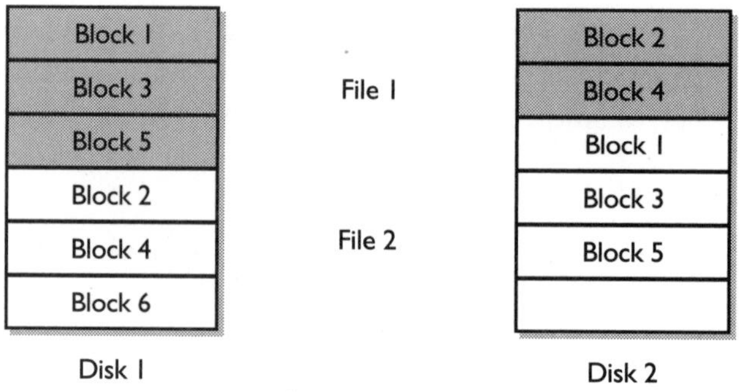

Disk 1
Block 1
Block 3
Block 5
Block 2
Block 4
Block 6

File 1

File 2

Disk 2
Block 2
Block 4
Block 1
Block 3
Block 5

Disk striping provides increased storage capacity, and can increase the drive's performance, since data read/write tasks are evenly divided between the disks. It is important to note that disk striping alone does not provide fault tolerance, since each block of data is written only once. The most common implementation of this type of disk striping is RAID-0 or disk striping without parity. RAID is an acronym for Redundant Array of Independent Disks. Stripe sets can be migrated to Windows 2000 from Windows NT Workstation or Server.

exam
ⓌatcH

Disk striping does not provide fault tolerance.

Stripe Set with Parity A stripe set with parity requires at least three hard disks, and provides both increased storage capacity and fault tolerance. In a stripe set with parity, data is interleaved across three or more disks, and includes parity (error checking) information about the data. As long as only one disk in the set fails, the parity information can be used to reconstruct the lost data. If the parity information itself is lost, it can be reconstructed from the original data. Figure 10-5 illustrates the interleaving of data and parity information across disks.

The parity information is a calculated result of the data in the original data blocks. For example, suppose that the blocks of file 1 in Figure 10-5 contain the numbers 4 and 8, respectively. The parity calculation for this data is 12, since $4 + 8 = 12$. If the first disk fails, the computer can use the parity information on the third disk to reconstruct the data; $n + 8 = 12$, so the missing data from block 1 must be 4. Because the parity information is simply a calculation of the data existing on the first two drives, it can also be reconstructed in the event of a disk failure ($4 + 8 = n$; n equals 12).

Using a stripe set with parity increases available capacity, since the three (or more) disks are treated as a single drive. Also, drive performance is enhanced since read/write tasks are divided among the available disks. Finally, the largest benefit of using a stripe set with parity is the fault tolerance it provides.

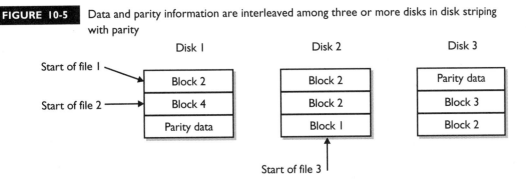

FIGURE 10-5 Data and parity information are interleaved among three or more disks in disk striping with parity

A disadvantage to this type of disk structure is the obvious increased cost of having three or more disks, and the fact that the parity information takes up space that could otherwise be used for regular data storage. A common implementation of a stripe set with parity is RAID-5, which can be migrated into Windows 2000 from Windows NT Server.

Now that you are familiar with the basic storage set and partition types, you should be able to answer the questions in the following table.

SCENARIO & SOLUTION

Set or Partition Type	How many disks?	Does it provide fault tolerance?	Other characteristics?
Primary or Extended Partition	One	No	One disk can contain many partitions and logical drives. Each is assigned a separate drive letter.
Volume Set	At least two	No	Increased capacity.
Mirror Set	Two	Yes	Provides a full backup of data. Write tasks can take much longer to perform.
Stripe Set	At least two	No	Read/write tasks are faster, increased capacity.
RAID-5 (Stripe Set with Parity)	At least three	Yes	Read/write tasks are faster, increased capacity.

Dynamic Storage

Windows 2000 supports a new storage type, called dynamic disk. This storage type is unique to Windows 2000, and cannot be used by other operating systems. Furthermore, it is the preferred storage type of Windows 2000, so many disk management features in Windows 2000, such as implementing fault tolerance, can only be performed on a dynamic disk.

Dynamic disks introduce conceptual as well as technical changes from traditional basic disk structure. Partitions are now called volumes, and these can be created or changed without losing existing data on the disk. Recall that when using basic disks, you must first create primary partitions (up to a maximum of four), then extended partitions (a maximum of one) with logical drives. Dynamic disks allow you to simply create volume after volume, with no limit on the number or type that can exist on a single disk (you are limited only by the capacity of the disk itself).

Another important feature of dynamic disks is that information about volume number and type is stored in a disk management database on the last 1MB of the disk, rather than in the first cluster. In multidisk systems, this database is automatically replicated to all other dynamic disks in the system. That is, each disk's management database contains the volume information of all other disks, up to approximately 512 disks. If the database on any disk becomes lost or corrupt, the information is automatically restored by the other disks. Note that this replication can only occur within a single computer; disk management databases cannot be replicated between different computers.

Dynamic disks are not supported by laptops or removable media, such as Jaz or Zip drives. It is also important to note that although you can create a dynamic disk in a single-disk computer, there are few benefits in doing so, since the 1MB management database has nowhere to replicate.

exam
Ⓦatch

Dynamic disks are not supported by removable media or laptops.

Volume Types on Dynamic Disks

Dynamic disks allow you to create a variety of configurations that can increase capacity, improve drive performance, and/or provide fault tolerance. The following sections describe the types of dynamic disk volumes, and their relationship to basic volumes.

Simple Volume   A simple volume is just that—it is a single volume that does not span more than one physical disk, and does not provide improved drive performance, extra capacity, or fault tolerance. One physical disk can contain a single, large simple volume, or several smaller ones. Each simple volume is assigned a drive letter, usually starting with C: simple; or the volume can be mounted to a folder using the new volume mount points feature of Windows 2000, removing limitations on the number of volumes.

Spanned Volume   When a dynamic volume includes the space on more than one physical hard drive, it is called a spanned volume. Spanned volumes can be used to increase drive capacity, or to make use of the leftover space on up to 32 existing disks. Like those in a basic storage volume set, the portions of a spanned volume are all linked together and share a single drive letter.

Mirrored Volume   Like basic disks, dynamic disks can also be mirrored, and are called mirrored volumes. A continuous and automatic backup of all data in a mirrored volume is saved to a separate disk to provide fault tolerance in the event of a disk failure or corrupt file. Note that you cannot mirror a spanned or striped volume.

Striped Volume   A striped volume is the dynamic storage equivalent of a basic stripe set, in which data is interleaved across more than one physical disk (up to 32 disks) to improve drive performance and increase drive capacity. Because each data block is written only once, striped volumes do not provide fault tolerance.

RAID-5 Volume   A RAID-5 volume on a dynamic drive provides disk striping with parity, and is similar to a basic stripe set with parity. This disk configuration provides both increased storage capacity and fault tolerance. Data in a dynamic RAID-5 volume is interleaved across three or more disks (up to 32 disks), and parity information is included to rebuild lost data in the event of an individual disk failure. Like a spanned or striped volume, a RAID-5 volume cannot be mirrored.

The following Scenario & Solution grid should help you determine which, if any, fault tolerance methods you should use.

SCENARIO & SOLUTION

I don't need fault tolerance, and I have only one disk.	Create primary and/or extended partitions on a basic disk, simple volumes on a dynamic disk.
I want fault tolerance, but I have only two disks.	Create a mirror set or mirrored volume.
I have a large number of disks, and I want a fault tolerance method that won't slow down my computer.	Create a RAID-5 set or volume.
I want fault tolerance that will restore lost data without interfering with the use of the computer.	Create a mirror set or mirrored volume; when data is missing, it is retrieved off the backup disk, and users won't even know it's happening.
I don't need fault tolerance, but I want to improve read/write operations.	Create a stripe set or striped volume.

Upgrading Basic Storage to Dynamic Storage

By default, Windows 2000 configures all disks as basic. However, you can upgrade from basic to dynamic storage at any time by using the Windows 2000 Disk Management tool. All disks to be upgraded to dynamic must have at least 1MB of free space at the end. This space is for the disk management database.

Before planning a basic to dynamic upgrade, you must make sure the physical disk conforms to a few limitations. You cannot upgrade removable media to dynamic. You also cannot upgrade disks whose sectors are larger than 512 bytes. Finally, if you plan to upgrade a basic disk that contains volumes on other disks, all other disks in the set must also be upgraded from basic to dynamic. For example, mirror, volume, and stripe sets all rely on the use of more than one physical disk. For the upgrade to work, all disks involved in the set must be upgraded to dynamic. To upgrade a basic disk to a dynamic disk, follow the steps in Exercise 10-1.

EXERCISE 10-1

Upgrading a Basic Disk to Dynamic

1. Close any applications running from the disk to be upgraded.

2. Open the Computer Management console by right-clicking My Computer, then selecting Manage, or by selecting Start | Administrative Tools | Computer Management.

3. In the Computer Management screen, expand the Storage icon, then click Disk Management. A listing of all attached disks, as well as the type and status of each disk, will appear in the right pane. This screen is shown:

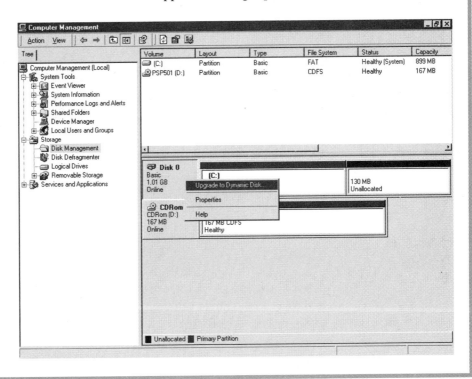

4. Right-click the basic disk you wish to upgrade, then select Upgrade to Dynamic Disk. This will start the Upgrade Wizard.

5. In the next screen, shown below, you will be prompted to select which disk (if there is more than one in the system) to upgrade. Place a check mark by each disk you wish to upgrade, then click OK.

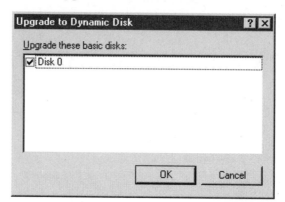

6. Select Upgrade from the next screen that appears, then confirm by choosing Yes. Choose Yes at the next prompt, informing you that file systems on any of the chosen disks will be force dismounted. If you are upgrading a boot volume, you will be prompted to restart your computer. Otherwise, the changes will take effect immediately, without a reboot.

When a disk is upgraded from basic to dynamic, any existing basic partitions are converted to dynamic simple volumes. The new properties of the upgraded disks are shown in Figure 10-6. Any mirror, stripe, volume, and RAID-5 sets are automatically upgraded to mirrored, striped, spanned, and RAID-5 dynamic volumes, respectively. It is important to note here that you can upgrade a basic disk containing the boot partition, but only if that disk does not also include partitions that are part of a volume, stripe, mirror, or RAID-5 set.

Now that you are familiar with different disk types, you should be able to identify the dynamic counterparts of basic partitions and sets in Table 10-1.

FIGURE 10-6 The partitions on the basic disk have been converted to dynamic simple volumes

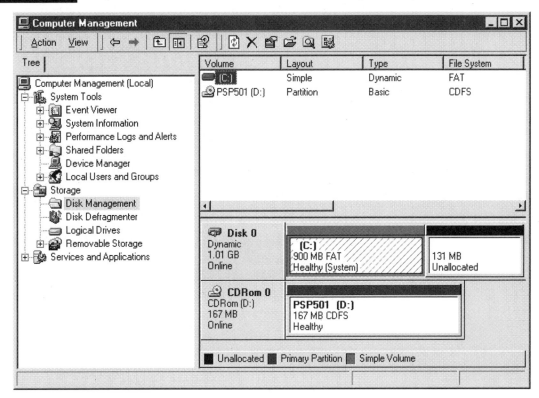

TABLE 10-1 Dynamic counterparts of basic partitions

Basic Storage Term	Corresponding Dynamic Storage Term
Partition	Volume
Primary Partition / Logical Drive	Simple Volume
Volume Set	Spanned Volume
Mirror Set	Mirrored Volume
Stripe Set	Striped Volume
Stripe Set with Parity	RAID-5 Volume

Reverting to a Basic Disk   Once a basic disk has been upgraded to dynamic, it is no longer accessible to older operating systems or in a dual-boot configuration. You may also find that some older or third-party disk utilities won't work. Fortunately, the upgrade from basic to dynamic is not one-way; you can revert to basic using the Revert to Basic Disk command in Computer Management.

To use the Revert to Basic Disk command, however, you must first delete all dynamic volumes on the disk. This means you will lose all of the data on the disk, even data that was originally converted from basic to dynamic in the initial upgrade process. Reverting a dynamic disk back to basic is not a very involved process for the user. Simply right-click the disk you wish to revert, then select Revert to Basic Disk. The disk will be reverted with no further selection dialog boxes.

File Systems

Once a partition, set, or volume is created, it must be formatted with a file system before it can store data. Windows 2000 Server supports a variety of file systems, including FAT16 and FAT32, as well as the newest file system, NTFS 5.

The file system you choose will depend on partition or volume size and the need for backward compatibility. The file system you use will affect the space efficiency and capabilities of the drive. Each time you create a new volume or partition, you are given the option to format it using any of the file systems described below.

FAT

FAT (File Allocation Table) is an older file system, and is supported by DOS, Windows 3.x, Windows 9.x, and Windows NT. It is a 16-bit file system, so it is often referred to as FAT16, to distinguish it from the newer FAT32.

The FAT file system allows the computer to use up to 4GB of disk space (DOS supports only 2GB), and as the storage capacity increases, so does the cluster size. This means less efficient use of storage space since files cannot share clusters. For example, on a FAT16 2GB hard drive, each cluster is 32KB. If a 4KB file is saved, 28KB are wasted! However, the FAT16 file system has the advantage of being read and accessed by all of the most popular operating systems, so you may decide to use it when backward compatibility is an issue.

FAT32

FAT32 was designed to eliminate the 4GB partition limitation and increase storage space efficiency. Introduced with Windows 95 OSR2, FAT32 can use up to 2TB (Terabytes) of space on a single drive, and keeps cluster sizes much smaller. A 32GB FAT32 drive has a cluster size of 16KB.

FAT32 is backward compatible with FAT16, so if you boot from a FAT32 drive, you will be able to access information on any FAT16 drives in the system. However, the reverse is not true. You cannot read a FAT32 drive if the computer is booted from a FAT16 drive. FAT32 is also not accessible by Windows NT or DOS without third-party utilities.

NTFS v5.0

The New Technology File System (NTFS) was first introduced with Windows NT. All versions of NTFS provide file and directory-level security, native file compression, the fault tolerance configurations described earlier, and support for large partitions or volumes. NTFS supports partitions up to 16 EXABYTES.

Windows 2000 improves on the NTFS file system with its new version, NTFS 5. Along with the features of NTFS 4, NTFS 5 also supports the Encrypting File System (described in Chapter 12), sparse file support, and disk quotas. NTFS drives are not accessible by operating systems running from FAT16 or FAT32.

exam
ⓦatch

NTFS 5 is the first Microsoft file system to support sparse file support, disk quotas, and EFS.

Converting to NTFS

When you install Windows 2000, all NTFS 4 drives are automatically upgraded to NTFS 5. You are also given the option to upgrade all FAT16 and FAT32 drives to NTFS. This conversion occurs without removing any data already existing on the drive.

If, however, you have chosen not to upgrade your FAT drives to NTFS during Setup, you can do so later using the NTFS conversion utility. Simply run CONVERT <driveletter> /FS:NTFS from a command prompt, and the selected partition or volume will be converted. Again, any data on the drive remains intact. An important note here is that the conversion utility only works one way; it will not convert NTFS drives to FAT16 or FAT32.

The Disk Management Tool

The Windows 2000 Disk Manager (introduced in Exercise 10-1) allows you to perform a large number of disk management tasks in an easy-to-use and intuitive interface. When you open the Disk Manager window, you will be presented with a screen. The upper-right-hand pane displays each partition or volume in the system, including information about the type of disk each resides on, and the file system, status, and capacity of each. Below that is information about each physical disk, and the partitions or volumes on each. This layout makes it easy to determine which volumes belong to which physical disks.

Aside from displaying disk and volume information, the Disk Manager allows you to create, format, and delete partitions or volumes. Exercise 10-2 demonstrates how to create a simple volume on a dynamic disk in Disk Manager (these steps can also be used to create a simple or striped volume).

EXERCISE 10-2

Creating a Simple Volume with the Disk Management Tool

1. Open the Computer Management window by right-clicking My Computer, then selecting Manage.

2. Expand the Storage icon, then click Disk Management to see information about the disks and volumes within the system.

3. In the lower-right-hand pane, right-click any unallocated space, then select Create Volume. The Create Volume Wizard will open.

4. In the Volume type section, select Simple, then click Next. You can also use this screen to select a spanned or striped volume. The following screen will appear:

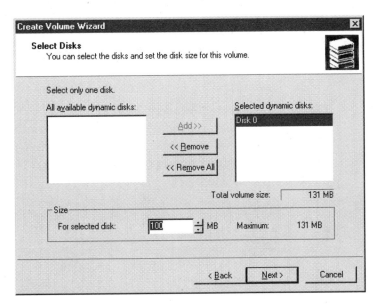

All dynamic disks in the system will be displayed here. Select the disk to be used in the simple volume in the All available dynamic disks section, then click Add (select at least two disks for a spanned or striped volume). The selected disk(s) will be shown in the space on the right.

5. In the Size area, select the size for the simple volume (the default setting is the combined available space on all of the selected disks). Click Next.

6. Assign a drive letter to the volume by selecting it from the drop-down list of available letters (only unused letters will be available here). Click Next.

7. Select to leave the volume unformatted, or choose to format it with NTFS, FAT, or FAT32. Click Next.

8. Following a confirmation dialog box, you will return to the Disk Management screen, and the simple volume will be created. The properties of the volume are displayed at the top right and its location on the disk is indicated in the disk section of the screen.

Aside from creating volumes, the Disk Management tool allows you to make changes to existing volumes. When you right-click a volume, you will be presented with a shortcut menu, with options to delete or reformat the volume, or change the drive letter. You can also use Disk Management to create fault tolerant volumes, described in more detail later in the chapter.

on the
J o b

The Disk Management window is pretty intuitive and easy to use. However, if you get stumped, use the Windows 2000 Help system. It's written in easy-to-understand language, provides thorough help, and includes tons of information on disk management and recovery.

FROM THE CLASSROOM

Windows 2000 Disk Management

Windows 2000 Disk Management makes it so easy to make changes! But beware, many changes and upgrades are one-way only, so you must plan, plan, and plan some more before you make changes to the disk or volume structure.

For example, recall that a disk can be upgraded to dynamic only if there is 1MB free at the end of the disk. If you choose to install Windows 2000 on a single partition that takes up the entire hard disk, you will not be able to upgrade it to dynamic. Because it is the system partition, you will not be able to remove and re-create the partition without losing your Windows 2000 installation.

Another important point to remember is that the conversion of a disk to dynamic is essentially one-way. You can upgrade from basic to dynamic without losing any existing

information, but you cannot revert back to basic in the same way. To do so, you must remove (delete) every volume on the dynamic disk (as well as any data on the volume), then revert it back to basic. The moral of the story is: Don't upgrade a basic disk (especially the one containing the system partition) unless you're absolutely sure you won't want to revert back to basic.

Finally, another one-way operation is the conversion of partitions or volumes to NTFS. This conversion does not remove any data from the volume, and enables you to use features like native compression, user quotas, and EFS. However, once a volume is converted to NTFS, it has to stay that way unless you remove the volume and re-create it (and lose all data on that volume).

—Amy Thomson, A+, MOUS Master

CERTIFICATION OBJECTIVE 10.02

Configure Data Compression

The NTFS file system includes native data compression (no external compression utility is required). You can select to compress specific folders and files on an NTFS volume, or the entire volume itself. The steps for compressing an NTFS folder are outlined in Exercise 10-3.

CertCam 10-3

EXERCISE 10-3

Compressing an NTFS Folder

1. In My Computer or Windows Explorer, right-click the folder to be compressed. From the shortcut menu, select Properties, then click Advanced. The Advanced Attributes dialog box will appear:

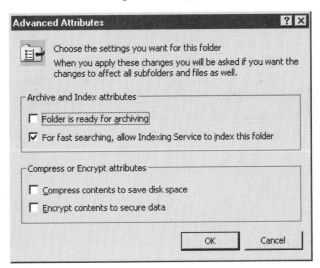

2. Select the option Compress contents to save disk space, then click OK.

3.   In the Properties dialog box, choose either OK or Apply to accept your changes.

4.   In the Confirm Attribute Changes dialog box (shown below), select to compress the current folder, or all files and subfolders within it. Click OK to complete the compression.

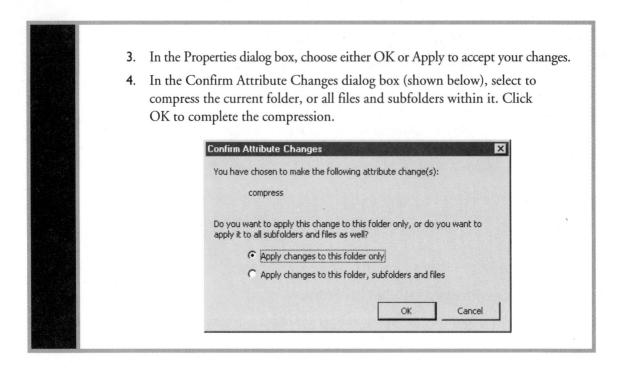

You can perform this type of compression only on volumes that have been formatted with NTFS. Any new file or subfolder that is added to the compressed folder will automatically be compressed as well.

You can compress any NTFS volume, including the system volume. You can also install Windows 2000 on a compressed volume, but only if it uses NTFS compression. While using NTFS native compression provides a quick method of increasing storage space, it can slow down disk read/write actions. All data must first be compressed before being written to the disk, or uncompressed in order to be read from the disk. Therefore, unless disk space is low, you may want to avoid compressing the system volume.

Furthermore, you cannot apply NTFS encryption to compressed files, folders, or volumes. Before encrypting a volume, folder, or file, you must first uncompress it. You can do this by returning to the properties windows for the compressed item. Once there, turn off the compression option, and the volume, folder, or file will be uncompressed as soon as you click OK.

exam
Watch

Windows 2000 will use native file compression and encryption on NTFS volumes only.

CERTIFICATION OBJECTIVE 10.03

Monitor and Configure Disk Quotas

Windows 2000 allows administrators to assign drive space limits (quotas) to all users of a system or to individual users. Quotas can be set only on entire volumes, and not on individual files or folders. For example, if a user moves files from one folder to another on the same volume, their volume usage stays the same. If, however, a user copies files from one folder to another, their usage doubles.

The term "disk quotas" is a bit of a misnomer, since quotas are set per user, per volume and are independent of disk layout. If a volume spans more than one disk, as in a spanned, mirrored, or striped volume, the user's quota is applied to the entire volume, not to each disk in the volume. For example, suppose a user has a quota of 50MB on volume D:. The user is limited to 50MB, regardless of whether volume D: resides on one physical disk or spans three disks.

Also, if a single physical disk contains more than one volume, quotas can be set on each. For example, suppose a user is given a quota on each of volumes D:, E:, and F:, all of which reside on one physical disk. Usage of volume D: will not affect usage of volumes E: and F: or vice versa.

exam
Watch

Disk quotas are set on volumes, not on physical hard disks.

Files are counted against a user's volume space every time the user saves, copies, or creates a file. Users are also "charged" for volume space whenever they take ownership of another user's file. If user 1 takes ownership of a 2MB file that was created by user 2, user 1's volume use increases by 2MB and user 2's volume use decreases by 2MB.

Setting, Assigning, and Configuring Disk Quotas

Administrators can set quotas either locally or on remote computers. Quotas can only be set on volumes formatted with the NTFS file system. Follow the steps in Exercise 10-4 to apply quotas for all users.

CertCam 10-4

EXERCISE 10-4

Creating Quotas for All Users

1. In the My Computer or Disk Management window, right-click the volume on which you want to create the quota, then click Properties.

2. In the Properties dialog box, select the Quota tab.

3. Click the Enable quota management check box. The grayed-out options in the dialog box will become available for selection. Select to Deny disk space to users exceeding quota limit.

on the !
job   *You can leave the Deny disk space...option off if you simply want to keep a log of all users who exceed their quota. This may help you study users' work habits and determine appropriate quota levels before you actually limit their disk usage.*

4. Click the Limit disk space to option, and type in the limit you want to apply. Use the drop-down arrow to select KB, MB, GB, and so on. Repeat the process to set warning levels for users who are getting near their limit. In the following example, users are limited to 1KB and will receive a warning at that level.

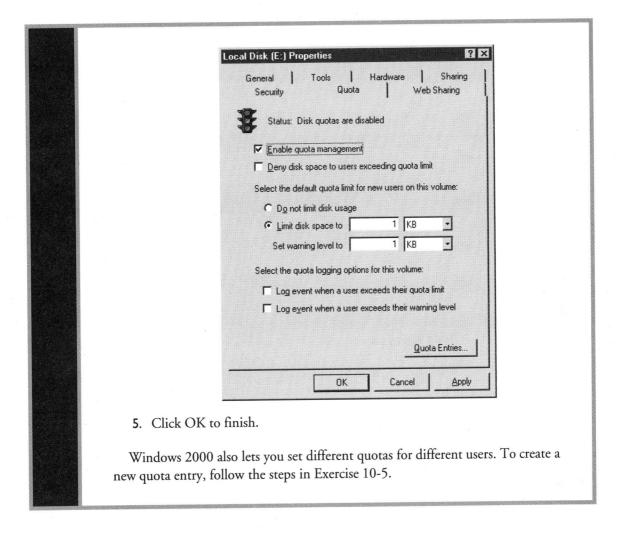

5. Click OK to finish.

Windows 2000 also lets you set different quotas for different users. To create a new quota entry, follow the steps in Exercise 10-5.

Create New Quota Entries

1. In the Quota tab, click Quota Entries. A dialog box displaying all previously set quotas will open:

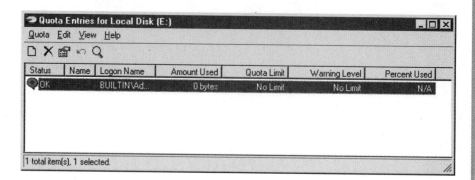

2. Select New Quota Entry from the Quota menu. A new dialog box will open, allowing you to select users:

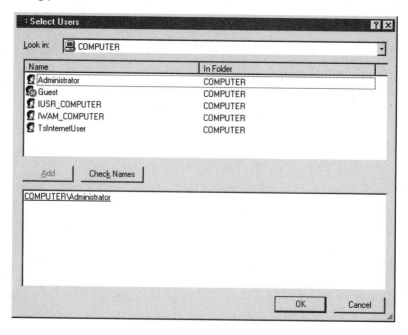

3. Select the user to whom you wish to apply the quota, then click Add. This dialog box will appear:

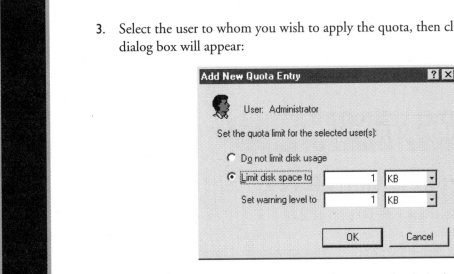

4. Click the Limit disk space to option, then enter the desired amount and unit. You can also set warning levels to users approaching the limit. When you are finished, click OK.

The Quota Entries dialog box will reappear, with the new quota in the list. Close the dialog box, then click OK to close the Properties dialog box and finish setting the quota.

Disk Quotas and Compression

Disk quotas are not affected by file, folder, or volume compression. That is, quotas are applied to the uncompressed size of files, whether they are compressed or not. For example, suppose a user has been assigned a quota of 10MB, and has already stored 9MB of data on the volume. If the user tries to save a 1.5MB file, the user will be denied access. Even if the user compresses the file to 1MB, he or she will still be denied access, since the uncompressed size of the file exceeds the user's quota.

Quotas can also be set on volumes that are compressed. When quotas are set, volume and file sizes are calculated in their uncompressed size. For example, suppose that a 2GB volume is compressed to 1.2GB. When you set the quotas on this volume, the total volume size will be reported as 2GB, not 1.2GB. If you divide the volume space equally between two users, each will be reported as having a 1GB limit, even though each user's volume space is actually being compressed to .6GB.

exam
ⓦatch

Quotas are set using the uncompressed size of files and folders.

CERTIFICATION OBJECTIVE 10.04

Recover from Disk Failures

You have already been introduced to some methods for preventing loss of data from disk failures, such as using mirrored or RAID-5 volumes. Also, recall that all dynamic disks in a system keep the management database of all other disks in the system. These forms of data redundancy won't prevent disk failures from happening, but can be used to restore data on a failed or new disk when a disk failure does occur. This section describes the steps for creating fault tolerant volumes, and how to recover data from these volumes if they fail.

Implementing Fault-Tolerant Volumes

Like simple, spanned, and striped volumes, fault-tolerant volumes are created in the Disk Management window. Remember that Windows 2000 Server will recognize and use fault tolerant drives that were created on basic disks in Windows NT 4, but will not allow you to create new fault tolerant drives on basic disks. To create new fault tolerant drives, you must first upgrade each disk to dynamic.

Creating Mirrored Volumes

To create a mirrored volume, there must be two disks in the system. Use the same steps outlined in Exercise 10-2. When creating the mirrored volume, simply select the Mirrored Volume option in the Create Volume Wizard. Use this method to create a *new* mirrored volume from the unallocated space on two disks.

Creating a RAID-5 Volume

A RAID-5 volume requires at least three, and up to 32 disks. Use the steps outlined in Exercise 10-2, but select the RAID-5 option in the Create Volume Wizard. RAID-5 volumes can be created only from the unallocated space on three or more disks.

Recovering a Failed Mirrored Volume

In the case of a disk failure, Windows 2000 Server is able to give you some clues as to the cause of the problem. The Disk Management window includes status descriptions for each disk and volume in the system. These descriptions can be your key to pinpointing the disk at fault and the cause of the problem.

Working volumes with the status Healthy are behaving normally, and there are no known failures of the disk on which the volume resides. Working disks are given the status Online. A healthy volume on an online disk should experience no problems.

Offline or Missing Disks

If a mirrored volume resides on one or more nonfunctional disks, the faulty drive becomes an orphan, and is temporarily removed from the mirrored volume. This means the volume will no longer be fault tolerant. If the disk displays the status Offline, but Windows 2000 still recognizes the name of the disk, the disk is partially corrupted or intermittently accessible. Right-click the disk in the Disk Management window, then select Reactivate. The disk's status should return to Online, and the mirrored volume will automatically be regenerated.

However, some disk problems are more serious. If Windows 2000 cannot locate a disk, or if the disk is completely unreadable, the disk's status will be Offline and unnamed, or Missing. In this case, you must repair the physical disk, check the cables, then select to Reactivate the disk. If this solves the problem, the disk's status will return to Online and the mirrored volume will return to Healthy.

If the disk cannot be repaired, it must be replaced, and the mirrored volume must be re-created. To add a mirror to an existing volume, follow the steps in Exercise 10-6.

CertCam 10-6

EXERCISE 10-6

Adding a Mirror to an Existing Volume

1. In the Disk Management window, right-click the volume you want to add the mirror to. From the shortcut menu that appears, select Add Mirror.

2. You will then be asked to select the disk to host the mirror. Select it from the available disks, then click Add Mirror.

3. Once the mirror is added, you will be returned to the Disk Management window, and the volume will display the status Regenerating until the mirror is established. The volume's status will then return to Healthy.

Online Disks (w/Errors)

When a disk is accessible, but contains underlying I/O errors, the disk's status will be Online (w/Errors). Simply reactivate the disk, and it should return to Online. The mirrored volume will automatically be regenerated and return to normal. However, keep a close eye on this disk, as the I/O errors may eventually lead to a total disk failure.

Re-establishing a Mirrored Volume

When an offline disk is reactivated, the mirrored volume should automatically return to Healthy. However, if it doesn't, you can use the Reactivate Volume command to fix the problem.

Not all mirrored volume failures occur because of underlying disk problems. If the volume itself is at fault, you can use Repair Volume to fix the problem. If the volume still doesn't return to Healthy, use the Resynchronize Mirror feature to synchronize the data on both disks in the volume.

If this doesn't work, as a last resort, you can remove part of the mirror, then add it again. To remove part of a mirror, right-click it, then select Remove Mirror. This part of the mirror will become unallocated space. You can then use Add Mirror to re-create the mirrored volume.

Recovering a Failed RAID-5 Volume

RAID-5 volume failures are a bit more serious than mirrored volume failures. RAID-5 volumes do not contain backup copies; rather, the data must be regenerated using the parity information on the remaining good disks. Fortunately, the recovery procedures for a RAID-5 volume are similar to those for a mirrored volume.

Offline or Missing Disks

An offline or missing disk must be returned to an online state before the RAID-5 volume can be accessed. Try reactivating the disk. If this doesn't work, repair the disk, then reactivate it. You have to select a new area of free space, which is the same size (or larger) as the members of the volume, on which to regenerate the data from the parity information. The volume's status should automatically change to Regenerating, then back to Healthy.

If the failed disk itself must be replaced, select Repair Volume. This feature will incorporate the new disk into the existing RAID-5 volume.

Online Disks (w/Errors)

When a RAID-5 volume resides on a disk with the status Online (w/Errors), the volume will be inaccessible. Reactivate the disk, and the RAID-5 volume should be automatically regenerated.

Regenerating a RAID-5 Volume

In some cases, a RAID-5 volume may not regenerate itself once a bad disk is brought back online. When this is the case, use the Reactivate Volume command.

If the volume itself is at fault, you can try to fix it using the Repair Volume command. If the volume is too badly damaged to be repaired, use the Regenerate Parity command.

For detailed information on working with fault tolerant disks, please visit **www.shinder.net/Win2000/disks.**

on the
Job

In all cases of volume failure, first check the status of the disk itself. Once the disk status is set to Online, the volume should automatically repair or regenerate itself. If it does not, or if the volume itself is at fault, use the Repair, or Reactivate Volume commands to fix the problem. More serious problems can sometimes be corrected by resynchronizing the mirrors or regenerating RAID-5 parity.

CERTIFICATION SUMMARY

Windows 2000 Server supports a large variety of disk configurations, including basic partitions and sets. Windows 2000 also introduces dynamic disks, with support for simple, spanned, and striped volumes. The new Disk Management tool allows you to easily upgrade from basic to dynamic disks, and to create or delete volumes without restarting the computer.

Also new to Windows 2000 is the NTFS 5 file system, which supports native file compression and user disk quota management. Files, folders, or even entire volumes can be easily compressed by enabling the compression option in the Properties window. Disk quotas can be set on NTFS volumes within the Quota tab in the Properties windows. A single quota can be set for all users who access a volume, or you may opt to set different quotas for different users.

Because a network's server is such a critical resource, fault tolerance methods can be configured to reduce data loss and server downtime. Windows 2000 Server allows you to create mirrored and RAID-5 volumes, each of which can be used to re-create or replace lost data. In the case of a disk or volume failure, the Disk Management tool provides easy troubleshooting tools to repair the disk or volume, and to recover the lost or damaged information.

TWO-MINUTE DRILL

Monitor, Configure, and Troubleshoot Disks and Volumes

- Windows 2000 supports traditional basic disks and introduces the use of dynamic disks.

- Windows 2000 allows you to create basic partitions, and will recognize existing fault tolerant sets, but does not allow you to create new basic fault tolerant sets.

- Dynamic simple volumes reside on a single physical disk, and spanned volumes use space on more than one disk to create a single drive letter. Striped volumes interleave data evenly among two or more disks.

- A mirrored volume includes two identical copies of all information on two separate disks to provide fault tolerance, and a RAID-5 volume uses striping with additional parity information.

- Windows 2000 Server supports FAT16 and FAT32 file systems, and can convert them to NTFS 5 using the Convert.exe utility.

- The Disk Management tool is the utility that allows you to create volumes, upgrade to dynamic disk, and configure fault tolerance.

Configure Data Compression

- The NTFS 5 file system supports native data compression for files, folders, or entire volumes.

- Compression is enabled within the Properties dialog box.

- Compressed data cannot be encrypted.

Monitor and Configure Disk Quotas

■ NTFS 5 supports disk quotas, which limit the amount of server disk space that can be used by the network's users.

■ Disk quotas are created in the Quota tab within a volume's Properties dialog box.

■ Quotas may be set that apply to all users, or you may select to set different quotas for different users.

■ Quotas are based on the uncompressed size of files and folders.

Recover from Disk Failures

■ Mirrored and RAID-5 volumes are created with the Disk Management tool.

■ Volume errors that stem from underlying disk problems will often fix themselves when the disk is reactivated or replaced.

■ If the volume does not automatically repair itself, or if there is a problem with the volume itself, use the Reactivate Volume command.

■ If reactivating the volume doesn't work, try the command Repair Volume, Regenerate Parity (for RAID-5 volumes), or Resynchronize (for mirrored volumes).

SELF TEST

The following questions will help you measure your understanding of the material presented in this chapter. Read all of the choices carefully, as there may be more than one correct answer. Choose all correct answers for each question.

Monitor, Configure, and Troubleshoot Disks and Volumes

1. Which of the following is the most accurate description of a striped volume?

   A. A volume that includes an exact duplicate of all data on a separate physical disk

   B. A volume that uses the available space on more than one physical disk

   C. A volume that interleaves data evenly across more than one physical disk

   D. A volume that interleaves data and parity information evenly across more than one physical disk

2. How many disks can be included in a single RAID-5 volume?

   A. Between 2 and 64

   B. Between 3 and 32

   C. Between 2 and 512

   D. Between 1 and 64

3. You are installing Windows 2000 Advanced Server on a laptop. Your first priority is disk failure recovery speed. Which fault tolerance method should you create?

   A. Mirroring

   B. Striping

   C. RAID-5

   D. None of the above

4. You have decided to create a dual-boot system with Windows 98 on one drive and Windows 2000 Advanced Server on another. How should you configure the hard disk(s) if you want each operating system to have access to the other's files?

   A. Use the NTFS file system.

   B. Use the FAT32 file system.

   C. You can't; no matter how you configure the disk, Windows 2000 will be able to access the Windows 98 volume, but not the other way around.

D. You can't; no matter how you configure the disk, neither operating system will be able to read the other's files.

5. When setting up Windows 2000 Advanced Server, you decide to implement disk fault tolerance. Your first priority is to create seamless user access in the event of a disk failure. Which volume type should you use?

A. Mirrored

B. Striped

C. RAID-5

D. Spanned

Configure Data Compression

6. Which file system(s) can support native file compression?

A. FAT16, FAT32, and NTFS

B. FAT32 and NTFS

C. FAT32

D. NTFS

7. You want to compress a folder so that all newly created files are also compressed. You also want to set up the automatic compression of all files that are moved into that folder from other volumes. Which of the following procedures will enable these features?

A. In the Folder Compression Options dialog box, select Automatically Compress new entries.

B. In the Confirm Attribute Changes dialog box, select Apply changes to this folder, subfolders, and files.

C. In the Compress: drop-down list of the Folder Compression Options dialog box, select All Current and Imported Files option.

D. In the Confirm Attribute Changes dialog box, turn off the Apply only to Existing Files option.

8. Which type(s) of volume cannot be compressed using NTFS compression?

A. System and RAID-5 volumes

B. System and encrypted volumes

C. Encrypted and Windows 98 volumes

D. RAID-5 and mirrored volumes

9. What are the proper steps (in order) for applying NTFS compression to a folder and all of its subfolders?

   A. Open the folder's Properties dialog box I select Compress contents to save disk space I select Apply changes to this folder, subfolders, and files.

   B. Remove all data from the folder I in the Properties dialog box, select Compress contents to save disk space I move all data back into the compressed folder.

   C. Open the volume's Properties dialog box I select Compress contents to save disk space I select the proper folder from the Select Folder drop-down list.

   D. You cannot compress a single folder.

Monitor and Configure Disk Quotas

10. Users have been assigned quotas on a particular server volume. For which of the following actions are users not "charged" with using server disk space?

   A. Creating a new file

   B. Uncompressing a file

   C. Moving a folder and its data into the volume

   D. Losing ownership of a file

11. You want to monitor each user's use of the server's disk space, but you do not want to limit their use. What should you do?

   A. Do not enable quota management.

   B. Enable quota management, but do not select to deny disk space to users exceeding their quota limit and enable disk space warning level event logging.

   C. Enable quota management, and select the Monitor Only option.

   D. Set each user's quota to Infinite, so that they never reach their maximum allotment.

12. When a new quota is set in the Add new quota entry dialog box, who is affected?

   A. All users who access that volume

   B. All users who currently have data on that volume

   C. The selected user(s) only

   D. Only users who are logged in at the time that the quota is set

13. A Windows 2000 Server volume is compressed from 100MB to 80MB. Two equal-sized quotas are set which take up all of the space on the volume. What size is each quota?

    A. 100MB

    B. 80MB

    C. 50MB

    D. 40MB

Recover from Disk Failures

14. What happens to each volume when you use the command Remove Mirror?

    A. Each volume becomes unallocated space.

    B. The last volume added to the mirror becomes unallocated space, and the original volume remains intact.

    C. Both volumes remain intact, but from then on will behave as separate unmirrored volumes, and each will be assigned a different drive letter.

    D. The selected volume becomes unallocated space, and the other volume remains intact.

15. A mirrored volume is inaccessible, so you look at its status in the Disk Management window. One disk included in the mirror has the status Offline and its corresponding volume is listed as Failed. What should you do first to recover the volume?

    A. Use the Resynchronize Mirror command.

    B. Use the Reactivate Disk command.

    C. Use the Reactivate Volume command.

    D. Use the Repair Volume command.

16. What is the normal working status of a RAID-5 volume, as shown in the Disk Management window?

    A. Normal

    B. Parity

    C. Healthy

    D. RAID-5

17. Which command do you use in the Disk Management window to create a RAID-5 volume?

A. Add Stripe volume

B. Add Parity volume

C. Create RAID-5

D. Create Volume

LAB QUESTION

You want to create a dual-boot system with the following features:

Windows 98 installed on drive C: (on Disk 0)

Windows 2000 Advanced Server installed on drive D: (on Disk 1)

You want each operating system to have access to the other's files.

Which of these goals can you achieve, and how can you best configure the computer's disks to provide the desired features?

SELF TEST ANSWERS

Monitor, Configure, and Troubleshoot Disks and Volumes

1. ☑ **C.** A striped volume is a volume that interleaves data evenly across more than one physical disk. Disk striping provides increased volume capacity, and can speed up read/write tasks.
    ☒ **A** is incorrect, because it suggests that a striped volume contains duplicate data on a separate disk. This is, in fact, the description of a mirrored volume. **B**, a volume that uses the available space on more than one disk, is also incorrect. Although disk striping makes use of more than one disk, it is the interleaving of data that differentiates a striped volume from a spanned volume. **D** is incorrect, because it suggests that parity information is included along with data. This is the description of a RAID-5 (striping with parity) volume.

2. ☑ **B.** Between three and 32 disks can be used in a single RAID-5 volume. RAID-5 uses disk striping with parity, and must contain space on at least three disks. Data is interleaved across the disks, and error-correction data (called parity) is included. The use of three disks enables the regeneration of data on a failed disk from the existing data on the other three disks. RAID-5 volumes, like striped or spanned volumes, can make use of the space on up to 32 disks.
    ☒ **A**, between 2 and 64, and **C**, between 2 and 512, are both incorrect, because RAID-5 requires at least three disks to work. Also, RAID-5 volumes cannot keep track of data on more than 32 separate disks. **D**, between 1 and 64, is also incorrect, because RAID-5 volumes require at least three disks, and can use no more than 32.

3. ☑ **D.** Laptops are limited to basic disks; that is, they cannot be upgraded to dynamic. However, Windows 2000 Advanced Server allows you to create fault tolerant volumes only on dynamic disks. The only way to create fault tolerance on a laptop using Windows 2000 Advanced Server is to create the fault tolerant set in an older operating system, then upgrade to Windows 2000. Windows 2000 will recognize legacy basic fault tolerant sets, even though it won't let you create new ones.
    ☒ **A**, mirroring, and **C**, RAID-5, are both incorrect, because, again, Windows 2000 does not allow you to create fault tolerant volumes on basic disks. **B**, striping, is incorrect, because you cannot create a striped volume on a basic disk. Furthermore, striping does not provide fault tolerance.

4. ☑ **B.** Use the FAT32 file system. It is one of the only file systems recognized by both Windows 98 and Windows 2000 (the other is FAT16). An important note here is that any disk upgraded to dynamic will be unreadable to Windows 98, so in this scenario, you must leave each operating system on a basic disk.

   ☒ **A,** use the NTFS file system, is incorrect, because Windows 98 cannot access data on NTFS partitions. **C** is incorrect, because it suggests that Windows 2000 can read files on the Windows 98 partition, but Windows 98 will never be able to read the Windows 2000 partition. Both Windows 98 and Windows 2000 can access data on any FAT16 or FAT32 partition. **D** is incorrect, because it states that neither operating system will be able to read the other's files, no matter what you do. This is incorrect, because Windows 2000 will always be able to read a Windows 98 partition (FAT16 or FAT32).

5. ☑ **A.** You should create a mirrored volume. This type of volume contains two exact copies of data on two separate disks. If one disk fails, the data is simply retrieved off the other. Although this method can take a longer time to set up, users will not even be aware of disk failures, as the data will simply be retrieved from the remaining good disk.

   ☒ **B,** striped, and **D,** spanned, are incorrect, because these volume types do not provide fault tolerance. Both methods use the space on more than one physical disk, but data is written only once within the volume. **C,** RAID-5, is incorrect, because when a disk in the volume fails, the missing information must be regenerated from the data on the remaining two or more disks. This process can be quite lengthy, since the missing data must be essentially rewritten.

Configure Data Compression

6. ☑ **D.** NTFS can support native file compression. You can leave data on an NTFS volume uncompressed, or you can select to compress a file, folder, or the entire volume itself.

   ☒ **A, B,** and **C** are all incorrect, because they suggest that the FAT16 or FAT32 file systems can support native file compression. This feature is exclusive to NTFS, and is not available in FAT16 or FAT32.

7. ☑ **B.** In the Confirm Attribute Changes dialog box, select Apply changes to this folder, subfolders, and files. This is a regular step for compressing a folder and all of its contents. NTFS native file compression will then automatically compress all new files created within that folder, and any files or subfolders moved into it from another volume.

   ☒ **A** and **C** are incorrect, because they suggest selecting options in the Folder Compression Options dialog box, which does not exist. The two dialog boxes you will see when compressing a folder are the Advanced Attributes and Confirm Attribute Changes dialog boxes. **D** is incorrect, because it suggests turning off the Apply only to Existing Files Option. This option does not exist in the Confirm Attribute Changes dialog box.

8. ☑ **C.** You cannot use NTFS compression on encrypted or Windows 98 volumes. NTFS volumes cannot be both compressed and encrypted. Windows 98 must reside on a FAT32 or FAT16 volume, since it cannot recognize NTFS. However, NTFS compression can only be performed on an NTFS volume. Since Windows 98 cannot run on an NTFS volume, it cannot use NTFS compression.

☒ **A** and **D** are both incorrect, because they suggest that you cannot use NTFS compression on system, RAID-5 or mirrored volumes. As long as these volumes are formatted with the NTFS file system, they can use NTFS compression. **B**, system and encrypted files, is also incorrect, because although you cannot compress encrypted volumes, you can compress system volumes.

9. ☑ **A.** This is the only proper method for compressing a selected folder and all of its contents.
☒ **B** is incorrect, because it suggests removing all data from the folder, compressing it, then moving all data back into the folder. Using the proper method described above will apply compression to all existing data in the folder, so there is no need to remove the data first. **C** is incorrect, because it states that you should apply compression from the *volume's* Properties dialog box, then select the appropriate folder. When you select compression from a volume's Properties dialog box, compression will be applied to the entire volume, and there is no option here to select an individual folder. To compress a single folder, use *that folder's* Properties dialog box. **D**, you cannot compress a single folder, is incorrect, because NTFS compression can be applied to an entire volume, or a specific folder or file.

Monitor and Configure Disk Quotas

10. ☑ **D.** Users are not charged with using server disk space when they lose ownership of a file. This occurs when another user takes ownership of the file. If, for example, user 1 takes ownership of a 4MB file previously owned by user 2, user1 is charged with 4MB, and user 2's used disk space decreases by 4MB.
☒ **A**, creating a new file, and **C**, moving a folder and its data into the volume, are both incorrect. Both of these actions mean that the user has placed data on the volume in question. That data is taking up space, so the user is charged against their quota (for example, if a user with a 5MB quota places 2MB worth of files on the volume, they now have only 3MB of space left on that volume). **B**, uncompressing a file, is also incorrect. Quotas are always created and reported based on the uncompressed size of files and folders. A user who is at the quota limit cannot recover extra space by compressing files.

11. ☑ **B.** Windows 2000 will then prepare reports about each user who has exceeded the set limit, but each user can continue to use server disk space. This is a good option to use in determining how high to set the quotas before actually implementing them.
☒ **A**, do not enable quota management, is incorrect, because you will not be able to monitor server disk space use unless this option is enabled. **C**, enable quota management, and select the Monitor Only option, is also incorrect. There is no Monitor Only option available when setting quotas. **D** is incorrect, because it states that you should set each user's quota to Infinite, so that none of them ever reaches the maximum allotment. When setting quotas, you cannot exceed the maximum available space on the volume in question.

12. ☑ **C.** In the Add new quota entry dialog box, you must select a user or users, then apply a quota and warning limit to that user or users only.

    ☒ **A,** all users who access that volume, is incorrect. It is possible to create a universal quota for all users, but this is done in the Quota tab of the volume's Properties dialog box, not in the Add new quota entry dialog box. **B,** all users who currently have data on that volume, and **D,** only users who are logged in at the time that the quota is set, are both incorrect. The only two options for setting quotas are to apply the quota to every user that accesses the volume, or to apply the quota to selected existing users. These options are applied whether the user is logged in or not, and regardless of whether the user has already stored data on the volume in question.

13. ☑ **C.** Each quota is 50MB. Quotas are reported in their uncompressed size. The uncompressed size of this volume is 100MB, and two equal-sized quotas are 50MB each. This is the value whether the volume is compressed or not.

    ☒ **A,** 100MB, and **B,** 80MB, are incorrect, because the total of all users' quotas cannot exceed the available uncompressed volume space. For these users to have 100MB or 80MB quotas, the volume would have to have a 200MB or 160MB capacity, respectively. **D,** 40MB, is incorrect, because this calculation is based on the compressed size of the volume.

Recover from Disk Failures

14. ☑ **D.** When you use the command Remove Mirror, the selected volume becomes unallocated space, and the other volume remains intact. However, the remaining volume will no longer be fault tolerant. You can add another mirror later by selecting Add Mirror.

    ☒ **A,** each volume becomes unallocated space, is incorrect, because only the "removed" part of the mirror becomes unallocated space. **B** is incorrect, because it suggests the last volume added to the mirror becomes unallocated space. When you use the Remove Mirror command, you select the disk to remove, regardless of which part of the mirrored volume existed first. **C** is incorrect, because it suggests that each part of the mirror remains intact, but from then on works independently of the other. This is the result of the command Break Mirror, not Remove Mirror.

15. ☑ **B.** Use the Reactivate Disk command. The mirrored volume problem in this case stems from an underlying disk problem. Reactivating the disk may return it to an Online status. If this is the case, the mirrored volume should automatically repair itself.

    ☒ **A,** use the Resynchronize Mirror command, **C,** use the Reactivate Volume command, and **D,** use the Repair Volume command, are all incorrect, because they suggest that the volume itself is at fault. However, in this case, the disk itself must be set back online before you can access the mirrored volume. The commands listed in answers **A, C,** and **D** can be used only if the volume resides on a working and online disk.

16. ☑ **C.** The normal working status of a RAID-5 volume is Healthy. In fact, the status of all functioning volumes is Healthy.

☒ **A,** normal, **B,** parity, and **C,** RAID-5, are all incorrect, because these are not valid Disk Management statuses, regardless of the functionality of the RAID-5 volume.

17. ☑ **D.** You use this command to create any type of volume. Once you have selected this command, you will be presented with a dialog box, where you then choose which type of volume to create (simple, striped, RAID-5, and so on). It is important to note that if you do not have unallocated space on at least three separate disks, the RAID-5 option will not be available in this dialog box.

☒ **A,** Add Stripe volume, **B,** Add Parity volume, and **C,** Create RAID-5, are all incorrect, because they are not real commands in the Disk Management window.

LAB ANSWER

Your knowledge about file systems should lead you to the conclusion that you cannot use the NTFS file system on drive C:, since it cannot be used by Windows 98. Also, you cannot upgrade Disk 0 to dynamic, since that would make it unreadable to Windows 98. Therefore, Disk 0 must be a basic disk, and drive C: must be formatted with either the FAT16 or FAT32 file system. Next, Windows 2000 Advanced Server works best when it is installed on a dynamic disk with an NTFS volume. However, one of the goals is to allow each operating system to have access to the other files. Remember, Windows 98 cannot read NTFS or dynamic disks. Therefore, Windows 2000 Advanced Server must be installed on a FAT16 or FAT32 partition on a basic disk.

To recap, these are the steps you must perform to achieve all of the goals in this scenario:

- Format drive C: as FAT16 or FAT32, then install Windows 98 on it.

- Format drive D: as FAT32, then install Windows 2000 on it.

- Do not upgrade the file system to NTFS or FAT32, and do not upgrade from basic to dynamic disk.

11

Configuring and Troubleshooting Windows 2000 Network Connections

CERTIFICATION OBJECTIVES

11.01	Installing, Configuring, and Troubleshooting Remote Access
11.02	Installing, Configuring, and Troubleshooting Network Protocols
11.03	Installing, Configuring, and Troubleshooting Network Adapters and Drivers
✓	Two-Minute Drill
Q&A	Self Test

Windows 2000 Server follows its predecessors in providing an integrated set of network services with which to build enterprise-level connectivity. Microsoft has added functionality and services to provide enhanced performance, security, and enterprise connectivity for the new Windows 2000 platform of products. These new services and features address deficiencies with the Windows NT 4.0 networking services platform. Some of the networking features that were installed in the previous versions of Windows NT are no longer installed by default in the new Windows 2000 platform due to the emphasis Microsoft has placed on making Windows 2000 Internet ready. The roles of some of the traditional services for networking have also changed in Windows 2000 in order to support organizations that utilize the Internet for their enterprise-level connectivity.

To provide shared access, remote access capability, and interoperability with existing network architectures, Windows 2000 incorporates the new network services with the existing NT traditional network services using new tool sets and operational methods. These tool sets and methodologies are designed to enable the NT administrator to migrate to the new network environment of Windows 2000 while still providing older network servers and workstations with services that maintain connectivity and interoperability.

CERTIFICATION OBJECTIVE 11.01

Installing, Configuring, and Troubleshooting Remote Access

Routing and Remote Access Service (RRAS) and *Network and Dial-Up Connections* are the main tools used to install, configure, and manage remote access to Windows 2000 Server. Network and Dial-Up Connections provide connectivity between the Windows 2000 server and the Internet, a private network, or another computer connected via either infrared or serial cable. Network and Dial-Up Connections combine the Windows NT 4.0 version of Dial-Up Networking (DUN) with network control panel features. Each connection in the Network and Dial-Up Connections folder contains the set of features that create and manage the links to other computers. RRAS provides the functionality for integrated routing, remote access from multiple computer types, and virtual private network (VPN) connections. In this chapter, we discuss the RRAS and network and dial-up functions and create and configure multiple modes of remote access.

Installing and Configuring RRAS

To install RRAS, you must make sure that all communications hardware is available and working correctly. Communications components used by RRAS include network interface cards (NICs), analog modems (both external and internal), the communications ports (COM1, COM2, etc.), and Integrated Services Digital Network (ISDN) modems. The status of all these components can be checked using the Device Manager.

1. Navigate to this dialog using Start | Settings | Control Panel | System.

2. In the System applet, choose the Hardware tab and select Device Manager. The Device Manager dialog box is shown in Figure 11-1.

3. If you right-click on a device, the properties for that device are displayed. Once you have installed all the appropriate devices, the network protocols that will

FIGURE 11-1   The Device Manager, used for viewing hardware configurations

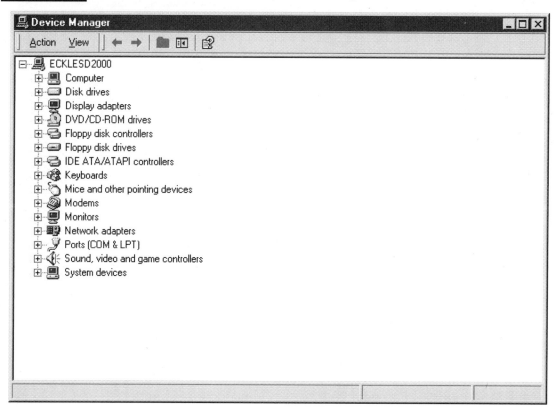

be deployed in your RRAS installation need to be configured. (We cover these protocols later in the chapter.) The next action is to activate RRAS.

exam
ⓦatch

The RRAS is installed by default, but it is not activated. In order to use RRAS, you need to activate it. A possible test question could involve a scenario in which the service is used without being activated. The outcome of this scenario would be that none of the options would work because the service was never activated.

4. To configure and activate RRAS, choose Start | Programs | Administrative Tools | Routing and Remote Access.

5. Select the RRAS server that you want to configure and activate. This dialog box is shown in Figure 11-2.

FIGURE 11-2   The Routing and Remote Access dialog box lets you activate and configure RRAS for your server

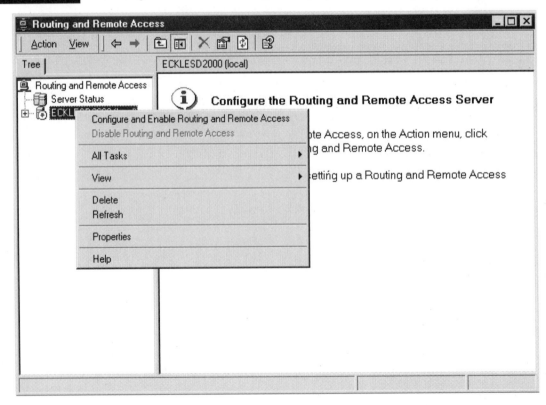

6. Once you have selected a server, a wizard process that configures the options for this server starts. You can edit these options later, but for the initial configuration, run the wizard.

7. Figure 11-3 shows the Server Setup wizard. There are several options from which to choose. These options determine how you will use RRAS. These common configurations make installation for most RRAS applications easier for the Windows 2000 administrator. Table 11-1 shows and briefly explains the various options for configuring RRAS for the most common applications.

8. Once a common option is selected, the wizard presents several prompts to guide the administrator to a more customized implementation of the common application. This feature allows most administrators to get RRAS up and running right away.

FIGURE 11-3   The Routing and Remote Access Server Setup wizard allows you to choose among common configuration options

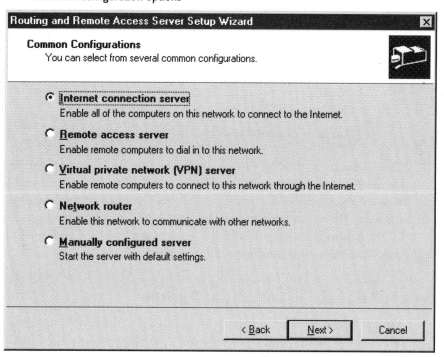

TABLE 11-1	Common Configuration	Description and Where to Use
The Options Available in the Remote Routing and Access Service	Internet Connection Server	This option is used to set up Internet connection sharing through a modem or a NIC as well as other communications devices.
	Remote Access Server	Allows remote users of the network to connect using a communications device such as a single modem, a modem pooling device, an ISDN modem, or the like.
	VPN Server	This option allows this computer to connect to the network remote users who are connected to the Internet through their own Internet service providers (ISPs).
	Network Router	The Windows 2000 server can function as a router between two networks that are both connected to the same Windows 2000 server.
	Manually Configured	If desired, RRAS can be manually configured with default starting settings. This is recommended for users with special configuration requirements or configurations not covered in the common configurations.

9. Once the configuration process is complete, the wizard presents the dialog box shown in Figure 11-4. The service can now be configured as necessary or used immediately, depending on the options chosen.

10. Click Finish to complete all the installation steps.

exam
ⓦatch

Administrators should be familiar with the remote access protocols that are available in Windows 2000. The features of each protocol and how they are mainly used are necessary in order to answer any scenario-based question. There are also two connection types: dial-up and access through a VPN. Knowing how each of these work is a plus when you must answer multiple-choice or scenario-based questions.

The Network Address Translation Option

Network address translation (NAT) can be enabled during the installation and configuration of RRAS. If you choose to set up a router with the NAT protocol, the wizard performs all configuration steps needed to complete the

FIGURE 11-4 The Server Setup Wizard gives you the option of obtaining immediate help to manage the remote access server that was just configured

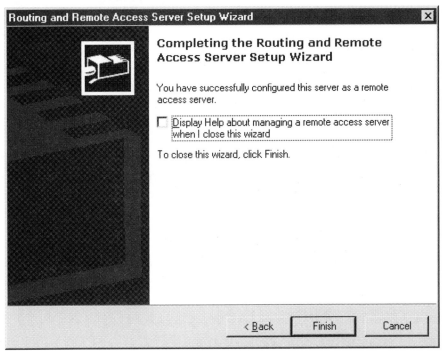

installation. Instances in which you need to perform an advanced configuration of NAT include IP addresses that were assigned by an outside authority or when services provided on the private network need to be accessed from an exterior or public network.

NAT is usually configured on a small network or home office network on which a number of workstations will share a single connection to the Internet. The small office/home office (SOHO) network is most likely to use private network addressing. The network on which these workstations are running needs to provide services from the Internet or the main office and still be able to maintain the private addressing and local services. The NAT service in Windows 2000 is used to provide that functionality. The workstations on the private network can share a single connection to the Internet to provide all the remote services of the Internet and/or the main office. The main components of NAT are translation, addressing, and name resolution.

The Windows 2000 computer on which network address translation is enabled translates the IP addresses and TCP/UDP port numbers for forwarded packets between the private network and the Internet. This network address translator effectively prevents the private network-addressing scheme from being exposed to the Internet or other exterior networks. This translation computer also provides an addressing component that provides the IP configuration to the computers on the SOHO network. The NAT computer uses a simplified DHCP allocator that allocates the IP address, the subnet mask, the default gateway, and the IP address of a DNS server. All computers on the SOHO network are configured as DHCP clients, which is a default in Windows 2000, Windows NT, Windows 95, and Windows 98 client workstations.

The last component provided is the DNS server that is used to provide responses to the SOHO network computers when they request name resolution. The NAT computer acts as a forwarder for these requests to a DNS server that provides Internet name resolution.

exam
⦿atch
NAT includes addressing and name resolution components that provide the DHCP and DNS services for the SOHO network. The hosts on the SOHO network cannot use the services of another computer running DHCP or DNS.

Configuring Inbound Dial-Up Connections

A RRAS server on Windows 2000 views all installed networking equipment as a collection of ports and devices. In order to understand what you are configuring for RRAS in Windows 2000, it is necessary to have an understanding of ports and devices and the tunneling protocols L2TP and PPTP, which we examine now.

Devices

Hardware and software installed in a Windows 2000 server can create physical and logical point-to-point connections. Such a connection is commonly referred to as a *device*. Devices can support single or multiple ports, such as a modem-pooling device. Point-to-Point Tunnel Protocol (PPTP) and Layer 2 Tunneling Protocol (L2TP) are examples of virtual multiport devices. Each of the protocols (PPTP or L2TP) supports multiple VPN connections. To see installed devices, you can view the properties using the RRAS tool.

Point-to-Point Tunneling Protocol

PPTP adds enhanced security for communications over the Internet. Using the new Extensible Authentication Protocol (EAP), data is secure through PPTP VPNs and is as secure as transferring the same data over a corporate LAN on a single segment. PPTP encapsulates IP, IPX, or NetBEUI protocols inside PPP packets. PPTP does not require a dial-up connection, but it does require IP connectivity to be established between the two points that are communicating. This means that in a dial-up connection to an ISP, the connection must be established and an IP address must be established before a dial-up client can create a PPTP tunnel. The tunnel server performs security checks, validations, and tunnel operations, so applications that are dependent on remote network protocols can be connected without having to provide the remote network protocol to the client.

Layer-Two Tunneling Protocol

A private network can be accessed through the Internet or other public network by creating a VPN with L2TP. This protocol is functionally equivalent to PPTP. Windows 2000 uses L2TP to provide tunneling services over Internet Protocol Security (IPSec)-based communications. L2TP tunnels can be set up to traverse data across intervening networks that are not part of the VPN being created. L2TP is used to send information across intervening and nonsecure networks. A remote access server could host a connection from a remote home user connected to the Internet through his or her own ISP using an L2TP tunnel.

Ports

A channel of a device that can support single point-to-point connections is known as a *port*. Devices can be single port, as in a modem. The modem is a single device with a single port for communications. For multiport devices, the device is divided using the port as the line of demarcation. On a BRI (Basic Rate Interface) ISDN adapter, multiple ports are available. The adapter itself is a device, and the B-channels of the adapter are separate ports. To see the dial-up ports in Windows 2000, you can view the list in the RRAS tool of Windows 2000.

Configuring Virtual Private Network Ports

Windows 2000 RRAS provides a multiprotocol VPN port capability for remote access clients using PPTP or L2TP protocols. VPN clients can be Windows 2000, Windows NT 4.0, Windows 95, or Windows 98 clients. The clients must be able to send TCP/IP packets to the remote access server. The client must have a NIC or a modem with a phone line (analog) or some type of WAN connection.

Non-Microsoft VPN clients using PPTP or L2TP with IPSec can access a Windows NT 4.0 or Windows 2000 RAS server. If you want secure VPN connections, you must take care to make sure the non-Windows VPN clients support the proper encryption. This means that for PPTP, Microsoft Point-to-Point Encryption must be supported, and for L2TP, IPSec encryption must be supported.

To configure PPTP or L2TP ports, use the RRAS dialog boxes, as before. Figure 11-5 shows a configured RRAS server dialog with the desired server chosen and the ports selection highlighted. Note that ports are already defined for this server. This is because the wizard that was run on this server has provided a starting configuration for these ports.

FIGURE 11-5 Routing and Remote Access provides default VPN-configured ports when the wizard is run to configure RRAS on Windows 2000 Server

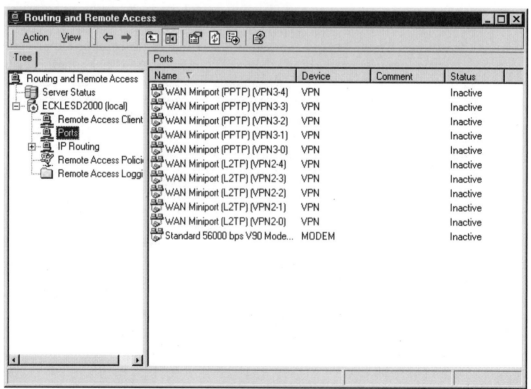

By right-clicking on the Ports selection and choosing Properties, you see the dialog box shown in Figure 11-6. Note that each of the types of ports on your server has been given a default number. Five PPTP and five L2TP ports are used by the RAS server.

1. By clicking Configure, you see a dialog box showing the options for the device highlighted. In this case, we are configuring the WAN Miniport (PPTP) device. The choices for this configuration appear in Figure 11-7.

2. If you wanted to limit the VPN connections to incoming only, you could check the box as shown. If you need to increase the maximum number of ports, this box is where you can change that option. If you do change the number of ports, the RRAS service must be restarted in order for you to be able to see these new ports created.

exam
ⓦatch

It is a good bet that one of the test questions will ask you to identify either the default number of ports assigned in this step or how to increase the number of ports. Knowing what each of these options controls and how it affects the users' capability will also help on scenario-based questions.

FIGURE 11-6

Ports Properties allows you to configure the devices used by RRAS, including the VPN ports for PPTP and L2TP connections

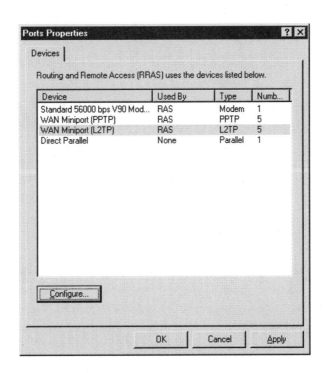

FIGURE 11-7

Configure the maximum number of ports of each type as well as routing options and phone number

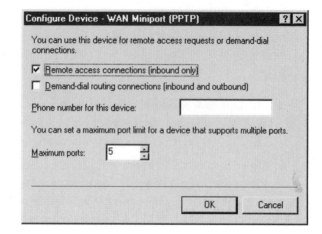

Configuring Modem Ports and Direct Cable Connections

To configure modem ports and direct cable connections, follow these steps:

1. Open the Remote Routing and Access tool by clicking Start | Programs | Administrative Tools | Routing and Remote Access.

2. To configure modem ports, choose Ports under the server name for which you are configuring access.

3. Right-clicking on Ports brings up the Ports Properties dialog box, as shown earlier in Figure 11-6. The dialog box mentions a Standard 56000bps V.90 modem to configure.

4. Highlight the modem device and click Configure to bring up the dialog box to configure a modem, as shown in Figure 11-8. Notice in this dialog box that the number of ports is grayed out so that it cannot be changed. Other than this difference, all the other options are the same for modems as they are for WAN miniports. You can configure the modem to accept inbound calls only and support demand-dial routing.

5. Click OK after making your changes and close the dialog box.

Configuring Modem-Pooling Equipment

To configure modem-pooling equipment, use a procedure similar to installing a new modem, as explained in the previous example. Modem-pooling equipment generates and accepts command strings as though it were a modem of the type found in the Install New Modem wizard. The equipment must also support RS-232 signaling in order to work properly. Configure the ports for remote access in the RRAS tool.

FIGURE 11-8

Configuring a
device for a
standard 56000
BPS V.90 modem

Configure Device - Standard 56000 bps V90 Modem

You can use this device for remote access requests or demand-dial connections.

☑ Remote access connections (inbound only)

☐ Demand-dial routing connections (inbound and outbound)

Phone number for this device:

You can set a maximum port limit for a device that supports multiple ports.

Maximum ports: 1

OK   Cancel

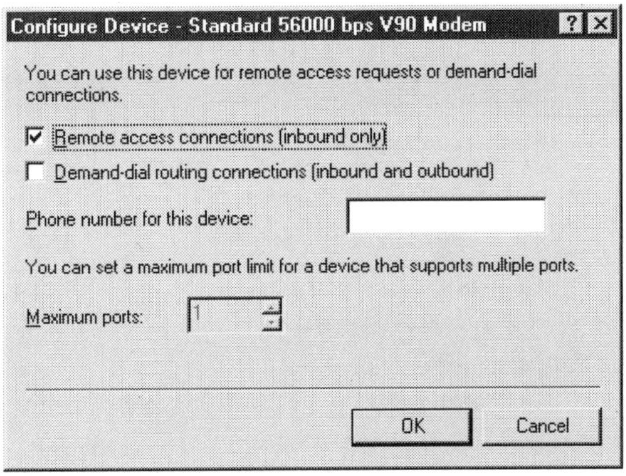

on the **Job**

If you want to save time configuring modem-pooling equipment, treat the equipment as though it were a Hayes-compatible modem, a widely known industry standard that will work with most modem-pooling equipment.

Configuring a Nonmodem Connection

You can connect two computers without modems through either an infrared connection or a direct connection. The direct connection eliminates the need for a network adapter, but it is a slow link, and you must consider the type of data that will be transmitted between the two computers.

Infrared Connections   To create an infrared connection between Windows 2000 systems or other Windows systems:

1. Open Network and Dial-Up Connections by clicking Start | Settings | Network and Dial-Up Connections.

2. Double-click Make new connections to start the Network Connection wizard. Figure 11-9 shows the dialog box that will be presented.

3. Choose the "Connect directly to another computer" option and click Next. Your Windows 2000 server can act as host or as a guest in the connection created. To receive connections, this server would be a host; to send files to another computer, use the guest setting.

4. The Network Connection wizard now presents a dialog box allowing you to choose the device available to make the connection. Choose the infrared port device. Figure 11-10 shows the dialog box in which you choose whether all users on the server or just yourself have rights to access this connection.

FIGURE 11-9 Use the Network Connection Wizard to quickly configure a variety of common connection types

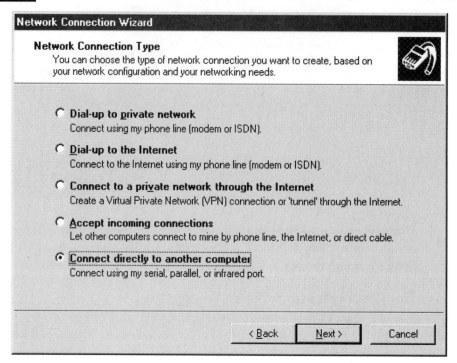

5. Name the connection, and then click Finish.

After you have added the device you may have to restart Windows 2000 to enable the device to work properly. If you want to change the properties later, open the Network and Dial-Up Connections tool and right-click on the icon representing the connection.

As with many other dialog boxes, you can open the Network and Dial-Up Connections tool by double-clicking Network and Dial-Up Connections in My Computer.

Creating a Remote Access Policy

Remote access policies allow you to create demand-dial connections to use specific authentication and encryption methods. In Windows NT versions 3.5x and Windows NT 4.0, authorization was much simpler. The administrator simply

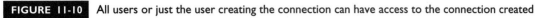

FIGURE 11-10   All users or just the user creating the connection can have access to the connection created

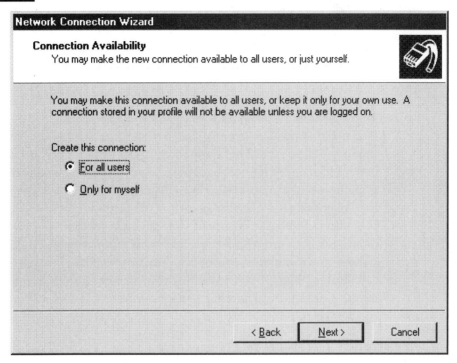

granted dial-in permission to the user. The callback options were configured on a per-user basis.

Starting with Windows 2000, authorization is granted based on properties of the user account and remote access policies. Remote access policies are settings that give the Windows 2000 administrator more options in authorizing connection attempts. Windows 2000 and RRAS and Internet Authentication Service (IAS) use the remote access policy to determine whether or not to grant access. Remote access policies allow the administrator flexibility in allowing user access based on time of day, day of week, the Windows 2000 group of which the user is a member, type of connection being requested, and other options. The session time can be limited, the type of encryption and authentication can be chosen, and Bandwidth Allocation Protocol (BAP) policies can be set.

exam

ⓌatcH

With remote access policies, a connection is only authorized if the settings of the connection attempt match at least one of the remote access policies. If the settings do not match any of the policies, the connection attempt is denied. The denial is made regardless of the dial-in properties of the user account.

There are three primary models for administering remote access permissions and connection settings:

- **Access by user**   The remote access permissions are determined on the Dial-In tab of the user account. The user can be enabled or disabled by choosing "Allow access" or "Deny access." The remote access permission is overridden on the remote access policy, but you can still modify the policy to configure other options such as encryption, idle time-outs, and so on. Each remote access policy has its own profile settings. These settings must be configured with care because a connection attempt can be rejected, even though the permission on the user account is set to allow access. In the access-by-user administrative model, three behaviors can be controlled, as described in Table 11-2. Configuring the server using this administrative model is equivalent to administering the remote access on a Windows NT 4.0 server.

exam

ⓌatcH

The access-by-user model on a remote access server is available if the server is a stand-alone server, a member of a Windows 2000 native-mode domain, a member of a Windows 2000 Mixed Mode domain, or a server that is a member of a Windows NT 4.0 domain.

- **Access by policy in a Windows 2000 Native Mode domain**   The remote access permission for every user is set to "Control access through Remote Access Policy." Permissions are determined by the remote access permission setting in the remote access policy. Again, three behaviors are controlled in this model, as illustrated in Table 11-3.

TABLE 11-2	Setting	Policy
Access-by-User Permissions Settings	Explicit allow	The remote access permission is set to allow access and the connection attempt matches the conditions of a policy subject to the settings of the profile and dial-in properties of the user.
	Explicit deny	The permission for the user account is set to deny access.
	Implicit deny	The attempt to connect does not match any of the remote access policies.

TABLE 11-3	Setting	Policy
Access-by-Policy Permissions Settings for a Native Mode Domain	Explicit allow	The remote access permission on the policy is set to grant remote access permission and the connection attempt matches the policy conditions and is subject to the settings in the dial-in properties of the user as well as the profile of the user.
	Explicit deny	The permission on the remote access policy is set to deny remote access permission and the attempt to connect matches the conditions of the policy.
	Implicit deny	The connection attempt does not match the conditions of any access policies.

exam

Watch

You cannot use the access-by-policy model for Windows 2000 Native Mode domain if you have Windows NT 4.0 RAS or IAS servers. The access-by-policy model for Windows 2000 Native Mode domain also applies to stand-alone remote access servers that are not members of a domain.

- **Access by policy in a Windows 2000 Mixed Mode domain**   The permission on every user account is set to allow access and the default remote access policy is deleted. Separate policies are created to define the connection types that will be allowed. On a Windows 2000 server running RAS that is a member of a Mixed Mode domain, "Control access through Remote Access Policy" is not available on the user account settings. If an attempt to connect matches the conditions of a policy, again subject to the profile and user account dial-in settings, the connection will be completed. This model also applies to a Windows 2000 server that is a member of a Windows NT 4.0 domain. In the access-by-policy administrator model, you can control the same three behaviors as in the other models already discussed, as outlined in Table 11-4.

on the

Job

If you do not delete the default remote access policy known as "Allow access if dial-in permission is enabled," all users will obtain a remote access connection. If you have any Windows NT 4.0 RRAS servers, you can use only the access by policy in a Windows 2000 Mixed Mode domain model for remote access. Furthermore, if your RRAS servers are configured as RADIUS clients to an Internet Authentication Service (IAS) server, you cannot use the access-by-policy Windows 2000 Mixed Mode administrative model for Windows NT 4.0 RAS servers.

TABLE 11-4	Setting	Policy
Access-by-Policy Permissions Settings for a Mixed Mode Domain	Explicit allow	The attempt to connect matches the policy conditions that are subject also to the settings of the access profile and dial-in properties of the user.
	Explicit deny	The attempt to connect matches the conditions of a policy but not the settings of the access profile. Explicit deny is enabled by using the restrict dial-in to this number-only setting. The administrator can enter a number that does not correspond to any dial-in number used by RRAS.
	Implicit deny	The attempt to access the server does not match any of the conditions of any remote access policies.

Each one of these options has an associated dialog box via which you configure the condition of the connection. Some of these attributes are self-explanatory, but some need more explicit definition. The reader is left to discover some of the details of each of these settings in order to use them in a particular environment. A number of combinations can be created and a number of settings and models will determine the complexity or the simplicity of granting the user remote access. Figure 11-11 contains a flow chart that describes the thought process in creating remote access policies.

The next section discusses the remote access profile, which is part of the decision tree process for accepting or rejecting a remote connection. The remote access policy is checked along with the remote access profile.

exam
⊕atch

The exam will probably include a very good scenario question based on users connecting and processing remote access policies. Remember this point: The user account and profile for the first matching policy are applied to the incoming connection. If an attempt does not match the profile and the user account settings of the first matching policy, the additional policies are not checked.

CertCam 11-1

Create Remote Access Policy

1. To create the access policy, open the Routing and Remote Access tool and double-click the server name.

2. Right-click the Remote Access Policies, and then click New Remote Access Policy.

3. The Add Remote Access Policy dialog box is presented. The attributes of the policy are blank. Click Add to bring up the choices shown:

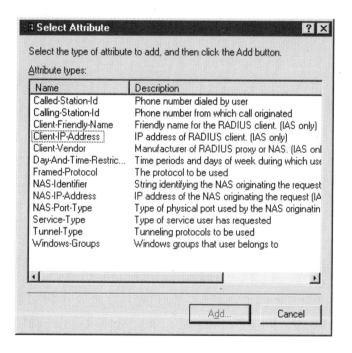

FIGURE 11-11 Remote Access Policy flowchart describing the decision process to accept a remote connection attempt

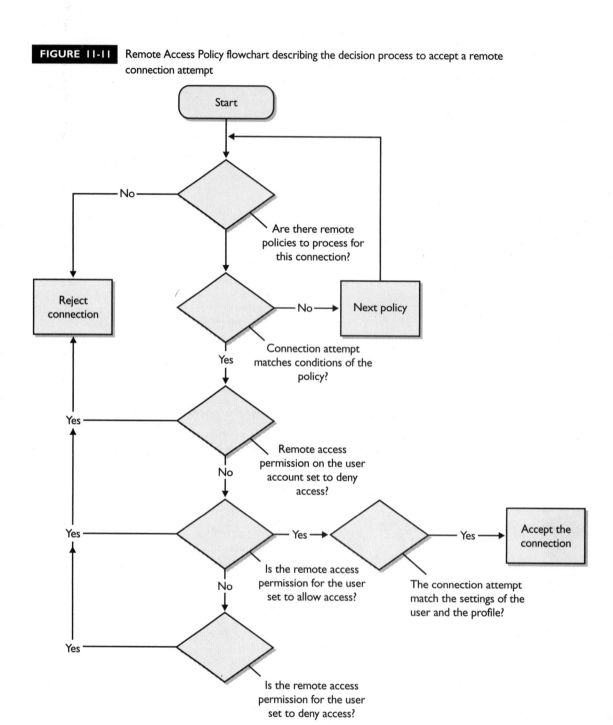

Creating and Configuring a Remote Access Profile

A *remote access profile* comprises the properties that are applied to a connection that has been authorized through user account permissions or the remote access policy. The profile consists of the groups of properties shown in Table 11-5.

TABLE 11-5	Property	Description
Remote Access Profile Property Settings	Dial-In Constraints	Idle disconnect Maximum session length Day and time limits Dial-in number Dial-in media
	IP	You can set properties that specify whether a client can request a particular IP address. By default, the remote access server allocates an IP address and the client is *not* allowed to request a specific address. You can also define remote access policy filtering. You can use profile packet filters to control IP traffic that is allowed out of this connection. Remote access policy profile filtering applies to all connections that match the remote access policy.
	Multilink	You can control whether the connection is allowed to utilize multilinking. You can also configure the BAP properties that determine BAP usage and when to add or drop BAP lines. By default, these properties are disabled. The remote access server must also have multilink and BAP enabled in order for this profile setting to be enforced.
	Authentication Type	Authentication properties enable the types of authentication protocols that will be allowed. The EAP can also be configured. By default, the MS-Chap and MS-Chap v2 are enabled.
	Encryption	Set the encryption properties to include: **None** When encryption *is* required, clear the No Encryption option. **Basic** PPTP-based VPN connections and Microsoft Point-to-Point Encryption (MPPE) with a 40-bit key are used. **Strong** MPPE uses 56-bit key; L2TP over IPSec uses 56-bit DES. **Strongest** MPPE with a 128-bit key is used; L2TP over IPSec uses a triple DES (3DES) encryption. This setting is available only in the North American version of Windows 2000.
	Advanced	Advanced properties specify the RADIUS attributes that are sent back to RADIUS clients by the IAS server. Default settings are Framed-Protocol set to PPP and Service-Type set to Framed.

On every remote access policy configuration dialog box is a button for editing the remote access profile for that policy. Figure 11-12 shows the dialog box that is presented when you click the Edit Profile button in the remote access policy.

As Table11-5 shows, there are a number of tabs and selections that can be made to constrain dial-in, define an IP address assignment policy for this particular profile, define IP packet filters, enable use of multilinks, and govern the use of BAP, set authentication and encryption methods and, under the advanced tab, set RADIUS properties. The profile is saved with the policy when the user chooses OK and closes the Edit Dial-in Profile screen.

on the **job**

Windows 2000 provides many more opportunities to make mistakes while installing and implementing RRAS. Make sure that you understand the new options available in RRAS. Your employer's or your customer's network will be much more accessible to the remote users with greater flexibility in the options available, but with that flexibility also comes complexity. Make sure that any connectivity you configure is tested to make sure you do not enable access to individuals or groups, either externally or internally, through improper configuration of options in RRAS.

FIGURE 11-12

The remote access profile for the default remote access policy

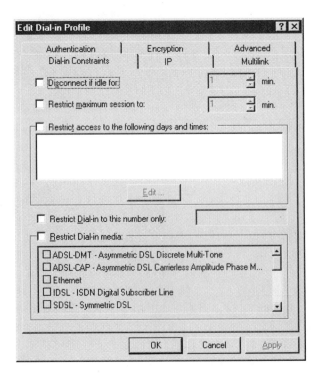

Configuring Outbound Dial-Up Connections

A dial-up connection allows you to communicate to a network that may or may not be on the Internet but is available only through a device that uses the telephone network. The devices used can be ISDN adapters, modems, modem-pooling devices, or an X.25 network. Typical uses involve one or two dial-up connections, mainly to the Internet and to a remote corporate network. You can also use Windows 2000 to configure dial-on-demand routing scenarios as well. It is easy to create multiple connections by making one representative model connection and then copying and renaming that connection and changing the attributes. This practice allows for easy administration of adds, moves, and deletes of multiple connection settings.

Dialing the Private Network   To configure a modem for a dial-up connection to a private network:

1. Open the Network and Dial-Up Connections dialog box. Clicking Start | Settings and choosing the Network and Dial-Up Connections tab brings up the dialog box shown in Figure 11-13.

2. Double-click Make New Connection. The dialog box presented is the same as the one shown in Figure 11-9. The Network Connection Wizard is launched.

3. Choose Next on this dialog box to continue.

4. Choose the radio button for "Dial up to private network" and click Next. The Network Connection wizard presents a dialog box in which you choose the phone number to dial and whether or not to use dialing rules. *Dialing rules* are options that you set when you configure operator-assisted dialing, special prefixes (such as the one used to disable call waiting), or Private Branch Exchange (PBX) codes to choose an outside line. If you enable dialing rules, make sure that the rules have been configured properly.

5. The Network Connection Wizard now presents the Connection Availability dialog box. The connection you are defining may be made available to all users or to only the user creating the connection. This connection will not be available unless you are logged on if you choose to make the connection available to yourself only.

6. Choose Next to continue. Internet Connection Sharing allows other computers on the network to access the resources of this connection. By enabling this option, you also make the decision whether to use on-demand

FIGURE 11-13 The Network and Dial-Up Connections dialog box allows creation of outbound dial-up connections

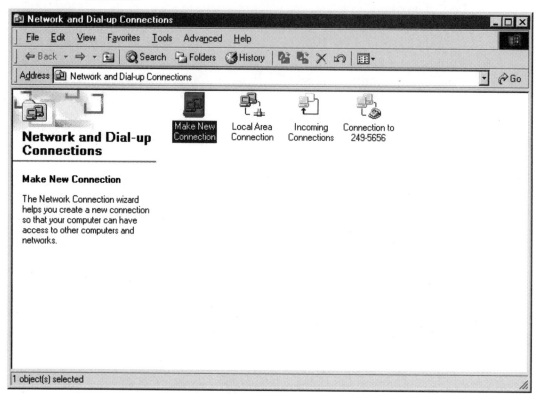

dialing. With on-demand dialing, the connection is made automatically when a computer on the network attempts to access the external resources available through this connection.

exam
ⓦatch

If you enable Internet Connection Sharing, your Windows 2000 machine will be forced to use the 192.168.0.1 address on the LAN adapter by default.

7. Clicking Next brings up the Completing the Network Connection Wizard dialog box. Name the connection that you just created. You also have the option to add an icon to the desktop, which will allow easier navigation to the connection.

Dialing the Internet   A dial-up connection to the Internet is very similar to dialing up to a private network. The main difference is that when you choose the dial-up to the Internet option in the Network Connection Wizard, the Internet Connection Wizard is launched.

Creating Connections to a Virtual Private Network

VPN connections are also known as *tunnels*. By creating a connection through the public Internet and then encapsulating the private network data inside the public packets, you are creating a "tunnel" through which the data can travel from one computer to another on opposite sides of an otherwise public connection. As discussed earlier, this connection is accomplished using PPTP and L2TP.

To create a VPN connection to another computer and use advanced security settings:

1. Open the Network and Dial-Up Connections dialog box.

2. Double-click Make New Connection. On the welcome screen, click Next.

3. Choose "Connect to a private network through the Internet" and click Next.

4. The dialog box presented allows the administrator to dial the network, if necessary. If the private network is available over a dial-up connection, the connection *must be* established before the VPN connection will be attempted. Choose the appropriate option and dial-up device, if necessary, and press Next.

5. Enter the name of the host or the dotted-decimal notation address (the IP address) of the host to which you are connecting. Click Next to continue.

6. Choose whether the connection is for all users or only the user creating the connection. Choose Next.

7. Other computers on the network can share VPN connections by choosing to enable Internet Connection Sharing. The on-demand dialing feature allows the Windows 2000 server to automatically dial the connection when necessary. Consider these options, choose the ones you want, and click Next.

8. In the completion dialog box, name the connection and decide whether you want an icon for it on the desktop. Click Finish. Figure 11-14 shows the dialog box that is presented when you create your connection.

FIGURE 11-14

The Connect Virtual Private Connection dialog box and associated options are presented on creation of or choosing to configure a VPN connection

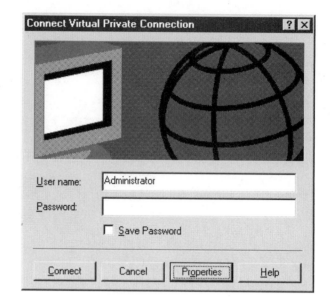

9. The name and password of the user on the remote system are entered on this dialog box. The properties button allows the administrator to configure the connection to conform to the remote computer requirements. Click Properties to continue.

10. Figure 11-15 shows the Virtual Private Connection properties dialog box. On the General tab, you can enter the name or IP address. There is also the option to dial another connection first. This connection can be chosen if the option to dial the connection was selected when the connection was created. You can also choose whether or not to display connection status on the taskbar. Click the Options tab to continue.

11. The Options tab allows the configuration of dialing options such as displaying progress while dialing, prompt for username and password, and certificate and whether to include logon to a Windows domain. There are also several options for redialing the connection. Choose the appropriate options for the connection being created or configured and click the Security tab.

12. The choice for security depends on the connection being made. The user can validate identity using the "Typical settings for most connections" option. A smart card can be used or a secured password chosen by selecting the option

FIGURE 11-15

The Virtual
Private
Connection
dialog box

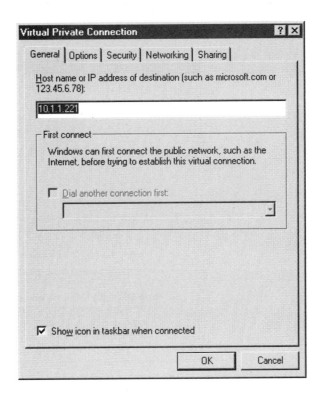

from the drop-down box. The connection is dropped by default if data encryption is required and there is no encryption available at the called host. The Advanced tab is for experienced users and presents a number of options, shown in Figure 11-16.

13. The dialog box is reached by selecting the radio button for Advanced (custom) settings and then clicking Settings. Under Data Encryption, the choices are:

■ **Required encryption**   The connection will not be made if the destination address does not support encryption.

■ **Optional encryption**   The connection will be made if the other side does not support encryption. Encryption may or may not be enabled.

■ **No encryption allowed**   The connection will not be made if the destination requires encryption.

FIGURE 11-16

The Advanced
Security Settings
dialog box

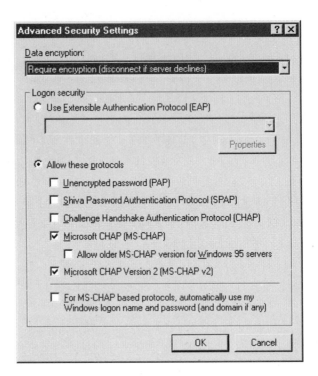

14. Select the data encryption properties for this connection. Once the selection is made, you see two radio buttons that control the logon security. These protocols are available when you check the appropriate boxes under "Allow these protocols." You can also choose to use EAP. Under the EAP choice is the option for MD5-Challenge and Smart Card. Figure 11-17 shows the dialog that allows the configuration of the smart card or other certificate options for logon security.

15. The dialog box allows for flexible options in setting the certificate server, connecting based on a string that matches all or a portion of the server name, and using a different name for the connection. Leave the settings set to their defaults and click OK. On the Advanced Security settings, choose "Allow these protocols."

16. You can choose as many of these protocols for your VPN connection according to the level of security you are trying to configure for this connection. If you are using the MS-CHAP protocols, your username and password as well as the domain can be supplied automatically. When you are done setting these protocols, click OK to continue.

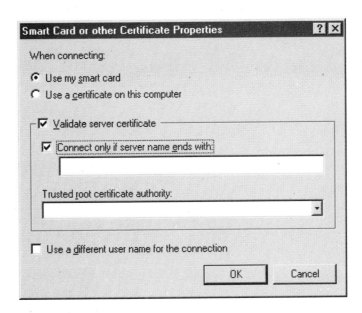

FIGURE 11-17

The Smart
Card or Other
Certificate
Properties
dialog box

17. Choose the Networking tab to continue the configuration of the VPN connection. The Networking tab allows a great deal of flexibility in creating the connection. Figure 11-18 shows the Virtual Private Connection Properties dialog box.

18. The type of VPN server can be either PPTP or L2TP. The type of VPN server is chosen automatically by default. Under either of these selections, you can configure the settings for the PPP protocol. By default, all of the settings for LCP, compression, and multilink are chosen.

19. Checking the boxes next to each selection chooses the components used by this connection. By checking the box, the Properties button might or might not be available. Clicking Properties can access the configurable properties for each of the components. These network properties are discussed in the next section of the chapter. Click the Sharing tab to access the Internet Connection Sharing properties of the VPN connection.

20. In this last dialog box, configure whether or not to enable ICS and whether or not to enable dial-on-demand services for the connection. Click OK to finish configuring the VPN connection.

FIGURE 11-18

The network choices in the Virtual Private Connection Properties dialog box

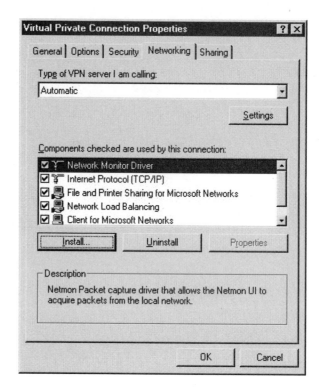

The following Scenario & Solution grid outlines some possible scenario questions that may come up during the exam and the answers that would be appropriate.

SCENARIO & SOLUTION

I have Windows NT 4.0 RAS servers in my domain and I want to configure the access-by-policy administrative model for my remote access policy. What should I do?	You cannot use the access-by-policy administrative model in a domain that contains Windows NT 4.0 RAS servers.
I want to configure 3DES encryption for a RAS server that is being deployed in our London, England, office, and I want to require that this encryption be used for every connection from the United States.	You cannot use the very strong encryption method for international versions of Windows 2000 due to export restrictions on the encryption code.
I am using the private address space of 10. 0.0.0 on my internal network where my RAS server resides, and I want to configure Internet Connection Sharing to use this address space for incoming client connections.	The address space of 10.0.0.0 will not be available to the clients using ICS due to the requirement of the 192.168.0.1 address on the RAS server. ICS is less configurable than NAT. If you don't want to use the predefined address range to share a connection, you can use NAT to accomplish the same thing. This allows the flexibility to change the address range.
My incoming connections are being dropped, even though the second and third remote access policies have matching conditions.	If the first access policy does not match the incoming connection, the connection is dropped.
I want to make sure that incoming connections have flexible options to connect and that more than one type of authentication protocol is acceptable as long as encryption is required.	Choose more than one authentication protocol for matching incoming connections, and make sure setting the data encryption to one of the available options in the RAS dialogs requires that encryption.

Installing, Configuring, and Troubleshooting Network Protocols

Windows 2000 users most likely belong to some network and are connected to that network either during or shortly after installing Windows 2000 Server. Windows 2000 detects a network and adapter and automatically starts a network connection. The LAN connection is created automatically; you do not have to start it manually for the connection to be available. If your Windows 2000 computer is physically connected to multiple LANs (multihomed), you need to add or enable all the clients, services, and protocols that are required for each LAN connection. These protocols are also configured and managed for all your VPN connections, direct cable connections, and outgoing connections as well.

This section discusses the network protocols available to Windows 2000 administrators in setting up network connections.

Transmission Control Protocol/Internet Protocol

TCP/IP is the most used protocol for Windows 2000 servers and is the basis for the Internet. On a TCP/IP network, all clients have several configurable properties used to communicate via TCP/IP. These properties are shown in Table 11-6.

TABLE 11-6	TCP/IP Protocol Properties	Description
Properties Used to Configure a TCP/IP Host	IP address	The dotted decimal notation *(x.x.x.x)* representation of the protocol address for TCP/IP hosts.
	Subnet mask	The portion of the IP address that represents what network the host is on.
	Default gateway	The IP address of the router on that subnet (or computer configured to function as a router). That address is not in any of the routing tables that the sending host uses to communicate on the network.
	WINS address(es)	In Windows NT 4.0 and previous networks, this is the address or addresses for the NetBIOS Name Server. In Windows 2000, WINS is still available in Mixed Node 2000 domains; however, the DNS address is now used by default.

TABLE 11-6	TCP/IP Protocol Properties	Description
Properties Used to Configure a TCP/IP Host (continued)	DNS address(es)	The Domain Name Server address is used for name resolution on a Windows 2000 server. The Windows 2000 server uses a new type of record to obtain host information.

Configuring the TCP/IP Protocol on Windows 2000 Server

To configure the settings for a Windows 2000 Server, perform the following steps:

1. Open the Network and Dial-Up Connections tool. Click Start | Settings | Network and Dial-up Connections.

2. Right-click the connection you want to configure, and then click Properties.

3. Do *one* of the following:

   ■ If the connection is for a LAN, under the heading Components that are used by this connection, click Internet Protocol and then click Properties.

   ■ If the connection is a dial-up, VPN, or incoming connection type, on the Networking tab under Network components used in this connection, click Internet Protocol and then click Properties.

4. Do *one* of the following:

   ■ If you want to use DHCP for assigning the properties to this connection automatically, click "Obtain an IP address automatically" and then click OK.

   ■ If you want to manually configure an IP address or DNS server, click "Use the following IP address," and in IP address area, type the IP address. Click the "Use the following DNS server addresses," and in Primary DNS server and Secondary DNS server, type the addresses of these servers. Click OK when finished.

5. To configure the DNS, WINS, and other options, click Advanced. Figure 11-19 shows the Advanced settings dialog box. The tabs at the top allow you to configure advanced options for IP addressing, advanced DNS address options, and WINS servers and whether or not to use LMHOSTS files for naming resolution.

6. Under the Options tab, IP security and TCP/IP filtering can be configured. These settings apply to all connections for which TCP/IP is enabled. You can

FIGURE 11-19

The options
familiar to most
administrators
of Windows
networks; the
new Options
tab allows for
IP security
and filtering

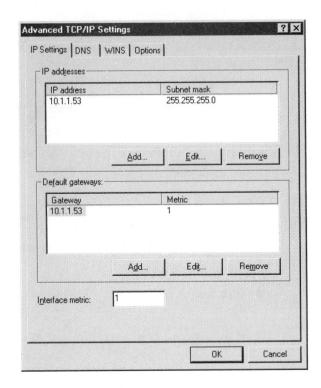

choose whether or not to use IPSec. If you do choose to use IPSec, you can
choose between Client (respond only), Secure Server (require security), or
Server (request security). Click OK when you are done reviewing or setting
these properties.

Troubleshooting the TCP/IP Protocol

You have now successfully configured your TCP/IP protocol for this server.
Let's review some scenario-based questions that could be on the exam that
deal with TCP/IP and some common connectivity problems. Table 11-7
has symptoms with some troubleshooting tips that would apply on any
exam dealing with IP addressing.

TABLE 11-7	Symptom	Possible Troubleshooting Steps
Troubleshooting TCP/IP Protocol Errors	You cannot connect to another computer or Web page.	Check the following to help determine the problem: **Default gateway settings** This is the most common reason for a failing connection to a computer on a different subnet. **DNS settings** Incorrect DNS settings will cause name resolution to fail. Make sure the DNS server address is correct. **WINS configuration settings** Pointing to a WINS server that is invalid or does not contain the names of your network workstations and servers will cause failures. **Check TCP/IP settings** Make sure the subnet mask and IP address settings are correct. If you have a DHCP server and you are not receiving a valid address, make sure the DHCP server is not out of leases or is up and running.
	Cannot ping a computer by name.	Check these settings to help determine if you have name resolution problems: Check your DNS settings to make sure you have the correct DNS address. If this is a DHCP client, run IPCONFIG to check the DHCP settings received.
	Cannot ping by IP address.	Check these settings to help determine the problem: **Check TCP/IP settings** Make sure you are using the correct IP address. If this is a DHCP client, run IPCONFIG to check your settings received from the server. **Use Event Viewer and check system log for errors with TCP/IP stack.** **Check the subnet mask.** **Trace the route to the address if it is on a different subnet and you can ping hosts on this subnet.** Use the TRACERT command to find out if the problem is in routing.

FROM THE CLASSROOM

Using the Subnet Mask in Client Networking

Whenever teaching someone about the TCP/IP protocol, the question always comes up about using the subnet mask in different ways to help with client networking configuration issues. In one scenario, a student described how his company had several privately addressed networks using a 172.20.0.0/16 network as the base network. For example, there are four subnets—172.20.1.0/24, 172.20.2.0/24, 172.20.3.0/24, and 172.20.4.0/24—connected through a single router to the 172.20.0.0 network. The subnet mask of "/24" means that the networks all use as the subnet mask 24 bits of the 32 bits available in the IP address. This means that the subnet mask for each network is 255.255.255.0 and the backbone is 255.255.0.0. The workstation address for the student was 172.20.2.25. The DHCP administrator had set the subnet mask to 255.255.0.0 for all workstations in the scope defined for all of these addresses (172.20.1.1–172.20.4.254) and had set the default gateway to 172.20.0.1. The student wondered how it was possible that the workstations could still connect and work properly.

It would seem that since the subnet mask was 255.255.0.0, the default gateway was on a different network than the student's workstation (the default gateway was 172.20.0.1). This may come up in some environments in which the TCP/IP network architects are using what is called the "natural mask" for the network. By setting the subnet mask to /16 on a network with a /24 definition, the TCP/IP network architect created a "supernet" of machines that can all connect to the network. Because the network mask of 255.255.0.0 was applied to all workstations, the TCP/IP stack actually operated as though the workstation at address 172.20.2.25 was on network 172.20.0.0, because the default gateway address of 172.20.0.1 was a valid configuration.

The problem is that some people who administer and install the workstations might not understand this concept and could assume that the configuration settings are wrong for either the mask or the default gateway. Some problems that can occur with this type of configuration include a very busy router handling requests from the workstations on one port and the broadcasts from hundreds of stations on another port. This situation could harm performance on the network. Even on a switched network with low collisions, a broadcast storm can cause real havoc for the network users and administrators.

—*Lance Ecklesdafer, MCSE, MCP+I, CNP, CNE*

Internet Packet Exchange

Internetwork Packet Exchange (IPX) and *Sequenced Packet Exchange (SPX)* are protocols used in Novell NetWare networks. They correspond to the IP and TCP protocols that are used in TCP/IP networking.

Windows 2000 implements these protocols using *NWLink IPX/SPX/NetBIOS Compatible Transport Protocol* (or simply *NWLink*). Windows 2000 users can use NWLink to access NetWare Servers, and NetWare clients can use NWLink to access resources on Windows 2000 servers. NWLink can also be used on small networks that use only Windows 2000 and other Microsoft client software. NWLink is a Network Driver Interface Specification (NDIS) compliant, native 32-bit protocol. The NWLink protocol supports Windows sockets and NetBIOS.

exam
ⓦatch

The IPX/SPX stack (or NWLink) can be used to network Microsoft computers when there is no need to connect to the Internet and the overhead of TCP/IP is undesirable.

Windows 2000 computers running NWLink can connect to client/server applications on a NetWare server and, with the added Client Service for NetWare or Gateway Service for NetWare, can connect to NetWare servers for file and print services.

exam
ⓦatch

By default, when configured for NWLink, the file and print sharing components of Windows 2000 use NetBIOS over IPX to send file and print sharing messages. In a process called direct hosting, you can disable NetBIOS so that file and print sharing are sent directly over IPX.

Installing and Configuring NWLink on Windows 2000 Server

You must perform the following steps in order to install and configure NWLink on your Windows 2000 server.

1. You must be logged in as a member of the Administrators group to continue.

2. Make sure your Windows 2000 computer has an NDIS compatible driver for proper connectivity. Check the documentation that came with your hardware or contact the manufacturer to determine the status of this requirement.

3. Open Network and Dial-Up Connections.

4. Right-click on the Local Area Connection icon and then click Properties.

5. Click the Install button. In the Select Network Component Type dialog box, click Protocol and then click Add.

6. In the Select Network Protocol dialog box, choose NWLink IPX/SPX/ NetBIOS Compatible Transport Protocol and click OK.

7. After the NWLink protocol is installed, you are returned to the Local Area Connection Properties dialog box. Figure 11-20 shows the two protocols that have been added to your Windows 2000 computer.

8. The NWLink NetBIOS protocol is not configurable, but removing the check from the associated box can disable it.

9. To configure the NWLink IPX/SPX Compatible transport, choose the protocol from the list shown in Figure 11-21 and then click Properties.

10. It is very important to configure an internal network number if you will run File and Print Services, IPX routing, or any other Service Advertising Protocol (SAP) agent. This number applies to all connections on the Windows 2000 computer. You might also want to set the frame type for the network to which you are connecting. The choices available are Ethernet 802.2, Ethernet 802.3, Ethernet II, and Ethernet SNAP. For most applications, allowing the Auto Frame Type is the best choice unless you have special applications or you need to have more than one frame type available. Click OK to return to the IPX/SPX Compatible Transport dialog box, and click OK to finish configuring IPX/SPX.

FIGURE 11-20

The Local Area Connection Properties dialog box after you add the NWLink protocol

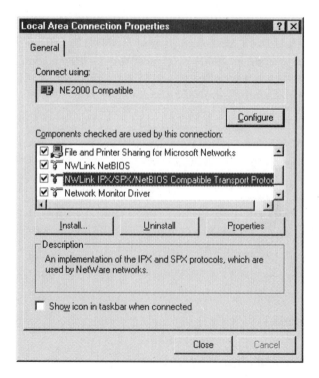

The General settings dialog box for network adapter properties

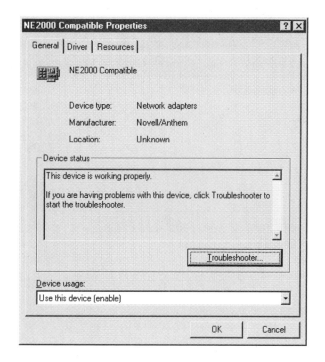

Troubleshooting IPX Protocol Connections

After successfully configuring the server for NWLink IPX/SPX connectivity, you should check your installation by trying to use the Windows 2000 server with another IPX/SPX client or server. Table 11-8 presents some possible scenarios and troubleshooting tips that deal with the IPX/SPX compatible transport.

NetBIOS Enhanced User Interface

NetBIOS Extended User Interface (NetBEUI) is suited for small workgroups and LANs. The NetBIOS gateway and the NetBEUI client protocol can be installed on remote access servers running Windows 2000 and most Windows networking clients. NetBEUI is not routable and requires only the computer name for configuration.

TABLE 11-8	Symptom	Possible Troubleshooting Steps
Troubleshooting IPX/SPX Errors	Entire Network under My Network Places does not show any NetWare servers or clients.	There are several possible causes for this situation. The most common is choosing the wrong frame type. Make sure the frame type you are using matches the network frame type. Other causes of this scenario can be: SAP not enabled on all router interfaces; Broadcast Type 20 frames not being propagated; or the protocol did not start; check the Event Viewer for messages.
	My RRAS Windows 2000 server cannot connect to other computers.	Verify that NetBIOS broadcast propagation is enabled on the router interfaces between the computers. A Windows 2000 remote access server, which is running RRAS, is an IPX router. Enable the setting in the RRAS Service tool.
	My computer has more than eight routers between two computers that are running Windows 2000.	Eight routers is the limit for the number of hops that can be crossed between two Windows 2000 computers over the NWLink protocol.

Troubleshooting the NetBEUI Protocol

Since NetBEUI only has one configuration option (the computer name), not much can go wrong with a connection using this protocol. The most common reasons for problems with the connection to another Windows computer running this protocol are:

- Bad network interface card
- Duplicate name error
- Destination computer is on a different network
- Bad physical hardware such as adapter card, hub, or switch and cable

By checking these items, you will most likely find the reason the connection is not working and be able to easily correct it.

CertCam 11-2

EXERCISE 11-2

Changing the Protocol Binding Order in a Windows 2000 Server

In this exercise, we change the protocol binding order for a Windows 2000 server running TCP/IP and NetBEUI. You would do this to optimize the server for TCP/IP connections:

1. Open Network and Dial-Up Connections.

2. Highlisght the connection to modify (in this case, Local Area Network Connection) and on the Advanced Toolbar option, click Advanced Settings.

3. The Advanced Settings dialog box contains the bindings and their order for all protocols installed in this computer, as shown in the illustration below. As you can see, the bindings are out of order.

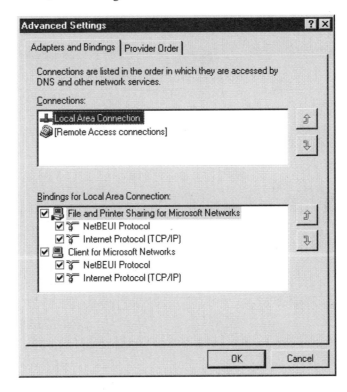

4. The bindings order for the client for Microsoft Networks and the File and Print Sharing service can be changed independently. Change the order for the client for Microsoft Networks by clicking TCP/IP and using the up and down buttons, moving the selection above the NetBEUI protocol. When you are done, your dialog box will look this:

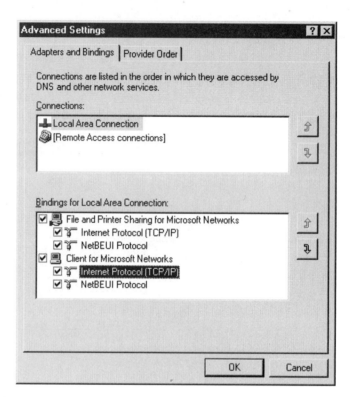

5. Click OK to accept the changes you have just made.

Installing, Configuring, and Troubleshooting Network Adapters and Drivers

Windows 2000 computers, as well as most other computers today, support a wide range of network adapter options. When Windows 2000 is installed for the first time in your computer, the OS detects whether a network adapter is present. The local area connection that results is always activated by default.

exam
ⓦatch

The local area connection is the only type of connection that is created and activated automatically.

If the LAN becomes unavailable for any reason, the connection is no longer automatically activated. This feature is very handy for the remote traveling computer user, because the user will not waste time waiting for LAN services to time out. The adapter in your computer will not even try to connect to the network if it is not active.

If changes are made to your network's configuration, you can modify the settings of the connection properties to reflect any of those changes. The Status menu in Windows 2000 allows you to view connection length of time, speed, data received, and transmitted totals as well as diagnostics available for any connection. If a new LAN adapter is installed in the computer at a later time, Windows 2000 detects this condition at the next restart of the OS. You can configure multiple NICs through the use of the Advanced Settings menu. You can change the order of the NICs in your configuration as well as the clients, services, and protocols used by each adapter.

Configuring Networking Settings

To configure connections in the Windows 2000 computer, you launch the Network and Dial-Up Connections tool and modify the settings for each installed connection:

1. Click Start | Settings | Network and Dial-Up Connections.

2. Right-click on the icon for the connection you want to modify.

3. Click Configure to configure the adapter settings. Figure 11-22 shows the General settings dialog box for an NE2000 adapter.

FIGURE 11-22

Modifying
resources for a
network adapter
in Windows 2000

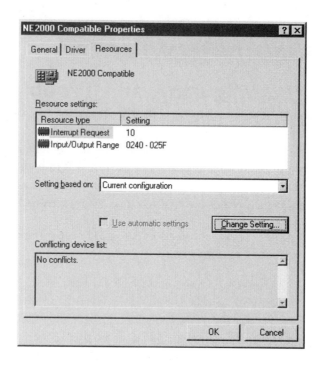

The three tabs in this dialog box allow you check the general settings of devices as well as give you the ability to disable devices. The troubleshooter feature is discussed in a moment. Under the Driver tab, the Driver Details option allows all files on the system associated with this adapter to be identified. The adapter driver can be uninstalled as well as updated from this dialog box. The resources for the adapter are shown in Figure 11-22. Clicking Change Setting allows the modification of the IRQ, I/O Range, and other settings. The settings you choose can be based on a number of configurable configuration options available under the Change Settings button.

To set advanced settings for network connections, open Network and Dial-Up Connections and choose Advanced from the menu. There are a number of features that can be configured; these features are described in Table 11-9.

The last choice on this menu is to configure optional networking components. The following section describes the process of configuring optional networking components.

Configuring Network Components

A number of optional networking components can be configured and installed to help the administrator with diagnostics as well as providing other services.

TABLE 11-9	Feature	Description
Advanced Network Connection Settings Options	Operator-assisted dialing	Toggle on or off to enable or disable operator-assisted dialing settings.
	Dial-up preferences	Allows the configuration of autodial and callback options for outgoing connections.
	Network identification	Allows the change of domain assignment, computer name, or primary DNS. Other nonnetwork settings are available in this dialog box for hardware profiles, advanced settings, and hardware wizards.
	Advanced settings	Allows change of the binding order of the adapters and protocols for the connection types on the Windows 2000 server. Choosing the Provider Order tab from this dialog box changes the provider order for network and printer services.

Table 11-10 presents all the optional components that are installed under the Windows Optional Networking Components Wizard, which is shown in Figure 11-23.

To configure any of these components after installation, use the Network Dial-Up and Connections tool and select the connection for which you want to modify the networking components used by the chosen connection. Click any of the components and then click Properties (if available; some components are not configurable). Depending on the components you choose, a different dialog box will be presented that will allow you to modify the configuration of this component.

Troubleshooting Network Adapter Problems

Occasionally things can go wrong with the network adapter or driver used for one of the Windows 2000 computer's connections. When this situation arises, the Windows 2000 troubleshooting tools are an excellent source of help. By navigating to the network adapter properties dialog box, you see the Troubleshooter button that was shown in Figure 11-21. Click the Troubleshooter button to launch the Windows 2000 help system and be automatically navigated to the Hardware Troubleshooter. In this dialog box are a number of hardware options the troubleshooter can affect. The selection of "My network adapter doesn't work" is an excellent place to start. Table 11-11 presents some problems that could arise and the possible answers for troubleshooting adapters and drivers in Windows 2000.

TABLE 11-10 Windows 2000 Optional Networking Components

Optional Component	Intended Use
Connection Manager components	Installs Connection Manager Administration Kit (CMAK) and Phone Book Service.
Network monitor tools	Packet analyzer (for this computer only).
Simple Network Management Protocol (SNMP)	Agents that monitor the network hardware and drivers and report to an SNMP manager.
COM Internet Services Proxy	Enables Distributed Component Object Model (DCOM) to travel over HTTP.
Domain Name Services (DNS)	Installs DNS.
Dynamic Host Configuration Protocol (DHCP)	Allows your computer to become a DHCP server.
Internet Authentication Service (IAS)	Enables authentication, authorization, and accounting of dial-up connections. IAS supports RADIUS protocol.
Quality of Service (QoS) Admission Control	Allows you to specify the quality of the network connection to each network segment.
Simple TCP/IP services	Character generator, day/time, echo, and quote of the day.
Site Server ILS services	Scans the TCP/IP stack and updates directories with current information for users.
Windows Internet Name Service	Sets up a NetBIOS name server on the Windows 2000 computer.
File Services for Macintosh	Enables resources of the Windows 2000 file system to be made available to Macintosh users.
Print Services for Macintosh	Enables resources of the Windows 2000 print spooler to be made available to Macintosh users.
Print Services for UNIX	Enables UNIX clients to print to the Windows 2000 printers.

FIGURE 11-23 The Windows Optional Networking Components Wizard

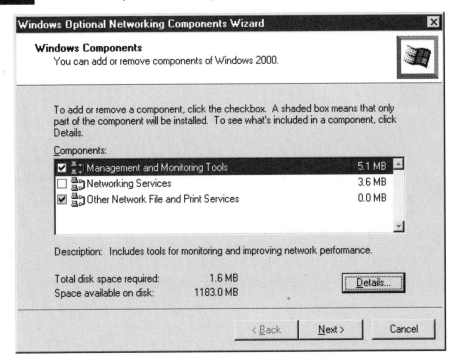

TABLE 11-11	**Problem**	**Resolution**
Windows 2000 Adapter and Driver Troubleshooting Tips	My network adapter does not work and it is not on the Hardware Compatibility List.	Contact the manufacturer for further assistance. The HCL is not always the most up-to-date list; it needs to be periodically reviewed. The best choice is to contact the manufacturer.
	My network adapter does not work and my device is on the Hardware Compatibility List.	Check the following: Is the network adapter faulty? Install and configure a new or replacement adapter. Is the driver corrupted? Reinstall the driver for this device and check the status again. Does the status show normal? In the network connection properties, check the status of the adapter, as explained earlier in the chapter. Is the adapter disconnected? Is the cable faulty? Replace the cable with a known working cable. Is the hub or switch faulty?

CertCam 11-3

EXERCISE 11-3

Installing and Configuring Microsoft Simple IP Components

Joe has been a fanatic user of the Quote of the Day service for his whole career in UNIX. Now that he is a trained MCSE, Joe wants to use some of his old UNIX tools. Joe has learned that some optional components of Windows 2000 include the Simple TCP/IP services in which Joe is interested. Joe installs these services on his Windows 2000 computer as follows:

1. Click Start | Settings | Network and Dial-Up Connections.

2. Choose Advanced from the menu and then click Optional Networking Components. In the dialog box, choose Networking Services and click Next.

3. Check the box for Simple TCP/IP services and click OK.

4. When the Windows Optional Networking Components Wizard returns, click Next.

5. If required, insert the Windows 2000 Advanced Server CD-ROM and click OK. The optional components will be installed.

6. The components can now be configured by right-clicking Local Area Connection and choosing Properties. Scroll down to the components to configure, and click Properties to change any settings for the installed components.

7. Change any of the properties and click OK to close the dialog box.

8. Click OK to finish installing and configuring the optional components.

CERTIFICATION SUMMARY

Windows 2000 Server networking adapters, services, and protocols are more complex in this version than they have ever been. Microsoft has built into the product many of these features in order to make it more Internet friendly. With a myriad of options to choose from for authentication, encryption, and filtering, the Windows 2000 server becomes more than just a file and print server. Drawing on the tradition set by the BackOffice product line, Windows 2000 Server offers Web services, e-mail services, database services, gateway and router services and, of course, remote terminal services.

Along with all this added functionality comes complexity. It is no longer an easy task to configure a number of services with proper connectivity and security options. Windows 2000 implements easy to use wizards for some of the most common applications of these features, but there is more to learn as you discover more sophisticated needs to which your network must respond.

It has never been easier to add and troubleshoot components to the system and install systems as it is with Windows 2000. Using "Plug-and-Play" technology, Windows 2000 adds adapters and configures them automatically for the administrator the first time. When you add additional components later as the network changes, the Windows 2000 computer can automatically configure and activate these adapters, too. The networking components are easily located and installed using the wizard applications. The troubleshooters in Windows 2000 help you easily locate, isolate, and correct most of the common problems you'll run into when working with networking services and protocols.

TWO-MINUTE DRILL

Installing, Configuring, and Troubleshooting Remote Access

- The Remote Routing and Access Service (RRAS) is installed by default, but it is not automatically activated. In order to use RRAS, you need to activate it. An exam question could involve a scenario in which the service is used without being activated.

- The Microsoft Windows 2000 RRAS provides a multiprotocol virtual private network (VPN) port capability for remote access clients using PPTP or L2TP protocols. VPN clients can be Windows NT 4.0 and later, Windows 95, or Windows 98 clients.

- Non-Microsoft VPN clients using PPTP or L2TP with Internet Protocol Security (IPSec) can access Windows NT 4.0 or Windows 2000 RAS servers. If you want secure VPN connections, you must take care to make sure the non-Windows VPN clients support the proper encryption.

- Network address translation (NAT) is usually configured on a small network or home office network on which a number of workstations share a single connection to the Internet.

- A remote access policy profile comprises the properties that are applied to a connection that has been authorized through user account permissions or the remote access policy.

- The user account and profile for the first matching policy are applied to the incoming connection. If an attempt does not match the profile and the user account settings of the first matching policy, the additional policies are not checked.

- By creating a connection through the public Internet and then encapsulating the private network data inside the public packets, you create a "tunnel" for the data to travel from one computer to another on opposite sides of an otherwise public connection.

Installing, Configuring, and Troubleshooting Network Protocols

■ Every TCP/IP connection requires an IP address, a subnet mask, and a default gateway to communicate on a LAN.

■ DHCP services provide for the automatic assignment of TCP/IP protocol settings.

■ In Windows 2000, WINS is still available in Mixed Node 2000 domains; however, the DNS address is now used by default.

■ IPX networks often have connectivity issues due to the fact that the network frame type is wrong or the network number that has been configured is wrong.

■ NetBEUI has no configuration options other than the name of the computer.

Installing, Configuring, and Troubleshooting Network Adapters and Drivers

■ The Status menu option in Windows 2000 allows you to view connection length of time, speed, data received, and transmitted totals as well as diagnostics available for any connection.

■ The local area connection is the only type of connection that is created and activated automatically.

■ You can configure multiple network interface cards (NICs) through the Advanced Settings menu.

■ The Windows 2000 troubleshooting tools are an excellent source of help when you run into difficulties.

SELF TEST

The following questions will help you measure your understanding of the material presented in this chapter. Read all of the choices carefully because there may be more than one correct answer. Choose all correct answers for each question.

Installing, Configuring, and Troubleshooting Remote Access

1. You are the security manager for an RRAS server that is being used by a number of clients from different companies using different methods of authenticating to your host. You want to provide incoming connections that support VPN connections from these remote locations. Which of the following steps do you take to enable the VPN clients? Choose all that apply.

   A. On the Incoming Connections Properties, check the box that allows others to make VPN connections to the computer.

   B. Edit the Network and Connections Properties and check all the protocols that you want to use for this connection.

   C. Edit the Dial-In Profile and check all the protocols that you want to use for this connection.

   D. Enable TCP/IP filtering on all adapters in the TCP/IP filtering dialog box.

2. What tool do you use to create a client connection to VPN servers when you are running a Windows 2000 server configured as a domain controller or member server?

   A. Routing and Remote Access

   B. Edit Dial-In Profile

   C. Network and Dial-Up Connections

   D. Performance Monitor

3. A user is attempting to connect to an RRAS server that is configured using the access-by-policy model. Which statement is true about the behavior of the explicit allow option when there are no Windows NT 4.0 RRAS servers in the domain?

   A. The remote access permission is set to allow access and the connection attempt matches the conditions of a policy subject to the settings of the profile and dial-in properties of the user.

   B. The attempt to connect matches the conditions of a policy but not the settings of the access profile. The administrator can enter a number that does not correspond to any dial-in number being used by RRAS.

   C. The remote access permission on the policy is set to grant remote access permission and the connection attempt matches the policy conditions and is subject to the settings in the dial-in properties of the user as well as the profile of the user.

   D. The remote access permission on the policy is set to grant remote access permission and the connection attempt does not match the policy conditions and is subject to the settings in the dial-in properties of the user as well as the profile of the user.

4. If you want to save time configuring a modem pool device in Windows 2000 RRAS, what should you do?

   A. Treat all modems as "Plug-and-Play" modems and let Windows 2000 configure them.

   B. Treat all modems as generic 56000 BPS V.90 modems.

   C. Treat all modems with a separate configuration and different ports (e.g., COM1, COM2, COM3…COM*x*).

   D. Treat all modems as Hayes-compatible modems.

Installing, Configuring, and Troubleshooting Network Protocols

5. Five users have called complaining that they have not been able to see any NetWare servers in My Network Places all day. The users cannot map drives, and they cannot log in to the NetWare servers. Since all these users are having the same problems, you call the network administrator, and he tells you that a new router was installed the night before. What are some of the possible reasons for the problems your users are having? Choose all that apply.

   A. The router has TCP/IP settings that are not correct.

   B. The router is not running IPX protocol.

   C. The router is running IPX protocol with the wrong frame type selected.

   D. The router is running IPX with the wrong network number configured.

6. Which of the following TCP/IP settings are required to communicate with computers on the same network segment? Choose all that apply.

   A. IP address

   B. Default gateway

   C. Subnet mask

   D. DNS address configured in TCP/IP protocol properties

7. Which of the following is true about the NetBEUI protocol? Choose all that apply.

   A. It is a nonroutable protocol.

   B. There are no configuration options for the NetBEUI protocol.

C. There are no configuration options except the host name for the NetBEUI protocol.

D. All of the above

8. Where do you configure the DNS and WINS information if there is no DHCP service available or none is used in your configuration?

A. The Routing and Remote Access tool

B. The Network and Dial-Up Connections tool

C. The IP Access Policy tool

D. The IP Filter tool

Installing, Configuring, and Troubleshooting Network Adapters and Drivers

9. John suspects that he is having trouble with the network adapter in his Windows 2000 computer. What tools can John use to diagnose the problem? Choose all that apply.

A. The "ping" utility

B. The troubleshooter built into the Windows 2000 Help files

C. The Troubleshooter button in the network adapter Properties dialog box

D. Performance Monitor

10. Which one of the following is an optional networking component that can be installed under Network and Dial-Up Connections?

A. QoS Admission Control

B. Microsoft Client

C. WINS

D. NetWare Client

11. How do you change the binding order of the adapters in Windows 2000?

A. There is no way; the system chooses the binding order.

B. The binding order is changed using the IP Policies dialog box and choosing Advanced options.

C. Go to the Advanced menu option in Network and Dial-Up Connections and choose Advanced Settings.

D. Go to the Tools menu option in Network and Dial-Up connections and choose Synchronize.

LAB QUESTION

You are the network administrator of a small company that has seven computers running on Windows-based computers and a single Windows 2000 computer. The owner of the company has asked you to install a single connection to the Internet through an ISP. The owner would like all the computers in the company to share the connection to the Internet to cut costs. The Windows 2000 server and the other seven workstations are currently using the private network address space of 192.168.0.0, and the Internet service provider has given your company the public address of 198.199.13.5.

Diagram and explain how the multiple private addresses on the 192.168.0.0 network are mapped to a single Web server that resides on a public network. Explain the different parts of the IP addressing and port usage. Additionally, what happens to packets that contain an IP payload that is not recognized by Windows 2000?

SELF TEST ANSWERS

Installing, Configuring, and Troubleshooting Remote Access

1. ☑ **A and C.** On the Incoming Connections Properties, check the box that allows others to make VPN connections to the computer, and edit the Dial-In Profile and check all the protocols that you want to use for this connection. In order to enable VPN connections, the box has to be checked in the Incoming Connections dialog box. The Dial-In Profile properties dialog box needs to be configured to allow the proper secure authentication methods.
☒ **B and D** are incorrect because enabling filtering is not part of VPN configuration, and checking protocols does not enable VPN connections.

2. ☑ **A.** The Routing and Remote Access tool is used to configure VPN servers.
☒ **B,C, and D** are incorrect because you cannot use Edit Dial-In Profile, Network and Dial-Up Connections, or Performance Monitor to create VPN connections.

3. ☑ **C** is correct because this describes the explicit allow behavior in a Native Mode Windows 2000 domain.
☒ **A** is incorrect because it describes explicit allow in a Mixed Mode Windows 2000 domain. **B** is incorrect because it describes attributes of the explicit deny behavior in a Native Mode Windows 2000 domain. **D** is incorrect because it incorrectly states the properties of explicit allow in a Windows 2000 domain. The connection attempt must match the policy conditions to satisfy the conditions for the explicit allow behavior.

4. ☑ **D.** Treat all modems as Hayes-compatible modems. This is the recommended way to configure a modem bank and provides for the greatest compatibility.
☒ **A** is incorrect because the configuration of the modems is not always automatic for all modem pools. **B** is incorrect because generic settings will not work for modem pooling equipment that uses different settings based on configuration. **C** is incorrect because although all ports are defined and enumerated by the system, they are not necessarily defined to COM ports in successive order.

Installing, Configuring, and Troubleshooting Network Protocols

5. ☑ **A, B, C, and D. A** is correct because the question does not indicate that the NetWare server is any certain version. The new version of NetWare supports TCP/IP as a connection method, and incorrect settings on the router would cause the server communications to be suppressed. **B** is correct because again, the version of NetWare server was not specified. The IPX protocol is required for versions of NetWare that bind IPX to the network adapter in the server. **C** is correct because the

wrong IPX protocol frame type will prevent the workstations from seeing the server if and only if they are not configured with the auto-frame detection. D is correct because if the server is running the wrong network number, the workstations and the server will have a routing error and there will be no communication to the server from the clients.

6. ☑ **A and C.** A, IP address, is correct because all IP workstations need TCP/IP to communicate with another IP device. C, subnet mask, is correct because the subnet mask allows the TCP/IP stack to determine what part of the address is the network number. With an incorrect subnet mask, a workstation will only be able to talk to its loopback address.
   ☒ **B** is incorrect because the default gateway is used when the TCP/IP protocol stack determines that the destination address is on a different network than any of the networks defined in the routing tables on that workstation. By default, the local segment has a route in the table; therefore, the default gateway will not be needed. **D** is incorrect because the DNS address is configured to provide name resolution to the client and is not necessary when an IP address is specified as the destination. When a name is used, the workstation will follow the name resolution steps as defined by the node-type setting of the TCP/IP protocol stack.

7. ☑ **A and C.** It is a nonroutable protocol, and there are no configuration options except the host name for the NetBEUI protocol. The NetBEUI protocol is a nonroutable protocol that uses the name of the computer to communicate with other hosts that are stored in the name cache. If the computer name is not in the cache, the NetBEUI protocol will do a NetBIOS name lookup to find the target computer on the current network. The NetBEUI has no information in the packet header for routing and therefore will only work on the current network segment.
   ☒ **B** is incorrect because NetBEUI needs the name of the machine in order to do host inquiries.

8. ☑ **B.** The Network and Dial-Up Connections tool. Configuring network protocol properties is always done in this tool.
   ☒ **A** is incorrect because RRAS is used to configure routing protocols and access by users. **C** is incorrect because the IP Access Policy tool is used to control security on network connections to and from the Windows 2000 computer. **D** is incorrect because the IP Filter tool is used to create different rules regarding IP traffic that is sent or received by the Windows 2000 computer.

Installing, Configuring, and Troubleshooting Network Adapters and Drivers

9. ☑ **B and C.** The troubleshooter built into the Windows 2000 Help files and the Troubleshooter button in the network adapter Properties dialog box. The troubleshooter in the Help files is easily located by entering the word *troubleshoot* as a keyword search. In the network adapter Properties, a Troubleshooter button actually calls up the proper document from Help as though you did the search yourself.

    ☒   A is incorrect because the ping utility only works to diagnose a problem with the TCP/IP protocol; it will not help you in an IPX or NetBEUI environment. D is incorrect because Performance Monitor will not diagnose an inoperative adapter.

10. ☑ C. The WINS server is installed as an optional networking component. The Advanced menu option on the Network and Dial-Up Connections tool presents an option in the "Other Network File and Print Services" selection. Click Details to select the component for installation.
    ☒   A, B, and D are incorrect because they are installed under Network and Dial-Up Connections as properties available in the various connection types that are defined.

11. ☑ C. Go to the Advanced menu option in Network and Dial-Up Connections and choose Advanced Settings. This is exactly how to make the changes in binding order. Use the arrows to move the highlighted selection up or down to increase or decrease priority for the selection.
    ☒   A is incorrect because the system must be able to change the binding order for the adapters installed in order to help performance by placing the most used adapter in the highest priority. B is incorrect because the IP Policy editor is not used to perform binding changes to the installed list of adapters. D is incorrect because the Tools menu does not provide for this functionality.

LAB ANSWER

If a private networked workstation using the address of 192.168.0.15 loads Microsoft Internet Explorer and attempts to connect to the public Web server at *w.x.y.z,* the workstation generates an IP packet with the following information, illustrated in Figure 11-24:

- Destination: w.x.y.z
- Source: 192.168.0.15
- Destination port: TCP port 80
- Source port: TCP port 1025

    The packet is forwarded to the network address translation computer, which is running Windows 2000 and RRAS, and Internet Connection Sharing is enabled, along with NAT protocol. The NAT protocol translates the packet information to the following:

- Destination: *w.x.y.z*
- Source: *a.b.c.d*
- Destination port: TCP port 80
- Source port: TCP port 5000

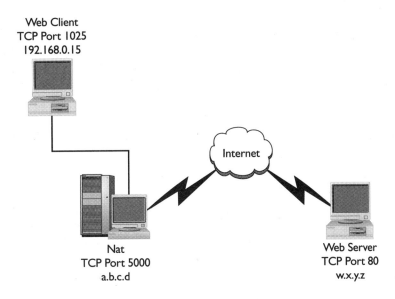

FIGURE 11-24

A NAT example

Web Client
TCP Port 1025
192.168.0.15

Internet

Nat
TCP Port 5000
a.b.c.d

Web Server
TCP Port 80
w.x.y.z

Network address translation keeps the internal mapping of the private address 192.168.0.15 TCP Port 1025 to *w.x.y.z* port 5000 in a table. This new packet is sent over the Internet to the destination Web host. The packet that is received back from the Web host contains the following address information:

■ Destination: *a.b.c.d*

■ Source: *w.x.y.z*

■ Destination port: TCP port 5000

■ Source port: TCP port 80

Network address translation checks the table and maps the public address to the private address and sends the packet to the workstation at address 192.168.0.15. The packet sent to the Web client contains the following information:

■ Destination: 192.168.0.15

■ Source: *w.x.y.z*

■ Destination port: TCP port 1025

■ Source port: TCP port 80

The outbound packets from the NAT protocol contain the mapping of the source IP address on the private network to the ISP address, and the port numbers are remapped to unique TCP/UDP port numbers.

Incoming packets to NAT are mapped so that the destination field contains the original private address, and the TCP/UDP port numbers are mapped back to their original port numbers.

Some NAT packets are not translated properly if there is an encapsulated packet that contains an IP address. This depends on the protocol being used with NAT. This potential error is best demonstrated using the example of PPTP tunneled data that does not use a TCP/UDP header. The packet is using a Generic Routing Encapsulation (GRE) header, and the tunnel ID stored in the GRE header identifies the data stream contents. NAT must properly translate the tunnel ID, or connectivity problems could occur.

12

User Security with Encryption, Policies, and Profiles

This chapter details user security with encryption, policies, and profiles. Windows 2000 has a new Encrypting File System (EFS) that can be used to encrypt data either on a user's personal hard drive or on a file server. EFS is an extra level of protection for files susceptible to theft (for example, laptops). Each user has the capability to encrypt a document that they have access to as long as it is not a shared document. Once the document is encrypted, only the user who encrypted it (and the Recovery Agent) have the ability to decrypt it. Even though encryption is an additional level of security, it should not be used instead of NTFS permissions, because anyone with appropriate access to the encrypted data could delete it even though they cannot decrypt and view the file.

Policies are the next level of user security. Windows 2000 has group policies, which are a vastly improved version of Windows NT policies. The two types of group policies are user configurations and computer configurations. They are used to configure software settings, Windows settings, and administrative templates for specific users or computers. In addition, group policies can be used for software deployment, following Microsoft's software deployment life cycle definition. This previously required a separate product such as Microsoft's System Management Server (SMS). Group policies can be applied to a site, domain, or organizational unit, and a specific order of inheritance is followed when they are applied.

User profiles are an additional level of security. They are used to configure desktop settings for each user who logs on to a computer. This insures that the next user to log on cannot see any changes that the previous user made. Windows 2000 user profiles are much more powerful than Windows NT 4 user profiles. Windows 2000 still has Local user profiles, Roaming user profiles, and Mandatory Roaming user profiles; however, they can now be used for several additional functions, such as bookmarks in the help system, My Network Places links, My Pictures, and printer connections.

CERTIFICATION OBJECTIVE 12.01

Encrypt Data on a Hard Disk by Using EFS

Microsoft's Encrypting File System (EFS) is used to encrypt Windows 2000 NTFS files and folders for added privacy beyond NTFS and share permissions. EFS is based on public key encryption, which encrypts each file with a randomly generated key that is separate from the user's public/private key pair. EFS is incorporated within the Windows 2000 NTFS file system. This makes it transparent to the user as it encrypts and decrypts in the background during normal read and write operations. When a user opens an encrypted file, EFS automatically locates the user's key from the system's key store to decrypt the file. EFS is very difficult to decipher, as it uses CryptoAPI architecture. CryptoAPI (CAPI) architecture is a collection of tasks that permit applications to digitally sign or encrypt data while providing security for the user's private key data. File encryption can be used only with information that is accessed by a single user, so EFS cannot be used with shared data. The user must also have sufficient NTFS permissions to the data in order to encrypt it.

To encrypt data, simply select the data that you would like to encrypt and check the Encrypt Contents to Secure Data check box on the folder properties advanced attribute dialog box. Figure 12-1 shows the Advanced Attributes dialog box with the encryption check box.

EFS uses two pairs of keys for the recovery policy:

- The user key pair, which is generated locally

- The recovery key pair that is issued by your Certificate Authority (CA)

Encrypting
data within
the Advanced
Attributes
dialog box

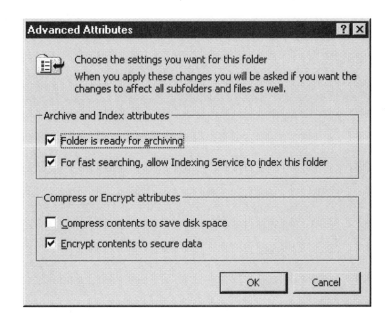

FROM THE CLASSROOM

Securing your Encrypted Data

When you use file encryption, it is a good idea to have the users encrypt their My Documents directory. This way, the files that they create (or have previously created) will be encrypted automatically. It is also recommended that users encrypt all Temp directories. Thus, temporary files that are created when a user is modifying an encrypted document are also encrypted, which prevents unauthorized access to the data while it is in use. These two things will keep your encrypted data as secure as possible without a great deal of additional effort for the user.

—Holly Simard, MCSE, MCP+I, A+

on the *Job*

A Certificate Authority (CA) is a public key certificate issuer (for example, Verisign). To use a public key certificate, you must trust the issuer (CA). This means that you have faith in the CA's authentication policies. The CA is used for doing things such as authorizing certification authenticity, revoking expired certificates, and responding to certification requests. Windows 2000 offers an alternative to a third-party CA. You can become a CA within your own Intranet. Thus you can manage your own certificates rather than relying on a third-party Certification Authority.

A random key called a file encryption key (FEK) is used to encrypt each file and is then itself encrypted using the user's public key. At least two FEKs are created for every encrypted file. One FEK is created with the user's public key, and one is created with the public key of each recovery agent. There could be more than one recovery agent certificate used to encrypt each file, resulting in more than two FEKs. The user's public key can decrypt FEKs created with the public key.

EFS uses public key cryptography and requires certificate-based services in order to encrypt data. EFS uses CryptoAPI architecture, so it can store keys on secure devices such as Smart Cards.

Each key is generated using a randomly generated key (FEK) separate from the user's public/private key pair. EFS encrypts any temporary files while encrypting and gets the key certified from a CA automatically or self-signs it if there is no CA. EFS automatically renews certificates for users when they come due.

You should be very careful with private keys, as they can be a security risk. You should either generate them on a computer that is physically secure or export the key and certificate into a .pfx file protected with a strong password and store it on a floppy in a secure location.

EFS uses DESX (Data Encryption Standard-X) encryption technology. EFS also uses a 40-bit encryption level outside North America, and either a 56-bit or 128-bit encryption level within the United States and Canada. You cannot switch between encryption levels when you encrypt or decrypt at this time, although future service packs may allow you to do so.

When you see an "E" in the attributes column of Windows Explorer it means that the data is encrypted. Figure 12-2 illustrates Windows Explorer with the attributes column enabled. To view the "E" attribute, you may need to add the attributes column by going into View, Choose Columns and adding a check mark to the attribute check box. Alternatively, you can use the Cipher command to view encryption settings from the command line. Cipher will be discussed later in the chapter.

Encryption/decryption attributes are not exposed on individual files graphically because Microsoft is trying to encourage users to turn encryption on at the folder level, not on individual files. This is a better way to protect user data, as temporary files created in encrypted folders will be encrypted automatically. Table 12-1 describes the various encryption tasks that you may perform and the status of each file after you perform the task.

TABLE 12-1   Various encryption tasks and subsequent file status

Encryption Task	Status
Moving an encrypted file or folder to a non-Windows 2000 NTFS volume	Encryption is lost.
Copying an encrypted file or folder to a Windows 2000 NTFS volume	Encrypted.
Copying an encrypted file or folder to a non-Windows 2000 NTFS volume	Encryption is lost.
Moving or restoring encrypted files or folders to a different computer	Encrypted - if you use the Windows 2000 Backup tool, regardless of target volume. Otherwise, Encryption is lost. NOTE: You cannot open the file on the other computer unless it has your private key.

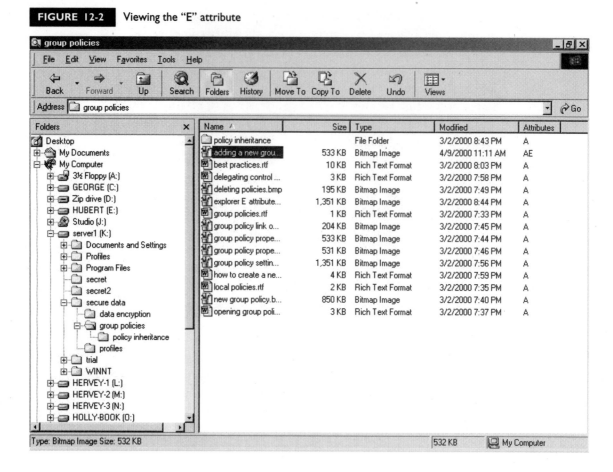

FIGURE 12-2   Viewing the "E" attribute

You can backup and copy encrypted files across systems, but they stay encrypted only if they are transferred to a NTFS version 5 system. Otherwise, the encrypted data is restored as plain text. File Encryption Keys (FEKs) cannot be exported across a network securely, so the remote copy will be encrypted with a new FEK.

As an integrated element of the operating system, Microsoft's Windows 2000 EFS is much better than other third-party encryption products, which require manual encryption and decryption on each use. This can cause security problems, as users may forget to encrypt their data after use, leaving the data vulnerable. These products also have potential leaks, as temporary paging files are left unencrypted during use. Third-party encryption utilities can also have weak security, as their encryption keys often use regular passwords that are easy to break. Most encryption products do not have the data recovery options provided by EFS. Only the user who encrypts the file and the recovery agent are capable of decrypting the document, because when a user encrypts a document, a private key is created that only the user has access to. The only other person who can decrypt the data is the administrator with the emergency recovery agent's private key. An administrator uses the recovery agent key only if a user's account has been deleted or the encryption key has been lost and the administrator requires access to the encrypted data. Once the recovery agent key is used to decrypt the data, the data cannot be reencrypted to the same state. Therefore, when users use EFS they will know for certain whether anyone else has decrypted and viewed their document.

exam
ⓦatch

Remember that the only person who can decrypt a file is the person who encrypted it. The only exception to this is when a recovery agent key is used.

The data recovery agent is defined by default the first time EFS is used on a domain or a stand-alone computer. The administrator group is defined as the recovery agent in a domain, and the local administrator account is defined as the recovery agent on a stand-alone computer.

EFS allows multiple recovery agents, which provides redundancy and flexibility with recovery procedures. EFS can also use scope-based enforcement of group policy to have different recovery agents for various parts of an organization. For example, the accounting staff may have a different recovery agent than the other staff for security reasons.

Users must obey the Encrypted Data Recovery Policy when they recover encrypted data. A default recovery policy is set up when Windows 2000 Server is installed on the first domain controller. This recovery policy designates the domain administrator as the recovery agent. Following that, a recovery policy is automatically set up when the administrator logs on to a system for the first time. This makes the administrator the recovery agent, as EFS enforces a recovery policy requirement.

You can define the following in the Encrypted Data Security Agents area of the Group Policy editor:

- No recovery policy, which allows the default local policy to be used
- Empty recovery policy, which turns EFS off
- Recovery policy with one or more X.509 v3 certificates belonging to recovery agents for that scope of administration. You can also add existing certificates or create new ones.

EFS requires that a data recovery policy be set up before EFS can be used. If a data recovery policy is set up and a user loses a private key, there are several ways to recover the encrypted file:

■ The recovery agent restores the encrypted file on a secure computer with its private recovery keys. The agent decrypts it using the cipher command line and then returns the plain text file to the user.

■ The recovery agent goes to the computer with the encrypted file, loads the recovery certificate and private key, and performs the recovery. It is not as safe as the first option, because the recovery agent's private key may remain on the user's computer.

Only the file's randomly generated encryption key, not the user's private key, is available when the recovery key is used. This insures that no other private information is revealed to the recovery agent accidentally. Only the data that falls in the range of authority of a recovery agent is recoverable by the agent.

A user without the private key to a file who attempts to access it will receive an access denied message. EFS also cannot be used with data with the read-only attribute, because you need to alter the file in order to encrypt it. You must have Write permission to encrypt any files that you own. You can also encrypt files that you don't own if you have Write permissions to them. This locks the owner of the files out, so as a file owner, you need to be especially careful to whom you give Write permissions. Administrators cannot encrypt system files, as these files are necessary for the system to boot. Windows 2000 insures that this doesn't happen by failing any encryption attempts on system files. You also cannot encrypt the %systemroot% folder or any files or folders within it.

Encrypt Folders and Files

All that a user needs to do to encrypt data is to right-click the file or folder and choose Properties. Then click Advanced and add a check mark to the "Encrypt contents to secure data" check box. Once a user does this, a unique file encryption key is created that is used when the user wants to decrypt the data. To guarantee the utmost security, the file encryption key is encrypted as well.

Folders are not actually encrypted; they are simply marked to indicate that they contain encrypted files. The list of file names within a directory is also left unencrypted. Consequently, users with the correct permissions can see the names of your encrypted files even though they will not be able to decrypt and view them. If you choose to add an encrypted marking to a folder, you will be prompted to choose whether you would like to encrypt the files and subfolders that are already within the folder as well as the folder itself. Figure 12-3 shows the Confirm Attribute Changes dialog box asking if you would like to encrypt the files and subfolders within the folder that you chose to encrypt. If you opt to encrypt the files and subfolders within the folder, any data that you add to the encrypted folder subsequently will also be encrypted.

Data on remote file servers can be encrypted, although you should keep in mind that the data is not automatically encrypted as it travels over the network. To insure the utmost security, you should implement protocol security (for example, SSL or IPSec) to encrypt the data as it crosses over the network. Users can encrypt files on a remote server only if the administrator has previously designated it as "trusted for delegation." Once the server is trusted for delegation, all users have the ability to encrypt their own documents that reside on the server. Once a file is encrypted, all reads and writes to the file are encrypted and decrypted transparent to the user. The only way a user can tell whether a file is encrypted is by checking the properties of the file. Data compression cannot be combined with encryption. They are mutually exclusive. If you rename a file or folder, it does not affect the encryption status, as it is the unique encryption key that defines the encryption status.

Exercise 12-1 shows you how to use EFS to encrypt a file or folder on an NTFS v5 partition.

FIGURE 12-3	

The Confirm Attribute Changes dialog box

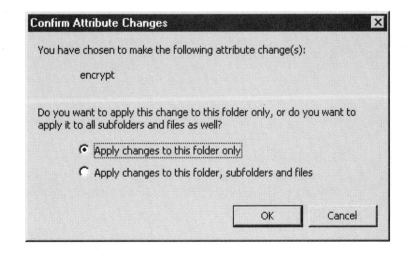

CertCam 12-3

EXERCISE 12-1

Using EFS to Encrypt Data

This exercise assumes that you are encrypting data on a partition that is formatted with NTFS v5.

1. Open Windows Explorer or My Computer and browse to the file or folder that you would like to encrypt.

2. Right-click the file or folder and choose Properties.

3. Click Advanced in the Properties dialog box.

4. Add a check mark to the "Encrypt contents to secure data" check box.

5. Click OK.

6. Click Apply.

7. If you are encrypting a file that is not in an encrypted folder, you will receive the Encryption Warning dialog box that is shown in the illustration below. Choose an option and click OK.

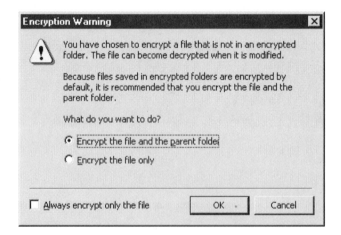

8. If you are encrypting a folder, you will receive a Confirm Attribute Changes dialog box as seen in the following illustration. It asks whether you would like to apply changes to the files and subfolders within the folder. Choose an option and click OK.

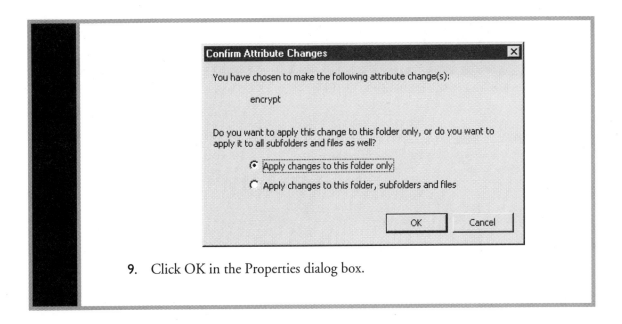

9. Click OK in the Properties dialog box.

Decrypt Folders and Files

Only the recovery agent and the person who initially encrypted it can decrypt a file
or folder. To decrypt a file, you must first decrypt the file encryption key (FEK).
To do this, the user's private key is matched up to the encrypted data's public key,
which decrypts the file encryption key (FEK). Then the FEK can be used to decrypt
the file. The only exception to this rule is when the emergency recovery agent's
private key is used. This is used only if the person who encrypted the key is
unavailable or if this person's account has been deleted and you must recover his
or her encrypted information. Once the data is decrypted with the recovery agent's
private key, only the original user can encrypt it back to the state it was in. The only
time you need to decrypt data yourself is if you want to share encrypted data with
other users. Encrypted data must be decrypted before other users can view it. To
decrypt data, simply select the data that you would like to decrypt and remove the
check mark from the encryption check box on the folder properties advanced
attribute dialog box.

Now that you have a better idea of EFS, see the following table for some possible
scenarios and solutions.

SCENARIO & SOLUTION

What file system must be you use in order to use EFS?	Windows 2000 NTFS version 5
What does EFS use to encrypt files?	CryptoAPI architecture
What is an FEK?	The File Encryption Key
Other than the person who encrypted the file, who else can decrypt a file?	The data recovery agent

The Cipher Command

The cipher command is another way to encrypt and decrypt data. It can be used from the command line and has many switches, so that you can define exactly what you want to have done. The Cipher.exe command syntax is simply CIPHER, followed by the switches that you would like to use, followed by the path and directory/file name. The most common switches are the /E switch, which encrypts the specified directories, and the /D switch, which decrypts the specified directories (for example, C:\>cipher /d "my documents"). You can use wildcards with the cipher command. For example, C:\>cipher /e /s *win* will encrypt all files and folders with "win" in the name and all files within them.

Pay attention to the CIPHER command line switches that follow. It is a good idea to practice using the CIPHER command so that you will be able to pick out the errors in CIPHER command examples.

The cipher command line syntax is CIPHER [/E | /D] [/S[:dir]] [/A] [/I] [/F] [/Q] [H] [K] [pathname [...]]. It has the following parameters:

- **/E** Encrypts the specified directories. Directories will be marked so that files added afterward will be encrypted.

- **/D** Decrypts the specified directories. Directories will be marked so that files added afterward will not be encrypted.

- **/S** Performs the specified operation on directories in the given directory and all subdirectories. Default "dir" is the current directory.

- **/A** Operation for files as well as directories. The encrypted file could become decrypted when it is modified if the parent directory is not encrypted. It is recommended that you encrypt both the file and the parent directory.

- ■ **/I** Continues performing the specified operation even after errors have occurred. By default, CIPHER stops when an error is encountered.

- ■ **/F** Forces the encryption operation on all specified objects, even those that are already encrypted. Already encrypted objects are skipped by default.

- ■ **/Q** Reports only the most essential information.

- ■ **/H** Displays files with the hidden or system attributes. These files are omitted by default.

- ■ **/K** Creates new file encryption key for the user running CIPHER. If this option is chosen, all the other options will be ignored.

- ■ **pathname** Specifies a pattern, file, or directory.

If you use the Cipher command without parameters, it displays the encryption status of the present directory and any files it contains. Figure 12-4 shows an example of the Cipher command. You are required to put spaces between multiple parameters, and you may use multiple filenames and wildcards with the Cipher command.

FIGURE 12-4 The CIPHER command displaying the status of the folders on the E:\drive

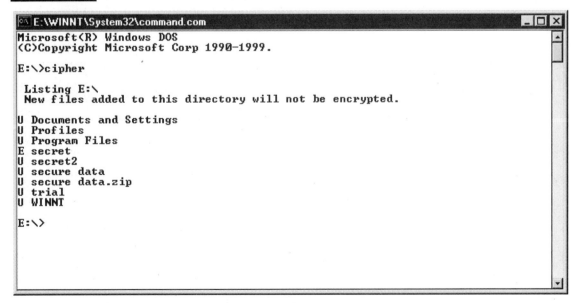

```
E:\WINNT\System32\command.com                                    _ □ ×
Microsoft(R) Windows DOS
(C)Copyright Microsoft Corp 1990-1999.

E:\>cipher

 Listing E:\
 New files added to this directory will not be encrypted.

U Documents and Settings
U Profiles
U Program Files
E secret
U secret2
U secure data
U secure data.zip
U trial
U WINNT

E:\>
```

Implement, Configure, Manage, and Troubleshoot Policies in a Windows 2000 Environment

Policies in Windows 2000 can be configured in many more ways than they could in Windows NT 4. There are local policies, system policies, and group policies that can be configured to allow you to manage your users more effectively.

Local Policy

A group policy stored locally on a Windows 2000 member server or a Windows 2000 professional computer is called a local policy. The local policy can be used to set up the configuration settings for each computer and for each user. Local policies are stored in the \%systemroot%\system32\grouppolicy folder on the local computer. Local policies include the auditing policy, user rights and privilege assignment, and various security options. Figure 12-5 illustrates the Local Security Settings console.

Local policies are the least significant of the various policies, as objects associated with sites, domains, and organizational units can overwrite them. Figure 12-6 shows the Policy Setting dialog box where you can enable or disable policy settings. Local policies are more influential in nonnetworked environments, because then they will not be overwritten by other group policies.

Local policies can be configured and analyzed using multiple options available from the security configuration and analysis tool set. If you import the local policy settings to a Group Policy Object (GPO) in Active Directory, they will have an effect on the local security settings of the computer accounts, which are associated with the GPOs.

System Policy

System policies have been mostly replaced by group policies, which extend their functionality, although there are still a few situations in which system policies are valuable. The system policy editor is used to provide user and computer

FIGURE 12-5   Local Security Settings

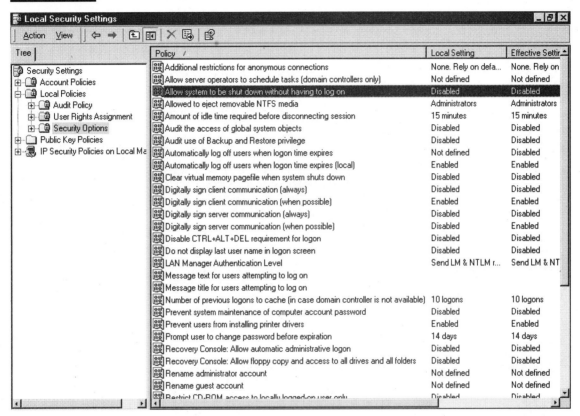

configuration settings in the Windows NT registry database. The system policy editor is still used for the management of Windows 9x and Windows NT server and workstations and stand-alone computers using Windows 2000. Windows 9x uses config.pol, and Windows NT Server and Workstation use ntconfig.pol.

Group Policy

Group policies are settings that can be applied to Active Directory objects to control users' operating environments. Unlike local policies, group policies can be used to

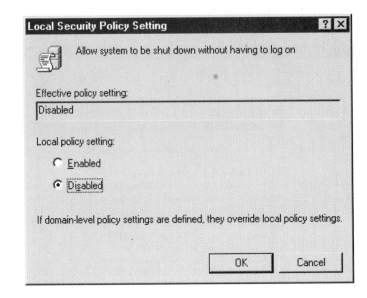

FIGURE 12-6

The Local
Security Policy
Setting policy
settings dialog
box. Remember
that domain-level
policies override
local policy
settings

set policies across site(s), domains, or organizational units (OUs) within Active
Directory. Group policies apply to users and computers within a certain container.
Table 12-2 lists and describes the types of group policies.

TABLE 12-2   Types of Group Policies

Type of Group Policy	Description
Software Settings	Determines which applications users have access to. Application assignment and Application publication.
Administrative Templates	Sets registry-based policies such as Disk quotas, offline files, and task scheduler options.
Scripts	Identifies batch files and scripts to be run at user logon or logoff and computer startup or shutdown.
Folder Redirection	Redirects special folders to network locations such as My Documents and My Pictures.
Security	Sets security settings such as file/folder access for account policies, local policies, public key policies, and IP security policies.
RIS	Controls Remote Installation Services options presented to the user, such as Automatic Setup options, Restart Setup option, and Custom Setup options.

Group policies define Microsoft certificate services, IP security, EFS, quality of service, user document management, user settings management, and software installation. You can also use group policies to set local disk quota limits. Only client computers that comprehend the Windows 2000 Active Directory (for example, Windows 2000 Professional) can utilize the Group Policy tool.

To set a group policy for a selected Active Directory object, you must have a Windows 2000 domain controller installed with Read and Write permission access to the system volume (SysVol) and Modify right to the currently selected directory object. The SysVol folder is a shared directory that is automatically created and later replicated between domain controllers. Figure 12-7 shows the SysVol folder contents.

FIGURE 12-7 The SysVol folder

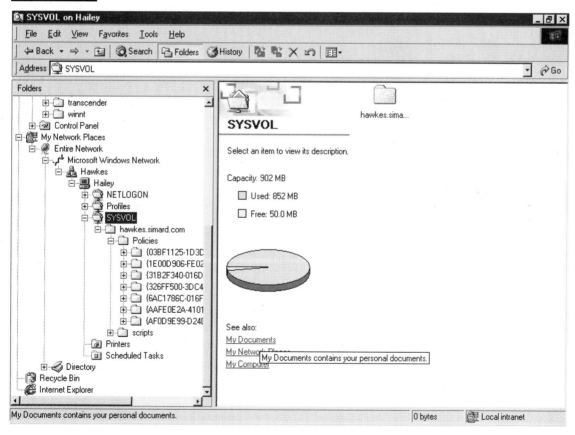

Group policies have an effect on all computers and users in a selected Active Directory container by default. You can filter the effects of a group policy based on user and computer security groups. You can also use security groups to set policies on users and computers within a site or organizational unit. In addition, you can use group policies to set policies on users and computers in a domain similar to Windows NT 4 with the System Policy Editor and poledit.exe. Group policies only pertain to users with at least Read permissions to that policy, so you can specify which groups are affected by a group policy by making sure that the groups that you want the policy applied to have the "Apply Group Policy" and read access to that Group Policy Object. Figure 12-8 shows the group policy's permissions.

The Group Policy container can be accessed via Active Directory Users and Computers, Active Directory Sites and Services, or the MMC if you have added the appropriate snap-ins. One object can have more than one group policy. For example, an object can have a user policy and a computer policy. Group policies are

FIGURE 12-8

Group Policy
Object
Permissions

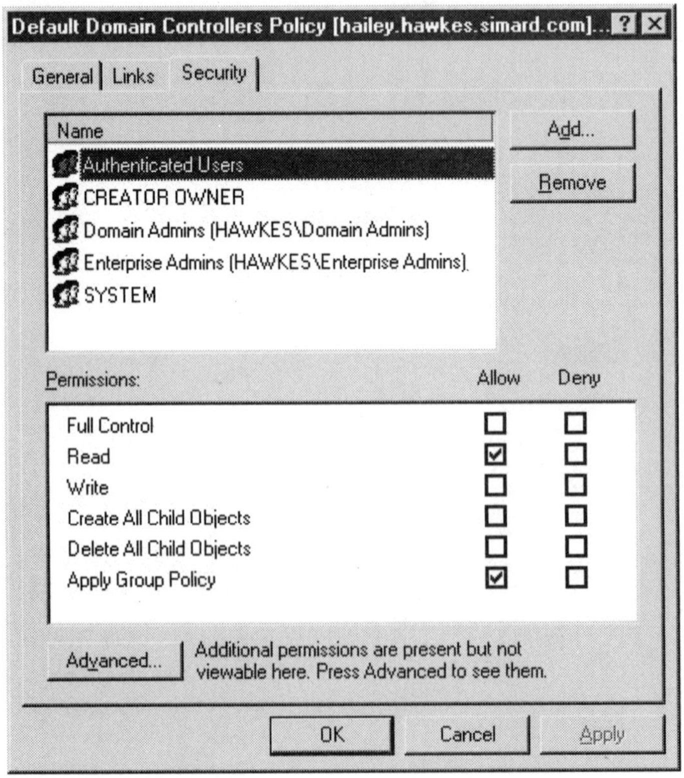

Default Domain Controllers Policy [hailey.hawkes.simard.com]...

General | Links | Security

Name	
Authenticated Users	Add...
CREATOR OWNER	Remove
Domain Admins (HAWKES\Domain Admins)	
Enterprise Admins (HAWKES\Enterprise Admins)	
SYSTEM	

Permissions:	Allow	Deny
Full Control	☐	☐
Read	☑	☐
Write	☐	☐
Create All Child Objects	☐	☐
Delete All Child Objects	☐	☐
Apply Group Policy	☑	☐

Advanced... | Additional permissions are present but not viewable here. Press Advanced to see them.

OK | Cancel | Apply

frequently used to enforce corporate policies. You can use them to do things such as defining the applications available to a user or computer, determine whether the network is accessible, lock down computers, disseminate applications, file replication, and script processing. A special group policy administrator typically manages the group policies to remove some of the numerous administrative duties from the system administrator. The only exception to this is that administrators can unlock a user account that a group policy has locked out even if they are not the group policy administrators. You should take into account the effect that group policies have on user accounts and groups.

Group policies affect subjects no matter where they are. Group policies are inherited by child containers within a domain. For example, an OU is a parent container that can contain several OU child containers. Policies are applied sequentially in order of priority settings and they apply to authenticated users by default.

There are three main group policy management models:

■ **Centralized model**   This model consolidates administrative control of group policies. A single team of administrators is responsible for managing all GPOs no matter where they are. This is usually applied by giving all the top-level OU administrators full control to all GPOs no matter where they are located. They give each second-level OU administrator Read permission only to each GPO. You can also decentralize other resources or keep all resources centralized, depending on the environment.

■ **Decentralized model**   This model is appropriate for companies that rely on delegated levels of administration. They decentralize the management of GPOs, which distributes the workload to a number of domains. To apply this model, simply give all OU administrators full control of their respective GPOs.

■ **Task-Based model**   This model is appropriate for companies in which administrative duties are functionally divided. This means that this model divides the management of GPOs by certain tasks. To apply this model, the administrators that handle security-related tasks will also be responsible for managing all policy objects that affect security. The second set of administrators that normally deploy the companies' business applications will be responsible for all the GPOs that affect installation and maintenance.

It is a good idea to limit the number of GPOs that affect any given computer or user, as the number of GPOs directly affects client performance. It can also become almost impossible to determine effective policy settings when many GPOs have been applied on top of each other. You should also use security groups to filter the effect of group policies. This reduces the number of GPOs that must be processed. User and computer portions of a GPO can also be disabled. You should disable the unused portions of GPOs, which speeds up user logons, as there are fewer policies for each logon to go through.

GPOs are inherited and cumulative. This means that they are processed hierarchically, starting with policies in the higher-level container in Active Directory. In addition, Group Policy naming conventions should reflect policy usage.

Group Policy Objects

After you create a group policy, it is stored in a Group Policy Object (GPO) and applied to the site, domain, or OU. GPOs are used to keep the group policy information; essentially, it is a collection of policies. You can apply single or multiple GPOs to each site, domain or OU. Group policies are not inherited across domains, and users must have Read permission for the GPO that you want to have applied to them. This way, you can filter the scope of GPOs by adjusting who has read access to each GPO.

You need to create one GPO before you can access the Group Policy Editor (GPE). Then you are required to open the GPE to make modifications to the group policy settings. You must also use the GPE to define the group policy settings for computer, user accounts, application and file deployment, security, scripts, and software. You can use the Active Directory Sites and Services Manager on a DC to edit a GPO for a site. Administrators with Read and Write permission to a GPO can make modifications to the group policy for that object and change who the group policy manager is.

You should limit how often group policies are updated, as updates require replication and the replication of group policies can take quite a long time. This is because the scope of a group policy may be huge. Think of it as regedit for the Active Directory. A single GPO may contain hundreds of settings. For security reasons, it is advantageous to limit the number of administrators who can edit GPOs. Also, don't bother making changes with profiles that group policies override, as it is simply redundant. By using GPOs, you can enforce and maintain the configuration settings, which can simplify computer management and lower the total cost of ownership (TCO). GPOs are a collection of settings that will affect a given user or computer. They are made up of a Group Policy Template (GPT) stored on SysVol and a Group Policy Container (GPC) stored in Active Directory.

Group Policy Containers

The Active Directory object Group Policy Containers (GPCs) store the information for the Folder Redirection snap-in and the Software Deployment snap-in. GPCs do not apply to local group policies. They contain component lists and status information, which indicate whether GPOs are enabled or disabled. They also contain version information, which insures that the information is synchronized with the GPT information. GPCs also contain the class store in which GPO group policy extensions have settings.

Group Policy Templates

The subset of folders created on each domain controller that store GPO information for specific GPOs are called Group Policy Templates (GPTs). GPTs are stored in the SysVol (System Volume) folder, on the domain controller. GPTs store data for Software Policies, Scripts, Desktop File and Folder Management, Software Deployment, and Security settings. GPTs can be defined in computer or user configurations. Consequently, they take effect either when the computer starts or when the user logs on.

Gpt.ini files are kept in the root folder of each GPT. Gpt.ini files contain two entries. The first entry is Version=x, where the x is the GPO version number. The GPO version number starts at 0 when you create a GPO initially and then it automatically adds a 1 each time the GPO is modified. The second entry is Disabled=y, where y is either 1 or 0 and indicates whether the local GPO is disabled or enabled.

You use the System Policy Editor to add policy templates. To add a policy template, copy any .adm files to the folder containing .inf files (usually C:\winnt\inf). Then open the System Policy Editor by clicking Run from the Start menu. Type in **poledit.exe** and click OK. Figure 12-9 illustrates the System Policy Editor. Once you have the System Policy Editor open, click the Policy Template option on the Options menu. Then click Add and specify the policy template that you would like to use. Figure 12-10 shows the Policy Template Options dialog box, where you can add a new GPT. Finally, click OK.

FIGURE 12-9   The System Policy Editor

FIGURE 12-10

Adding a policy
template

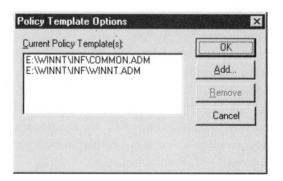

SCENARIO & SOLUTION

Where are local policies stored?	On the local computer
What is a GPO?	Group Policy Object
Who manages group policies?	The Group Policy administrator

You acquire policies from the Active Directory. To configure policies on a member server, you must use the Group Policy Editor, which is a snap-in to the MMC. It is launched from the property page of a site, domain, or OU.

When you make a group policy, several folders are added to the SysVol folder share of the DC that you are connected to. The top folder in this structure is called the GUID (global unique identifier of the GPO). The other folders store the policy object's user and computer settings. They are stored in the /SysVol share, so it can be replicated to all DCs in a domain.

Now that you have a better idea of policies, see the table, above, for some possible scenarios and solutions.

Applying Policies

To apply a group policy, simply open the group policy with either Active Directory Users and Computers or Active Directory Sites and Services. Then right-click the site, domain, or organizational unit in which you want to set a group policy and select Properties. Then select the Group Policy tab. Click New and choose Edit to define the settings. Figure 12-11 shows the group policy properties box. Group policies can also be managed in the Group Policy Management Console snap-in of the Microsoft Management Console. Use it as an interface to edit the registry. It is better to use administrative templates for group policies instead of administrative templates for system policies as in Windows NT 4. You can also delegate who controls each Group Policy. To do this, you need to first create and save Group Policy Management Consoles. Then you need to set Read and Write permissions for the appropriate administrators for each of the Group Policies.

Policy Inheritance

Group policies have an order of inheritance in which the policies are applied. Local policies are applied first, then group policies are applied to the site, then the domain,

FIGURE 12-11

Adding a new
Group Policy
Object

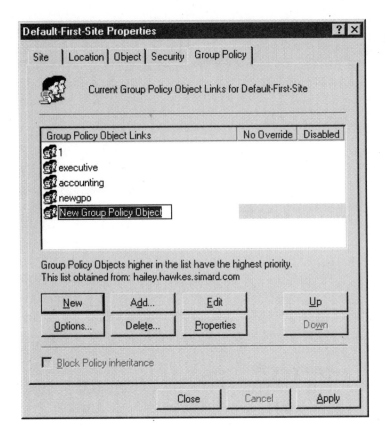

and finally the organizational unit (OU). Policies that are applied first are overwritten by policies applied later. Therefore, group policies applied to a site overwrite the local policies and so on. When there are multiple GPOs for a site, domain, or OU, the order in which they appear in the properties list applies. This policy inheritance order works well for small companies, but a more complex inheritance strategy may be essential for larger corporations.

Further customization is accessible in the form of overriding inheritance and blocking inheritance. To block inheritance in a site, right-click the site, domain, or OU in the Users and Computers MMC. Then click on the Group Policy tab and add a check mark to the Block Policy inheritance check box. Figure 12-12 shows the domain controllers properties dialog box where you can add a Block Policy inheritance check mark. Blocking policy inheritance allows a child container to block policy inheritance from parent containers. The Block Policy inheritance setting only applies to sites, domains, and OUs, not on particular Group Policy

Objects. This is a beneficial option to have when an OU requires unique settings. To override inheritance, simply click Options. Then add a check mark to the No Override check box in the Link Options dialog box, as shown in Figure 12-13. The No Override check box can be used to force a policy onto the child containers beneath it. Essentially, it is used to cancel any Block Policy Inheritance settings that may have been made. If there is a conflict, the No Override option wins over the block policy inheritance.

on the **Job**

It is a good idea to keep the number of group policies to the bare minimum necessary to get the job done. The more group policies you have, the longer it takes each user to log on. It can also get complicated to keep up with the administrative tasks involved with all the different policies. One way to decrease the number of group policies is to associate group policies objects through group membership instead of just by individual users.

FIGURE 12-12

The Group Policy properties with the Block Policy inheritance check box

Domain Controllers Properties   ? X

General | Managed By | Object | Security | Group Policy |

Current Group Policy Object Links for Domain Controllers

Group Policy Object Links	No Override	Disabled
Default Domain Controllers Policy		

Group Policy Objects higher in the list have the highest priority.
This list obtained from: hailey.hawkes.simard.com

New	Add...	Edit	Up
Options...	Delete...	Properties	Down

☑ Block Policy inheritance

OK   Cancel   Apply

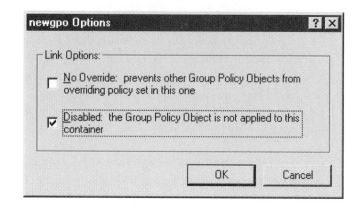

User Versus Computer Policies

There are two parent nodes at the root of the group policy snap-in:

- **User Configuration**   User policies define all user-related policies that specify operating system behavior, desktop settings, application settings, security settings, assigned and published application options, user logon and logoff scripts, and folder redirection options. User policies are applied when users log on to a computer.

- **Computer Configuration**   Computer policies define all computer-related policies that specify operating system behavior, desktop behavior, application settings, security settings, assigned application options, and computer startup and shutdown scripts. Computer policies are applied when a computer first starts up.

Both user and computer policies have Software settings, Windows settings, and Administrative Templates that can be configured. Figure 12-14 shows the User and Computer configurations.

exam
ⓦatch

If there is a conflict between a user policy and a computer policy, the user policy setting overrides the computer policy.

Modifying Group Policy

There are two ways to modify group policies. You can select the site, domain, or organizational unit in Active Directory that you wish to modify and choose the

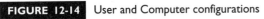

FIGURE 12-14   User and Computer configurations

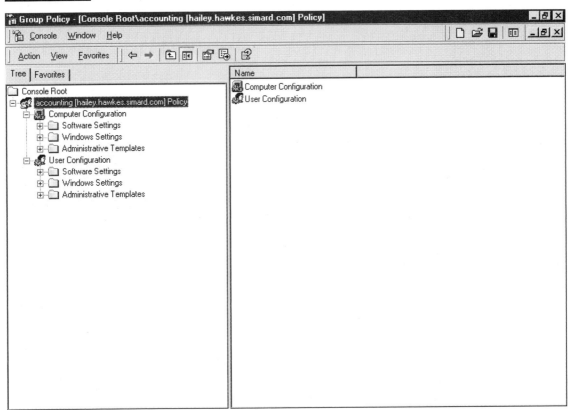

group policy tab from the properties page. Alternatively, you can use the Group Policy Management snap-in. In the Group Policy tab, you can choose from several buttons. There is a New button that you can use to add and create a brand-new policy. The Add button can be used to add a previously configured policy. The Edit button starts the Group Policy Object editor so that you can modify the policy object settings. The Options button is used to specify whether you want the object disabled for this container and whether you want to specify the No Override attribute, as shown in Figure 12-15. This prevents other Group Policy Objects from overriding that policy. You can use the Delete button to remove any of the group policies specified.

FIGURE 12-15

Group Policy
Options

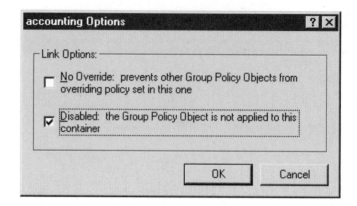

When you choose to delete a policy, you will be prompted to choose whether you simply want the policy removed from this object, or whether you would like to delete the policy entirely. Figure 12-16 shows the Delete dialog box. Be extremely careful that you do not select the latter if other objects use the policy. The Properties button allows you to modify the group policy properties. It has General, Links, and Security tabs, each with configuration settings that can be adjusted. Finally, there are Up and Down buttons that are used to determine the priority of each Group Policy Object. These only apply if you have multiple Group Policy Objects. The first policy in the list takes priority over the remaining policies.

Exercise 12-2 will show you how to modify a Group Policy Object.

FIGURE 12-16

Deleting a policy. Be careful when deciding whether to remove the GPO along with the link

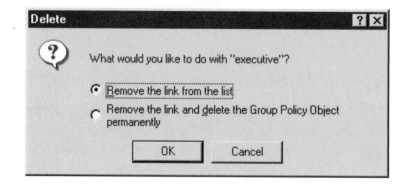

CertCam 12-2

EXERCISE 12-2

Modifying a GPO

You can modify a GPO using MMC with a Group Policy snap-in on a Windows 2000 member server.

1. Open the MMC with a Group Policy snap-in.

2. Browse to the GPO that you would like to modify. In the illustration below, we have chosen to modify the Password Policy within Computer Configuration>Windows Settings>Security Settings>Account Policies.

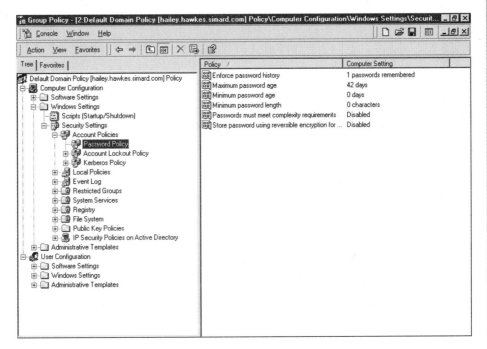

3. Right-click the policy that you would like to modify and choose Security.

4. Make the changes that you would like to make. The illustration below shows where you can modify the Password must meet complexity requirements policy setting. You can choose to enable or disable this setting.

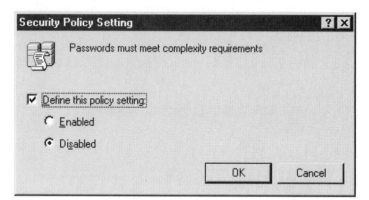

5. The illustration below shows where you can modify the Minimum password length policy setting. Here you can decide how many characters the password must be.

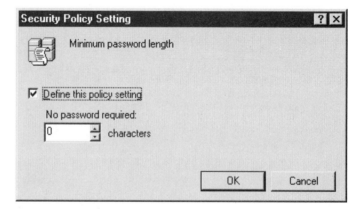

6. Once you make your changes, click OK to apply them.

Close the MMC and choose to save the settings.

Using Group Policy for Software Distribution

Group policies can be used for software distribution. There are two distinct types of software deployment:

- **Application assignments**   Use to provide limited software distributions to a desktop. Once applications are installed, they cannot be deleted or modified without the user having the correct policy settings. Application assignments help to enforce standard desktop settings.

- **Application publications**   Use to authorize a user or computer to install or uninstall software or software updates from a distribution list at their convenience. This allows the users to manage their hard-drive space more efficiently, as they can add and remove programs as they require them.

Troubleshooting Local and Group Policies

Some common problems that you may come across include not being able to modify GPOs and GPOs that are not taking effect. There are several things that you should check when you troubleshoot policies. You should verify that authentication did not fail or that the user did not log on with cached information. You should make sure that the user belongs to a domain (unless it is a local policy problem). You should check to see whether the policy is being modified by someone else, check permissions, and check to see that the convergence time has passed (that the changes you have made have replicated). You could also be having problems because child-level GPOs are blocking policy inheritance or a GPO has been disabled. Last, you should confirm that your domain controllers are up to date and that there aren't any parent-level entries in the GPO taking precedence over your new GPO entries. The Group Policy and Active Directory troubleshooter can help walk you through some of these steps.

on the *Job* *The convergence time is the amount of time that it takes for changes that you have made to be replicated to the other domain controllers (DCs). DCs require the latest directory information, but at the same time you do not want to reduce their efficiency by having them replicating all the time. The replication frequency can be configured in Active Directory Sites and Services.*

CERTIFICATION OBJECTIVE 12.03

Create and Manage User Profiles

User profiles are collections of data and folders that are used to configure the desktop settings, applications settings, and personal data for each user. Thus when multiple users share a computer, each can have a unique desktop and connections when it logs on. This also provides consistency for each user. Desktop settings incorporate things like mapped network connections, files in My Documents, icons on the desktop, wallpaper, and Start menu items. As illustrated in Figure 12-17, profiles are defined on the Profile tab for each user's properties. This is where you assign a path to the user's profile.

FIGURE 12-17

The User
Properties dialog
box. This is where
you type in the
user profile path

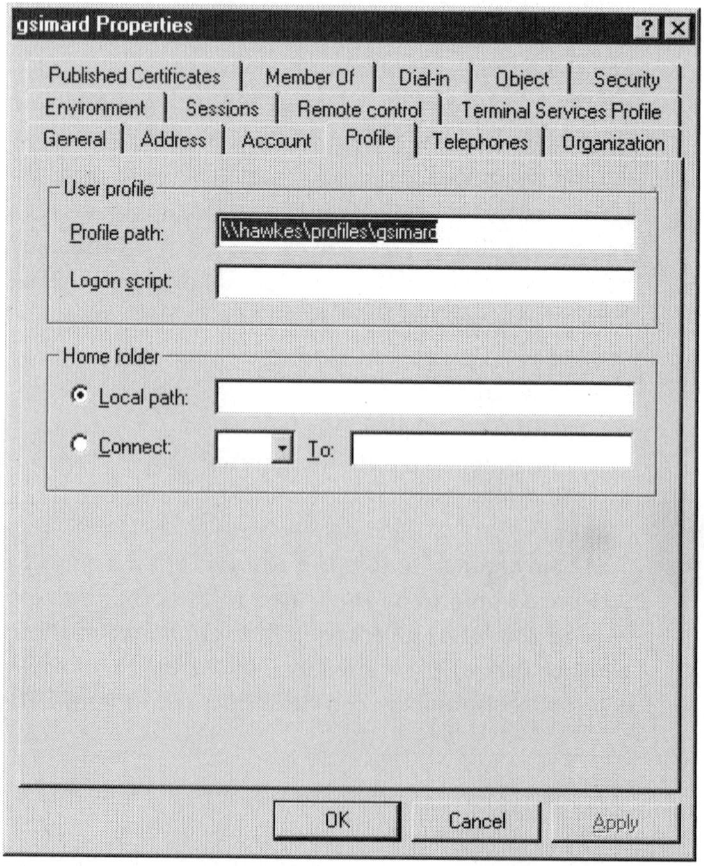

There are three types of user profiles:

■ **Local profiles**   Local user profiles are kept on one local computer hard drive. When a user initially logs on to a computer, a local profile is created for them in the \%systemdrive%\Documents and Settings\<username> folder (for example,: C:\Winnt\Documents and Settings\gsimard). When users log off the computer, the changes that they made while they were logged on will be saved to their local profile on that client computer. This way, subsequent logons to that computer will bring up their personal settings. When users log on to a different computer, they will not receive these settings, as they are local to the computer in which they made the changes. Therefore, each user that logs on to that computer receives individual desktop settings. Local profiles are ideal for users who only use one computer. For users that require access to multiple computers, the Roaming profile would be the better choice.

exam
ⓦatch   *Remember that Local profiles are always stored on the local computer. They are created in the |%systemdrive%\Documents and Settings\<username> folder on the local computer by default.*

■ **Nonmandatory Roaming profiles**   Roaming user profiles are stored on the network file server and are the perfect solution for users who have access to multiple computers. This way their profile is accessible no matter where they log on in the domain. When users log on to a computer within their domain, their Roaming profile will be copied from the network server to the client computer and the settings will be applied to the computer while they are logged on. Subsequent logins will compare the Roaming profile files to the local profile files. The file server then copies only any files that have been altered since the user last logged on locally, significantly decreasing the time required to logon. When the user logs off, any changes that the user made on the local computer will be copied back to the profile on the network file server. If a user attempts to log on to a computer with a Nonmandatory Roaming user profile and the profile is not available, the user can still log in. A user who has logged on to the particular computer previously receives a locally cached copy of the Roaming profile. Unfortunately, none of the changes that they make to the local Roaming profile will be saved if the file server is still unavailable when the user logs off. The changes will be saved back to the file server if it is back online by the time the user logs off. If the user has never logged on to the computer before and the file server is unavailable, the computer gives the user a temporary profile created from the workstations default user profile. The temporary file is then stored in the \%systemroot%\ Documents and Settings\Temp directory. As soon as the user logs off, the temp directory is deleted, and none of the changes are saved to the profile.

To make a Nonmandatory Roaming profile Mandatory, a hidden file called ntuser.dat in the user profile must be renamed to ntuser.man.

■ **Mandatory Roaming profiles** Mandatory user profiles are Roaming profiles that cannot be changed by the user. They are usually created to define desktop configuration settings for groups of users in order to simplify administration and support. Users can make changes to their desktop settings while they are logged on, but these changes will not be saved to the profile, as Mandatory profiles are read-only. The next time they log on, their desktop will be set back to the original Mandatory profile settings. The downside to Mandatory user profiles is that a user who tried to log on when the Mandatory Roaming profile was not available would not be permitted to log on at all. The user would receive an error message and would not be allowed to log on until the profile could be loaded. You can have a different Mandatory Roaming profile for each user, for each group of users, or for all users. If you assign a Roaming profile to groups of users or all users, make sure that they are Mandatory. This is because more than one user uses it; you don't want any of them to make changes to it, because this would change the profile that everyone else receives.

on the
Ö o b

Mandatory Roaming user profiles are very handy to use from the help desk support perspective. The user support staff will be able to determine the causes of user problems more quickly, as they will see any changes to the profile immediately. They can also be used to lock down users' systems so that they are limited in the "damage" that they can do.

SCENARIO & SOLUTION

What are the three profile types?	Local user profiles, Roaming user profiles and Mandatory Roaming user profiles.
What kind of profiles are stored on file servers?	Roaming user profiles and Mandatory Roaming user profiles.
Where are Local profiles stored?	On the local computer.
What happens if a user tries to log on and the user's Mandatory Roaming profile is unavailable?	They will not be permitted to log on.

Now that you have a better idea of the various profile types, the table, above, offers some possible scenarios and solutions.

To switch between a Local profile and a Roaming profile on a particular computer, simply go into the System Properties for the computer and click the User Profiles tab. Figure 12-18 shows the User Profiles tab of System properties. Choose the user that you would like to change the profile type for and then click Change Type. Choose the profile type (Roaming or Local) that you would like the user to have and click OK twice to accept the changes you have made. Figure 12-19 shows the Change Profile Type dialog box.

All new profiles are a copy of the default user profile. You can have them modified initially by an administrator or allow the users to log in and make changes themselves. To copy a user profile, go into the System Properties and choose the User Profiles tab. Next select the profile that you would like to copy and click Copy To. In the Copy To dialog box, you can either type in or click Browse to look for the profile that you would like to copy to (for example, \\hawkes\profiles\gsimard). Figure 12-20 shows the Copy To dialog box. You also need to change the Permitted to use user to the person whose profile you are copying to. Simply click Change and find the user or group that you want to have access to the profile and click OK. Click OK two more times to complete the profile copy.

User profiles include the My Documents folder, which Windows 2000 automatically creates on the desktop where users can store their personal files. The My Documents folder is the default location for File Open and File Save As

FIGURE 12-18

The User Profiles
tab of System
Properties

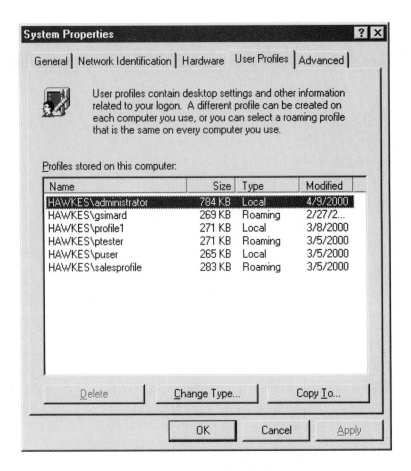

FIGURE 12-19

The Change
Profile Type
dialog box

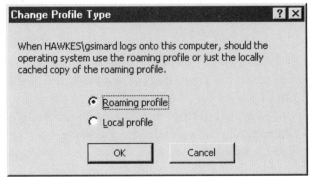

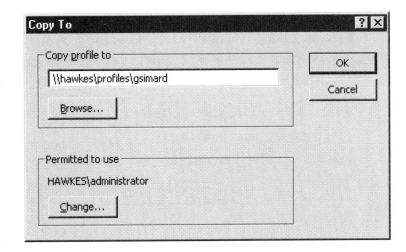

FIGURE 12-20

The Copy To
dialog box. Be
sure to give the
appropriate
permissions to
the user to whom
you are copying
the profile

commands. Users can change their profiles by doing things such as adding an icon
to the desktop, changing their screen saver, making a new network connection, or
adding files to their My Document folder. These settings are then saved back to
their profile on the server. The next time the user logs in, their profile changes
are there.

You can create a customized Roaming user profile to give specialized profiles to
users, depending on which department they are in. You can then add or remove
any applications, shortcuts, and connections according to what each department
requires. Customized Roaming user profiles are also helpful for troubleshooting and
for technical support. They make technical support easier, as the technical support
staff would know what programs and exact shortcuts should be there, so they will
notice any deviations immediately. To create a customized Roaming user profile, set
up a desktop environment and connections for a user as a template. Once you have
the template profile set up, you can copy the template profile to the user's Roaming
profile location. Note: Windows 2000 does not support the use of encryption with
Roaming user profiles.

exam
ⓦatch

*When you use Roaming user profiles with Terminal Services clients, the
profiles are not replicated to the server until the user logs off.*

Exercise 12-3 demonstrates how to assign a customized Roaming profile to
another user profile.

EXERCISE 12-3

How to Create a Customized Roaming User Profile and Copy and Assign It to a User Profile

You can complete the following on any Windows 2000 member server.

1. Create an account called Profile1.

2. Log on with the Profile1 account.

3. Configure the desktop settings and network connections as you would like them to appear for the future users.

4. Log off the computer.

5. Log on as Administrator and click Start, Settings, Control Panel, and then choose the System icon.

6. Click on the User Profiles tab.

7. Select the Profile1 profile under Name and then click Copy To, as shown:

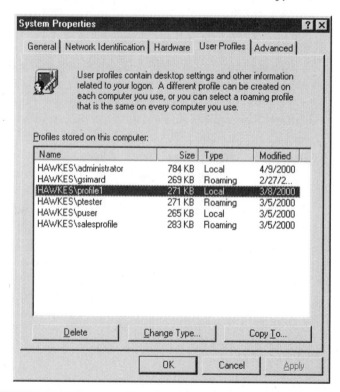

8. In the Copy To dialog box, you can either type in the profile path or click Browse to look for the profile that you would like to copy to. In the illustration below, we chose to copy the profile to E:\Profiles\gsimard and give permissions to HAWKES\gsimard.

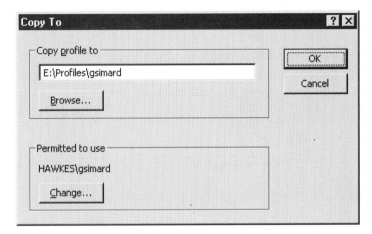

9. Click Change and then find the user or group that you want to have access to the profile, and then click OK.

10. Click OK two more times to complete the profile copy.

on the Job *Local profiles can be customized, but customizing Local profiles is inefficient because you would have to change the local profile for every computer that the client logs on to.*

CERTIFICATION SUMMARY

The Windows 2000 Encrypting File System can be used to encrypt data on a hard drive. EFS is an extra level of security that can be used only on data that is accessed by a single user. Only the user who encrypted the data and the recovery agent have agent have the ability to decrypt the data. Take into account that this can only be used once, as the emergency recovery agent cannot encrypt the data again apart from encrypting it with the recovery agent's own file encryption key.

Group policies are used to configure a user's computer settings such as the numerous software settings, windows settings, and administrative templates. Finally, user profiles are used to configure desktop settings for each user who logs on to a computer. There are Local user profiles, Roaming user profiles, and Mandatory user profiles which can perform things such as saving any user-specific program settings, user-definable settings for Windows Explorer, and all user-defined settings made in Control Panel. All of these items combined can increase the level of user security on your Windows 2000 network.

TWO-MINUTE DRILL

Encrypt Data on a Hard Disk by Using Encrypting File System (EFS)

❑ Only the person who encrypted the data and the holder of the recovery agent private key can decrypt the data.

❑ Data encryption and data compression are mutually exclusive.

❑ Shared files/folders cannot be encrypted.

❑ NTFS should be used in addition to EFS permissions because any user who has the permissions to access the encrypted data can delete it even without being able to read/decrypt it.

❑ Only Windows 2000 NTFS volumes support EFS.

Implement, Configure, Manage, and Troubleshoot Policies in a Windows 2000 Environment

❑ The two configuration types of group policies are user settings and computer settings.

❑ Group policies can be set for sites, domains, and organizational units (SDOU).

❑ Group Policy Objects (GPOs) are used to store configuration information.

❑ GPOs can be stored in Group Policy Templates (GPTs) or Group Policy Containers (GPCs).

❑ The group policy applied closest to the computer or user takes precedence over the group policies applied further toward the organizational unit.

Create and Manage User Profiles

❑ Local user profiles are used to save any personal desktop settings made by a user on a particular computer and are stored locally on that computer.

❑ Roaming user profiles are used to save a user's settings to be used on any computer in the domain. These profiles are stored on a network file server.

❑ Mandatory profiles are read-only Roaming profiles.

❑ Default user profiles can be created as a basis for users' settings.

❑ Ntuser.dat in the user profile must be renamed to ntuser.man to make a Nonmandatory Roaming profile Mandatory.

SELF TEST

The following questions will help you measure your understanding of the material presented in this chapter. Read all of the choices carefully, as there may be more than one correct answer. Choose all correct answers for each question.

Encrypt Data on a Hard Disk by Using Encrypting File System (EFS)

1. What file system is required on your Windows 2000 partition in order to use EFS?

   A. HPFS

   B. NTFS

   C. FAT

   D. NTFS v5

2. You want to add extra security via EFS to your laptop users. What are some things that you can do to use EFS in the most effective way? (Choose all that apply.)

   A. Have the users encrypt their My Documents directory so that all of their files are automatically encrypted.

   B. Have the users encrypt all of their shared documents.

   C. Have the users apply the read-only attribute to their files as well as encrypting them.

   D. Have the users encrypt their Temp directories so that when they are using a file, all of the temporary files are encrypted.

3. What type of encryption does Windows 2000 EFS use?

   A. DESZ

   B. DES+X

   C. DESX

   D. DES+Z

4. A user has four files that she would like to encrypt. One has the read-only attribute applied, one is a system file, one is a shared file, and one is compressed. Which files cannot be encrypted? (Choose all that apply.)

   A. The compressed file

   B. The system file

C. The shared file

D. The read-only file

5. One of your users has left the company and you require access to his encrypted data. What is the best way to recover the data?

A. Go to the computer with the encrypted data and log on as Administrator. Use your own private key to decrypt the data.

B. Have the recovery agent go to the computer with the encrypted data and load her recovery certificate and private key. She can then perform the data recovery.

C. Have the recovery agent restore the encrypted data from backup onto a secure computer with the private recovery keys. She can then decrypt it using the CIPHER command.

D. Have another user who has access to the encrypted data decrypt it for you.

6. You want to encrpt a folder and its subdirectories, and you want the CIPHER command to stop when it comes across an error. What switches would you use?

A. /D, /S, and /I

B. /E and /I

C. /E, /S, and /I

D. /E and /S

Implement, Configure, Manage, and Troubleshoot Policies in a Windows 2000 Environment

7. Which of the following can be performed by Group Policies? (Choose all that apply.)

A. Set scripts to run at startup and shutdown.

B. Add folders to a user's desktop.

C. Distribute a new piece of software to each user's machine.

D. Security settings such as automatically logging off users when their logon time expires.

8. Your company has several administrators. Each is responsible for a certain function such as security, new users, or data. What group policy management model would you use?

A. Decentralized model

B. Frequency-based model

C. Task-based model

D. Centralized model

9. You have eight main departments in your company, and you are the main administrator. What is the best way to assign who should apply and configure the group policies for each department?

   A. All users should configure their own group policies within their department.

   B. The Administrator should always administer the group policies for all departments.

   C. You should assign eight Group Policy Administrators and have each one configure the group policies for their own department.

   D. The Printer Operators should configure the group policies for each department.

10. Users are complaining that it takes too long to log on. What can you do to decrease the length of time it takes for users to log on to their computers? (Choose all that apply.)

    A. Disable unnecessary GPOs.

    B. Enable the Quick Logon group policy for all users.

    C. Remove the Process All Policies Before User Can Log On option for the Site.

    D. Delete unnecessary GPOs.

11. In what order are policies applied?

    A. NT 4 style policies, site group policies, domain group policies, OU group policies, and then local policies

    B. Site group policies, domain group policies, OU group policies, local policies, and then NT 4 style policies

    C. NT 4 style policies, local policies, site group policies, domain group policies, and then OU group policies

    D. OU group policies, domain group policies, site group policies, NT 4 style policies, and then local policies

Create and Manage User Profiles

12. Which of the following are types of User Profiles? (Choose all that apply.)

    A. Mandatory user profiles

    B. Local user profiles

    C. Primary user profiles

    D. Group user profiles

13. What kinds of profiles are stored on a file server?

    A. Local user profiles

    B. Mandatory and Nonmandatory Roaming user profiles

    C. Local and Roaming user profiles

    D. Mandatory Roaming profiles and Local user profiles

14. What is the difference between a Roaming user profile and a Local user profile?

    A. A Local profile is stored on a user's computer, and a Roaming user profile is stored on a file server.

    B. A Local user profile can be stored on a user's computer or a file server, and a Roaming user profile is stored on a file server.

    C. A Local user profile is stored on a file server, and a Roaming user profile is stored on a user's computer.

    D. A Local user profile is stored on a user's computer, and a Roaming user profile can be stored on a user's computer or on a file server.

15. A user logs in and makes the following changes. Which changes will be saved to the user's Roaming profile? (Choose all that apply.)

    A. Network printer connections

    B. Bookmarks that the user placed in the Windows 2000 Help system

    C. Shortcuts that the user created on the desktop

    D. User-definable settings in Windows Explorer

16. You run a company that offers computer help desk support. Which of the following profile types would aid in client help desk support?

    A. Have users use Local profiles.

    B. Have users use Mandatory Roaming profiles.

    C. Have users use Roaming profiles.

    D. Have users use group profiles.

17. Your art department users require the same computer settings no matter where they log on. What can you do to simplify this process? (Choose all that apply.)

    A. Set the users up with identical Local profiles.

    B. Set up Local and Roaming user profiles for each user.

    C. Set up a Mandatory profile for the users in the art department.

    D. Assign a customized Roaming user profile.

LAB QUESTION

You start working as the head administrator at a large company with several domains. You need to improve the way things are done, as you do not have time to do everything yourself. What could you implement to simplify and distribute your numerous administrative duties and user support workload?

SELF TEST ANSWERS

Encrypt Data on a Hard Disk by Using Encrypting File System (EFS)

1. ☑ **D.** Windows 2000 requires NTFS v5 in order for EFS to work.
   ☒ **A, B,** and **C** are incorrect, because EFS will not work with them, as they are older file systems that are not compatible with EFS.

2. ☑ **A** and **D.** They are both ways to insure that all of the users' files and also their temp files are encrypted at all times. Temporary files are often left unencrypted and are therefore vulnerable to attack.
   ☒ **B** is incorrect, because you cannot encrypt shared documents. This may be something that is improved upon in a future Windows 2000 Service Pack. **C** is incorrect, because read-only data cannot be encrypted because a file needs to be changed in order to encrypt it.

3. ☑ **C.** It is the encryption method used in Windows 2000 EFS.
   ☒ **A, B,** and **D** are incorrect, as they are not encryption methods.

4. ☑ **A, B, C,** and **D. A** is correct, because file compression and file encryption are mutually exclusive. Windows 2000 will allow you to choose only one of the check boxes. **B** and **D** are correct, because system files and read-only files cannot be encrypted. This is because they require changes to be made to the file, which can't be done, due to their attributes. **C** is correct, because files used by more than one user cannot be encrypted at this time. Future service packs may allow encryption of shared files.

5. ☑ **C.** It insures that the recovery agent's private key is never compromised.
   ☒ **A** is incorrect, because the administrator's private key cannot decrypt someone else's data. Although **B** is effective, it is not the best choice, because the recovery agent's private key is left vulnerable, as it is loaded on a user's machine. There is always the chance that it may be left on the computer by mistake. **D** is incorrect, because shared data cannot be encrypted, so no one else will be able to encrypt the encrypted data even if with NTFS permissions to the data.

6. ☑ **D.** The /E switch tells the CIPHER command to encrypt the specified directories, and the /S switch tells the CIPHER command to perform the encryption on all subdirectories as well. The CIPHER command automatically stops when it comes across an error, so a third switch is not required.
   ☒ **A** is incorrect, because the /D switch would decrypt the directory instead of encrypting it and the /I switch prevents the CIPHER command from stopping when it comes across an error. **B** is incorrect, because the /I switch prevents the CIPHER command from stopping

when it comes across an error. It also would not encrypt the subdirectories because it is missing the /S switch. **C** is incorrect, because the /I switch prevents the CIPHER command from stopping when it comes across an error.

Implement, Configure, Manage, and Troubleshoot Policies in a Windows 2000 Environment

7. ☑ A, B, C, and D are all functions that can be performed by the various Group Policies.

8. ☑ C. Your company already divides administrative responsibility by functions, so the task-based model would be the ideal model for you to use. The model divides the management of GPOs by certain tasks and gives them to the administrator that deals with that area.
☒ A is incorrect, because this divides the tasks up by the different domains, so each domain administrator controls the tasks in his or her own domain. B is incorrect, because it is not a model. D is incorrect, because it would put all the administrative duties on one central administrator, which your company does not have.

9. ☑ C. It is a good idea to distribute the administration of group policies to each department, as the group policy administrators in each department will know what is required for each department better than the main administrator. This also lessens the work for the main administrators so that they can concentrate on other tasks.
☒ A and D are incorrect, because users cannot administer their own group policies and Printer Operators do not have the correct permissions to administer group policies by default. B is incorrect, because it is not the most effective way to administer group policies in a large organization, although it is possible for one administrator with group policy administrator access to administer all the group policies.

10. ☑ A and D. Often GPOs are repeated at the different levels (Site, Domain, or OU) and are not all necessary. A is the preferred solution, because you can speed up logins by simply disabling unnecessary GPOs. This way if you change your mind and decide that you need that GPO again, you can simply enable it. You can also delete unnecessary GPOs if you are certain that you will no longer need them.
☒ B is incorrect, because there is no Quick Logon group policy. C is incorrect, because there is no Process All Policies Before Users Log On option.

11. ☑ C. This is the order in which policies are applied. The only exception to the results of the order of inheritance is when either the block policy inheritance or enforce policy from the options listed above have been set.
☒ A, B, and D are incorrect, because they are simply not the correct order of application for policies.

Create and Manage User Profiles

12. ☑ **A and B.** Mandatory user profiles and Local user profiles are two of the three types of user profiles. Roaming user profiles is the third type.
    ☒ **C and D** are incorrect, because Group user profiles and Primary user profiles are not profile types.

13. ☑ **B.** All Roaming user profiles (whether Mandatory or Nonmandatory) are kept on a file server. This way, users can log on to any computer in the domain and receive their profile settings.
    ☒ **A, C, and D** are incorrect, because Local user profiles are stored on the local computer, not on a file server. A user who uses Local profiles needs to make changes to each computer that he or she logs on to the profile setting changes will not apply to any other computer than the one the user made the changes on.

14. ☑ **A.** Local profiles are always stored on the user's local machine, and Roaming user profiles are always stored on a file server. When using a Roaming user profile, a user can log on to any computer in the network and still receive the same profile. Local user profiles must be created on each machine that a user logs on to.
    ☒ **B, C, and D** are all incorrect, because Local user profiles are stored on the local user computer and Roaming user profiles are stored on the file server. Neither Local nor Roaming user profiles can be stored on both local computers and a file server.

15. ☑ **A, B, C, and D** are correct as long as you haven't set any policies to prohibit users from doing any of them.

16. ☑ **B.** Mandatory Roaming profiles do not save users' changes back to the server. If a user deletes a printer connection or an icon, the help desk support staff would be able to figure that out immediately as it would be different from the regular profile. They can simply ask the user to log off and log back on to return their desktop to the way it should be.
    ☒ **A, C, and D** are incorrect, because they would not aid your help desk staff in supporting the users. Local profiles would be different on every computer that a client logs on to, which might cause confusion. Roaming profiles that are not Mandatory can be changed and saved back to the server; therefore, the help desk staff will not be able to gauge what is wrong by what they have on their desktop, and so on, as every user's desktop is different. There is no such thing as group profiles, so they would not aid for help desk support.

17. ☑ **C and D.** C is the ideal solution, because Mandatory profiles will insure that the users always have access to the same data. D is also correct, because a customized Roaming user profile would set up all art department users with the same settings. With customized Roaming

user profiles, users can change their desktop settings and they are saved to the file server. Therefore, they are not as easy to troubleshoot as Mandatory profiles as the customized settings you defined can be altered by the users.

☒ **A** is incorrect, because configuring identical Local profiles is a lot of work and they apply only to the one local computer. A user who changes computers will no longer have the same Local profile. **B** is incorrect, because users cannot have both Local and Roaming user profiles.

LAB ANSWER

First, you can delegate and distribute the group policy management to the other administrators within the company. The ideal solution in this case would be to use the Decentralized Model. This model distributes the management of GPOs to each domain's administrator. This insures that the Group Policy Objects are applied in the most efficient manner as the domain administrators generally have the majority of the knowledge about their own domain. To apply this model, simply grant all of the administrators full control to the GPOs that apply to their domain.

Second, you can enforce Mandatory Roaming user profiles, which will greatly simplify user support. If you configure all the users' desktop settings identically, then when a user has a problem, you will be able to identify it immediately. You can also copy the profile on top of a corrupt profile if necessary. This will insure that the user can get back to work (with a familiar desktop) immediately.

Last, you can assign multiple administrators as emergency recovery agents, perhaps one recovery agent per domain. The administrators' group is the recovery agent by default, but this can be changed at your discretion. This can save you a lot of work if EFS is used regularly within your company and there is another administrator available to take on this task. Of course, there are many other things that can be done to simplify your administrative tasks.

13

Implementing, Monitoring, and Troubleshooting Security

CERTIFICATION OBJECTIVES

T his chapter will look at one of the most talked-about elements in computing today; security. In order for your organization to protect its resources and data it is essential that you understand the security components in Windows 2000 and how to implement them. This operating system greatly enhances your ability to provide your organization with protection against unauthorized access, both from within and from outside intrusion.

The key to a successful security system is careful planning. Windows 2000 provides several levels of defense that range from the way you set up local accounts, to account policies, to the use of the Security Configuration Toolset. Establishing standards that utilize the security options Windows 2000 provides not only a smart use of the technology; it's good business. This chapter will give you the information you need to make effective choices where the security of your organization is concerned.

CERTIFICATION OBJECTIVE 13.01

Implement, Configure, Manage, and Troubleshoot Auditing

With Windows 2000, administrators can deny, allow, or simply monitor access to specific objects in Active Directory or to specific files or folders. You can also track events like user logons, failed logon attempts, logoffs, and the use of special privileges that you may have granted. This type of security is called auditing. For Microsoft, auditing is defined as a process that tracks the activities of users by recording selected types of events in the security log of a server or workstation. Using auditing is an effective security policy in that it leaves behind a trail of breadcrumbs that for an administrator can mean the difference between finding or not finding a major security violation. Auditing not only detects unauthorized access to objects; it provides a log of that detection should an intruder be caught and prosecuted.

Configuring Auditing

Before Windows 2000 will audit access to files and folders, you must use the Group Policy Snap-in to enable the Audit Object Access setting in the Audit Policy. If you do not, you will receive an error message when you set up auditing for files and folders, and no files or folders will be audited. To audit files and folders you must be logged on as a member of the Administrators Group or have been granted Manage Auditing and Security Log right in Group Policy. Note that you can set auditing only on files and folders that reside on an NTFS partition. Once Auditing is enabled in Group Policy and you have configured auditing for the desired events, view the security log in Event Viewer to review successful or failed attempts to access the audited files and folders. Exercise 13-1 details how to add the Group Policy Snap-in and set up auditing files and folders.

EXERCISE 13-1

Adding the Group Policy Snap-in and Setting Up Auditing Files and Folders

1. Click Start, click Run, type **mmc /a**, and then click OK.

2. On the Console menu, click Add/Remove Snap-in, and then click Add.

3. Under Add Standalone Snap-in, click Group Policy, and then click Add.

4. In Select Group Policy Object, accept the default Group Policy Object of Local Computer, click Finish, click Close, and then click OK. If you were choosing to use a group policy that was the default domain policy, you would click the browse button and navigate to the location of that policy rather than using the local policy.

5. From Local Computer Policy, expand Computer Configuration, then Windows Settings, then Security Settings, then Local policies and finally Audit Policy.

6. In the details pane, right-click Audit Object Access, and then click Security. The illustration below shows where to select Audit Policy in the Console 1 window.

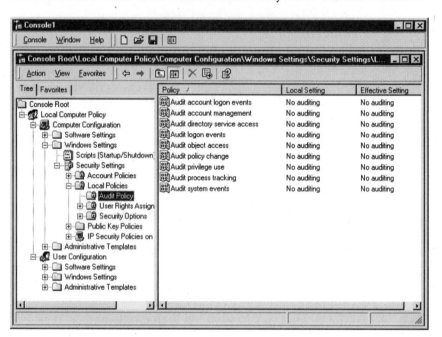

7. In Local Security Policy Setting, select the Success check box and then click OK:

on the
job

You have to use the Group Policy Snap-in to enable the Audit Object Access setting in the object policy before you can audit files or folders.

Setting an Audit Policy

Now that you have configured the Group Policy snap-in to enable file and folder auditing, you should develop a policy that determines the security events to be reported, or what is called an audit policy. Windows 2000 can track a variety of events and you will need to decide which of those events will be most important for you to monitor. Auditing changes to group policy do not take effect immediately. User and computer group policy is refreshed periodically (every 90 minutes by default). It is also refreshed when users log on and when computers are started. You can also use the Secedit Command Line Tool with the /refresh policy switch to refresh policy settings manually. (Secedit is covered in more detail later in this chapter.) You will use your audit policy to select which events to audit, and those events will then be added as an entry in the computer's Security log. You will use the Event Viewer snap-in to view that Security log to track your audited events. You should keep in mind that the Security log is limited in size so you should select the events you choose to audit carefully. You should also decide how much disk space you are willing to give up for the Security log. The maximum size of your Security log is defined in the Event Viewer.

exam
Watch

Remember that you can set auditing only on files and folders that reside on an NTFS partition.

Auditing Access to Files and Folders

Once your system is configured to allow you to audit, you can actually start tracking events such as the access of files and folders by various users and groups. This is a relatively simple process that is done using Windows Explorer. In order to audit a file or folder, you simply navigate to the file or folder through Windows Explorer and right-click on it to display the properties. Select the Security tab and click the Advanced button. Click the Auditing tab and add the user or group whose access to the object you wish to track. Now you can select which events you want to audit that relate to that user or group.

on the

Üob

You should keep in mind that after you set up auditing on a parent folder, new files and subfolders created in the folder inherit the auditing by default. If you do not want them to inherit the auditing, in the Auditing Entry dialog box, select This Folder Only in the Apply onto list when you set up auditing for the parent folder.

Auditing Access to Active Directory Objects

Using Windows 2000, administrators can monitor access to specific objects in Active Directory—for example, printers. You may be concerned that users are accessing printers outside work hours to print personal documents, or you may be concerned that users without privileges to a certain printer are attempting to use that printer. Using auditing, you could track the successful and failed attempts to use that printer. Using the Active Directory Users and Computers Snap-in, you can monitor use of special privileges by users and groups as well as user logons, failed logon attempts, and logoffs. Each object has a set of security information attached to it. Part of this information specifies the groups or users that can access that object and the types of access that have been granted to those users or groups. In addition to the security information, objects also have auditing information. This information includes which users or groups to audit when accessing the object, the access events to be audited for each group or user, and success or failure in accessing each object. Auditing access to objects in Active Directory can be useful for looking at trends in the use of a particular object or tracking access to a certain object for security reasons. Before you can audit any objects in Active Directory, you must first enable auditing of the Directory Service Access Event. Exercise 13-2 details how to do that.

CertCam 13-2

EXERCISE 13-2

Enabling Auditing of the Directory Service Access Event

1. Start the Active Directory Users and Computers Snap-in (Start—Programs—Administrative Tools).

2. On the View menu, click Advanced Features.

3. Right-click on the Domain Controllers Container and choose Properties.

4. Click the Group Policy tab.

5. Click Default Domain Controller Policy, then click Edit. The illustration below shows the Default Domain Controllers Policy window.

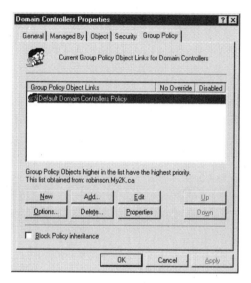

6. Double-click the following items to open them: Computer Configuration, Windows Settings, Security Settings, Local Policies, Audit Policy. The illustration below shows where to find the Audit Policy in the Group Policy Window.

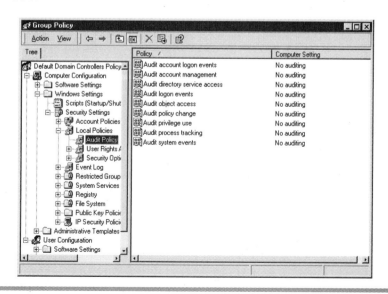

7. In the right pane, double-click Audit Directory Services Access. You can also right-click this item and select Security.

8. Click the appropriate options(s): Audit Successful Attempts and/or Audit Failed Attempts, and click OK.

9. Open the Security log in Event Viewer to view logged events.

The following scenarios and solutions address events you can record and audit in Windows 2000.

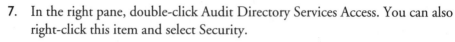

SCENARIO & SOLUTION

How is Account Logon triggered?	It is triggered when a logon request is received by a domain controller.
How is Account Management triggered?	It is triggered when a user or group account is created or modified, or when a user password is changed or initially set.
How is Directory Service Access triggered?	It is triggered when an object in Active Directory level is accessed. (You would need to define this more at the level of the actual object.)
How is Logon Events triggered?	It is triggered when a user logs on or off a computer.
How is Object Access triggered?	It is triggered when a user accesses a file, folder, or printer. This differs from Directory Service Access. Directory Service Access is for specific Active Directory objects, while Object Access is for auditing users' access to files, folders, and printers.
What triggers Policy Change?	It is triggered when security options, user rights, or audit policies are altered.
What triggers Privilege Use?	It is triggered when a user right is used to perform an action.
What triggers Process Tracking?	It is triggered when an application performs an action that is purposefully being tracked by a programmer.
What triggers System Events?	It is triggered when an event occurs that affects security, or when a user restarts or shuts down a computer.

Implement, Configure, Manage, and Troubleshoot Local Accounts

Users and groups are important because they allow the administrator to limit the ability of users and groups to perform certain actions by assigning them rights and permissions. On Member Servers you can create and manage local users and groups using Computer Management Users and Groups. A local user or group is an account that can be granted permissions and rights from your computer. Local Users and Groups is not available on Domain Controllers, as Active Directory is used to manage users and groups on Domain Controllers.

Creating and Managing User Accounts

Windows 2000 creates some users by default on a Member Server: the Administrator account and the Guest account (which is disabled by default). User Accounts that you create can have usernames that contain up to twenty uppercase or lowercase characters excluding the following; " / \ [ ] : ; | = + * ? < >. A username cannot consist solely of periods or spaces and cannot be the same as any other user or group name on the computer being administered. When creating a User Account, you will also need to assign the user a password, which the user will be prompted to change the first time he or she logs into the system. Windows 2000 passwords can be up to 127 characters long; however, Windows 98 and Windows 95 support only 14 character passwords, so if you are working in a mixed environment, you will want to keep that in mind. Exercise 13-3 shows you how to add a new user.

CertCam 13-3

EXERCISE 13-3

Adding a New User

1. Click Start, Programs, Administrative Tools, Computer Management. Open Local Users and Groups.

2. In the left pane, highlight the Users folder.

3. From the Action menu, select New User.

4. Give the user a username based on your organization's conventions. It is common to use the first initial and last name of the user. You should also give the user a description so that you and future administrators will be able to easily identify the user. You will also need to give the user a password. Note that the user will be prompted to change this password the first time he or she logs on. You may also disable the account at this screen if it is not needed immediately. The New User window is shown:

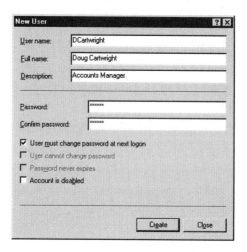

5. Click Create, then click Close. Note that in the following illustration, the new user appears in the list of users.

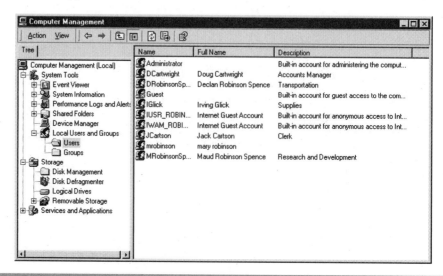

6. Now you can manage the new user account by double-clicking the new user in the right pane. Note that there are now four tabs associated with the properties of the user account.

7. Click the Member Of tab. Note that by default the user is only a member of the Users Group. Click Add.

8. From the top pane of the Select Groups Windows, highlight Backup Operators and click Add. Note that the Backup Operators group now appears in the lower pane and is associated with the computer on which it was created: Robinson. Click OK.

The Profile tab is used to map the user to the location of the profile, to give the user a login script, and to map the user to the home directory. In the Profile Path you would enter the location in which you want the user's profile to be stored. This profile can be stored locally or on another server. Figure 13-1 shows the Properties windows for the user.

FIGURE 13-1

The User
Properties
window.

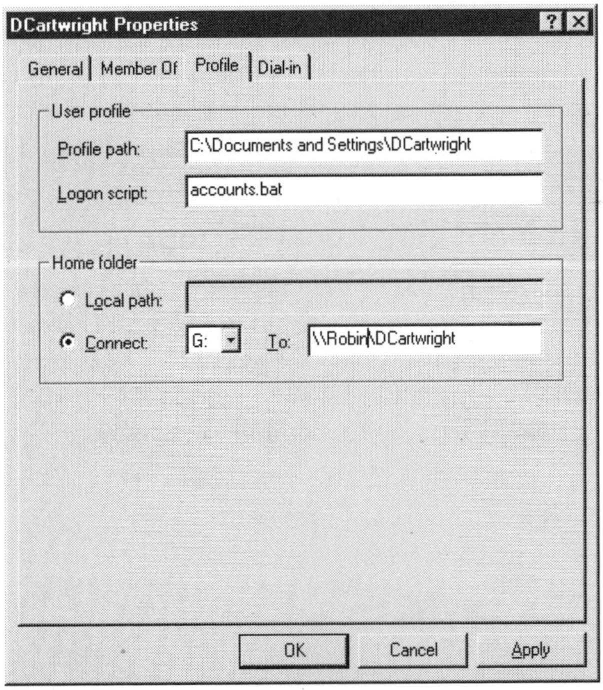

Figure 13-1 — DCartwright Properties

Tabs: General | Member Of | Profile | Dial-in

User profile
Profile path: C:\Documents and Settings\DCartwright
Logon script: accounts.bat

Home folder
○ Local path:
● Connect: G: To: \\Robin\DCartwright

OK   Cancel   Apply

If a user complains that it is taking an extremely long amount of time to log on to his or her computer, check the size of the profile. Each time a user logs on to a machine, the entire profile is downloaded to that particular machine. If the user has a large amount of data stored in the profile, this download will obviously take longer.

The Login Script will map the user to whatever network drives you choose as the administrator. This is written as a batch file using the Net Use command.

The user's home folder is generally a place where users are allowed to keep their own data. In many organizations, the only people with rights to this folder are the user and the administrator. If the folder is kept locally, use Local Path to enter its location. If the user's folder is kept on another server, connect it as a mapped drive using the \\servername\sharename convention.

The Dial-in tab is used to give the user permissions for a dial-in account to your network.

Creating Users on a Domain Controller is a very similar process to creating them on a Member Server except that the operations are performed in Start, Programs, Administrative Tools, Active Directory Users and Computers.

Creating and Managing Computer Accounts

A computer account is an account that is created by an administrator and uniquely identifies the computer on the domain. The newly created account is used so that a computer may be brought into a Windows 2000 Domain.

Exercise 13-4 shows you how to add a computer to your domain.

Creating and Managing Local Groups

On a Member Server, a local group is one that can be granted rights and permissions from its own computer and, if the computer participates in a domain, user accounts and global groups from its domain. Like local users, local groups are created in the Local Users and Groups portion of Computer Management in the Administrative Tools. By selecting Groups from the console tree, you can select New Group from

EXERCISE 13-4

Adding a Computer to the Domain

1. Log on as a member of the Domain Admins Group.

2. Open the Active Directory Users and Computers Snap-in.

3. From the Action menu, choose New, then choose Computer. The New Object—Computer window will open.

4. From the New Object—Computer window, add the name of the new computer. Adding a computer, named Scott, to the domain:

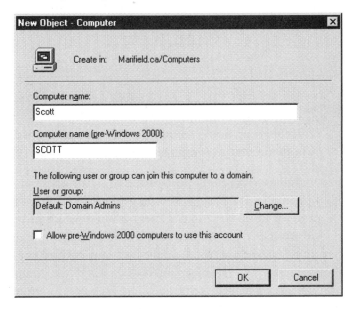

5. When you have entered the name of the computer, click OK.

In order to manage tasks such as disk management or services on the computer you have added, highlight the computer and choose Manage from the Action menu.

the Action Menu. You will give the group a name and use the Add button to add members to your group. Figure 13-2 shows the members of the group Researchers.

FIGURE 13-2

Group members

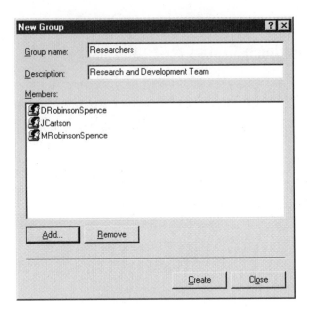

on the **Job**

A local group name cannot be the same as any other group name or username on the computer being administered.

A user who belongs to a group has all the rights and privileges assigned to that group. If a user is assigned to more than one group, then the user has all the rights and permissions granted to every group to which he or she belongs. If a user is a member of two groups, one of which has more restricted access to a particular file or folder, the user will have the least restrictive access provided by his or her group membership. (The exception is when any of the groups to which the user belongs is specifically denied permission. The deny permission overrides all others.)

Windows 2000 provides several groups for you. By default, the following groups are placed in the built-in folders for Active Directory Users and Computers: Account Operators, Administrators, Back-up Operators, Guests, Printer Operators, Replicator, Server Operators, and Users.

Security Groups

Windows 2000 allows you to organize users and other domain objects into groups for easy administration of access permissions. Defining your security groups is a major task for your distributed security plan.

FROM THE CLASSROOM

User Rights

Administrators can assign specific rights to group accounts or to individual user accounts. These rights authorize users to perform specific actions such as logging on to a system interactively or backing up files and directories. User rights are different from permissions, because user rights apply to user accounts and permissions are attached to objects. User rights define capabilities at the local level. Although user rights can apply to individual user accounts, they are best administered on a group basis. This ensures that the user logging on automatically inherits the rights associated with that group. It also eases the amount of administration necessary.

A new user who joins your organization and is part of the Personnel Department can be put in the group you have already created for that department and will automatically be able to access all the files and folders the rest of the users in the Personnel Department can access.

There are two types of user rights: privileges and logon rights. Privileges are activities like changing the system time, generating security audits, and shutting down the system. Logon rights are activities like logging on as a service and logging on locally to a machine.

—Mary Robinson, MCP

The Windows 2000 Security Groups allow you to assign the same security permissions to large numbers of users in one operation. This ensures consistent security permissions across all members of a group. Using Security Groups to assign permissions means the access control on resources remains fairly static and easy to control and audit. Users who need access are added or removed from the appropriate security groups as needed, and the access control lists change infrequently.

Windows2000 supports both Security Groups and Distribution Groups. The Security Groups can have security permissions associated with them and can also function as mailing lists. The Distribution Groups are used for mailing lists only; they have no security function.

There are three types of Security Groups: Domain Local, Global, and Universal.

Domain Local Groups are used for granting access rights to resources such as file systems or printers that are located on any computer in the domain where common access permissions are required. The advantage of Domain Local Groups being used to protect resources is that a member of the Domain Local Group can come from both inside the same domain and from outside as well.

Global Groups are used for combining users who share a common access profile based on job function or business role. Typically organizations use Global Groups for all groups in which membership is expected to change frequently. These groups can have as members only user accounts defined in the same domain as the Global Group.

Universal Groups are used in larger, multidomain organizations, in which there is a need to grant access to similar groups of accounts defined in multiple domains. It is better to use Global Groups as members of Universal Groups to reduce overall replication traffic from changes to Universal Group membership. Users can be added and removed from the corresponding Global Groups with their account domains, and a small number of Global Groups are the direct members of the Universal Group. Universal Groups are used only in multiple domain trees or forests. A Windows 2000 domain must be in native mode to use Universal Groups.

CERTIFICATION OBJECTIVE 13.03

Implement, Configure, Manage, and Troubleshoot Account Policy

Another way of making your system more secure is to implement policies that protect your data from unauthorized access. An Account Policy encompasses several different means to accomplish a more secure organization. Account Policies are those enforced against the user accounts you have created for your users to gain access to data. There are three parts to an Account Policy: Password Policy, Account Lockout Policy, and Kerberos Policy.

Password Policy

A password policy regulates how your users must establish and manage their passwords. This includes password complexity requirements and how often passwords must change. There are several settings that can be used to implement a successful password policy. You can enforce password uniqueness so that users cannot simply switch back and forth between a few easy to remember passwords. This can be set to low, medium, or high security. With low security, the system remembers the user's last 1–8 passwords (it is your choice as administrator to decide how many); with medium, it remembers the last 9–16 passwords; with high, it remembers the last 17–24 passwords.

The following Scenarios & Solutions grid presents some possible settings and their results.

As in the last section, you must have added the Group Policy Snap-in in order to manage account policies. (See Exercise 13-1.) Once you have the Group Policy Snap-in installed, you can manage your account policies. Exercise 13-5 details how to make changes to your password policy.

Account Lockout Policy

The Account Lockout Policy dictates the behavior for locking and unlocking user accounts. This includes Account lockout threshold and how long to lock accounts. There are three configurable parameters: Account lockout threshold determines how many times users can attempt to log on before their accounts are locked. This can range from low (five attempts) to high (one or two attempts). The Account lockout duration parameter controls how long an account is locked after the Account lockout threshold parameter is triggered. The Reset account lockout counter after parameter is a counter for unsuccessful logon attempts which increments for x

SCENARIO & SOLUTION	
Maximum Password Age	This is the time period that the user is given to use a new password.
Minimum Password Age	Setting this parameter higher prevents users from reverting back to their previous passwords for X number of days.
Passwords must meet complexity requirements of installed password filter.	Installing a password filter allows you to define more complex password requirements. For example, you can install a password filter that requires users to make passwords that consist of lowercase, uppercase, and numeric characters.
User must log on to change password.	Enabling this forces users to log on to change their passwords when they expire.

EXERCISE 13-5

Changing Password Policies

1. From Start, Programs, Administrative Tools, select the Group Policy Snap-in you have already added in Exercise 13-1.

2. Double-click on Computer Configuration, then Windows Settings, then Security Settings, then Account Policies, then Password Policy. The Console window with the Security Settings is shown:

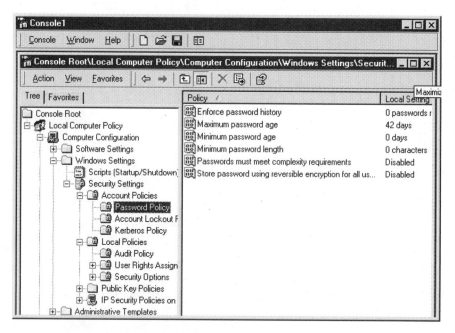

3. In the right pane, double-click Enforce password history.

4. In the Keep Password History box, select the number of passwords you wish the security settings to remember. Click OK. The following illustration shows the password policy being set for enforcing a password history.

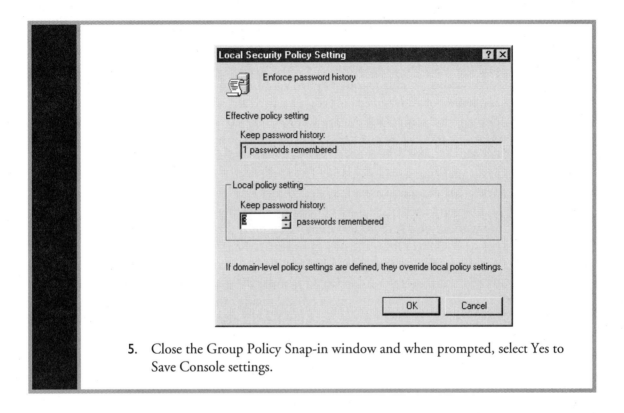

5. Close the Group Policy Snap-in window and when prompted, select Yes to Save Console settings.

number of minutes before returning its value to zero. Account Lockout Policy is configured in the same place as the password policy: the Group Policy Snap-in. This policy is very useful in the sense that someone who is trying to gain unauthorized access to your system may try logging on using a username and password they think might work. If the intruder tries three different passwords, for example, and you have configured your account lockout policy to lock users out after three unsuccessful login attempts, your intruder is now out of chances.

Kerberos V5 and Kerberos Policy

Using the Group Policy Snap-in, you can also configure the Kerberos Policy. Kerberos V5 is the primary security protocol for authentication with the Windows

2000 domain. Kerberos is an industry-standard, platform-independent security protocol developed at the Massachusetts Institute of Technology (MIT). Kerberos network authentication enhances security because network servers and services need to know that the client requesting the access is actually a valid client and the client also knows that the servers it is connecting to are valid. The central component of Kerberos is the Key Distribution Center. The KDC runs on each Windows 2000 domain controller as a part of Active Directory, which stores passwords and other sensitive account information. The Kerberos V5 protocol verifies both the identity of the user and network services. The Kerberos V5 authentication method issues tickets for accessing network services. A ticket is a set of identification data for a security principal, issued by a domain controller for the purposes of user authentication. These tickets contain encrypted data, including an encrypted password that confirms the user's identity to the requested service. If a client wants to communicate with a server, the client sends the request to the KDC, and the KDC in turn issues a session key so that the client and server can authenticate with each other. The session key has a limited lifetime that is good for a single logon session. After the login session is terminated, the session key is no longer valid. The copy of the session key that the server receives is contained in a session ticket, which also contains information about the client. Now the client and the server can communicate.

exam
Ⓦatch

Kerberos requires that both the Client and the Server be running the Windows 2000 operating system. If one of the two systems in a pair trying to authenticate is running an operating system other than Windows 2000, NTLM is the protocol that is used.

Using Kerberos Policy, you can set rules for how the tickets are handled by the system. Kerberos Policy is set at the domain level and is stored within Active Directory and may be accessed on a server in the Group Policy Snap-in. Only members of the Domain Admins Group have permission to change the policy. Kerberos Policy can define the following parameters: Maximum lifetime for user ticket renewal, Maximum lifetime for service ticket, Maximum tolerance for computer clock synchronization, and Maximum lifetime for user ticket. Enforce user logon restrictions is enabled by default and is used to validate every request for service tickets by making sure that the client has the correct user rights for logging on the requested server.

on the

ⓘob *The Enforce user logon restrictions portion of Kerberos Policy takes the server extra time to perform and can slow down your network. This setting can be disabled so if you are experiencing these problems, you may consider disabling this function.*

The Maximum lifetime for service ticket parameter is set in minutes. A service ticket is the same thing as a session ticket. The setting for the lifetime of the service ticket cannot be more than the time specified in the Maximum User Ticket lifetime or less than ten minutes. It is advisable to make this setting the same as the Maximum User Ticket lifetime.

■ The Maximum lifetime for user ticket parameter is set in hours. The default setting is ten hours.

■ The Maximum lifetime for user ticket renewal parameter is set in days. The default setting is seven days.

■ The Maximum tolerance for computer clock synchronization parameter determines how much difference in the clocks is tolerated. This setting is in minutes, and five minutes is the default.

exam

ⓦatch *Policies may be set for the domain or for the local machine. Any time a local policy and a domain policy conflict, the domain policy will go into effect.*

CERTIFICATION OBJECTIVE 13.04

Configure, Manage, and Troubleshoot Security with the Security Configuration Toolset

The Security Configuration Toolset is a set of snap-ins for MMC that is designed to provide a central place for security-related tasks. With the Security Configuration Toolset, you will be able to use an integrated set of tools to configure and analyze security on one or more Windows 2000 machines in your network. It is intended to answer the need for a central security configuration tool. Most important, it provides a single place where the entire system's security can be viewed, analyzed, and adjusted, as necessary. The components of the Security Configuration Toolset are as follows:

- Security Configuration and Analysis Snap-in
- Security Settings Extension to Group Policy
- Security Templates Snap-in
- The command line tool, Secedit.exe

Security Configuration and Analysis Snap-in

The Security Configuration and Analysis Snap-in allows you to configure and analyze your system. By comparing what your system currently looks like in terms of security against a Security Template that you load into a personal database, the system's security setup is analyzed. The template contains the settings for how you want your system's security to be managed. If the analysis finds discrepancies between the template and the current state of your system, it will point out those discrepancies and make recommendations based on the template. Exercise 13-6 details how to set up the personal database and analyze your system's security.

CertCam 13-6

EXERCISE 13-6

Setting Up the Personal Database and Analyzing System Security

1. First you need to set a working database. Open the MMC console into which you have loaded the Security Configuration and Analysis Snap-in.

2. Right-click Security Configuration and Analysis under the Console Root and select Open Database.

3. If this is your first personal database, type in the name you want to give it and click Open.

4. You will be prompted to select a Security Template to import. For the purposes of this exercise we will use the basicsv file, as it is the default template for Windows 2000 servers that aren't Domain Controllers. Double-click Basicsv. Templates available by default:

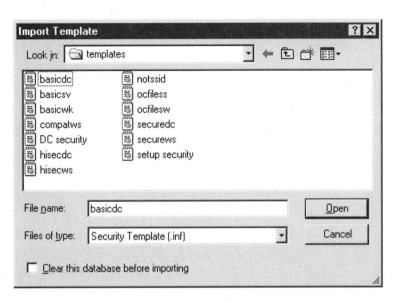

5. Now the system's security can be analyzed. Right-click Security Configuration and Analysis under Console Root and select Analyze Computer Now. Make a note of or change the location of the log file, as this is where you will view the results of the analysis. Click OK. The analysis will now run. The illustration below shows the analysis in progress:

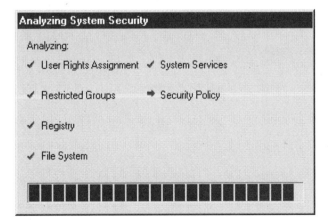

6. Go to the location of the log file and view the results.

Security Setting Extensions to Group Policy

The Security Configuration Toolset also includes an extension snap-in to the Group Policy Editor to configure local security policies as well as security policies for domains and organizational units. Local security policies only include the Account Policy and Local Policy. Exercise 13-7 details how to view your local security policy.

CertCam 13-7

EXERCISE 13-7

Viewing Local Security Policy

1. Log on to your Windows 2000 Server computer as a user with administrative privileges.

2. Click Start, Programs, Administrative Tools, Console 1, which is the Group Policy Snap-in you added earlier in this chapter.

3. Click the + next to Computer Configuration, then Windows Settings, then Security Settings, and then Local Policies to expand these folders.

4. Click the Security Options folder under Local Policies. Your screen should look like the following:

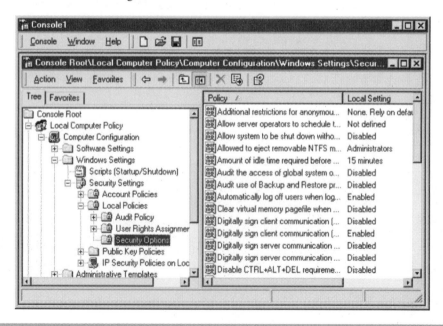

Templates

The Security Templates Snap-in allows you to create a text based template file that can contain security settings for all of the security areas supported by the Security Configuration Toolset. You can then use these template files to configure or analyze system security using other tools.

Windows 2000 comes with several predefined Security Templates. These templates address several security scenarios. Security Templates come in two basic categories: Default and Incremental. The Default or Basic templates are applied by the operating system when a clean install has been performed. They are not applied if an upgrade installation has been done. The incremental templates should be applied after the Basic Security Templates have been applied. There are four types of incremental templates: Compatible, Secure, High Secure, and Dedicated Domain Controller.

The Compatible Template Security Level is used to alter the default permissions for the Users Group so that legacy applications can run properly.

The Secure template will increase the level of security for Account Policy, certain Registry keys, and Auditing. Permissions to file system objects are not affected with this configuration, but it removes all members from the Power Users group.

The High Secure templates add security to network communications. Legacy clients will not be able to communicate if this level is used.

The Dedicated Domain Controller template optimizes security for local users on domain controllers that do not run other server applications.

The Secedit.exe Command Line Tool

The Secedit.exe Command Line tool offers much of the functionality of the Security Configuration and Analysis Snap-in, only from the command line. Secedit.exe, when called from a batch file or from an automatic task scheduler, can be used to automatically create and apply templates and analyze system security. It can also be run dynamically from the command line. Secedit.exe allows the administrator to analyze system security, configure system security, refresh security settings, export security settings, and validate the syntax of a Security Template. There are many switches the administrator can use with secedit. Figure 13-3 shows the syntax used to refresh security settings for the local machine with the machine name Robinson.

FIGURE 13-3

Using Secedit.exe
to refresh
security settings

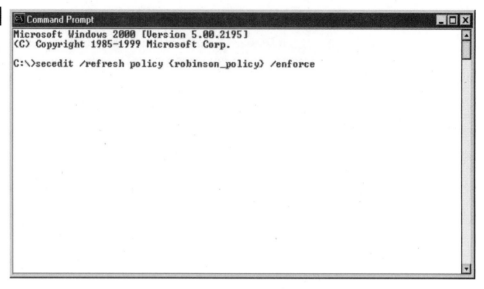

FIGURE 13-3

Using Secedit.exe
to refresh
security settings

exam

ⓦatch

*The Secedit Command Line Tool, when used with the /refresh policy switch,
is a very useful way of quickly updating any changes you have made to your
security policies.*

The following Scenarios & Solutions grid shows some of the Secedit.exe switches
and their uses.

The Secedit.exe command line tool will allow you to schedule regular security
audits of local policies on the machines in any domain and organizational unit. By
running scripts that call on the secedit.exe program, you can update each computer's

SCENARIO & SOLUTION

Initiate Security Analysis.	Use Secedit /analyze. You would use this syntax with additional switches like /DB *filename* to inform secedit what database to apply the security analysis results to.
Apply a Template using the Configure Switch.	Use Secedit /configure. You would also use switches like /CFG *filename* where filename is the location of the template that will be applied to the database.
Export the template stored in the database to an .inf file.	Use Secedit /export with the switch /DB *filename*, for example, to inform secedit what database to extract the template from.

personal database with the results of your security analysis. You can then later use the Security Configuration and Analysis Snap-in to analyze the results of your automated analysis.

Use extreme caution in employing any of the tools in the Security Configuration Toolset in a live environment. Make sure you have thoroughly tested your security configurations before applying them.

CERTIFICATION SUMMARY

Given the current buzz over newly created viruses, not to mention Denial of Service attacks on major organizations, having a handle on the security of your system is clearly a vital component of your Windows 2000 plan. In order to protect your data from unauthorized access, it is essential that you learn as much as possible about implementing effective security.

Using Auditing, you can track the activities of users in order to find security violations that need to be addressed. The log that is provided by event auditing will help you retrace the steps of an intruder so that you can close that security hole. You can audit access both to files and folders and to Active Directory objects.

With Local Accounts, you, as the administrator, can limit the ability of users and groups to perform certain actions and access certain objects. By creating accounts for users, groups, and computers, you can tighten your grip on what actually gets accessed in your system and uniquely identify these objects on your network.

Implementing policies such as Account, Password, and Kerberos Policies are excellent steps that you can take in developing a tight security system. Depending on how concerned you are about access to your data, you can impose a variety of policies that will help keep your system as secure as you want it to be.

The Security Configuration Toolset allows you to configure security for local machines, domains, or organizational units. Using the Security Configuration and Analysis Snap-in you can apply a number of different security scenarios. With Templates, you can create files that contain security settings for export to other computers in your domain or used on the local machine. The Secedit.exe Command Line Tool allows you much of the functionality of the Security Configuration Toolset, but from the command line so that you can schedule the application of Security Templates.

Defining an easy-to-use, effective security policy is a vital undertaking and shouldn't be taken lightly. Once you have this in place however, you can feel safer knowing you have a thorough understanding of your potential vulnerabilities and that you have addressed them.

TWO-MINUTE DRILL

Implement, Configure, Manage, and Troubleshoot Auditing

❑ Use the Group Policy Snap-in to configure Auditing.

❑ Auditing can only be set on an NTFS partition.

❑ Use Windows Explorer to audit files and folders.

❑ Subfolders and files inherit auditing set on parent folders by default.

Implement, Configure, Manage, and Troubleshoot Local Accounts

❑ New Users are created in Computer Management, Users, and Groups.

❑ You have to be a member of the Domain Admins Group to create a computer account in a domain.

❑ Users get all the rights and permissions granted to them by their group membership.

Implement, Configure, Manage, and Troubleshoot Account Policy

❑ Password Policy regulates how users establish and manage their passwords.

❑ Account Lockout Policy can be used to set how many times a user can try logging in with the incorrect login information and how long the account will stay locked once the lockout is enforced.

❑ Kerberos Policy is set for the domain level.

❑ Only members of the Domain Admins Group have permission to alter Kerberos Policy.

Implement, Configure, Manage, and Troubleshoot Security by Using the Security Configuration Toolset

❑ The Security Configuration and Analysis Snap-in uses a personal database to store computer-specific system Security Templates.

❑ Security Templates can be used to analyze your computer's current security settings and determine whether there are discrepancies between the template and your settings.

❑ Secedit.exe is a command line version of the Security Configuration Toolset and can be run dynamically or scheduled.

SELF TEST

The following questions will help you measure your understanding of the material presented in this chapter. Read all of the choices carefully, as there may be more than one correct answer. Choose all correct answers for each question.

Implement, Configure, Manage, and Troubleshoot Auditing

1. What event is triggered when a user right is used to perform an action?

   A. Policy Change

   B. System Event

   C. Process Tracking

   D. Privilege Use

2. Your company has a lot of secure data, and the CEO is very concerned about infiltration from within the company. What can you do to monitor the folders and files on the network? (Choose all that apply.)

   A. Apply restrictive permissions to the folders and files in question.

   B. Create groups to manage who has access to the files.

   C. Audit access to the files to make sure no one without permissions is attempting to access the files and folders.

   D. Create an account lockout policy.

3. Where can failed attempts to access folders that have been audited be viewed? (Check all that apply.)

   A. Audit Policy

   B. Event Viewer

   C. Security Configuration Toolset

   D. Group Policy Snap-in

4. What do you use to enable auditing for files or folders? (Check all that apply.)

   A. Windows Explorer

   B. Security Templates

   C. Audit Policy

   D. Account Policy

Implement, Configure, Manage, and Troubleshoot Local Accounts

5. In order to create a computer account in a domain, you must be logged on as a member of which group? (Check all that apply.)

A. Domain Admins

B. Administrators

C. Domain Users

D. Backup Operators

6. Several users from the Accounting Department will be working on a project with users from the Programming Department, and they need to share documents with each other but don't want other users from the rest of the Accounting or Programming Departments to have access to them. How can you facilitate this? (Check all that apply.)

A. In the Local Users and Groups section of Computer Management, create a group with those users as members. Give that group rights to the data they need to access and deny access to all other users.

B. In Active Directory, create a group with the users in it who need access to the files.

C. Create a single logon for all the users who need access to the data to use. Tell all those working on the project the username and password.

D. In the Group Policy Snap-in, give the users who need it rights to the folders

7. A user complains to you that it is taking a long time to log in each morning. You check the size of his profile on the server and find that it is 30MB. What can you do to speed up the user's login time? (Choose all that apply.)

A. Put the profile on the user's local machine.

B. Move the user's profile to another server.

C. Have the user keep some data in a personal folder on the server rather than in the profile.

D. Delete the user's profile.

8. What are some examples of login rights? (Check all that apply.)

A. Logon as a Service

B. Shut down the system

C. Generate Security Audits

D. Logon Locally

9. Which utility would you use to create new User Accounts?

   A. User Manager for Domains

   B. Computer Management Users and Groups

   C. Account Manager

   D. System Information

Implement, Configure, Manage, and Troubleshoot Account Policy

10. Your users keep using their pets' names as passwords and you are concerned that this is not very secure. What can you do to make them use more complex passwords? (Check all that apply.)

    A. Lock out their accounts until they use longer passwords.

    B. Impose a Password Policy that requires a minimum length for passwords.

    C. Have users change their passwords once a week.

    D. Impose a Password Policy that requires users to use both upper- and lowercase characters in their password.

11. A new employee has started working at your organization and has been given a username and password, but the new employee's supervisor doesn't want her to be able to log on until she has been trained on your company's software applications. How can you temporarily deny the user access to the network?

    A. Delete the user's account and re-create it when the supervisor gives you the go-ahead.

    B. Select the Account is disabled check box on the properties for the user's account.

    C. Use the Password Policy to change the user's password so she can't log on.

    D. Prompt the user to change her password the first time she logs on.

12. What does the Minimum Password Age setting define?

    A. How long a user's password lasts before it has to be changed

    B. When a user can reuse an old password

    C. How many characters must be in a user's password

    D. How many hours a user's account will be locked if the user uses the wrong password

13. How can Kerberos Authentication be used?

    A. Between all Microsoft operating systems only

    B. Between Windows 2000 Servers and NT 4.0 Servers only

C. Between Windows 2000 Servers only

D. Between all Windows 2000 computers

14. Your company uses software that processes large amounts of data between servers and workstations and requires a highly secure connection between the two. What can you do to make a secure connection between the two computers that won't time out?

A. Use Kerberos to implement a secure session between the machines and set your Maximum user ticket lifetime to as long as the processing takes.

B. Require users to log on as Domain Admins to start the processes.

C. Run processes after hours when users have gone home.

D. Impose a password policy for running the processes.

15. If policies between the local computer and domain conflict, which of the following will happen?

A. The local computer policy will go into effect.

B. The domain policy will go into effect.

C. The most restrictive of the two policies will go into effect.

D. The least restrictive of the two policies will go into effect.

16. What can you use to stop intruders from logging on by trying multiple passwords?

A. Account Lockout Policy

B. Kerberos Policy

C. Password Policy

D. Secedit.exe

Implement, Configure, Manage, and Troubleshoot Security by Using the Security Configuration Toolset

17. You aren't sure that your original security policies are still in place after a new Network Administrator you hired has been making some changes to the system. How can you make sure everything is still set up the way you want it?

A. Look in the Security Configuration and Analysis Snap-in to see what your settings are.

B. Run an analysis to compare the Security Template you want to have against what your system actually has and view the discrepancies.

    C. Use the Security Settings Extensions to Group Policy to analyze your system's security.

    D. Create a new Security Template and copy it to your local computer.

18. You need to schedule regular analysis of your system's security. How can this be done?

    A. Use Secedit.exe, the command line tool with the scheduler.

    B. You can't schedule an analysis.

    C. Use the Security Configuration and Analysis Snap-in.

    D. Use an audit policy to schedule an analysis.

19. You need a Security Template that will work in an environment that is running Windows 2000 Professional, Windows 98, and Windows NT Workstation; which of the following would you use?

    A. Dedicated Domain Controller

    B. Compatible

    C. High Secure

    D. Legacy

20. What can you use to view Local Security Account Policy?

    A. Security Settings Extension to Group Policy

    B. Active Directory Users and Computers

    C. Event Viewer

    D. Security Templates Snap-in

LAB QUESTION

You have recently taken a new position as a Network Administrator in a company whose former Network Administrator was very lax in developing and implementing security policies. Due to the lack of enforcement of security of any kind, users have been allowed access to files and folders that should have been protected. You also feel the system is extremely vulnerable to outside intrusion. The former Network Administrator also failed to document what, if any, Security Templates have been imposed. Detail how you would straighten things out in terms of the security of this organization. Discuss what policies you would impose and why, and what else you might do to tighten things up.

SELF TEST ANSWERS

Implement, Configure, Manage, and Troubleshoot Auditing

1. ☑ **D.** One of the events you can track using an audit policy is when users take advantage of special privileges they have been granted, such as access to certain files and folders.
   ☒ **A** is incorrect, because the Policy Change event is triggered when security options, user rights, or audit policies are used. **B** is also incorrect, because the System Event is triggered when an event occurs that affects security, or when a user restarts or shuts down a computer. **C** is incorrect, because this event is triggered when an application performs an action that is purposely being tracked by a programmer.

2. ☑ **C.** By applying auditing to files and folders that you need to keep secure, you can ensure that no one without authorized access is getting to those files. By setting an audit policy that monitors successful as well as failed attempts at accessing the data, you will be able to tell who may be attempting to breach your security policy.
   ☒ **A**, while a good idea, won't help you keep an eye on the folders; it will simply make it difficult for anyone to break past your security plan. **B** is also a good idea, but won't help you keep an eye on the folders. By creating groups, however, you can more easily manage granting and denying permissions to folders and files. Finally, **D** wouldn't be appropriate in this case, because what you are trying to do is watch who is trying to get to data that they aren't supposed to access. This may sound like spying or not trusting employees, but when important data is at risk, sometimes policies have to be set that will ensure the safety of your data.

3. ☑ **B.** In order to view failed or successful attempts to folders and files that have that sort of auditing set on them, you would view the Security log in Event Viewer. Remember that the size of your log can be limited, so bear that in mind when you determine what events to audit.
   ☒ **A** is incorrect, because Audit Policy is where the actual auditing is set, not where it is viewed. **C** is incorrect, because the Security Configuration Toolset is used for activities like setting Security Templates and analyzing and configuring system security settings. **D** is incorrect, because the Group Policy Snap-in is the console where the Audit Policy is found so that you can indeed set auditing up on files or folders.

4. ☑ **A.** Once you have used the Group Policy Snap-in to enable the Audit Object Access setting in the Audit Policy, auditing of files and folders is done using Windows Explorer by right-clicking on the folder, selecting Properties, and then setting up auditing.
   ☒ **B** is incorrect, because Security Template, part of the Security Configuration Toolset, is used to set certain security policies for your entire machine. **C** is incorrect, because the Audit

Policy needs to be set up in order to do the actual auditing, but the auditing of specific files and folders is done with Windows Explorer. **D** is incorrect, because Account Policy is used to set Password, Account Lockout, and Kerberos Policies.

Implement, Configure, Manage, and Troubleshoot Local Accounts

5. ☑ **A.** Domain Admins are the only group with rights to add computers to the domain as a whole.

☒ **B** is incorrect, because the Administrators Group is allowed access only to add new user or group accounts to a local machine. **C** is incorrect, because the only way a Domain User would be able to add a computer account to a domain would be if this user were also a member of the Domain Admins Group. **D** is incorrect, because Backup Operators are not permitted to perform this role.

6. ☑ **A.** Creating a group with the users who are members of the new team is a good way to keep things well organized rather than giving all the individual users special access to the data. Local Users and Groups is where this would be done. You also need to give that group access to the data and make sure the rest of the users don't have access to the data.

☒ **B** is partially correct, if the files reside on a server in an Active Directory domain. However, you also need to give that group rights to the data they need to access and deny access to all other users. **C** would work, but it is not a very secure policy to give a large number of users a single logon name and password to use, as this is information that could easily be passed on to those who shouldn't have access. It also makes it easier on users to only have to remember one username and password. Finally, you would also need to give that single user account access to the data and deny access to other user accounts. **D** is incorrect, as the Group Policy Snap-in is not used for creating users and groups; it is used for creating security policies, among other things.

7. ☑ **A and C.** If the user's profile is on the local machine, the user will no longer have to download it each morning. The only stipulation would be that you are probably not backing up the user's machine, so the data may be prone to being lost. Also, by having users keep data in a personal directory on the server rather than in their profile, you eliminate the downloading time.

☒ **B** is incorrect, because by moving the data to another server you do not solve the problem of the length of time it takes to download the profile. **D** is incorrect, because you may not want to be around when the user comes in and finds that you have deleted all the information the user has stored in his or her profile, including Internet Favorites and any data stored on the user's desktops, both part of the profile.

8. ☑ **A** and **D**. Both Logon as a Service and Logon Locally are considered user rights that are Logon rights.

   ☒ **C** is incorrect, because Generate Security Audits is considered a Privilege User right. **B**, Shut down the system, is also considered a Privilege.

9. ☑ **B**. Computer Management Users and Groups would be used to create new User Accounts.

   ☒ **A** is incorrect, because this is the place where in Windows NT 4.0 Server users accounts were created; this is one of the changes made in Windows 2000 Server. **C** is also incorrect, because there is no Account Manager in Windows 2000 Server, nor is there a **D**, System Information.

Implement, Configure, Manage, and Troubleshoot Account Policy

10. ☑ **B** and **D**. You are right to be concerned that your users are using their dog's, cat's, or kid's names as passwords, as this is not a secure system. By imposing a Password Policy that requires a minimum length, you ensure that, in most cases, users will at least have to add additional characters to their passwords. In addition, you can impose a policy that requires both upper- and lowercase characters to be used throughout the password, lessening the threat of an intruder figuring out a password that is easy to remember.

    ☒ **A** is incorrect, because while you may want to lock users out for creating vulnerabilities in your security plan, your organization won't run very well if no one can access data they need to do their jobs. **C** is incorrect, because if all users have to do is change their password once a week, they can easily go back and forth between their dog's and cat's names on a weekly basis.

11. ☑ **B**. A user who checks this box won't have to remember another password, and you'll save yourself work. When the supervisor is ready, you can simply uncheck the box and the user will be allowed into the system.

    ☒ **A** is incorrect, because while it would technically do the job, it only causes you more work and forces the user to remember another password. If you have added the user to any groups, you will also have to redo that if you delete and re-create the account. **C** is incorrect, because Password Policy is not used to change a user's password. **D** is also incorrect, because by default, all users are prompted to change their passwords the first time they log on. This doesn't mean they can't log on, however.

12. ☑ **B**. By setting this parameter higher, you can prevent users from going back to old passwords that they have used recently.

    ☒ **A** is incorrect, because this setting refers to Maximum Password Age. **C** is incorrect, because it refers to the complexity requirements settings. **D** is incorrect, because this actually refers to the Account Lockout Policy.

13. ☑ **D.** Kerberos Authentication can be used between all Windows 2000 computers.
    ☒ **C** is incorrect, because Kerberos can be used between Windows 2000 Servers as well as between Windows 2000 Server machines and Windows 2000 Professional machines. In the case of other Microsoft operating systems, NTLM is used, so **A** and **B** are both incorrect.

14. ☑ **A.** By using Kerberos, you require that both the client and the server machines use session tickets to authenticate with one another, providing the security you need. The Maximum user ticket lifetime is a useful setting, as you can have the ticket expire as soon as you think the process will be done, thus ending the session between the two machines.
    ☒ **B** is incorrect, because it is not necessary for users to log on in this way. **C** is incorrect, because it is not practical to have processes run when their users are not able to check that nothing has gone wrong with the processing. **D** is incorrect, because it is not necessary to impose a password policy to run the process. With Kerberos, you can provide a highly secure connection that can be terminated when necessary.

15. ☑ **B.** The domain policy will go into effect if policies between the local computer and domain conflict.
    ☒ **A** is incorrect, because the domain policy always overrides that of the local machine, so. **C** and **D** are both incorrect, because the domain policy may be more or less restrictive than that of the local machine and it will still override the local settings.

16. ☑ **A.** Using the Account Lockout Policy, you can set the number of chances users will have to enter their password correctly. The fewer the chances, the higher your security.
    ☒ **B** is incorrect, because Kerberos Policy is used to determine settings such as how long the session between the two computers will last. **C** is incorrect, because Password Policy is used for settings such as how long a user's password needs to be and how often it will expire. **D** is incorrect, because the Secedit.exe command line tool is used to run activities like Security Configuration and Analysis from the command line.

Implement, Configure, Manage, and Troubleshoot Security by Using the Security Configuration Toolset

17. ☑ **B.** By running an analysis, you can compare the settings you want to the settings you actually have and then make changes as necessary.
    ☒ **A** is incorrect, because looking in the Security Configuration and Analysis Snap-in may be deceiving, as your local policies may be being overridden by domain policies. **C** is incorrect, because the Security Setting Extensions to Group Policy are used to do the actual configuration of local security policy, not analyze the policy. **D** is incorrect, because creating a new Security

Template is a good idea and it does need to be copied to the computer, but that doesn't mean it's been applied.

18. ☑ **A.** The Secedit.exe command line tool can be used with the scheduler to run analysis so that you don't have to do them yourself. It can also be run dynamically.

☒ In light of that, **B** is clearly incorrect. **C** is incorrect, because you can use the Security Configuration and Analysis Snap-in to run an analysis of your system, but you can't schedule it from there. **D** is incorrect, because Audit policy is used for auditing access to files, folders, and Active Directory objects, not for running an analysis of your security system.

19. ☑ **B.** The Compatible Template Security Level is used to alter the default permissions for the Users Group so that legacy applications can run properly.

☒ **A** is incorrect, because the Dedicated Domain Controller template is for optimizing security for local users on domain controllers only. **C** is incorrect, because the High Secure template is used to add security to network communications. Legacy clients will not be able to communicate if this level is used. **D** is incorrect, because there is no Legacy Security Template.

20. ☑ **A.** You can use the Security Settings Extension to Group Policy to view Local Account Policies.

☒ **B** is incorrect, because this is where you would add a computer account to a domain. **C** is incorrect, because you would use the Security Log in the Event Viewer to look at events that you have audited. **D** is incorrect, because the Security Templates Snap-in is used to configure templates that determine the security configuration of your system.

LAB ANSWER

It is always difficult to take over a position that someone else has been doing, especially if there is no documentation to lead you in trying to figure out the current state of things. A good start in this case would be to use the Security Configuration and Analysis Snap-in. By selecting even the most basic template, such as Basicsv, you will be able to detect glaring security holes in your system. You will also be able to make some decisions about where you want to go next with your security plan. You may wish to continue using the Basicsv template or create a template of your own that addresses your specific needs. Once you have started creating your security plan you would also be wise to start putting the individual users into groups so that security on files and folders and objects can be more easily managed. By managing users in groups that you have created rather than as individual users you can more easily assign rights to the users as necessary. You will also want to apply protective permissions to files and folders so that data that should be kept securely is no longer vulnerable.

Once you have the users in groups and have assigned rights to files, folders and objects, you may want to set up an auditing policy. After so much freedom, some users may still be testing what they have access to and establishing auditing on protected data would assist you in detecting that potential breach.

You could also impose a Password Policy that would make your system more secure by having users change their passwords often, or requiring passwords of a certain length. You may wish to use a Password Policy in tandem with an Account Lockout Policy to keep your system from being vulnerable to outside intrusion.

All of these steps really add up to having a good security plan in mind so that you are not taken by surprise. Plugging up as many of the security holes as possible is part of your job as a Network Administrator, and with the aid of the Windows 2000 Security system, you can successfully accomplish that.

MICROSOFT CERTIFIED SYSTEMS ENGINEER

14

Terminal Services and Internet Information Services

Not so long ago, "thin was in." It was speculated that *thin clients*—computers or devices that rely on "fat" servers to get the job done—would overtake the personal computer-centric world. Consequently, a great deal of energy was channeled toward producing thin clients. In subsequent years, personal computer prices plummeted dramatically, and the excitement surrounding the thin-client movement died down. However, many companies, including Microsoft, continued to work on their thin-client initiatives.

By no means is Microsoft trying to replace the personal computer with its thin-client initiatives. It is trying to supplement the personal computer by incorporating the power of thin clients into the PC with Terminal Services and Internet Information Services. Terminal Services and Internet Information Services allow clients to do all their application processing on a server computer, greatly reducing the resources needed by the client computers. This ability allows the client to do processing with software that is installed on the server but not on the client. As a consequence, the lifetime and usefulness of client computers are greatly extended.

exam
ⓦatch

A client does not have to be a "thin" terminal to use Terminal Services. Often a "fat" PC acts as the client accessing Terminal Services and Internet Information Services.

Terminal Services were available in a special edition of Windows NT 4.0, but Microsoft has improved it a great deal and made it an integral part of the entire Windows 2000 Server family. It comes with and can be installed on any Windows 2000 Server using one of the following modes:

- Application server mode
- Remote administration mode

Application server mode was the only mode in which Terminal Services was implemented in Windows NT 4.0. It allows clients to simultaneously access Windows-based applications that run on the server. When installed on the server, they can be available to all clients who connect to the server and can run with all the resources that the server has to offer. Generally speaking, the applications that run on a terminal server must be modified to some extent in order to function optimally when Terminal Services is in application server mode.

Being able to use Terminal Services in remote administration mode is new to Windows 2000. It should prove a very powerful and pervasive tool to administer the Windows 2000 Server family. Remote administration mode provides administrators with secure remote graphical administration of the Windows 2000 Server family.

With Terminal Services in remote administration mode, an administrator can connect, monitor, and troubleshoot servers from almost any location.

Internet Information Server (IIS) provides interfaces that can understand HTTP and FTP to interact with clients around the world. Whereas Terminal Services brings the Windows 2000 interface to client computers, IIS typically delivers an HTML interface to client computers. Once again, this ability allows client computers to offload resource-intensive processing to a server and allows clients to do processing with software that exists on the server.

CERTIFICATION OBJECTIVE 14.01

Understanding Terminal Services

Terminal Services provides the Windows 2000 graphical user interface (GUI) to any device that can run a Terminal Services client locally. Microsoft produces client software for the following operating systems:

- Windows CE-based terminals and handheld professional devices
- 16-bit Windows-based PCs running Windows for Workgroups 3.11 with MS TCP/IP-32
- 32-bit Windows-based PCs running Windows 95, Windows 98, Windows NT 3.51, Windows NT 4.0, or Windows 2000 Professional

Terminal Services is designed to allow a client to do all its application processing on a server, giving existing computers additional functionality provided by terminal servers. As long as the client is able to use Terminal Services, it can do almost anything that the server can do. For instance, a Windows for Workgroups 3.11 client connecting to Terminal Services has access to the Windows 2000 look and feel and all the 32-bit software that would not run on the older operating system. In this way, the older client can run the modern software without having to upgrade the client's hardware. The potential longevity of the client is greatly extended with this approach.

Terminal Services is able to support such a large variety of clients because it is built on two industry-standard protocols:

- Transmission Control Protocol/Internet Protocol (TCP/IP)
- Remote Desktop Protocol (RDP)

Terminal Services uses *Transmission Control Protocol/Internet Protocol (TCP/IP)* as the transport protocol between the client and the server for Terminal Services. This protocol allows sessions to exist over a local area network (LAN), a wide area network (WAN), the Internet, or any other method in which TCP/IP is used. Microsoft provides only support for TCP/IP communication, which allows Terminal Services connections to be implemented through any sort of network that supports TCP/IP, including virtual private networks (VPN) and wireless networks.

Remote Desktop Protocol (RDP) is the application protocol between the client and the server. It informs the server of the client's keystrokes and mouse movement and returns to the client the Windows 2000 graphical display from the server. Microsoft RDP 5.0 is based on the International Telecommunications Union (ITU) T.120 protocol, a multichannel, standard protocol that provides various levels of compression so that it can adapt to different connection speeds and encryption levels from 40 bits to 128 bits. TCP/IP is the courier that carries the messages, and RDP is the language in which the messages are written. Both are needed to use Microsoft's implementation of Terminal Services.

exam
ⓦatch

In addition to the graphical interface, it is also possible to return audio to the client.

Now that you have an understanding of Terminal Services, the following scenarios and solution grid gives scenarios and solutions you should know.

SCENARIO & SOLUTION

In what modes can Terminal Services be run on a Windows 2000 server?	Terminal Services can be run in either application server mode or remote administration mode.
What network protocol is needed for the Microsoft client to use Terminal Services?	TCP/IP is required to run Terminal Services with the Microsoft client. Third-party vendors do sell add-ons that allow other network protocols to be used.
What information is transmitted to the Terminal Services server from the client?	The keystrokes and mouse movements are sent from the client to the server, and the Windows 2000 GUI is returned from the server to the client.

EXERCISE 14-1

Connecting to a Terminal Server with Terminal Services Client

1. From the Start menu, go to Programs | Terminal Services Client | Terminal Services Client.

2. Choose the server to which you want to connect and the screen resolution. You can either type in the name of the terminal server and then click Connect, or you can double-click a server name from the available servers list.

3. Provide your login and password in the Terminal Services window.

4. From the Start menu in the Terminal Services client window, go to Log Off. It is important that you log off your Terminal Services session; *clicking the control box on the Terminal Services window will not close your session.*

5. Close Terminal Services Client.

Remote Administration Versus Application Server

When Terminal Services is configured to run in remote administration mode, it is designed to carry a very small footprint. It installs only the needed components and uses them only when they are required, leaving out components and scripts that optimize Windows applications for the Terminal Services environment. If no one is connected to Terminal Services, Terminal Services consumes a minuscule amount of resources on the server. Because running Terminal Services in remote administration mode does not consume resources from critical servers, there is no real penalty to using Terminal Services to administer all the Windows 2000 servers. Microsoft allows the use of remote administration mode with Terminal Services with no additional licenses or fees, but you are limited to two concurrent remote administration sessions.

on the
Job

A terminal server in application mode should not be run on a domain controller or another dedicated server. However, you should consider running Terminal Services in remote administration mode for each of your Windows 2000 servers, including domain controllers.

Application server mode consumes a great deal more overhead, in both installation and in operation. This mode allows Terminal Services to run applications remotely for many users, letting the Terminal Services server do all the application processing. Application server mode has a much a larger footprint and is intended to be run as an application server. Most applications, including Microsoft Word and Excel, require special installation scripts to perform well in Terminal Services. These scripts are provided and should be installed when Terminal Services is installed in application server mode but not in remote administration mode.

exam
ⓦatch

A Windows 2000 server must be in either application server or remote administration mode; it cannot be in both.

Remote Control Versus Remote Access

Remote access is the common way of using Terminal Services. An individual uses a Terminal Services client to connect to a server and conduct application processing on it instead of on his or her local device. All the client keystrokes and mouse movements within the Terminal Services client are sent to the server, and the graphical Windows 2000 display that is a result of the client actions on the server is passed back to the client.

Remote control is a way to monitor an existing session. With remote control, a user can connect to an existing session, see everything that the client sees, and send keystrokes and mouse movements to that session. In order to initiate remote control of a session, a user with full control must log in to the server using the Terminal Services client and then use the Terminal Services Manager to take remote control of a session. It is important to understand that you cannot use the Terminal Services Manager outside a Terminal Services client session to join a session; in order to join a session, you must be connected to the Terminal Services server using a Terminal Services client. When you are about to join the session, the user is notified that his or her session is about to be remotely controlled when you join, unless you disable the warning in the RDP-TCP properties dialog box, as shown Figure 14-1.

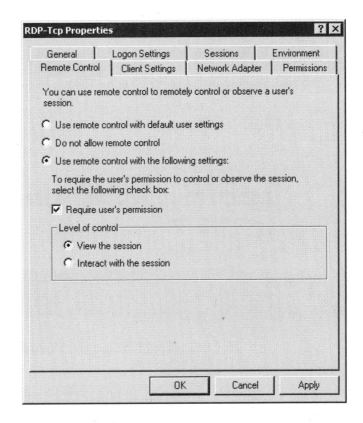

FIGURE 14-1

Setting whether
you can join a
user session with
or without
permission

CERTIFICATION OBJECTIVE 14.02

Installing and Configuring Terminal Services

As mentioned earlier, Terminal Services must be installed in either application server
mode or remote administration mode. It cannot be in both at one time. Microsoft
has decided to make Terminal Services a core part of Windows 2000, so can you
install Terminal Services using the Windows Components wizard in the
Add/Remove Programs application in the Control Panel. If you are installing
Terminal Services in application server mode, you need to install Terminal Services
Licensing if it is not already installed (we'll do this in Exercise 14-3).

Installing in Remote Administration Mode

1. Log the computer in to the Windows 2000 Server as an administrator.

2. From the Start menu, go to Settings | Control Panel and choose Add/Remove Programs.

3. Choose Add/Remove Windows Components, and the Windows Components wizard appears, as shown:

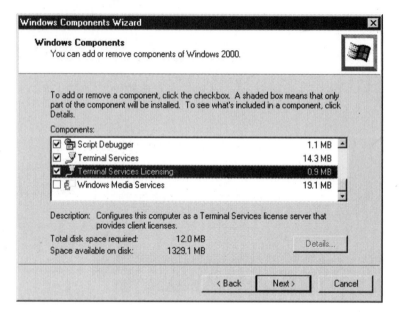

4. Select Terminal Services and click Next.

5. Choose to run Terminal Services in remote administration mode, as shown in the next illustration, and then click Next.

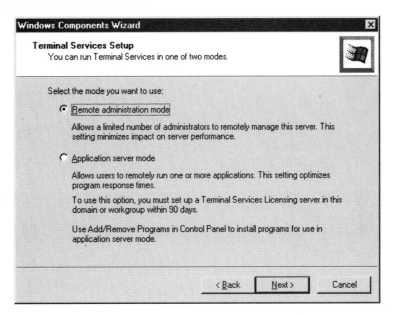

6. Click Finish, and then restart the computer when prompted.

CertCam 14-3

EXERCISE 14-3

Installing in Application Server Mode

1. Log the computer in to the Windows 2000 Server as an administrator.

2. From the Start menu, go to Settings | Control Panel and choose Add/Remove Programs.

3. Choose Add/Remove Windows Components, and the Windows Components wizard appears.

4. Select Terminal Services and Terminal Services Licensing.

5. Choose to run Terminal Services in application server mode, and then click Next.

6. The next screen prompts you to select default permissions for application compatibility. You can choose "Permissions compatible with Windows 2000 Users" to run in the most secure mode or "Permissions compatible with Terminal Server 4.0 Users" to run in a less secure mode that is compatible with Terminal Server 4.0.

7. Next you see a list of applications that are already installed and might not work correctly when Terminal Services is enabled. You will have to reinstall them later to ensure that they function properly.

8. Next you are asked to provide information to set up the computer as a license server. You need to specify the role of the license server (whether the license server is available to your entire enterprise or just your domain or workgroup) and the file path for the license server database. Click Next to begin the installation.

9. Click Finish, and then restart the computer when prompted.

After you have completed your installation of Terminal Services, a number of applications are available to you inside the Administrative Tools menu:

- Terminal Services Licensing
- Terminal Services Manager

- Terminal Services Client Creator

- Terminal Services Configuration

With *Terminal Services Configuration,* you can change most of the choices that you made during installation. For instance, you can change Terminal Services from application server mode to remote access mode and permission compatibility mode. In addition, you can configure other server settings as follows:

- Delete temporary folders on exit

- Use temporary folders per session

- Use Internet connector licensing

- Use Active Directory

You can also create, modify, and delete connection properties such as encryption level, remote access, and client settings.

Terminal Services Manager, shown in Figure 14-2, allows you to monitor, kill, and join sessions. Terminal Services Licensing communicates with a licensing server that holds all the Terminal Services Client Access Licenses (TS CAL).

FIGURE 14-2

Terminal Services Manager allows you to monitor and manage all the available terminal servers

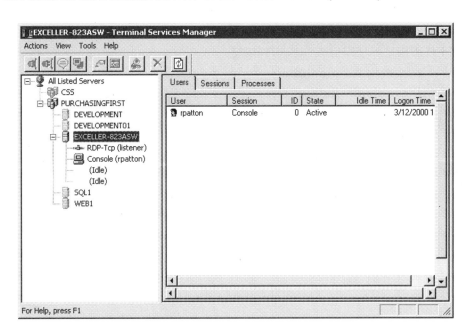

Terminal Services Client Creator, shown in Figure 14-3, allows you to create a floppy disk installation program for:

- Sixteen-bit Windows
- Thirty-two-bit Windows on x86

In addition to being able to install the Terminal Services client from floppy disk, you can also install Terminal Services over the network. The network installations are stored in:

```
\\%systemroot%\\system32\clients\tsclient\net\
```

You need to establish a unique home directory for each user who will connect to the server using Terminal Services. If no home directory is specified for a user, the profile directory will be \Documents and Settings\Username.

All Microsoft Terminal Services clients must be running a 32-bit version of TCP-IP and have at least a 33MHz 386 processor, 4MB or RAM, and 500KB of disk space. If you want to use the bitmap caching feature, you need more available disk space. Like most applications, the Terminal Services Client runs better if the client computer has more RAM.

Terminal Services Licensing

In the past, licensing for Terminal Services was not easily understood, and this is still fairly true with Terminal Services in Windows 2000. You do not need licenses for Terminal Services when it is in remote administration mode. Remote administration

FIGURE 14-3

Terminal Services
Client Creator
allows you to
create installation
floppy disks

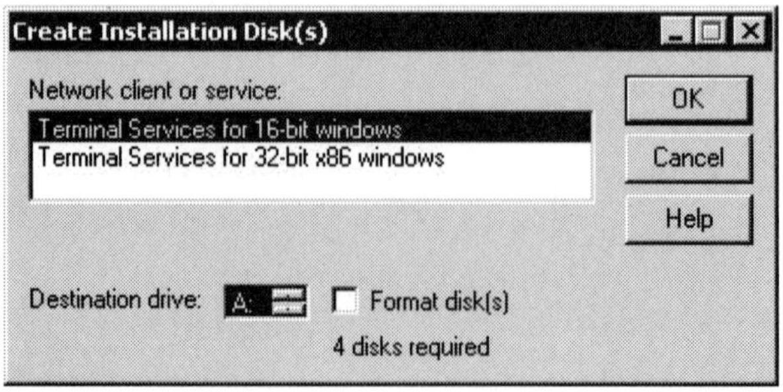

Create Installation Disk(s)

Network client or service:

Terminal Services for 16-bit windows
Terminal Services for 32-bit x86 windows

OK
Cancel
Help

Destination drive: A: ☐ Format disk(s)

4 disks required

mode can—and most of the time should—be used for every Windows 2000 server that is not in application server mode. Remote administration mode is free and, as detailed before, tremendously effective.

Licensing in application server mode is somewhat confusing because it is separate from licensing for the clients for a Windows 2000 server. Licenses, which are needed when a server is in application server mode, are available in several types:

- Terminal Services Client Access License (TS CAL) is a purchased license for a device that does not have Windows 2000 Professional installed. When a client tries to connect to a terminal server for the first time, a license is issued to the client device.

- The licensing server issues temporary TS CALs to client devices that are trying to connect when there are no licenses available. A client is able to receive a Temporary Terminal Services Client Access License only once, and the license is valid for 90 days.

- Each copy of Windows 2000 Professional has a valid license to be a Terminal Services client.

- The Internet Connector License permits up to 200 anonymous Internet concurrent user connections. This license can be useful for demonstrating Windows-based applications to groups of Internet users for short periods; it cannot be used by employees of your company.

Licenses are stored locally on a licensing server. A single server can contain the licenses for many servers running Terminal Services in application server mode.

Microsoft Clearinghouse is the organization that can activate a licensing server and issue terminal server client licenses to licensing servers. Microsoft Clearinghouse can be accessed using the Terminal Services Licensing wizard, directly through TCP-IP. If that cannot be done, the clearinghouse can also be accessed through a Web page, by telephone, or by fax machine.

Remotely Administering Servers Using Terminal Services

You can perform almost any administrative task on a server using Terminal Services: You can defragment the hard drives, edit the registry, add COM+ components, administer print sharing, and even conduct tasks that require a reboot. However, you should not reboot an important server unless you can gain physical access to the server in case a problem occurs during rebooting, such as a floppy disk left in the disk drive.

One of the nice features of Terminal Services is that you can transfer information using the Windows Clipboard. You can seamlessly copy information from a document on the client and paste it in the server, or vice versa. This feature is called *clipboard redirection*. However, clipboard redirection does not work with files. If you want to exchange files between the client and server, you must use either a shared network device or the file-copy utilities available in the Windows 2000 Server Resource Kit.

Configuring Terminal Services for Application Sharing

Terminal Services requires a Pentium or higher processor and a minimum of 128MB RAM. Additional RAM must be added to support each concurrent user on the server. The *Windows 2000 Terminal Services Capacity and Scaling* white paper suggests an additional 3.4MB RAM for each light user and up to 9MB RAM for each power user. Other sources recommend greater amounts of RAM per user type, and for the most part, having more RAM on a server is not a bad thing.

Configuring Applications for Use with Terminal Services

After Terminal Services is installed in application mode on the server, you need to install the applications that will be used by the clients via Terminal Services. The best way to handle application installation is through the Add/Remove Programs application in the Control Panel. If applications are installed this way, Terminal Services will be able to replicate the needed registry entries or configuration files for each user per program. The Add/Remove Programs application in the Control Panel is the recommended way to install the applications, but you could achieve a similar result by installing the applications with the CHANGE USER /INSTALL command from the command line. You put the server in install mode through the command line by typing **change user /install**, perform your installation, and exit install mode from the command line by typing **change user /execute**.

Most applications need to have additional application compatibility scripts to be run after their installation is complete. It is important to run the scripts after the programs are installed but before any client session is initiated. The scripts alter the way that the applications function so that they better coexist under Terminal Services.

on the Job *Some applications do not complete installation until after the Terminal Services server is rebooted. Once the server is rebooted, log on with the same administrator logon with which you performed the installation and let the installation finish.*

In order for Terminal Services to replicate the necessary registry entries or .INI files for each user, the user must install the application in install mode. This installation is accomplished using Add/Remove Programs in the Control Panel.

Terminal Services can automatically connect local client printers at logon. When the client logs on to the server, the local printer is detected and the appropriate printer driver is installed on the terminal server. If multiple printers are connected, you can also default all print jobs to the main client printer. You can also specify an initial application through Terminal Services Configuration, but this application will be the only application available to all users.

on the Job *If you decide to disable Terminal Services while in application server mode, the applications that you installed and configured to run on a terminal server will not run when you enable Terminal Services again. You will have to configure or install the applications again in order for them to function correctly.*

Now that you have a better idea of configuring applications for use within Terminal Services, here are some possible scenarios and solutions.

SCENARIO & SOLUTION

What is the best way to install applications on a terminal server in application server mode?	Use the Add/Remove Programs application in Control Panel.
How can I install an application without using Add/Remove Programs?	Run the CHANGE USER /INSTALL command from the command line.
What should I do after I install an application on a terminal server in application server mode?	Run any applicable application compatibility scripts for the program that you have installed.

CERTIFICATION OBJECTIVE 14.03

Monitoring and Troubleshooting Terminal Services

Through Terminal Services Manager, an administrator can monitor all the user sessions, their processes, and all processes on the machine. With Terminal Services Manager, you can see all the processes running on a server or look at just the process for a single session. In addition to seeing the user sessions and processes, an administrator can disconnect user sessions and kill processes, providing a powerful mechanism to find and terminate a user who is consuming too many resources.

If a user is having problems, an administrator can join a session with Terminal Services Manager to help the user. In this mode, the administrator sees what the user sees and is able to send his or her own keystrokes and mouse movements to the session. In addition, administrators can send messages to users in sessions using the Terminal Services Manager.

on the Job *You can monitor the overall performance of a Terminal Server using the Performance application (formerly Performance Monitor), just as you would any other server. In addition to the traditional counters available for such things as Disk, CPU, memory and network usage, there are also special Terminal Services counters available.*

In the event that a terminal server needs to be rebooted remotely, it is best to do it via the TSSHUTDN command. This is a special command built to provide the most graceful shutdown possible. You could simply tell a server to reboot with the Start menu REBOOT command, but some complexities in the multisession environment might not be accounted for with the traditional REBOOT command.

FROM THE CLASSROOM

Shutting Down the Terminal Services Server

Shutting down a Terminal Services Server through Terminal Services can be done from the Start menu, just as you would do with an ordinary workstation, but it shouldn't be handled this way. The multisession Terminal Services environment is a little more complicated than the

FROM THE CLASSROOM

running applications from your local console. It would not be good practice to have it appear to users that the terminal server simply disappears from time to time.

The preferred way to shut down a Terminal Services server in a controlled manner is with the TSSHUTDN command from the command line. The easy way to remember this command is TS (Terminal Services) SHUT DN (down). Using TSSHUTDN notifies users who are connected through Terminal Services that the machine will be shut down. With this command come a few switches:

> WAIT_TIME
> /SERVER:*servername*
> /REBOOT
> /POWERDOWN
> /DELAY
> /V

When you use TSSHUTDN, all connected users, whether they are at the console or in a Terminal Services session, receive a message telling them that the Terminal Services server will shut down in X seconds. The default is 60 seconds, but that number can be tweaked with the WAIT_TIME parameter. This time period allows users to save their work and, if necessary, you to cancel the shutdown. The /DELAY parameter is the amount of time between the

point when all users are logged off and the shutdown starts.

The most important switch to remember is the /REBOOT switch. Without it, the computer goes down but does not come back up. If you do not have physical access to the Terminal Services Server, you are unable to bring the server back up for users until you can reboot it. The /POWERDOWN switch takes the Terminal Services server all the way down to the powered-off state; without using this switch, you arrive at the screen telling you it is safe to power off the computer. If you use /POWERDOWN with /REBOOT, the computer reboots instead of ending up in a powered-down state.

The /SERVER switch allows you to run TSSHUTDN on another machine, but TSSHUTDN is installed only on machines that have installed Terminal Services Server; you will not find it installed on a machine running Windows 2000 Professional. You can use Terminal Services Client to run a session on a machine with Terminal Services Server and, from the command line of that session, use TSSHUTDN.

Note that only administrators can run TSSHUTDN.

—Robert Patton, MCDBA, MCSD, MCSE+I, MCP+I

An administrator is not limited to the functionality of Terminal Services Manager to inspect and correct problems; an administrator can use any of the ordinary tools, even in application server mode.

on the
Job

Even if an administrator is doing only remote administration work on a terminal server in application mode, he or she must have a TS CAL to connect to the terminal server. If it is a one-time-only operation, a temporary TS CAL is issued, but if the administrator is trying to administer a server for a long period of time from a machine that is not running a licensed version of Windows 2000 Professional, a TS CAL must be obtained.

CertCam 14-3

EXERCISE 14-4

Remote Control of a Terminal Services Session

1. From the Start menu, go to Programs | Terminal Services Client | Terminal Services Client.

2. Choose the server that you want to connect to, as shown in the next illustration, and choose screen resolution. You can type the name of the terminal server and then click Connect, or you can double-click a server name from the available servers list.

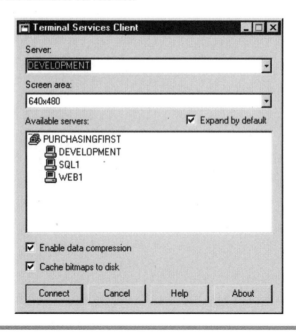

3. Provide your login and password in the Terminal Services window.

4. From the Start menu, go to Programs | Settings | Control Panel | Administrative Tools | Terminal Services Manager.

5. In Terminal Services Manager, as shown in the next illustration, right-click on the session on the server that you want to join.

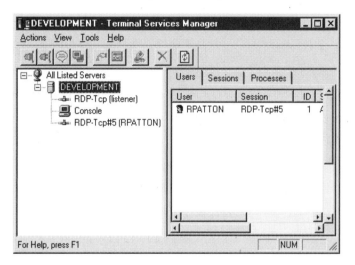

6. In the Remote Control dialog box, choose the keyboard combination that will allow you to end the joined session.

7. If you configured Terminal Services to allow the user to deny remote control, wait until they either accept or deny your attempt. Otherwise join the session.

8. Use your keyboard connection to exit the session.

9. Choose the Remote Control Menu option.

10. From the Start menu in the Terminal Services client window, go to Log Off. It is important that you log off your Terminal Services session; *clicking the control box on the Terminal Services window will not close your session.*

11. Close Terminal Services Client.

A Windows 2000 server in application server mode does not preclude an administrator from doing anything that he or she can do in remote access mode.

Establishing Policies for Terminal Services

You can determine feature selection or deselection at run time based on settings about the user in the registry. In Windows 2000 Server, you can use the Group Policy MMC Snap-in to configure which features are available for which users; these policies can also be configured for their terminal server sessions only .

It is much easier to maintain user preferences and privileges through groups, so create Terminal Services-specific user groups. Likewise, using Terminal Services-specific profiles allows you to prevent waste of server resources by resource-intensive screen savers and background images. By assigning a specific profile to users, as shown in the Terminal Services Profile tab in Figure 14-4, you can conserve the resources of the server.

In order to set up a Terminal Services user account, the user must have an account either on the server or in a domain on the network. Terminal Services user accounts can be set up for a specific server using Local Users and Groups or for the domain using Active Directory Users and Computers. The Terminal Services user accounts contain additional information about the user, including where to retrieve desktop settings in varying circumstances.

Terminal Services Environment Versus Local Environment Settings

The Terminal Services environment can be very different from the local environment settings that a user sets up. You can configure new network and printer connections for a user to access during his or her session. You can restrict the applications that a user can access from the Start menu, and you can limit the user to a single application.

FIGURE 14-4

Establishing the
Terminal Services
profile for a user

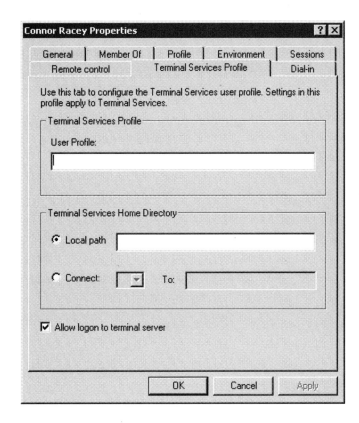

The Environment tab, shown in Figure 14-5, contains settings for creating the environment of a user connected to Terminal Services. If you specify a starting application, it automatically opens every time the user connects to a terminal server, and it is the only application that the user will be able to access through Terminal Services. In addition, if the user closes the application, the connection to the terminal server closes.

FIGURE 14-5

Establishing the
environment for
a Terminal
Services user

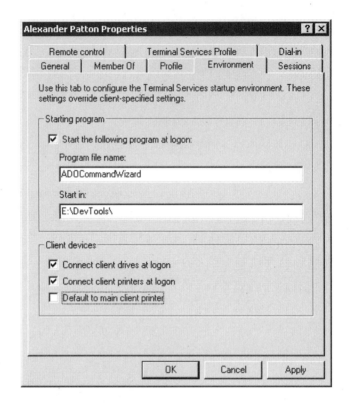

CERTIFICATION OBJECTIVE 14.04

Understanding Internet Information Services 5.0

Internet Information Services has been updated for Windows 2000 to perform
better, be easier to manage, and be more reliable. IIS 5.0 interacts with clients using
the HTTP and FTP protocols. One of the most important improvements in
Windows 2000 Server is that multiple Web sites and FTP sites can be hosted on one
PC without multihoming. Now, by choosing a different IP address, a different port,
or a different host header name for a Web site, you can make a second Web site run
on the same computer. In addition to making IIS easier to use, Microsoft emphasizes
making it easier to install. In Windows 2000, IIS can be installed using the Windows
Components wizard. There is no need to get the Option Pack in order to add IIS to
a Windows 2000 Server.

EXERCISE 14-5

Installing Internet Information Services

1. Log the computer in to the Windows 2000 Server as an administrator.

2. From the Start menu, go to Settings | Control Panel and choose Add/Remove Programs.

3. Choose the Add/Remove Windows Components, and the Windows Components wizard appears.

4. Select Internet Information Services, as shown in the following illustration, and then click Next.

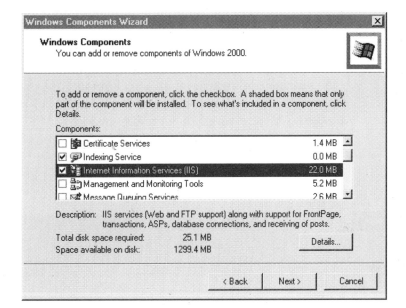

5. The installation process begins copying files.

6. Click Finish.

After you complete your IIS installation, a number of applications are available to you inside the Administrative Tools menu:

- Server Extensions Administrator
- Internet Information Services MMC Snap-in

exam
ⓦatch

The Internet Information Services MMC Snap-in was formerly known as the Internet Services Manager.

Monitoring, Configuring, and Troubleshooting Access to Web Sites

In addition to Server Extensions Administrator and the Internet Information Services MMC Snap-in, "good old" Performance Monitor (called simply *Performance* under Windows 2000) is still an excellent tool to monitor a Web site. With Performance, you can closely monitor the CPU, RAM, and disk usage of the server. In addition, Performance has many specific counters, as shown in Figure 14-6, for Web Service, Internet Information Service Global, and Active Server Pages that will allow you to tap into almost any metric you need to monitor relating to your server's performance.

Analyzing the data provided by the Performance application, you should be able to tune your existing Web site thoroughly with the power of the Server Extensions Administrator and Internet Information Services MMC Snap-in. A new option to audit Web server performance has been added to IIS 5. This option is called *process accounting.* You can turn it on for a Web site with the IIS MMC Snap-in by clicking the extended log file format on the Extended Properties tab. With process accounting, you can record the information about how a Web site uses its CPU.

FIGURE 14-6

Choosing counters in the performance application to monitor a Web server

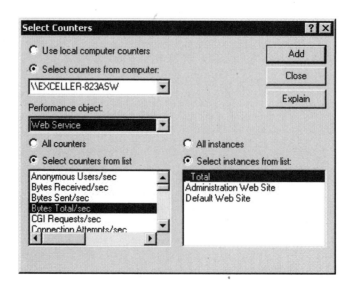

This information is very useful when you are trying to isolate a single process that might need to be optimized.

Windows 2000 is a much more scriptable operating system than its predecessor; in its \Scripts directory, Microsoft provides scripts for many common management tasks for IIS. In a push for greater reliability in Windows 2000, Microsoft has built *reliable restart* into its services, allowing the automatic restart of its services in case of failure once, twice, or an unlimited number of times. In addition to being able to restart the service in event of a failure, you can also configure the system to run a file or reboot the server. The services associated with IIS can be set to automatically restart in event of failure in order to provide the greatest possible uptime.

Accessing Files and Folders via Web Services

Windows 2000 implements a *distributed file system (Dfs)* that allows files residing in multiple network locations to reside in a single namespace. From an outside view, it is not even apparent that the files are residing in different computers, because they appear to be in one place on the network. IIS can use the Dfs available in Windows 2000.

Administration Tools

IIS can be administered using the IIS MMC Snap-in or an HTML interface. The HTML interface offers much of the functionality of the Snap-in, but not everything. The HTML interface was intended for remote use. However, with Terminal Services, you can use IIS MMC Snap-in effectively from a remote location.

The Server Extensions Manager allows you to configure a number of parameters, including the number of expected hits for your Web site, how mail should be sent, cache sizes, and security settings for authoring. The Server Extensions Manager is available by itself in the Administrative Tools program group, but it is also incorporated within the IIS MMC Snap-in.

The World Wide Web Publishing Service

The World Wide Web Publishing Service is perhaps the most important component of IIS because most people use IIS as a Web server. The World Wide Web Publishing Service is a service that is automatically installed with IIS 5.0 that provides Web administration and connectivity through the IIS Snap-in. Like other services in Windows 2000, the World Wide Web Publishing Service in IIS 5.0 can be configured to automatically restart the service in case of failure, as shown in Figure 14-7.

The World
Wide Web
Publishing Service
Recovery tab

FTP Services

HTTP is synonymous with the Internet because of its use in Web browsers, but FTP is still an important and widely used protocol to transfer files efficiently on the Internet. IIS continues to include an FTP service, which it has improved. In IIS in Windows 2000, Microsoft has included the FTP Restart protocol. To clients that support it, this protocol provides the ability to continue, from the point of interruption, a download that has been interrupted.

TCP/IP is the protocol that FTP uses to transfer the information, whereas FTP is the protocol used on top of TCP/IP to execute and understand FTP. All the FTP servers can be administered from the Internet Service Manager.

Administrative Tasks

Many administrative tasks are needed to keep a Web server and its sites running optimally. You must ensure that each file and directory has the appropriate permissions. You need to set the proper cache sizes. The routine administrative tasks can be performed with the IIS MMC Snap-in and the Windows 2000 Performance Monitor. Between the two, an administrator can tune a Web server for optimal performance.

Server-Level Administration

At the server level, you can set a great number of parameters for IIS and the Server Extensions that will apply to each site running on the server, such as:

- How files are mapped via MIME
- The server extensions (document or image and including cache sizes)
- Bandwidth throttling
- Master properties for the Web site

Bandwidth throttling is provided with IIS 5. This feature allows you to set a limit on how much of the network bandwidth the IIS can consume at a given time. The Master properties allow you to set the defaults for new and existing FTP and Web sites. If an existing value is different from a value you set in the master, you are asked whether you want that value to overwrite the existing value. To edit server properties, right-click on the server (the root) in the IIS MMC Snap-in and choose Properties.

Site-Level Administration   To edit a site, right-click on the site in the IIS MMC Snap-in and choose Properties. At the site level, you can configure a great many things, including:

- The IP addresses, ports, and HTTP headers
- The type of logging that is done for the site
- Custom error messages
- Directory security
- ISAPI filters and more
- Directory-level administration—at the directory, you can set many permissions, including:
    - Access to the directory (*Read* and *Write*)

- Whether directory browsing is permitted
- Execute permissions (*None, Scripts only, Scripts and Executables*)
- To edit directory properties, right-click on the directory in the IIS MMC Snap-in and choose Properties; anything you apply to a directory can also apply to all the subdirectories of the directory

- File-Level Administration—set the access for the file (anonymous, secured, etc.) if it requires SSL; you can also set whether the file is marked for read, write, or logged; set the expiration of the file; or set any of the custom errors
- Access to the directory (*Read* and *Write*)
- Whether there is anonymous access
- Authenticated access (*Basic, Digested, Integrated*)

In order to have two sites on a single server, one of these three properties must be different from other sites on the server: IP addresses, ports, and host name headers. Two sites can share two of the properties, but as long as one is different, it responds to the outside world. Custom error messages allow you to set Web pages to respond to common predefined IIS errors. For instance, you could replace *Error 404* with a message that gives the user the impression that the error is handled better and is more consistent with the look and feel of your site.

To edit file properties, right-click the filename in the IIS MMC Snap-in and choose Properties.

In order to aid the administration of security management in IIS, Microsoft has included some new wizards:

- Permission wizard
- Web Server Certificate wizard

The Permission wizard aids an administrator in creating and maintaining the *needed* permissions to the files and directories that should be restricted to some degree. The Web Server Certificate wizard helps with the installation, removal, and administration of certificates. This wizard makes it much easier to set up Web sites that use Secured Socket Layer (SSL) to handle the transfer of secure information. Both are available from the IIS MMC Snap-in .

Now that you have a better idea of how to conduct IIS administration, here are some possible scenarios and their solutions.

SCENARIO & SOLUTION

If you want a change to apply to all Web sites on a server, where should you set the property?	You should change the Master values for the Web service and, when prompted to overwrite existing value, respond "Yes."
If I set all files to be read only at the site level, can I override this setting at the file level?	Yes, you can overwrite it on a file-by-file basis, but all new files will follow whatever you set at the site level. If you want them to be different, you must edit either the file or the directory properties in which the file resides.
How do I set custom error messages in IIS 5?	On the Custom Error tab of the site, you can attach a specific file to respond in event of an error.

Preventing Unauthorized Access to a Web Site   A great deal of the HTML generated by IIS is dynamic and generated by Active Server Page (ASP) scripts. A common method for an intruder to gain unauthorized access to a Web site is by uploading scripts or an executable to the server and then having IIS execute them, giving the intruder the security privileges of the Internet Information Server. You can prevent that scenario by denying execute permissions to scripts and executables in directories where files are placed and denying write privileges to directories in which execute permissions to scripts and executables are allowed.

CERTIFICATION SUMMARY

The Microsoft Windows 2000 Server family has made great strides in unleashing the power of remote computing using client software. With either a Terminal Services client or a Web browser, clients with limited resources can do anything that powerful servers in remote locations can do.

Terminal Services for Windows 2000 greatly simplifies remote administration of back-office servers; because it is free and an integral component of Windows 2000, Terminal Services should become quite pervasive. Running Terminal Services for Windows 2000 as an application server has the potential to extend the capabilities of existing hardware, bringing the Windows 2000 interface to clients running other operating systems.

Internet Information Services provides powerful tools to provide and administer information over the Internet, building on the familiar tools of Windows 2000. Likewise, Windows 2000 has greatly simplified the management of IIS by consolidating it into a single MMC Snap-in.

TWO-MINUTE DRILL

Understanding Terminal Services

- Terminal Services can be configured to run in either remote administration mode or in application server mode.

- Terminal Services Configuration allows you to change Terminal Services to run in remote administration mode or in application server mode.

- To use Terminal Services with the Microsoft Client software, you need to use TCP/IP and RDP.

- Third-party companies offer add-ons to Terminal Services that allow other network protocols and client operating systems.

Installing and Configuring Terminal Services

- Terminal Services client software can be installed over the network or with floppy disks.

- Terminal Services Client Creator creates installation disks for 16- and 32-bit Microsoft network clients.

- Microsoft recommends 128MB of RAM for Terminal Services in application server mode, plus 3.4MB of RAM for each data entry worker, 7.5MB for each knowledge worker, and 9MB of RAM for each structured task worker.

- Add applications using the Add/Remove Programs application in the Control Panel in order to ensure that the user can correctly access his or her configuration settings in the Registry and in .INI files.

- You can also add applications from the command line by running the CHANGE USER /INSTALL command.

Monitoring and Troubleshooting Terminal Services

- Terminal Services Manager is the primary tool to monitor and administer client sessions.

- Terminal Services Configuration allows you to create, modify, and delete sessions and to change high-level Terminal Services parameters.

- Through Terminal Services, you can use any standard network administration tool that is on the Terminal Services server, including Task Manager and the Performance application.

- You can join sessions to help users, sharing keystrokes, mouse movements, and the Windows 2000 GUI.

Understanding Internet Information Services

- The two primary communication protocols in Internet Information Services are HTTP and FTP.

- Windows 2000 Server allows multiple Web and FTP sites to be hosted on a single machine by giving the machine a unique IP, port, or host name header.

- Internet Information Services can be administered using the IIS MMC Snap-in.

- Any property you set at one level of the IIS MMC Snap-in can be inherited at a lower level. You are prompted as to whether you want those changes to apply.

SELF TEST

The following questions will help you measure your understanding of the material presented in this chapter. Read all the choices carefully because there might be more than one correct answer. Choose all correct answers for each question.

Understanding Terminal Services

1. You have configured a Windows 2000 Terminal Services server to function in remote administration mode. How many client connections can be supported at one time?

   A. One

   B. Two

   C. Three

   D. Four

2. You are unable to connect to a server using Terminal Services Client because of too many connections. How can you discover who is currently connected? Choose all that apply.

   A. Use Terminal Services Manager from your local PC.

   B. Use Terminal Services Manager for Domains from your local PC.

   C. Use Terminal Services Manager from the server.

   D. Use Terminal Services Manager for Domains from the server.

3. You believe that your company can leverage a great deal of its existing hardware by using Terminal Services in application mode, and you have permission to run a pilot program to test its effectiveness. How long can you run Terminal Services clients connecting to a terminal server running in application server mode without Terminal Services Client Access Licenses (TS CAL) for your pilot project?

   A. You cannot connect to Terminal Server in application server mode without TS CAL

   B. 30 days

   C. 60 days

   D. 90 days

4. You are a network administrator for Dominion Technologies Group and you would like to administer local users and groups using the Computer Management Microsoft Management Console Snap-in application from home over a 56kb modem. You need to ensure that all your

actions are secure. What installation of Terminal Services should you choose for a Windows 2000 server that you are setting up?

A. Terminal Services SSL Edition in application server mode

B. Terminal Services SSL Edition in remote administration mode

C. Terminal Services in application server mode

D. Terminal Services in remote administration mode

Installing and Configuring Terminal Services

5. You have just completed the installation of Terminal Services on a Windows 2000 server. What utilities will be added to the server's Administrative Tools menu group? Choose all that apply.

A. Terminal Services Licensing

B. Terminal Services Manager

C. Terminal Services Client Creator

D. Terminal Services Configuration

6. You would like to create a set of installation diskettes for a 32-bit Windows client using Terminal Services Client Creator. How many floppy disks will you need to create the installation?

A. 2

B. 4

C. 8

D. 16

7. You would like to run Terminal Services on your Windows 2000 Advanced Server. Which of the following modes are valid choices?

A. Application server mode

B. Remote control mode

C. Remote administration mode

D. Hybrid mode

Monitoring and Troubleshooting Terminal Services

8. You have performed a software installation using Terminal Services on a back-office server that requires a reboot. What is the most graceful way to reboot the server using Terminal Services?

    A. Go to the Start menu and select Shut Down.

    B. Use the TSSHUTDN command-line utility.

    C. Select Reboot from the File menu in the Terminal Services Manager.

    D. Select Reboot from the File menu in the Terminal Services Configuration.

9. Using the Windows 2000 Performance application, you can see that the CPU usage of your application server, APP01, is almost 100 percent, whereas typically it is around 30 percent. Which tools could you use to determine which process is using a high degree of the CPU?

    A. Through Terminal Services, you could use Task Manager on APP01.

    B. Through Terminal Services, you could use the Performance application on APP01.

    C. From a remote computer, you could use the Performance application.

    D. You could use Terminal Services Manager from a remote computer.

10. Using the Windows 2000 Performance application, you can see that the CPU usage of your application server, APP01, is almost 100 percent, whereas typically it is around 30 percent. Which tools could you use to determine in which session is the process that is using a high degree of the CPU? Choose the best answer.

    A. Through Terminal Services, you could use Task Manager on the APP01.

    B. Through Terminal Services, you could use the Performance application on the APP01.

    C. From a remote computer, you could use the Performance application.

    D. You could use Terminal Services Manager from a remote computer.

11. You work for a software company that has decided to use Terminal Services with the Internet Connector license to demonstrate your product to clients over the Internet. One of your clients using a modem is trying to use your software and is have difficulty with a particular aspect of it. You seem unable to explain it to him over the phone because he cannot see the application while he's disconnected. What is the best way that you can help the client through this problem?

    A. Dispatch a representative to the client in the morning.

    B. Have the client take screen captures of the area with which he is having trouble.

    C. E-mail the client the most up-to-date .CHM help file for the application.

    D. Use Terminal Services Manager to join the user's session.

12. You would like to use Terminal Services in application server mode for your call center employees. They should use only one application, Help Master 2000, and you would like to prevent them from using any other application, such as Solitaire. What is the best way to ensure that the users do not use any application other than Help Master 2000 through Terminal Services? Choose the best answer.

A. Set Help Master 2000 as the application for the user to use in the Environment tab of the group of call center users.

B. Using User Manager for Domains, specify Help Master 2000 on the Application tab.

C. Using Terminal Services Configuration, remove all applications except Help Master 2000 from the Start menu.

D. Using Terminal Services Configuration, set Terminal Services into single application mode and specify that application as Help Master 2000.

13. You would like to have your network administrator remotely administer your terminal server in application server mode over the Internet for the next six months. Currently, all the TS CALs are in use. What type of additional license (if any) is needed for the administrator to do this? Choose the best answer.

A. You do not need any license to remotely administer a terminal server in application server mode.

B. Internet connector license

C. Terminal Services Client Access License (TS CAL)

D. Temporary Terminal Services Client Access License (TS CAL)

Understanding Internet Information Services

14. You have completed a default installation of Windows 2000 Server on WEB01. You need to install Internet Information Services (IIS) 5.0 on WEB01 in order for it to be used for its intended purpose. What do you need to do to install IIS on the server?

A. Contact Microsoft Clearinghouse and purchase the IIS Server addition license.

B. Go to the Windows Components wizard and add Internet Information Service to the installation of Windows 2000.

C. Purchase the IIS 5 Resource Kit CD from Microsoft and run SETUP.EXE for Internet Information Services.

D. Do nothing. Internet Information Services are installed by default with Windows 2000.

15. Your CIO has told you that your company's Web server must be available as close to 24/7 as possible. How should you configure the World Wide Web Publishing Service to ensure that the Web server is up as often as possible?

    A. Configure the World Wide Web Publishing Service to automatically restart one minute after each time it fails.

    B. Use the Internet Service Manager to run all scripts in safe mode.

    C. Configure the World Wide Web Publishing Service to automatically restart to run the IIS self-repair script that is distributed with the IIS Resource Kit one minute after each time it fails.

    D. Use the Internet Service Manager to run each ASP script in its own package.

16. Windows 2000 allows you to host multiple Web sites on a single server, and you would like to host a new site on your company's Web server, WEB01. Which of the following properties would need to be different from the existing Web site in order to host a second on the web server? Choose the best answer.

    A. The port number

    B. The IP address

    C. Host header name

    D. Any of the above

17. Because of some security concerns, you need to change all the directories on your Web site to allow read-only access. What is the easiest way to change all the files in the Web site to read-only access?

    A. Using Windows 2000 Explorer, visit each file on the server and set the NTFS permissions to read only, and then select each virtual drive using the Internet Information Services MMC Snap-in and set the NTFS permission to read only.

    B. Using the IIS MMC Snap-in, change the properties of the root directory to read-only and, when prompted, tell it to change all subdirectories.

    C. Using the IIS MMC Snap-in, change the properties of the root file to read only and, when prompted, tell it to change all subdirectories.

    D. Using the Server Extensions Manager, use the lock-down function to commit all the files in the Web site to read only.

LAB QUESTION

In addition to being a Web applications developer, you are the primary administrator for your company's e-commerce Web site. Some of your company's important clients have complained about the site's performance in general; at times it even times out. The CIO has assigned you to discover the bottleneck so that your team can attempt to resolve it. Your Web server runs both IIS 5 and SQL Server 7. What could you do to try to isolate the performance problems with your Web site?

SELF TEST ANSWERS

Understanding Terminal Services

1. ☑ **B.** Two. When Terminal Services is in remote administration mode, only two client connections are supported. In addition to the two client sessions, a single console session is also allowed simultaneously with the two client sessions. The client connections for remote administration mode do not require licenses.
    ☒ **A** is incorrect because one is too few, and **C** and **D** are incorrect because three and four are too many. Only two client sessions are allowed in remote administration mode.

2. ☑ **A and C.** Terminal Services Manager allows you to monitor, reset, connect to, and disconnect sessions. In addition, you can send messages to users, log them off, or terminate processes running on the server. In this case, we are concerned with knowing who is occupying all the sessions for which Terminal Services Manager will allow us to connect.
    ☒ **B** and **D** are incorrect because there is no Terminal Services Manager for Domains.

3. ☑ **D.** 90 days. You can run Terminal Services in application server mode for 90 days before client licenses are required. This time span gives a great deal of flexibility to organizations for trying out application server mode.
    ☒ **A** is incorrect because Microsoft does provide a grace period before licenses are needed, and **B** and **C** are incorrect because the grace period is 90 days, not 30 or 60.

4. ☑ **D.** Terminal Services in remote administration mode allows the network administrator to accomplish what he needs. Terminal Services has built-in encryption that can be set from 40 bits to 128 bits to provide secure connections and can scale its compression to be used in high-speed LAN or slow-dial connections.
    ☒ **C** is incorrect because application server mode is meant to run standard applications for large groups of individuals simultaneously. **A** and **B** are incorrect because there is no SSL Edition; Terminal Services has built-in encryption for secured connections.

Installing and Configuring Terminal Services

5. ☑ **A, B, C, and D** are all correct. Terminal Services Licensing, Terminal Services Manager, Terminal Services Client Creator, and Terminal Services Configuration will each be added to the Administrative Tools menu group. Each of them accomplishes a separate task. Terminal Services Licensing is used to add and monitor Terminal Services client licenses. Terminal Services Manager supervises Terminal Services sessions, users, and processes on the network.

Terminal Services Client Creator creates floppy disk installations for client computers. Terminal Services Configuration controls the configuration of Terminal Services and the Terminal Services connections.

6. ☑ **A. 2.** You need two floppy disks if you use the Terminal Services Client Creator to create an installation.

   ☒ For a 32-bit Windows client, **B** is incorrect because you need only two disks for the software. However, if you were creating the installation disks for a 16-bit Windows client, you need all four disks. **C** and **D** provide enough capacity for the installation, but they also provide a great deal more than the four floppy disks that are needed.

7. ☑ **A** and **C**. Application server mode and remote administration mode. You can run Terminal Services in either application server mode or remote administration mode at one time.

   ☒ **B** is incorrect because remote control is a type of a session, not a Terminal Services mode. **D** is incorrect because there is no hybrid mode. Terminal Services must be in either remote administration or application server mode. You can switch a server from one to another, but it can be in only one mode at a time.

Monitoring and Troubleshooting Terminal Services

8. ☑ **B.** The most graceful way to reboot Terminal Services is to use the TSSHUTDN command-line utility.

   ☒ **A** is incorrect because it is not the most graceful way to reboot the server, but it can be used. **C** and **D** are incorrect because neither of them exists. If a server is mission critical, it is important to be able to physically access the server that you are rebooting in case there are problems, such as a floppy disk being left in the disk drive.

9. ☑ **A** and **D**. With Terminal Services, you can use the Task Manager on APP01 to see which process is consuming most cycles. Terminal Services Manager allows you to monitor all the processes on a terminal server.

   ☒ **B** and **C** are incorrect because the Performance application cannot isolate CPU usage by individual processes.

10. ☑ **D.** Terminal Services Manager allows you to monitor all the processes on a terminal server, and it allows you to break them down by session.

    ☒ **A** is incorrect because, although the Task Manager on APP01 allows you to see which process is consuming the most cycles, it will not identify the session to which that process belongs. **B** and **C** are incorrect because the Performance application cannot isolate CPU usage by individual processes.

11. ☑ **D.** Terminal Services Manager allows you to join sessions in progress. Once part of the session, you can see everything that the user sees and communicate with the user to help him or her through the problem.

☒ **A** is incorrect because dispatching a representative is not as immediate and is much more expensive than joining the session. **B** is incorrect because it will consume more time, and there is no guarantee that the user will send the most important information. **C** is incorrect because it is unlikely that the help file will provide the answer and because it does not make the client feel that his problem is valid.

12. ☑ **A.** You can set Terminal Services to allow only a single application for a user or a group of users. When the Terminal Services client connects, that application starts. When that application closes, the session automatically disconnects.

☒ **B** is incorrect because there is no Application tab. **C** is incorrect because removing the applications from the Start menu will not prevent the user from using an application. **D** is incorrect because you cannot put a terminal server into single application mode where it will run only one application.

13. ☑ **C.** The administrator needs a Terminal Services Client Access License (TS CAL) in order to administer the terminal server for the next six months. If the administrator needed to connect to the server for less than 90 days, a Temporary TS CAL would be sufficient.

☒ **A** is incorrect because you need a license to connect to a terminal server in application server mode, even when just doing administration. **B** is incorrect because the Internet connector licenses are not valid for the employees of a company. The users of these licenses must be anonymous outside users. **D** is incorrect because the question states that the administrator needs access for more than 90 days.

Understanding Internet Information Services

14. ☑ **B.** Go to the Windows Components wizard and add Internet Information Service to the installation of Windows 2000. Internet Information Services comes with the Windows 2000 Server family; no additional license is needed. You can install it on your Windows 2000 server using the Windows Component wizard.

☒ **A** is incorrect because no additional licenses are needed, and Microsoft Clearinghouse is an entity used for licensing Terminal Services clients. **C** is incorrect because there is no IIS Resource Kit. **D** is incorrect because Internet Information Services are *not* installed by default with Windows 2000; you must choose to install them through the Windows Components wizard.

15. ☑ **A.** Configure the World Wide Web Publishing Service to automatically restart one minute after each time it fails. IIS 5.0 allows you to configure the World Wide Web Publishing Service to automatically restart after it fails. You can set the number of minutes, and one minute is the lowest interval that you can choose.

    ☒ **B** is incorrect because there is no script safe mode. Even if there were, that would not guarantee that the World Wide Web Publishing Service would never crash due to external influences. **C** is incorrect because there is no IIS Resource Kit. **D** is incorrect because, although you can run components in their own package (which reduces the risk of bringing down the server), you cannot run scripts in their own packages. If you could, that would do nothing to bring the World Wide Web Publishing Service back up in the event that an external influence crashed it.

16. ☑ **D.** Any of the above. By changing any of the above parameters, you can create a new Web site on the existing server, responding to its new identity. All of these properties are configurable at the site level using the Internet Information Services MMC Snap-in.

17. ☑ **B.** Using the IIS MMC Snap-in, change the properties of the root directory to read-only and, when prompted, tell it to change all subdirectories. Any time you change a property at one level, you are asked if you want the changes to be inherited at the lower levels. By selecting the root directory, all the files and directories in the Web site could inherit the permissions you set up.

    ☒ **A,** visiting each file on the server and set the NTFS permissions to read only, and then selecting each virtual drive using the Internet Information Services MMC Snap-in and set the NTFS permission to read only, is incorrect because it is far more difficult than the correct choice. **C** is incorrect because a file has no children, and **D** is incorrect because there is no lock-down option as part of the Server Extensions Manager.

LAB ANSWER

The first thing you should do is try to isolate the resource that is the bottleneck and the process that is eating up all those resources. You can do this by setting up counters within the performance application to capture empirical data about what is happening on the Web server. In addition to the standard resource counters for memory, network, disk, and CPU, you should also set up the IIS and SQL Server specific counters. Ideally, you should capture information at the times of day when the bottlenecks are happening.

    Analyze the information captured in the performance logs for clues about what is hampering your server. The type of resource that is the bottleneck might be obvious from the standard resource counters for memory, network, disk, and CPU. Sometimes those counters will tell you what the problem is. For instance, heavy disk usage generally indicates a SQL Server bottleneck, not an IIS one. However, if you are experiencing heavy usage of memory and CPU, either process could be causing your problems, and you need to closely analyze the counters for those processes.

If you are able to isolate the problem to be IIS's use of the CPU, you can turn on Process Accounting from the Internet Information Services MMC Snap-in. This will allow you to isolate which IIS process is consuming large slices of the CPU's resources. You should be able to find out which page or application running from IIS is the source of your CPU saturation.

A

About the CD

This CD-ROM contains the CertTrainer software. CertTrainer comes complete with ExamSim, Skill Assessment tests, CertCam movie clips, the e-book (electronic version of the book), and Drive Time. CertTrainer is easy to install on any Windows 98, NT, or 2000 computer and must be installed to access these features. You may, however, browse the e-book directly from the CD without installation.

Installing CertTrainer

If your computer CD-ROM drive is configured to autorun, the CD-ROM will automatically start up upon inserting the disk. From the opening screen you may either browse the e-book or install CertTrainer by pressing the Install Now button. This will begin the installation process and create a program group named "CertTrainer." To run CertTrainer use START | PROGRAMS | CERTTRAINER.

System Requirements

CertTrainer requires Windows 98 or higher, Internet Explorer 4.0 or above, and 600MB of hard disk space for full installation.

CertTrainer

CertTrainer provides a complete review of each exam objective, organized by chapter. You should read each objective summary and make certain that you understand it before proceeding to the SkillAssessor. If you still need more practice on the concepts of any objective, click the In Depth button to link to the corresponding section from the Study Guide or the CertCam button to view a short .avi clip illustrating various exercises from within the chapter.

Once you have completed the review(s) and feel comfortable with the material, launch the SkillAssessor quiz to test your grasp of each objective. Once you complete the quiz, you will be presented with your score for that chapter.

ExamSim

As its name implies, ExamSim provides a simulation of the actual exam. The number of questions, the types of questions, and the time allowed are all intended to be an accurate representation of the exam environment. Figure A-1 shows the screen you will see when you are ready to begin ExamSim.

When you launch ExamSim, a digital clock display will appear in the upper left-hand corner of your screen. The clock will continue to count down to zero unless you choose to end the exam before the time expires.

There are three types of questions on the exam:

- **Multiple Choice** These questions have a single correct answer that you indicate by selecting the appropriate check box.

FIGURE A-1

The ExamSim opening page

■ **Multiple-Multiple Choice** These questions require more than one correct answer. Indicate each correct answer by selecting the appropriate check boxes.

■ **Simulations** These questions simulate actual Windows 2000 menus and dialog boxes. After reading the question, you are required to select the appropriate settings to most accurately meet the objectives for that question.

Saving Scores as Cookies

Your ExamSim score is stored as a browser cookie. If you've configured your browser to accept cookies, your score will be stored in a file named "History". If your browser is not configured to accept cookies, you cannot permanently save your scores. If you delete this History cookie, the scores will be deleted permanently.

E-Book

The entire contents of this Study Guide are provided in HTML format, as shown in Figure A-2. Although the files are optimized for Internet Explorer, they can also be viewed with other browsers including Netscape.

FIGURE A-2
Study Guide contents in HTML format

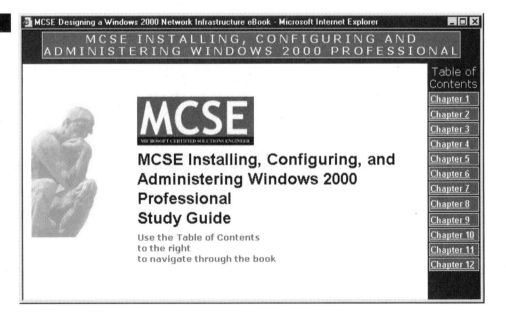

CertCam

CertCam .avi clips provide detailed examples of key certification objectives. These clips, narrated by Thomas Shinder, M.D., MCSE, MCT, walk you step-by-step through various system configurations. You can access the clips directly from the CertCam Table of Contents (shown in Figure A-3) or through the CertTrainer objectives.

The CertCam .avi clips are recorded and produced using TechSmith's Camtasia Producer. Since .avi clips can be very large, ExamSim uses TechSmith's special AVI Codec to compress the clips. The file named **tsccvid.dll** is copied to your Windows\ System folder when you install CertTrainer. If the .avi clip runs with audio but without video, you may need to reinstall the file from the CD-ROM. Browse to the "bin" folder, and run TSCC.EXE.

FIGURE A-3

The CertCam Table of Contents

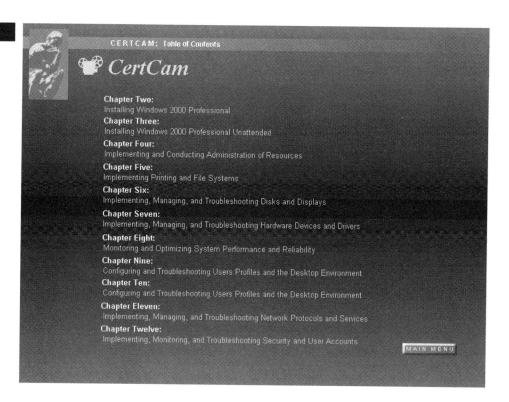

DriveTime

DriveTime audio tracks will automatically play when you insert the CD-ROM into a standard CD-ROM player, such as the one in your car stereo. There is one track for each chapter. These tracks provide you with certification summaries for each chapter and are the perfect way to study while commuting.

Help

A help file is provided through a Help button on the main CertTrainer screen in the lower right-hand corner.

Upgrading

A button is provided on the main ExamSim screen for upgrades. This button will take you to the Syngress web site at **www.syngress.com** where you can download any available upgrades.

B

About the
Web Site

A t Access.Globalknowledge, the premier online information source for IT professionals (**http://access.globalknowledge.com**), you'll enter a Global Knowledge information portal designed to inform, educate, and update surfers on issues regarding IT and IT education.

Get *What* You Want *When* You Want It

At the Access.Globalknowledge site, you can:

- Choose personalized technology articles related to your interests. Access a news article, a review, or a tutorial, customized to what you want to see, regularly throughout the week.

- Continue your education, between Global courses, by taking advantage of chat sessions with other users or instructors. Get the tips, tricks, and advice that you need today!

- Make your point in the Access.Globalknowledge community by participating in threaded discussion groups related to technologies and certification.

- Get instant course information at your fingertips. Customized class calendars show you the courses you want, and when and where you want them.

- Obtain the resources you need with online tools, trivia, skills assessment, and more!

All this is available now on the Web at **http://access.globalknowledge.com**. Visit today!

Glossary

Account Lockout Policy   The Account Lockout Policy dictates the behavior for locking and unlocking user accounts. There are three configurable parameters: Account lockout threshold determines how many times users can attempt to log on before their accounts are locked. This can range from low (five attempts) to high (one or two attempts). The Account lockout duration parameter controls how long an account is locked after the Account lockout threshold parameter is triggered.

ACPI   *See* Advanced Configuration and Power Interface.

Active Directory   The Active Directory is implemented on Windows 2000 domain controllers, and the directory can be accessed from Windows 2000 Professional as an Active Directory client. The Active Directory arranges objects—including computer information, user and group information, shared folders, printers, and other resources—in a hierarchical structure, in which domains can be joined into trees (groups of domains that share a contiguous namespace). Trees can be joined into forests (groups of domain trees that share a common schema, configuration, and global catalog).

Active Directory Service   This service provides the means for locating the Remote Installation Service (RIS) servers and the client computers on the network. The RIS server must have access to the Active Directory.

Administration   The word *administer* is generally used as a synonym for *manage,* which in turn means to exert control. One of the many enhancements to Windows 2000—both the Professional and Server incarnations—is the ability Microsoft has given administrators to apply the degree of control desired, in a flexible and granular manner.

Add Printer Wizard   All clients running a version of the Windows operating system (Windows 2000, Windows NT, Windows 98, and Windows 95) can use the Add Printer Wizard to create a printer entry on the client. This Add Printer Wizard can create and share a printer on a print server. The Windows 2000 version of the

Add Printer Wizard has more options than the wizard in other versions of Windows, but many of the same methods can be used to get the printer set up on the client.

Advanced Configuration and Power Interface (ACPI)   ACPI combines Plug-and-Play (PnP) capability with Power Management and places these functions under complete control of the operating system.

Advanced Power Management (APM)   An Intel/Microsoft application programming interface (API) allowing programs to indicate their requirements for power to regulate the speed of components.

Alerts   Alerts allow some action to be performed when a performance counter reaches a particular threshold. A common action is to log the event in the application event log. You can also send a network message to a specified computer. You can have the alert start a performance log to start logging when the alert occurs. And finally, you can configure the alert to start a program.

Analysis   Analysis is the process of comparing, contrasting, diagnosing, diagramming, discriminating, and/or drawing conclusions.

Answer file   An answer file is a file containing the information you would normally have to key in during the setup process. Answer files help automate the installation process as all the queries presented to you during installation are answered by the answer files. With careful planning, you can prepare answers that eliminate the possibility of incorrect answers being typed in by the person performing the installation, thus reducing the chances of setup failure. You can use the Setup Manager wizard to create a customized answer file. This technique minimizes the chances of committing syntax-related errors while manually creating or editing the sample answer files.

APIPA   *See* Automatic Private Internet Protocol Addressing.

APM   *See* Advanced Power Management.

AppleTalk   The AppleTalk protocol suite was developed by Apple Computer for use in its Macintosh line of personal computers. AppleTalk is a local area networking system that can run over a variety of networks that include Ethernet, FDDI, and Token Ring as well as Apple's proprietary media system LocalTalk. Macintosh computers are very popular in the education and art industries, so familiarity with the way they communicate using their native protocol is very useful.

AppleTalk printing device   Another type of remote printer is the AppleTalk printing device. Like a Transmission Control Protocol/Internet Protocol (TCP/IP) printer, an AppleTalk printer can be connected directly to an AppleTalk network or shared across the network through an AppleShare print server. Like the TCP/IP printers, a large number of modern, high-capacity PostScript printers can be configured to communicate with an AppleTalk network as well as a TCP/IP network. In fact, many Hewlett-Packard LaserJet printers have JetDirect cards that will speak TCP/IP and AppleTalk at the same time.

Application (software)   A program designed to perform a specific function directly for the user or for another application program. An application would be, for example, word processors, database programs, graphics/drawing programs, Web browsers, e-mail programs.

Application Service Provider (ASP)   ASPs are companies that manage applications and provide organizations with application hosting services. Analysts expect the ASP market will be a six billion dollar industry by the year 2001. The application-hosting model offers organizations the option of outsourcing application support and maintenance.

ASP   *See* Application Service Provider.

Auditing   Windows 2000 gives the ability to audit security-related events, track access to objects and use of user rights, and detect attempted and successful access (authorized and unauthorized) to the network. Auditing is not enabled by default, but once enabled, a security log is generated that provides information in regard to specific activities performed on the computer.

Automatic Private Internet Protocol Addressing (APIPA)   APIPA, or Automatic Client Configuration, is a new feature initially available in Windows 98. The feature has been extended to Windows 2000 and allows Dynamic Host Control Protocol (DHCP) client computers to self-configure their IP addressing information in the event a DHCP server is not available when the computer issues a DHCPDISCOVER message. It also allows self-configuration when it senses that it has been moved from a previous network via Windows 2000 media sensing capabilities.

Backup Domain Controller (BDC)   A backup file or copy of the Primary Domain Controller (PDC). Periodically, the BDC is synchronized with the PDC.

Backup Logs   Windows Backup generates a backup log file for every backup job. These files are the best place to review the backup process in case the program encounters some problem. The backup log is a text file that records all the events during the backup process.

Basic Input/Output System (BIOS)   A set of programs encoded in ROM on IBM PC-compatible computers. These programs handle startup operations such as Power On Self Test (POST) and low-level control for hardware such as disk drives, keyboards, etc.

BDC   *See* Backup Domain Controller.

BIOS   *See* Basic Input/Output System.

Boot   The process of loading an operating system into the computer's memory (RAM) so those applications can be run on it.

Boot ROM   A boot ROM is a chip on the network adapter that helps the computer boot from the network. Such a computer need not have a previously installed operating system. The BIOS of the computer that has a PXE-based boot ROM must be configured to boot from the network. Windows 2000 Server RIS supports PXE ROM versions 99 or later.

Bottleneck   A bottleneck in computer terms is also a component of the system as a whole that restricts the system from operating at its peak. When a bottleneck occurs, the component that is a bottleneck will have a high rate of usage and other components will have a low rate of usage. A lack of memory is a common cause of bottleneck when your computer doesn't have enough memory for the applications and services that are running.

CA   *See* Certificate Authority.

CAL   *See* Client Access License.

CAPI   *See* CryptoAPI.

Centralized model   This model consolidates administrative control of group policies. A single team of administrators is responsible for managing all Group Policy Objects (GPOs) no matter where they are. This is usually applied by giving all the top-level Organizational Unit (OU) administrators full control to all GPOs no matter where they are located. They give each second-level OU administrator Read permission only to each GPO. You can also decentralize other resources or keep all resources centralized, depending on the environment.

Certificate Authority (CA)   An authority/organization that produces digital certificates with its available public key. A Certificate Authority (CA) is a public key certificate issuer (for example, Verisign). To use a public key certificate, you must trust the issuer (CA). This means that you have faith in the CA's authentication policies. The CA is used for doing things such as authorizing certification authenticity, revoking expired certificates, and responding to certification requests. Windows 2000 offers an alternative to a third-party CA. You can become a CA within your own Intranet. Thus you can manage your own certificates rather than relying on a third-party Certification Authority.

Certificate service   Provides security and authentication support, including secure e-mail, Web-based authentication, and smart card authentication.

Change Permission   You can use this permission to allow users the ability to change permissions on files and folders without giving them the Full Control permission. You can use this permission to give a user or group access to modify permissions on file or folder objects without giving them the ability to have complete control over the object.

CIPHER command   The CIPHER command is another way to encrypt and decrypt data. You can use it from the command line and it has many switches, so that you can define exactly what you want to have done. The Cipher.exe command syntax is simply CIPHER, followed by the switches that you would like to use, followed by the path and directory/file name. The most common switches are the /E switch (encrypts the specified directories) and the /D switch (decrypts the specified directories). You can also use wildcards with the CIPHER command. For example, C:\>cipher /e /s *win* will encrypt all files and folders with "win" in the name and all files within them.

CIW   *See* Client Installation Wizard.

Client Access License (CAL)   The CAL allows clients to access the Windows 2000's network services, shared folders, and printers. There are two types of CAL modes: Per Seat and Per Server. It important to understand the difference between the two modes: Per Seat and Per Server. When you use the Per Seat mode, each computer that accesses the server must have a CAL. The Per Server mode requires a CAL for each connection to the server. This is a subtle but significant difference. In addition, the CAL allows clients to access the Windows 2000 Server's network services, shared folders, and printers. The licensing modes are the same as under Windows NT 4.0.

Client Installation Wizard (CIW)   When a client computer boots using either the Remote Boot Disk or the PXE-based Boot ROM, it tries to establish a connection to the Remote Installation Service (RIS) server. If the RIS server is preconfigured to service the RIS clients, it helps the client get an Internet Protocol (IP) address from the Dynamic Host Control Protocol (DHCP) service. The CIW is then downloaded from the RIS server. This wizard has four installation options. The options that are presented to the user depend on the group policy set in the Active Directory. A user may get all four options, or may not get any of the options starting an automatic setup.

Cloning   *See* Disk imaging/cloning.

Comprehension   The process of distinguishing between situations, discussing, estimation, explaining, indicating, paraphrasing, and giving examples.

Computer account   A computer account is an account that is created by a domain administrator and uniquely identifies the computer on the domain. A newly created account is used so that a computer may be brought into a Windows 2000 Domain.

Configuration   Configuration of an operating system involves specifying settings that will govern how the system behaves.

Container Object   Container objects can contain other objects. A special type of container object you can create in the Active Directory is the Organizational Unit (OU).

Containers   Containers are used to describe any group of related items, whether they are objects, containers, domains, or an entire network.

Control Panel Accessibility Options   These are options that include StickyKeys, FilterKeys, ToggleKeys, SoundSentry, ShowSounds, High Contrast, MouseKeys, and SerialKeys.

Cooperative multitasking   An environment in which an application relinquishes its use of the computer's Central Processing Unit (CPU) so that another application can use the CPU.

Copy backup   This type of backup simply copies the selected files. It neither looks for any markers set on the files nor does it clear them. The Copy backup does not affect the other Incremental or Differential backup jobs and can be performed along with the other types of backup jobs.

Counter logs   Counter logs are maintained in a similar fashion as they were in Windows NT 4.0, but the procedure for configuring the Counter logs is a bit different. Trace logs are much easier to configure in Windows 2000 because you now can set them up from the console, rather than having to edit the registry as you had to do in Windows NT 4.0.

CryptoAPI (CAPI)   CryptoAPI (CAPI) architecture is a collection of tasks that permit applications to digitally sign or encrypt data while providing security for the user's private key data.

Daily backup   This type of backup does not use any markers to back up selected files and folders. The files that have changed during the day are backed up every day at a specified time. This backup will not affect other backup schedules.

Data Backup   A backup and disaster protection plan is an essential part of a network administrator's duties. Windows 2000 provides a built-in Backup utility used to back up data to tape or file, or to create an Emergency Repair Disk (ERD). An ERD can be used to repair a computer with damaged system files.

Data compression   Windows 2000 offers the capability of compressing data on a file-level basis, so long as the files and folders are located on an NT File System (NTFS) formatted partition or volume. Compression saves disk space; however, NTFS compression cannot be used in conjunction with file encryption.

Data Link Control (DLC)   DLC is a nonroutable protocol used for connecting to IBM mainframes and some network-connected laser printers.

Debugging Mode   This is the most advanced startup option of all. To use this option you will need to connect another computer to the problematic computer through a serial cable. With proper configuration, the debug information is sent to the second computer.

Decentralized model   This model is appropriate for companies that rely on delegated levels of administration. They decentralize the management of Group Policy Objects (GPOs), which distributes the workload to a number of domains. To apply this model, simply give all Organizational Unit (OU) administrators full control of their respective GPOs.

Dedicated Server   A dedicated print server is a Windows 2000 server whose only role is to provide printing services. The server does not provide directory space for users other than storage for spooled print jobs. It does not provide authentication services, does not host database services, does not act as a Domain Name System (DNS) server, and so on. A dedicated print server can host several hundred printers and print queues, however. Though it may not be obvious, the printing process does have an impact on the performance of the server providing the printing services. An environment with a large number of printers or print jobs should strongly consider using at least one dedicated print server.

Defragmentation   The task of finding fragmented files and moving them into contiguous space is called defragmentation.

Deny Permissions   Unlike the Allow permission, the Deny permission overrides all other permissions set for a file or folder. If a user is a member of one group with a Deny Write permission for a folder and is a member of another group with a Allow Full Control permission, the user will be unable to perform any of the Write permission tasks because it has been denied. The Deny permission should be used with extreme caution, as it can actually lock out all users, even administrators, from a file or folder. The proper way to remove a permission from a user or group on a file or folder is to uncheck the Allow permission for that user or group, not to check the Deny permission.

Dfs   *See* Distributed File System.

DHCP   *See* Dynamic Host Configuration Protocol.

Differential backup   The Differential backup checks and performs a backup of only those files that are marked. It does not clear the markers after the backup, which means that any consecutive differential backups will backup the marked files again. When you need to restore from a differential backup, you will need the most current full backup and the differential backup performed after that.

Digital Subscriber Line (DSL)   There are many variants of digital subscriber line (xDSL). All versions utilize the existing copper loop between a home and the local telco's Central Office (CO). Doing so allows them to be deployed rapidly and inexpensively. However, all DSL variants suffer from attenuation, and speeds drop as the loop length increases. Asymmetrical DSL (ADSL) and Symmetrical DSL (SDSL) may be deployed only within 17,500 feet of a CO, and Integrated Services Digital Network emulation over DSL (IDSL) will work only up to 30,500 feet. All DSL variants use Asynchronous Transfer Mode (ATM) as the data-link layer.

Direct Memory Access (DMA) DMA is a microprocessor capable of transferring data between memory units without the aid of the Central Processing Unit (CPU). Occasionally, built-in circuitry can perform this same function.

Directory A directory is a database that contains information about objects and their attributes.

Directory service The directory service is the component that organizes the objects into a logical and accessible structure, and provides a means of searching and locating objects within the directory. The directory service includes the entire directory and the method of storing it on the network.

Directory Services Restore Mode This startup mode is available on Windows 2000 Server domain controller computers only. This mode can be used to restore the SYSVOL directory and Active Directory on the domain controller.

Discover A Dynamic Host Control Protocol (DHCP) client begins the lease process with a DHCPDISCOVER message. The client broadcasts this message after loading a minimal Transmission Control Protocol/Internet Protocol (TCP/IP) environment. The client does not know the address of the DHCP server, so it sends the message using a TCP/IP broadcast, with 0.0.0.0 as the source address and 255.255.255.255 as the destination address. The DHCPDISCOVER message contains the clients network hardware address, its computer name, a list of DHCP options the client supports, and a message ID that will be used in all messages between the client and server to identify the particular request.

Disk compression This compression allows you to compress folders, subfolders, and files to increase the amount of file storage, but slows down access to the files.

Disk Defragmenter   Disk Defragmenter can analyze your volumes and make a recommendation as to whether or not you should defragment it. It will also give you a graphical display showing you the fragmented files, contiguous files, system files, and free space. Disk Defragmenter does not always completely defragment free space; instead, it often moves it into just a few contiguous areas of the disk, which will still improve performance. Making the free space one contiguous space would have little added benefit.

Disk imaging/cloning   The deployment of a new operating system is one of the most challenging and time-consuming tasks that a network administrator has to perform. The disk duplication methods are particularly useful when you need to deploy Windows 2000 Professional on a large number of computers. This is also known as disk imaging or cloning. These tools make the rollout fast and easy.

Disk quota   Windows 2000 comes with a disk quota feature that allows you to control users' disk consumption on a per user/per partition basis. To begin setting disk quotas for your users, right-click any partition in either Windows Explorer or the My Computer object. Click Properties and then click the Quota tab. Also, a disk quota allows you to limit the amount of disk space used by each user.

Distributed File System (Dfs)   The Windows 2000 Distributed File System provides you a method to centralize the organization of the shared resources on your network. In the past, shared resources were most often accessed via the Network Neighborhood applet, and users would have to wade through a number of domains and servers in order to access the shared folder or printer that they sought. Network users also had to remember where the obscure bit of information was stored, including both a cryptic server name and share name. The Distributed File System (Dfs) allows you to simplify the organization of your network resources by placing them in central shares accessed via a single server. Also, the Dfs allows you to create a central share point for shared resources located through the organization on a number of different servers.

Distribution Server   This is a server on which the Windows 2000 installation files reside. When you install the operating system over the network, the client machine does not need a CD-ROM drive. The first requirement for network installation is a distribution server that contains the installation files. The distribution server can be any computer on the network to which the clients have access.

DLC *See* Data Link Control.

DMA *See* Direct Memory Access.

DNS *See* Domain Name System.

Domain A collection of connected areas. Routing domains provide full connectivity to all end systems within them. Also, a domain is a collection of accounts and network resources that are grouped together using a single domain name and security boundary.

Domain controller Domain controllers validate logons, participate in replication of logon scripts and policies, and synchronize the user account database. This means that domain controllers have an extra amount of work to perform. Since the Terminal Server already requires such heavy resources, it is not a good idea to burden a Terminal Server with the extra work of being a domain controller. Also, all user accounts, permissions, and other network details are all stored in a centralized database on the domain controllers.

Domain Local Groups Domain Local Groups are used for granting access rights to resources such as file systems or printers that are located on any computer in the domain where common access permissions are required. The advantage of Domain Local Groups being used to protect resources is that a member of the Domain Local Group can come from both inside the same domain and from outside as well.

Domain Name System (DNS) Because the actual unique Internet Protocol (IP) address of a Web server is in the form of a number difficult for humans to work with, text labels separated by dots (domain names) are used instead. DNS is responsible for mapping these domain names to the actual Internet Protocol (IP) numbers in a process called resolution. Sometimes called a Domain Name Server.

Domain restructure   Domain restructure, or domain consolidation, is the method of changing the structure of your domains. Restructuring your domains can allow you to take advantage of the new features of Windows 2000, such as greater scalability. Windows 2000 does not have the same limitation as the Security Accounts Manager (SAM) account database in Windows NT. Without this limitation, you can merge domains into one larger domain. Using Windows 2000 Organizational Units (OUs), you have finer granularity in delegating administrative tasks.

Domain Tree   A domain tree is a hierarchical collection of the child and parent domains within a network. The domains in a domain tree have contiguous namespaces. Domain trees in a domain forest do not share common security rights, but can access one another through the global catalog.

Driver signing   One of the most frustrating things about Windows operating systems is that any software vendors can overwrite critical system level files with their own versions. Sometimes the vendor's version of a system level file is buggy or flawed, and it prevents the operating system from functioning correctly, or in the worst case, prevents it from starting at all. Windows 2000 uses a procedure called Driver Signing that allows the operating system to recognize functional, high-quality files approved by Microsoft. With this seal of approval, you should be confident that installing applications containing signed files will not disable your computer. Windows 98 was the first Microsoft operating system to use digital signatures, but Windows 2000 marks the first Microsoft operating system based on NT technology to do this.

DSL   *See* Digital Subscriber Line.

Dynamic disks   Dynamic disks introduce conceptual as well as technical changes from traditional basic disk structure. Partitions are now called volumes, and these can be created or changed without losing existing data on the disk. Recall that when using basic disks, you must first create primary partitions (up to a maximum of four), then extended partitions (a maximum of one) with logical drives. Dynamic disks allow you to create volume after volume, with no limit on the number or type that can exist on a single disk; you are limited only by the capacity of the disk itself.

Dynamic Host Configuration Protocol (DHCP)   A software utility that is designed to assign Internet Protocol (IP) addresses to clients and their stations logging onto a Transmission Control Protocol/Internet Protocol (TCP/IP) and eliminates manual IP address assignments.

EAP   *See* Extensible Authentication Protocol.

EFS   *See* Encrypting File System.

Encrypting File System (EFS)   Unlike Windows NT 4.0, Windows 2000 provides the Encrypting File System (EFS) that allows you to encrypt and decrypt data on a file-by-file basis without the need for third-party software, as long as it is stored on an NTFS formatted partition or volume. EFS is based on public key cryptography.

Encryption   Scrambling of data so as to be unreadable; therefore, an unauthorized person cannot decipher the data.

Ethernet   A networking protocol and shared (or switched) media Local Area Network (LAN) access method linking up to 1K nodes in a bus topology.

Evaluation   Evaluation is the process of assessing, summarizing, weighing, deciding, and applying standards.

Extended Partitions   Although extended partitions cannot be used to host operating systems, they can store other types of data and provide an excellent way to create more drives above the four-partition limit. Extended partitions do not represent one drive; rather, they can be subdivided into as many logical drives as there are letters in the alphabet. Therefore, one extended partition can contain several logical drives, each of which appears as a separate drive letter to the user.

Extensible Authentication Protocol (EAP)   EAP allows the administrator to "plug in" different authentication security providers outside of those included with Windows 2000. EAP allows your organization to take advantage of new authentication technologies including "smart card" logon and Certificate-based authentication.

FAT   *See* File Allocation Table.

Fault tolerance   Fault tolerance is high-system availability with enough resources to accommodate unexpected failure. Fault tolerance is also the design of a computer to maintain its system's performance when some internal hardware problems occur. This is done through the use of back-up systems.

FEK   *See* File Encryption Key.

File Allocation Table (FAT)   A FAT is an area on a disk that indicates the arrangement of files in the sectors. Because of the multiuser nature of Terminal Server, it is strongly recommended that the NTFS file system be used rather than the FAT file system. FAT does not offer file and directory security, whereas with NTFS you can limit access to subdirectories and files to certain users or groups of users.

File Allocation Table 16 (FAT16)   The earlier version of the FAT file system implemented in MS-DOS is known as FAT16, to differentiate it from the improved FAT32.

File Allocation Table 32 (FAT32)   FAT32 is the default file system for Windows 95 OSR2 and Windows 98. The FAT32 file system was first implemented in Windows 95 OSR2, and was supported by Windows 98 and now Windows 2000. While FAT16 cannot support partitions larger than 4GB in Windows 2000, FAT32 can support partitions up to 2TB (Terabytes) in size. However, for performance reasons, the creation of FAT32 partitions is limited to 32GB in Windows 2000. The second major benefit of FAT32 in comparison to FAT16 is that it supports a significantly smaller cluster size—as low as 4K for partitions up to 8GB. This results in more efficient use of disk space, with a 15 to 30 percent utilization improvement in comparison to FAT16.

File Encryption Key (FEK)   A random key called a file encryption key (FEK) is used to encrypt each file and is then itself encrypted using the user's public key. At least two FEKs are created for every encrypted file. One FEK is created with the user's public key, and one is created with the public key of each recovery agent. There could be more than one recovery agent certificate used to encrypt each file, resulting in more than two FEKs. The user's public key can decrypt FEKs created with the public key.

File Transfer Protocol (FTP)   Transfers files to and from a computer running an FTP server service (sometimes called a daemon).

FireWire   Also known as IEEE 1394. An Apple/Texas Instruments high-speed serial bus allowing up to 63 devices to connect; this bus supports hot swapping and isochronous data transfer.

Forest   A forest is a grouping of one or more domain trees that do not share a common namespace but do share a common schema, configuration, and global catalog; in fact, it forms a noncontiguous (or discontiguous) namespace. The users in one tree do not have global access to resources in other trees, but trusts can be created that allow users to access resources in another tree.

Forward Lookup Query   A forward lookup query occurs when a computer needs to get the Internet Protocol (IP) address for a computer with an Internet name. The local computer sends a query to a local Domain Name System (DNS) name server, which resolves the name or passes the request on to another server for resolution.

FQDN   *See* Fully Qualified Domain Name.

FTP   *See* File Transfer Protocol.

Fully Qualified Domain Name (FQDN)   A full site name of a system rather than just its host name. The FQDN of each child domain is made up of the combination of its own name and the FQDN of the parent domain. The FQDN includes the host name and the domain membership of that computer.

Gateway   In networking, gateway refers to a router or a computer functioning as one, the "way out" of the network or subnet, to get to another network. You also use gateways for software that connects a system using one protocol to a system using a different protocol, such as the Systems Network Architecture (SNA) software (allows a Local Area Network (LAN) to connect to an IBM mainframe). You can also use Gateway Services for NetWare to provide a way for Microsoft clients to go through a Windows NT or Windows 2000 server to access files on a Novell file server.

Global Groups   Global Groups are used for combining users who share a common access profile based on job function or business role. Typically organizations use Global Groups for all groups in which membership is expected to change frequently. These groups can have as members only user accounts defined in the same domain as the Global Group.

Globally Unique IDentifier (GUID)   The Globally Unique IDentifier (GUID) is a unique numerical identification created at the time the object is created. An analogy would be a person's social security number, which is assigned once and never changes, even if the person changes his or her name, or moves.

GPC   *See* Group Policy Container.

GPO   *See* Group Policy Object.

GPT   *See* Group Policy Template.

Graphical User Interface (GUI)   An overall and consistent system for the interactive and visual program that interacts (or interfaces) with the user. GUIs can involve pull-down menus, dialog boxes, on-screen graphics, and a variety of icons.

Group policy   Group Policy provides for change management and desktop control on the Windows 2000 platform. You are familiar with the control you had in Windows NT 4.0 using System Policies. Group Policy is similar to System Policies but allows you a much higher level of granular configuration management over your network. Some of the confusion comes from the change of names applied to different groups in Windows 2000. You can apply Group Policy to sites, domains, and organizational units. Each of these represents a group of objects, so Group Policy is applied to the group of objects contained in each of these entities. Group

Policy cannot be directly applied to Security Groups that are similar to the groups you are used to working with in Windows NT 4.0. However, by using Group Policy Filtering, you can successfully apply Group Policy to individual Security Groups.

Group Policy Container (GPC)   The Active Directory object Group Policy Containers (GPCs) store the information for the Folder Redirection snap-in and the Software Deployment snap-in. GPCs do not apply to local group policies. They contain component lists and status information, which indicate whether Group Policy Objects (GPOs) are enabled or disabled. They also contain version information, which insures that the information is synchronized with the Group Policy Template (GPT) information. GPCs also contain the class store in which GPO group policy extensions have settings.

Group Policy Object (GPO)   After you create a group policy, it is stored in a Group Policy Object (GPO) and applied to the site, domain, or Organizational Unit (OU). GPOs are used to keep the group policy information; essentially, it is a collection of policies. You can apply single or multiple GPOs to each site, domain or OU. Group policies are not inherited across domains, and users must have Read permission for the GPO that you want to have applied to them. This way, you can filter the scope of GPOs by adjusting who has read access to each GPO.

Group Policy Template (GPT)   The subset of folders created on each domain controller that store Group Policy Object (GPO) information for specific GPOs are called Group Policy Templates (GPTs). GPTs are stored in the SysVol (System Volume) folder, on the domain controller. GPTs store data for Software Policies, Scripts, Desktop File and Folder Management, Software Deployment, and Security settings. GPTs can be defined in computer or user configurations. Consequently, they take effect either when the computer starts or when the user logs on.

GUI   *See* Graphical User Interface.

GUID   *See* Globally Unique IDentifier.

HAL   *See* Hardware Abstraction Layer.

Hardware Abstraction Layer (HAL)   The Windows NT's translation layer existing between the hardware, kernel, and input/output (I/O) system.

Hardware Compatibility List (HCL)   The Hardware Compatibility List is published by Microsoft for each of its operating systems, and is updated on a monthly basis. There is a copy of the HCL on the Windows 2000 Professional CD, located in the Support folder and named Hcl.txt.

Hardware profile   A hardware profile is a set of instructions that tells your computer how to boot the system properly, based on the setup of your hardware. Hardware profiles are most commonly used with laptops. This is because laptops are frequently used in at least two different settings: stand-alone and in a docking station on a network. For example, when the laptop is being used at a docking station, it requires a network adapter. However, when the laptop is used away from the network, it does not. The hardware profile dialog manages these configuration changes. If a profile is created for each situation, the user will automatically be presented these choices on Windows startup.

HCL   *See* Hardware Compatibility List.

HKEY_CLASSES_ROOT   Contains information used for software configuration and object linking and embedding (OLE), as well as file association information.

HKEY_CURRENT_CONFIG   Holds data about the current hardware profile that is in use.

HKEY_CURRENT_USER   Has information about the user who is currently logged on.

HKEY_LOCAL_MACHINE   Stores information about the hardware, software, system devices, and security information for the local computer.

HKEY_USERS   Holds information and settings for the environments of all users of the computer.

HTML *See* HyperText Markup Language.

HTTP *See* HyperText Transfer Protocol.

HyperText Markup Language (HTML) The format used to create documents viewed on the World Wide Web (WWW) by the use of tags (codes) embedded within the text.

HyperText Transfer Protocol (HTTP) HTTP is an Internet standard supporting World Wide Web (WWW) exchanges. By creating the definitions of Universal Resource Locators (URLs) and their retrieval usage throughout the Internet.

IAS *See* Internet Authentication Services.

ICS *See* Internet Connection Sharing.

IDE *See* Integrated Drive Electronics (IDE) drive.

IIS *See* Internet Information Service.

Incremental backup This backup process is similar to the Differential backup, but it clears the markers from the selected files after the process. Because it clears the markers, an incremental backup will not back up any files that have not changed since the last incremental backup. This type of backup is fast during the backup but is very slow while restoring the files. You will need the last full backup and all of the subsequent incremental backups to fully restore data. The positive side of this backup type is that it is fast and consumes very little media space.

Indexing service Provides indexing functions for documents stored on disk, allowing users to search for specific document text or properties.

Industry Standard Architecture (ISA) A PC's expansion bus used for peripherals plug-in boards.

Integrated Drive Electronics (IDE) drive   An IDE drive is a hard-disk drive for processors containing most controller circuitry within the drive. IDE drives combine Enhanced System Device Interface (ESDI) speed with Small Computer System Interface (SCSI) hard-drive interface intelligence.

Integrated Services Digital Network (ISDN)   Integrated Services indicates the provider offers voice and data services over the same medium. Digital Network is a reminder that ISDN was born out of the digital nature of the intercarrier and intracarrier networks. ISDN runs across the same copper wiring that carries regular telephone service. Before attenuation and noise cause the signal to be unintelligible, an ISDN circuit can run a maximum of 18,000 feet. A repeater doubles this distance to 36,000 feet.

Internet Authentication Services (IAS)   IAS performs authentication, authorization, and accounting of dial-up and Virtual Private Networking (VPN) users. IAS supports the Remote Access Dial-In User Service (RADIUS) protocol.

Internet Connection Sharing (ICS)   ICS can be thought of as a less robust version of Network Address Translation (NAT lite). ICS uses the same address translation technology. ICS is a simpler version of NAT useful for connecting a few computers on a small Local Area Network (LAN) to the Internet or useful for a remote server through a single phone line and account.

Internet Information Service (IIS)   Windows NT Web browser software that supports Secure Sockets Layer (SSL) security protocol from Netscape. IIS provides support for Web site creation, configuration, and management, along with Network News Transfer Protocol (NNTP), File Transfer Protocol (FTP), and Simple Mail Transfer Protocol (SMTP).

Internet Packet eXchange (IPX)   Novell NetWare's built-in networking protocol for Local Area Network (LAN) communication derived from the Xerox Network System protocol. IPX moves data between a server and workstation programs from different network nodes. Sometimes called an Internetnetwork Packet eXchange.

Internet Protocol Security (IPSec)   IPSec is a new feature included in Windows 2000 and provides for encryption of data as it travels between two computers, protecting it from modification and interpretation if anyone were to see it on the network.

Internet Service Provider (ISP)   The organization allowing users to connect to its computers and then to the Internet. ISPs provide the software to connect and sometimes a portal site and/or internal browsing capability.

Interrupt ReQuest (IRQ)   An electronic signal that is sent to the computer's processor requiring the processor's attention. Also, a computer instruction designed to interrupt a program for an Input/Output (I/O).

IPSec   *See* Internet Protocol Security.

IPX   *See* Internet Packet eXchange.

IRQ   *See* Interrupt ReQuest.

ISA   *See* Industry Standard Architecture.

ISDN   *See* Integrated Services Digital Network.

ISP   *See* Internet Service Provider.

Kerberos   Kerberos guards against username and password safety vulnerability by using tickets (temporary electronic credentials) to authenticate. Tickets have a limited life span and can be used in place of usernames and passwords (if the software supports this). Kerberos encrypts the password into the ticket. It uses a trusted server called the Key Distribution Center (KDC) to handle authentication requests. Kerberos speeds up network processes by integrating security and rights across network domains and also eliminates workstations' need to authenticate themselves repeatedly at every domain they access. Kerberos security also makes maneuvering around networks using multiple platforms such as UNIX or NetWare easier.

Knowledge   Knowledge is the very lowest level of learning. It is, of course, important that a network administrator have this knowledge. Knowledge involves the processes of defining, location, recall, recognition, stating, matching, labeling, and identification.

L2TP   *See* Layer-Two Tunneling Protocol.

Last Known Good Configuration   This mode starts the system using the configuration that was saved in the registry during the last system shutdown. This startup option is useful when you have changed some configuration parameters and the system fails to boot. When you use this mode to start the system, all changes that were made after the last successful logon are lost. Use this option when you suspect that some incorrect configuration changes are causing the system startup failure. This mode does not help if any of the installed drivers have been corrupted or any driver files are deleted by mistake.

Layer Two Tunneling Protocol (L2TP)   L2TP offers better security through the use of IPSec and creates Virtual Private Networks (VPNs). Windows 2000 uses L2TP to provide tunneling services over Internet Protocol Security (IPSec)-based communications. L2TP tunnels can be set up to traverse data across intervening networks that are not part of the VPN being created. L2TP is used to send information across intervening and nonsecure networks.

LDAP   *See* Lightweight Directory Access Protocol.

Legend   The legend displays information about the counters that are being measured. It is the set of columns at the bottom of System Monitor.

Lightweight Directory Access Protocol (LDAP)   A simplified Directory Access Protocol (DAP) accessing a computer's directory listing. LDAP is able to access X.500 directories.

Line Printer Daemon (LPD)   LPD is the server process that advertises printer queues and accepts incoming print submissions, which are then routed to the print device.

Line Printer Remote (LPR)   A process that spools a print job to a remote print spool that is advertised by the Line Printer Daemon (LPD).

Load balancing   The fine tuning process of a system (computer, network, etc.) to allow the data to be distributed more efficiently and evenly. Load balancing is an add-on feature of MetaFrame that must be purchased separately from the base product. Load balancing allows the administrator to group servers in a server farm which can act as a single point of access for clients accessing published applications.

Local policy   A group policy stored locally on a Windows 2000 member server or a Windows 2000 Professional computer is called a local policy. The local policy is used to set up the configuration settings for each computer and for each user. Local policies are stored in the \%systemroot%\system32\grouppolicy folder on the local computer. Local policies include the auditing policy, user rights and privilege assignment, and various security options.

Local printer   A print device that is directly attached, via a parallel or serial cable, to the computer that is providing the printing services. For a Windows 2000 Professional workstation, a local printer is one that is connected to the workstation. For a Windows 2000 Server, a local printer is one that is connected to the server. Drivers for the print device must reside on the computer that connects to the printer.

Local user profiles (local profiles)   Local user profiles are kept on one local computer hard drive. When a user initially logs on to a computer, a local profile is created for them in the \%systemdrive%\Documents and Settings\<username> folder. When users log off the computer, the changes that they made while they were logged on will be saved to their local profile on that client computer. This way, subsequent logons to that computer will bring up their personal settings. When users log on to a different computer, they will not receive these settings, as they are local to the computer in which they made the changes. Therefore, each user that logs on to that computer receives individual desktop settings. Local profiles are ideal for users who only use one computer. For users that require access to multiple computers, the Roaming profile would be the better choice.

LogicalDisk object   The LogicalDisk object measures the transfer of data for a logical drive (i.e., C: or D:) or storage volumes. You can use the PhysicalDisk object to determine which hard disk is causing the bottleneck. Then, to narrow the cause of the bottleneck, you can use the LogicalDisk object to determine which, if any, partition is the specific cause of the bottleneck. By default, the PhysicalDisk object is enabled and the LogicalDisk object is disabled on Windows 2000 Server.

LPD   *See* Line Printer Daemon.

LPR   *See* Line Printer Remote.

Mandatory Roaming profiles   Mandatory roaming profiles are mandatory user profiles the user cannot change. They are usually created to define desktop configuration settings for groups of users in order to simplify administration and support. Users can make changes to their desktop settings while they are logged on, but these changes will not be saved to the profile, as Mandatory profiles are read-only. The next time they log on, their desktop will be set back to the original Mandatory profile settings.

Master File Table (MFT)   The MFT stores the information needed by the operating system to retrieve files from the volume. Part of the MFT is stored at the beginning of the volume and cannot be moved. Also, if the volume contains a large number of directories, it can prevent the free space from being defragmented.

Master image   After configuring one computer with the operating system and all the applications, Sysprep is run to create an image of the hard disk. This computer serves as the master or model computer that will have the complete setup of the operating system, application software, and any service packs. This hard disk image is the master image and is copied to a CD or put on a network share for distribution to many computers. Any third-party disk-imaging tool can then be used to replicate the image to other identical computers.

MCSE   *See* Microsoft Certified Systems Engineer.

Message queuing service   Provides a communication infrastructure and a development tool for creating distributed messaging applications. Such applications can communicate across heterogeneous networks and with computers that might be off-line. Message queuing provides guaranteed message delivery, efficient routing, security, transactional support, and priority-based messaging.

MFT *See* Master File Table.

Microsoft Certified Systems Engineer (MCSE) An engineer who is a technical specialist in advanced Microsoft products, specifically NT Server and NT Workstation.

Microsoft Management Console (MMC) The MMC provides a standardized interface for using administrative tools and utilities. The management applications contained in an MMC are called Snap-ins, and custom MMCs hold the Snap-ins required to perform specific tasks. Custom consoles can be saved as files with the .msc file extension. The MMC was first introduced with NT Option Pack. Using the MMC leverages the familiarity you have with the other snap-ins available within MMC, such as SQL Server 7 and Internet Information Server 4. With the MMC, all your administrative tasks can be done in one place.

Mini-Setup Wizard The purpose of this wizard is to add some user-specific parameters on the destination computer. These parameters include: End-user license agreement (EULA); Product key (serial number); Username, company name, and administrator password; Network configuration; Domain or workgroup name; and, Date and time zone selection.

Mirror Set In a mirror set, all data on a selected partition or drive is automatically duplicated onto another physical disk. The main purpose of a mirror set is to provide fault tolerance in the event of missing or corrupt data. If one disk fails or contains corrupt files, the data is simply retrieved and rebuilt from the other disk.

Mirrored Volume Like basic disks, dynamic disks can also be mirrored, and are called mirrored volumes. A continuous and automatic backup of all data in a mirrored volume is saved to a separate disk to provide fault tolerance in the event of a disk failure or corrupt file. Note that you cannot mirror a spanned or striped volume.

Mirroring Also called RAID 1. RAID 1 consists of two drives that are identical matches, or mirrors, of each other. If one drive fails, you have another drive to boot up and keep the server going.

Mixed Mode   When in Mixed Mode, the domain still uses master replication with a Windows 2000 (DC). The Windows NT Backup Domain Controllers (BDCs) replicate from the Windows 2000 server, as did the Windows NT Primary Domain Controller (PDC). When you are operating in Mixed Mode, some Windows 2000 functionality will not be available. You will not be able to use group nesting or transitive trusts. Mixed Mode is the default mode.

MMC   *See* Microsoft Management Console.

NAT   *See* Network Address Translation.

Native Mode   Native Mode allows only Windows 2000 domain controllers to operate in the domain. When all domain controllers for the domain are upgraded to Windows 2000 Server, you can switch to Native Mode. This allows you to use transitive trusts and the group-nesting features of Windows 2000. When switching to Native Mode, ensure you no longer need to operate in Mixed Mode, because you cannot switch back to Mixed Mode once you are in Native Mode.

NDS   *See* NetWare Directory Service.

NetBEUI   *See* NETwork Basic Input/Output System Extended User Interface.

NetBIOS   *See* Network Basic Input/Output System.

NetWare Directory Service (NDS)   NDS (created by Novell) has a hierarchical information database allowing the user to log on to a network with NDS capable of calculating the user's access rights.

Network Address Translation (NAT)   With NAT, you can allow internal users to have access to important external resources while still preventing unauthorized access from the outside world.

Network Basic Input/Output System (NetBIOS)   A program in Microsoft's operating system that links personal computers to a Local Area Network (LAN).

NETwork Basic Input/Output System Extended User Interface (NetBEUI)   The transport layer for the Disk Operating System (DOS) networking protocol called Network Basic Input/Output System (NetBIOS).

Network   Two or more computers connected together by cable or wireless media for the purpose of sharing data, hardware peripherals, and other resources.

Network Interface Card (NIC)   A board with encoding and decoding circuitry and a receptacle for a network cable connection that, bypassing the serial ports and operating through the internal bus, allows computers to be connected at higher speeds to media for communications between stations.

Network printer   A print device that has a built-in network interface or connects directly to a dedicated network interface. Both workstations and servers can be configured to print directly to the network printer, and the network printer controls its own printer queue, determining which jobs from which clients will print in which order. Printing clients have no direct control over the printer queue and cannot see other print jobs being submitted to the printer. Administration of a network printer is difficult. Drivers for the print device must reside on the computer that connects to the printer.

NIC   *See* Network Interface Card.

Nondedicated server   A nondedicated print server is a Windows 2000 server that hosts printing services in addition to other services. A domain controller, database server, or Domain Name System (DNS) server can provide printing services as well, but should be used only for a smaller number of printers or for printers that are not heavily used. Anyone setting up a nondedicated print server should monitor the performance of the printing process and the other tasks running on the server and be prepared to modify the server configuration if the performance drops below acceptable levels.

Nonmandatory Roaming profiles   Roaming user profiles are stored on the network file server and are the perfect solution for users who have access to multiple computers. This way their profile is accessible no matter where they log on in the domain. When users log on to a computer within their domain, their Roaming profile will be copied from the network server to the client computer and the settings will be applied to the computer while they are logged on. Subsequent logins will compare the Roaming profile files to the local profile files. The file server then copies only any files that have been altered since the user last logged on locally, significantly decreasing the time required to logon. When the user logs off, any changes that the user made on the local computer will be copied back to the profile on the network file server.

Normal backup   This is the most common type and is also known as a full backup. The Normal backup operation backs up all files and folders that are selected irrespective of the archive attributes of the files. This provides the easiest way to restore the files and folders but is expensive in terms of the time it takes to complete the backup job and the storage space it consumes. The restore process from a Normal backup is less complex because you do not have to use multiple tape sets to completely restore data.

NT File System (NTFS)   The NT File System (with file names up to 255 characters) is a system created to help the computer and its components recover from hard disk crashes.

NTFS   *See* NT File System.

NWLink IPX/SPX/NetBIOS Compatible Transport Protocol (NWLink)   Microsoft's implementation of Novell's Internet Packet eXchange/Sequenced Packet eXchange (IPX/SPX) protocol stack, required for connecting to NetWare servers prior to version 5. NWLink can also be used on small networks that use only Windows 2000 and other Microsoft client software. NWLink is a Network Driver Interface Specification (NDIS) compliant, native 32-bit protocol. The NWLink protocol supports Windows sockets and NetBIOS.

ODBC   *See* Open DataBase Connectivity.

Offer   After the Dynamic Host Control Protocol (DHCP) server receives the DHCPDISCOVER message, it looks at the request to see if the client configuration request is valid. If so, it sends back a DHCPOFFER message with the client's network hardware address, an IP address, a subnet mask, the length of time the lease is valid, and the IP address of the server that provided the DHCP information. This message is also a Transmission Control Protocol/Internet Protocol (TCP/IP) broadcast, as the client does not yet have an Internet Protocol (IP) address. The server then reserves the address it sent to the client so that it is not offered to another client making a request. If there are more than one DHCP servers on the network, all servers respond to the DHCPDISCOVER message with a DHCPOFFER message.

Open DataBase Connectivity (ODBC)   A database programming interface that allows applications a way to access network databases.

Open Systems Interconnection (OSI) model   This is a model of breaking networking tasks into layers. Each layer is responsible for a specific set of functionality. There are performance objects available in System Monitor for analyzing network performance.

Organizational Units (OUs)   OUs in Windows 2000 are objects that are containers for other objects, such as users, groups, or other organizational units. Objects cannot be placed in another domain's OUs. The whole purpose of an OU is to have a hierarchical structure to organize your network objects. You can assign a group policy to an OU. Generally, the OU will follow a structure from your company. It may be a location, if you have multiple locations. It can even be a department-level organization. Also, OUs are units used to organize objects within a domain. These objects can include user accounts, groups, computers, printers, and even other OUs. The hierarchy of OUs is independent of other domains.

OSI   *See* Open Systems Interconnection (OSI) model.

OU   *See* Organizational Units (OUs).

Paging   When enough memory is not available for the running applications, pages of memory can be swapped from physical memory to the hard disk. This is also known as paging because pages of memory are swapped at a time.

Windows 2000 separates memory into 4KB pages of memory to help prevent fragmentation of memory. Swapping can even get bad enough that you can hear your hard disk running constantly.

Paging file   A file on the hard disk (or spanning multiple disks) that stores some of the program code that is normally in the computer's RAM. This is called virtual memory, and allows the programs to function as if the computer had more memory than is physically installed.

Password policy   A password policy regulates how your users must establish and manage their passwords. This includes password complexity requirements and how often passwords must change. There are several settings that can be used to implement a successful password policy. You can enforce password uniqueness so those users cannot simply switch back and forth between a few easy to remember passwords. This can be set to low, medium, or high security. With low security, the system remembers the user's last 1–8 passwords (it is your choice as administrator to decide how many); with medium, it remembers the last 9–16 passwords; with high, it remembers the last 17–24 passwords.

PCMCIA   *See* Personal Computer Memory Card Interface Adapter.

PDC   *See* Primary Domain Controller.

Peer-to-peer network   A workgroup is also referred to as a peer-to-peer network, because all the computers connected together and communicating with one another are created equal. That is, there is no central computer that manages security and controls access to the network.

Performance logging   Performance logging has many features. The data collected is stored in a comma-delimited or tab-delimited format, which allows for exportation to spreadsheet and database applications for a variety of tasks such as charting and reports. The data can also be viewed as collected. You can configure the logging by specifying start and stop times, the name of the log files and the maximum size of the log. You can start and stop the logging of data manually or create a schedule for logging. You can even specify a program to run automatically when logging stops. You can also create trace logs. Trace logs track events that occur rather than measuring performance counters.

Permissions Inheritance   By default, all permissions set for a folder are inherited by the files in the folder, the subfolders in the folder, and the contents of the subfolders. When the permissions on a folder are viewed in the Security tab of the file or folder Permissions window, inherited permissions are indicated with a gray check box.

Personal Computer Memory Card Interface Adapter (PCMCIA)

An interface standard for plug-in cards for portable computers; devices meeting the standard (for example, fax cards, modems) are theoretically interchangeable.

Physical memory   Physical memory is the actual Random Access Memory (RAM) on the computer. When the physical memory becomes full, the operating system can also use space on the hard disk as virtual memory. When memory becomes full, rather than locking up the computer, the operating system stores unused data on the hard disk in a page file (also called paging or swap file). Data is swapped back and forth between the hard disk and physical memory as needed for running applications. If memory is needed that is in virtual memory, it is swapped back into physical memory.

PhysicalDisk object   The PhysicalDisk object measures the transfer of data for the entire hard disk. You can use the PhysicalDisk object to determine which hard disk is causing the bottleneck. By default, the PhysicalDisk object is enabled and the LogicalDisk object is disabled on Windows 2000 Server.

Plug-and-Play (PnP)   A standard requiring add-in hardware to carry the software to configure itself in a given way supported by Microsoft Windows 95. Plug-and-Play can make peripheral configuration software, jumper settings, and Dual In-line Package (DIP) switches unnecessary. PnP allows the operating system to load device drivers automatically and assign system resources dynamically to computer components and peripherals. Windows 2000 moves away from this older technology with its use of Kernel-mode and User-mode PnP architecture. PnP autodetects, configures, and installs the necessary drivers in order to minimize user interaction with hardware configuration. Users no longer have to tinker with IRQ and I/O settings.

PnP   *See* Plug-and-Play.

Point-to-Point Protocol (PPP)   A serial communication protocol most commonly used to connect a personal computer to an Internet Service Provider (ISP). PPP is the successor to Serial Line Internet Protocol (SLIP) and may be used over both synchronous and asynchronous circuits. Also, PPP is a full-duplex, connectionless protocol that supports many different types of links. The advantages of PPP made it the de facto standard for dial-up connections.

Point-to-Point Tunneling Protocol (PPTP)   One of two standards for dial-up telephone connection of computers to the Internet. It offers better data negotiation, compression, and error corrections than the other Serial Line Internet Protocol (SLIP), but costs more to transmit data. PPTP is unnecessary when both sending and receiving modems can handle some of the procedures.

Policy Inheritance   Group policies have an order of inheritance in which the policies are applied. Local policies are applied first, then group policies are applied to the site, then the domain, and finally the Organizational Unit (OU). Policies applied first are overwritten by policies applied later. Therefore, group policies applied to a site overwrite the local policies and so on. When there are multiple Group Policy Objects (GPOs) for a site, domain, or OU, the order in which they appear in the Properties list applies. This policy inheritance order works well for small companies, but a more complex inheritance strategy may be essential for larger corporations.

Ports   A channel of a device that can support single point-to-point connections is known as a port. Devices can be single port, as in a modem.

Power options   Power options are dependent on the particular hardware. Power options include Standby and Hibernation modes. Standby mode turns off the monitor and hard disks to save power. Hibernation mode turns off the monitor and disks, saves everything in memory to disk, turns off the computer, and then restores the desktop to the state in which you left it when the computer is turned on.

PPP   *See* Point-to-Point Protocol.

PPTP   *See* Point-to-Point Tunneling Protocol.

Preboot eXecution Environment (PXE)   The PXE is a new Dynamic Host Control Protocol (DHCP)-based technology used to help client computers boot from the network. The Windows 2000 Remote Installation Service (RIS) uses the PXE technology along with the existing Transmission Control Protocol/Internet Protocol (TCP/IP) network infrastructure to implement the RIS-based deployment of Windows 2000 Professional. The client computer that has the PXE-based ROM uses its Basic Input/Output System (BIOS) to contact an existing RIS server and get an Internet Protocol (IP) address from the DHCP server running on the network. The RIS server then initializes the installation process on the client computer.

Preemptive multitasking   An environment in which timesharing controls the programs in use by exploiting a scheduled time usage of the computer's Central Processing Unit (CPU).

Primary Domain Controller (PDC)   Performs NT security management for its local domain. The PDC is periodically synchronized to its copy, the Backup Domain Controller (BDC). Only one PDC can exist in a domain. In an NT 4.0 single domain model, any user having a valid domain user account and password in the user accounts database of the PDC has the ability to log onto any computer that is a member of the domain, including MetaFrame servers.

Primary Domain Name System (DNS) Server   The Primary DNS server maintains the master copy of the DNS database for the zone. This copy of the database is the only one that can be modified, and any changes made to its database are distributed to secondary servers in the zone during a zone transfer process. The server can cache resolution requests locally so a lookup query does not have to be sent across the network for a duplicate request. The primary server contains the address mappings for the Internet root DNS servers. Primary servers can also act as secondary servers for other zones, as described below.

Primary Partitions   Primary partitions are typically used to create bootable drives. Each primary partition represents one drive letter, up to a maximum of four on a single hard disk. One primary partition must be marked as active in order to boot the system, and most operating systems must be loaded on a primary partition to work.

Print Device   The hardware that actually does the printing. A print device is one of two types as defined in Windows 2000: local or network-interface. A local print device connects directly to the print server with a serial or parallel interface. A network-interface print device connects to the printer across the network and must have its own network interface or be connected to an external network adapter.

Print Driver   A software program used by Windows 2000 and other computer programs to connect with printers and plotters. It translates information sent to it into commands that the print device can understand.

Print Server   A print server is a computer that manages printing on the network. A print server can be a dedicated computer hosting multiple printers, or it can run as one of many processes on a nondedicated computer.

Printer permissions   Printer permissions are established through the Security tab in the printer's Properties dialog. The security settings for printer objects are similar to the security settings for folder shares.

Protocols   Protocols are sets of rules that computers use to communicate with one another. Protocols usually work together in stacks, so called because in a layered networking model, they operate at different layers or levels. These protocols govern the logic, formatting, and timing of information exchange between layers.

Publishing resources   Resources, such as folders and printers, which are available to be shared on the network, can be published to the Active Directory. The resources are published to the directory and can be located by users, who can query the directory based on the resource's properties (for example, to locate all color printers).

PXE   *See* Preboot eXecution Environment.

QoS   *See* Quality of Service (QoS) Admission Control.

Quality of Service (QoS) Admission Control   Admission control allows you to control how applications are allotted network bandwidth. You can give important applications more bandwidth, less important applications less bandwidth.

RAID   *See* Redundant Array of Inexpensive Disks.

RAS   *See* Remote Access Service.

RDP   *See* Remote Desktop Protocol.

Recovery agent   The recovery agent restores the encrypted file on a secure computer with its private recovery keys. The agent decrypts it using the CIPHER command line and then returns the plain text file to the user. The recovery agent goes to the computer with the encrypted file, loads the recovery certificate and private key, and performs the recovery. It is not as safe as the first option because the recovery agent's private key may remain on the user's computer.

Recovery Console   The Recovery Console is a new command-line interpreter program feature in Windows 2000 that helps in system maintenance activities and resolving system problems. This program is separate from the Windows 2000 command prompt.

Redundant Array of Inexpensive Disks (RAID)   Although mirroring and duplexing are forms of RAID, most people think of RAID as involving more than two drives. The most common form of RAID is RAID-5, which is the striping of data across three or more drives, providing fault tolerance if one drive fails. For the best disk performance, consider using a SCSI RAID (Redundant Array of Independent Disks) controller. RAID controllers automatically place data on multiple disk drives and can increase disk performance. Using the software implementation of RAID provided by NT would increase performance if designed properly, but the best performance is always realized through hardware RAID controllers.

Redundant Array of Inexpensive Disks 5 (RAID-5) Volume   A RAID-5 volume on a dynamic drive provides disk striping with parity, and is similar to a basic stripe set with parity. This disk configuration provides both increased storage capacity and fault tolerance. Data in a dynamic RAID-5 volume is interleaved across three or more disks (up to 32 disks), and parity information is included to rebuild lost data in the event of an individual disk failure. Like a spanned or striped volume, a RAID-5 volume cannot be mirrored.

Registry   The Registry is the hierarchical database that stores operating system and application configuration information. It was introduced in Windows 9*x* and NT and replaced much of the functionality of the old initialization, system, and command files used in the early versions of Windows (.ini, .sys, and .com extensions). The registry is also a Microsoft Windows program allowing the user to choose options for configuration and applications to set them; it replaces confusing text-based .INI files.

Remote   The word "remote" can take on a number of different meanings depending on the context. In the case of an individual computer, the computer you are sitting in front of is sometimes referred to as being "local" while any other computer is considered "remote." In this context any machine but your own is considered a remote computer. In discussions related to network configuration and design, "remote" may refer to segments and machines that are on the far side of a router. In this context, all machines on your physical segment are considered "local" and machines located on other physical segments are referred to as remote.

Remote Access Policy   Remote access policies allow you to create demand-dial connections to use specific authentication and encryption methods. In Windows NT versions 3.5x and Windows NT 4.0, authorization was much simpler. The administrator simply granted dial-in permission to the user. The callback options were configured on a per-user basis.

Remote Access Service (RAS)   Remote Access Service is a built in feature of the Microsoft NT operating system. It allows users to establish a connection to an NT network over a standard phone line. Remote Access allows users to access files on a network or transfer files from a remote PC, over a Dial-Up Networking connection. The performance of transferring files over a dial-up connection is very similar to the performance you would get if you were downloading a file from the Internet.

Remote Desktop Protocol (RDP)   Remote Desktop Protocol (RDP) is the application protocol between the client and the server. It informs the server of the keystrokes and mouse movement of the client and returns to the client the Windows 2000 graphical display from the server. RDP is a multichannel, standard protocol that provides various levels of compression so that it can adapt to different connection speeds and encryption levels from 40 to 128 bit. Transmission Control Protocol/Internet Protocol (TCP/IP) carries the messages, and RDP is the language in which the messages are written. Both are needed to use Microsoft's implementation of Terminal Services.

Remote Installation Preparation (RIPrep)   RIPrep is a disk duplication tool included with Windows 2000 Server. It is an ideal tool for creating images of fully prepared client computers. These images are the customized images made from the base operating system, local installation of applications such as Microsoft Office, and customized configurations.

Remote Installation Preparation (RIPrep) Wizard   The RIPrep wizard enables the network administrator to distribute to a large number of client computers a standard desktop configuration that includes the operating system and the applications. This not only helps in maintaining a uniform standard across the enterprise; it also cuts the costs and time involved in a large-scale rollout of Windows 2000 Professional.

Remote Installation Service (RIS)   The RIS, part of Windows 2000 Server, allows client computers to install Windows 2000 Professional from a Windows 2000 Server with the service installed. The Remote Installation Services (RIS) facilitates installation of Windows 2000 Professional remotely on a large number of computers with similar or dissimilar hardware configurations. This not only reduces the installation time but also helps keep deployment costs low. Also, the Windows 2000 Remote Installation Services allow you a way to create an image of Windows 2000 Professional you can use to install Windows 2000 Professional on your network client systems. This image actually consists of the installation files from the Windows 2000 Professional CD-ROM.

Remote local printer   A print device connected directly to a print server but accessed by another print server or by workstations. The queue for the print device exists on the server, and the print server controls job priority, print order, and queue administration. Client computers submit print jobs to the server and can observe the queue to monitor the printing process on the server. Drivers for the print device are loaded onto the client computer from the print server.

Remote network printer   A network printer connected to a print server that is accessed by client workstations or other print servers. Like the remote local printer, the printer queue is controlled by the print server, meaning that the client computers submit their print jobs to the print server, rather than to the print device directly. This allows for server administration and monitoring of the printer queues. Drivers for the print device are loaded onto the client computers from the print server.

Request   After the client receives the DHCPOFFER message and accepts the Internet Protocol (IP) address, it sends a DHCPREQUEST message out to all Dynamic Host Control Protocol (DHCP) servers indicating that it has accepted an offer. The message contains the IP address of the DHCP server that made the accepted offer, and all other DHCP servers release the addresses they had offered back into their available address pool.

Reverse Lookup Query   A reverse lookup query resolves an Internet Protocol (IP) address to a Domain Name System (DNS) name, and can be used for a variety of reasons. The process is different, though, because it makes use of a special domain called in-addr.arpa. This domain is also hierarchical, but is based on IP addresses and not names. The subdomains are organized by the *reverse* order of the IP address. For instance, the domain 16.254.169.in-addr.arpa contains the addresses in the 169.254.16.* range; the 120.129.in-addr.arpa domain contains the addresses for the 129.120.*.* range.

RIPrep   *See* Remote Installation Preparation.

Rollback Strategy   As with any upgrade, problems can sometimes require going back to the previous state. This possibility also applies to upgrading your domain to Windows 2000. You need to create a plan to roll back your network to its previous state if the upgrade to Windows 2000 fails. When upgrading the domain controllers, do not upgrade the Backup Domain Controller (BDC) that has the current directory database. Make sure the BDC is synchronized with the Primary Domain Controller (PDC), and then take it offline. Leave the BDC as is until the upgrade is successful. If you run into problems during the upgrade, you can bring the BDC back online, promote it to the PDC, and recover the Windows NT state. If this process is successful, you can upgrade the BDC to Windows 2000.

Routing and Remote Access (RRAS)   Within Windows NT, a software routing and remote access capability combining packet filtering, Open Shortest Path First (OSPF) support, etc.

RRAS   *See* Routing and Remote Access.

Safe Mode   Safe Mode starts Windows 2000 using only some basic files and device drivers. These devices include monitor, keyboard, mouse, basic VGA video, CD-ROM, and mass storage devices. The system starts only those system services that are necessary to load the operating system. Networking is not started in this mode. The Windows background screen is black in this mode, and the screen resolution is 640 by 480 pixels with 16 colors.

Safe Mode with Command Prompt   This option starts the operating system in a safe mode using some basic files only. The Windows 2000 command prompt is shown instead of the usual Windows desktop.

Safe Mode with Networking   This mode is similar to the Safe Mode, but networking devices, drivers, and protocols are loaded. You may choose this mode when you are sure that the problem in the system is not due to any networking component.

SAM   *See* Security Accounts Manager.

Scripted method   This method for Windows 2000 Professional installation uses an answer file to specify various configuration parameters. This is used to eliminate user interaction during installation, thereby automating the installation process. Answers to most of the questions asked by the setup process are specified in the answer file. Besides this, the scripted method can be used for clean installations and upgrades.

SCSI   *See* Small Computer System Interface.

Secondary Domain Name System (DNS) Server   Secondary DNS servers provide fault tolerance and load balancing for DNS zones. Secondary servers contain a read-only copy of the zone database that it receives from the primary server during a zone transfer. A secondary server will respond to a DNS request if the primary server fails to respond because of an error or a heavy load. Since secondary servers can resolve DNS queries, they are also considered authoritative within a domain, and can help with load balancing on the network. Secondary servers can be placed in remote locations on the network and configured to respond to DNS queries from local computers, potentially reducing query traffic across longer network distances. While there can be only one primary server in a zone, multiple secondary servers can be set up for redundancy and load balancing.

Security Accounts Manager (SAM)   The Security Accounts Manager (SAM) is the portion of the Windows NT Server registry that stores user account information and group membership. Attributes that are specific to Terminal Server can be added to user accounts. This adds a small amount of information to each user's entry in the domain's SAM.

Security Groups   The Windows 2000 Security Groups allow you to assign the same security permissions to large numbers of users in one operation. This ensures consistent security permissions across all members of a group. Using Security Groups to assign permissions means the access control on resources remains fairly static and easy to control and audit. Users who need access are added or removed from the appropriate security groups as needed, and the access control lists change infrequently.

Security Templates   Windows 2000 comes with several predefined Security Templates. These templates address several security scenarios. Security Templates come in two basic categories: Default and Incremental. The Default or Basic templates are applied by the operating system when a clean install has been performed. They are not applied if an upgrade installation has been done. The incremental templates should be applied after the Basic Security Templates have been applied. There are four types of incremental templates: Compatible, Secure, High Secure, and Dedicated Domain Controller.

Segment   In discussions of Transmission Control Protocol/Internet Protocol (TCP/IP), segment often refers to the group of computers located on one side of a router, or sometimes a group of computers within the same collision domain. In TCP/IP terminology, "segment" can also be used to describe the chunk of data sent by TCP over the network (roughly equivalent to the usage of "packet" or "frame").

Sequenced Packet eXchange (SPX)   The communications protocol (from NetWare) used to control network message transport.

Server   The word "server" can take on a variety of meanings. A server can be a physical computer. Such as "Check out that Server over in the Accounting Department". A server can also represent a particular software package. For example, Microsoft Exchange 2000 is a mail and groupware Server application. Often server applications are just referred to as "servers," as in "Check out what the problem is with the mail server." The term "server" is also used to refer to any computer that is currently sharing its resources on the network. In this context, all computers, whether Windows 3x or Windows 2000, can be servers on a network.

Service pack   A service pack typically contains bug fixes, security fixes, systems administration tools, drivers, and additional components. Microsoft recommends installing the latest service packs as they are released. In addition, as a new feature in Windows 2000, you do not have to reinstall components after installing a service pack, as you did with Windows NT. You can also see what service pack is currently installed on a computer by running the WINVER utility program. WINVER brings up the About Windows dialog box. It displays the version of Windows and the version of the service pack you are running.

Setup Manager   The Setup Manager is the best tool to use when you have no idea of the answer file syntax or when you do not want to get into the time-consuming task of creating or modifying the sample answer file. When you choose to use the Setup Manager for unattended installations, you need to do a lot of planning beforehand. It is understood that you will not be using Setup Manager for automating installations on one or two computers; that would be a waste of effort. Setup Manager is useful for mass deployments only.

SETUPACT.LOG   The Action log file contains details about the files that are copied during setup.

SETUPAPI.LOG   This log file contains details about the device driver files that were copied during setup. This log can be used to facilitate troubleshooting device installations. The file contains errors and warnings along with a time stamp for each issue.

SETUPCL.EXE   The function of the SETUPCL.EXE file is to run the Mini-Setup wizard and to regenerate the security IDs on the master and destination computers. The Mini-Setup wizard starts on the master computer when it is booted for the first time after running SysPrep.

SETUPERR.LOG   The Error log file contains details about errors that occurred during setup.

SETUPLOG.TXT   This log file contains additional information about the device driver files that were copied during setup.

Shared Folders   Sharing folders so that other users can access their contents across the network is easy in Windows 2000, as easy as right-clicking on the folder name in Windows Explorer, selecting the Sharing tab, and choosing Share This Folder. An entire drive and all the folders on that drive can be shared in the same way.

Shared Folders Permissions   As only folders, not files, can be shared, shared folder permissions are a small subset of standard NT File System (NTFS) permissions for a folder. However, securing access to a folder through share permissions can be more restrictive or more liberal than standard NTFS folder permissions. Shared folder permissions are applied in the same manner as NTFS permissions.

Shared printers   The process for sharing a printer attached to your local computer is similar to that for sharing a folder or drive. If the users who will access your printer will do so from machines that don't run the Windows 2000 operating system, you will need to install drivers for the other operating system(s).

Shared resource   A shared resource is a device, data, or program that is made available to network users. This can include folders, files, printers, and even Internet connections.

Simple volume   A simple volume is a volume created on a dynamic disk that is not fault tolerant, and includes space from only one physical disk. A simple volume is just that—it is a single volume that does not span more than one physical disk, and does not provide improved drive performance, extra capacity, or fault tolerance. One physical disk can contain a single, large simple volume, or several smaller ones. Each simple volume is assigned a separate drive letter. The number of simple volumes on a disk is limited only by the capacity of the disk and the number of available letters in the alphabet.

Single-Instance-Store (SIS) Volume   When you have more than one image on the Remote Installation Service (RIS) server, each holding Windows 2000 Professional files, there will be duplicate copies of hundreds of files. This may consume a significant hard drive space on the RIS server. To overcome this problem, Microsoft introduced a new feature called the Single-Instance-Store, which helps in deleting all the duplicate files, thus saving on hard drive space.

SIS   *See* Single-Instance-Store (SIS) Volume.

Site Server Internet Locator Server (ILS) Service   This service supports Internet Protocol (IP) telephony applications. Publishes IP multicast conferences on a network, and can also publish user IP address mappings for H.323 IP telephony. Telephony applications, such as NetMeeting and Phone Dialer in Windows Accessories, use Site Server ILS Service to display user names and conferences with published addresses. Site Server ILS Service depends on Internet Information Services (IIS).

Small Computer System Interface (SCSI)   A complete expansion bus interface that accepts such devices as a hard disk, CD-ROM, disk drivers, printers, or scanners.

SMP   *See* Symmetric Multiprocessing.

SMS   *See* Systems Management Server.

SNA   *See* Systems Network Architecture.

Spanned volume   A spanned volume is similar to a volume set in NT 4.0. It contains space from multiple disks (up to 32), and provides a way to combine small "chunks" of disk space into one unit, seen by the operating system as a single volume. It is not fault tolerant. When a dynamic volume includes the space on more than one physical hard drive, it is called a spanned volume. Spanned volumes can be used to increase drive capacity, or to make use of the leftover space on up to 32 existing disks. Like those in a basic storage volume set, the portions of a spanned volume are all linked together and share a single drive letter.

SPX   *See* Sequenced Packet eXchange.

Stack   A data structure in which the first items inserted are the last ones removed, unlike control structure programs that use the Last In First Out (LIFO) structure.

Static Internet Protocol (IP) address   A static IP address allows users to use a domain name that can be translated into an IP address. The static IP address allows the server to always have the same IP address, so the domain name always translates to the correct IP address. If the address was assigned dynamically and occasionally changed, users might not be able to access the server across the Internet using the domain name.

Stripe Set   The term "striping" refers to the interleaving of data across separate physical disks. Each file is broken into small blocks, and each block is evenly and alternately saved to the disks in the stripe set. In a two-disk stripe set, the first block of data is saved to the first disk, the second block is saved to the second disk, and the third block is saved to the first disk, and so on. The two disks are treated as a single drive, and are given a single drive letter.

Stripe Set with Parity   A stripe set with parity requires at least three hard disks, and provides both increased storage capacity and fault tolerance. In a stripe set with parity, data is interleaved across three or more disks, and includes parity (error checking) information about the data. As long as only one disk in the set fails, the parity information can be used to reconstruct the lost data. If the parity information itself is lost, it can be reconstructed from the original data.

Striped volume   Like a stripe set in NT 4.0, a striped volume is the dynamic storage equivalent of a basic stripe set and combines free space from up to 32 physical disks into one volume by writing data across the disks in stripes. This increases performance but does not provide fault tolerance. A striped volume improves drive performance and increases drive capacity. Because each data block is written only once, striped volumes do not provide fault tolerance.

Striping   Striping is when the data are striped across the drives and there is parity information along with the data. The parity information is based on a mathematical formula that comes up with the parity based on the data on the other drives.

Subnetting   Using several data paths to reduce traffic on a network and avoid problems if a single path should fail; usually configured as a dedicated Ethernet subnetwork between two systems based on two Network Interface Cards (NICs).

Symmetric Multiprocessing (SMP)   SMP is a system in which all processors are treated as equals, and any thread can be run on any available processor. Windows 2000 also supports processor affinity, in which a process or thread can specify which set of processors it should run on. Application Programming Interfaces (APIs) must be defined in the application.

Synthesis   The process of design, formulation, integration, prediction, proposal, generalization, and show relationships.

SYSPREP.INF   SYSPREP.INF is an answer file. When you want to automate the Mini-Setup wizard by providing predetermined answers to all setup questions, you must use this file. This file needs to be placed in the %Systemroot%\Sysprep folder or on a floppy disk. When the Mini-Setup wizard is run on the computer on which the image is being distributed, it takes answers from the SYSPREP.INF file without prompting the user for any input.

System Preparation (Sysprep)   SysPrep provides an excellent means of saving installation time and reducing installation costs. Sysprep is the best tool to copy the image of a computer to other computers that have identical hardware configurations. It is also helpful in standardizing the desktop environment throughout the organization. Since one Sysprep image cannot be used on computers with identical hardware and software applications, you can create multiple images when you have more than one standard. It is still the best option where the number of computers is in hundreds or thousands and you wish to implement uniform policies in the organization.

System Monitor   The System Monitor is part of the Administrative Tools utility, and allows you to collect and view data about current memory usage, disk, processor utilization, network activity and other system activity. The System Monitor replaces the Performance Monitor used in Windows NT. System Monitor allows you to collect information about your hardware's performance as well as network utilization. System Monitor can be used to measure different aspects of a computer's performance. It can be used on your own computer or other computers on the network.

System policy   Group policies have mostly replaced system policies since group policies extend the functionality of system policies. A few situations still exist in which system policies are valuable. The system policy editor is used to provide user and computer configuration settings in the Windows NT registry database. The system policy editor is still used for the management of Windows 9x and Windows NT server and workstations and stand-alone computers using Windows 2000.

Systems Management Server (SMS)   This Windows NT software analyzes and monitors network usage and various network functions.

Systems Network Architecture (SNA)   Systems Network Architecture (SNA) was developed by IBM in the mainframe computer era (1974, to be precise) as a way of getting its various products to communicate with each other for distributed processing. SNA is a line of products designed to make other products cooperate. In your career of designing network solutions, you should expect to run into SNA from time to time because many of the bigger companies (i.e., banks, healthcare institutions, government offices) bought IBM equipment and will be reluctant to part with their investment. SNA is a proprietary protocol that runs over SDLC exclusively, although it may be transported within other protocols, such as X.25 and Token Ring. It is designed as a hierarchy and consists of a collection of machines called nodes.

Take Ownership Permission   This permission can be given to allow a user to take ownership of a file or folder object. Every file and folder on an NT File System (NTFS) drive has an owner, usually the account that created the object. However, there are times when ownership of a file needs to be changed, perhaps because of a change in team membership or a set of new responsibilities for a user.

Task-based model   This model is appropriate for companies in which administrative duties are functionally divided. This means that this model divides the management of Group Policy Objects (GPOs) by certain tasks. To apply this model, the administrators that handle security-related tasks will also be responsible for managing all policy objects that affect security. The second set of administrators that normally deploy the companies' business applications will be responsible for all the GPOs that affect installation and maintenance.

TCP/IP   *See* Transmission Control Protocol/Internet Protocol (TCP/IP).

Terminal Services   In application server mode, Terminal Services provides the ability to run client applications on the server, while "thin client" software acts as a terminal emulator on the client. Each user sees an individual session, displayed as a Windows 2000 desktop. The server manages each session, independent of any other client session. If you install Terminal Services as an application server, you must also install Terminal Services Licensing (not necessarily on the same computer). However, temporary licenses can be issued for clients that allow you to use Terminal servers for up to 90 days. In remote administration mode, you can use Terminal Services to log on remotely and manage Windows 2000 systems from virtually anywhere on your network (instead of being limited to working locally on a server). Remote administration mode allows for two concurrent connections from a given server and minimizes impact on server performance. Remote administration mode does not require you to install Terminal Services Licensing.

TFTP   *See* Trivial File Transfer Protocol.

Token Ring   A Local Area Network (LAN) specification that was developed by IBM in the 1980s for PC-based networks and classified by the (Institute of Electrical and Electronics Engineers) IEEE as 802.5. It specifies a star topology physically and a ring topology logically. It runs at either four Mbps or 16 Mbps, but all nodes on the ring must run at the same speed.

Transmission Control Protocol/Internet Protocol (TCP/IP)   A set of communications standards created by the U.S. Department of Defense (DoD) in the 1970s that has now become an accepted way to connect different types of computers in networks because the standards now support so many programs.

Trees   Trees are groups of domains that share a contiguous namespace. It allows you to create a hierarchical grouping of domains that share a common contiguous namespace. This hierarchy allows global sharing of resources among domains in the tree. All the domains in a tree share information and resources with a single directory, and there is only one directory per tree. However, each domain manages its own subset of the directory that contains the user accounts for that domain. So, when a user logs into a domain, the user has global access to all resources that are part of the tree, providing the user has the proper permissions.

Trivial File Transfer Protocol (TFTP)   A simplified version of the File Transfer Protocol (FTP), associated with the Transmission Control Protocol/Internet Protocol (TCP/IP) family, that does not provide password protection or a user directory.

Trust   The users in one tree do not have global access to resources in other trees, but trusts can be created that allow users to access resources in another tree. A trust allows all the trees to share resources and have common administrative functions. Such sharing capability allows the trees to operate independently of each other, with separate namespaces, yet still be able to communicate and share resources through trusts.

Trust relationship   A trust relationship is a connection between domains in which users who have accounts in and log on to one domain can then access resources in other domains, provided they have proper access permissions.

UDF   *See* Unique Database File.

UDP   *See* User Datagram Protocol.

Unattended method   The unattended method for Windows 2000 Server installation uses the answer file to specify various configuration parameters. This method eliminates user interaction during installation, thereby automating the installation process and reducing the chances of input errors. Answers to most of the questions asked by the setup process are specified in the answer file. In addition, the scripted method can be used for clean installations and upgrades.

UNATTEND.TXT file   The creation of customized UNATTEND.TXT answer files is the simplest form of providing answers to setup queries and unattended installation of Windows 2000. This can either be done using the Setup Manager or by editing the sample UNATTEND.TXT file using Notepad or the MS-DOS text editor. The UNATTEND.TXT file does not provide any means of creating an image of the computer.

UNATTEND.UDF   This file is the Uniqueness Database File, which provides customized settings for each computer using the automated installation.

UNC   *See* Universal Naming Convention.

UNICODE   UNICODE is a 16-bit character encoding standard developed by the Unicode Consortium between 1988 and 1991 that uses two bytes to represent each character and enables almost all of the written languages of the world to be represented using a single character set.

Uninterruptible Power Supply (UPS)   A battery that can supply power to a computer system if the power fails. It charges while the computer is on and, if the power fails, provides power for a certain amount of time allowing the user to shut down the computer properly to preserve data.

Unique Database File (UDF)   When you use the WINNT32.EXE command with the /unattend option, you can also specify a Unique Database File (UDF), which has a .UDB extension. This file forces Setup to use certain values from the UDF file, thus overriding the values given in the answer file. This is particularly useful when you want to specify multiple users during the setup.

Universal Groups   Universal Groups are used in larger, multidomain organizations, in which there is a need to grant access to similar groups of accounts defined in multiple domains. It is better to use Global Groups as members of Universal Groups to reduce overall replication traffic from changes to Universal Group membership. Users can be added and removed from the corresponding Global Groups with their account domains, and a small number of Global Groups are the direct members of the Universal Group. Universal Groups are used only in multiple domain trees or forests. A Windows 2000 domain must be in native mode to use Universal Groups.

Universal Naming Convention (UNC)   A UNC is an identification standard of servers and other network resources.

Universal Serial Bus (USB)   A low-speed hardware interface (supports MPEG video) with a maximum bandwidth up to 1.5 MBytes per second.

UPS   *See* Uninterruptible Power Supply.

USB   *See* Universal Serial Bus.

User account   The information that defines a particular user on a network, which includes the username, password, group memberships, and rights and permissions assigned to the user.

User Datagram Protocol (UDP)   A Transmission Control Protocol/Internet Protocol (TCP/IP) normally bundled with an Internet Protocol (IP) layer software that describes how messages received reached application programs within the destination computer.

Value bar   The value bar is positioned below the graph area. It displays data for the selected sample, the last sample value, the average of the counter samples, the maximum and minimum of the samples, and the duration of time the samples have been taken over.

Virtual Private Networking (VPN)   VPNs reduce service costs and long distance/usage fees, lighten infrastructure investments, and simplify Wide Area Network (WAN) operations over time. To determine just how cost-effective a VPN solution could be in connecting remote offices, use the VPN Calculator located on Cisco's Web site at www.cisco.com.

Volume Set   The term "volume" indicates a single drive letter. One physical hard disk can contain several volumes, one for each primary partition or logical drive. However, the opposite is also true. You can create a single volume that spans more than one physical disk. This is a good option when you require a volume that exceeds the capacity of a single physical disk. You can also create a volume set when you want to make use of leftover space on several disks by piecing them together as one volume.

VPN   *See* Virtual Private Networking.

WDM   *See* Windows32 Drive Model.

Windows 3x   Windows 3 changed everything. It was a 16-bit operating system with a user interface that resembled the look and feel of IBM's (at that time not yet released) OS/2, with 3D buttons and the ability to run multiple programs simultaneously, using a method called cooperative multitasking. Windows 3 also provided virtual memory, the ability to use hard disk space to "fool" the applications into behaving as if they had more RAM than was physically installed in the machine.

Windows 9x   In August of 1995, Microsoft released its long-awaited upgrade of Windows, Windows 95. For the first time, Windows could be installed on a machine that didn't already have MS-DOS installed. Many improvements were made: the new 32-bit functionality (although still retaining some 16-bit code for backward compatibility); preemptive multitasking (a more efficient way to run multiple programs in which the operating system controls use of the processor and the crash of one application does not bring down the others that are currently running); and support for filenames longer than the DOS-based eight-character limit.

Windows32 Driver Model (WDM)   The Win32 Driver Model (WDM) provides a standard for device drivers that will work across Windows platforms (specifically Windows 98 and 2000), so that you can use the same drivers with the consumer and business versions of the Windows operating system.

Windows 2000   Microsoft's latest incarnation of the corporate operating system was originally called NT 5, but the name was changed to Windows 2000 between the second and third beta versions—perhaps to underscore the fact that this is truly a *new* version of the operating system, not merely an upgrade to NT.

Windows 2000 Control Panel   The Control Panel in Windows 2000 functions similarly to the Control Panel in Windows 9*x* and NT, except that "under the hood" there are now two locations that information is stored, which is modified by the Control Panel applets. The Control Panel in previous operating systems was a graphical interface for editing Registry information.

Windows Backup   Windows Backup is a built-in Backup and Restore utility, which has many more features than the backup tool provided in Windows NT 4.0. It supports all five types of backup: Normal, Copy, Differential, Incremental, and Daily. Windows Backup allows you to perform the backup operation manually or you may schedule it to run at a later time in unattended mode. Included with the operating system, it is a tool that is flexible and easy to use.

Windows Internet Name Service (WINS)   WINS provides name resolution for clients running Windows NT and earlier versions of Microsoft operating systems. With name resolution, users can access servers by name, instead of having to use Internet Protocol (IP) addresses that are difficult to recognize and remember. WINS is used to map NetBIOS computer names to IP addresses. This allows users to access other computers on the network by computer name. WINS servers should be assigned a static IP address, which allows clients to be able to find the WINS servers. Clients cannot find a WINS server by name because they need to know where the WINS server is in order to translate the name into an IP address.

Windows Internet Name Service (WINS) Name Registration   Each WINS client has one or more WINS servers identified in the network configuration on the computer, either through static assignment or through DHCP configuration. When the client boots and connects to the network, it registers its name and IP address with the WINS server by sending a registration request directly to the server. This is not a broadcast message, since the client has the address of the server. If the server is available and the name is not already registered, the server responds with a successful registration message, which contains the amount of time the name will be registered to the client, the Time To Live (TTL). Then the server stores the name and address combination in its local database.

Windows Internet Name Service (WINS) Name Release   When a WINS client shuts down properly, it will send a name release request to the WINS server. This releases the name from the WINS server's database so that another client can use the name if necessary. The release request contains the WINS name and address of the client. If the server cannot find the name, it sends a negative release response to the client. If the server finds the matching name and address in its database, it releases the name and marks the record as inactive. If the name is found but the address does not match, the server ignores the request.

Windows Internet Name Service (WINS) Name Renewal   As with Dynamic Host Control Protocol (DHCP), WINS name registrations are temporary and must be renewed to continue to be valid. The client will attempt to renew its registration when half (50 percent) of the Time To Live (TTL) has elapsed. If the WINS server does not respond, the client repeatedly attempts to renew its lease at ten-minute intervals for an hour. If the client still receives no response, it restarts the process with the secondary WINS server, if one is defined. The client will continue attempting to renew its lease in this manner until it receives a response from a server. At that time, the server sends a new TTL to the client and the process starts over.

Windows Internet Name Service (WINS) Proxy agent   A WINS Proxy agent is similar to a Dynamic Host Control Protocol (DHCP) Relay Agent. It listens for requests for non-WINS network clients and redirects those requests to a WINS server. A WINS proxy operates in two modes.

Windows Internet Name Service (WINS) Snap-in   With the snap-in, you can view the active WINS entries under the Active Registrations folder. In addition, you can supply static mappings for non-WINS clients on the network through the snap-in. To configure a static mapping, select the Active Registrations folder and the select New Static Mapping from the Action menu. Once a static mapping is entered into the WINS database, it cannot be edited. If you need to make changes to a static mapping, you must be delete and recreate the entry.

Windows NT   The NT kernel (the core or nucleus of the operating system, which provides basic services for all other parts of the operating system) is built on a completely different architecture from consumer Windows. In fact, NT was based on the 32-bit preemptive multitasking operating system that originated as a joint project of Microsoft and IBM before their parting of the ways, OS/2. NT provided the stability and security features that the "other Windows" lacked, albeit at a price, and not only a monetary one; NT was much pickier in terms of hardware support, did not run all of the programs that ran on Windows 9*x* (especially DOS programs that accessed the hardware directly), and required more resources, especially memory, to run properly.

WINNT.EXE program　The WINNT.EXE program is used for network installations that use an MS-DOS network client. The WINNT32.EXE program is used to customize the process for upgrading existing installations. The WINNT32.EXE program is used for installing Windows 2000 from a computer that is currently running Windows 95/98 or Windows NT.

WINS　*See* Windows Internet Name Service.

Workgroup　A workgroup is a logical grouping of resources on a network. It is generally used in peer-to-peer networks. This means that each computer is responsible for access to its resources. Each computer has its own account database and is administered separately. Security is not shared between computers, and administration is more difficult than in a centralized domain.

Zones of Authority　The Domain Name System (DNS) namespace is divided into zones, and each zone must have one name server that is the authority for the name mapping for the zone. Depending on the size of the namespace, a zone may be subdivided into multiple zones, each with its own authority, or there may be a single authority for the entire zone. For instance, a small company with only 200-300 computers could have one DNS server handle the entire namespace.

INDEX

D

E

S

Custom Corporate Network Training

Train on Cutting Edge Technology   We can bring the best in skill-based training to your facility to create a real-world hands-on training experience. Global Knowledge has invested millions of dollars in network hardware and software to train our students on the same equipment they will work with on the job. Our relationships with vendors allow us to incorporate the latest equipment and platforms into your on-site labs.

Maximize Your Training Budget   Global Knowledge provides experienced instructors, comprehensive course materials, and all the networking equipment needed to deliver high quality training. You provide the students; we provide the knowledge.

Avoid Travel Expenses   On-site courses allow you to schedule technical training at your convenience, saving time, expense, and the opportunity cost of travel away from the workplace.

Discuss Confidential Topics   Private on-site training permits the open discussion of sensitive issues such as security, access, and network design. We can work with your existing network's proprietary files while demonstrating the latest technologies.

Customize Course Content   Global Knowledge can tailor your courses to include the technologies and the topics which have the greatest impact on your business. We can complement your internal training efforts or provide a total solution to your training needs.

Corporate Pass   The Corporate Pass Discount Program rewards our best network training customers with preferred pricing on public courses, discounts on multimedia training packages, and an array of career planning services.

Global Knowledge Training Lifecycle   Supporting the Dynamic and Specialized Training Requirements of Information Technology Professionals

- Define Profile
- Assess Skills
- Design Training
- Deliver Training
- Test Knowledge
- Update Profile
- Use New Skills

College Credit Recommendation Program   The American Council on Education's CREDIT program recommends 53 Global Knowledge courses for college credit. Now our network training can help you earn your college degree while you learn the technical skills needed for your job. When you attend an ACE-certified Global Knowledge course and pass the associated exam, you earn college credit recommendations for that course. Global Knowledge can establish a transcript record for you with ACE, which you can use to gain credit at a college or as a written record of your professional training that you can attach to your resume.

Registration Information

COURSE FEE: The fee covers course tuition, refreshments, and all course materials. Any parking expenses that may be incurred are not included. Payment or government training form must be received six business days prior to the course date. We will also accept Visa/MasterCard and American Express. For non-U.S. credit card users, charges will be in U.S. funds and will be converted by your credit card company. Checks drawn on Canadian banks in Canadian funds are acceptable.

COURSE SCHEDULE: Registration is at 8:00 a.m. on the first day. The program begins at 8:30 a.m. and concludes at 4:30 p.m. each day.

CANCELLATION POLICY: Cancellation and full refund will be allowed if written cancellation is received in our office at least six business days prior to the course start date. Registrants who do not attend the course or do not cancel more than six business days in advance are responsible for the full registration fee; you may transfer to a later date provided the course fee has been paid in full. Substitutions may be made at any time. If Global Knowledge must cancel a course for any reason, liability is limited to the registration fee only.

GLOBAL KNOWLEDGE: Global Knowledge programs are developed and presented by industry professionals with "real-world" experience. Designed to help professionals meet today's interconnectivity and interoperability challenges, most of our programs feature hands-on labs that incorporate state-of-the-art communication components and equipment.

ON-SITE TEAM TRAINING: Bring Global Knowledge's powerful training programs to your company. At Global Knowledge, we will custom design courses to meet your specific network requirements. Call 1 (919) 461-8686 for more information.

YOUR GUARANTEE: Global Knowledge believes its courses offer the best possible training in this field. If during the first day you are not satisfied and wish to withdraw from the course, simply notify the instructor, return all course materials, and receive a 100% refund.

In the US:

CALL: 1 (888) 762-4442

FAX: 1 (919) 469-7070

VISIT OUR WEBSITE:

www.globalknowledge.com

MAIL CHECK AND THIS FORM TO:

Global Knowledge

Suite 200

114 Edinburgh South

P.O. Box 1187

Cary, NC 27512

In Canada:

CALL: 1 (800) 465-2226

FAX: 1 (613) 567-3899

VISIT OUR WEBSITE:

www.globalknowledge.com.ca

MAIL CHECK AND THIS FORM TO:

Global Knowledge

Suite 1601

393 University Ave.

Toronto, ON M5G 1E6

REGISTRATION INFORMATION:

Course title ——————————————————————————

Course location ——————————————————— Course date —————

Name/title —————————————————— Company ——————

Name/title —————————————————— Company ——————

Name/title —————————————————— Company ——————

Address ———————————— Telephone ————— Fax ——————

City —————————— State/Province ————— Zip/Postal Code—————

Credit card ————— Card # ———————————— Expiration date —————

Signature ——————————————————————————

LICENSE AGREEMENT

THIS PRODUCT (THE "PRODUCT") CONTAINS PROPRIETARY SOFTWARE, DATA AND INFORMATION (INCLUDING DOCUMENTATION) OWNED BY THE McGRAW-HILL COMPANIES, INC. ("McGRAW-HILL") AND ITS LICENSORS. YOUR RIGHT TO USE THE PRODUCT IS GOVERNED BY THE TERMS AND CONDITIONS OF THIS AGREEMENT.

LICENSE: Throughout this License Agreement, "you" shall mean either the individual or the entity whose agent opens this package. You are granted a non-exclusive and non-transferable license to use the Product subject to the following terms:

(i) If you have licensed a single user version of the Product, the Product may only be used on a single computer (i.e., a single CPU). If you licensed and paid the fee applicable to a local area network or wide area network version of the Product, you are subject to the terms of the following subparagraph (ii).

(ii) If you have licensed a local area network version, you may use the Product on unlimited workstations located in one single building selected by you that is served by such local area network. If you have licensed a wide area network version, you may use the Product on unlimited workstations located in multiple buildings on the same site selected by you that is served by such wide area network; provided, however, that any building will not be considered located in the same site if it is more than five (5) miles away from any building included in such site. In addition, you may only use a local area or wide area network version of the Product on one single server. If you wish to use the Product on more than one server, you must obtain written authorization from McGraw-Hill and pay additional fees.

(iii) You may make one copy of the Product for back-up purposes only and you must maintain an accurate record as to the location of the back-up at all times.

COPYRIGHT; RESTRICTIONS ON USE AND TRANSFER: All rights (including copyright) in and to the Product are owned by McGraw-Hill and its licensors. You are the owner of the enclosed disc on which the Product is recorded. You may not use, copy, decompile, disassemble, reverse engineer, modify, reproduce, create derivative works, transmit, distribute, sublicense, store in a database or retrieval system of any kind, rent or transfer the Product, or any portion thereof, in any form or by any means (including electronically or otherwise) except as expressly provided for in this License Agreement. You must reproduce the copyright notices, trademark notices, legends and logos of McGraw-Hill and its licensors that appear on the Product on the back-up copy of the Product which you are permitted to make hereunder. All rights in the Product not expressly granted herein are reserved by McGraw-Hill and its licensors.

TERM: This License Agreement is effective until terminated. It will terminate if you fail to comply with any term or condition of this License Agreement. Upon termination, you are obligated to return to McGraw-Hill the Product together with all copies thereof and to purge all copies of the Product included in any and all servers and computer facilities.

DISCLAIMER OF WARRANTY: THE PRODUCT AND THE BACK-UP COPY OF THE PRODUCT ARE LICENSED "AS IS." McGRAW-HILL, ITS LICENSORS AND THE AUTHORS MAKE NO WARRANTIES, EXPRESS OR IMPLIED, AS TO RESULTS TO BE OBTAINED BY ANY PERSON OR ENTITY FROM USE OF THE PRODUCT AND/OR ANY INFORMATION OR DATA INCLUDED THEREIN. McGRAW-HILL, ITS LICENSORS, AND THE AUTHORS MAKE NO GUARANTEE THAT YOU WILL PASS ANY CERTIFICATION EXAM BY USING THIS PRODUCT. McGRAW-HILL, ITS LICENSORS AND THE AUTHORS MAKE NO EXPRESS OR IMPLIED WARRANTIES OF MERCHANTABILITY OR FITNESS FOR A PARTICULAR PURPOSE OR USE WITH RESPECT TO THE PRODUCT. NEITHER McGRAW-HILL, ANY OF ITS LICENSORS, NOR THE AUTHORS WARRANT THAT THE FUNCTIONS CONTAINED IN THE PRODUCT WILL MEET YOUR REQUIREMENTS OR THAT THE OPERATION OF THE PRODUCT WILL BE UNINTERRUPTED OR ERROR FREE. YOU ASSUME THE ENTIRE RISK WITH RESPECT TO THE QUALITY AND PERFORMANCE OF THE PRODUCT.

LIMITED WARRANTY FOR DISC: To the original licensee only, McGraw-Hill warrants that the enclosed disc on which the Product is recorded is free from defects in materials and workmanship under normal use and service for a period of ninety (90) days from the date of purchase. In the event of a defect in the disc covered by the foregoing warranty, McGraw-Hill will replace the disc.

LIMITATION OF LIABILITY: NEITHER McGRAW-HILL, ITS LICENSORS NOR THE AUTHORS SHALL BE LIABLE FOR ANY INDIRECT, SPECIAL OR CONSEQUENTIAL DAMAGES, SUCH AS BUT NOT LIMITED TO, LOSS OF ANTICIPATED PROFITS OR BENEFITS, RESULTING FROM THE USE OR INABILITY TO USE THE PRODUCT EVEN IF ANY OF THEM HAS BEEN ADVISED OF THE POSSIBILITY OF SUCH DAMAGES. THIS LIMITATION OF LIABILITY SHALL APPLY TO ANY CLAIM OR CAUSE WHATSOEVER WHETHER SUCH CLAIM OR CAUSE ARISES IN CONTRACT, TORT, OR OTHERWISE. Some states do not allow the exclusion or limitation of indirect, special or consequential damages, so the above limitation may not apply to you.

U.S. GOVERNMENT RESTRICTED RIGHTS: Any software included in the Product is provided with restricted rights subject to subparagraphs (c), (1) and (2) of the Commercial Computer Software-Restricted Rights clause at 48 C.F.R. 52.227-19. The terms of this Agreement applicable to the use of the data in the Product are those under which the data are generally made available to the general public by McGraw-Hill. Except as provided herein, no reproduction, use, or disclosure rights are granted with respect to the data included in the Product and no right to modify or create derivative works from any such data is hereby granted.

GENERAL: This License Agreement constitutes the entire agreement between the parties relating to the Product. The terms of any Purchase Order shall have no effect on the terms of this License Agreement. Failure of McGraw-Hill to insist at any time on strict compliance with this License Agreement shall not constitute a waiver of any rights under this License Agreement. This License Agreement shall be construed and governed in accordance with the laws of the State of New York. If any provision of this License Agreement is held to be contrary to law, that provision will be enforced to the maximum extent permissible and the remaining provisions will remain in full force and effect.

MCSE Windows® 2000 Study Guide

A COMPLETE STUDY PROGRAM BUILT UPON
PROVEN INSTRUCTIONAL METHODS

Self-study features include:

Expert advice on how to take and pass the test:

One or more graphical elements are sometimes used to help present or clarify an exam question. These elements may take the form of a network diagram, pictures of networking components, or screen shots from the software on which you are being tested.

Step-by-Step Certification **Exercises** focus on the specific skills most likely to be on the exam. The **CertCam** icon guides you to the graphical animation that demonstrates this skill set on CD-ROM.

CertCam 1-1

Special warnings prepare you for tricky exam topics:

exam Watch

It is important to remember that you can also access Device Manager by right-clicking My Computer and selecting Properties. Once the Properties page pops up, select the Hardware tab and then the Device Manager button.

MCSE Windows 2000 Server **"On The Job Notes"** present important lessons that help you work more efficiently:

on the Job

If the member server you are upgrading is a DHCP server, you must authorize the DHCP Server service in Active Directory or the service will not start. Authorization is not automatically granted when you upgrade to Windows 2000.

Two-Minute Drills at the end of every chapter quickly reinforce your knowledge and ensure better retention of key concepts:

Roaming user profiles are used to save a user's settings to be used on any computer in the domain. These profiles are stored on a network file server.

Scenario & Solution sections lay out problems and solutions in a quick-read format. For example:

I don't want to continuously run logs, but I do want to know when my resources reach certain levels. How can I accomplish this?

You can use alerts. Alerts can be configured to automatically start logs and notify you when a threshold is reached.

More than 230 realistic practice questions with answers help prepare you for the real test!

What is the difference between a forest and a tree?

A. A forest is a group of domains, and a tree is a group of forests that share the same namespace.

B. A tree is a group of domains with the same namespace, and a forest is a group of trees that also share the same namespace.

C. A tree is a group of domains with the same namespace, and a forest is a group of trees that do not share the same namespace.

D. A forest is a group of domains with the same namespace, and a tree is a group of forests that do not share the same namespace.

☑ **C.** A tree is a group of domains that share a DNS namespace. A forest is a group of trees that allow transitive trusts between the trees.

☒ **A** *is not correct because a tree is not a group of forests, it is a group of domains.* **B** *is not correct because the trees in a forest do not necessarily share a namespace. Each tree can have its own separate namespace.* **D** *is not correct because a forest is a group of trees, not domains.*